MILO L. CHAPMAN

Professor of Old Testament, Warner Pacific
College, Portland, Oregon. Th.B., Anderson
College; B.D. and Th.D., Pacific School of
Religion.

W. T. PURKISER

Editor of *Herald of Holiness*, Church of the
Nazarene, and Associate Professor of Eng-
lish Bible (part-time), Nazarene Theological
Seminary, Kansas City, Missouri. A.B., D.D.,
Pasadena College; M.A., Ph.D., University
of Southern California.

FIFTH PRINTING, 1971

COPYRIGHTED 1967 BY
BEACON HILL PRESS OF KANSAS CITY
KANSAS CITY, MO.

LIBRARY OF CONGRESS
CARD NUMBER 64-22906
ISBN: 0-8341-0302-8

Printed in the United States of America

BEACON
BIBLE COMMENTARY

In Ten Volumes

Volume III

The Poetical and Wisdom Literature

JOB
    Milo L. Chapman, B.D., Th.D.

PSALMS
    W. T. Purkiser, M.A., Ph.D.

PROVERBS
    Earl C. Wolf, A.B.

ECCLESIASTES, SONG OF SOLOMON
    A. F. Harper, M.A., Ph.D.

BEACON HILL PRESS OF KANSAS CITY
Kansas City, Missouri

BEACON BIBLE COMMENTARY

In Ten Volumes

I. Genesis; Exodus; Leviticus; Numbers; Deuteronomy

II. Joshua; Judges; Ruth; I and II Samuel; I and II Kings; I and II Chronicles; Ezra; Nehemiah; Esther

III. Job; Psalms; Proverbs; Ecclesiastes; Song of Solomon

IV. Isaiah; Jeremiah; Lamentations; Ezekiel; Daniel

V. Hosea; Joel; Amos; Obadiah; Jonah; Micah; Nahum; Habakkuk; Zephaniah; Haggai; Zechariah; Malachi

VI. Matthew; Mark; Luke

VII. John; Acts

VIII. Romans; I and II Corinthians

IX. Galatians; Ephesians; Philippians; Colossians; I and II Thessalonians; I and II Timothy; Titus; Philemon

X. Hebrews; James; I and II Peter; I, II, and III John; Jude, Revelation

Preface

"All scripture is given by inspiration of God, and is profitable for doctrine, for reproof, for correction, for instruction in righteousness: that the man of God may be perfect, throughly furnished unto all good works" (II Tim. 3:16-17).

We believe in the plenary inspiration of the Bible. God speaks to men through His Word. He hath spoken unto us by His Son. But without the inscripted Word how would we know the Word which was made flesh? He does speak to us by His Spirit, but the Spirit uses the written Word as the vehicle of His revelation, for He is the true Author of the Holy Scriptures. What the Spirit reveals is in agreement with the Word.

The Christian faith derives from the Bible. It is the Foundation for faith, for salvation, and sanctification. It is the Guide for Christian character and conduct. "Thy word is a lamp unto my feet, and a light unto my path" (Ps. 119:105).

The revelation of God and His will for men is adequate and complete in the Bible. The great task of the Church, therefore, is to communicate the knowledge of the Word, to enlighten the eyes of the understanding, and to awaken and to illuminate the conscience that men may learn "to live soberly, righteously, and godly, in this present world." This leads to the possession of that "inheritance [that is] incorruptible, and undefiled, and that fadeth not away, reserved in heaven."

When we consider the translation and interpretation of the Bible, we admit we are guided by men who are not inspired. Human limitation, as well as the plain fact that no scripture is of private or single interpretation, allows variation in the exegesis and exposition of the Bible.

Beacon Bible Commentary is offered in ten volumes with becoming modesty. It does not supplant others. Neither does it purport to be exhaustive or final. The task is colossal. Assignments have been made to thirty-nine of the ablest writers available. They are trained men with serious purpose, deep dedication, and supreme devotion. The sponsors and publishers, as well as the contributors, earnestly pray that this new offering among Bible commentaries will be helpful to preachers, teachers, and laymen in discovering the deeper meaning of God's Word and in unfolding its message to all who hear them.

—G. B. WILLIAMSON

Acknowledgments

Permission to quote from copyrighted material is gratefully acknowledged as follows:

Abingdon Press, *The Interpreter's Bible,* edited by George A. Buttrick, *et al.,* Volumes 3, 4, and 5; and *The Interpreter's Dictionary of the Bible,* edited by George A. Buttrick, *et al.*

Doubleday and Co., Inc., Mitchell Dahood, *Psalms I,* "The Anchor Bible."

Gerald Duckworth and Co., Ltd., T. H. Robinson, *The Poetry of the Old Testament.*

A. J. Holman Co., *The Biblical Expositor,* edited by Carl F. H. Henry.

The Jewish Publication Society, Julius H. Greenstone, *Proverbs with Commentary.*

John Knox Press, *The Layman's Bible Commentary,* edited by Balmer H. Kelly, *et al.*

The Macmillan Company, Edgar Jones, *Proverbs and Ecclesiastes* ("Torch Bible Commentaries").

Moody Press, *The Wycliffe Bible Commentary,* edited by Charles F. Pfeiffer and Everett F. Harrison.

Fleming H. Revell Company, G. Campbell Morgan, *An Exposition of the Whole Bible.*

SCM Press, Norman Snaith, *Hymns of the Temple.*

Society for the Propagation of Christian Knowledge, W. O. E. Oesterley, *The Psalms.*

Tyndale Press, Derek Kidner, *The Proverbs* ("The Tyndale Old Testament Commentaries," D. J. Wiseman, general editor).

Westminster Press, Lawrence E. Toombs, *The Old Testament in Christian Preaching.*

Scripture quotations have been made from the following copyrighted sources:

The Amplified Old Testament. Copyright 1964, Zondervan Publishing House.

The Berkeley Version in Modern English. Copyright 1958, 1959, Zondervan Publishing House.

Quotations and References

Boldface type in the exposition indicates a quotation from the King James Version of the passage under discussion. Readings from other versions are put in quotation marks and the version is indicated.

In scripture references a letter (*a, b,* etc.) indicates a clause within a verse. When no book is named, the book under discussion is understood.

Bibliographical data on a work cited by a writer may be found by consulting the first reference to the work by that writer, or by turning to the bibliography.

The bibliographies are not intended to be exhaustive but are included to provide complete publication data for volumes cited in the text.

References to authors in the text, or inclusion of their books in the bibliography, does not constitute an endorsement of their views. All reading in the field of biblical interpretation should be discriminating and thoughtful.

How to Use "Beacon Bible Commentary"

The Bible is a Book to be read, to be understood, to be obeyed, and to be shared with others. *Beacon Bible Commentary* is planned to help at the points of understanding and sharing.

For the most part, the Bible is its own best interpreter. He who reads it with an open mind and receptive spirit will again and again become aware that through its pages God is speaking *to him.* A commentary serves as a valuable resource when the meaning of a passage is not clear even to the thoughtful reader. Also after one has seen his own meaning in a passage from the Bible, it is rewarding to discover what truth others have found in the same place. Sometimes, too, this will correct possible misconceptions the reader may have formed.

Beacon Bible Commentary has been written to be used with your Bible in hand. Most major commentaries print the text of the Bible at the top of the commentary page. The editors decided against this practice, believing that the average user comes to his commentary from his Bible and hence has in mind the passage in which he is interested. He also has his Bible at his elbow for any necessary reference to the next. To have printed the full text of the Bible in a work of this size would have occupied approximately one-third of the space available. The planners decided to give this space to additional resources for the reader. At the same time, writers have woven into their comments sufficient quotations from the passages under discussion that the reader maintains easy and constant thought contact with the words of the Bible. These quoted words are printed in boldface type for quick identification.

ILLUMINATION FROM RELATED PASSAGES

The Bible is its own best interpreter when a given chapter or a longer section is read to find out what it says. This book is also its own best interpreter when the reader knows what the Bible says in other places about the subject under consideration. The writers and editors of *Beacon Bible Commentary* have constantly striven to give maximum help at this point. Related and carefully chosen cross-references have been included in order that the reader may thus find the Bible interpreted and illustrated by the Bible itself.

Paragraph Treatment

The truth of the Bible is best understood when we grasp the thought of the writer in its sequence and connections. The verse divisions with which we are familiar came into the Bible late (the sixteenth century for the New Testament and the seventeenth century for the Old). They were done hurriedly and sometimes missed the thought pattern of the inspired writers. The same is true of the chapter divisions. Most translations today arrange the words of the sacred writers under our more familiar paragraph structure.

It is under this paragraph arrangement that our commentary writers have approached their task. They have tried always to answer the question, What was the inspired writer saying in this passage? Verse numbers have been retained for easy identification but basic meanings have been outlined and interpreted in the larger and more complete thought forms.

Introduction to Bible Books

The Bible is an open Book to him who reads it thoughtfully. But it opens wider when we gain increased understanding of its human origins. Who wrote this book? Where was it written? When did the writer live? What were the circumstances that caused him to write? Answers to these questions always throw added light on the words of the Scripture.

These answers are given in the Introductions. There also you will find an outline of each book. The Introduction has been written to give an overview of the whole book; to provide you with a dependable road map before you start your trip—and to give you a place of reference when you are uncertain as to which way to turn. Don't ignore the flagman when he waves his warning sign, "See Introduction." At the close of the commentary on each book you will find a bibliography for further study.

Maps and Charts

The Bible was written about people who lived in lands that are foreign and strange to most English-speaking readers. Often better understanding of the Bible depends on better knowledge of Bible geography. When the flagman waves his other sign, "See map," you should turn to the map for a clearer understanding of the locations, distances, and related timing of the experiences of the men with whom God was dealing.

This knowledge of Bible geography will help you to be a better Bible preacher and teacher. Even in the more formal presentation of the sermon it helps the congregation to know that the flight into Egypt was "a journey on foot, some 200 miles to the southwest." In the less formal and smaller groups such as Sunday school classes and prayer meeting Bible study, a large classroom map enables the group to see the locations as well as to hear them mentioned. When you have seen these places on your commentary maps, you are better prepared to share the information with those whom you lead in Bible study.

Charts which list Bible facts in tabular form often make clear historical relationships in the same way that maps help with understanding geography. To see listed in order the kings of Judah or the Resurrection appearances of Jesus often gives clearer understanding of a particular item in the series. These charts are a part of the resources offered in this set.

Beacon Bible Commentary has been written for the new-comer to Bible study and also for those long familiar with the written Word. The writers and editors have probed each chapter, each verse, every clause, phrase, and word in the familiar King James Version. We have probed with the question, What do these words mean? If the answer is not self-evident we have charged ourselves to give the best explanation known to us. How well we have succeeded the reader must judge, but we invite you to explore the explanation of these words or passages that may puzzle you when you are reading God's written Word.

Exegesis and Exposition

Bible commentators often use these words to describe two ways of making clear the meaning of a passage in the Scriptures. *Exegesis* is a study of the original Greek or Hebrew words to understand what meanings those words had when they were used by men and women in Bible times. To know the meaning of the separate words, as well as their grammatical relationship to each other, is one way to understand more clearly what the inspired writer meant to say. You will often find this kind of enriching help in the commentary. But word studies alone do not always give true meaning.

Exposition is a commentator's effort to point out the meaning of a passage as it is affected by any one of several facts known to the writer but perhaps not familiar to the reader. These facts may be (1) the context (the surrounding verses or chapters), (2) the historical background, (3) the related teaching from other parts of the Bible, (4) the significance of these messages from God as they relate to universal facts of human life, (5) the relevance of these truths to unique contemporary human situations. The commentator thus seeks to explain the full meaning of a Bible passage in the light of his own best understanding of God, man, and the world in which we live.

Some commentaries separate the exegesis from this broader basis of explanation. In *Beacon Bible Commentary* writers have combined the exegesis and exposition. Accurate word studies are indispensable to a correct understanding of the Bible. But such careful studies are today so thoroughly reflected in a number of modern English translations that they are often not necessary except to enhance the understanding of the theological meaning of a passage. The writers and editors seek to reflect a true and accurate exegesis at every point, but specific exegetical discussions are introduced chiefly to throw added light on the meaning of a passage, rather than to engage in scholarly discussion.

The Bible is a practical Book. We believe that God inspired holy men of old to declare these truths in order that the readers might better understand and do the will of God. *Beacon Bible Commentary* has been undertaken only for the purpose of helping men to find more effectively God's will for them as revealed in the Scripture—to find that will and to act upon that knowledge.

Helps for Bible Preaching and Teaching

We have said that the Bible is a Book to be shared. Christian preachers and teachers since the first century have sought to convey the gospel message by reading and explaining selected passages of Scripture. *Beacon Bible Commentary* seeks to encourage this kind of expository preaching and teaching. The set contains more than a thousand brief expository outlines that have been used by outstanding Bible teachers and preachers. Both writers and editors have assisted in contributing or selecting these homiletical suggestions. It is hoped that the outlines will suggest ways in which the reader will want to try to open the Word of God to his class or congregation. Some of these analyses of preachable passages have been contributed by our contemporaries. When the outlines have appeared in print, authors and references are given in order that the reader may go to the original source for further help.

In the Bible we find truth of the highest order. Here is given to us, by divine inspiration, the will of God for our lives. Here we have sure guidance in all things necessary to our relationships to God and under Him to our fellowman. Because these eternal truths come to us in human language and through human minds, they need to be put into fresh words as languages change and as thought patterns are modified. In *Beacon Bible Commentary* we have sought to help make the Bible a more effective Lamp to the paths of men who journey in the twentieth century.

A. F. Harper

Abbreviations and Explanations

The Books of the Bible

Gen.	Job	Jonah	I or II Cor.
Exod.	Ps.	Mic.	Gal.
Lev.	Prov.	Nah.	Eph.
Num.	Eccles.	Hab.	Phil.
Deut.	Song of Sol.	Zeph.	Col.
Josh.	Isa.	Hag.	I or II Thess.
Judg.	Jer.	Zech.	I or II Tim.
Ruth	Lam.	Mal.	Titus
I or II Sam.	Ezek.	Matt.	Philem.
I or II Kings	Dan.	Mark	Heb.
I or II Chron.	Hos.	Luke	Jas.
Ezra	Joel	John	I or II Pet.
Neh.	Amos	Acts	I, II, or III John
Esther	Obad.	Rom.	Jude
			Rev.

Vulg.	The Vulgate
LXX	The Septuagint
ASV	American Standard Revised Version
RSV	Revised Standard Version
Amp. OT	Amplified Old Testament
NASB	New American Standard Bible
NEB	New English Bible
Berk.	The Berkeley Version
BB	The Basic Bible Containing the Old and New Testaments in Basic English
Anchor	*The Anchor Bible,* translation
Harrison	*The Psalms for Today:* A New Translation from the Hebrew into Current English, by Roland Kenneth Harrison
IB	Interpreter's Bible
IDB	The Interpreter's Dictionary of the Bible
ISBE	International Standard Bible Encyclopedia
NBC	The New Bible Commentary
NBD	The New Bible Dictionary
BBC	Beacon Bible Commentary
HDB	Hastings' Dictionary of the Bible

c.	chapter	OT	Old Testament
cc.	chapters	NT	New Testament
v.	verse	Heb.	Hebrew
vv.	verses	Gk.	Greek

Table of Contents

VOLUME III

The Book of

JOB

Milo L. Chapman

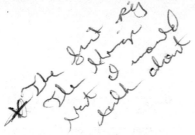

Introduction

Men have grappled long and seriously with the problem and meaning of human suffering. The Book of Job is the most brilliant of all such efforts which are recorded in the literature of mankind.

The narrative concerns a man whose name furnishes the title of the book. It opens with a prose prologue which describes Job as a wealthy and upright man. Through a series of calamities, all of his possessions, together with his children, are stripped from him. The question raised in the prologue is whether or not Job will retain his integrity in the face of such suffering. We are informed that he came out victorious—"In all this did not Job sin with his lips" (2:10).

In addition to setting the stage for further discussion as to the meaning and significance of suffering, the prologue also furnishes the cast of characters. God is the Hebrew *Yahweh*, who is the Lord of heaven and earth.[1] Satan appears in the role of Job's adversary. Job, the hero, is a wealthy citizen of the land of Uz. He is joined by three of his friends: Eliphaz from Teman, Bildad from Shuah, and Zophar from Na'ameh. These men come to bring comfort to their old friend.

The main body of the book is made up of dialogue between the four friends. The "comforters" are certain that Job's suffering is caused by some sin which their friend has been harboring. They are sure that humility and repentance will clear up the matter. Job on his part insists that, while he has the normal weaknesses of humanity, he has committed no sin which would cause such misfortune as that which he suffers. He does not agree with his friends that sin and suffering are invariably linked together in direct cause-and-effect sequence. It would appear at this point that the poet-author intends that Job should be the victor in the argument with his comforters.

A youthful bystander named Elihu has been silent and unmentioned. After three rounds of disputation by the others he intervenes in the discussion. He is outraged at Job for his im-

---

[1]*Yahweh* is regularly used in the prologue and epilogue for the name of Deity. Elsewhere in the book God is referred to by the use of *El* or its derivatives. In several instances in the dialogues, *Shaddai*, Almighty, is used, usually as a parallel alternative term to *El*.

pious attitude toward the providence of God. He is equally indignant at the three friends for their inability to convince Job of his guilt. Through four discourses, never answered by Job, Elihu expresses his strong opposition to the sentiments of Job and disagrees with him with regard to the meaning of suffering. Elihu, although maintaining the basic position of Job's other counselors, emphasizes the providence of God in all human events and the disciplinary value of suffering. Thus he extols the greatness of God. Against this background he affirms that the affliction of man is for his instruction. If Job were humble and trusting, he would find that God is leading him into a good life.

Then the Lord speaks out of the storm. At last Job's repeated request that God would appear and give meaning to his suffering is answered. However, God does not mention Job's individual problem, nor does He address himself directly to the problems which Job has raised. Rather, He makes clear who He is and the relationship which Job, or any man, should have to Him. In light of God's glory and power Job is overwhelmed and humbled. When he sees God in His true light, Job repents of his impudent words and attitude.

The epilogue describes how the repentant and humbled Job is restored to double his former prosperity. With friends and family restored to him, Job lived a long and happy life—in fact, an additional 140 years. Then he died, "being old and full of days" (42:17).

A. Historicity of the Book

Very often the questions are asked, Is Job a real man? or, Is the Book of Job real history? These two questions need not be given the same answer.

That there was a Job with the reputation of being righteous is attested by a reference to him in Ezek. 14:14. In all likelihood the basic narrative in the book is based upon a real character by this name.

One need not assume by virtue of this fact, however, that the Book of Job is describing historical event throughout. Only by special revelation could the author have had access to information concerning the two scenes in heaven described in cc. 1 and 2. Further, it is evident that the prologue sets the stage for the discussion which the author has in mind. The dialogue between the friends is highly stylized poetry, not at all like spontaneous discussion.

These and other factors have led to the general opinion that the basic narrative of the book is an old story of a real man who suffered immensely. An unnamed author used this material to discuss the meaning of human suffering and God's relationship to it. This the author has done brilliantly.

B. The Text

One of the primary problems presented to the serious student of the Book of Job is the condition of the original text. At many places the meaning of the text is difficult if not impossible to ascertain, and so lacking in continuity that translators are forced to make some conjectural emendations in order to make sense of the material. That this is true can be readily seen by comparing the variety of meanings given some sections by modern translators.

It is also acknowledged that the vocabulary employed by the author of this book is the broadest found in the Old Testament. Numerous words appear once in this book and nowhere else in the Bible. Comparison with languages of similar origin helps to some extent in discovering these meanings. Discoveries at Ugarit of some ancient texts have given assistance in understandin some of the terms. But the problem still remains to such an extent that this is one of the most difficult books in the Old Testament to translate.[2]

C. Integrity of the Text

The composite nature of the Book of Job is generally accepted.[3] The prologue (1:1—2:13), as well as the introduction to the Elihu speeches (32:1-5), and the epilogue (42:7-17) are in prose. The remainder is in poetic form. This fact is readily seen by the English reader in a modern translation such as Moffatt or the RSV, which put both prose and poetry in proper form. While this alternation of prose and poetry in itself does not prove the composite character of the text, it does suggest it. Perhaps what occurred was that the poet-author used an ancient

[2]For a more complete discussion of the language and the text of Job see Marvin H. Pope, "Job," *The Anchor Bible,* ed. William Foxwell Albright and David Noel Freeman (Garden City, New York: Doubleday & Company, Inc., 1965), XV, xxxix ff. In this commentary the King James Version is used, since it is the translation most commonly in use. In the comments upon the text, however, appropriate attention will be given to more recent translations and information which help to give understanding of the text.

[3]Edward Young, although stoutly affirming that "any view which would destroy the unity of the book must be rejected," admits that "certain portions . . . may exhibit . . . linguistic revision" (*Introduction to the Old Testament* [Grand Rapids: Wm. B. Eerdmans Publishing Co., 1949], p. 313).

narrative concerning Job to furnish the setting for the discussion between Job and his friends. If so, the old story is represented by the prose prologue and perhaps the epilogue.

It is commonly held that the epilogue does not belong to the major argument of the book. Job has spent much of his time denying that material prosperity is the reward of righteousness. Therefore, to have the book end with the Lord giving Job "twice as much as he had before" (42:10) seems incongruous. When this view is held, it is assumed that the hand of a later editor devised this ending to suit his own convictions concerning the issues raised.

However, Gray[4] argues strongly that the epilogue rightfully belongs to the original material on the basis that the real purpose of the author is simply to maintain that man can be good without being rewarded for it. It is at this point that Job is the victor. He accepts both good and ill from God without rebelling against Him, even though he does ask why, and sometimes bitterly assumes that God is against him without cause. Job did not demand restoration of his prosperity as a condition of serving God. That which he asked was a vindication of his character. When this is achieved, it is not inconsistent with the author's purpose and argument to permit the narrative to have a materially happy ending for Job. The sufferings inflicted upon him were for a particular purpose. There was no need for the suffering to be made perpetual after the purpose had been achieved.

Another portion of the book, though beautiful in poetic structure and lofty in thought, is frequently rejected as not being an which constitutes c. 28. As it stands, it is interjected between original part of the book. That is the poem in praise of wisdom two portions of Job's speech in which he complains bitterly of his lot. Furthermore, the attitude of the wisdom poem, if truly coming from Job, would make unnecessary much of that which God says to him later in the book.

The Elihu speeches (32:6—37:24) may also be an addition to the original book. In support of this view it may be noted briefly that Elihu is not introduced among the friends of Job at the beginning of the narrative, nor is he recognized among them in the epilogue. Furthermore, his observations add little that is new to the discussion. They are primarily an impassioned

    [4]George Buchanan Gray and Samuel R. Driver, *The Book of Job*, I ("The International Critical Commentary"; New York: Charles Scribner's Sons, 1921), lxii.

reiteration of the same principles which have been advocated by the three other friends.[5]

Another portion of the book which is most frequently held to be an interpolation is the description of Behemoth and Leviathan (40:15—41:34). Evidence offered is that these descriptions are unusually detailed in relationship to the rest of the speech and that they reflect ideas about creatures taken from popular thought.[6] The case against this portion of the book is not decisive.

D. Authorship

It is generally agreed among Old Testament scholars that a search for the author of this book is doomed to failure. Nowhere in the book itself is there any indication as to the identity of the man who created this literary masterpiece. Not only is the book silent as to its origin, but there is no independent biblical suggestion made concerning its authorship. Ezekiel (14:14, 20) speaks of the man Job as one who has a reputation for righteousness; and James (5:11) knows him as a paragon of patience. Both of these references are concerning the individual named Job. They do not deal with the identity of the author of the book.

Numerous suggestions have been made concerning those who could have written the book. Among these are Job himself, Moses, and a variety of unnamed persons ranging in time from the period of the patriarchs to the third century B.C.

Even though the author's name may never be known to us, some qualities of the man can be ascertained through the work which he has left. Whoever he may have been, he was one of the world's great literary figures. Any list of great masterworks of literature would certainly contain the Book of Job. In fact, many would place it first on the list. Alfred Tennyson spoke of Job as the greatest poem in ancient or modern times, while Thomas Carlyle said there was nothing either in or out of the Bible of equal literary worth.

The author of Job must either have suffered greatly in his

[5]Admitting the composite nature of the book as it has come down to us does not destroy its value nor does it need to lessen the reader's confidence in its divine inspiration. If the Spirit of God could inspire one author, He could certainly inspire and direct other writers or compilers. See on this issue in general the very fine statement of Samuel A. Cartledge, *A Conservative Introduction to the Old Testament* (Athens: University of Georgia Press, 1944), p. 44.

[6]For further discussion see Samuel Terrien, "Job" (Exegesis), *The Interpreter's Bible,* ed. George A. Buttrick, *et al.,* III (New York: Abingdon-Cokesbury Press, 1954), 1186.

own life or have had unusual capacity for sympathy and empathy with those who have suffered. Along with this great sensitivity he was deeply religious. He had unusual insight into human nature and was well acquainted with the world in which he lived—the world of nature, of ideas, and of literature.

It is not certain that the author was an Israelite, although this point is contested. Those who believe that he was not a Jew[7] point to the fact that the name of the God of Israel, Yahweh, is rarely mentioned except in the prose prologue and epilogue, while in the poetic dialogue terms are employed which were of general use among the neighboring peoples surrounding Israel. In addition to this, it is pointed out that no characteristically Jewish institution or custom is referred to, and that the setting of the story is Uz (Edom, see map 1), a land of the East (1:3).

On the other hand, those who see the author as being an Israelite point to the fact that it is Israel's sacred literature in which the story is preserved and canonized. Furthermore, even though "wisdom" literature is known from ancient times throughout the Near East, the theological ideas of the Book of Job fit better into a biblical background and frame of reference than anywhere else.

We may assume that the unknown author of the book used a historical man "of Uz" named Job, well-known to all for his reputation of suffering and integrity, to be the hero of his dialogue. Other questions of authorship must of necessity remain unresolved.

E. Date of Writing

The time of writing of this book remains as perplexing a problem as that of authorship. Dates have been suggested which range from about the eighteenth century to the third century B.C.

The man Job as described in the book represents a type of life and culture which is most nearly matched in the patriarchal period. For example, it is stated that Job lived after the restoration of his health and wealth for 140 years, this in addition to the years which he had lived prior to his misfortune. No such life expectancy as this appears in the biblical narrative after the patriarchal period. Job's wealth was largely in terms of flocks and herds, as was true of the patriarchs. Job himself offers sacrifice for the family, as was the custom with the patriarchs. However, the offering for sin and other Mosaic practices he does not seem to know.

[7] Cf. Robert H. Pfeiffer, *Introduction to the Old Testament* (New York: Harper & Brothers Publishers, 1941), pp. 678 ff.

24

This kind of consideration causes many scholars to believe that the prologue (1:1—3:1) and epilogue (42:7-16) where this information is given reflects an older record which formed the basis for the poetic dialogue which was composed much later.

There is no allusion in the Book of Job that gives help in ascertaining a date for its composition. Therefore the only means to fix a date would be its literary relationship to other datable materials. Unfortunately there is not much of this kind of material to give precise aid. Ezekiel (14:14-20) knows of the man by this name, but it is not certain that he knows of the Book of Job. Jeremiah's curse on the day of his birth (20:14) and that of Job (3:1-26) are strikingly similar, but it is impossible to say which poet may have had the other's work in mind. Malachi 3:13-18 could easily have been written with the Book of Job in mind. Robert H. Pfeiffer argues that Job is earlier than the suffering-servant poem of Isaiah (52:13—53:12) on the basis that the vicarious suffering in Isaiah is theologically more advanced than Job in its understanding of the meaning of undeserved suffering,[8] but this is an argument based on a dubious premise. The discovery of a Targum of Job from the Qumran Caves proves that the book was in circulation for some time prior to the first century B.C.

The date of the Book of Job remains an open question with most opinions currently placing the dialogue in the seventh century B.C.[9]

F. Place in the Canon

The Book of Job comes in the third section of the Hebrew canon, the *Kethubim, Hagiographa,* or Writings. The order within this section has varied in different traditions. Presently Job is placed between Proverbs and the Song of Songs (Song of Solomon) in the Hebrew canon. Our English translations place Job between Esther and Psalms, making Job the first of the three great poetic books. This is the order used by Jerome in his Vulgate translation, and was subsequently fixed by the Council of Trent (1545-63) in its pronouncement on the canon of scripture.

[8]*Op. cit.,* p. 476. He dates this portion of Isaiah at about 540 B.C. at the close of the Babylonian exile.

[9]For a more detailed discussion of the evidences see Pfeiffer, *op. cit.,* pp. 675 ff.; Pope, *op. cit.,* pp. xxx ff. Young, *op. cit.,* p. 309, contends for a date during the reign of Solomon. However, his arguments are weak and inconclusive.

Outline

Section I Prologue: Job's Calamities

Job 1:1—3:26

The Book of Job begins with a prose prologue which introduces the hero and victim of the book along with the friends who come to give him comfort and advice. Included in the prologue are two scenes where the heavenly beings are assembled. Opportunity is given for the reader to gain information about Job and his relationship to God, which set forth the conditions against which further discussions take place.

A. Job's Fame and Righteousness, 1:1-5

The derivation of the name **Job** (*'iyyobh*) is not certain, but it is most frequently equated with a root which means "to hate" or "to be an enemy." It is possible that the passive sense, "to be persecuted," is the best meaning of the noun form used here. The Arabic form of the name seems to come from the root meaning "to return or repent"—the penitent one or, by extension of idea, the pious one.

Job lived in the **land of Uz** (1). Again, it is not possible to achieve certainty as to geographic location, but it would seem according to such biblical passages as Gen. 10:23 and Jer. 25:23 that Uz is to be associated with Aram. In an addition to the Book of Job which the Septuagint preserves, it is stated that Job lived in the land of Uz on the borders of Edom and Arabia (see map 1).

The Hebrew term (*tam*) used in the statement, **That man was perfect,** is one which is of a great deal of interest to the holiness theologian. The primary meaning of the root term is completeness of character. In Job's case it does not mean perfect in an absolute sense. Job claims that he is *tam* (27:5), but he also admits to the common frailty of humanity (9:1 ff.; 13:26). That which Job maintains is the basic integrity of his character. It is all of one piece. He has a single eye and heart (cf. Matt. 6:22; Acts 2:46). Job's heart is not divided (Ps. 12:2). Job's will belongs to God, and this he will not give up (2:9-10; 27:5).[1] In

---

[1]See Johs. Pedersen, *Israel, Its Life and Culture* (London: Oxford University Press, 1946), I, 336 ff. Also Driver, *op. cit.*, pp. 2 ff.

addition to being perfect, it is affirmed that Job **was upright, and one that feared God, and eschewed** (turned away from) **evil.** There was no lack in Job. He met all of the requirements in his day of being a model man. In the narrative these qualities in Job are not cast in terms of one man's evaluation of another, but are the regard with which God holds Job.

Job's possessions, including his **sons and . . . daughters,** are listed to give proof of the righteousness of the man (2-3). The major point of discussion between Job and his friends will be the meaning of material prosperity. It was popularly believed that family and flocks were blessings of God upon a righteous person. Job's wealth classified him as being in God's good graces to an exceptional degree. The numbers used (seven, three, and five) enumerating Job's children and his flocks are further expressions of his completeness and perfection.

Each son had his own house. The daughters probably lived in their father's house. Each son held a feast, **every one on his day** (4). It is not clear here whether a birthday feast is intended or whether, since there were seven sons, the author is describing a life so ideal that Job's children were constantly feasting and entertaining each other in harmonious fellowship. In any event, Job's piety is illustrated by the fact that he customarily **offered burnt offerings** (5) to make atonement for his children, just in case they might have sinned inadvertantly or secretly. The phrase **and sanctified them** illustrates a common OT use of sanctification as a ceremonial hallowing or setting apart (cf. BBC, II, 34).

B. THE DISCUSSION BETWEEN GOD AND SATAN, 1:6—2:10

After the description of total happiness, prosperity, and piety which Job enjoyed the author shows a scene in heaven. The divine court convenes. One may imagine God surrounded by celestial beings ready to "do his pleasure" (Ps. 103:21). Into this group comes one named the Adversary, who is cynical about the reasons for Job's piety.

1. God Trusts Job's Uprightness (1:6-12)

The sons of God (6) were conceived of as divine beings or angels as in contrast to human beings. Their function in general was to minister to God and perform His purposes. In the Book of Job they are described as being those to whom a person might turn for sympathetic understanding (5:1); they form the council of God (15:8); they are interpreters or messengers between

God and man (33:23). They seem to have been present at the
beginning of the creation of the world (38:7). They are referred
to as being "saints" (lit., holy ones), understood as referring
primarily to their attendance upon God (5:1; 15:15). When contrasted with God they are not wise nor are they entirely dependable (4:8; 15:15). That is, they are definitely of a lower order.
They are not gods.

Satan came also (6). In the Hebrew the definite article
accompanying the word for **Satan** would imply that the term had
not yet become a proper name. The literal meaning is "the Adversary," as appears in the marginal reading. It is the function
of testing which he performs here. Some have understood the
Satan of Job to be one of God's messengers who represents God
in His trying or sifting providence,[2] and not the independent
tempter of men nor the "prince of devils" of the New Testament
(Matt. 12:24). He would not then be the one going through the
earth "as a roaring lion . . . seeking whom he may devour" (I Pet.
5:8). **Came also among them** is literally "in the midst of them."
Satan (the satan) was not particularly out of place among the
other celestial beings, although the term **also** is used in relation
to both of his appearances. He is singled out as being different in
function, but here he appears in the heavenly court, presumably
to report upon his activities along with the others.

God's question to Satan, **Whence comest thou?** (7) was not
in surprise at his coming but as an introduction to the conversation between them for the benefit of the reader. His words to
Adam, "Where art thou?" are similar in purpose.

The scope of Satan's (the satan's) activity is described as
going to and fro in the earth. He has been assiduous and faithful
to his duties. The same phrase is used with reference to the eyes
of the Lord in describing His rapid and complete survey of men
(II Chron. 16:9). Angelic emissaries elsewhere sent to report on
conditions go "to and fro through the earth," or as the RSV translates it, "These are they whom the Lord has sent to patrol the
earth" (Zech. 1:10-11).

Hast thou considered my servant Job? (8) calls Satan's
attention to Job as an example of one who is upright. The
author's estimate of Job's character and his reputation among his
fellows is here confirmed by the Lord.

The key to understanding the argument of the book lies in

[2]A. B. Davidson, *The Book of Job* ("The Cambridge Bible for Schools
and Colleges"; Cambridge: University Press, 1899), p. 7.

the question phrased by Satan, **Doth Job fear God for nought?** **(9)** Will a man serve God in righteousness without reward?

Satan not only raises the above question, but he observes that Job has been rewarded with everything possible—**Hast not thou made an hedge about him?** **(10)** He and his household have been protected from every conceivable danger, everything that he has done has been **blessed,** and **his substance is increased.** Unusual success is indicated in all that Job has undertaken. Such prosperity, Satan charges, is the reward which God has given to Job for his fidelity.

After accusing God of buying the loyalty of Job, Satan makes the charge that a reversal in Job's happy condition would cause his defection: **But put forth thine hand . . . and he will curse thee to thy face (11).** That is, he would make a complete and open renunciation of God and the pious way of life.

God does not abandon Job to Satan, but He gives permission for him to test Job's willingness to remain loyal and devoted: **All that he hath is in thy power** (12). Note, however, that a limit of testing is set. **Only upon himself put not forth thine hand.** With such a commission Satan quickly sets out to accomplish his purposes, no doubt with great confidence in the success of his venture.

2. *Job's Possessions Taken* (1:13-22)

The first trial of Job has to do with stripping him of all his possessions. The reader has been prepared for that which is about to occur, but Job had not. He knew nothing of the conversation between God and Satan. His only knowledge was that which servants brought to him.

In the first instance a sole survivor from an attack by the **Sabeans** (15) informs Job that all of his **oxen** and **asses** have been stolen by the marauders, and in addition the slaves in attendance upon the herds were killed. The Sabeans were an Arab tribe living in the southwest section of the Arabian peninsula which roughly corresponds to the area of modern Yemen. They traded in spices, gold, and a variety of precious stones. An encampment of Sabeans near the borders of Edom, the general area in which Job lived, would not be unlikely.[3]

---

[3]For a good summary of available information about Saba see the article by G. W. Van Beeck, "Sabeans," *The Interpreter's Dictionary of the Bible*, ed. George A. Buttrick, *et al.* (Nashville: Abingdon Press, 1962), IV, 144 ff.

The second stroke of misfortune is a **fire of God** (16), probably lightning, which destroyed all of his **sheep, and the servants who attended them.** Notice that a pattern is established in describing the loss. First a servant appears who says, **I only am escaped alone to tell thee;** and **while he was yet speaking, there came also another** (16-17). The destruction described in each case is complete. The sequence of events is rapid.

The third misfortune is the taking of **the camels** by **three bands** of **Chaldeans** (17). These represent marauding nomad bands from the country to the east of Job's home. Thus he was being attacked from every quarter. Again, complete and sudden calamity is described. The Chaldeans divided themselves into three bands and surrounded the servants of Job. There was no means of escape for man or beast, save one who reported to his master.

Camels have long been associated with the desert and semi-desert regions of Arabia. They were used as beasts of burden and for wool. The Mosaic law does not permit the use of the camel for food (Lev. 11:4; Deut. 14:7), but they were used for both meat and milk by the Arabs. It is not known exactly when they were domesticated, but there is evidence of their use early in the second millennium B.C. The loss to Job of 3,000 camels would represent a serious loss indeed.

The fourth disaster is announced as the others. Job's children were all together in one of their celebrations (cf. 4-5). **There came a great wind** (19) which struck **the four corners of the house** where they were. This would seem to describe a whirlwind or hurricane coming out of the desert. The storm was so severe that the house was destroyed and all of its inhabitants were killed. Thus Job in rapid sequence is stripped of wealth and family. One needs only to reflect upon the anguish of women such as Sarah, Rachel, and Hannah in their childlessness to understand something of the loss represented by this last tragic event. It goes beyond the natural grief at the loss of family. Job in this case was cut off from the future. No son would bear his name. There would be none to remember him, and no one close to mourn his passing.

Job now had lost all of his possessions and his children. Satan had been certain that no one would remain steadfast in his devotion and worship of God under such circumstances. He was mistaken. Job went through all of the normal expressions of grief. **He rent his mantle** (20), the outer garment worn especially by nobility or men in high positions. This action perhaps symbolized his broken heart (Joel 2:13). He **shaved his head**—part of the usual practice in mourning rites, as shown in passages such as Isa. 15:2; Jer. 7:29; Ezek. 7:18; Amos 8:10. There is, however, some limitation to this kind of practice contained in the law (Lev. 19:27-28; Deut. 14:1). **He fell down upon the ground, and worshipped;** that is, he prostrated himself in an attitude of humility and submission.

Verse 21 shows the complete acquiescence to the will of God which characterizes Job, and which is a mark of the fundamental integrity which he maintains. Even though this statement from his lips may be a "a formula of submission,"[4] it represents Job as blessing God instead of cursing or rebelling against Him. Man is in the hands of God. God is to be honored in evil times as well as in the good.

In all this (22)—both in that which happened to Job and in that which Job said and did—there was no expression of wrongdoing: **Job sinned not, nor charged God foolishly** ("attributed folly to God," marg.). He found in God no inappropriate, reproachable, or blameworthy action.

In 1:18-22 we find "Sorrow That Worships." (1) The vindication of sorrow, 20; (2) Loss and sorrow as the law of life, **Naked came I out of my mother's womb,** 21; (3) Recognition of God in the law, **The Lord gave, and the Lord hath taken away,** 21; (4) Thankful resignation to God's loving administration, **Blessed be the name of the Lord,** 21 (A. Maclaren).

3. *The Final Test of Job's Integrity* (2:1-10)

The previous scene in heaven (1:6-12) is repeated. Satan (the satan; see comments on 1:6-7) had failed in his initial attempt to prove Job's selfish interest in fidelity to God. Now a conversation is again held between God and Satan regarding that which should follow. Both recognize that Job has passed the first test. He remains **perfect and . . . upright** (3). One interesting variation from the first celestial scene is what God says regarding His own motivation in permitting Job to be tested. **Thou** (Satan) **movedst me against him, to destroy him without cause.** Job's innocence now demonstrates that fact.

The expression **Skin for skin** (4) would appear to be a part of an old proverbial saying whose derivation cannot be deter-

---

[4]Pope, *op. cit.*, p. 16.

mined. Its meaning, however, is made clear by the remaining portion of Satan's statement: **All that a man hath will he give for his life.** That which has gone on before is not sufficient to test a man thoroughly. Job himself has been untouched. **Touch his bone and his flesh** (5), strike him in his own physical being, and the outcome will be entirely different. Satan here reasons that not only is Job pious because it pays him to be, but now he also charges that Job is completely selfish. Strike him in that which is uniquely his—his healthy body—and **he will curse thee to thy face.**

Again God permits Job to be tested. Satan may do as he pleases so long as he saves Job's life. The test may be real and it may be extreme, but it must fall short of killing Job.

With this permission, Satan **smote Job with sore boils** (7). In times past the most generally agreed identification of the affliction described by this statement was that it is a kind of leprosy, elephantiasis. The conjecture is made because the Hebrew term, *shehin,* in the Bible represents a very serious skin disease. It is the same malady described in Deut. 28:35: "The Lord shall smite thee in the knees, and in the legs, with a sore botch that cannot be healed, from the sole of thy foot unto the top of thy head." N. H. Tsur-Sinai says, "Our text, however, does not mean to describe any known illness—which is why commentators have tried in vain to identify Job's ailment from references in the book—but an unidentified disease, the disease of diseases, comprising in fact every suffering in the world."[5]

The extent of Job's affliction can be understood more easily by observing the descriptive statements from the book itself regarding his suffering, although it is to be remembered that these are poetic rather than scientific descriptions. The infection must have created intense itching, which Job attempted to alleviate by scraping himself with broken pieces of pottery (8).[6] He was so disfigured by the disease that his friends did not recognize him (2:12). The sores, which apparently bred worms, alternately crusted over and broke open and ran (7:5). He was bothered with recurring dreams and terror (7:14), so that he could not sleep (7:4). His skin became gangrenous (30:30). Pain gnawed at his bones until they seemed to be on fire (30:17,

[5]*The Book of Job* (Jerusalem: Kiryath Sepher, Ltd., 1957), p. 25.

[6]M. H. Pope, *op. cit.,* p. 21, thinks that the scraping with a potsherd was a form of flagellation expressing grief.

30). With such torment death would have been welcome, but his life was maintained even against his will (3:20 f.).[7]

He sat upon the ashes, literally, **among the ashes** (8). Probably he sat upon the *mazbalah,* the place outside of the village where rubbish and dung were thrown. From time to time this would be burned over. As time went on, such practice would create a mound. Beggars and those stricken with infectious disease would congregate there to beg for alms from those who passed by.

Then said his wife . . . curse God, and die (9). Job's wife had personally survived the calamities which so nearly destroyed her husband. A variety of reactions have been recorded by those who comment upon her attitude toward Job's affliction. Some see in her a second Eve tempting her husband to his destruction. Some think her expression represents scorn and ridicule designed to deepen the suffering already endured by Job. Others see in her a woman who has also suffered the torture of losing everything which gives meaning to life and therefore she strikes out at Job as the cause of her misfortune. Perhaps, however, she is motivated by kindness. Maintaining integrity is of no value, she reasons, when God has apparently abandoned Job. Therefore Job should turn against God in the hope that He might withdraw completely from Job and let him die—get it over with mercifully.

If this does represent additional temptation, Job resisted it as well. His wife's words are **foolish** (10). God is sovereign. Therefore one may expect **evil** at God's hands as well as **good.** This affirmation is made against the common assumption that God is responsible for all that takes place in the world (see I Sam. 16:14; Isa. 45:6). Thus Job **did not sin with his lips;** he remained faithful and trusting, thereby proving once more his spiritual integrity.

C. Job's Friends Come to Condole Him, 2:11-13

His **three friends** (11) eventually heard of the serious plight of Job. They came from their respective places to give what comfort they could. There was **Eliphaz,** a name which could mean either "God is fine gold" or "God crushes"; he came from Teman. This area is generally referred to as Edom and is known for its great wisdom (cf. Gen. 36:4, 10-12; Jer. 49:7; see map 1).

---

[7]Cf. Davidson, *op. cit.,* p. 14.

There was **Bildad**—"beloved of the Lord"—who came from the tribe of Shuah, associated with Aramean nomads who migrated into the southeast of Palestine (Gen. 25:1-6). Also there was **Zophar**—the meaning of which is uncertain. It may have meant "twittering bird," perhaps "goatlike jumper," or "sharp nail." He came from Na'ameh, which may be Djebel-el-Na'ameh in the northwestern portion of Arabia. This term is used in the OT only in connection with Zophar.

They knew him not (12) when they first saw him sitting outside the village on the refuse heap, so marred was his appearance from the effects of his disease. Seeing his misery, their immediate reaction was to show their grief and sympathy through the age-old custom of tearing their clothes and sprinkling **dust upon their heads.** So stunned and overwhelmed were the friends at the turn in the affairs of Job that they sat with him for **seven days** without saying **a word.** In this fashion they expressed their concern and deep sympathy for him in the same manner that the dead are mourned (Gen. 50:10; I Sam. 31:13).

D. Job Laments the Day of His Birth, 3:1-26

1. *He Curses the Day He Was Born* (3:1-10)

After seven days of mourning with his friends it is Job who breaks the silence. He **cursed his day** (1), that is, the day of his birth. The words Job speaks do not seem to be addressed either to his friends or to God. Rather they are a soliloquy of despair. Both **day** and **night** (3)—the day of his birth and the night of his conception—are personified and wished out of existence. Then follows a series of curses against both the day and the night in question.

Let not God regard it (4) is, literally, seek after it. It is Job's wish that his birthday be cast completely from the mind of God and therefore be banished from existence. **Darkness** and **death** (5) are here, as elsewhere in Scripture, used as being symbolically equivalent to each other. In the curse, **Let the blackness of the day terrify it,** the word for **blackness** is in the plural form. This would suggest that all of the means for making darkness appear during the daytime were in mind, such as an eclipse of the sun, terrifying dark storms, and perhaps magical or supernatural ways of hiding the sun.

The night of Job's conception should have a similar fate. **Let it not be joined** (6) is better rendered, Let it not rejoice

35

among **the days of the year** (see RSV), nor be numbered in **the months. Let that night be solitary** (7) is, literally, Let it be sterile or barren. **Let no joyful voice come therein** is the exact outcome envisioned in v. 3, where the conception and the birth of a male child are decried. That the author speaks throughout this portion of his poem as though conception and birth take place at the same time should be considered poetic license. **Let them curse** (8) refers to the popular belief that magicians or sorcerers had the ability to put a curse or a charm into effect (see the story of Balaam, Num. 22:6, 12). **Raise up their mourning** is an obscure allusion. The Hebrew refers to Leviathan. Probably the author had in mind the popular mythology of his day. Leviathan belonged to the world of chaos. It was thought that he was capable of creating an eclipse by covering or swallowing the sun and moon. This verse then would refer to those who are capable of cursing days and arousing Leviathan to bring about darkness and therefore effectively destroying the day. Verse 9 then is a repetition of this wish for the elimination from existence of the fateful day-night of his birth-conception, because **the doors of my mother's womb** (10) were not **shut.** It would have been better that everything had ceased rather than that he should have been born and lived to see such anguish and destruction in his life.

2. *He Wishes That He Had Been Born Dead* (3:11-19)

Lacking the ability to roll back time and cancel out the events which led to his birth, Job turns to the next phase of his lament, **Why died I not from the womb?** (11) Many babies are stillborn; why could he not have had the good fortune to be one of them? The **knees** of the midwife and **breasts** (12) of his mother should have failed to preserve the newborn child. Had death been his lot from the very beginning, then his highest hopes now would have been achieved long ago—**then had I been at rest** (13).

From vv. 14 through 19 observations are made upon the fact that all men are equal when death strikes them. **Kings** (14), the rich (15), **the wicked** (17) all are past trouble and **the weary be at rest.** Moffatt renders the thought of **desolate places** (14) as "kings . . . who build pyramids for themselves." No prisoner is any longer bothered by those who would oppress him (18), and even the slave is free from his **master** (19). In his despair Job can only hope for the release which death would bring. Even

36

with death-desiring expressions as strong as these, Job never contemplates suicide. God is the Giver and Sustainer of life, and man is powerless to act against God's providence in this matter. That this is true is shown in the portion of his lament which follows.

3. *He Wonders Why Life Is Maintained* (3:20-26)

Job was given **light,** he was brought into **life** (20), he is lost and God has him **hedged in** (23), all against his will or at least with no opportunity for him to exercise choice in the matter. In his misery he longs **for death.** Death would be like **hid treasures** for which to search, or something over which to **rejoice exceedingly** (21-22). But even this is denied to Job. Moffatt interprets the first part of 23, "Why does God give light to a man at his wits' end?" Job's misery has become so great that his **roarings** (expressions of agony) **are poured out like the waters** (24) in a broad, unbroken stream. So difficult has his life become that all he need do is to fear additional agony, and it happens (25). Thus Job had no surcease from trouble. He had no opportunity for safety, for rest, nor for quiet. **Yet trouble came** (26) can properly be translated, "Trouble keeps on coming."

Job's soliloquy comes at the beginning of the disputation in which he engages with his friends. The depth of his suffering is matched by the power of the poem. Rarely has a poet achieved such beauty of expression and revealed such depth of feeling and emotion as that portrayed here. Job is a human being pressed to the limit of his endurance. Bitterly he complains of his lot and eagerly yearns to be done with life.

Section II Job Debates the Meaning
of His Suffering

Job 4:1—31:40

The major argument of the book takes the form of formal discourses by Job and his friends. These are organized into cycles. Each of the friends speaks and is in turn answered by Job. This happens three times, with the exception that in the third cycle there is some incompleteness, either as an indication that Job has been the victor or that the text as it now stands does not preserve the original order.

A. The First Cycle of Speeches, 4:1—14:22

1. *The First Speech of Eliphaz* (4:1—5:27)

The friends of Job, out of Oriental courtesy and sympathy, had been quiet until Job broke the silence. Now after seven days **Eliphaz the Temanite** is driven to speech by the lament of Job in which he has shown his inability to accept his fate with equanimity and patience. The fact that Eliphaz speaks first suggests that he is the oldest or that for some unstated reason his wisdom is held in higher regard by the others.

a. Eliphaz chides Job for his dismay (4:1-6). Eliphaz begins by being gentle and kindly. Tactfully he asks Job to listen to him, as **we assay to commune with thee** (2). He knows that anyone afflicted as Job had been must of necessity be under extreme emotional and physical pressure. Therefore he asks permission to speak. **Wilt thou be grieved?** is better translated, "Will you be offended?" (RSV) There is a rather humorous implication in the translation by J. M. P. Smith in which the characters of the story sit silent for seven days only to have Eliphaz inquire, "If one should venture a word with you, would you be bored?" It is a permissible translation of the Hebrew, but it is not likely that Eliphaz intended to be funny.[1] **Who can withhold himself from speaking?** Some comment is necessary. Sympathy and concern have been demonstrated and Job's outburst cannot go unan-

---

[1]*The Bible, An American Translation,* J. M. P. Smith and Edgar J. Goodspeed, et al. (Chicago: University of Chicago Press, 1939), p. 471.

swered. Job should understand this, for he has himself been the successful instructor of **many** (3). With tact Eliphaz begins to chide Job for his lack of patience.

Job had given comfort—he had **strengthened the feeble knees** (4)—but now that trouble had come upon him he had forgotten the truth contained in his own advice (5). Fear of God in Hebrew thought is the basis of wisdom and religion (see 1:9; Exod. 14:31; Lev. 19:14, 32; 25:17; Eccles. 12:13), and as such may be equivalent to reverence. Hence Eliphaz' question, **Is not this thy fear, thy confidence?** (6) Job's basic religious convictions should hold him steady in this stormy period of his life. Not only so but **the uprightness of thy ways**—better, your integrity of character—should be the basis of hope for Job. This is no time for him to give in to despondency and dejection.

b. Men reap as they sow (4:7-11). In order to prove that trust in God and righteous living bring good results, Eliphaz points to that which he believes to be self-evident truth. **Who ever perished, being innocent?** (7) The expected answer to this question is that the righteous are not driven to destruction by trouble. On the contrary, destruction is the fate of the wicked. Against the wicked comes **the blast of God . . . the breath of his nostrils** (9), i.e., the destructive, fierce wind of God's judgment. Furthermore, there is a divine principle at work. It is the law of harvest. Those who **sow** evil **reap** evil (8).

The destruction of the wicked is further described in 10-11 by another graphic figure—the breaking up of a den of lions. Davidson notes that there are five words used for **lion** in these verses; **roaring** lion, **fierce** lion, **young** lion, **old** (strong) lion, and the **whelps** of the lioness. Eliphaz sees a parallel between the wicked and the lion at two points: first, their strength; and secondly, their violent nature. It shall be with the wicked as when the strong lion's roaring and the taking of his prey are suddenly stopped and his **teeth . . . are broken,** so that he dies from lack of food. The **whelps,** now helpless, **are scattered** because they have no provider of food. In like manner disaster or judgment falls upon evil men whose violent nature is similar to that of the lion (see 5:2-5).[2]

c. Job should seek God (4:12—5:16). Eliphaz next appeals to a supernatural authority to substantiate his position: **Now a thing was secretly brought to me** (12); literally, There came to

---

[2]Davidson, *op. cit.,* p. 30.

me a word stealthily. This is not like the coming of the word of
the Lord to the prophet (see Jer. 1:4; 2:1, 4; etc.), nor is this the
manner in which the prophets describe their experience of vision.
Eliphaz' experience came in the middle of **the night** (13); a
terror seized him (14). In 15, **Then a spirit passed,** it is better
to translate *ruach* by "wind" rather than by **spirit.** *Ruach* may
mean either, but as Terrien points out, the masculine form as
used here always refers to a breath of air.[3] Eliphaz is not describing a ghost or apparition. *Ruach* is never used that way in the
OT. The description is that of a presence which he felt and
heard (16).[4] **There was silence, and I heard a voice** (16), is,
literally, There was a stillness and a voice, perhaps a whisper
—cf. **a little thereof** (12), and I Kings 19:12.

The message is in the form of two questions: **Shall mortal
man be more just than God? and shall a man be more pure than
his maker?** (17) This construction in the KJV is an admissible
translation but the sense is strange and impossible unless it is
intended to be a hyperbolic statement. It is also possible to
translate this passage, as is done almost universally, by making
it read, "Can mortal man be righteous before God? Can a man
be pure before his maker?"[5] These questions introduce the
human situation which Eliphaz observes all around him.

Man is incapable of being perfect, Eliphaz states. At this
point he is gently correcting Job, who seemed on the verge of
placing himself in a role equal to that of the Creator as he complained about his birth and the life-sustaining power of God.
Job may have been a very good man according to human standards, but compared to God, no mortal could claim innocence.
In order to illustrate this great difference between man and God,
Eliphaz uses some of God's other creatures as examples. He
points out that God's finite servants are not to be trusted im-
plicitly, and even the angels are **charged with folly** (18). The
word translated **folly** (*teholah*) is unique in the OT. It may have
the sense of "error." The poet does not seem so much to be dis-
crediting the heavenly beings as he is magnifying the perfection

[3]*Op. cit.,* p. 939.

[4]This quality of the supernatural is that which has caused H. Wheeler
Robinson to call him "Eliphaz the Mystic." Bildad is the traditionalist, and
Zophar is the dogmatist. See *The Cross in the Old Testament* (Philadelphia:
Westminster Press, 1955), pp. 36 ff.

[5]See RSV and *The Holy Scriptures* (Philadelphia: The Jewish Publication Society of America, 5706—1946), *ad. loc.*

of God. If even celestial beings are imperfect in God's sight, and do not merit His putting full trust in them, **how much less in them that dwell in houses of clay?** (19) This obviously refers to mortal man, whose body is dust (Gen. 2:7; 3:19; II Cor. 5:1). The reference to man's being earthbound is amplified by the expression **whose foundation.** Man is made from the earth; he is bound to the earth; he will return to the earth. Not only so, but man's life is transitory; it is **crushed** like a **moth.** There is only the brief span **from morning to evening** (20) which marks his existence. **They perish for ever without any regarding it.** Man is born; he lives briefly; he dies and is forgotten.

Verse 21 is obscure. The verb translated **go away** means "to pull out." Consequently the text is frequently emended to read, "Their tent-cord [or tent peg] is plucked up within them" (RSV). However, if **excellency** and **wisdom** are placed alongside each other as parallel terms, then the meaning might well be that man's excellence, whatever he may have, is torn from him and he dies without attaining wisdom.[6]

The foregoing is the broad base of conviction which Eliphaz has concerning the nature of man's existence upon the earth. He now proceeds to apply this directly to Job.

Call now, if there be any that will answer (5:1). The inference is that there is none to hear an accusation from Job against God. **The saints,** or "holy ones," are the angels—heavenly beings who are presumed to be helpful to man. Eliphaz mocks Job with the fact that he is unable to find any of these to intercede with God on his behalf. This, then, is a strong statement of the idea that the holy God is unapproachable and far distant from mortal creatures.

In v. 2 a proverbial statement regarding the destruction of **the foolish man** is included to warn Job that continued fretting over his condition will only add to his peril. In the experience of Eliphaz, there had been opportunity to watch such a fool as he seemed to be **taking root** (3) and prospering. However, suddenly everything collapsed around him and his **habitation** was **cursed.** Moffatt translates it, "A senseless man may strike root—I have seen it—but suddenly his branches rot." Not only so, but **his children** lack security—**they are crushed in the gate** (4). The town gate was the place where the elders of the village met to hear complaints and to pass judgment. The children of the foolish

[6]See Terrien, *op. cit.*, p. 940.

have no recourse open to them in seeking to have their possessions restored. There is none **to deliver them.** The Hebrew of
taketh it even out of the thorns (5) is obscure, but the meaning
of the verse seems clear. Hunger and **thorns** dog their way, and
even that which they may chance to have is easily taken from
them by those who would rob and plunder. Thus the foolishness
of the father is visited upon the children with disastrous effect.

In spite of the fact that evil seems to permeate the world,
it is not a product of the nature of things as they are: **Affliction
cometh not forth of the dust** (6). It is not accidental nor is it
entirely beyond man's control. **Man is born unto trouble** (7);
that is, he attracts evil as surely as **sparks fly upward.** It is man's
nature, through his own sin, to bring trouble upon himself.[7]
Thus, gently but pointedly, Eliphaz attempts to show Job the
cause of his suffering.

Having set forth the cause, Eliphaz proceeds to show how a
cure for suffering may be effected. **I would seek . . . God, and
unto God . . . commit my cause** (8). He is a Being of great
power and worthy of being trusted (9-10), for He providentially
lifts up **those that be low** (11) and brings to safety **those which
mourn.** Not only so, but He also confounds the way of **the crafty**
and **the froward**—those who trust in human wisdom (12-14).
Verse 13*a* is the only portion of Job to be quoted in the NT.[8] It
is noted by Paul in I Cor. 3:19 to show that even the greatest
wisdom of the world is as nothing compared to the wisdom of
God.

d. Suffering is God's instruction (5:17-27). Not only is God
to be trusted in affliction, but He should be praised in it. Suffering is evidence of God's correction and **chastening** (17). It is true
that God permits man to endure pain, but He also supplies the
means for healing (18).

With this premise stated clearly, Eliphaz proceeds to list the
many **troubles** from which trust in God will save a person (19-
26). **Six . . . seven** (19) is an example of the use of numbers in
an indefinite sense to refer to several or many. "The meaning is,
that six would be a large number, but it is increased to seven."[9]
When one attempts to find the seven evils alluded to it is impos-

---

[7]Davidson, *op. cit.*, p. 37.

[8]Other portions of the NT contain language which is similar to passages
from Job, but are not exact quotations.

[9]Gray, *op. cit.*, p. 54.

sible to make up a precise list from the present text. Those distresses listed include: **famine** and **war** (20), **the scourge of the tongue** (slander) and **destruction** (21), wild **beasts** (22), and perhaps drought (23). In addition to escaping from these plagues, he who trusts in God will live **in peace** (24), he shall have numerous **offspring** (25), and shall live to a **full** and satisfying **age** (26). The KJV translators seem to have missed the meaning in 24b. The ASV renders the verse: "And thou shalt know that thy tent is in peace; and thou shalt visit thy fold, and shalt miss nothing" (cf. Berk. and RSV).

Eliphaz concludes with the affirmation that his remarks are true; they have been tested and tried. Job should, therefore, listen to them **for** his own **good** (27).

In 17-27 may be seen "The Peaceable Fruits of Sorrows Rightly Borne." (1) An afflicted man may be happy, 17; (2) God wounds in order to heal, 18; (3) God can deliver the righteous, 19-21; (4) The universe is in league with God's man, 22; (5) Righteousness brings blessings to the home, 24-25; (6) The righteous live and die well, 26-27 (A. Maclaren).

2. Job's Reply to Eliphaz (6:1—7:21)

Job's reply may be divided into three basic sections. First, he justifies his complaints in c. 3, and defends himself against the chiding of his friend while insisting as before that death remains his only hope (6:1-13). Second, he registers deep sorrow and disappointment over the attitude his friends are taking toward him (6:14-30). And third, he bitterly laments his great suffering and implores God to leave him alone and let him die (7:1-21).

Eliphaz made no direct charge that Job had sinned. This will come later. He had only expressed surprise at Job's despair and impatience. Job seizes upon this criticism as the basis for his reply.

a. Job justifies his complaints (6:1-13). Job cries out, **Oh that my grief were throughly weighed!** (2) He feels that his friends see only the external evidences of suffering. Physical pain and loss of property are but a small measure of the agony which he has experienced. If some means could be found to bring together in one situation the sum of all his suffering, then it would be clear that Job's calamity **would be heavier than the sand of the sea** (3). With everything thus considered, who could accuse

43

him of speaking rashly? (This is a better translation of **Therefore my words are swallowed up.** See RSV.)

Not only has Job reached a state of utter desolation, but he affirms that **the arrows of the Almighty are within me** (4). Perhaps this is the real reason for his intense suffering. He believes that his misfortunes have come from God, but he cannot understand why God should treat him this way. **The arrows of God** are the plagues, diseases, pains, etc., with which He assails men (see 16:13-17; Deut. 32:23-27; Ps. 38:2-8). To Job these arrows are poisoned and **the terrors of God** are so numerous it is as though they are an attacking army **in array against** him.

At times it seems true that the arrows of the Almighty fly at a man where he has no defense, inflict severe wounds in the soul, and strike terror to his mind. But this seeming truth is based upon a conception of God which is superseded by the understanding of His nature which Jesus brings. God is able in everything to work for good (Rom. 8:28), and in the cross of Jesus the knowledge is given that He suffers with men. Had Job been able to see that God suffered too, instead of thinking that God was the cause of his sorrow, his problem would have been much less—perhaps completely solved.

In the question, **Doth the wild ass bray when he hath grass?** (5) Job continues to defend his right to complain. His complaints are proof of his pain, just as "braying" and "lowing" are the result of dissatisfaction among the beasts. When well-fed and comfortable they are silent. Job's desperation is as natural as that of hungry animals. On the other hand, his sufferings are compared to repulsive food which is **unsavory** or tasteless, like **the white of an egg** (6). The **soul,** in Hebrew psychology, is the seat of desire and appetite. Thus **the things that my soul refused** (7) expresses here that man wants more from life than tasteless food. He wants a decent and satisfying existence. When denied the opportunities for this, he protests, and rightfully so.

Having thus defended himself, Job reiterates his desire for death—**Oh that I might have my request . . . the thing that I long for!** (8) If God would **let loose his hand** (9), then a man could die.

Job's **comfort** (10), he thinks, is to be found only in the insensibility of the grave. **Harden myself in sorrow** has been rendered, "I would even exult in pain unsparing" (RSV). He

has not yet **concealed,** i.e., denied, **the words of the Holy One.**
But Job seriously questions how much longer he can hold out.
His **strength** is not that of **stones,** nor is his **flesh** like **brass** (12).
There is no longer any meaning in **life,** no **hope,** no purpose (11).
He is convinced that there is no **help** (13) left to him. All of his
resources are gone (RSV).

b. Job is disappointed in his friends (6:14-30). In this
section Job turns upon his friends. He feels that they should
have come to help him in his hour of need. Now he knows, even
though Eliphaz had been rather gentle about it, that they are
really his critics. To a man who is afflicted as Job has been, a
friend should show pity even though the man's misery should
drive him to the extremity of forsaking God (14).[10]

Far from being comforting and helpful, Job charges that his
friends **have dealt deceitfully** (15) with him. They have been as
deceitful and disappointing as a **brook** which has vanished. In
the heat of the desert **they are consumed out of their place** (17).
The words translated **paths** (18) and **troops** (19) are the same
in Hebrew and should be translated "caravan." The picture is
that of caravan travelers following paths which should lead to
water, but which end in disappointment. Job's friends have been
this kind of disappointment to him (15-21).

In his dilemma Job did not ask for material aid (22) nor
deliverance from an enemy nor **from the hand of the mighty** (23).
He needed sympathy and understanding. He wanted his friends
to retain their confidence in him. This would have helped him
to remain strong. They have not shown him **wherein I have
erred** (24). If they had spoken **right words** (25)—if they had
been honest and straightforward—then they would have been
helpful to him. But their words so far have been as nothing—
What doth your arguing reprove? Job's words have been the
words of a despairing man, and perhaps they have been **as wind**
(26). But his comforters' actions show that they "would cast
lots over the fatherless, and bargain over your friend" (27, RSV).
These are harsh and retaliatory words. Job has been deeply offended at the seemingly unsympathetic attitude shown him.

---

[10]The text here is obscure. A comparison of the various translations
will show the variety of meanings which have been assigned to this passage.
The sense followed here has the advantage of not employing any basic
alteration of the text, yet giving reasonable consistency to the pattern
of thought in the general context of the passage.

Now he, as humans are prone to do, lashes out in order to inflict similar pain upon his friends.

Many have supposed that the words, **Return, I pray you** (29), imply that Eliphaz has started to leave. This may well be. In any event Job does not wish **iniquity** (30), or wrong, to be done. Perhaps he is saying, "Return again; my cause is righteous." He does ask, **Is there iniquity in my tongue?** In the last portion of this verse the figure of the tongue tasting represents the tongue as an organ of perception rather than of speech. Job is asking a rhetorical question in order to affirm that he is perfectly capable of discerning the truth and that he is honest with them and with himself. He insists that right is on his side.

c. *Job still feels that death is his only remaining hope* (7:1-21). Having affirmed his competency to evaluate his own condition, Job turns to generalizing upon the condition of mankind. Life is always hard. **Is there not an appointed time to man upon earth?** (1) is better rendered, Is there not a time of service, or hard labor? The life of man is like the **days of an hireling** or **as a servant** (2) wanting shade in the heat of the day. So Job has found his life to be. The **months** of his life are **vanity** and emptiness (3). His nights are endless and full of misery (4). His **skin** is full of putrescence (5). His **days** are fleeting and **without hope** (6), doomed to vanish away as a **cloud is consumed** (9). The sense of 8b is, Even "while thy eyes are upon me, I shall be gone" (RSV). Life ends in **the grave,** and beyond this there is nothing. The dead man does not **return . . . to his house** and is no longer known by the living (10).

For this reason Job feels that it is proper for him to **speak** out in his **anguish of . . . spirit** (11). Turning from his friends, he again complains bitterly to God that he is permitted to live. Does God consider him to be some kind of sea monster who needs to be plagued constantly in order to keep him from doing damage to the world? (12) Then follows a list of plagues which are used to destroy him: he finds no rest in his **bed** (13); he is frightened with horrible nightmares (14) until he once more pleads with God to let him die (15-16). Then pathetically he inquires why God should set any store by man. Why should He set His **heart upon him?** (17) It seems that God is constantly at him, trying him **every moment** (18). Why does not God **let me alone till I swallow down my spittle?** (19) seems to be a proverbial expression signifying a short time. In 9:18, Job asks for time to catch his breath. The two expressions apparently have the same meaning.

I have sinned (20) should read, "If I sin." He is not here admitting wrong done. He is inquiring of God concerning the significance of sin. What does it matter to God even if Job had sinned? What has God seen in him that causes such unusual attention? If there is some wrong, then why does not God **pardon my transgression?** (21) Job does not fully comprehend the meaning of sin and forgiveness, but he does envision God as the Seeker after man. The statement, **Thou shalt seek me,** is one word in Hebrew. It is a strong word meaning to make diligent, persistent, and earnest search. In spite of Job's accusation against God, he still believes that He is a God of love. He therefore anticipates the day when God will again hold him in His favor and wish to establish communion with His old servant. He knows that if God does this it will have to be quickly, for soon **I shall not be.** Job appears to believe that in the grave he will be beyond the cognition of God, just as he will be removed from relationship with men. When he has passed into Sheol, God's search for him will be too late!

Seldom, indeed, does one find in literature such a powerful and haunting description of utter despair.

3. *The First Speech of Bildad* (8: 1-22)

Bildad, the traditionalist, holds to a position which is very similar to that of Eliphaz. However, his method of reasoning and his approach to Job are different. He reacts in anger to what he considers to be complete irreverence on Job's part.

Bildad takes hold of the general trend of Job's arguments and attempts to contradict the conclusions to which his friend had come. Job had asserted that right was on his side (6: 29-30). This implied that God was unjust. Job also had bitterly charged that the life of man is cruelly shaped by the unbearable pressures brought upon him by an unrelenting and inescapable God (7: 1-7, 17-18). To both of these charges Bildad asserts that God is eminently just—so much so that He rewards the righteous and punishes the wicked. He supports his position by appealing to the traditions of the fathers.

a. Bildad affirms that God is just (8: 1-7). **How long wilt thou speak these things?** (2) Bildad is surprised that Job would permit himself to speak in such an irresponsible manner con-

cerning God. Job's words are **like a strong wind;** they are violent in nature and empty of truth.

Doth God pervert judgment? (3) This is the key question
which Bildad asks of Job. God is **the Almighty** one. He cannot,
would not, act unjustly. Bildad is not depreciating the gravity
of Job's position, nor is he minimizing the extent of his suffering.
He simply cannot accept Job's premise that his calamities represent unjust action on the part of God. If God has done it, then
it is just, because it comes from God.

The proposition **If thy children have sinned** (4) is made by
Bildad in a hypothetical statement, but the intention is not
hypothetical. In a cruel fashion, considering Job's bereavement,
he charges that the death of Job's children is a natural result of
their **transgression.** To Bildad sin carries its own punishment—
death. To a man of his mentality the situation is all black or
white. The fate of Job's children proved their guilt. Their death
proved the magnitude of their sin. This same kind of reasoning
is then applied to his friend. Job's affliction, in like manner,
proved his guilt; but since Job's life was spared, it was evident
that his sin was not so grievous. Therefore, **if thou wouldest seek
unto God** (5), there was hope for him.

Bildad hopes that Job will profit from his experience and
show adequate evidence of repentance and humility; in short,
that he will become **pure and upright** (6). Then God **would
awake for thee** is better, He would arouse himself on your behalf and **make the habitation of thy righteousness prosperous.**
The key words here are **habitation** and **prosperous.** What Bildad
envisions is that the home, health, wealth, and peace of Job are
to be restored if Job will only follow his instructions. Such restoration would be proof of his righteousness. It is even possible
that Job's latter years would **greatly increase** over the former
years (7). This, in fact, does occur (42:10-17), but not for the
reason nor in the manner in which Bildad anticipated it.

b. *Bildad points to the wisdom of the fathers* (8:8-22). Bildad has expressed the principle to which he subscribes. Now he
invites Job to reflect upon this truth and test it against available
knowledge to see that it is true. For this purpose the wisdom **of
the former age, and . . . their fathers** (8) is ideally suited. Bildad
is not referring merely to the previous generation. He refers to
antiquity. The life-span of a man is so short that he cannot
attain to adequate understanding based upon his own experi-

ence. There is available the long experience of generations of men from the past who will **teach** those who will be attentive to their wisdom (9-10). **Words out of their heart** (10) are words of understanding in contrast to the empty and hasty words of Job (2). Bildad's position is that "what is true is not new, and what is new is not true; that Job is wrong, because he is propounding a monstrous new doctrine; and Bildad is right, because he is simply repeating an old doctrine, so old that it must be true."[11]

One wonders why Bildad thought that wisdom based upon experience and then filtered through the past into the present was any more true than that observed from experience in the present. After all, the ancients had only one lifetime to make their observations, just as men in the present have.

The teaching of the ancients is given in poetic imagery. **The rush** (11) is likely the papyrus plant, which at one time grew abundantly in the marshlands of lower Egypt. It is an aquatic reed sometimes growing to a height of ten or twelve feet. **The flag** refers to marshland grass (see Gen. 41:2). These plants require an abundant water supply for growth. When they are in their **greenness,** that is, when they are in full flower but not ready for cutting, they wither **before any other herb** if water is withdrawn from them (12).

The application of this simile is given: **So are the paths of all that forget God** (13). Men perish suddenly, they wither and die, when His sustaining power is taken from them. The word translated **hypocrite's** does not mean hypocrisy in the usual sense of that word. Rather, it refers to one who is a profane person. He is godless because he has denied or rebelled against his proper mission in life. For such a person any basis for the future is as flimsy as **a spider's web** (14), literally, the spider's house. He will **lean upon** such a house but it will not support him; **it shall not endure** (15).

In 16-19 another figure of sudden destruction is given: a luxuriant plant is suddenly destroyed, leaving no trace of itself. While such a plant was still alive, its branches filled the **garden** and its roots spread everywhere among the **stones,** seeking nourishment. When it was destroyed, however, it was as though the place where it had been could say, **I have not seen thee** (18). Not only so, but where it was, **others grow up** (19).

[11]Gray, *op. cit.,* p. 78.

Bildad applies these lessons from nature to the relationship which exists between God and man. **God will not cast away a perfect man (20).** The word **perfect** is the one which has already been applied to Job by the author (1:1). On the other hand, God will not **help the evildoers.** Bildad finds both hope and cause for warning in this age-old truth. Job's evident difficulties prove that something is wrong. But that Job has not been destroyed completely gives hope that God will yet give him **laughing** and **rejoicing (21).** Those who have turned against Job—who **hate** him—will themselves be put to **shame (22).** Bildad has not explicitly accused Job of wickedness yet, but the warning he gives to his friend has that implication. If Job persist in his wickedness, he will be completely destroyed—**the dwelling place of the wicked shall come to nought (22).**

It may be noticed at this point that the author permits Bildad some prophetic insights, even though Bildad himself does not recognize it. His reference to those who have turned against Job being themselves put to shame comes true in the experience of the friends at the conclusion of the book.

Bildad began his speech to Job in a harsh, even cruel manner, but some kindness and concern for his friend is evident in the latter portion of this discourse. Bildad contradicted the assumptions of c. 8, in which Job saw no evidence of a moral government in the world. His friend insists that this is in no wise the case. History and the judgment of the ages prove otherwise. If Job will humble himself and accept the counsel of those who are wiser than he, then he shall be comforted and restored.

4. *Job's Reply to Bildad* (9:1—10:22)

a. Job admits that the wicked suffer (9:1-35). The words, **I know it is so (2),** follow readily upon that which Bildad has been saying. But it is also a further reply to what Eliphaz had said. Job rather impatiently admits that there is some truth in the arguments of his friends. The problem is that they do not concede the possibility that Job is correct when he affirms his innocence. Therefore he asks, **How should man be just with God?** The question does not concern itself so much with how a man acts as with how one can present himself before God in a manner that will demonstrate his innocence. This wording reflects what Eliphaz asked in 4:17, but Job uses the idea in a different fashion. Eliphaz had contrasted the finite with the infinite. Job here questions one's ability to substantiate his righteousness and to maintain his claim to innocence in the face of the overwhelming action of God against them.

In a contest between man and God the outcome is obvious. **If . . . he contend** (3) is legal terminology meaning to enter a plea as in a lawcourt. In such a situation man is doomed to failure, for he has not the ability to answer **one of a thousand** of the questions God in His infinite wisdom could ask. Not even one who is **wise in heart, and mighty in strength** could with impunity be stiff-necked against God (4; cf. II Chron. 36:13). Man is certainly no match for an omnipotent God.

Job acknowledges God's power as it is observed in various phenomena of the physical world. God **removeth the mountains** (5) in His great power. This may be a reference to any of a number of situations in which a mountain is seen to crumble under the impact of lightning, earthquakes, or torrential rains causing landslides. **And they know not** may refer to the suddenness with which such upheavals occur. Some, however, see God as the subject in this phrase. If this is the proper inference, then He destroys the mountains without knowing it, so easily does He act in relation to His great power.[12] But this interpretation does not fit into the thought structure of the last portion of the verse. God removes mountains as a result of **his anger,** not as an accidental consequence of mammoth power. He also **shaketh the earth . . . and the pillars thereof** (6). This is poetic description, but it may have a quite literal background of thought. No doubt this is specifically a description of an earthquake. The flat earth was conceived of as resting upon pillars or upon the roots of the mountains (38:6; Ps. 75:3).

God **commandeth the sun, and it riseth not; and sealeth up the stars** (7). Natural phenomena such as heavy thunderstorms, sandstorms, and eclipses would conceal the sun and the stars. The ancients viewed these events as evidence of the severe displeasure of the gods.

God's power is so great that He **alone spreadeth out the heavens** (8). The same description of power and activity is contained in Isa. 40:12 and 44:24. Isa. 40:22 says that God is the One "that stretcheth out the heavens as a curtain, and spreadeth them out as a tent to dwell in." The meaning of **treadeth upon**

[12]*Ibid.*

the waves of the sea is uncertain. Amos 4:13 speaks of God treading upon the heights of the earth. Perhaps the thought of omnipresence is in the mind of our author here. God is exalted above all the grandeur of nature. Thus He is the absolute Sovereign over the entire earth. He is also the Creator of the constellations—**Arcturus, Orion, and Pleiades** (9). **The chambers of the south** must be a general reference to the heavenly bodies in the southern sky.

In v. 10, Job's conclusion from his consideration of these marvels from nature is given. He finds that God's activity is beyond the ability of man to comprehend. The thought is the same as expressed by Eliphaz in 5:9. In the case of Eliphaz, this observation was made in the context of God's orderly control over the affairs of man and the achievement of His purposes in goodness. With Job, however, these words are used as a summary of his contention that God's tremendous power has no moral significance. It is sheer force before which man is helpless, a theme which Job undertakes to explore next.

The normal standards used to measure the morality of human beings are not applicable to One of such power. The power of God is far outside the realm of man. It is invisible (11); it cannot be controlled nor questioned by man (12). **Taketh away** is an expression used in connection with a wild animal carrying off its prey.

Before a Being such as this, man is helpless. **God will not withdraw his anger** (13) until His purposes are accomplished. Man cannot turn back God's wrath, and God does not do so himself. Therefore the only course of action left to one who is found suffering His displeasure is to submit to His anger. This is what was done by the mighty beings of ancient lore. **The proud helpers** (better, "the helpers of Rahab") **do stoop under him.** This may be a reference to the Babylonian creation myth as it deals with conflict between Marduk and Tiamat. After Marduk had destroyed Tiamat, he then dealt with her helpers, those who aided and abetted her:

> *After he had slain Tiamat, the leader,*
> *Her band was shatered, her troupe was broken up;*
> *And the gods, her helpers who marched at her side,*
> *Trembling with terror, turned their backs about,*
> *In order to save and preserve their lives.*

> *Tightly encircled, they could not escape.*
> *He made them captive and he smashed their weapons.*
> *Thrown into the net, they found themselves ensnared;*
> *Placed in cells, they were filled with wailing;*
> *Bearing his wrath, they were held imprisoned.*[13]

Thus Job sees that even the primeval forces are under the control of God. It should no tbe surprising that the poet-author made use of popular myths existing in the mind of his age to illustrate his point.

With creatures such as these impotent against God, what chance does Job have? But even though he believes his case to be hopeless he continues to think of the possibilities of meetin God face-to-face and presenting his case to Him. This idea of a trial scene dominates his thought and is the key to understanding much of what he says.[14] Such is the case when Job says, **How much. less shall I answer him?** (14) That is, he could not bring a rebuttal to the charges which God apparently has brought against him. **Choose out my words** involves a plea against God in which it would certainly be advisable to select well the words **to reason with him.** But how can this be possible in the light of God's overpowering might and majesty? **Though I were righteous** (15), that is, in the right, there would still be no possibility of getting a decision against God. With such an Opponent, Job could only **make supplication to my judge** (adversary or accuser). All that would be possible would be to ask for mercy (RSV). If Job's cause against God were to be judged, and God were actually to appear, Job says that even then he cannot believe that God would actually listen **unto my voice** (16).

In vv. 17-19, Job describes both his present condition and that which would happen in the suit against God which he has been imagining. The verbs used describe the destruction which would take place in such a meeting: break or crush, multiply **wounds,** withhold **breath,** fill **with bitterness.** In a contest of strength or in a matter of justice there is none who can match God. T. H. Robinson translates verses 20-21 well to show the hopelessness which Job feels in the situation:

[13]James B. Pritchard, *Archeology and the Old Testament* (Princeton: University Press, 1958), p. 189.

[14]T. H. Robinson, *Job and His Friends* (London: SCM Press, Ltd., 1954), p. 89.

> *I may be in the right, but my own mouth would condemn me,*
> *Though I were faultless, he would prove me a rogue.*
> *Though I were perfect I would not know myself,*
> *I would spurn my life.*[15]

No matter how good his case, the contrast between him and God would be so great that he would be overpowered and be made to look as though he were in the wrong.

Job has stated his case presenting the nonmoral nature of God's supreme power in strong language. Now he goes even further in making application of this principle to life as he observes it. He makes no effort to soften his language in answering the arguments of his friends. Bildad had asserted that God slays the wicked (8:11-19). Job declares, **He destroyeth the perfect and the wicked** (22). The assertion **This is one thing** means that God treats both alike. Job is saying that God's terrifying power is indiscriminate. This, of course, means that justice is perverted, which Bildad had denied (8:3).

Not only is God indiscriminate in His destruction of men, but He mocks those whom He destroys through some form of catastrophe: **He will laugh at the trial of the innocent** (23). Thus Job believes that **the earth is given into the hand of the wicked** (24). He charges that God is the One who is responsible for this condition, since He is the Sovereign of all nature and of mankind as well. If God is not responsible, then who is? (Cf. 24, RSV.)

Job has reached the lowest point in his feeling of separation and alienation from God. The charges made here are far removed from the Christian conception of the nature of God and His relationship to the suffering of humanity. To understand these reactions properly the twentieth-century reader must remember that in Job's day there was no conception of secondary causes, of natural law, nor perhaps even of a general providential scheme of events. Men in that period considered God to be the immediate and direct Cause of all that occurred. With this understanding of God's relationship to events, and given the confidence that there was no real lack of piety in himself, Job could only conclude that God had afflicted him without cause. If this were true, then it would also follow that God exercised His power in an indiscriminate and unjust fashion.

[15]*Ibid.*

In a somewhat calmer mood but with continued pessimism, Job turns from the world in general to himself and complains of the brevity of his life and of his inability to find any satisfactory relationship with God. The speed with which his life is coming to an end is described in three different figures. The first is that of the **post** or courier running swiftly to deliver his message (25). The second is that of **swift ships** (26)—better, "skiffs of reed" (RSV). These were constructed of wooden keels and reeds and so were light. They carried only one or two persons and were very swift.[16] The third is the picture of **the eagle that hasteth to the prey;** it swoops down from the sky in a lightning-quick attack upon its victim.

Job next examines what would occur if he bravely decided to stop complaining and to cheer up (27). But he knows this will be of no use. The suffering will continue, and these things so difficult to bear are evidence that God still will **not hold me innocent** (28). Therefore any effort on Job's part to improve his attitude is of no avail (29). It is even useless to go through the process of thorough cleansing **with snow water** (30) and lye (see RSV), because God will **plunge** him **in the ditch,** from which he will emerge so filthy that even his **clothes shall abhor him** (31). The figure here is a strong one envisioning Job, naked but cleansed, thrown into foul mire. His clothing is personified and described as then refusing to cover such abominable filth.

These verses have described how futile Job's efforts are to justify himself in light of the fact that God is bent on holding him to be guilty. Now Job returns to his major difficulty—man has no capability of contending with God. Since Job is honest in the conviction of his innocence, it appears that God is dealing with him in a terribly unfair manner. **He is not a man, as I am** (32)—i.e., they are not equals in the conflict—and there is no **daysman** (arbitrator or umpire) between them in order that equal requirements might be laid upon both (33). If God would take away **his rod** (34; this inequality) and let Job's terror subside, then he would be able to **speak, and not fear him** (35). But such is not the case. The fear is there. The suffering is there. The knowledge of God's apparent displeasure is constantly and strongly with him. Job is certain that God does not and will not hold him innocent. Yet he has no way of finding out the cause of this displeasure.

[16]Davidson, *op. cit.,* p. 72.

b. Job searches for meaning in God's actions (10:1-22). Chapter 10 follows easily after the observations of c. 9, although there is a transition to different subject matter. In c. 9, Job has affirmed his innocence in spite of the fact that God seems determined to hold him guilty. It is no wonder under these circumstances that he feels completely helpless and hopeless in his misery. However Job continues in his search to find meaning for his existence. He does so by trying to reason logically from what he knows to be the nature of God.

Job's initial reaction is that of despair. **My soul is weary of my life** (1), but this in itself gives him a certain measure of courage. He has nothing more to lose. Death could only liberate him from suffering. He says, **I will leave** ("give free utterance to," RSV) **my complaint.** So out of this **bitterness of . . . soul** he dares to make inquiry of God concerning His motives in the treatment of His servant. Job felt that his suffering was adequate evidence of God's displeasure with him. God had "made him guilty" by his afflictions. Rather than such arbitrary condemnation Job wishes to know the reason God has for the contention against him (2).

Addressing the Lord, Job reasons that it is illogical for God to **oppress** and **despise the work of** His **hands** (3). And God does not **shine upon** ("favor," RSV) **the counsel of the wicked.** What pleasure could He find in destroying that which He had created? Surely the Almighty knew what was happening. It was common knowledge in Job's age that God was spirit and not **flesh,** so that He was not limited as human vision is limited (4). Neither is God's life to be measured **as the days of man** (5). Therefore it is not the pressure of time that causes God to exert such effort to discover some **sin** in Job's life (6). On the contrary, God knows full well that Job is **not wicked** (7). Why then should He torture him? **None that can deliver** reechoes the previous reflection of Job with regard to his helplessness. Job has come to an impasse in his thought. He is caught without a means of escape in the displeasure of a God who is unapproachable. God has afflicted him with horrible suffering without permitting him to know the cause of such antagonistic action.

In contrast to the strange treatment that God inflicts upon him, Job notes that it is God who has **fashioned** (8) him. The figure is that of a potter carefully molding clay to create his work of art. Why should the Creator **bring . . . into dust again** (9) that over which He has labored so carefully? Verses 10-12 speak of God's activity in bringing Job to life from conception to full growth (cf. Ps. 139:13). God gives **life and favour** (12) and He has **preserved** his **spirit.** Job remembers with nostalgia the loving-kindness God has shown to him in times past.

Job next investigates what he considers to be the secret purposes of God: **These things hast thou hid in thine heart** (13). In vv. 14-15 there are three hypothetical situations to test the case: **If I sin . . . If I be wicked . . . if I be righteous.** Job is not making any claims for himself. Rather he is saying that regardless of his conduct his fate is the same. This leaves him **full of confusion** at the increase of his afflictions and at the fact that God seems to hunt him down as though He were **a fierce lion** (16). The words **shewest thyself marvellous upon me** do not refer to the creative and providential marvels of God, but rather to torment and enmity. Job feels that God's intentions are to renew His plagues and afflictions against him as a witness to his guilt (17).

With God acting in this fashion, Job wonders why He ever brought him birth, or having been born, why he was not permitted to die immediately (18-19; cf. 3:11-16). He reminds God that at best his **days** are **few** (20), and pleads for his tormentor to **let** him **alone,** so that he might **take comfort a little** before he dies and goes to the **land of darkness,** from which he **shall not return** (21).

5. *The First Discourse of Zophar* (11:1-20)

Zophar, the dogmatist, defends the justice of God as both Eliphaz and Bildad have done. However, in cc. 9—10, Job has been far more explicit in his claims of innocence than he had been before. In c. 3 he did not claim innocence. He lamented his fate. Eliphaz could assume Job's guilt without making an issue of it. In cc. 6—7, Job rather casually claims innocence while concerning himself with other matters. Bildad could disregard these claims as being somewhat natural but unimportant. But in cc. 9 and 10, Job made strong claims of innocence. By doing so he forces the friends to consider this question seriously. Zophar knows that he must make some reply to Job's claim. His speech falls into three short sections: (*a*) Job's sin (11:1-6); (*b*) God's wisdom (11:7-12); (*c*) Exhortation to humility and repentance (11:13-20).[17]

---

[17]*Ibid.,* p. 81.

a. Job's sin (11:1-6). **Should not the multitude of words be answered?** (2) The question is Zophar's defense for speaking to Job. This is probably not a complaint against a long speech on Job's part so much as it is against the irresponsibility of Job's allegations against God. What Eliphaz and Bildad have already said should have given Job adequate reason to pause and to reflect upon the error of his thought. This in turn should have produced respectful and humble silence, but it has not. Therefore, more is necessary. **A man full of talk** is literally "a man of lips." The insinuation is that Job could not really be serious in his rantings against God. His words come from the lips rather than from the heart. As a result Job's words are **lies** and **mockery** (3).

Zophar directs his attention to Job's claim of a pure **doctrine** and cleanness in his relationship with God (4). He agrees that it would be well if Job could receive his desire and **God would speak** (5). But if this should happen, the result would be far different from what Job expects. Rather than being exonerated, Job would find that his present suffering was small in comparison to the enormity of his sin: **God exacteth of thee less than thine iniquity deserveth** (6). Zophar gives no proof that this charge is true. He dogmatically makes the affirmation. **Job's** suffering is from God, but Job's attitude shows that the measure of punishment he has received does not yet equal the degree of his sin.

b. God's wisdom (11:7-12). Zophar does not believe that man can discover the nature of God (7). Job has questioned God's motives in dealing so treacherously with him, and in so doing he has attempted to inquire into the divine character. God's omniscience reaches beyond the boundaries of both **heaven and hell** (*Sheol;* 8). By this Zophar affirms that God knows everything throughout the earth, the regions above the earth, and the regions below the earth. Man cannot possibly comprehend Him in His character or in His works (7-9). Job had been correct when he realized that no one **can hinder him** (10; see 9:11-12) or turn Him back from His purposes, whatever they may be. But Job had charged that God did not distinguish between the righteous and the wicked in His dealings with men. To this Zophar will not agree. **God knoweth vain men** (11). He will not observe wicked action without taking it into consideration. Zophar then quotes an old proverb concerning stupidity:

> *But an insane man will get intelligence,*
> *When a wild ass's colt is born a man* (Smith-Goodspeed).

Zophar, no doubt, applied it to the stubbornness of Job. The modern reader, however, is more apt to apply it to Zophar.

c. Exhortation to humility and repentance (11:13-20). Zophar has been blunt, even harsh, in his treatment of Job. But he has not given his old friend up as a hopeless case. There is yet opportunity for Job to recover from his terrible condition. Since he is sure that some sin of Job lies at the root of his condition and that Job's suffering results from that sin, the answer is simple. Job should be open and humble about his wrongdoing. This calls for reformation. It will include a proper preparation of his **heart** (13) to bring it into a right relationship with God. **Stretch out thine hands toward him** indicates supplication in prayer to remove **iniquity** from his life and from his home (14). When this is done, Job will be able **to lift up** his **face without spot** (15). He will be held innocent before God. **Fear** and **misery** will be forgotten (15-16). His life will be brighter and happier than before. All of the causes for fear shall be removed and in their place will be security and **hope** (17-19). For **thine age** (17) read "your life" (RSV). For **dig about thee** (18) read "look around" (Berk.). **Many shall make suit unto thee** (19) means, "Many will appeal to you for favor" (Berk.).

6. *Job's Reply to Zophar* (12:1—14:22)

Like Job's previous speeches, this one is addressed only in part to the three friends. The remainder is addressed directly to God. The ever-increasing criticism from his friends angers Job to the point where he employs biting sarcasm in his rejoinder to Zophar. The friends had rather piously claimed superior knowledge of God's wisdom and ways with men. Each in turn asserted that Job's suffering was adequate proof of his sin. Job turns upon them fiercely and condemns the superficial manner in which they have viewed the evidence. Their presentation has been shallow and biased. Their views do not show sincerity. After castigating his friends, Job again challenges God to meet him and answer the questions which he raises. The challenge goes unanswered and Job sinks once more into melancholy over the fate of man.

a. Job mocks the wisdom of his friends (12:1-25). Job sarcastically compliments his friends for their great wisdom: **No**

doubt but ye are the people (2). They have been supporting the opinions generally held during much of the biblical period. Job has been forced by his own experience to dissent from this opinion. In his mockery he declares that they are the very embodiment of wisdom, so that when they die, **wisdom shall die** also. Zophar's sharp comment concerning Job's chances of gaining understanding (11:12) must have cut deeply. Job claims that he already has that kind of **understanding,** and is in no way **inferior** to them (3). But even so, it is no occasion for boasting. Who is there that **knoweth not such things as these?**

Verses 4-6 may be viewed as a partial listing of those things which everyone knows. First, Job has become a "laughingstock" (RSV) to his neighbors. Yet he is one **who calleth upon God** and one who has been an **upright man.** Even so, he has been **laughed to scorn (4).** The second observation is that when a person who has once been in an enviable position slips, or has· some misfortune, then those who are yet secure despise him. They reason that, since God has abandoned the unfortunate one, why should not they do the same (5)? The meaning of **as a lamp despised** is not clear. The RSV translates it, "Contempt . . . is ready for those whose feet slip." The third readily observable fact is that the **tabernacles of robbers prosper (6).** Here Job denies categorically that it is only the righteous man who prospers. A casual glance at life will show that it is the wicked man who gets along best.

The friends may brag of their knowledge of the wisdom and power of God, but anyone who takes the trouble to look around can discover these truths. Even creatures of the earth—the **beasts** of the field, **the fowls of the air (7), the fishes of the sea** (8)—know that these things are true. The **breath of all mankind (10)** is in the hands of God! His power is complete. All creation knows this, but it does not follow that only the righteous benefit from His sustaining power. The wicked man and even lower forms of life also receive from Him.

Bildad had urged Job to listen to the wisdom which comes from **the ancient (12,** the aged). In 13-25, Job had followed this advice, but he could not accept their conclusions. It seemed to him that history shows God using **wisdom and strength (13)** indiscriminately. If one follows the logic of the friends, then **judges (17), kings (18), princes,** better "priests" **(19),** elders, and the chiefs of the people would all certainly deserve the unqualified blessing of God, but history does not support such a theory. On the contrary, there are examples of all of these kinds of people who were brought low. God causes them **to grope in the dark without light** (25). Deposed from their exalted positions, they **stagger like a drunken man** in their foolishness.

  b. *Job's friends have proven false* (13:1-28). Job here reaffirms his equality in knowledge with his friends: **What ye know, the same do I know also** (2). He observes that it is more to his liking to deal directly with God: **I would speak to the Almighty** (3). The friends have dealt in **lies** and are likened to **physicians of no value** (4). Under these circumstances the wisest thing that they could do would be to remain silent (5)!

  Actually, Job believes, the reasoning of his counselors has been inherently wicked. They have spoken falsely and have professed to be speaking on behalf of **God** (7), thus perverting the very basis of truth. Furthermore, they have shown partiality —this is the meaning of **Ye accept his person**—in putting themselves in the position as contenders **for God** (8). The friends had no knowledge of Job's guilt from firsthand information. In judging between him and God they had already decided for God with only superficial and incomplete evidence. To Job this kind of reasoning is the very essence of hypocrisy. In order to follow Job's thought, one must remember that his words are uttered against the background of his desire for an arbitrator between himself and God. For the moment he had thought of the friends performing that function, only to find that they are already unfairly committed to his Opponent. Consequently they cannot be fair to him.

  Having come to this conclusion, Job knows that the friends themselves stand in peril. If God should **search** them **out** (9), surely they would be subject to severe reproof because of their partiality (9-10). They should be in great **dread** (11). Their **remembrances**—the traditional sayings remembered from antiquity—**are like unto ashes** (12) and their arguments (not **bodies**) are likened to a shield made of **clay** rather than of metal.

  At v. 13, Job turns from his friends and addresses his remarks to God. The friends are instructed, **Hold your peace . . . that I may speak** to God, no matter what the risk may be. He knows that his daring may well result in his complete destruction—**I . . . put my life in mine hand** (14)—but he has become so desperate that the risk is worth taking. **Though he slay me** (15; better, "Behold, He will slay me") expresses the extremity to which Job thinks his condition has progressed. **Yet will I trust**

in him is one of the most sublime utterances recorded in the KJV. Unfortunately the Hebrew text does not support this translation. It was taken with some modification from the marginal notes of the Masoretes. Admittedly the text here is very difficult, but the best reading is that followed by RSV and others: "Behold, he will slay me; I have no hope." Job no longer anticipates any way in which his life and good fortune can be restored. In spite of this he courageously insists, **I will maintain mine own ways before him.**

He also shall (16) is better rendered, "This also shall." Job is referring to the fact that he is about to state, rather than referring to God. That which shall be his **salvation** in this situation is the fact that a **hypocrite** or godless man would not dare **come before** God and attempt to plead his case. This statement matches the grandeur of thought found in the KJV mistranslation of 15. Job had lost all hope for life, but at the very moment in which he reached this nadir of despair, a glimmer of hope appeared. His unfailing conviction of his own integrity makes him realize that he still has faith that his former peaceful relationship with God must be restored. For this Job earnestly yearns. It is at this point that Blackwood contrasts the experience of Job with that of Paul as described in Phil. 1:19-26. Paul knew that God, in the cross of Jesus Christ, took the suffering of the world to himself. Job had not achieved this knowledge of God's concern for man. Rather he sees Him as sitting serene and untouched by man's woe.[18]

Job has determined to take his case directly to God, if this privilege be permitted him, but he wants his dubious friends to pay close attention: **Hear diligently my speech** (17). Job had been accused of being a voluble liar in his claims of innocence (11:1 ff.). But now, as a result of his appeal to God, he affirms, **I shall be justified** (18). In 19 he asks, **Who is he that will plead with me?** That is, Who is there who can oppose me with any valid argument to prove my guilt? If there is just proof against his innocence, Job is willing to **hold** his **tongue** and die.

Turning to God, after this great reaffirmation of innocence, Job makes a request that two things may be granted to him. First, he asks that God will not terrify him so that he cannot

---

[18]Andrew Blackwood, *Devotional Introduction to Job* (Grand Rapids: Baker Book House, 1959), pp. 81 ff.

speak (21; see 9:34-35). **Withdraw thy hand** has been inter-preted, "Lift off thy heavy hand" (Moffatt). Second, Job asks that God will, indeed, speak to him (22). With these conditions stipulated, he is ready to plead his cause before God.

His first request of God is, **Make me to know my trangres-sion and my sin** (23). He no doubt refers to sins that are sig-nificant enough in number or nature to warrant the severity of his affliction. Job here agrees with his friends at a critical point: God is the Cause of his suffering. The friends believe that Job's wrongdoing causes God to inflict punishment. Job is sure that this cannot be the cause; but if it should be so, he demands to know from God exactly what it is of which he is guilty. Feeling his estrangement from God, he asks, **Wherefore hidest thou thy face, and holdest me for thine enemy?** (24) Using the figures of a **leaf driven** in the wind and **dry stubble** (25), Job shows how insignificant he really feels in the sight of God. Therefore he is surprised that God pursues him so relent-lessly. The verse has been translated: "Wilt thou frighten a drifting leaf? Wilt thou chase dry stubble?" (Berk.)

Thou writest (26) means to pass sentence upon. Why does God hold such an attitude towards him? Is it because of some forgotten sin in his **youth?** If this were the case, then why has God waited so long to punish him? As things stand, God has Job completely hedged in. His **feet** are **in the stocks** (27); he is closely watched in all of his movements. The last part of 27 may be read, "Thou . . . settest bounds to my footsteps" (Berk.). Job refers to himself in the third person in his next statement. **And he,** that is, Job, "wastes away as a rotten thing" (28, RSV).[19]

c. Frail man (14:1-22). Job continues his line of reasoning through 14:1-6. He not only wonders at God's concern over one as insignificant as he is, but now he notes that the entire human race is of such low estate that it is surprising that God would be overly concerned with any one of them.

It is the common lot of mankind, so frail as to be **born of a woman,** to experience **trouble** (1) in the few days which are assigned to him. His life is like a briefly blooming **flower;** it **fleeth also as a shadow** (2) and is quickly over. Why should God **open** His **eyes** (look so carefully) **upon such an one?** He is so much greater than man that it is beneath Him to watch him

---

[19]See Davidson, *op. cit.,* p. 101.

so carefully. Applying this fact to himself, Job questions why such scrutiny should end in bringing him **into judgment** (3).[20]

Continuing to think about the general frailty of mankind, Job affirms that not one of them can really be **clean** in the sight of God (4). Since man's life is so thoroughly circumscribed by **his bounds** (5) which God has **appointed** him, God should **turn from him**, literally, "look away." God should relent in His persistent punishment in order that man might have at least the measure of contentment that **an hireling** (6) has in his day's work.

The request for at least a brief span in which enjoyment of life might be experienced is based upon the belief that man has no opportunity for enjoyment after death. Man is not like **a tree** (7) that can spring again to life even though it may be cut off close to the ground. Though the **root is old in the earth** (8), yet at **the scent of water** (9) it will send out new shoots and thus be restored to life. Man is not like this. When he dies he is gone. He **wasteth away . . . as the waters fail from the sea** (10-11). Any inland pool or body of water could be described as a "sea." In hot and arid climates, these evaporate and rapidly become extinct. He is like **the flood** (stream or river) that **decayeth and drieth up.** The verse is a graphic figure describing complete extinction. **So a man lieth down** (12), as though to sleep, but he shall never be awakened. Many of the burial customs dating to very ancient times indicate some kind of hope or consciousness of existence beyond the grave, and elsewhere this hope is seen in the OT. However, Job here denies that he sees any such hope for a man. It must always be kept in mind that it was Christ who finally "brought life and immortality to light through the gospel" (II Tim. 1:10).

Having denied that there is any reason to hope that a man can live again, Job immediately expresses a deep desire that it might be true. If God could only **hide me away in the grave** (13) and **keep me secret,** perhaps His anger would subside. After this perhaps God would **remember** him again with kindness. Surely

---

[20]RSV and other modern translations follow the Greek, Syriac, and Vulgate texts in saying "bringing *him* into judgment." This use of the third person is consistent with the reference to humanity in general in the preceding verses. However, the Hebrew reads "bringeth me." It is not inappropriate for Job to think from the general to himself specifically. This he has done before and does so hereafter.

God, who can rejuvenate a tree, could bring a man back from the grave. A seed of hope lies buried in Job's sorrow.

To understand these verses it is helpful to remember the Hebrew conception of death. To them death was not the cessation of being. There was a kind of existence, albeit a weakened and even an undesirable kind. Man was not alive, but he had not ceased to exist. His existence in death was a shadowy type of his former life. He was completely cut off from the living and from God (see 3:12-19; 10:21-22; 14:20-22). Elsewhere it is affirmed that the power of death is overcome by God on behalf of those who trust in Him (see Ps. 16:10; 49:15; 73:23-26). The Psalmist speaks out of a sure relationship with God. Job speaks from the fear that God has rejected him and that the divine anger will pursue him to the grave.[21]

Job's question, **If a man die, shall he live again?** (14) is ambivalent in that both doubt and hope are contained within it. If Job dared to hope for a life beyond the grave, he would endure his present condition and **wait** with equanimity God's **call** to him (15). But Job is not yet able to rise above his immediate dilemma to a strong faith in God's concern for him. Therefore he turns once more to the despair which is forced upon him by the tragedy of his life. It seems to him that God **numberest my steps** (16). It is as though God had written out all of Job's transgression and had **sealed** the record **up in a bag** (17), to be brought out at the time for judgment. When even the **mountain and the rock** (18) are worn away, what hope does frail man have? He has none, for God **prevailest for ever against him** (20). He dies and loses contact with the living, not knowing the **honour** or loss that may come to **his sons** (21). His lot is to **have pain** and to **mourn** (22).

B. The Second Cycle of Speeches, 15:1—21:34

In the first cycle of discussion the friends completely misunderstood the cause of Job's trouble, and they misconstrued Job's attitude toward his suffering. They earnestly urged him to humility and repentance because they honestly believed that he was not beyond the help of God. Their advice was based on experience which to them had proved true time and again.

But Job's impassioned insistence on his innocence convinced them that he was adding bigotry, if not blasphemy, to his suspec-

---

[21]Davidson, *op. cit.*, pp. 103 ff. Cf. Pedersen, *op. cit.*, III, 477 ff.

ted hidden sin. They now became convinced that they were dealing with a stubborn and proud man who would go to any lengths to justify himself. From this point on, plain and powerful language must be used. He must be made to realize that he is the kind of wicked person they have been describing in general terms. Perhaps by this method they will be able to stab his conscience awake, so that he can see himself in a true light. This second round of dialogue is pointed and at times cruel as the friends try to cut through Job's defenses.

If Job has not convinced his critics, at least he has reinforced his own conviction concerning his innocence. He is certain that God's attack upon him has been unjustified. Therefore he responds in equally harsh terms against the criticism of his friends. Perhaps he had hoped that his protestation of innocence would convince his friends of his integrity. When this failed, and his counselors are even more certain of his sinfulness, Job sinks to a new depth of despair. Much that he says in this second cycle reflects the feeling that both God and man have deserted him. In his last speech he turns his attention to the actual argument which the friends have used against him, and answers the position which they hold.

1. *The Second Speech of Eliphaz* (15:1-35)

Eliphaz, as before, takes the lead in the discussion. In doing so he sets the pattern of the discourse for the other members of the group. He makes particular use of Job's last speech (cc. 13—14) in order to show how Job has maligned his friends and has been completely irreverent towards God. This convinces him that Job is even more wicked than he formerly had suspected him to be. Therefore Eliphaz describes the fate of the wicked in the hope that he can shock Job into a sensible appraisal of his condition.

A wise man (2) such as Job claims to be should know better than to speak in this **vain** manner. Rather than having spoken from the heart—the seat of intelligence and understanding—Job has filled **his belly with the east wind**—a violent, hot, and harmful wind. Job has used **talk** that is **unprofitable** and **can do no good** (3). As a result, the **fear** (4) of God and **prayer** to God, which are the very essence of religion, are destroyed. Thus by his own words Job has done more to condemn himself than any of the arguments of his friends. Eliphaz observes, **Thine own lips testify against thee** (6). He believed that arguments such as Job had used in 12:6 were merely crafty pretenses to cover his guilt.

Job also claimed to possess wisdom equal to or superior to that of his friends. Eliphaz sarcastically asks concerning the basis of this claim: **Art thou the first man that was born?** (7) Job had admitted that wisdom came with age (12:12). Ironically Eliphaz inquires if Job thinks himself a super being, one who had **heard the secret of God** (8) at the beginning of time. He asks, **Dost thou restrain** (draw) **wisdom to thyself? Wisdom** as used here is the divine wisdom. The question is whether Job, as a member of the heavenly council, had access to knowledge of the mysteries of God. Eliphaz answers the question he has raised by implying that Job is in fact no wiser than they: **What knowest thou, that we know not?** Indeed, there is one in their midst (could it be Eliphaz himself?) who is old enough to be Job's **father** (10). If there is a relationship between age and wisdom, Job is far outclassed. Eliphaz also claimed in his first speech to have received wisdom by divine revelation (4:12-17). In v. 11 he asks, "Are God's consolations too trivial for you, or the word that treats you gently?" (Berk.) On what basis did Job choose to disregard such counsel?

Eliphaz next turns from Job's assertion of superior wisdom and rebukes him for his irreverent attitude towards God: **Thine eyes wink** (12); rather, They flash as a sign of temper. **Turnest thy spirit** (13) may be translated "breath," standing for anger or fury (Judg. 8:3, marg.; Prov. 16:32). Even the average man, **born of a woman** (14), is not capable of being **clean** in God's sight; how much less Job, who **drinketh iniquity like water** (16). Eliphaz declares that "God puts no trust in his holy ones, and the heavens are not clean in his sight" (15, RSV). Therefore how can Job be clean?

With Job thus classified as an evil man, Eliphaz proceeds to describe the fate of the wicked. Verses 17-19 are a difficult prefatory statement which Moffatt translates:

> Listen, let me tell you this,
>   let me relate what I have learned—
> a truth that wise men handed down,
>   imparted to them by their fathers,
> who had the land all to themselves,
>   untainted by a foreigner.

Pain dogs **the wicked man** (20) "all of his life" (Berk.). The last
part of 20 is obscure. The RSV relates it to the first statement
thus:

> The wicked man writhes in pain all of his days,
>> through all the years that are laid up for the ruthless.

The wicked man has **a dreadful sound** (of terror) constantly
in his ears (21); **the destroyer** (robber) pursues him. He lives
in constant fear and danger (22). **Trouble and anguish . . .
prevail against** the one who persists in wickedness, as though
they were a successful attacking army (24). Such men have
defied God and have given themselves completely to sensual
pleasures in their stubborn resistance to Him. Moffatt clarifies
the passage thus:

> For he challenged God,
>> he matched himself against the Almighty,
> charging at him haughtily,
>> behind stout bossed shields—
> so swollen in prosperity,
>> so bloated in his wealth.
> He rebuilt ruined cities for himself,
>> places that no man ought to dwell in (25-28).

But no such rebellion shall prove to be of any help, for the
wicked man will not be permitted to flourish **upon the earth**
(29). **Darkness** and destruction will overtake him (30-31). The
death of the wicked shall occur **before his time** (32), like the
falling of the **unripe grape** (33) or the **olive** failing to mature
before some blight hits it. It is impossible in God's economy for
hypocrites (34) to prosper. "They conceive mischief and produce unfairness; their hearts bring forth deception" (35, Berk.).

Thus the prosperity of the wicked man is only apparent.
Promises of success are unfulfilled. His life is cut off before
it reaches a successful fruition.

2. Job's Reply (16:1—17:16)

This reply to Eliphaz, like the others, is directly addressed
to the friends only in part. God is addressed, and also there is a
kind of introspective conversation which Job holds with himself.
Job's previous appeal to God (13:20-28) remained unanswered.
God seemingly refused to answer Job or show himself to him.
Job had hoped that his honest appeal to heaven would convince
his friends of his integrity. Instead he is accused of crafty use of

words to hide his sin (15:5-6). Eliphaz convinces Job that his friends have abandoned him, and Job reacts in anger prompted by deep hurt.

Miserable comforters are ye all (2) is literally "comforters of trouble." They add to the trouble that Job already has instead of helping through sympathy and understanding. Their **vain words** (3) do not **end.** They persist in hurting him further. He has difficulty in understanding what **emboldeneth** Eliphaz to speak at all, since he has nothing of value to say (cf. 13:5).

With contempt Job affirms that it would be easy indeed for him to **heap up words** (4) against his friends if their situation were reversed. Verse 5 should probably be read as a continuation of Job's sarcasm. If he were in their place he could do lip service to their friendship by mouthing insincere words of condolence. Whether he speaks or is silent, Job's pain continues, so he may as well speak plainly concerning the way he feels (6).

In the form of a soliloquy Job once more describes the pathetic condition which God's enmity towards him has produced. God has made him **weary** (7), i.e., exhausted him. His relentless pursuit has **made desolate all my company** (7). Even his best friends are now alienated from him. His **wrinkles** and **leanness** (8) witness against him. The ravages of disease are obvious and are interpreted by those who see him as evidence of his guilt. These statements are an echo of the attitude shown by Job's comforters and are exactly the kind of evidence which they have used to condemn him. God's hostility is further described as being like a beast of prey that **gnasheth upon me with his teeth** (9). Smith translates the expression **sharpeneth his eyes** as, "My enemy looks daggers at me" (Smith-Goodspeed).

The figure moves from beasts to men who have **gaped upon** Job with derision and **have smitten** him in their hatred (10). Thus God has betrayed Job **into the hands of the wicked** (11). When he **was at ease** (12) God shook **me by my neck,** as a terrier shakes a rat. **Archers** (13) used him as a target until they spilled his **gall upon the ground.** "The Oriental speaks of gall and gall-bladder where we might refer to the blood and the heart."[22] God is described as **a giant** warrior (14) who makes **breach upon breach** against Job, as an army breaks down the walls of a besieged city. As a consequence Job, in complete humility, has sewn together a garment of **sackcloth** (15). **Defiled my horn**

[22]*Ibid.,* p. 121

may be read "bowed my glory to the dust" (Moffatt). His **face is foul** (red or inflamed) **with weeping** (16) over the humiliation and hopelessness of his condition.

Once more, after pouring out his grief, Job seems to rally enough to renew his basic claim: all of this evil has happened to him, but **not for any injustice in mine hands** (17). Consequently he calls, **O earth, cover not thou my blood** (18). Spilled blood called for vengeance (Gen. 4:10-11) and continued to do so until it was covered properly (Ezek. 24:7-8). Although Job is not being murdered, he believes that his death is unjustified and wants his cry for justice to continue to be heard: "Let . . . it go wandering through the world" (Moffatt). Even though he expects to die, he hopes for justice.

Job's cry for vindication seems to arouse hope within him, and he affirms that he has a **witness . . . in heaven,** and his **record is on high** (19). At a later time (19:25) Job will make a stronger claim upon God for vindication. For the present he is able only to express the desire to have someone intercede for him **with God, as a man pleadeth for his neighbour** (21). He has little to anticipate now except **a few years** (22) before his death—"the path along which I shall not return" (Berk.).

Chapter 17 continues the thought at the end of 16. **My breath is corrupt** is better translated, "My life is destroyed." The Hebrew (*ruach*) occasionally carries the idea of breath, but it is a term having to do with the essence of life itself. Parallel to this thought Job adds that his **days are extinct,** almost over, and **the graves are ready**—that is, the grave awaits him (1).

Job is conscious of the fact that **mockers** (2; his friends) are watching him as he slowly dies. The closer he comes to death, the more certain they are that they have been correct in their diagnosis of his case. RSV translates the last part of 2, "My eye dwells on their provocation." Job cannot follow their delusive counsel. He turns to God and makes an additional appeal for help in achieving the little satisfaction that might yet be available to him.

His request is that God will vouch for him. **Lay down now** (3) means, "Give me a pledge" (Berk.). **Put me in a surety with thee** expresses the same idea, while **striking hands** was a method of sealing a bargain. Making pledges and going a bond (suretyship) are actions which have strong implications for the future. This confidence is not ready to blossom, but the seeds of hope have been planted well.

In the immediate context Job wishes God to confound his friends for their obstinate refusal to recognize his integrity. They have no **understanding** (4), and have in some way betrayed him (5) "for a price" (Berk.). They have also made him a **byword** (added to his ill reputation) among **the people** (6). **Tabret** in KJV is a mistranslation. The RSV renders the last part of 6, "I am one before whom men spit." As a result of this mistreatment Job's **eye . . . is dim** (7) and he wastes away.

However Job believes that there is some moral justice yet. **Upright men** (8) at least will show amazement at the terrible state of affairs, and **the innocent** shall stand **against the hypocrite.** Men like Job who are truly **righteous** (9) will not permit themselves to be swayed from their convictions. As a consequence the man who is upright and **clean** shall grow **stronger and stronger.** Job has come a long way back toward confidence in the moral order!

Having established this truth, he turns to his friends and invites them to **return** (10)—a word frequently translated "repent." But even as he extends the invitation he realizes that there is not one of his friends **wise** enough to profit from his advice.

Once more Job subsides into gloom over his hopeless plight. His **days are past** (11) and his "plans" (RSV) are **broken off.** The Hebrew of 12 is obscure but it seems to express frustration and despair.

> *Night is a day to me,*
> *and light is darkness* (Moffatt).

Job cannot do anything except **wait** for **the grave** (13) and embrace the worms of decay as though they are his closest relatives (14). Even the **hope** that he has managed to muster (8-9) is useless, for **who shall see it?** (15) Job and his hope will **rest together . . . in the dust** (16). **The pit** is *Sheol,* the grave.

Job has returned to his earliest conclusion. His life is so far destroyed and his health so completely lost that his only hope is to make *Sheol* his home. There at last he can find some peace and rest from his physical suffering and his spiritual anguish.

3. *The Second Speech of Bildad* (18:1-21)

Bildad as a traditionalist is uneasy when his pat answers to the questions raised by Job's suffering are not accepted. He is even more disturbed when "self-evident" truth is contradicted and it is demonstrated that it is not so self-evident after all.

In Job's last discourse he had not been kind to his friends. He had called them unkind and troublesome comforters. They had, according to Job, been scornful and mocking, and were themselves blind and devoid of understanding. Indeed, there was not one of them who had any wisdom.

Job's impious attitude was yet another matter that annoyed Bildad. Job had accused God of treating him as a beast, tearing him to pieces in unjustified anger.

Briefly Bildad deals with these rash charges (18:1-4), and then proceeds to describe in some detail the true fate of the wicked (5:21). Unlike the first discourse, this one has no invitation to Job to repent and take a humble attitude. Bildad seems to be convinced now that Job's case is hopeless. To him Job is an excellent example of the wicked one whom he describes. Job's misfortunes obviously prove his case.

Ere ye make an end of words (2) is literally "set snares for words." Bildad believes Job has been so feverishly hunting for arguments that he has produced nothing but words with no meaning. **Mark** means "Think over the situation carefully," **and afterwards we will speak** together, in order to come to a true understanding.

With Job the friends had been **counted as beasts, and reputed vile** (3; cf. 17:4, 10). Bildad wants to know why Job should malign them so. The reference to being **vile** is probably an accusation of stupidity rather than uncleanness, for Job had not accused his friends of being dirty. The reference to beasts reminds Bildad that Job had accused God of tearing him like a beast (16:9). The fact is quite contrary to this, for it is Job who **teareth himself** (4) in his own impassioned rage against God. Such outbreaks only serve to destroy the man who utters them. Besides, who does Job think he is? Would he have the **earth . . . forsaken** on his behalf or **the rock . . . removed out of his place?** These expressions are commonly interpreted as symbols used to describe the moral universe. Would Job have the undergirding principle of punishment for sin abrogated in order that he might be able to maintain his righteousness? (Cf. Lev. 26:43; Isa. 6:12.)

In Bildad's mind these questions can have only one answer. There is no further need to debate the issue. Job is guilty. His suffering proves his wickedness. It now remains only to paint a lurid picture of the fate of the sinner. This Bildad proceeds to do. He traces the downfall of the unrighteous through five stages:

(a) Darkness overtakes him (5-6).

(b) Snares are laid for his feet (7-11).

(c) He is given over to the king of terrors (12-15).

(d) His name and memory are obliterated from the earth (16-19).

(e) He becomes a symbol of horror to other men (20-21).

Light is universally used to symbolize life, vitality, warmth, and cheer. Here Bildad declares, **The light of the wicked shall be put out** (5). The figures used are those of the nomad tent dwellers. The flame of **his fire** and the **candle** (6; lamp) in his tent are extinguished. The Lord says through Jeremiah, "I will take from them the voice of mirth, and the voice of gladness, the voice of the bridegroom, and the voice of the bride, the sound of the millstones, and the light of the candle" (Jer. 25:10). Bildad agrees that this is the consequence of wickedness. Such a person can only expect to grope darkly as he walks in a path which is full of obstacles, while **his own counsel** (7; deluded judgment) leads him to his downfall.

Bildad adds figure to figure to describe the result of iniquity. There is **a snare** hidden to catch the sinner as **his own feet** (evil conduct) carry him on (8-10). Note the various terms used for seizing a man: the **net**, the **gin**, the **snare**, the **trap**. Thus **terrors** (11) are all around him. He cannot move without being caught. Standing still, he is terrorized at that which will befall him.

His strength shall be hungerbitten (12); i.e., dissipated in the same way that one becomes feeble from starvation. **The first-born of death** (13) is descriptive of epidemics which shall overtake the man who persists in wrongdoing. When these epidemics strike, the wicked man's **confidence** will be destroyed. Not even in his own **tabernacle** (14; tent) will he find consolation. The personal application of these allusions could scarcely escape Job. It is as though Bildad deliberately describes him.

Bildad returns to the figure used in 8:15, where the individual attempts to maintain himself by leaning upon his house. The **king of terrors** (14) is death. Strangers, those that are **none of his** (15), shall dwell in his tent after it has been disinfected by **brimstone** (sulphur). Or perhaps brimstone is a figure of utter desolation—a mark of the curse of God which makes his

73

dwelling unfit for occupancy forever. It may also be reminiscent of the fire of God which destroyed Job's cattle and the servants attending them.

Bildad has carried the progress of the wicked man to the point of death. Is there more? Yes! His memory and his race shall also be blotted out. **His roots** and **his branch (16)** are both destroyed. Job had received just a spark of hope upon reflecting that a tree cut off at the ground could live again. Bildad makes sure that Job understands there is no such hope for him. The wicked man's **name** is no longer **in the street (17).** It is out of memory. In many regards this is the worst fate that can befall the Oriental. The wicked man, and all that pertains to him, are **chased out of the world (18)** with **no son** or other relative **remaining (19).** These statements no doubt reminded Job of the loss of his sons and daughters which he had already suffered.

One would think that Bildad had exhausted the list of horrors to befall the sinner, but he has yet another. Those **that come after him shall be astonied (20)** at the completeness of his downfall and shall use him as a frightening example of the consequence of wickedness. Bildad seems to have forgotten that he had just said that the wicked are to be unremembered.

Bildad's description follows the course of Job's trouble so exactly that one is tempted to conclude that he consciously used Job for his model. If so, the latter portion of his speech is a direct prediction of what will soon overtake Job. Job's actual death is all that is required to make the case complete and prove decisively that Bildad is correct.

4. *Job's Reply to the Second Speech of Bildad* (19:1-29)

Bildad's speech had been ruthless in its denunciation of Job. In the first round of dialogue all three friends agree that there is a remedy for Job's dilemma. But now the situation has changed. With only Zophar left to speak in the second round, it is plain that the friends agree that Job is terribly guilty of wrongdoing. Job is still capable of reacting with some heat to their cynicism, but even this ultimately gives way to a cry of deep anguish (19:21). He is driven once more to the extremity of despair but finds something within him which refuses to admit that he will be completely abandoned by God. He is presently abandoned by both God and man, but in the future God will appear to vindicate him.

At the outset of this reply to Bildad, Job complains about the unkind attitude of his friends. **How long will ye vex my soul?** (2) But there is more than annoyance. The condemnation of the friends threatens to **break** him **in pieces.** Job is crushed. They have not only failed to alleviate his pain with their consolations (16:4-6), but they have actually added to it. Had Job been able to accept their interpretation of his condition, he could have accepted their solution of repentance. But since he has not done anything for which he should repent, their repeated condemnation of him merely adds to his burden. **These ten times** (3) is not to be taken literally but as a round number to express frequent and repeated reproach levied against him. The remainder of the verse is obscure but Smith gives it meaning consistent with Job's mood when he translates it, "You wrong me shamelessly" (Smith-Goodspeed).

Verse 4 is obscure. However, on the basis of the kind of statements Job has made up to this point the words must be taken as further denial of the offenses of which the friends have constantly accused him. The second clause, **Mine error remaineth with myself,** may mean that whatever wrong Job has committed is so insignificant that it is of no concern to anyone other than himself. God could not be interested in punishing any such small infraction of His will, and the friends should therefore mind their own business.[23]

Be that as it may, Job wishes his friends to know that he agrees with them at one cardinal point: It is **that God hath overthrown me** (6). He does not agree that God's action against him is justified. Job says that he cries **out of wrong** and that **there is no judgment** (7). God has afflicted him in a completely unjustified manner. He further contradicts the claims made by Bildad in 18:8 that Job's own feet have led him into a snare. Rather, he affirms, God has **compassed me with his net** (6), i.e., thrown the net around him.

From this position Job proceeds to describe the severe hostility which God has shown to him. The figure in v. 6 pictures Job as being caught in a trap like a helpless animal. When he calls out for help, there is no one who answers him, not even God (7). No escape is possible, for God has **fenced up my way** and has created a thick **darkness** (8). God has taken from him his

---

[23]For a rather complete discussion of the possible meanings of this verse see Pope, *op. cit.,* pp. 130 ff. and Terrien, *op. cit.,* pp. 1041 ff.

glory and his **crown** (9). These terms are related to righteousness and godliness (see 29:14). It may be also that **glory,** with its association with brilliance, is a conscious contrast to the darkness Job has just described. With this taken from him, his reputation for being a righteous man is destroyed, so that he is considered by his friends and neighbors to be a sinner. Job's **hope** was **removed like a tree** (10) that had been torn up by its roots. Had the tree been cut off, there might be hope for new growth (14:7), but in this instance it is described as being totally destroyed.

Next Job describes God as a vindictive enemy who assaults him like an army laying siege against his encampment. Already the attacks have been so severe that Job is nearly annihilated and his resources are almost gone. The question is, How much longer can he hold out? (11-12) At this point Job forgets that he has already indicated on several other occasions that he wants to die and get it over with.

God's hostility has destroyed Job's human contacts. He is **estranged** from people and is abhorred by them. This develops as one of the deepest hurts in his experience. The description moves from various relationships which a man enjoys and depends upon and finally concludes with the plaintive cry, **Have pity upon me, have pity upon me, O ye my friends** (21).

Brethren (13) are not necessarily blood relatives but may refer to members of his general community. **Acquaintance** is used in much the same way as in modern usage. **Kinsfolk and familiar friends** (14) are those closest to him. **They that dwell in mine house** (15) are his guests, while **maids** are his female slaves. All of these plus his **servant** (16) and the "sons of my mother" (17; following RSV, since Job's children are already dead) have been alienated from him and have deserted him in his time of trial. Even his **wife** is included in the list. **His breath is strange** to her (17). The word translated **breath** (*nephesh*) is frequently used in the reflexive sense to stand for the individual himself. This is another way in which Job describes the attitude which she has toward him. She has come to despair of Job's very self. Indeed, she had already advised him to "curse God, and die" (2:9). **Young children** (18) and his **inward** (intimate) **friends** (19) are repulsed by the ravages of his disease (20). It is no wonder that Job felt utterly desolate and pleaded so plaintively, **Have pity upon me, O ye my friends** (21). Is it necessary for them to treat him **as God** has done? Why cannot they be **satisfied** (22) with what has already been done and cease from their painful accusations?

At this, another low point in the experience of Job, he once more looks to the future. He wishes that his **words were now written** (23), so that succeeding generations might hear his protests of innocence. Ordinary writing would not be sufficient. This should be done with an **iron pen and lead in the rock** (24), so that it would endure **for ever.**

Thinking of an enduring witness causes Job to achieve the greatest insight thus far in the search for meaning in his situation. He suddenly realizes deep within him that he has a living **redeemer** (25). The word is *goel,* which usually stands for the next of kin. Such a person is charged with taking blood revenge in case murder has been committed; he "redeems" the estate of a dead man, or he raises up posterity for a deceased brother in the levirate marriage. Thus he is the defender, avenger, the one who saves from oppression, the deliverer. God is this to Israel in a fashion that no one else could ever be (Exod. 6:6; 15:13; Ps. 74:2; *et al.*). Job finally sees God standing up to defend his honor and setting the record straight.

He also affirms, **Yet in my flesh shall I see God** (26). These lines have received a variety of interpretation which ranges from a denial that a resurrection is intended to affirmation that resurrection is exactly what is meant.

To support the negative view it is pointed out that Job has positively stated that there is no hope for life after death (14: 7-14), that he is a man who hast lost all hope. It is also argued that such hope at this juncture of the argument precludes any necessity for further discussion and that it fails to account for the discouragement and hopelessness which Job will yet express. It is further affirmed that the text of these verses is quite corrupt.[24]

On the other hand, it has been noted that Job fluctuates in his emotions from despair to some vestige of hope. And even though he has often expressed despair and confusion, he ha` resolutely refused to abandon his integrity in his relationship to God. In spite of his depths of despair Job comes back. These moments seem to grow stronger and finally climax in Job's cry of

---

[24]Among those who support this view and who give rather detailed interpretations of this passage are: Pope, *op. cit.,* p. 135; Terrien, *op. cit.,* p. 1056; Tsur-Sinai, *op. cit.,* pp. 304 ff. See also James K. Zink, "Impatient Job," JBL, LXXXIV (June, 1965), 147-52.

faith that he shall see God as his Redeemer (*goel*) with his own eyes (27; see comments on 14:14-15; 16:17-20).[25]

It may be, as some suggest, that immortality in the sense of unending existence after death is not here affirmed. But it cannot be denied that Job has come to the point of faith where he knows that there must be some relationship between himself and God even after death. Up to this point in the discussion death has been the barrier past which Job could not look. Now he can see beyond it with the certainty that ultimately he will receive satisfaction.[26]

Having come to this remarkable conclusion, Job is overcome with desire to see his hope come to fruition. The KJV margin reads, "My reins within me are consumed with earnest desire." In the Hebrew psychology the **reins** (kidneys) were considered to be the seat of emotions and intense feeling.

Finally in vv. 28-29, Job turns again to his friends and warns them against persecuting him further lest they, completely in the wrong, be themselves destroyed, for surely they will discover **there is a judgment.** There is yet justice in the world.

5. *The Second Speech of Zophar* (20:1-29)

Zophar's first speech had been answered by Job in a sarcastic manner. Zophar also has fresh in his mind the fact that Job threatened his friends with severe judgment from God because of their criticism of him. Like the others, he holds Job guilty; and despite all of Job's protests to the contrary, this conviction has grown instead of being dissipated. As a result, Zophar explodes with fiery language.

Therefore (2) has reference to what has preceded. Zophar has been maintaining his silence with difficulty, and he can do so no longer—**My thoughts cause me to answer.** The assertion, **I make haste,** means, in this connection, "I am stirred up" (Berk.). Zophar is not willing to be ridiculed by Job and does not appreciate being likened to a dumb beast (12:7). Nor does he like to be called a blow-hard (16:3). Therefore he affirms his **understanding** (3) of life. Verse 3 has been rendered, "I have heard your presumptuous warning to censure you no more; but a spirit prompts me to inquire of you" (Berk.). Having defended

---

[25]Davidson, *op. cit.*, pp. 142 ff. supports this position and in general also Gray, *op. cit.*, pp. 171 ff.

[26]See T. H. Robinson, *op. cit.*, p. 100.

himself in this manner, he launches an attack upon the position
held by Job.

Zophar quickly passes to his dogmatic interpretation of the
moral order of the world. **Since man** has lived **upon earth** (4)
it is common knowledge that any **triumphing of the wicked** (5)
is brief. Job should know this and mark it well, for it is the
foundation of the argument. Job had claimed that the prosperity
of the wicked nullified his friends' contention that suffering is
a result of sin. Zophar reaffirms this truth, explaining that no
matter how grand the wicked man conceives himself to be—even
if **his head reach unto the clouds** (6)—his apparent success is
not lasting.

The fact is that the greater the achievement, the greater the
fall of the sinner. Though the expression is indelicate, the figure
of speech is expressive. The haughty man shall perish **like his
own dung** and men will one day look around and realize that
he no longer exists (7). He will have no more substance and
reality than a bad **dream** (8). His wealth will be restored to the
rightful owners by **his children** (10). Nothing of his ill-gotten
gain will remain, and in addition to this he shall die young,
while **his bones are full of the sin of his youth** (11).

Zophar believes that sin has its own punishment within it.
He speaks of it as a sweet-tasting food which one holds **in his
mouth** (12) in order to savor it fully, yet it turns to poison in
his stomach—**it is the gall of asps within him** (14). The figure
is extended to include all manner of rich foods that are pleasant
to eat but when consumed they are vomited back again. Sin can
never be like an inexhaustible supply of **honey and butter** (17).

The sinner may work hard for his possessions, but he will
not be able to enjoy them as he had anticipated because he has
oppressed . . . the poor and **hath violently taken** (19) what he
wanted. Such gain will turn sour and be like food that will not
digest in the stomach. At the very time that a man is full, he
shall become sick with the poison of it. This is God's **wrath upon
him** (23).

The figure of destruction changes from poisonous food to
that of the sword. The doer of iniquity shall be forced to **flee
from the iron weapon** (24) but he will be run through by an
arrow with a **glittering** shaft (not **sword,** 25) shot from a **bow
of steel** (rather, brass). Thus shall the **terrors** of death overtake
him.

The idea of terror is expanded to include the **darkness** of calamities that hide in **secret places** (26). **A fire not blown** is one that is not kindled by man. It is a fire of God that consumes him. Destruction is not sufficient terror for the wicked person. **His iniquity** (27) will be revealed to everyone by the observable results of judgments levied against him. Consequently **the earth** (all of his fellowmen) **Shall rise up against him.** All that he gained will be destroyed in the **day of . . . wrath** (28). This is the way of God, and it is as certain as a **heritage** given to him **by God** (29).

Like Bildad, Zophar has used Job as his model for describing the fate of the wicked. He has not supported his contention with new evidence. He simply uses the weight of dogmatism to defend his view.

6. *Job's Second Reply to Zophar* (21:1-34)

Following his great affirmation of faith in 19:25-27, Job is able to achieve a remarkable degree of equanimity. Even after the sharp implications of Zophar's speech he does not react with the same kind of emotional tension that characterized his previous discourses. In this chapter he begins to think more clearly upon the issues at stake rather than to expend his energies in emotional outbreaks describing his suffering and frustration.

In the first cycle of dialogue Job's concern was with the fact that he felt God had become his enemy. Next he was crushed over the fact that his friends had deserted him to the point where they actually turned against him. But now Zophar's speech causes Job to take a positive position concerning the arguments of his friends. He attacks these arguments with empirical evidence which contradicts them. He notes that prosperity and righteousness do not invariably go together. It is also evident from observation of life that wickedness is not always punished.

Prior to launching the major issues of his argument Job makes some introduction statements. The first of these is to request the attention of his friends—**Hear diligently my speech** (2). The expression **let this be your consolations** means, "Your thoughtful attention will bring me consolation" (Berk.). After he has spoken they may **mock on** (3) if they wish. In the meantime they should listen carefully to what he has to say, because his **complaint** (4) is not against **man**; it is against God! His friends may well be **astonished** (5), and he himself is seized with **trembling** (6) when he thinks about it. But what he is about to say is truth in spite of their reaction to it.

The truth is quite contrary to the picture which the friends have drawn. Eliphaz (15:17 ff.), Bildad (18:5 ff.), and Zophar (20:4 ff.) have each described the fate of the wicked man as being certain punishment from the hand of God. Job now points out that this does not always occur. He asks, How is it that **the wicked live** and grow **mighty in power?** (7) Rather than God's punishing judgment being evident in their lives, **their seed (children) is established in their sight** (8), their **houses are safe from fear** (9), their cattle multiply (10), and there is happiness in their homes (11). They spend their times pleasantly with **the timbrel and harp** (12) and **sound of the organ** (pipe or flute). When it is their natural time to die, **in a moment** they **go down to the grave** (13). It is no wonder, therefore, that they feel no need of God nor any desire for the **knowledge of His ways** (14). They get along very well without Him. There is no need even for such a man to **pray (15)**!

The question which Job's answer raises is pertinent for any age. Why do men pray? Is it for gain? The Christian perspective will dictate quite another answer, even though much praying heard today has a great deal of the "give me" type of request. Jesus' story of the wayward son comes strongly to mind. The boy was prodigal when he said to his father, "Give me." He was a penitent son when he asked, "Make me" (Luke 15:12, 19).

In v. 16, Job underscores the great problem which the prospering wicked man presents. His prosperity is not a result of his own doings—**Their good is not in their hand.** The inference is that God prospers the wicked man as well as the righteous, and Job continues to ask why. The meaning of 17-18 is clarified if question marks replace the exclamation marks in KJV (cf. Moffatt, Smith-Goodspeed). Job asks, How often does one see the judgments of God come upon the evildoer—judgments such as a shortened life, calamity or destruction, sorrow and pain, or resources being driven away like **chaff** or **stubble?** The implication is that one seldom sees it.

Job anticipates objections from the friends on the grounds that God will inflict His punishment upon the **children** (19-20) of the wicked man (cf. Exod. 20:5; Jer. 31:29-30). He insists that this is no punishment for wickedness. To be real and effective punishment, the evildoer must himself **drink of the wrath of the Almighty** (20). An evil man has little concern about the suffering of **his house after him** (21).

Verse 22 furnishes a transition in thought which is not entirely clear. Is it the friends who are trying to **teach God** how His providence rules in the affairs of men? If so, then Job holds them in derision, for God is exalted above all of the earth. That this is true is demonstrated by the fact that He **judgeth those that are high.** Or is Job musing to himself concerning his own effort to determine the meaning of life and the operation of God in the moral universe? If so, then Job is apologetic in his effort to assess God's motives. No mere mortal is capable of doing this.

In any event Job continues to draw upon observable detail in man's life to learn of God's ways. Death is especially instructive. As Job has watched in what circumstances men die, he has not been able to discern any meaningful pattern that would distinguish between the righteous and the wicked. One dies in the **full strength** (23) of his manhood, while everything seems to be going well. The phrase, **His breasts are full of milk** (24), has a marginal alternative that makes better sense: His "milk pails are full." The reference is to the richness and plenty which a man receives from his herds. **His bones are moistened with marrow** means, "His health is sound" (Moffatt). Such a person dies in the midst of health and plenty and in peace (23-24). Yet another person dies **in the bitterness of his soul** (25), without having the opportunity to experience any of the normal pleasures of life. When death strikes, both of these individuals are alike. **They shall lie down alike in the dust** (26) and are consumed by **worms.** Thus two very dissimilar lives suffer the same fate and are treated in identical fashion. If God is responsible for the death of both, as Job and his friends agree that He is, then Job believes that God is unjust in His treatment of men.

Job knows what his friends are thinking—**Behold, I know your thoughts** (27). They have told him plainly enough. The friends have said that the wicked disappear from the earth without leaving any trace of themselves—**Where is the house of the prince? and where are the dwelling places of the wicked?** (28; cf. 18:14-18; 20:26-28.) But they have not considered the evidence which any world traveler would give to them.

> *Well, talk to travellers,*
> *learn what they have to tell:*
> *of how an evil man is spared calamity,*
> *how he goes scatheless from the wrath of God.*
> (29-30, Moffatt)

Job continues: "Who rebukes a [wicked] man to his face, or who repays him for his behavior? When he is borne to the grave, a watch is kept over his tomb. Softly the clods of the valley cover him" (31-33, Berk.).

How then comfort ye me in vain? (34), Job asks. He feels that he has completely refuted the arguments of his friends. He has demonstrated that in their **answers there remaineth falsehood.** That which they have said cannot be documented from real life. Consequently their testimony is not true.

C. THE THIRD CYCLE OF SPEECHES, 22:1—31:40

The third cycle of discourse is to be viewed as another stage in the argument of the book. This is true even though at times the characters seem to be only repeating themselves.

In the first cycle the discussion basically centered around the meaning of suffering as it relates to the nature of God. In the second cycle the speakers were concerned about the operation of divine providence in the world as demonstrated especially by the fate of the wicked. Since Job very forcefully denied that the fate of the wicked illustrated any providential principle operating in history, the only thing left to the friends is to be specific about the charges which they have been making concerning Job. In this cycle they undertake to name clearly the sins of which they consider him guilty.

1. *The Third Speech of Eliphaz* (22:1-30)

The gentle mystic of the first cycle (cf. comments on 4:1-6) now makes his charge against Job. In his second discourse Eliphaz had accused Job of impious attitudes against God. Now, in addition to commenting upon some of Job's claims, he accuses him of specific sins against his fellowman.

In reply to Job's charge that there is no moral order in the world, Eliphaz asks, **Can a man be profitable unto God?** (2) He declares that God is unaffected by man's conduct, whether it be good or bad. Any righteousness on Job's part is of no advantage to God. The advantage is only to the man **himself** (2-4). He will not **reprove thee for fear of thee** (4) is better translated "because of your fear of Him"—your religion. Since God derives no advantage or disadvantage from man's actions, it follows that His judgment is for the good of the individual. This brings Eliphaz back to his original contention. Job suffers greatly; therefore, **Is not thy wickedness great? and thine iniquities infinite?** (5)

It remains for Eliphaz to show Job precisely where his sin lies. He charges that while Job was living a life of plenty he refused to help those who were **naked** (6) and **hungry** (7). He had joined with **the mighty man** (8) in oppressing the poor, such as the **widows** and the orphans. **The arms of the fatherless** (9) expresses the right that the orphan has to expect help from those who are wealthy. These rights Job has **broken** by not fulfilling them. These are the reasons that there are **snares** (10) for Job's feet, **fear** is upon him, and he is surrounded with **darkness** (11). Eliphaz believes that Job does not understand the meaning of the calamities—**the abundance of waters**—which have befallen him.

Even though Eliphaz pretends to be explicit in his charges against Job, he names sins that could be laid at the door of any rich man—the inequities that exist in any society. Those who are able to help the poor and refuse to do so should not be excused from their obligation. But so far as Job is concerned, he should not be punished any more than others in like circumstances.

Eliphaz turns next to describe the feeling toward God which he imagines Job must have had in committing these sins. Both men agree upon the transcendence of God; He is **in the height of heaven** (12), and this is very high. Then, seeming to quote, he says that Job had claimed that God was so far removed that He could not see or care what men did. **He walketh in the circuit of the heaven** (14; the arch of the skies which spans the earth) and therefore cannot be much concerned with minutiae upon the earth. This is not Job's position in c. 21. He did not claim that God was ignorant of conditions on the earth, but rather that the wicked prosper just like or even more than the righteous. This means that, although God knows, He does not differentiate between the good man and the wicked one in allowing them the blessings of life.

Eliphaz uses his twisted reference to Job's argument to reason further from **the old way** (15; history). He refers to the sinful men who were destroyed by the **flood** (16)—probably in the time of Noah—to prove that God does, after all, visit judgment upon the wicked. These men had refused to acknowledge God in spite of the fact that he had **filled their houses with good things** (18). The wicked were ungrateful for the blessings which God had given them. It was for this reason that they were cut off. Verses 19-20 reflect the satisfaction that good men in the OT found in the vindication of God's moral world. When **the righ-teous see** the destruction of the wicked, they **are glad.**

From v. 21, Alexander Maclaren discusses "Knowledge and Peace." (1) What is acquainting oneself with God? (2) The peace of acquaintance with God; (3) The true **good** from acquaintance with God.

In his final speech to Job, Eliphaz does not end upon a note of condemnation. Once more he kindly and urgently invites Job to repent—to **return to the Almighty** (23). He beautifully describes the blessing which will follow the restoration to God's favor which repentance will produce (21-30).

Maclaren[27] finds in 23-29 "What Life May Be Made." (1) Life may be full of delight and confidence in God, 26; (2) Life can be blest with the fullest communion with Him, 27; (3) Such a life will know neither failure nor darkness, 28; (4) Such a life will be always hopeful, and finally crowned with deliverance, 29.

2. *Job's Third Reply to Eliphaz* (23:1—24:25)

In replying to his friends Job does not immediately respond to the direct charges that Eliphaz made concerning his conduct. Rather, he continues to reflect upon his misery and tries to find some meaning in what has befallen him. These two chapters are more a monologue than a dialogue, since Job does not really address the friends directly. Chapter 23 shows that Job is yet very much confused over God's treatment of him. In c. 24 he questions God's treatment of mankind in general.

Some have felt that the words **Even to day** (2) indicate that the debate had been carried on over a period of many days. Perhaps originally the division of the book was according to days, with each response being given in a day.[28] A literal translation of the Hebrew text of v. 2 makes no sense. It reads, "Even today is my complaint rebellion; my hand is heavy upon my groaning." Very little emendation is necessary in order to make the first half of the verse read, "Today again my complaint becomes rebellious" (Berk.). The second part is then changed so that the text is made to read, "His hand is heavy in spite of my groaning" (RSV).

The friends have urged Job to return to God. He counters, saying he wishes he might know where He could be found. If

[27]*Exposition of Holy Scripture* (Grand Rapids: Wm. B. Eerdmans Publishing Co., 1944), III, 58-63.

[28]Tsur-Sinai, *op. cit.*, p. 351.

so, he would certainly go **to his seat** (3; judgment seat), and lay his case before Him, even to the point of **arguments** (4). Under these circumstances Job would be glad to find out what God **would say unto me** (5). If Job were able to plead his cause directly, how would God treat him? Would He overwhelm him **with his great power?** (6) No. "He would give heed to me" (6, RSV). Surely the righteous, of whom Job considers himself to be one, could find justice at such a tribunal.

Verses 8 and 9 constitute a passage of great pathos. Job would like to find God but he **cannot.** His face is hidden from Job in every direction. God eludes him no matter which way he goes in his search for Him.

Once more, however, the low point which Job reaches sparks a hope within him. He is confident that, even though he cannot find God, God knows where Job is—**He knoweth the way that I take** (10). Further, he now is convinced that **when** (rather, if) **he hath tried me, I shall come forth as** (refined) **gold.** The reason for this confidence is clear. It is because Job has walked circumspectly in **his way** (11) and has kept His **commandment** (12).

Unfortunately, Job feels that God has disregarded his innocence even though He knows of it. God seems to be **in one mind** (13); i.e., He does just as He pleases. At the moment **the thing that is appointed to me** (14; Job's death) appears to be what He desires. This troubles Job (15) because God has no reason for treating him in this fashion. He uses His power arbitrarily. This makes Job's **heart soft** (16; faint or afraid) and is the real cause of the **darkness** (17) in his life. The cause is not the judgment of God against sin in his life, as Eliphaz charged (22: 10-11). Moffatt renders 17:

> I am appalled at his dark mystery,
> and its black shadow has bewildered me.

Chapter 24 continues the argument over the manner in which God is involved in man's life. Job's friends claimed that suffering is the retributive action of God against sin. Job has all along insisted that this cannot be true. In this chapter he offers further proof to support his position.[29]

---

[29]Chapter 24 has been considered by many as an interpolation. The reasons are: (1) alleged differences in the poetic form, and (2) the content of the chapter. These arguments are not conclusive, but the chapter is difficult to relate logically to what has preceded it. For further discussion of this matter see Gray, *op. cit.*, pp. 205 ff.

The first verse seems to be a statement of Job's major complaint. The verse should read:

Why are times not laid up by the Almighty?
And why do not they that know Him see His days?

God, the Judge of the world, should, in Job's opinion, make a regular and known schedule for trial. But even those who know Him, those who are righteous, are unable to see **his days. Times** and **days** for Job are court days "for sitting in judgment and dispensing right among men."[30]

In vv. 2-12, Job describes situations to be found everywhere among men in which God's beneficent judgment cannot be discerned. *The Berkeley Version* gives a clear and vivid description: "There are evil men who remove landmarks, rustle flocks, and pasture them. They drive away the orphan's donkey, and take the widow's cow in pawn. They push the needy off the road; the wretched of the earth all huddle out of sight. Like wild donkeys in the desert, they go out to work, looking for prey which the wilderness may yield as food for their children. They gather provender from the field and glean the wicked man's vineyard. They pass the night naked for lack of clothes, having no covering against the cold; drenched by the rains in the mountains and lacking shelter, they cling close to the shelter of overhanging rocks. Some wrest fatherless infants from their mothers' breasts and hold them as security for unpaid debts. Having no clothes they are made to go about naked; and though hungry themselves, they are forced to carry sheaves. Between the rows of olive trees of the wicked they press oil and they are compelled to tread the wine presses, while dying of thirst" (2-11).

In these circumstances Job charges that God pays no attention to what is going on. He **layeth not folly** (12); i.e., He does not regard it enough to charge them with their crimes.

Job points out in the remainder of this chapter that evil is triumphant throughout the earth. Moffatt renders 13:

Others evade the daylight,
caring not for the ways of God,
refusing to pursue his paths.

The murderer (14), the adulterer (15), and **the robber (16)** range the earth under the cover of darkness.

[30]Davidson, *op. cit.*, p. 173.

Job's friends say (RSV introduces v. 18 by "you say") that a man like this is punished. He is **cursed** in his efforts to make a living (18), and **the grave** (19) consumes those who **have sinned.** The wicked shall die at an early age, unremembered even by his mother (20). Thus **wickedness shall be broken as a tree** and destroyed. But Job again denies that this is always the case, observing that "God prolongs the life of the mighty by his power" (22, RSV). Some seem to live **in safety** (23) and happiness, even though God's **eyes are upon their ways.** They prosper for a time, even if they are ultimately **brought low** and are **cut off as the tops of the ears of corn** (24).[31]

Job has refuted the arguments of his friends and has considered some of the exceptional cases. He is certain of his position and challenges his friends to prove his **speech** (25) unsound.

3. *The Third Speech of Bildad* (25:1-6)

The third speech of Bildad as it appears in the Masoretic (the standard Hebrew) text is a brief effort to magnify God. No new thought is proposed, and Job's most recent allegation (cc. 23—24) concerning God's rule of the world is ignored.

The brevity of Bildad's last statement has suggested to many that he considers the argument to be exhausted—that he really has nothing more to say. All he wishes to do is to make one final protest against Job's impious attitude. He does this by reaffirming the majesty of God in an effort to show how small and impure man is. Some believe that the brevity of this portion is due to mutilation of the text. Frequently 26:5-14 is credited to Bildad.

The speech opens abruptly with praise of the divine omnipotence—**Dominion and fear are with him** (2). No one rules save God alone, and His majesty inspires fear. **He maketh peace** (imposes His will) **in his high places,** i.e., the heavens where He dwells. This may refer to His control of natural phenomena such as storms, or to the heavenly beings who surround Him.

He is able to call upon innumerable **armies** (3). These may be the "host of heaven" who fight for God (I Sam. 17:45; I Kings

---

[31]Some scholars, seeing that 18-24 seem to be contrary to that which Job has characteristically maintained, suggest that this portion is a part of the missing third speech of Zophar or a part of Bildad's third speech. They suggest that it has been lifted from its original place by an orthodox editor who places it in the context of Job's speech in order to make him conform more happily to the position that he thought Job should espouse.

22:19). However, the fact that **armies** (or host) is parallel to **light** suggests that this refers to the stars, which were frequently regarded as being animated and were sometimes identified as angels (Deut. 4:19; 17:3).

Bildad reiterates a basic principle held by the friends: man is not **clean** (4; impure, sinful). It cannot be otherwise when even **the moon, and . . . the stars are not pure in his sight** (5), i.e., compared to the majesty and the purity of God. Finite man is nothing more than a **worm** (6) alongside the heavenly bodies. Two different words are used for **worm.** The first of these is the worm of corruption and decay (7:5; 17:14; 21:26; 24:20). The second is a word describing extreme abasement (see Ps. 22:6). The distinction between these words is retained in the RSV:

> *How much less man, who is a maggot,*
> *and the son of man, who is a worm.*

4. *Job's Third Reply to Bildad* (26:1—27:6)

Job had heard before all that Bildad said in his brief speech magnifying God. Consequently he begins his reply with biting sarcasm levied against the irrelevant statements made by Bildad.

Job asks, **How hast thou helped?** (2) The arguments achieve nothing by way of either logic or aid to the one in need. Job needs **power . . . strength . . . wisdom** (2-3), and truth. These are not supplied by Bildad's discourse. **To whom hast thou uttered words?** (4) Does Bildad seriously think that he has been talking to Job's situation? Job already knows what Bildad had affirmed, and is in agreement with it. The debate is not over God's power and majesty, but over His use of it. God has used His power to mistreat Job. **Whose spirit came from thee?** means, "Who was it that inspired you?" (Moffatt)

In order to demonstrate that he is not in need of Bildad's admonition, Job launches into a discourse lauding God's greatness, which is far superior to that coming from his friend.[32]

Dead things (5) are literally "shades" or departed persons who reside in *Sheol*. The meaning seems to be: "The shades below quake, the waters and their inhabitants" (5, Berk.). **From under the waters** indicates that *Sheol* was thought of as underneath the waters of the sea or at the base of the earth (Isa. 14:9;

---

[32]See Davidson, *op. cit.*, p. 182. Others consider 26:5-14 as more naturally coming from Bildad, and therefore add this portion to his third speech.

cf. Exod. 20:4; Deut. 4:18; 5:8). **Hell** (6) is literally *Sheol.* The idea of hell as a place of punishment such as is found in the NT does not appear here. *Sheol* is the netherworld. **Destruction,** literally *Abaddon,* is a synonym of *Sheol,* a place where the dead congregate. Even this place beneath the earth **hath no covering** —it is not beyond the vision and power of God.

God's creative power is lauded in language which reveals something of the cosmology of the day. **Stretcheth out the north (7)** means that as far as the eye can see into the horizon of the north there is an **empty place.** The flat plain of **the earth** He has **hung upon nothing.** How far the ancients envisioned limitless space surrounding the earth is impossible to ascertain. The power of the Almighty is further illustrated by His control of nature. The clouds seem to hold vast amounts of **the waters** (8), yet they are not **rent** apart by their load. To those who knew nothing about evaporation and other causes of rainfall, the torrents of rain that pour forth from the clouds would seem marvelous indeed.

The divine presence is invisible to men below because God has enshrouded **his throne** with **his cloud** (9). In His creative power He has **compassed the waters with bounds** (10). The ancients considered the earth to be a flat disc surrounded by water. The boundary (our horizon) was thought to be the limits of **day and night. The pillars of heaven** (11) were the mountains on the horizon which held up the vault of the sky. The thunder, God's voice of **reproof,** made these pillars tremble.

Verses 12 and 13 may have for their general background the thought pattern of the Babylonian myth of creation where Tiamat, representing primeval chaos, was subdued. **The proud** (12) is literally Rahab, the primeval sea monster. *The Berkeley Version* translates 12: "By His power the sea is stilled, and by His understanding He smites through proud Rahab." God through His great power is able to subdue the sea, as a monster, in its wild raging. **Garnished the heavens** (13) is a description of the **spirit** (breath) of God clearing away the dark and ominous storm clouds. The reference to the **crooked serpent** is probably an allusion to the popular notion that a great dragon caused the darkness produced by storms or an eclipse. Job says it is God who controls all of these natural forces.

Having described only **parts** (some) **of his ways** (14), Job says that in reality man knows but a **little . . . portion** of God. Man cannot understand the full measure of His power. As translated in RSV the contrast is between a "whisper" that man knows as over against the thunder which he does not know.

How small a whisper do we hear of him!
But the thunder of his power who can understand?

The expression **Moreover Job continued** (27:1) is unusual. If the pattern established in the earlier portions of the book were followed, this would be superfluous, since 26:1 identifies Job as the speaker and no interruption is noted. It is quite clear that the text has been disturbed. However, we shall consider vv. 1-6 a continuation of Job's reply to Bildad. In this portion he simply but strongly reaffirms his innocence. **Parable** (1) should read "discourse" (RSV).

As God liveth (2) is the form of a solemn oath. It is the first time that Job has employed it in affirming his integrity. God has **taken** from Job his **judgment** (rights) and has **vexed** his **soul.** In spite of this, while Job is still alive (3) he will continue to maintain his truthfulness with his friends (4). He will not **remove** his **integrity** (5) in order to agree with his friends concerning the cause of his suffering. Instead he will **hold fast** (6) to his position because it is right. In so doing he will retain a good conscience—**My heart shall not reproach me so long as I live.**

5. *The Third Speech of Zophar* (27:7-23)

The Masoretic text (cf. comment on 25:1-6) does not identify a third speech for Zophar. This may indicate that the author considers Job to have won the argument and uses this method to show that the friends have given up in their effort to convince him of sin. However, the text seems to have been disturbed. Furthermore, these verses are strange coming from Job. They more adequately fit the line of thought followed by the friends. For these reasons we have chosen to treat this section as though it constitutes a portion at least of a third discourse by Zophar.

If these are, indeed, words from Zophar, he attempts to reassert dogmatically his former position in spite of what Job has said by way of refutation.

Let mine enemy be as the wicked (7) is a type of curse wished upon those who oppose the speaker. He then argues against Job's affirmation that **the hypocrite** (the godless) gets along in this life as well as anyone. He asks, What good does this prosperity do if **God taketh away his soul?** (8) **Will God hear**

the **cry** (9) of one such as this? Indeed, will he even **call upon God?** (10) The intended answer is, No. These truths seem to Zophar to be as self-evident as those which Job has advocated. If Job can support his argument from real life, so can Zophar— "The almighty's program I will not hide" (11, Berk.).

Verses 13-23 are the kind of description of the fate of the wicked with which we have already met. All of the calamities described are the judgment of God upon the **wicked man** (13). He shall raise **children** (14) only to have them slaughtered or starved. Unmourned **death** (15) shall be the fate of those who associate with him. Any **silver** or **raiment** (16) that he may accumulate will do him no good, for the wealth will be used by another. The **house** (18) that he builds is as temporary as "a spider's web" (RSV).

> *He lies down rich—it is the end!*
> *he opens his eyes, to find that all is over!* (19, Moffatt)

The **terrors** (20) of death will overtake him and throw him about as a great **storm** (21), with none to deliver him from its power.

> *God pelts him without pity,*
> *he opens his eyes, to find that all is over!* (19, Moffat)

When he is gone, **men shall clap their hands at him** to express their complete contempt for him and their joy at his demise (23).

6. Job's Third Reply to Zophar (?) (28:1—31:40)

Job's final speech is a summation of his basic position rather than a new argument against his three friends. It is difficult to assess the rightful position of c. 28, but here we view it as an answer to the friends' claim that wisdom has been granted them in asertaining the cause of Job's suffering.

Chapters 29—31 are in the nature of a monologue, inasmuch as Job no longer takes any note of his "comforters." He is concerned with himself and with God's treatment of him. These chapters furnish three basic issues which Job discusses. Chapter 29 constitutes a sad look at the good life Job lived prior to the calamities which befell him. God blessed him and he in turn was honored by his fellowmen, whom he treated kindly. Chapter 30 describes the tragic difference between the past and the present. God is Job's Antagonist, men despise him, and he is completely humiliated. Chapter 31 is a detailed defense of his integrity, in which he denies being guilty of the sins commonly observed in the lives of other men. Because of his innocence he fails to find any cause for God's treatment of him. Having built his case again to this point, he reaffirms his willingness and strong desire to meet God.

These chapters furnish an adequate introduction to those in which God appears and replies to Job. However, in the present arrangement of the text Elihu's speeches (cc. 32—37) intrude upon the logical sequence and thus, to some, spoil the symmetry and finesse of the argument.

a. Wisdom is beyond the reach of man (28:1-28). It is generally questioned whether or not c. 28 should be considered a part of the original poem. It is even more seriously questioned as to whether it is a part of the answer which Job gives to the friends. The reason is that this poem on wisdom does not fit into a logical sequence of ideas in relationship to the dialogue. It is also pointed out that much of the reason for God's conversation with Job is eliminated if this chapter is considered to be authentic.

On the other hand, there is wide agreement that the style and quality of this poem match those of the rest of the book. It may also be observed that there is a major thought in this chapter which fits into the general theme of Job's contention: Wisdom cannot be reached by man. A number of different ways are found to illustrate this fact. In spite of the difficulties it is assumed here that this poem possesses some direct connection with the debate. Job never has been bound by the necessity of direct and immediate comment upon the argument of the others. In this case perhaps some transitional passages are missing which would make the relationship clear.

In vv. 1-14 the author explores the mining activities of men. **Fine** (1) means to refine. They go into the depths of **the earth** (2) to discover metals and precious stones. The mining process is described rather precisely in vv. 3-11. The modern translations make this more clear than KJV. Setting **an end to darkness** (3), men go into the depth of the earth as though it were light. Man can by his industry and invention discover the hidden treasure— **the stones of darkness.** The meaning of 3-5 is thus clarified: "Men search the limits of dark places, venturing into their remotest bounds to obtain the ore. They drive deep shafts in valleys, in remote places seldom visited by anyone, and descend into them, hanging to ropes that swing back and forth. From the

93

earth man obtains his daily bread; but underneath its surface there is blasting as with fire" (Berk.). This activity takes place beyond the view of sharp-eyed birds (7) and beyond paths of wild beasts (8). Man is able to overcome **the mountains** (9) and **he cutteth out rivers** (10), i.e., makes canals and builds dams, or perhaps seals water veins with lime in order to prevent them from leaking into the mine (11).

Man's activity and ingenuity are marvelous, but in all of this achievement **wisdom** (12) is not discovered. It is not to be **found in the land of the living** (13). It is not in the **depth** nor in the **sea** (14).

The poet-author next envisions the price of wisdom. How much would it cost to purchase it? No price can be fixed. It cannot be **weighed** (15), or **valued with the gold of Ophir** (16). No amount of precious stones can equal it (17-19). Wisdom and understanding are beyond the reach of the **living** (21). Even **destruction and death** (22) have **heard** of wisdom but they do not know where to find it.

God (23) alone knows the way of wisdom because He sees everything **under the whole heaven** (24). He controls the forces of nature (25-26). God is able to find wisdom because He is the Author of it; **he prepared it** (27). Then He instructs man in its way: **Behold, the fear of the Lord, that is wisdom** (28).

b. *Job reflects upon his past prosperity* (29:1-25). Job opens this survey of the happiness of his former life by wishing that he might be as he was in those days. For **parable** (1) read "discourse" (RSV). His words **in the days when God preserved me** (2) are even more poignant when it is remembered that Job believed his suffering to be due to God's enmity. In those good days God's presence was like a **candle** or a **light** (3). Note how often **darkness** has been used by both Job and his friends as a symbol of frustration and judgment. It is also true that the lamp or **light** of God is often a symbol of God's beneficent presence.

In the days of my youth (4) is literally "my autumn days" (RSV). Job is not so much describing a given age as he is picturing a time of fulfillment in his life. This was a time of joy and intimate friendship with the Creator—**the secret of God was upon my tabernacle.**

Job also reflects upon those happy days when his **children were about** him (5). At that time his life overflowed with blessings. It was as though he had **washed his steps with butter**

(6) and as though even barren rocks were a source of **rivers of oil.** The word translated **butter** here is treated in a variety of ways by more recent translators. They range from "milk" through "cream" and on to "curds." Fat and oil were signs of wealth and luxury. The **rock** that gave oil may have been "terraces between rock curbs, forming olive groves" (Berk., fn.).

The pleasure that Job felt in the respect shown him by his fellows is described under the figure of the old men sitting **in the street** (7). It was probably a place near the city **gate** where social intercourse and judgment in civil affairs took place. In Job's case **young men . . . hid themselves** (8) and even the old men **stood up** in his presence. Both the young and old showed him deference. Even **princes** (9) and **nobles** (10) waited for him to speak before they would vouch an opinion. His reputation spread far, and those who heard about him honored him. Those who actually observed how he lived **gave witness** (11) to the truth of what he was now claiming.

There was just cause for the respect in which Job was held. He helped **the poor** (12) and those who were orphaned and widowed (13). **Righteousness . . . clothed me** (14) is literally, "Righteousness clothed itself with me." Job was the human embodiment of kindness and justice. He aided the **blind** and the **lame** (15) and opposed evil wherever he found it (16-17). Verse 17 has been translated, "I broke the grinder teeth of the unfair and forced them to drop their prey" (Berk.).

Job lived in complete and happy security. He anticipated nothing but a continuation of such goodness until in due time he should **die in my nest** (18). His **days** would be innumerable **as the sand.** His life was like the well-watered **root** (19) and the **branch** of a flourishing tree with **the dew** keeping it fresh and green.

My glory (20) is an expression of the honor in which Job was held. It was **fresh,** literally "new," and need not diminish. Likewise "my bow [was] as vigorous as ever in my hand" (Berk.).

Verses 21-25 follow the same line of thought as that found in 7-11. They are a reflection upon what Job seems to have cherished most, namely, his place of honor among his fellows. Now that it was gone, he felt greatly impoverished.

After my words they spake not (22) probably indicates deference for this great man and also the wisdom with which he spoke. His **speech dropped upon them,** gently and beneficently like **rain** (23). Those who heard drank in his words like the parched ground absorbed **the latter rain,** which falls in April and May and determines the productivity of the ripening crops.

When men needed advice Job was able to give it.

When I smiled, it encouraged them,
  my cheerful gaze put heart into the hopeless (24, Moffatt).

In this fashion Job was **chief** (25) among his fellows. He was like a **king** or the commander of an **army.** At the same time he was **as one that comforteth the mourners.** Job was a leader of men who **chose out the way** for others to go.

If this chapter is poetic exaggeration, Job's boasting needs the charity of the reader. We recall that he was a sufferer contemplating in retrospect the heights from which he had fallen and the depths to which he had sunk. If the chapter is not exaggeration, then of course Job needs no excuse for recording the facts.

c. *Job contrasts his present with his past* (30:1-31). This chapter throughout is a contrast to c. 29. Where Job used to enjoy the respect and honor of the elders of the city and the great among men, he now is despised by the lowest element of society.

But now (1) introduces the change from what preceded to that which now exists. Chapter 29 ended with Job remembering how in former times he was like a king among men. Now even younger men, **whose fathers** Job would not have considered fit to be shepherds **with the dogs,** hold Job in derision.

This class of men were so miserable a lot that they were virtual outcasts from the society of ordinary people. They had **no strength** (2) because they were gaunt with hunger (3). The only food they could get was the sparse produce of the desert areas. They were forced to eat the leaves of the **mallows** (4), a scrubby bush that grows in the salt marshes of Palestine, and **juniper roots,** likewise a wilderness bush (broom) rather than the juniper tree.

These unfortunate men are **driven** (5) from the society of others as though they were thieves and were therefore forced to live **in caves** and among the **rocks** (6). **Among the bushes they brayed** (7), living like the ass and eating the food common to the wild ass. Thus they were **children of fools** (8), literally "sons of a worthless one." They were **children of base men,** i.e., unnamed persons. **Viler than the earth** is better translated "whipped out of the land" (RSV).

And now (9) Job finds himself the butt of their derision! He is like a **byword** to them. Their abhorrence of him is so great that they **spit in** his **face** (10). Because God has **afflicted** (11) Job, they are unrestrained in their animosity toward him. Young men **push** (12) him aside and obstruct his **path** (13) and thus add to his **calamity**. The action of these outcasts is no incidental thing. It comes upon Job like **a wide breaking in of waters** (14). They terrify him with their persistent abuse until his **welfare** evaporates like **a cloud** (15).

Once more Job turns to a description of the horrors of his disease. His **bones** (17) ache and pain gnaws at his **sinews**. His whole appearance has been altered by the **disease** (18), even as it chokes him like a tight-fitting **collar** about the neck.

However Job is constantly aware of the fact that God lies behind all that has happened to him. He is the One who has attacked him with such great severity. It is as though God has **cast** him **into the mire** (19). God will not listen to Job when he prays nor take any notice of him (20). He cries in anguish, **Thou art become cruel to me** (21). God causes him to be dissipated in all of his substance as though he were caught up and blown away by a whirlwind (22). As a consequence, Job can anticipate nothing but death and a departure into *Sheol*, **the house appointed for all living** (23).

In v. 24, Job returns to the idea of the injustice of God's treatment of him. He reminds God that he had shown compasion for those who were **in trouble** (25) and **poor**. But such action on his part has done him no good. He has **looked for good** (26) and gets **evil** instead. He is completely torn emotionally—his **bowels boiled** (27)—and unexpected **affliction** has overtaken him.

Verse 28 is difficult to interpret. RSV associates this passage with the results of Job's disease as described in 29. Hence, "I go about blackened, but not by the sun," and cry for help but no one is there to answer. Consequently Job likens himself to **dragons** and **owls** (29), probably better translated "jackals" and "ostriches," whose mournful sounds in the night make them appropriate symbols for his melancholy. With **skin** (30) blackened by the ravages of his disease and his **bones** burning in pain, Job's comfort and joy are stripped from him. There is nothing left to him but **mourning** (31) and weeping. **Organ** is better flute or pipe.

d. Job defends his integrity (31:1-40). Job reviews various categories of sin which might have been the cause of his misfortune and solemnly swears that he is innocent of any misdeed. Occasionally along with his protests of innocence he includes a statement of why he chose to be virtuous. He also includes a curse upon himself if he has not spoken the truth.

First Job denies that he is guilty of the sensual sins which are so common among men. He **made a covenant with** his **eyes** so that he would not lust after **a maid** (1). Here Job recognizes that temptation comes through observation of that which might be desirable. He has an agreement with his eyes that they shall not lead him astray. **What portion** (2) would he have with **God** if guilty of such crimes? Surely God punishes **the wicked** and those who are **workers of iniquity** (3). Not only so, but Job asks, **Doth not he see?** (4) **He** is emphatic, underscoring the idea that God looks closely at man and punishes his **vanity** and **deceit** (5). Verses 6-8 are an oath of innocence and a curse for any falsehood which Job may have spoken in the preceding verses.

Job has also been innocent of adultery (9-10). In this instance Job wishes upon himself, through his wife, retaliation in kind if he has been guilty of coveting a neighbor's wife (see Deut. 22:22; John 8:5). In his mind adultery is a **heinous crime** (11). It is like a fire that **consumeth to destruction** (12). The word for **destruction** is *Abaddon,* a parallel to *Sheol.* The figure, then, is of a fire so fierce that it follows one to the grave (see Prov. 6:24-35).

Job denies, further, that he has misused his power or position to mistreat anyone. His **manservant** and **maidservant** (13) have received fair treatment from him. Job's description of his relationship to his servants is one of the most remarkable of the book. He has treated his servants as persons, defending their personal dignity. The reason given for this treatment is that God made both **me** and **him** (15). Therefore there is a kind of equality between them. Unfortunates have also received aid from Job. **The poor . . . the widow** (16), the **fatherless** (17) are mentioned. The reason offered for this kindness to others is that Job was raised with boys and girls of this sort (18). The picture suggests that he was raised in an influential family which took good care of the needy—perhaps slaves—around them. In this connection Job denies that he has knowingly permitted anyone to go destitute of adequate **clothing** (19) or in any way deprived the **poor** of his rights (20-21). Again he invites a curse upon himself—**Let mine arm fall . . . and mine arm be broken from the bone** (22)—if he has lied in this regard. This is in contradiction to that with which Eliphaz charged him in c. 22. In v. 23, Job notes that "calamity from God and dread of His judgment have always restrained me" (Berk.).

Job denies that he has been an idolater. He has not made **gold** his **hope** (24) nor has he exulted over his great **wealth** (25). He has not **kissed** his **hand** (27), worshipped **the sun** or **the moon** (26; see Jer. 44:17-19; Ezek. 8:16), for this would **be an iniquity to be punished** (28). In so doing he would have **denied the God that is above.**

Job has not even been guilty of mistreating his enemies. He did not rejoice at their **destruction** (29) nor seek to put **a curse** upon them (30). It was thought that the curse had the power in itself to work evil (see Num. 22:5-6). This concern over the welfare of an enemy shows the high moral level which Israel achieved at a relatively early period. (For additional material on this theme see Prov. 24:17-18; 25:21-22.)

Selfishness was never a part of Job's character. Even the servants, **the men of my tabernacle** (31), witnessed, "There never was a man whom I did not generously supply with meat" (Berk.). They pictured Job as a man seeking out those with whom he could share his table. Likewise **a stranger did not lodge in the street** (32). He was invited into the home of Job.

Job was not a hypocrite. He did not hide his **transgressions as Adam** (33) from the view of others. Adam did not hide his sin; he hid himself. The figure, therefore, is not exact. Perhaps the general meaning of **Adam** (namely, mankind) should be followed in this instance. Nor did Job permit the attitude and opinions of others to deter him from performing his duty or cow him into pretending something that was not true (34).

Finally Job turns once more to the urgency of the continuing cry of his heart throughout all of the dialogue, **Oh that one would hear me!** (35) God was silent and distant. Job desperately needed the opportunity to plead his case. The charges God had placed against him should be plainly **written** for Job to see and take note of (35-36). Then it would be possible to answer and to tell God just how he had walked. God would see that he had been a **prince** in his conduct (37).

Job next calls the **land** (38) itself to be a witness on his behalf. He has treated the earth and its produce and **the owners** (39) of land fairly. If not, he invites a curse upon his land in the form of noxious weeds, **thistles** and **cockle** (40).

With this final protest of innocence Job rests his case—**The words of Job are ended.**

Section **III** *The Speeches of Elihu*

Job 32:1—37:24

The speeches of Elihu break the pattern of dialogue that characterize the book up to this point. He is introduced to the reader and then four speeches are identified by the formula, **Elihu . . . said.** None of these is answered by Job or commented upon by any of the characters of the book. Thus the speeches stand as a separate unit within the book without literary antecedent or inscription at the end.

This portion of the book is widely considered to be the work of someone other than the poet-author of the rest of the book. Among the arguments offered supporting this opinion are (*a*) lack of mention of Elihu anywhere else in the book, (*b*) difference in poetic style and language, and (*c*) the fact that in some places Elihu seems to have read the arguments of the friends instead of having heard them.[1]

A. ELIHU INTRODUCED, 32:1-5

As a part of the prose introduction of Elihu's speeches, note is made that the three friends have **ceased to answer Job** (1). It can easily be assumed that their silence was induced by the fact that they had been bested in the debate. The reason offered here for their silence suggests their frustration because **he was righteous in his own eyes.**

At this point a young man who had been standing by silently is introduced. He is **Elihu** (My God is He) **the son of Barachel the Buzite, of the kindred of Ram** (2). This is a more complete genealogy than is given for any of the other persons involved in the book and identifies him as being more closely related to Job than the others (cf. Gen. 22:21 and Job 1:1, where Elihu's ancestor Buz is mentioned as the brother of Job's progenitor Huz or Uz). **Barachel** and **Ram** are not mentioned elsewhere in the Scriptures.

Elihu is an angry young man. His anger is caused by the self-righteousness of Job and the complete failure of the three

[1]Cf. Davidson, *op. cit.*, pp. xl ff.

friends in their effort to convince Job of his guilt. What was
equally bad was that they had failed to answer Job's charges
against the rectitude of God. Verse 4 should be read, "Now
Elihu had waited to speak to Job because they were older than
he" (RSV). Out of deference to the age of the others he had
remained silent, but he had not been calm. **His wrath was kindled (5).**

B. THE FIRST SPEECH OF ELIHU, 32: 6—33: 33

1. *Elihu Has Proper Authority to Speak* (32: 6-22)

Elihu's youthful timidity gave way to his anger, but in the
process he discovered some additional truth. Wisdom does not
always accompany age; it is also a gift of God. **The inspiration of
the Almighty giveth . . . understanding (8). Judgment** is not a
possession unique to **the aged (9).** Therefore, since he possesses
the Spirit of God, Elihu requests the older men to listen atten-
tively to him, even though he lacks years. He has an **opinion**
he feels compelled to express (10).

Elihu is apologetic for the intrusion he makes in the conversation. He points out that he had listened carefully to their
words and **reasons (11)** to persuade Job of the right, but they
were unable to do so **(12).** He chides the three friends:

> *Say not, "We found him too clever for us!*
> *It must be God, not man, who puts him down!"*
> (13, Moffatt)

Elihu disagrees. There is a great deal left to say, but it is different from **your** speeches **(14).** He is so full of words after having
listened to their ineffective arguments that he is about to **burst
(18-19).** He warns them that he will not flatter any of them **(21-
22).** "Elihu intends to speak as an umpire, not as a partisan; Job
had longed for an arbiter" (9: 33-34; Berk., fn., *ad loc.*).

2. *Elihu and Job Meet on Common Terms* (33: 1-7)

Unlike the other speakers, Elihu addresses **Job** by name **(1).**
He has complete confidence in himself, and claims to be upright
and capable of speaking truth **clearly (3).** This attitude in Elihu
suggests bigotry to the Western mind, but probably did not have
such connotation in its own setting (cf. the attitude of Job in
c. 29). Perhaps this kind of self-evaluation was necessary, for
he next points out that he was created by the **spirit of God (4),**

but like other men he was **formed out of the clay** (6). Having
the inspiration of God, but also being a man like Job, he is able
to discuss Job's problem under conditions of equality for both
of them.

Job had asked for an audience with God; Elihu says that he
has come **in God's stead** (6). Job had expressed concern lest,
meeting with God, he should be so terrified that he could not
speak. Elihu assures him that he need not worry about God's
representative—**My terror shall not make thee afraid** (7).

3. *The Implications of Job's Position* (33:8-13)

Elihu makes it clear that he has heard all that Job has said
to the others, and that which he addressed directly to God. Then
he selects a specific complaint of Job's with which to deal. He
observes that Job claims to be **innocent** of any **transgression** and
iniquity (9), yet God has treated him as an **enemy** (10-11).
According to Elihu, Job is wrong at that point. **God is greater
than man** (12); therefore it is wrong to try to bring Him to
account for His action—**to strive against him** (13). The RSV
clarifies 13 thus:

> *Why do you contend against him,*
> *saying, "He will answer none of my words"?*

Thus the stage is set for Elihu to deal specifically with one of the
basic issues in Job's argument.

4. *God Does Speak to Men* (33:14-33)

One reason Job felt that God was an enemy was that he
couldn't get any response from Him. Elihu says that **God speaks
to men once, yea twice** (14), if men are wise enough to take
notice. The first way He speaks is through dreams—**in a vision
of the night** (15). At such a time God **openeth the ears of men**
(16) so that they can hear His words, and then He **sealeth their
instruction**; i.e., He confirms the moral communication thus
given. God speaks so that the sinner may be turned **from his
evil purpose** (17) and be preserved **from the pit** (death; 18).
This is also the reason man is **chastened . . . with pain** (19-21) of
various sorts. By warning the individual of the consequence of
his premeditated sin through dreams and pain, God saves him
from the **destroyers** (22)—perhaps the death angel (see II Sam.
24:16; II Kings 19:35; Ps. 78:49).

The second way that God speaks to men is through the

heavenly **messenger** who is also called **an interpreter** (23). The purpose of this one is to explain God's ways, so that the individual may be upright. **He is gracious** (24). If the sinner heeds God's warning and is repentant, God will **deliver him from . . . the pit** (24). Verse 26 has been interpreted, "He prays to God, and He accepts him; he beholds God's face and is joyful; the man is restored to his normal living" (Berk.). Verses 27-28 constitute the testimony of the redeemed man:

> *I sinned, I went astray,*
> *but he has not punished me;*
> *he saved my soul from death,*
> *and let me see the dear light of the living* (Moffatt).

Elihu says that he has more to say—**Hold thy peace, and I will speak** (31)—but if Job has **any thing to say** in reply, he should by all means do so (32). **If not . . . hold thy peace, and I shall teach thee wisdom** (33).

C. THE SECOND SPEECH OF ELIHU, 34:1-37

In his first discourse, Elihu replied to Job's charges that the affliction from God demonstrated God's arbitrary enmity against him. In this chapter Elihu denies that God has been unjust in His treatment of Job. God, the Creator of all, is above any requirement which man may place upon Him; therefore it would be impossible for Him to do wrong.

1. *Further Consideration of Job's Claims* (34:1-9)

Verses 1 to 4 constitute an introduction in which Elihu invites **ye wise men** (2)—probably others standing about rather than the three friends—to join with him in search after **judgment**, in order that they might **know among ourselves what is good** (4).

Then he addresses himself to another aspect of Job's problem. Job had claimed, "I am innocent" (5, RSV), and, furthermore, that there was no profit in serving God (9). Job had rather piously asserted that he would not **lie against** himself in order to appear humble (6). Such an attitude on Job's part is impossible for Elihu to accept. He says that Job is a man **who drinketh up scorning like water** (7) and is in the habit of walking **with wicked men** (8). Job has come to this woeful condition because of the attitude which he holds. Elihu cannot accept the judgment of such a man.

2. God's Justice Is Defended (34:10-20)

Again Elihu appeals to **men of understanding** (10) to hear his defense of God's righteousness. How could God **commit iniquity?** God rewards **every man . . . according to his ways** (11). He will not, indeed could not, **pervert judgment** (12). This would be contrary to His very nature.

Elihu sees two basic reasons why wicked action is impossible for God to perform. The first is that God is the Creator of all that exists. He did not receive His power and authority from anyone. He is the One who has given life and the One who sustains it. Therefore there is no point in His doing wrong (13-15).

Moffatt finds the argument based, not upon God's power, but upon His concern for man:

> No, never will God do an evil deed,
>   never will the Almighty act unjustly—
> he is no viceroy lording it on earth!—
>   his heart and hand are on the universe,
> and were he to withdraw his spirit,
>   were he to gather in his breath,
> the human race would perish in a moment,
>   man would return to the dust (12-15).

The second proposition supporting God's justice is given in the form of a question. **Shall . . . he that hateth right govern?** (17) Justice is a prerequisite for ruling. It is unthinkable for a subject to question the authority of his **king** (18). Much more is man completely out of place in questioning God's actions. Furthermore, God has no motive for injustice, since He is the One who has created the **rich** and the **poor** as well as commoners and **princes** (19). He shows no partiality in His administration of justice. This is the reason that all men **die . . . and pass away** alike (20). **Without hand** means "by no human hand" (RSV). Job had used this fact to illustrate indiscriminate action on the part of God. Elihu uses it to illustrate God's equal treatment of men.

3. Consequences of Rebellion Against God (34:21-37)

There is no way to hide from God. **His eyes are upon . . . man** (21). **He seeth all** reflects omniscience and means that God deals in an absolutely just fashion with every man. **He will not**

lay upon man more than is right (23), so there is no need for a
man to enter into judgment with God, as Job has done. Since
God knoweth their works (25), His judgment upon the wicked
is unerring, whether against a nation, or against a man only
(29). It is impossible under these circumstances for hypocrisy
to be successful (30). Verse 29 seems again to assert the sovereignty of God. It has been translated:

If he keep quiet, who can condemn?
And if he hide his face, who can see him? (Smith-Goodspeed)

The wise man, knowing God's omniscience and unerring
justice, surely will accept chastisement (31) as a warning from
God and repent of his sin. He would ask God, Teach thou me
(32), and, Speak what thou knowest (33). But Job has spoken
without knowledge (35). His answers to the problems raised
have been wrong and if left unchallenged will lead men astray.
Therefore he should be tried unto the end (36) for his rebellious
words against God (37).

In 31-33 we see "The Righteous Response to Divine Discipline." (1) Recognition that God has given us chastisement, 31;
(2) Promise to amend our ways, I will not offend any more,
31-32; (3) Request for divine guidance, Teach thou me, 32;
(4) Deliberate choice to trust when we cannot see, "You yourself must choose," 33, Berk. (A. F. Harper).

D. The Third Speech of Elihu (35:1-16)

Elihu was especially perturbed at Job's claim that neither
his sin nor his piety made a difference, either to himself or to
God. He has already referred to this in 34:9 but he feels the
necessity of treating it further. He expresses surprise that Job
could ever put himself in the position of claiming that his righteousness is more than God's (2). Such a claim cries for a reply.
Elihu says: I will answer thee, and thy companions (the three
friends) with thee (4).

At one critical point Elihu and Job are in agreement. A look
at the heavens (5), where God sits enthroned, will convince
anyone that He is beyond man's capacity to affect, either by sin
or by righteousness. Elihu affirms that man takes nothing away
from God when he sins (6) and gives Him nothing when he is
righteous (7). What happens is that the man himself and other
men may be hurt or may profit (8).

Job had said that the cry of suffering was unheard by God, thereby claiming that God was unconcerned. Elihu here recognizes that there are a **multitude of oppressions** (9) over which men cry. However, he points out that in many cases it is only because of pain that **they cry out** "for rescue from the tyrant's arm" (Moffatt). It does not come from true religious intent— **None saith, Where is God my maker?** (10) When men cry out, it should be more than instinctive reaction to pain. God has created man superior to **the beasts** (11). He should therefore respond to the problems of his life on a level higher than animal instinct. If the cry of man is not heard, it is **because of the pride of evil men** (12) or because men have prayed in **vanity** (13; presumption, or falsehood). God can be trusted to hear an honest appeal. **Therefore doth Job open his mouth in vain** (16). He has been completely wrong in claiming that God is indifferent to the suffering of mankind. In 15-16, Elihu charges Job with presumption: "And now, because God has not visited you in His anger and does not attend to your transgression, Job uselessly opens his mouth" (Berk.).

One of the most beautiful passages of the book is in v. 10. The phrase **who giveth songs in the night** is one to stretch the imagination. Truly one of the marvels of God's creativity is the fact that He has placed hope within man's heart. No matter how dark it may be, man has the capacity to see a glimmer of light. He can sing a song of joy in the midst of sorrow. When hope like this is gone, life is gone. Elihu reaches his highest point of religious understanding and awareness in this great insight.

E. THE FOURTH SPEECH OF ELIHU, 36:1—37:24

1. *Introduction in Defense of God's Justice* (36:1-4)

Elihu claims there is more to say and requests the attention of his audience. He promises to **fetch** his **knowledge from afar** (3) and assures his hearers that they have the great privilege to have one in their midst who is **perfect in knowledge** (4). This may be either, as Moffatt understands it, a claim something less than modest, or, with *The Berkeley Version,* an allusion to the unseen presence of God in the midst.

2. *The Reason Men Suffer* (36:5-14)

Elihu's major premise has been that **God is mighty . . . in strength and wisdom** (5). He is certain that God gives to every

man that which he justly deserves. He does not show favor to
the wicked (6) nor forget **the poor,** as Job has charged. He especially cares for **the righteous** (7), whom He exalts to the
highest position—**with kings . . . on the throne** (7). If by chance
the righteous are in **affliction** (8), suffering serves as instructive discipline to cause them to **return from iniquity** (10) which
they may be contemplating. **If they obey . . . him** (11), they
shall prosper; but **if they obey not** (12), they will be destroyed
as they perform their wicked intentions. The **hypocrites** (godless) **in heart** (13) get angry at God for the divine discipline,
thereby missing the benefit of the whole experience (14).

3. *The Reason Job Suffers* (36:15-25)

In v. 15, Elihu states the principle of instructive discipline:
God **openeth their ears in oppression.** In 16 he applies it to Job.
God would have brought Job into happiness—**a broad place** and
on thy table . . . fatness—instead of oppression. **Straitness** recalls Job's references to snares, stocks, and circumscribed paths,
in 19:6-8. But Job has not accepted the instruction of chastisement. Instead he has joined with the **judgment of the wicked**
(17) and has been angry with God (18). Job should be warned
that no **ransom** or **forces of strength** (19) can deliver him under
these circumstances of rebellion.

Job had requested death as an answer to his problem, but
Elihu admonishes, **Desire not the night** (20). God sometimes
cuts off people in this manner as a part of His judgment. But this
attitude shows that Job is really rebelling against God's ways
rather than humbly accepting His instruction. It shows that Job
has chosen **iniquity . . . rather than affliction** (21). Instead of
complaining he should acknowledge God's great **power** (22) and
magnify his work (24). The marvelous work that God does is
easy for **men** to **behold** (24-25), but Job has presumed to teach
God rather than to learn from Him.

4. *God Is to Be Praised for His Majesty* (36:26—37:13)

Elihu is reminded of the greatness of God as seen in the
marvels of nature. Although this theme has been exploited well
by both sides of the discussion already, Elihu feels he must join
with them. He points to the many evidences of God's majestic
power. In doing so he wishes to impress Job with God's transcendence.

Elihu invites Job to consider the raindrop and the clouds
(27-28) and the awesome thunderstorm (36:28—37:5). **The
noise of his tabernacle** (29) is the thunder from the pavillion of
the sky. Verse 30 has been interpreted: "See how He disperses
lightning around Him and covers the tops of the mountains"
(Berk.). Moffatt connects v. 31 with the gift of rain in 27-28 and
renders it:

> *Therewith he sustains the nations,*
> *and provides food for mankind.*

Verse 33 is difficult. It clearly refers to the thunder, but interpreters differ on its function intended here. *The Berkeley Version* has, "His thunder announces His presence; the cattle feel
warned of the storm" (cf. Smith-Goodspeed). RSV has:

> *Its crashing declares concerning him,*
> *who is jealous with anger against iniquity* (cf. Moffatt).

In 37:6-10, Elihu considers the helplessness of man in coping
with ice and snow. Verses 6-7 may be read:

> *He bids the snow fall on the earth,*
> *also the heavy rains,*
> *that keep men within doors—*
> *to let all mortals feel his power* (Moffatt).

Verse 10 has been translated:

> *By the breath of God ice is given,*
> *and the broad waters are frozen fast* (RSV).

In 11-13, Elihu returns to a consideration of the clouds,
which, along with the wind, obey God's **counsels** (12) to go anywhere over the earth. They achieve whatever purpose He has in
mind for them, **whether for correction . . . or for mercy** (13).
Verse 11 is clarified in the RSV:

> *He loads the thick cloud with moisture;*
> *the clouds scatter his lightning.*

5. *Exhortation to Humble Submission* (37:14-24)

Elihu is so thrilled at the revelations he has been unfolding
that he cannot understand how Job could do anything but bow
down before such a God in humble reverence and awe.

To Elihu, Job has been trying to play at being God in his
condemnation of God's treatment of men. In anticipation of the
kind of question that God will ask Job (cf. 38:4), Elihu asks:
"When God works, do you know how?" (15) and, **Hast thou with**

him spread out the sky? (18) **The bright light** (21) refers to the sun. The meaning is clarified thus:

> *And now men saw not the light;*
> *It was obscure in the skies;*
> *But the wind passed over and cleared them.*
>   (Smith-Goodspeed)

It should be obvious to anyone, Elihu thinks, that the author of those marvels in nature is **terrible** in **majesty** (22). Man **cannot find him out** (23), but He can be depended upon in **judgment** and in **justice**. God respects those who are humble. Only the proud—those that are **wise of heart**—do not merit His favor (24).

Elihu has not said much that is new. Primarily he took the position of the three friends, but he elaborated this position with fervor and enthusiasm. He represents a devout attitude but does not produce any unusual or new position. Any bid for uniqueness on Elihu's part must rest on his statement of the instructive power of suffering, and the extension of this principle to the idea that suffering is an expression of God's goodness, even though it be in disguise. These ideas, however, are inherent in the concepts of the others.

Some scholars feel that Elihu furnishes a necessary literary interlude between Job's impassioned plea and the next scene—the whirlwind out of which God speaks to him.

Section **IV**   *God's Conversation with Job*

Job's greatest wish, expressed many times, was that God would grant him an audience in order that the whole question of his integrity and his suffering might be resolved. In this portion of the book Job's desire is finally satisfied, but not in the manner that he had anticipated.

The major question raised in the book is, "Doth Job fear [serve] God for nought?" (1-9) It is ultimately a question about the kind of relationship that exists between man and God.

Satan (the satan; see comments on 1:6) and the friends of Job agree essentially on the answer to this question. Satan does not believe that Job will "retain his integrity" without a reward. The friends believe the material prosperity enjoyed by a man is the reward for integrity and that, therefore, the lack of reward is *prima facie* evidence of sin. The poet-author has Job come out as victor over these enemies. Satan is proved wrong because Job does not "curse God" at the loss of health and wealth. Job defeats the friends in their contention. He argues persuasively from the realities of life that wealth and blessedness do not always result from righteousness.

However, Job has not survived his trial without being marked by it. His relationship to God has not been clarified. Job's own attitude is his problem. In defending his integrity he impugned the integrity of God and made Him appear to be unjust. God does not seem to show observable consistency in His moral jurisdiction of the world. This is the issue which must be resolved now.

Job had wished for an opportunity to face God in order that he might justify himself before Him. He seemed to think that he could appeal to the moral nature of God to counteract the enmity which God apparently held towards him. It is this issue to which God addresses himself. He does not enter into a judicial dispute with Job, but shows him the true relationship that must always exist between God and man. between the infinite and the finite.

111

A. God's First Answer to Job, 38:1—40:5

1. *The Opening Challenge* (38:1-3)

The Lord (1)—this is *Yahweh,* the Hebrew God. **Out of the whirlwind** is literally "out of the storm" or "tempest." It is not clear whether the author intended to be literal or figurative in the language which he uses. However it is the biblical language of theophany (see Ps. 18:8-16; Ezek. 1:4, 28; but see also I Kings 19:11-12).

The Lord challenges Job by asking, **Who is this that darkeneth counsel?** (2) The question implies that some kind of confusion had been caused. **Counsel** suggests the plan or reason of things. Job had made obscure the purposes of God in the world by his argument and complaint, especially in his claim that God acted unjustly in the affairs of men.

Gird up now thy loins (3) is an expression urging preparation for action. Job had repeatedly challenged God to meet him. Now God is ready to acquiesce in this request. Job must enter into the argument with God thoroughly prepared for what is coming, and it was not what Job expected. He had wished to quiz God about His attitude and actions. Instead God says, **I will demand of thee, and answer thou me.** When God asked His questions, Job is not ready for the interview as he had previously imagined (40:3-5).

2. *Inanimate Nature Speaks of God's Wisdom* (38:4-38)

God overwhelms Job with reference to orderly systems within nature which are beyond Job's power to control. He cannot even comprehend them completely.

First He asks Job, **Where wast thou** (4) at the beginning of creation? This emphasizes both Job's limited intelligence and the transitory nature of his existence. **Declare** refers to v. 3 and also to the questions which follow immediately. The questions show that Job has no firsthand knowledge of how the earth is made. He knows *who* made it, but he was not present to see *how* it was done. The creation of the earth is likened to the construction of a well-designed building plumbed with a **line** (5) and leveled carefully with strong **foundations** and a **corner stone** (6). **The morning stars** (stars personified) and **the sons of God** (7; angels) are described as expressing great **joy** over the grandeur of the earth as they watched God construct it. They were there but Job was not.

God also inquires into Job's relationship to the creation of the oceans. The basic question is still, Where were you? The figure is that of a giant being born from **the womb** (8) of the universe, and wrapped in a **swaddlingband** of **cloud** (9). As the sea grew, boundaries were placed upon it, so that it was restrained within a given territory (8-11).

Days and nights are the creation of God. Every morning **the dayspring** (12; dawn) breaks forth. It sends light to **the ends of the earth** (13). In its light the evil perpetuated under the cover of darkness can be overcome (13, 15). Verse 14 describes the effect of the morning sun upon the appearance of the world.

> *Earth stands out clear like clay, stamped by a seal,*
>   *in all its colours like a robe* (Moffatt).

The mysteries of land and sea are next explored. **Hast thou entered?** (16) is the same kind of question as that posed in v. 4. Has Job discovered from whence come the **springs of the sea?** Here **the depth** refers to the netherworld which was assumed to exist under the ocean. In v. 17 **gates of death** and **doors of the shadow of death** refer to *Sheol*. Has Job passed through the gates of *Sheol* to discover the secrets it holds within its depths? Does he know the **breadth of the earth** (18) or what lies beyond the flat plain of the earth?

In like manner God shows Job that he is ignorant of the source of **light** and **darkness** (19). The **number of thy days** (21) is an allusion to the dialogue with the friends concerning the relationship between age and wisdom.

The causes of natural phenomena such as **snow and hail** (22) are beyond Job's knowledge. Yet God keeps them in His storehouse to use at His will—even in **battle** (23; see Josh. 10: 11). **Wind** (24), **lightning** (25), **rain** (26-28), **ice** (29c-30) have no source which Job can control. **Hid as with a stone** (30) is better rendered "became hard like a stone" (RSV). Job cannot **bind the sweet influences** (bonds) or **loose the bands**[1] or **bring forth** the constellations in the sky (31-33). Nor can he command **the clouds** to do his bidding (34-38). All of these fulfill the purpose of God, but they are beyond man's knowledge and control.

---

[1] "The Pleiades were Seven Sisters, a conspicuous constellation of stars, thought to be fastened in their place. Orion, in mythology was one of the giants, who because of rebellion against the gods was lashed to the sky" (Berk., fn.).

3. *Examples from Animate Nature* (38:39—39:30)

Examples of wildlife are here brought in word pictures before Job. His utter lack of any direct responsibility for bringing into existence or sustaining these marvels is emphasized. The **lion** (38:39) and the **raven** (38:41) are completely opposite as far as nature is concerned, yet both are fed by God in His providential care for them. **Wild goats** and **hinds** (39:1; female of the red deer) breed, have their young, raise them to independent maturity without the aid of man. **Knowest thou** and **mark** (1-2) refer to jurisdiction and control as much as to knowledge of the habits of these creatures. **Cast out their sorrows** (3) is better rendered "give birth to their offspring"; it is a parallel construction to **bring forth their young ones.**

The wild ass (5) is a hardy and independent animal. Who set him **free?** He can live in the **wilderness** and exist where other animals cannot (6-8). Likewise **the unicorn** (9; wild ox) with its untamable nature, defies the effort of man to harness him (10-12). The beauty of the **peacocks** (13) is not the result of man's effort. Even the foolish lack of care which the **ostrich** gives to its young is a kind of unfathomable **wisdom** that escapes Job (14-17). **What time she lifteth herself on high** (18) is better translated, "When she rouses herself to flee" (RSV). The marvelous courage of the war **horse** (19) is contrasted with that of the **grasshopper** (20). **Thunder** (19) is better "strength"; the Hebrew meaning is obscure. In his fierce **strength** (21) it seems that **he swalloweth the ground** (24) as he rushes into battle. For **neither believeth he** read, "He cannot stand still at the sound of the trumpet" (RSV). **The hawk** (26) flies by instinct as she migrates **south.** Likewise it is instinct which causes the **eagle** to **make her nest . . . upon the crag of the rock** (27-28), where she raises her young and from which she looks to find **the prey** (29).

4. *Job Is Silenced* (40:1-5)

The point of all the foregoing illustrations is emphasized by the question that God next asks of Job: **Shall he that contendeth with the Almighty instruct him?** (2) These examples have spoken eloquently of the sharp contrast between the God who created all and Job, who is only one of God's creatures. But as Davidson points out, it is not the ineffable mystery that lies behind the **Creator's** works that impresses Job so much. It is God himself

who is paraded before him.[2] Everywhere he looks there is eloquent speech about the Creator. Job had said that he looked
before, behind, and on both sides but could not find God. This he
has learned is completely wrong. God is all about him if he will
only take the time to see Him. Job had been so preoccupied
with himself that he lost his perspective and was therefore missing God's self-revelation which exists in every corner of the
universe.

The development of the thought in this section is superb,
but rivaling the sequence of idea is the beauty of its expression.
These vignettes are unsurpassed poetry and they mark the
author as an astute and perceptive student of nature.

God's first communication with Job finds its mark. In humility Job admits that he has spoken unwisely—**I am vile** (4).
This is not a moral term. Job is saying that he is too small to
answer God. It is true that God has not explained the cause of
Job's suffering, but Job is beginning to see that his religion—his
integrity—must be more than self-interest. There is, therefore,
nothing to do but to **lay mine hand upon my mouth . . . and . . .
proceed no further** (5) in this dispute with God.

B. God's Second Answer to Job, 40:6—42:6

The first speech of God addressed itself to the fact that Job
had been presumptuous in his desire to dispute with God. The
display from creation put Job in his place, but it has not yet
dealt with Job's flagrantly impious attitude. Job had charged
God with unrighteousness in His rule of the world. It is to this
issue that the second speech gives attention.

God first challenges Job's criticism of Him (40:6-14) and
ironically invites Job to sit, if he can, in God's place and govern
the world. There follows a description of Behemoth and Leviathan,[3] probably representations of the victory of God over the
chaotic forces in the universe. If one may reason backward from
what is achieved to the purpose of these descriptions, this revelation serves to bring Job to repentance rather than to mere submission as in 39:1—40:6. At this point Terrien argues well that

---

[2]*Op. cit.*, pp. 276 ff.

[3]There is general dispute over the authenticity of the description of
these two beasts. But the commentator must ultimately deal with the text
as it is. For good discussions of the problems of the text see Terrien,
op. cit., pp. 1183 ff.; Pope, *op. cit.*, pp. 268 ff.; Gray, *op. cit.*, pp. 351 ff.

the time interval between Job's submission and his penitence is psychologically and theologically sound.[4]

1. *The Challenge to Job Is Renewed* (40:6-14)

Gird up thy loins (7) is an introductory formula almost exactly like that found in 38:1, 3. As before, God speaks out of the **whirlwind** or stormy tempest (6). He asks Job, **Wilt thou also disannul my judgment?** (8) The word translated **judgment** (*misphat*) has a broad meaning in the OT. It may refer to the act of upholding justice or right. It is also an ordinance or system of correct teaching to be followed. Sometimes it refers to one's legal rights or privileges. It may also refer to what is proper or fitting, as in manners or customs. In this context, it would seem to mean the principles by which God rules the world. Job had said that no such moral control was in evidence. The attitude that God probed was Job's wish to maintain his own righteousness at the expense of God's rectitude (8).

To show the absurdity of this position, Job is asked if he has **an arm like God** (9) or can **thunder with a voice like him.**

In his criticism of God's administration, Job had by inference placed himself as God's equal. Ironically God asks if he has the ability to match the claim. Assuming that Job might claim such ability, God next invites him to demonstrate this by donning the robes of divine **majesty** and **glory** (10). He is challenged to send abroad his **wrath** in order to humble the **proud** (11) and **tread down the wicked** (12), hiding **them in the dust** (13). If Job can do this, God will **confess unto thee** (14; concede) that Job is able to save himself. The heavy irony of these propositions is self-evident. Terrien rightfully sees here the pivotal verse of the book.[5] Satan had raised the question of Job's willingness to remain in his place as a servant of God without reward (1:9-11; 2:4-5). This verse raises the question whether Job has, indeed, elevated himself to the point where he does not need God. Will Job remember who he is and in humble faith let the Lord be God?

2. *Behemoth* (40:15-24)

In order to aid further in making distinction between God and man the poet has God described **behemoth** (15). The name of this beast is simply the transliteration of the Hebrew word which

[4]*Op. cit.*, p. 1184.   [5]*Ibid.*, p. 1186.

is used. As described, he was **made with thee** (created at the beginning of time along with mankind?). He is herbivorous, and of immense strength. Even his tail **moveth . . . like a cedar** tree (17). His muscles are hard as **stones** and his bones . . . **like bars of iron** (18). No other beast is like him in strength. Moffatt interprets 19,

> *He is God's very masterpiece,*
> *made to be lord of his fellows.*

Nature serves him by giving him **food** (20), a place to **play,** and **shady** (21-22) comfort. He is so huge that even **Jordan** at flood stage does not bother him—**He drinketh up a river** (23). Who could trap him with any kind of **snares** (24)?

Behemoth is often taken as a description of the hippopotamus, even though its tail hardly matches the cedar tree in size or strength. Tsur-Sinai considers **behemoth** to be an "imaginary animal" who represents all great grass-eating cattle created by God.[6] Terrien sees him as having mythological significance—a primeval beast.[7] Pope sees a parallel between behemoth and the great buffalo which, according to Ugaritic myth, were hunted by Baal in the Lake Huleh region in the marshy area of the upper Jordan.[8]

Whatever the identification, **behemoth** was created by God and serves to contrast the power of God with that of man. It may have had mythical overtones for the author, in which case he is not merely repeating the theme of cc. 38 and 39. He may be alluding to that world of spirit which, to the popular mind of his day, was populated with great and terrifying creatures. Even these, the poet says, are subject to God and were created by Him.

3. *Leviathan* (41:1-34)

There follows immediately a rather lengthy description of **leviathan**—which is also a transliteration of the Hebrew term. It is generally considered that the description best fits the crocodile, although there may very well be mythical overtones with regard to him, as already noted in 3:8 and 26:13. In any case, as with "behemoth," the emphasis is upon the superior strength of **leviathan** compared to man's ability to cope with him.

[6]*Op. cit.,* p. 557.   [7]*Op. cit.,* pp. 1186 ff.
[8]*Op. cit.,* pp. 268 ff.

It is impossible to capture leviathan **with an hook** (1). Being impossible to capture, he is also incapable of being tamed. Almost whimsically God paints a picture of Job attempting to do so. Can he **put an hook into his nose** (2) or bridle **his jaw?** Who would visualize such a creature speaking softly or making **a covenant with** his captor (3-4)? Certainly he would never be a plaything one would give to his **maidens** (female slaves) as a pet (5).

This sea monster is not one to be taken for food at **a banquet** (6), because there is no method of catching him. He is impervious to any kind of **barbed irons** or **fish spears** (7). One who gets close enough to put his **hand upon him** (8) will long remember the ferocious struggle he puts up and will never try such a thing again. "The man who hopes to master him will be disillusioned; at the sight of him a person is paralyzed!" (9; Berk.)

The moral of this illustration is given in the middle of the description. **None . . . dare stir him up** (10). Since no man is strong enough to do combat with **leviathan,** how much less is anyone qualified to **stand before me! Everything under the whole heaven is mine** (11). Job has no claim against a God who is of the stature of the One being described here.

Once more the author moves to a consideration of leviathan. He is tremendous in **power** and of **comely proportion** (12). His hide, covered with scales like close-fitting armor, cannot be penetrated. Verse 13 may be read:

> *Who can strip off his outer garment?*
> *Who can penetrate his double coat of mail?* (RSV)

The doors of his face (14) would be his jaws. **His teeth are terrible.** The expression **By his neesings** (sneezing) **a light doth shine** (18) may refer to the light shining upon the **vaporized** water blown from his nostrils. Verses 19-21 describe the popular notion that a sea monster breathes **fire** and **smoke, as out of a seething pot or caldron.**

Leviathan's great strength is described under the figures of the power of **his neck** (22), his **hard flesh** (23), and his **heart of stone** (24). Moffatt clarifies 22 thus:

> *Strength is seated in his neck—*
> *all creatures twitch in terror at him.*

Verse 25 may be read, "When he raises himself up, the mighty are afraid; beside themselves with panic" (Berk.). Leviathan makes their weapons of **iron** seem like **straw** and those of **brass** appear as **rotten wood** (27). No **arrow** (28) can bother him, while **slingstones** (28) and **darts** (29) are no better than throwing stalks of straw at him. "His nether parts are like potsherds; they leave threshing-sledge grooves in the mire" (30, Berk.). He laughs at a **spear** (29), and when he gets angry he **maketh the deep to boil like a pot** (31). He swims through the water so swiftly that he leaves **a path** (a shining wake) in the water after him (32). Nowhere is there anything like him (33). **He is a king** (34) over even the proudest of all beasts.

4. Job Repents (42:1-6)

Job is convinced of God's great majesty and wisdom. He admitted after God's first discourse that he had gotten out of place. Now he realizes that his rebellious thought has been terribly wrong.

Thou canst do every thing (2). Job has been impressed with God's incomparable power. Nothing is beyond His ability. **No thought can be withholden from thee** means that God can do anything He plans to do.

Job repeats God's words to him regarding hiding **counsel without knowledge** (3). By doing so he admits that he has been guilty as charged. He has spoken in such a manner and about things that are far beyond his knowledge and experience.

I have heard of thee (5) indicates that Job's knowledge of God has been far too limited. It had been academic. His friends and religious teaching had told Job *about* God. He himself had passed on this kind of information to others. On the basis of what he had heard he had engaged in a great deal of speculative discussion about the nature of God. But the conceptions held by his friends were inadequate to fit his circumstances. Those held by himself led him to make charges against God which were rebellious and blasphemous. He had now been changed—**Mine eye seeth thee.** It is no longer hearsay truth that Job relies upon. He had been confronted by God on a Person-to-person basis.

What are the results of such a confrontation? Repentance. **I abhor myself** (6). The word translated **abhor** means to melt, dissolve, waste away. God had accused Job of making too much of himself. Now Job is saying, I have become nothing (see Ps. 58:8). Seeing God, he realized how insignificant he really was (cf. Isa. 6:5). Job saw himself as God must have seen him, but he also went beyond self-depreciation—**I repent in dust and ashes.** Of what did Job repent? Of the sins of which his friends accused him? Of claiming an integrity that he did not have? No. He repented of his presumptuous accusations against God and especially of the pride which these accusations demonstrated.

This must be the answer to which the author of the book has been steadily moving. Job's misery is still with him. His friendships have been destroyed or severely strained. None of the misfortunes and tragedies perpetrated by Satan have been removed. God has not granted Job's desire for a debate over the divine justice in administering the world. What Job has come to know is that God's ways are beyond man's ability to comprehend. Therefore God is not to be criticized nor questioned under any circumstance of life.

But Job learned more. He found in his own experience that, no matter how low one may sink under the pressure of suffering, hope rises in the soul and can produce a persistent faith. His conversation with God proved that a humble trust in Him is the only reasonable position for man to take. He, and He alone, is God. He is eminently worthy of absolute trust. But such trust does not go unrewarded. When Job had walked this path, he found God himself. He saw Him, the Creator and Sustainer of the universe.

Section V *Prose Epilogue*

Many people believe that the work of the poet-author stops with Job's confession and repentance. Some object to the restoration of Job's goods as an anticlimax which, after all, supports the position of the friends. That this is not necessarily true has already been shown (see Intro., "Integrity of the Text").

A. JOB INTERCEDES FOR HIS FRIENDS, 42:7-9

God did not approve of the attitude that Job held toward Him, but neither did He approve of the attitude of the three friends in their disputation with Job. God addresses Eliphaz: **My wrath is kindled against thee, and against thy two friends** (7), because you have been even more seriously wrong than Job. He then instructs them to request **Job** to **pray** (8) to Him on their behalf. This was done, **according as the Lord commanded them** (9).

In 1-10 we see "The End of the Lord." (1) The omnipotence of God, 1-2; (2) Man's incapacity to judge God's providence, 3-6; (3) Intercession for one's opposition, 7-10 (A. Maclaren).

B. JOB IS RESTORED TO HEALTH AND WEALTH, 42:10-17

The captivity of Job (10) refers to all of the suffering that had come to him. Friendship and honor were restored (11). His wealth was doubled (cf. 1:3 and 42:12). He gained a like number of children (cf. 1:2 and 42:13). The names of his three daughters are given (14). It is stated that **in all the land were no women so fair as the daughters of Job** (15). It is also noted that they were granted a share of the **inheritance** along with the sons. Job's life was crowned by long days after his trial—**an hundred and forty years** (16)—so that he saw a succession of **four generations**. His death was a happy one because his life had been so well lived. **So Job died, being old and full of days** (17).

This book does not really tell why men suffer in our world. It can help those who suffer to do so with patience, and to maintain faith in the ways of God even when those ways are obscure. But it took Another, bearing a cross, to show the world clearly what can be achieved through undeserved suffering.

Bibliography

I. COMMENTARIES

BLACKWOOD, ANDREW W. *Devotional Introduction to Job.* Grand Rapids: Baker Book House, 1959.

DAVIDSON, A. B. *The Book of Job.* "The Cambridge Bible for Schools and Colleges." Cambridge: University Press, 1899.

DRIVER, SAMUEL ROLLES, and GRAY, GEORGE BUCHANAN. *The Book of Job.* "The International Critical Commentary." New York: Charles Scribner's Sons, 1921.

MOULTON, RICHARD G. *The Book of Job.* "The Modern Readers' Bible." New York: The Macmillan Co., 1927.

POPE, MARVIN H. "Job," *The Anchor Bible.* Edited by WILLIAM FOXWELL ALBRIGHT and DAVID NOEL FREEDMAN, Vol. XV. Garden City: Doubleday and Co., Inc., 1965.

ROBINSON, T. H. *Job and His Friends.* London: SCM Press, Ltd., 1954.

TERRIEN, SAMUEL. "Job" (Exegesis), *The Interpreter's Bible.* Edited by GEORGE A. BUTTRICK, et al., Vol. III. New York: Abingdon-Cokesbury Press, 1954.

TUR-SINAI, N. H. *The Book of Job.* Jerusalem: Kiryath Sepher, Ltd., 1957.

WARD, WILLIAM B. *Out of the Whirlwind.* Richmond: John Knox Press, 1958.

II. OTHER BOOKS

ALBRIGHT, WILLIAM FOXWELL. *From the Stone Age to Christianity.* Baltimore: The Johns Hopkins Press, 1946.

ANDERSON, BERNHARD W. *Understanding the Old Testament.* Englewood Cliffs: Prentice-Hall, Inc., 1957.

BAKER, WESLEY C. *More than a Man Can Take.* Philadelphia: The Westminster Press, 1966.

BEWER, JULIUS A. *The Literature of the Old Testament.* New York: Columbia University Press, 1933.

CARTLEDGE, SAMUEL A. *A Conservative Introduction to the Old Testament.* Athens: University of Georgia Press, 1944.

FERRE, NELS F. S. *Evil and the Christian Faith.* New York: Harper Brothers Press, 1947.

GOTTWALD, NORMAN K. *A Light to the Nations.* New York: Harper and Brothers Pub., 1959.

MACLEISH, ARCHIBALD. *Job.* Boston: Houghton Mifflin, 1956.

MOULD, ELMER W. K. *Essentials of Bible History.* New York: The Ronald Press Co., 1951.

NAPIER, B. DAVIE. *Song of the Vineyard.* New York: Harper and Brothers Pub., 1962.

PEDERSEN, JOHS. *Israel*, 4 vols. Copenhagen: S. L. Moller, 1946.

PFEIFFER, ROBERT H. *Introduction to the Old Testament.* New York: Harper and Brothers Pub., 1941.

PRITCHARD, JAMES B. *Archeology and the Old Testament.* Princeton: Princeton University Press, 1958.

PURKISER, W. T. (ed.). *Exploring the Old Testament.* Kansas City: Beacon Hill Press of Kansas City, 1961.

ROBINSON, H. WHEELER. *The Cross in the Old Testament.* Philadelphia: Westminster Press, 1955.

SILVER, MAXWELL. *There Was a Man . . .* New York: Union of American Hebrew Congregations, 1965.

YOUNG, EDWARD J. *An Introduction to the Old Testament.* Grand Rapids: Wm. B. Eerdmans Publishing Co., 1949.

III. ARTICLES

BECK, H. F. "Shuah," *The Interpreter's Dictionary of the Bible,* Vol. R-Z. Edited by GEORGE A. BUTTRICK, *et al.*, New York: Abingdon Press, 1962, p. 341.

DAHLBERG, B. T. "Zophar," IDB. Vol. R-Z, p. 963.

FINE, HILLEL A. "The Tradition of a Patient Job," *Journal of Biblical Literature,* LXXIV (March, 1955), 28-32.

GASTER, T. H. "Satan," IDB, Vol. R-Z, pp. 224-28.

GOLD, T. R. "Teman," IDB, Vol. R-Z, p. 534.

GUTHRIE, JR., H. H. "Bildad," IDB, Vol. A-D, pp. 437-38.

HICKS, L. "Eliphaz," IDB, Vol. E-J, p. 91.

HONTHEIM, JOSEPH. "Job," *Catholic Encyclopedia,* Vol. VIII. Edited by CHARLES G. HERBERMANN, *et al.* New York: The Gilmary Society, 1910.

KLOSTERMANN, AUGUST. "Job," *The New Schaff-Hertzog Encyclopedia of Religious Knowledge,* Vol. VI. Edited by SAMUEL MACAULEY JACKSON, *et al.* Grand Rapids: Baker Book House, 1963, pp. 186-93.

LAKS, H. JOEL. "The Enigma of Job: Maimonedes and the Moderns," *Journal of Biblical Literature,* LXXXIII (December, 1963), 345-64.

NAPIER, B. D. "Uz," IDB, Vol. R-Z, p. 741.

POPE, MARVIN H. "Job," IDB, Vol. E-J, pp. 911-25.

SARNA, NAHUM M. "The Mythological Background of Job," *Journal of Biblical Literature,* LXXXII (September, 1963), pp. 315-18.

VAN BEEK, G. W. "Sabeans," IDB, Vol. R-Z, pp. 144-46.

ZINK, JAMES K. "Impatient Job," *Journal of Biblical Literature,* LXXXIV (June, 1965), 147-52.

The Book of

PSALMS

W. T. Purkiser

Introduction

The Book of Psalms stands as the first book in the third division of the Hebrew Bible. Known as the *Kethubhim* or Writings, this third division was popularly called by the name of the first book, i.e., "The Psalms." Thus Jesus included the entire Old Testament when He spoke of the prophecies concerning himself in "the law of Moses, and in the prophets, and in the psalms" (Luke 24:44).

Our English title comes from the Greek Septuagint translation, made about one hundred fifty years before Christ. *Psalmoi,* the Greek term, means "songs" or "sacred songs," and is derived from a root meaning "impulse, touch," as of the chords of a stringed instrument. The Hebrew title is *Tehillim,* meaning "praises" or "songs of praise."

The Psalms has a place of special importance in the Bible. Luther spoke of the book as "a Bible in miniature."[1] Calvin described it as "an anatomy of all the parts of the soul," since, as he explained, "there is not an emotion of which any one can be conscious that is not here represented as in a mirror."[2] Johannes Arnd wrote, "What the heart is in man, that the Psalter is in the Bible."[3] W. O. E. Oesterley described the Psalms as "the grandest symphony of praise to God ever composed on earth."[4] Theodore H. Robinson said,

> The Hebrew Psalter holds a unique position in the religious literature of mankind. It has been the hymnbook of two great religions, and has expressed their deeper spiritual life through the centuries. It has ministered to men and women of widely different races, languages and cultures. It has brought comfort and inspiration to the sorrowing and to the faint-hearted in all ages. Its words have shown themselves to be adaptable to the needs of people who

[1]Quoted by J. G. S. S. Thompson, "Psalms," *The New Bible Dictionary,* ed. J. D. Douglas, *et al.* (Grand Rapids, Michigan: Wm. B. Eerdmans Publishing Co., 1962), p. 1059.

[2]*Commentary on the Book of Psalms;* quoted by W. Stewart McCullough, "The Book of Psalms" (Introduction), *The Interpreter's Bible,* ed. George A. Buttrick, *et al.,* IV (New York: Abingdon Press, 1955), 16.

[3]Quoted by Franz Delitzsch, *A Commentary on the Book of Psalms,* translated by Eaton and Duguid, I (New York: Funk and Wagnalls, n.d.), 1.

[4]*The Psalms,* translated with text-critical and exegetical notes (London: S. P. C. K., 1953), p. 593.

have no knowledge of its original form and little understanding of the conditions under which it was produced. No other part of the Old Testament has exercised so wide, so deep, or so permanent an influence on the life of the human soul.[5]

The place given to the Psalms in the New Testament clearly testifies to the value of this great book. Of approximately 263 Old Testament passages quoted in the New Testament, slightly more than one-third, or a total of 93, are drawn from the Book of Psalms. Some of them, most notably Psalm 2 and Psalm 110, are quoted several times. In the words of W. E. Barnes, "Only the existence of a true spiritual continuity between the Psalms and the Gospel can explain the deep affection with which the Christians of every age have clung to the Psalter."[6]

One of the most important values in the Psalms for the study of the Old Testament is the insight given into the true nature of Old Testament religion. Unfortunately, we have too often associated the religion of the Old Testament with the Phariseeism and legalism described in the Gospels and in the writings of Paul. The psalms show clearly that in Old Testament times piety was a living, spiritual, joyful, and intensely personal faith. The psalms reflect a level of spirituality which many in the more favored Christian dispensation fail to reach or rise to only rarely. As A. F. Kirkpatrick noted:

> The Psalms represent the inward and spiritual side of the religion of Israel. They are the manifold expression of the intense devotion of pious souls to God, of the feeling of trust and hope and love which reach a climax in such Psalms as 23, 42-43, 63, 84. They are the many-toned voice of prayer in the widest sense, as the soul's address to God in confession, petition, intercession, meditation, thanksgiving, praise, both in public and private. They offer the most complete proof, if proof were needed, how utterly false is the notion that the religion of Israel was a formal system of external rites and ceremonies.[7]

A. STRUCTURE OF THE BOOK

From very ancient times the Book of Psalms in Hebrew has been subdivided into five "books" or divisions which are indicated in most of the modern translations although they do not

[5]*The Poetry of the Old Testament* (London: Gerald Duckworth and Co., Ltd., 1947), p. 107.

[6]*The Psalms: With Introduction and Notes* (New York: E. P. Dutton and Company, Inc., n.d.), I, xli.

[7]*The Book of Psalms* ("The Cambridge Bible for Schools and Colleges"; Cambridge: University Press, (1894), I, lxvii.

appear in the King James Version. Book I comprises **Psalms** 1—41. Book II includes Psalms 42—72. Book III is **Psalms 73—** 89. Book IV takes in Psalms 90—106, and Book V, Psalms 107— 50. The Jewish *Midrash* or commentary on the Psalms compares these five books to the five books of Moses. The division is probably related to the three-year cycle for the reading of the law which prevailed in ancient Palestine. The Book of Genesis was read for the first forty-one Sabbaths. The reading of Exodus began on the forty-second Sabbath, Leviticus on the seventy-third, Numbers on the ninetieth, and Deuteronomy on the one hundred seventh—corresponding with the first psalm in each book.[8]

It is also probable that our present Book of Psalms is in fact a collection of collections. This is seen in both the nature and groupings of the titles (cf. below) and the statement in 72:20, "The prayers of David the son of Jesse are ended."

A survey of the titles of the psalms in Book I reveals that all are credited to David with the exceptions of 1, 2, 10, and 33. Book I was probably the first official psalter. It freely uses the sacred covenant name for God, the Hebrew *Yahweh,* translated "Jehovah" in the ASV, "the Lord" in the KJV and RSV, and printed in small capitals.

A second collection, apparently made later, is found in Book II, Psalms 42—72. Of this number, seven (42; 44—49) are inscribed "for the sons of Korah," one is identified with Asaph (50), eighteen with David, one with Solomon (72), and four are without titles (43, 66, 67, 71). That this collection was originally separate from the first book is indicated by the repetition of Psalm 14 in Psalm 54, and part of Psalm 40 in Psalm 70: and by the fact that the term *Elohim* (translated "God") is consistently used as the divine name rather than *Yahweh.* The Asaph psalms of Book III, 73—83, also use *Elohim* in preference to *Yahweh,* although the remaining psalms in the book refer to God as *Yahweh.* No good reason can be given for the different usage. It was apparently deliberate, and carefully done. It is true that later Judaism regarded the name *Yahweh* as too sacred to use, but this attitude arose long after the psalms were completed.[9]

Of Book III, the basic core is a group of psalms (73—83)

---

[8]Norman Snaith, *Hymns of the Temple* (London: SCM Press, Ltd., 1951), pp. 18-19. The full citation is given by Mitchell Dahood, *Psalms I (1—50)* ("The Anchor Bible," ed. William Foxwell Albright and David Noel Freedman; Garden City, New York: Doubleday and Company, Inc., 1966), pp. xxx-xxxi.

[9]Kirpatrick, *op. cit.,* pp. xxxix-xli.

attributed to Asaph, who was David's choirmaster (I Chron. 16: 4-7). From the mention of Hezekiah's revival of the psalmnody of David and Asaph (II Chron. 29:30), Delitzsch surmises that the collection represented by Book III may have been added in Hezekiah's time.[10] The remainder of the psalms in this shortest of the five books are attributed in their titles to (or for) the sons of Korah (84, 85, 87, perhaps 88), David (86), Heman the Ezrahite (88; cf. II Chron. 35:15), and Ethan the Ezrahite (89; cf. I Chron. 2:6). Heman and Ethan are characterized in I Kings 4:31 as men of notable wisdom. I Chron. 2:6 would indicate that they were grandsons of Judah, but II Chron. 35:15 shows that there was also a Heman who was one of the sons of Asaph.

The psalms in the last two books are largely without superscriptions, although the titles relate Psalm 90 to Moses; fifteen of this group are attributed to David, one to Solomon (127), and Psalm 96 and part of Psalm 105 to David in I Chron. 16:7-33. There are three discernible groupings of psalms in Book IV. Psalms 90—99 are a group of ten Sabbath psalms, and Psalm 100 is the traditional psalm for the weekday. Psalms 103—4 are the two Blessing Psalms, built on the refrain, "Bless the Lord, O my soul." Psalms 105—6 comprise a pair of Hallelujah Psalms.[11]

In Book V we have two Davidic groups, 108—10 and 138—45, in addition to two others attributed to David (112, 133). Psalms 113—18 are known as the Egyptian Hallel (from the reference to the Exodus in Psalm 114). A "Hallel" is a song of praise, "Praise ye the Lord" being *Hallelu-Yah* ("hallelujah!") in the original Hebrew. The Egyptian Hallel is traditionally used in connection with the observance of Passover. Psalms 120—34, "songs of degrees" or "ascents," are a group of pilgrim songs commemorating the return from exile and used by the devout on their annual pilgrimages to Jerusalem. These fifteen psalms comprise a miniature psalter, divided into five groups of three psalms each. Psalms 146—50 are known as the Great Hallel. Each of the five psalms begins and ends with the Hebrew *Hallelu-Yah*, translated, "Praise ye the Lord."

While noting the exceptions to the rule, Kirkpatrick points out that the psalms of Book I are chiefly personal; those of Books II and III are chiefly national; and Books IV and V are in the main liturgical, or designed for use in public worship.[12]

[10]*Op. cit.,* pp. 22-23. Cf. Prov. 25:1 for an example of Hezekiah's interest in the religious literature of his people.

[11]Cf. Snaith, *op. cit.,* pp. 14-17.   [12]*Op. cit.,* I, xlii.

B. The Titles

Reference has frequently been made to the titles of many of the psalms. In all, about two-thirds of the psalms have titles, which are generally printed in the English translation just before verse 1 in each case. While the titles were not part of the original text of the psalm, they are very ancient. This is seen in the fact that the translators of the Septuagint, or Greek version of the Hebrew Bible, found them attached to the psalms, but so obscure in meaning that they were unable to understand even their general import. The Septuagint version (abbreviated, LXX) of the Psalms became current about 150 B.C.[13]

In general, there are five types of titles. There are those which describe the character of the poem, e.g., psalm, song, *maschil, michtam, shiggaion,* prayer, praise. Others are connected with the musical setting or performance of the psalms. Typical of these are "to the chief musician; on *Neginoth; upon Nehiloth, Alamoth, Sheminith,* or *Gittith* (probably the names of musical instruments); and set to *Muth-labben, Aijeleth Shahar,* etc. (representing tunes).

A third kind of title refers to the liturgical use of the psalms —for example, dedication (30), for the Sabbath (92), and the songs of ascents (120—34). Other titles relate to authorship, or possibly to dedications. The Hebrew phrase found in the headings of some seventy-three of the psalms, *le-David,* and translated "of David," might equally well be translated "to" or "for David," "belonging to David," or "after the manner or style of David."[14] Titles of this sort, in addition to the seventy-three psalms which name David, are found attached to Psalm 90 (Moses); Psalms 72 and 127 (Solomon); Psalms 50, 73—83 (Asaph); Psalm 88 (Heman); Psalm 89 (Ethan); and ten or eleven referred to "the sons of Korah."

A final sort of title has reference to the occasion attributed to the composition of the psalm. These are found principally in connection with psalms credited to David: e.g., 3, "when he fled from Absalom his son"; 7, "which he sang unto the Lord, concerning the words of Cush the Benjamite"; 18, "who spake unto the Lord the words of this song in the day that the Lord delivered him from the hand of all his enemies, and from the hand of

---

[13]*Ibid.,* p. xxvii.

[14]Cf. Barnes, *op. cit.,* pp. xxiii-xxiv; and Sigmund Mowinckel, *The Psalms in Israel's Worship,* trans. by D. R. Ap-Thomas (New York: Abingdon Press, 1962), II, 95-103.

Saul: and he said";[15] 34, "when he changed his behaviour before Abimelech; who drove him away, and he departed"; etc.

Where the titles require explanation, it is given in the commentary dealing with that particular psalm.

C. Classification of the Psalms

There are many attempted classifications of the psalms, none of which is entirely satisfactory. A number of psalms contain material of more than one type, making any classification necessarily tentative. The following classification, drawing on a number of standard sources, at least illustrates the breadth and variety to be found in this hymnal of the Bible:

1. Wisdom Psalms and Psalms of Moral Contrast: 1, 9—10, 12, 14, 19, 25, 34, 36—37, 49—50, 52—53, 73, 78, 82, 92, 94, 111—12, 119.

2. Royal and Messianic Psalms: 2, 16, 22, 40, 45, 68, 72, 89, 101, 110, 144.

3. Songs of Lament, Individual and National: 3—5, 7, 11, 13, 17, 26—28, 31, 39, 41—44, 54—57, 59—64, 70—71, 74, 77, 79—80, 86, 88, 90, 140—42.

4. Penitential Psalms: 6, 32, 38, 51, 102, 130, 143.

5. Psalms of Adoration, Worship, Praise, and Thanksgiving: 8, 18, 23, 29—30, 33, 46—48, 65—67, 75—76, 81, 85, 87, 91, 93, 103—8, 135—36, 138—39, 145—50.

6. Liturgical Psalms: 15, 20—21, 24, 84, 95—100, 113—18, 120—34.

7. Imprecatory Psalms: 35, 58, 69, 83, 109, 137.

The titles given to the psalms as listed in the Contents provide additional evidence of the wide range of subjects considered in these ancient songs.

A special note should be given to the final class. These psalms have come to be characterized as "imprecatory" from the curses they invoke upon the wicked in general and the enemies of the Psalmist in particular. It has widely been asserted that the imprecatory psalms are sub-Christian and unworthy of a place in the Holy Bible. That they appear to fall far short of the standard given by Jesus in the Sermon on the Mount (particularly Matt. 5:43-48) may readily be admitted.

However, there are some points which should be kept in mind as these psalms are read. First, they have never been used

[15]This title is identical with II Sam. 22:1, from which it was no doubt taken. Psalm 18 is found also in II Samuel 22 with minor revisions.

in the worship of the synagogue, and have never become part of the ritual of Judaism. The destruction of the wicked has been traditionally understood by the Jews as meaning that God would destroy, not the sinners, but the sin itself. There is a well-known story of a famous rabbi of the second century after Christ who was provoked by the lawless behavior of some of his neighbors. He prayed that they would die. His wife reproved him: "How can you act thus? The Psalmist says: Let sins cease on the earth. And then he continues: And the wicked shall be no more. This teaches that as soon as sin vanishes there will be no more sinners. Therefore do thou pray, not for the destruction of these wicked men, but for their repentance." The story hinges on the fact that it is possible to read "sins" for "sinners" in the Hebrew.[16]

Second, while personal retaliation is contrary to the spirit of the New Testament, the entire Bible makes it clear that all men must ultimately reap the consequences of their choices. As Franz Delitzsch states:

> The kingdom of God does not come only by the way of grace, but also by the way of judgment; the coming of God's kingdom is what is longed for by the suppliant of the Old Testament as well as the New (*vid.* 9:21; 59:14, etc.); and in the Psalms also every imprecation of judgment upon those, who set themselves to oppose the coming of this kingdom, is made upon the assumption of their persistent impenitence (*vid.* 7:13 f.; 109:17).[17]

Third, it is difficult to distinguish grammatically between the forms "Let this happen" and "This will happen." That is, we cannot be sure the Psalmist may not have intended his bitter words as predictions of what must inevitably come to the godless.[18]

Fourth, the Psalmist's words do not necessarily reflect any personal spite or cruelty. These men were concerned with the enemies of God as well as their own enemies, or better, they regarded their own enemies as such because of enmity toward God. Ps. 139:21 expresses this point: "Do not I hate them, O Lord, that hate thee?" A zeal for God rather than a desire for personal revenge lay behind many of the imprecatory passages.

[16]Cited by William W. Simpson, *Jewish Prayer and Worship* (Naperville, Ill.: SCM Book Club, 1965), p. 61.

[17]*Op. cit.*, p. 99.

[18]Leslie M'Caw, "Psalms," *The New Bible Commentary*, ed. Francis Davidson (Grand Rapids, Michigan: Wm. B. Eerdmans Publishing Company, 1956), p. 414.

Finally, the imprecatory psalms express a strong sense of the moral law which governs the universe. As C. S. Lewis wrote:

> If the Jews cursed more bitterly than the Pagans this was, I think, at least in part because they took right and wrong more seriously. For if we look at their railings we find they are usually angry not simply because these things have been done to them but because these things are manifestly wrong, are hateful to God as well as to the victim. The thought of the "righteous Lord"—who surely must hate such doings as much as they do, who surely therefore must (how terribly He delays!) "judge" or avenge, is always there, if only in the background.[19]

There is, of course, danger in a too casual equation of one's personal interests with the kingdom of God. That the psalmists themselves were not unaware of this is seen in the words which immediately follow the exclamation of Ps. 139:21-22, "Do not I hate them, O Lord, that hate thee? and am not I grieved with those that rise up against thee? I hate them with perfect hatred: I count them mine enemies." But the prayer continues, "Search me, O God, and know my heart: try me, and know my thoughts: and see if there be any wicked way in me, and lead me in the way everlasting" (vv. 23-24).

D. The Dating of the Psalms

The fashion of biblical criticism in the past has been to date the psalms much later than their traditional association with David would indicate. Some scholars have purported to find postexilic and even Maccabean dates for most of the psalms (e.g., 520-150 B.C.). Some of the dating was done on the basis of linguistic considerations such as vocabulary and grammatical forms. Other conclusions were drawn from a supposed evolutionary development of the thought forms expressed in the psalms.

The picture, however, has radically changed with a more intensive study of the Ras Shamra or Ugaritic texts. The full impact of these discoveries is yet to be felt.[20] Coupled with this is the even later evidence of the Qumran texts (the Dead Sea Scrolls). Mitchell Dahood summarizes the newer trends in psalm chronology: "An examination of the vocabulary of these psalms reveals that virtually every word, image, and parallelism are

---

[19]*Reflections on the Psalms* (New York: Harcourt, Brace and Company, 1958), pp. 30-31.

[20]Cf. the discussion in Dahood, *op. cit.*, pp. xv-xxxii.

now reported in Bronze-Age Canaanite texts. . . . If they are poems composed shortly prior to the LXX, why is it that the Alexandrian Jewish translators understood them so imperfectly? Roughly contemporary works should fare better than they did in translation."[21] Again Dahood states, "Though direct evidence enabling us to date the completion of the entire collection is lacking, the vast difference in language and prosody between the canonical Psalter and the Qumran Hodayot makes it impossible to accept a Maccabean date for any of the Psalms, a position still maintained by a number of critics. Nor is a Hellenistic date more plausible. The fact that the LXX translators were at a loss before so many archaic words and phrases bespeaks a considerable chronological gap between them and the original psalmists."[22]

[21]*Ibid.*, p. xxix.

[22]*Ibid.*, p. xxxii. Cf. the discussion of this point in Moses Buttenwieser, *The Psalms Chronologically Treated with a New Translation* (Chicago: The University of Chicago Press, 1938), pp. 1-18.

Outline

Section I Book One: Psalms of David

The forty-one psalms of Book One are all ascribed to David with the exception of Psalms 1, 2, 10, and 33, which are without titles. Only Book V is longer. There is no particular order of arrangement to be found in the collection. A number of the titles relate individual psalms to events in the life of David, but these are not arranged in chronological order.

Psalm 1: A STUDY IN CONTRASTS, 1:1-6

The first psalm is in the nature of a prelude to the entire collection. It is quite possible that it was composed for that purpose. It has no title, but was apparently written and known before the times of Jeremiah, since Jer. 17:5-8 seems to be a paraphrase and expansion of a portion of it.

The psalm would be classified as a wisdom psalm. It draws the sharp contrast between the righteous and the wicked that is found in the wisdom literature. It sets forth what has been called "the doctrine of rewards." The righteous prosper and are happy. The wicked are troubled and of short life. That there are glaring exceptions in individual cases to this rule was well-known. But the general principle was accepted as true and valid.

1. The Blessing of the Saint (1:1-3)

The godly man is described first in terms of what he does not do. He is **blessed** (1; *asher*) or happy. The LXX uses *makarios,* the same Greek term found in the Beatitudes of Matt. 5:3-11.

The righteous man is happy in what he does not do. Religion is more than negatives, but it involves the negative. There can be no building without excavation, and there can be no holy living without renunciation of evil. The happiness of the pious consists first in the fact that he does not walk **in the counsel of the ungodly** (Heb., *rashaim,* the wicked). Kirkpatrick suggests that, "if the primary notion of the Hebrew word *rasha* is unrest (cp. Job iii.17; Isa. lvii.20, 21), the word well expresses the disharmony which sin has brought into human nature, affecting man's relation to God, to man, to self."[1] Nor does he stand **in the way of sinners.** The intensive form of the term translated **sinners** indicates that habitual and determined transgressors are in mind. **The scornful,** often described in the Book of Proverbs, are "the worst of the godless; they are arrogant, quarrelsome, and mischief-making, foes of peace and order among men and in their communities, and mockers of goodness."[2]

There is unmistakable progress here, describing the path which the pious carefully avoid. **Walketh** suggests a casual or passing association with those who are out of touch with God. **Standeth** is a continued fellowship with persons consistently sinful in attitude and act. **Sitteth** implies being quite at home with those who mock God and religion. The godly person refuses to take even the first step on this downward path.

The character of the righteous is next described positively. This is what the person does who is truly happy. He finds **his delight . . . in the law of the Lord** (2), the teaching or instruction of Yahweh. The Hebrew term *torah* has a much broader meaning than is suggested by **law.** It stands for the whole revealed way of life contained in the teachings of Moses and the prophets, and is used in parallel construction with "the word of the Lord," to which it is virtually synonymous. The Hebrew term for **meditate** comes from a root which suggests the murmuring of one who is studying half-aloud the words of a book.[3] "True happiness is to be found not in ways of man's own devising, but in the revealed will of God."[4] The Christian is "Bible-bred, Bible-led, and Bible-fed."

The results of godliness are described in familiar symbols. Such a man is **like a tree planted by the rivers of water** (3). The imagery is of a well-watered tree, advantageously placed ("transplanted," Anchor) by a stream or irrigation canal, cultivated and cared for and consequently fruitful. This is not a wild growth, surviving by chance. The mention of evergreen leaves and the abundance of water suggests that the valuable date palm was in mind. In the words **whatsoever he doeth** the Psalmist drops the figure of the tree, and refers directly to the righteous

[1]*Op. cit.,* p. 2.

[2]William R. Taylor, "Psalms 1—71, 93, 95—96, 100, 120—28, 140—50" (Exegesis), *The Interpreter's Bible,* ed. George A. Buttrick, *et al.,* IV (New York: Abingdon Press, 1955), 20.

[3]*Ibid.*   [4]Kirkpatrick, *op. cit.,* p. 3.

man himself. Implied, of course, is the idea that such a man will do those things in which the Lord can prosper him.

2. The Burden of the Sinner (1: 4-6)

The sinner is in complete contrast with the righteous. **The ungodly** (4) are the *rashaim* of 1. Unlike the deep-rooted tree, they **are like the chaff which the wind driveth away.** This is a reference to the threshing floor on which the chaff was beaten from the wheat. The floor was usually on a hilltop or high place to catch the breeze. Wheat and chaff together were thrown into the breeze with shovels. The heavier wheat dropped to the ground to be carefully gathered, but the light and worthless chaff was blown away.

The chaff-like ungodly ones, without root or fruit, are unable to **stand in the judgment** (5). The wicked can survive neither the judgment of the last day nor the continual judgment of God's providential sifting of human character. **Nor** shall **sinners** stand **in the congregation of the righteous.** These **sinners** are persistent and habitual, as in v. 1. **The congregation of the righteous** is the biblical ideal for the true community of faith. The purpose of God's present judgments as well as His final future judgment (Matt. 13:24-30, 36-43) is to remove evil and evildoers from His Church.

A summary of the total contrast in Psalm 1 is given in the last verse. The first line, **For the Lord knoweth the way of the righteous,** summarizes vv. 1-3. The second line summarizes 4-5. **The Lord knoweth,** not in the abstract sense of awareness of or information about, but in the concrete and personal sense of caring, approving, guiding, regarding. It is possible, in some contexts, to translate *yada,* "know," with the English "care." Conversely, **the way of the ungodly shall perish,** end in ruin, "the ways of death" (Prov. 14:12). The first and last words of the psalm epitomize the contrast it draws between the righteous and the wicked: *blessed* and *perish.*

Psalm 2: MAN'S SINFUL REBELLION AGAINST THE LORD, 2:1-12

Psalm 2, like the one which precedes it, is without a title. It belongs to the very important class of psalms known as "royal" or "Messianic." There has been a great deal of debate over the significance of these psalms. Some have held that they are to be understood in relation to Israel's kings only, and that at least some of them may have been used in an annual enthronement ceremony. It may be objected to this that the NT persistently relates most of these psalms to Christ, and that any supposed annual enthronement festival in Israel is purely hypothetical. No such festival is known from any source other than these psalms and a supposed parallel with Babylonian customs.

It may readily be conceded that the royal psalms could have had an immediate occasion in the life of David or some other Israelite king. But as Samuel A. Cartledge points out, "At times a Psalm relating to one of the natural kings shades into a description of the King of kings; at times a description of contemporary blessedness leads to a description of the greater bliss of the times of the Messiah."[5] Harold H. Rowley says of such psalms: "They held before the king the ideal king, both as his inspiration and guide for the present, and as the hope of the future."[6]

Psalm 2 may have had its local occasion in a revolt of subject nations against Solomon in the early days of his reign.[7] Yet the fact that the psalm is applied in the NT no less than five times to Christ and His kingdom (Matt. 3:17; Acts 4:25-26; 13:33; Heb. 1:5; 5:5) points to the universal rebellion against the divine rule which is the essential nature of sin.

The psalm consists of four stanzas of three verses each. Three speakers are represented: the Psalmist himself, the Lord, and the king. In vv. 1-3, the Psalmist views the revolt of the nations against the Lord and His anointed. In 4-6, he sees the futility of the revolt in the light of God's sovereign power, and hears Him declare that He has set His king upon His holy hill of Zion. In vv. 7-9, the king recites the decree that has established his authority, and receives the answering assurance of God that he will be victorious. In 10-12, the Psalmist draws the lessons to be learned by the rebellious peoples, and exhorts them to make their peace with God.

1. Rebellion of the Nations (2:1-3)

Why do the heathen rage? (1) refers to the *goyim,* "Gentiles," "nations," non-Israelites as distinguished from the people

---

[5] *A Conservative Introduction to the Old Testament;* 2nd ed. (Atlanta, Georgia: University of Georgia Press, 1944), p. 185.

[6] *The Faith of Israel: Aspects of Old Testament Thought* (Philadelphia: The Westminster Press, 1956), p. 192.

[7] Cf. Kirkpatrick, *op. cit.,* pp. 5-7.

of Israel. **Rage** would better be translated, "assemble in tumult," that is, for the purposes of insurrection. The nations of Gentiles in antagonism to the true God may properly be called **heathen.** **The people imagine** means "the peoples [Heb. is plural] *meditate";* the same word as used in 1:2, but here with the connotation of plotting an evil deed. The **vain thing** is an irrational and hopeless rebellion.

The rebellion is viewed as more than political. It is **against the Lord, and against his anointed** (2)—Hebrew, *Meshiach* or Messiah. When translated into Greek, *Meshiach* becomes *Christos,* from which our English term "Christ" is derived. This is the justification for a Messianic interpretation of the psalm, together with the application made in the NT to Jesus. The rebels are determined to **break their bands** (3)—possibly the fastenings which secure the yoke to the animal—and **their cords**—which may represent the reins used for controlling a plowing ox. "Throw off their yoke" (Anchor).

Whatever the immediate circumstances may have been, these verses represent the most typical OT description of sin. Sin is not mere human or finite imperfection. It is moral rebellion, a revolt against the laws of God. Sin is putting man's will at the center of life instead of God's will. The revolt of the nations is a picture of the sin of the individual soul.

2. *Response of the Lord* (2:4-6)

God's response is pictured by the Psalmist in terms of derision and human scorn. The Bible frequently attributes to God features, attitudes, and actions drawn from human experience. This is done without thought of lowering the Infinite to the level of the human, but in the interest of presenting truth in terms we are able to understand. The Lord is viewed as **he that sitteth in the heavens** (4), "throned in the heavens" (Perowne). He need not even rise to meet the insurrection. **The Lord** is not the more usual *Yahweh* (translated LORD in the KJV and RSV) but *Adonai* (Lord, indicated by the use of the lower-case letters after the initial capital). "God is spoken of as the sovereign ruler of the world, rather than as the covenant God of Israel."[8]

Then shall he speak (5) pictures the power of the word of God. He has but to speak the word to bring confusion to His enemies. **And vex them** means bringing to nought their efforts,

---

[8]*Ibid.,* p. 9.

troubling, confounding, filling them with terror. **Sore displeasure** is literally a wrath which consumes, or fiery wrath (cf. Exod. 15:7).

Just as the first stanza ends with the defiant words of the rebels, the second closes with the words of the Lord. The **king** who rules upon the **holy hill of Zion** (6)—literally, "Zion, the mountain of my holiness"—is God's appointed and anointed. Since He reigns by the authority and in the name of God, resistance to Him is resistance to God. Christians rightly apply this truth to Jesus. "He that receiveth me receiveth him that sent me" (Matt. 10:40; John 13:20).

3. *Reassurance of the King* (2:7-9)

The king now speaks. **I will declare the decree** (7), i.e., set forth the constitution of the Kingdom in the will of God. **The Lord** (*Yahweh*) had said, **Thou art my Son; this day have I begotten thee.** These words are applied to the resurrection of Jesus by Paul in his Antioch sermon (Acts 13:33), and by the writer to the Hebrews both to the sonship of Jesus as superior to angels (Heb. 1:5) and to Christ's having been made a High Priest by God's own action (Heb. 5:5). Only here in the OT is the term **begotten** used with the Lord as its subject. In relation to Christ, **this day** has variously been interpreted as the "day" of His eternal generation, the day of His conception by the Virgin, the day of His resurrection (Rom. 1:4), or the whole of His incarnate state viewed as His "day."

God answers the declaration of His King with a promise of universal dominion. **The heathen** (8), are, as in 1, the *goyim*, "nations" or "Gentiles." **Uttermost parts of the earth**—literally, "the ends of the earth." **Inheritance** and **possession** are terms frequently used of the gift of Palestine to Israel.

In the expression **Thou shalt break them** (9), the Hebrew verb with different vowel markings may be read either "break" or "rule." The LXX translators understood the term to mean "rule," and it is so quoted in Rev. 2:27 and 12:5. However, **dash them in pieces** surely means destruction. It has been suggested that the two lines be read, "Thou shalt rule these with a rod of iron; thou shalt dash those in pieces like a potter's vessel." That is, those who submit to the Christ's authority will be His subjects, while those who resist shall be destroyed.[9]

[9]Cf. Barnes, *op. cit.*, I, 9-10.

4. *Repentance Demanded of the Rebels* (2:10-12)

In the last stanza, the Psalmist speaks directly to the rebels. **Now therefore** (10) stands first in the Hebrew text, as indicating the conclusion drawn from the preceding verses. **Be instructed,** or "admonished." **Judges** is a term used of rulers in general, including the King's subordinates.

Instead of pursuing their hopeless rebellion, the people are urged to **serve the Lord with fear** (11). More than political submission is in mind here, since **serve** and **fear** are used constantly throughout the OT with religious meanings. "The fear of the Lord" is the reverent awe with which man must regard the sovereign God. It is the nearest OT synonym for "religion." Such service will enable men to **rejoice with trembling.** There is no contradiction in this clause. It represents the blending of "the joy of the Lord" with "the fear of the Lord." Both emotions are proper for man before his Maker.

Just as the rebellion expressed itself as against the Lord and against His anointed, so the repentance must embrace both the sovereign God and His kingly Son. **Kiss the Son** (12), as yielding homage to Him. This reading has been disputed, but no better has been suggested, so the traditional interpretation may well be retained. "Bow to the ground before Him" (Harrison). There are frequent examples of the kiss as representing submission and obedience (I Sam. 10:1; I Kings 19:18; Job 31:27; Hos. 13:2). The Hebrew for **when his wrath is kindled but a little** is literally "for his anger may kindle quickly."

A beatitude closes the psalm. **Blessed are all they that put their trust in him** is literally, "Oh, the blessings of all those seeking refuge in Him!" "How blest are all who trust in him!" (Anchor) To trust the Lord is to put oneself in His care, under His protection. As sin and rebellion lead to certain destruction, trust and submission bring divine blessing. "Many sorrows shall be to the wicked: but he that trusteth in the Lord, mercy shall compass him about" (32:10).

Psalm 3: A MORNING PRAYER OF TRUST, 3:1-8

Psalm 3 is the first to bear a title: "A Psalm of David in his flight from the face of Absalom his son." The poem is to be classified as a song of lament. The term "psalm" in the title is *mizmor,* a word found only in the titles of the psalms, where it occurs fifty-seven times, usually followed by the name of an author, generally David. It means "a song with instrumental accompaniment."

Psalms 3 and 4 are closely related, since Psalm 3 is a morning prayer and Psalm 4 a prayer for evening. Psalm 3 is one of many written against a background of religious dissension and persecution. In the face of the hostility of those about him, the Psalmist expresses his supreme faith in God. As Oesterley comments, "For the expression of sublime trust in God this psalm is not surpassed in the Psalter."[10]

The psalm may be divided into four stanzas. (Cf. RSV or other translations that show the poetic form.) With the exception of the third, each stanza ends with *Selah*. The first two verses state the Psalmist's distress. Verses 3-4 relate his desire for the Lord's intervention. Verses 5-6 refer to the nature of the danger. The last two verses glory in the deliverance wrought by the Lord.

1. *Distress* (3:1-2)

The Psalmist's distress takes on new poignancy in light of the immediate circumstances indicated in the title. David apparently had little or no advance information of Absalom's plot. The first word he received is reported in II Sam. 15:12-13, "And the conspiracy was strong; for the people increased continually with Absalom. And there came a messenger to David, saying, The hearts of the men of Israel are after Absalom." The same descriptive word is used in the psalm, **How are they increased!** (1) The expression **that trouble me** is literally "my adversaries." Many were rising up in insurrection against their king.

That the rebellion had religious overtones would seem to be indicated in the reaction of the opposition, **There is no help for him in God** (2). *Ha-Elohim* is the generic term for Deity in Hebrew rather than *Yahweh* ("the Lord"), the personal name of the covenant God of Israel. Absalom's pagan mother (II Sam. 3:3) and the young prince's three-year exile with his grandfather in Geshur (II Sam. 13:37-38) may have given him a desire to supplant the worship of the true God with that of one of the gods of the Canaanites.

Selah is a term of uncertain meaning. It is found seventy-one times in the Psalter and three times in Habakkuk 3. All of the psalms in which it occurs with the exception of two are attributed

---

[10]*Op. cit.*, p. 129.

by title to David or to one of the Levitical singers such as Asaph, the sons of Korah, Ethan, or Heman. The remaining two have no titles. Most of the psalms in which **Selah** occurs are also inscribed, "For the chief musician," and frequently contain notes concerning the use of accompanying instruments. From these facts, **Selah** would seem to be a musical term, perhaps indicating a pause in the chanting of the hymn while instruments played. There are no clearly evident principles connecting its use to the thought of the psalms in which it occurs, but it generally ends a stanza or occurs before the introduction of some new and important thought. For modern readers, the most profitable interpretation would seem to be, "Pause—and meditate."

2. *Desire* (3:3-4)

Hard-pressed by opposition and danger, David expresses his longing for the Lord's intervention and tells of his prayer for help. He prefaces it with an acknowledgment of what the Lord had already been to and done for him. God had been **a shield** (3) about him, his **glory,** and **the lifter up of** his **head.** A soldier would quite naturally think of the protection of a shield against the power of his enemies. The Lord had also given the king **glory,** or honor. "To lift up the head" was an expression which meant "to provide deliverance for" (II Kings 25:27).

Previous answers to prayer encourage faith for the present. The Hebrew of **I cried** (4) is in the imperfect tense, and indicates repeated or habitual action: "As often as I cried, He answered me." "When I cry loudly to the Lord, He answers me" (Harrison). God's answers are given more readily to the habit of prayer than to the single act. It is those who "wait upon the Lord" who are rewarded (Isa. 40:31) much more than those who come as strangers in an hour of need. **Out of his holy hill,** as in 2:6, means "from the mountain of His holiness." God manifested His special presence in and help from His Temple on Mount Zion. For **Selah,** cf. comment on 2.

3. *Danger* (3:5-6)

The third stanza recounts the Psalmist's trust in the face of great danger. The note which constitutes this "a morning prayer" is found in 5: **I laid me down and slept; I awaked.** It is a rare faith indeed which can sleep soundly facing the threat of imminent destruction (cf. Acts 12:6-7). The tense of **sustained** in the

Hebrew suggests continual action, "sustains" or "will sustain me."

Prayer and trust produce courage: **I will not be afraid** (6). The masses of people were arrayed against the king. **Ten thousands** in Hebrew is "myriads." The right way can never be determined by "a count of noses." But "one with God is a majority." The Psalmist's faith might have been expressed in the words his friend Jonathan had spoken long before, "There is no restraint to the Lord to save by many or by few" (I Sam. 14:6). **Round about** suggests that the king's danger is so desperate he speaks of himself as already surrounded by his foes. This stanza does not end with a "selah," possibly because the situation is still unresolved, and the note of trust about to be sounded anew.

4. *Deliverance* (3:7-8)

The Lord his God is now called upon to deliver David from those who had made themselves his enemies. **Arise** (7) is frequently used in the OT as a call for the manifestation of God's power in salvation or judgment. In **thou hast smitten . . . thou hast broken,** the Hebrew perfect tenses relate both to the experience of the past and the confidence that the deliverance has as good as come. It is so certain that the writer can express it as already done. There is always this sense of "the presence of the future" in real faith: "What things soever ye desire when ye pray, believe that ye [do now] receive them, and ye shall have them" (Mark 11:24). To strike **the cheek** was to show contempt for, and to break **the teeth**—as for example of a ravaging lion—was to render powerless.

Salvation (8; *ha-yeshuah*) is the great word of deliverance in the OT. It may be used in a temporal sense, as initially here, to mean a deliverance from physical danger, the threat of death or defeat in war. But it deepens throughout the OT to take on more and more the meaning of deliverance from man's most bitter enemy, his sin and rebellion against the Lord. All such deliverance comes from God alone. It is the chief blessing accruing to the people of God.

It is important to note that David prays not only for the few who had been loyal to his cause. He invokes divine blessing upon the entire nation, which would include the rebels. This reminds us of the prayer of David's greater Son for those who crucified Him: "Father, forgive them; for they know not what they do" (Luke 23:34). For **Selah,** cf. comment on v. 2.

149

Psalm 4: AN EVENING PRAYER, 4:1-8

As Psalm 3 may be titled "A Morning Prayer," its companion piece, Psalm 4, is a prayer for the evening hour (vv. 4, 8). It is identical in structure with Psalm 3, differing only in the absence of a closing "selah." There are eight verses, divided into four stanzas of two verses each. The title, in addition to ascribing the psalm to David, dedicates it "to him that is over," that is, the chief musician, "on *Neginoth.*" The term *natsach,* translated "chief musician," is found in the titles of fifty-five psalms, all but two of which bear the name of David or one of the other singers such as Asaph or the sons of Korah. It is frequently combined, as here, with a musical designation. *Neginoth* means "stringed instruments." It appears in the titles of five other psalms (6, 54, 55, 67, 76), and apparently relates to the accompaniment.

Some commentators find in Psalm 4 a background of distress due to crop failures. Oesterley says, "Written at a time when there was famine, or at any rate shortage of food, in the land owing to a bad harvest, the psalmist glories in the spiritual satisfaction of joy within him through his love and faithfulness to God; compared with this, material wants do not trouble him."[11]

1. *Trial* (4:1-2)

The Psalmist speaks of God's former deliverance, and prays for present help in the face of continued opposition. **O God of my righteousness** (1) speaks of the Lord as the One who vindicates or justifies His servant's cause. **Thou hast enlarged me** is literally, "Thou hast made room for me," "opened a way for me" (Harrison). From being constrained or bound in limited circumstances, the Psalmist has been brought into ample room. **Ye sons of men** (2) is *bene ish,* men of power, rather than *bene adam,* men of weakness—but still men in contrast with God, who brings deliverance. **Vanity** is emptiness, delusion. **Leasing** is an obsolete English word for lying or falsehoods. For **Selah,** cf. comment on 3:2.

2. *Teaching* (4:3-4)

The second stanza is addressed to the same opposers described in 2. It affirms David's confidence in the Lord's protecting care. **The Lord hath set apart** (3) expresses the idea of

[11]*Ibid.,* pp. 131-32.

consecration in which the Lord separates the godly from the common or unclean and to himself. **Stand in awe, and sin not (4)** is given in the LXX as, "Be ye angry, and sin not," and is so quoted in Eph. 4:26. Either translation of the Hebrew is possible, for the same term may suggest either fear or anger. On **commune with your own heart,** Kirkpatrick writes: "The voice of conscience, unheeded in the turmoil and excitement of the day, or silenced by fear of men and evil example, may make itself heard in the calm solitude of the night, and convince you of the truth."[12]

3. *Trust* (4:5-6)

The true source of prosperity and happiness is not in men and their ways, but in the Lord above. **The sacrifices of righteousness (5)** are the sacrifices required by God's righteous law, and further, offered in the right spirit. **Who will shew us any good? (6)** is the cynical and despairing question of unrighteous men. The answer is found in the favor of God. **Lift thou up the light of thy countenance** is an expression used often for the favorable regard of the Lord for His chosen people.

4. *Triumph* (4:7-8)

There is a lilt of victory in the final stanza, as so often in such psalms of lament. The Psalmist's faith takes told. He finds a **gladness (7)** in his **heart** greater than that of the ungodly in times of bountiful harvest. Harvesttimes for the Hebrews and other ancient peoples were times of great celebration and rejoicing. The gladness of the Lord is greater. **For thou, Lord, only makest (8)** means that the Lord alone could make it possible for him to live **in safety,** or security.

Psalm 5: PRAYER FOR THE MORNING SACRIFICE, 5:1-12

Psalm 5 is also a morning prayer (v. 3) associated with the Temple worship (v. 7). It reflects the same background of peril and controversy found in Psalms 3 and 4. The title ascribes it to David, and it is dedicated to the chief musician "upon *Nehiloth*," that is, "upon wind instruments." It has been argued that the psalm must be later than David, since it mentions the Temple (v. 7). However, we find the same Hebrew term here translated "temple" applied to the Tabernacle sanctuary at Shiloh

---

[12]*Op. cit.,* p. 19.

(I Sam. 1:9; 3:3). It is therefore possible that it might have been used for the Tabernacle housing the ark of the Lord in David's time.

The psalm divides into four stanzas. Stanza one is the Psalmist's appeal to the Lord for a hearing (1-3). Verses 4-7 express the confidence that God will not tolerate the wicked. The third stanza describes the unfaithfulness of the Psalmist's enemies (8-10). The closing verses (11-12) voice David's confidence in the Lord's vindication of his cause.

1. Request (5:1-3)

The writer prays that God will hear his **words,** and **consider my meditation** (1). The Hebrew term translated **meditation** is a rare word, used again only in Ps. 39:3. It may mean either an unspoken prayer or the low voice of brooding sorrow.[13] Prayer is fitting at any time, but particularly appropriate **in the morning** (3).

2. Righteousness (5:4-7)

David is convinced that God's righteousness is such that He cannot and will not tolerate evil. Therefore **the foolish (5),** literally, boasters, or the arrogant, cannot stand in His sight. **Thou hatest all workers of iniquity** in their evildoing, although in love the Lord works for their repentance. **Leasing (6)** is lying or falsehood. **Bloody** is literally "man of blood"—bloodthirsty. In contrast, the Psalmist himself will worship the Lord in memory of **the multitude of thy mercy (7).** The Hebrew for **worship toward** is, "I will bow down toward." Even in private worship in a home, the Psalmist would turn his face toward the sanctuary of the Lord as representing God's presence with and favor toward His people (cf. Dan. 6:10).

3. Retribution (5:8-10)

Evil cannot go unpunished. The Psalmist combines a prayer for deliverance for himself with a note of imprecation against those who were both God's enemies and his (cf., Intro., "Classification of the Psalms"). **Make thy way straight (8),** that is, Lead me in the straight or plain way. **No faithfulness (9)** means no steadfastness or truth. **Inward part** refers to the core of per-

---

[13]*Ibid.,* p. 21.

sonality, the heart or very self. In Hebrew **very wickedness** means "destruction," in the sense of bent on destruction. **Their throat is an open sepulchre** is cited by Paul in Rom. 3:13 as part of his demonstration of the universal wickedness of man apart from God. An open grave would be particularly offensive to the Hebrews, to whom contact with death brought ceremonial defilement (Num. 19:11). **Destroy thou them** (10) is, in Hebrew, "Charge them with guilt," and therefore punish them. **Let them fall by their own counsels** suggests that their own evil plans will "backfire," and bring about their destruction. The attitude of the Psalmist toward the wicked is not based on personal spite or vindictiveness, but because **they have rebelled against thee.**

4. *Reward* (5:11-12)

Justice requires not only the punishment of wickedness, but the reward of righteousness. Those who **put their trust** (11) in the Lord and love His name shall **rejoice** and **be joyful,** for they have a sure defense. God will **bless the righteous** (12) and **compass him** (surround or protect him) **as with a shield.** The word used here meant a "buckler," a large shield sufficient to protect the entire body.

Psalm 6: A Prayer for Deliverance, 6:1-10

Psalm 6 is the first of a special class known as "penitential" psalms, expressing repentance and sorrow for sin. There are seven of these (6, 32, 38, 51, 102, 130, 143), and since the early days of Christianity they have been related to "the seven deadly sins." G. Campbell Morgan comments concerning Psalm 6: "It is somewhat weak in its note of true penitence and in this respect is not to be compared with some which follow. It is rather a cry for deliverance from the pain and the sorrow and chastisement than from the sin which causes it."[14] Its immediate occasion seems to have been a prolonged and dangerous illness. It is titled "A Psalm of David," and inscribed to the chief musician on *Neginoth,* "stringed instruments" (cf. introductory comment on Psalm 4). The added words in the title, "upon *Sheminith,*" mean "the eighth" or an octave—a musical notation the significance of which is not clear.

---

[14]*An Exposition of the Whole Bible* (Westwood, New Jersey: Fleming H. Revell Company, 1954), p. 223.

The psalm divides into three sections. Verses 1-5 present the Psalmist's painful illness. The second section continues his description of suffering and grief (6-7). The final division sounds a note of confident trust.

1. *Cry* (6:1-5)

The Psalmist calls on the Lord for mercy in the face of possible death. Although he is a man who fears the Lord, he sees his affliction as a divine chastisement for sin, which gives the poem its classification as a penitential psalm. The Bible elsewhere shows that sickness is not necessarily a divine infliction in punishment for personal sin. Nevertheless, it is clear that in some cases illness may be used as a chastening rod designed to turn a wanderer back to God (cf. I Cor. 11:30; Jas. 5:15). **Hot displeasure** (1), Hebrew, "wrath." **I am weak** (2), literally, "withered," or languishing. **My bones are vexed** (Heb., "troubled"; cf. 2:5, comment). The bones were regarded as fundamental to the health of the whole body (Prov. 16:24). The poet's bones are troubled, but his **soul is . . . sore vexed** (3; "greatly troubled"). **In death there is no remembrance of thee: in the grave** (Heb., "Sheol") **who shall give thee thanks?** (5) It must be remembered that only Jesus Christ "brought life and immortality to light through the gospel" (II Tim. 1:10). The OT nowhere regards death as an end of existence; but *Sheol,* the place of the dead, was not a place to be anticipated with joy. Occasionally men of OT times were given a glimpse of a happier eternity (e.g., Job 19:25-27; Ps. 16:10-11; 49:15; 73:23-26). But for the most part, death was dreaded as an interruption of the worship of and walk with God.

2. *Complaint* (6:6-7)

David's anguish is vividly described, **I am weary with my groaning** (6). Great grief is exhausting, and the Psalmist was coming to the end of his endurance. **All the night make I my bed to swim; I water my couch**—copious tears through the long night flooded the poet's bed. **Mine eye is consumed** (7); red and lusterless eyes betrayed both his illness and grief. **It waxeth,** that is, "gradually becomes." The unceasing opposition of **all mine enemies** kept up even during the serious sickness. His enemies were without pity.

3. Confidence (6:8-10)

As in so many psalms of this sort, the bitterness of the poet's circumstances is relieved by his trust in the Lord. Those who learn to pray in all conditions of life can find reason to give praise for the hope of God's help. David pictures his enemies as standing around, hoping the worst for him. He bids them be gone, declaring that **the Lord hath heard** (8). Although the circumstances have not yet changed, the Psalmist is confident that **the Lord will receive**—with favor—his **prayer** (9). As a result, his enemies will **be ashamed and sore vexed** (10)—abashed and greatly troubled, "humbled and greatly shaken" (Anchor). The verbs in 10 are best translated as simple future: "My enemies shall be ashamed . . . they shall be turned back."

Psalm 7: A Cry for Help, 7:1-17

Psalm 7 is another song of lament, entitled *"Shiggaion* of David." *Shiggaion* occurs only here in the OT, and in a different form ("Upon Shigionoth") in Hab. 3:1. No certain meaning can be given for it, although it could possibly be defined as "a passionate or intense song." Nor is anything known about "Cush the Benjamite," named in the title. It is possible that he was a close associate of King Saul who brought false charges of disloyalty against David. This psalm is the first of eight traditionally associated with David's flight from Saul. The others in this category are 34, 52, 54, 56, 57, 59, and 142.

After a brief invocation (1-2), the Psalmist protests his innocence of any wrongdoing (3-10). The last seven verses are less personal and more general. They deal with God's wrath against the iniquity of the Psalmist's foes.

1. Invocation (7:1-2)

David affirms his faith in God, and prays for deliverance from a bitter enemy. **In thee do I put my trust** (1)—Hebrew, "In Thee I took refuge." **Them that persecute me** is literally "those who pursue me." The antecedent to the pronoun in **lest he** (2) is either Cush or Saul himself. **My soul** (*nephesh*) may be used for the person, the individual life, or in place of a simple first-person "me."

2. Innocence (7:3-10)

Apparently subject to false charges, David protests his innocence of the wrongdoing. The Lord God is called upon to

155

permit the direst of calamities if the writer is guilty. **If I have done this** (3) would refer to the specific crimes with which Cush had charged him. In addition, the Psalmist protests his innocence of any **iniquity** (*avel,* "moral evil," "perverseness," "unrighteousness," "wickedness"). **Rewarded evil** (4) would be "returned evil for good." Conversely, David claims to have delivered the one who **without cause** was his **enemy.** Two clear examples of this occurred during David's flight from Saul (I Sam. 24:1-22; 26:1-25). **Persecute my soul, and take it** (5) is in the Hebrew, "Let my enemy pursue and overtake me." For **Selah,** see comment on 3:2.

Arise . . . lift up thyself . . awake for me (6), is a prayer expressed in terms of human experience and action. God's justice must manifest itself as anger against persistent evil. **Compass thee about** (7) means "gather around Thee." The Hebrew of the last half of v. 7 is difficult. We should probably picture the congregation of the people gathered in the presence of the Lord, who sits over them as their Judge. The Psalmist is confident of his own integrity. He is conscious of no wrongdoing which would in any sense justify the persecution he receives. He is willing to have God himself judge the case (8). God in His righteousness **trieth the hearts and reins** (9), or tests the hearts and consciences of men. "The searcher of mind and heart is God the just" (Anchor). **Reins** (*kelayoth*) means "kidneys." Its usage throughout the OT suggests that it is the Hebrew equivalent of what we should call the conscience.[15] **My defence** (10) is literally "my shield."

3. *Indignation* (7:11-17)

With the exception of the last verse, this stanza of the psalm deals with the iniquity of man and God's wrath against the evildoers. It is expressed in general terms, rather than in the personal terms of the first two sections. **God judgeth the righteous** (11) is literally, "God is a righteous Judge." As indicated by the italics in the KJV, there is nothing in the Hebrew corresponding to the words **with the wicked.** The object of God's wrath, although unspecified in the original, is undoubtedly the evils of which men are guilty. **If he turn not** (12) means, "If he does not repent." The Hebrew term *shub,* **turn,** is the OT equivalent

[15]C. Ryder Smith, *The Bible Doctrine of Man* (London: The Epworth Press, 1951), p. 23.

of repentance in the NT. Failure to repent will bring swift judgment. God **will whet** (sharpen) **his sword; his bow** is already **bent** and ready to discharge the arrows of judgment. **He ordaineth his arrows against the persecutors** (13) is in the Hebrew, "He will make His arrows into flaming missiles," "shafts of fire" (Harrison). God as a Warrior-Judge will use arrows tipped with pitch and set afire in order to burn the besieged city.

Verses 14-16 turn from the wrath of God to the evils of the wicked man. In vivid imagery the Psalmist describes the schemes of the wicked as conceiving **mischief** (14, perverseness, misery), **travailing with iniquity** (evil, perversity), and bringing forth lies. Like a careless hunter who digs **a pit** in which to trap his prey, the evil man falls into his own snare (15). The **mischief** (16) he has plotted for others will come back upon him. **His violent dealing** (*chamas,* "violence," "damage," "cruelty") will fall back upon **his own pate** (top of the head). Here is a vivid description of the recoil, the boomerang action of evil. "Chickens come home to roost" is a popular proverb expressing the same biblical truth.

Verse 17 is a closing doxology, an ascription of praise to God. **According to** means "because of." To **sing praise** (*zamar*) is "to sing psalms or songs." Praise is often associated with singing in the Bible. **Most high** (*Elyon*) is used only in poetry by the Hebrew writers (twenty-one times in the Psalms). It is also used by non-Israelites quoted in the Bible as a title for the Supreme God.

Psalm 8: THE PARADOX OF MAN BEFORE GOD, 8:1-9

Psalm 8 is a perfect gem of adoration, praise, and worship. It is full of the sense of man's degradation and dignity as one of the most insignificant yet highly honored creatures of God's world. Although placed in a nature setting, it is man and not the universe which is the Psalmist's theme. It has been called "Genesis 1 set to music,"[16] and "the best commentary" on Genesis 1.[17] It calls to mind Immanuel Kant's much-quoted statement: "Two things fill the mind with ever-renewed wonder and reverence the more often and persistently thought is occupied with

---

[16]Arnold B. Rhodes, *Layman's Bible Commentary,* ed. Balmer Kelly, *et al.* (Richmond, Va.: John Knox Press, 1959), I, 64.

[17]Edmond Jacob, *Theology of the Old Testament* (New York: Harper and Brothers, 1958), p. 170.

them: the star-lit heavens above me, and the moral law within me."[18]

Oesterley writes of Psalm 8: "Full of instructive beauty is the twofold thought of man's insignificance in the sight of God, and yet of man's dignity as God's highest creation."[19] Vriezen says, "A Psalm such as Psalm viii is one of the finest instances of a deeply human feeling of dependence and unworthiness linked with the consciousness that man has been called to a great, an independent task. These two go together in a striking way in the Old Testament."[20]

The psalm, credited to David, is inscribed "to the chief musician upon Gittith." "Gittith" is also found in the titles of Psalms 81 and 84. The meaning of the term is unknown. It is an adjective derived from the word *Gath*, and has variously been supposed to indicate accompaniment on a kind of instrument which originated in the Philistine city of Gath, a Gittite melody perhaps associated with the march of the Gittite guard (II Sam. 15:18),[21] or since *gath* also means "winepress" in Hebrew, it may have been the tune of a vintage song.[22]

The psalm begins and ends with the same seven Hebrew words which we translate, **O Lord our Lord, how excellent is thy name in all the earth!** (1, 9) It divides into two sections of unequal length. The first two verses speak of the majesty of God. The last section, 3-9, describes the measure of man.

1. *The Majesty of God* (8:1-2)

O LORD our Lord (1; *Yahweh Adoninu*) *Yahweh* is the sacred personal name of the God of the Covenant. *Adonai* is the Hebrew term for "lord," "master," "sovereign." **The heavens** reveal the majesty and **glory** of the Lord. **Babes and sucklings** (2) is in Hebrew "children and babes." For **hast thou ordained strength** the LXX reads, "thou hast perfected praise." Jesus quotes it thus in Matt. 21:16. In the expression **that thou mightest still the enemy and the avenger,** "the general sense is plain. Jehovah has ordained that even the feeblest representatives of

---

[18]*Critique of Practical Reason, and Other Writings in Moral Philosophy,* trans. Louis White Beck (Chicago: University of Chicago Press, 1949), p. 258.

[19]*Op. cit.,* p. 141.

[20]*An Outline of Old Testament Theology* (Boston, Mass.: Charles T. Branford Company, 1958), p. 313.

[21]Kirkpatrick, *op. cit.,* p. xxiii.   [22]McCullough. *op. cit.,* 4:Q

humanity should be His champions to confound and silence those who oppose His kingdom and deny His goodness and providential government."[23]

2. *The Measure of Man* (8:3-9)

In comparison with the span of the heavens and the heavenly bodies, man can but confess his insignificance. **When I consider** (3)—many are strangely unmoved by the grandeur of creation. There are important lessons to be learned by considering the heavens at night. **Hast ordained** is literally "established." **What is man** (4, *enosh*), man in his weakness and frailty? **Son of man** (*ben-adam*), "son of man in his earthly origin." *Adam* (man) also means "earth" in Hebrew. **Visitest him**—that is, to care for and provide for him. **Thou hast made him a little lower** (5) is literally, "Thou hast made him lack little of." The Hebrew term for **the angels** (*Elohim*) may mean "God," "gods," or "supernatural beings in general." The revised versions translate it here as "God." The usual OT designation for angels is either *malakhim,* "messengers," or *ben-Elohim,* "sons of God." It should be noted, however, that the LXX translates *Elohim* here by *par' angelous,* "than the angels," and it is so quoted in Heb. 2:7 in a great Christological passage. **Crowned him with glory and honour** indicates the attributes of royalty. In his intended dominion over the works of God's hands, man was to be king.

Have dominion over (6) means to "rule over." There is a parallel in this verse with Gen. 1:26, 28. The listing of the various areas of man's dominion is given only by way of example: domestic and wild animals, birds and fish, and denizens of the deep. Our scientific age is witnessing the extension of man's dominion through understanding and utilizing the laws of nature. Let it be remembered, however, that even what we call "space" constitutes the work of God's hands.

The psalm closes with the same seven Hebrew words with which it opens: "O Yahweh, our Master, how excellent is Thy name in all the earth!" (lit.)

Psalm 9: THANKSGIVING AND TRUST, 9:1-20

Psalms 9 and 10 are generally thought to have been originally a single composition. There is no title at the beginning of Psalm 10

---

[23]Kirkpatrick, *op. cit.,* p. 38.

as there is in all the other psalms of Book I except 1, 2, and 33. Psalms 9 and 10 are found as one psalm in the LXX, Jerome's Latin Version, and the Latin Vulgate. Yet the relation between the two is in part one of contrast. Psalm 9 glories in the sovereignty of God, particularly in relation to the heathen enemies of the nation. Psalm 10 rather deals with the problem of infidelity and wickedness within the nation itself. Both are constant and pressing problems for the Christian nations of the West today. There is both the bitter foe without, and the malignant growth of secularism and irreligion within.

Psalm 9 bears the title, "To the chief Musician upon Muth-labben. A psalm of David." The meaning of "Muth-labben" is obscure. The words themselves might be translated, "Death to the son," or even, "Upon the death of a son."[24] The most reasonable suggestion is that we have a familiar tune-title here, meaningful to those for whom the title was written but unknown to us.

The Hebrew text shows evidence of an original acrostic arrangement, different verses beginning with successive letters of the Hebrew alphabet. However, the arrangement does not follow through consistently.

The psalm alternates between prayer to God and address to or discourse about those who oppose the nation.

1. *Thanksgiving* (9:1-6)

Even in the face of the enemy's threat, the Psalmist praises God for the deliverances He has given. Faith faces the future without fear because it has behind it a past that testifies to the trustworthiness and power of the Lord. The **heart** (1, *leb*) in the OT means the essential self, the personality, the thinking, feeling, choosing being. No less than wholehearted praise is due the Lord for all His **marvellous works. Most high** (2) is *Elyon;* cf. 7:17, comment. The very presence of the Divine is sufficient to rout the foe; they shall **fall and perish at thy presence** (3). **Thou hast maintained . . . my cause** (4), means, "Thou hast judged in favor of my case." Here is the symbolism of a courtroom trial. **Thou satest,** "thou hast sat" (RSV). **Judging right** (*tsedeq*), "righteousness." The word comes from a root which means "straight," hence "just" and "right." **Put out their name** (5), Hebrew, "blotted out their name." The ancients set great store by the preservation of their names for posterity. To have one's

---

[24]*Ibid.*, p. 43.

name blotted out was viewed as a great calamity. Some commentators, feeling that direct address to the enemy would be out of place, translate, **O thou enemy** (6), etc., "The enemy are consumed, left desolate forever." The enemy's cities had been destroyed. **Their memorial is perished**—literally, "Their remembrance has perished."

2. Teaching (9:7-12)

The sovereignty and justice of God are proclaimed as the basis for the trust and confidence of God's people. **Shall endure** (7) is in Hebrew "shall sit (enthroned)." "God is still on the throne!" His throne is both a throne of sovereignty and a throne of judgment and justice. His judgments are righteous and true (8). **A refuge** (9) is literally "a high place," in the sense of a fortified tower.

Know thy name (10) implies those who have come by personal acquaintance to know the character of God. Knowledge in the OT is always more than "information about"—it is "acquaintance with." **Name** (*shem*) is often used in the Bible for the nature, the character, of God or of men. Trust is followed by the shout of triumph to God who **dwelleth in Zion** (11). God's special presence was symbolized by the ark of the covenant in the Tabernacle and later the Temple on Mount Zion in Jerusalem. **Maketh inquisition for blood** (12) is translated, "He who avenges blood [shed] is mindful of them" (RSV); or, "The avenger of death bears them in mind" (Harrison).

3. Trouble (9:13-14)

The Psalmist interjects a plea for personal deliverance from those who oppose him, in order that he may praise God and rejoice in the Lord's salvation. **From the gates of death** (13) is contrasted with **in the gates of the daughter of Zion** (14). Snatched from the very portals of destruction, the poet would praise God at the Tabernacle or Temple. *Sheol,* the place of the dead, is often described as a fortified city, with gates that swing only inward. (Cf. Matt. 16:18, where "gates of hell" is "gates of hades" in the Gk., *hades* being the Gk. equivalent of *Sheol.*)

4. Transgression (9:15-18)

The wickedness and destruction of **the heathen** (15) are contrasted with the hope and prospect of the righteous needy. The truth earlier voiced in 7:15-16 is here repeated: wicked men

161

are destroyed by their own evil schemings and doings. **Higgaion (16)** is probably a musical note indicating an instrumental interlude for meditation. The same term occurs in connection with the music of the harp in 92:3, where it is translated "a solemn sound." For **Selah,** cf. comment on 3:2.

The wicked shall be turned into hell (17) is a solemn warning of the fate of wicked men and nations. **Hell** is *Sheol;* and in the case of the godless, it was represented as a hopeless existence cut off from God and life. The full revealed truth about the afterlife awaited the coming of Christ and the apostles. But enough is said in the OT to warn the wicked to turn from their sins lest they go down to *Sheol* without hope. **The needy and the poor (18)** are not vindicated because of their poverty but because of their defenseless piety (cf. Luke 16:19-31).

5. *Triumph* (9:19-20)

The scope of the Psalmist's prayer testifies to his faith in the triumph of righteousness. Human wickedness will not prevail. The Hebrew word for **be judged (19)** also means "condemned." All must finally recognize that the Lord alone is God. **The nations** (Heb., *goyiim,* translated "heathen" in 19) **shall know themselves to be but men (20).**

Psalm 10: PRAYER FOR THE DEFEAT OF THE WICKED, 10:1-18

For the relationship between this psalm and the preceding, see the comments at the beginning of Psalm 9. G. Campbell Morgan says, "The psalm opens in complaint, it closes in confidence."[25] The author vividly describes the character and conduct of the wicked, and cries for divine deliverance from them.

1. *Complaint* (10:1-2)

The Psalmist feels that God stands **afar off (1),** as an idle spectator or disinterested bystander, while **the wicked in his pride doth persecute the poor (2).** To the poet it seems that God hides himself **in times of trouble,** destitution or extremity. Job experienced the same feeling (Job 13:24). When **the wicked** prosper and the righteous suffer, God seems afar off. But the wicked will **be taken in the devices that they have imagined**

---

[25]*Op cit.,* p. 225.

(Heb., thought out), "snared by the schemes which they have hatched" (Harrison).

2. Character (10:3-6)

The evil character of the wicked is drawn in bold, strong strokes. Pride, irreverence, unbelief, materialism, and a sense of false security are characteristic of the godless life. **Blesseth the covetous, whom the Lord abhorreth** (3) may be translated as by *The Berkeley Version,* "The greedy one curses and spurns the Lord." His covetousness is idolatry (Col. 3:5), spurning God for mammon. The attitude expressed in v. 4 is not necessarily theoretical atheism but practical atheism or secularism: **God is not in all his thoughts.** "He thinks in his insolence, 'God never punishes'; his thoughts amount to this, 'There is no God at all' " (Moffatt). Instead of the true security of those who trust in God, the wicked cling to a false security, sniffing at their foes and boasting that they will never come to **adversity** (5-6).

3. Conduct (10:7-11)

The character of the wicked manifests itself in their conduct. Their sins mar every area of life, and are committed in the false assumption that God does not know or care. They are bold and blasphemous in speech (7), **lurking** in ambush to strike down the defenseless (8), taking **the poor** like a ravening beast or a hunter with a **net** (9). Moffatt interprets v. 10: "He hunts the helpless till they drop, unlucky victims in his clutches." The wicked man says **in his heart, God hath forgotten: he hideth his face; he will never see it** (11). But the Word stands true: "God shall bring every work into judgment, with every secret thing, whether it be good, or whether it be evil" (Eccles. 12:14).

4. Cry (10:12-15)

In the face of such danger, the righteous can only cry out to God for vindication and the overthrow of the wicked. The Psalmist calls upon God to rise in judgment and remember the plight of the defenseless and **humble** (12). He wonders why the Lord has so long tolerated the blasphemies of the enemies of His kingdom (13). **Contemn God** means to spurn or despise the Lord. **Hath said in his heart** points out the special emphasis of this psalm on the secret thoughts that motivate the godless conduct of the unrighteous (cf. 6, 10). **Thou wilt not require it** means, "There will be no accounting required for the evil deeds done." But there will.

God has not ignored the evils men do. The righteous poor who commit themselves to Him will find Him **the helper of the fatherless (14)**. **The arm** (power) **of the wicked** must be broken. **Seek out his wickedness till thou find none** means that the judgments of God will so destroy the power of the unrighteous to do evil that their wickedness will finally cease. Harrison trans- lates it, "Break the power of the guilty and wicked; punish his iniquity till You have completely obliterated it."

5. *Confidence* (10:16-18)

As in the case of so many songs that begin in a minor strain, this psalm ends in an expression of confidence and faith in the ultimate triumph of righteousness. **The Lord is King for ever and ever (16)**, and His purposes shall prevail. The sovereignty of God is best expressed in the OT concept of kingdom. The sovereign is not one who controls the actions of his subjects in minute detail, but one who wins their loyalty or crushes their revolt. Faith rests either on the fact that the Canaanite nations had been destroyed or anticipates the final destruction of the rebels: **The heathen are perished out of his land.** Because the Psalmist is sure his prayer is heard, he is confident that God will **prepare** (establish) the hearts of the humble. **The fatherless and the oppressed** will be vindicated, and **the man of the earth may no more oppress (18)**, or, "Mortal man no more may be a terror" (Moffatt).

Psalm 11: THE COURAGE OF FAITH, 11:1-7

Psalm 11 is another inscribed "to the chief Musician" and credited to David. G. Campbell Morgan comments: "This psalm is the answer of faith to the advice of fear. Both alike are con- scious of immediate peril. Fear sees only the things that are near. Faith takes in the larger distances. If the things fear sees are indeed all, its advice is excellent. When the things which faith sees are realized, its determination is vindicated."[26]

1. *Trust in Face of Treachery* (11:1-3)

The Psalmist is beset by his foes, yet avows his firm faith in the Lord's protection. His friends (or his scornful enemies) counsel him to **flee as a bird to your mountain (1)**. "The 'moun-

---

[26]*Ibid.*

tain' or 'hill-country' with its caves and strongholds was the natural place of retreat for fugitives. . . . Possibly 'to flee to the mountain' may have been a proverbial phrase, taken from the narrative of Gen. xix. 17 ff., for the last resource in extremity of peril."[27] The reason given for such flight is that the wicked have already fitted their arrows to the bow **that they may privily (secretly and treacherously) shoot at the upright in heart** (2).

If the foundations be destroyed, what can the righteous do? (3) When the decay of society is such that these things can take place, the righteous are in serious danger. Delitzsch interprets this verse as continuing the counsel of the timid. They justify their advice to flight by the sad state into which the administration of justice had fallen.[28] This assumes that the psalm was written during David's hazardous final days in Saul's court, beset by the treacheries of the king's jealous retainers. Or it may be the Psalmist's own despair of the situation from the human standpoint.

2. *Trial and Triumph* (11: 4-7)

Faith's answer to fear is the confidence that **the Lord is in his holy temple, the Lord's throne is in heaven** (4). God reigns sovereign in the heavens, and yet dwells in the midst of His people in His holy temple (or tabernacle). **His eyelids try,** as one narrows his eyes to peer more intently at an object of interest. **The Lord trieth the righteous** (5) in the sense of proving them, testing their loyalty. The contrasting attitudes of the Lord toward the righteous and the wicked are displayed. Love of righteousness implies hatred of evil. It is the fate of the **wicked** to be exposed to **snares, fire and brimstone, and an horrible tempest** (6)—literally, "a wind of burning heat," the parching, searing wind from the desert. **Fire and brimstone** (sulphur) are often associated with the judgments of God throughout scripture (Gen. 19:24; Deut. 29:23; Isa. 30:33; 34:9; Ezek. 38:22; Luke 17:29; Rev. 9:17; 14:10; 19:20; 20:10; 21:8). **Portion of their cup,** i.e., their appointed lot, what they justly deserve.

God's love for righteousness is not arbitrary. He is himself **righteous.** Therefore **his countenance doth behold** (look with favor upon) **the upright** (7). The last clause would be more accurately translated, "The upright shall behold His face." "They that are upright shall behold His face" (Perowne); "The upright

[27]Kirkpatrick, *op. cit.,* p. 58.   [28]*Op. cit.,* p. 239.

will finally see Him" (Harrison). Dahood comments "The vision of God mentioned here is doubtless that of Pss. xvi 11, xvii 15, xli 13, xlix 16, lxxiii 26, which suggest a belief in an afterlife in the presence of Yahweh. If perfect justice is not attained in this life, it will be in the next; this seems to be the ultimate motive for the psalmist's confidence."[29] Dahood believes that in the light of the Ras Shamra texts (cf. Intro.), "the opinion of Sigmund Mowinckel that 'neither Israel nor early Judaism knew of a faith in any resurrection nor is such a faith represented in the psalms' will not survive serious scrutiny."[30]

Psalm 12: GOD'S HELP IN AN UNGODLY WORLD, 12:1-8

This is a psalm of David inscribed to the chief musician "upon Shiminith," a term which means "eighth" and may be used here to indicate a lower octave, as for bass singers. The contrast of righteous and wicked and the high estimate placed on "the words of the Lord" classify Psalm 12 as a wisdom psalm. The cry for divine help (1-2), the condemnation of the evil (3-4), and the confidence of God's keeping power (5-7) express faith that looks beyond circumstances to a heavenly Helper.

1. Cry (12:1-2)

David's cry for help is wrung from him because of the low estate of religion and morals he sees about him. **The godly man** (1; Heb., *chasid;* lit., the saint) and **the faithful** have all but vanished from society. On every hand, people **speak vanity** (2; falsehood) one to another. Insincerity and hypocrisy abound. Any society marked by the breakdown of confidence in common honesty is headed for disaster. Suspicion and cynicism destroy the very fabric of human relationships. **With a double heart do they speak** means thinking one way and speaking another. "Their speech is flattering, their mind deceitful" (Harrison). This is the very antithesis of the holiness and truth that God requires.

2. Condemnation (12:3-4)

Two things a holy God cannot tolerate are flattery and pride (3). Both attitudes are further described in 4. The world has unbounded confidence in the power of words. It is as if they were saying, "Flattery will get you anything." Their arrogant pride is seen in a sneering rejection of the sovereignty of God:

[29]*Op. cit.,* p. 71.   [30]*Ibid.,* xxxvi.

Who is lord over us? The same prideful independence of God is seen in Rev. 3:17.

3. Confidence (12:5-8)

In such a crisis of morals and religion, the Psalmist hears the Lord speak: **For the oppression of the poor, for the sighing of the needy, now will I arise** (5). God has not forgotten His own. **I will set him in safety from him that puffeth at him** is literally, "I will put him in the safety that he pants for." The only real security human life knows is that which comes from strong faith in God.

God's word of assurance and guidance is both **pure** and precious (6; cf. 19:8, 10). **Silver** refined **seven times** is without dross and costly. That the word of the Lord is compared to silver and gold suggests the labor of mining and smelting. But the yield is well worth the effort.

The wicked walk on every side (8; in circles, as Augustine translated it); "parade about" (Harrison); "prowl" (Anchor). When unworthy men **are exalted,** wickedness is encouraged, and righteousness is imperiled. But the **Lord** will **keep** and **preserve** those who put their trust in Him (7).

Psalm 13: FEARFUL BUT NOT FORSAKEN, 13:1-6

Here is a psalm of David inscribed to the chief musician. This psalm of lament passes through the familiar stages of despair, desire, and deliverance. Kirkpatrick relates the psalm to the period in David's life when he was a hunted fugitive fleeing from the jealousy of King Saul (I Sam. 27:1). In vv. 2 and 4, one enemy stands out above all others as both powerful and relentless.[31] But the psalm expresses the dark night of the soul through which many of God's people pass.

1. Despair (13:1-2)

The Psalmist utters his sense of forsakenness in a series of four questions: **How long** will God **forget . . . for ever? how long** will He **hide** His **face?** (1) **How long** must the Psalmist carry his sorrow within him? **How long shall** his **enemy be exalted?** (2) The first two questions are God-centered. The second two are related to the poet's feelings and circumstances. For **take counsel** read "bear pain" (RSV).

[31]*Op. cit.*, p. 63.

2. *Desire* (13:3-4)

In such turmoil of spirit, David makes his appeal to God for help. **Lighten mine eyes** (3), is a prayer to "revive and quicken me," as the eye reflects the physical vitality of the entire body. **The sleep of death** does not suggest what is now known as "soul sleeping," since the OT view of the life after death is expressed in the idea of *Sheol*, in which persons were conscious of one another. This metaphor of sleep represents death as it seems to those who look on. The Psalmist prays that his **enemy** and those who **trouble** (4) him may not have the privilege of glorying in his downfall and destruction. For **moved** read "overthrown" (Berk.).

3. *Deliverance* (13:5-6)

Faith rises as the poet prays. He affirms his trust in the mercy of God, and his confidence that the **heart** now sorrowful (2) **shall rejoice** in the Lord's **salvation** (5). God's bountiful dealing will yet be the theme of his song. Oesterley says: "Very short as this psalm is, it brings out forcibly the great truth that trouble, though long-drawn-out, does not mean that God has no care for those who trust in Him. The reason why relief does not come is doubtless often hidden . . . but the psalm teaches the beautiful lesson that the true believer in God will not be shaken in his faith, however severe the stroke."[32]

Psalm 14: THE BITTER FRUIT OF GODLESSNESS, 14:1-7

This psalm is virtually identical with Psalm 53, except that the latter substitutes *Elohim* as the term for God instead of *Yahweh* as here. In 53, the title indicates that the psalm is a *Maschil* (cf. comment on title of Psalm 32), a teaching psalm, and shows that it was set to a tune known as *Mahalath*. Most of vv. 1-3 are quoted by Paul in Rom. 3:10-12 as showing the universal corruption of the unredeemed human heart. The poem is composed of two stanzas of three verses each, and a concluding verse. It describes the folly and fear of the godless, and the faith of the truehearted.

1. *Folly* (14:1-3)

The psalm starts with a statement about **the fool** (1). Folly in the Bible is not a matter of intellectual limitation, but of moral

---

[32]*Op. cit.*, p. 152.

wrong. Morgan notes: "Here the psalmist utters his own consciousness of the meaning of godlessness. In its essence it is folly.
The word 'fool' here stands for moral perversity rather than
intellectual blindness. This is repeated in the declaration, 'They
are corrupt,' and in the statement that their works are abominable."[33] Leslie M'Caw writes: "*Fool* or 'vile person' (Isa. xxxii.
5); i.e., a man wholly indifferent to the moral standards of the
law, and who daily adopts as his own principle the belief that
deity cares nothing about the differences between men's behaviour. Such persons cannot but live a dissolute life and be
incapable of 'doing good.' "[34]

There is no God indicates not chiefly theoretical atheism, but
the kind of unbelief that resides in the heart. It is the practical
direction of life with no thought of God or eternity. Mankind
without God is described as corrupt, given to abominable works
and incapable of good. The Lord looked down from heaven upon
the children of men (2; lit., the sons of Adam). God looks for
signs of spiritual understanding and for hearts inclined toward
Him. There are, alas, none. "All we like sheep have gone astray;
we have turned every one to his own way" (Isa. 53:6). They are
all together become filthy (3) is derived from a word which
means "tainted, gone bad, turned sour"; "depraved" (Anchor).
One of the most penetrating biblical insights into the nature of
sin is its definition as corruption, the spoiling and misuse of what
is or could be good.

2. Fear (14:4-6)

The end result of folly is great fear (5). It is the Lord who
speaks: Have all the workers of iniquity no knowledge? who
eat up my people as they eat bread, and call not upon the Lord
(4). The implication is that the workers of iniquity do have a
rudimentary knowledge of the moral law. "For the invisible
things of him from the creation of the world are clearly seen,
being understood by the things that are made, even his eternal
power and Godhead; so that they are without excuse" (Rom.
1:20). The result of their guilt is fear (5). There may mean
"there in God's presence." The presence of God in the generation of the righteous is the guarantee of sure vindication of right
and condemnation of evil. Generation (dor) may also mean
dwelling or posterity.

[33]*Op. cit.*, p. 226.   [34]*Op. cit.*, p. 422.

Ye have shamed (6) may mean derided, or more probably defeated or frustrated, **the counsel of the poor** (the afflicted). This is so much the more blamable in view of its religious considerations: they have done it **because the Lord is his refuge.**

3. *Faith* (14:7)

Again faith sings its song of triumph. **The salvation of Israel** will not be found in human might or wisdom. It will **come out of Zion,** the place of God's abode. Some have dated this psalm in the period of the Exile because of the phrase **bringeth back the captivity of his people.** But in Job 42:10 we have the same phrase, "The Lord turned the captivity of Job," simply in the sense of restoring the fortunes of Job. And even if the verse should mean a literal captivity, Kirkpatrick points to the use of the same phrase by both Hosea (6:11) and Amos (9:14) long before the Babylonian captivity.[35] God's action will bring rejoicing and gladness to **Jacob** (taken as a synonym for the nation as a whole) and **Israel.**

Psalm 15: The Life of Holiness, 15:1-5

This psalm, identified by title as "A Psalm of David," is the first of a type known as "liturgical," that is, connected with public worship. There are approximately thirty which fall into this class (cf. Intro.). Psalm 15 is a perfect little gem of devotion, and like a gem can scarcely be divided without being spoiled. The poem describes both positively and negatively the characteristics of the one who abides in the Lord's tabernacle and dwells in His holy hill. The life of holiness has both of these sides. It involves some abstinences, some denials of self. It also calls for some positive characteristics, some active service. A merely passive, negative goodness will never meet the vast needs of human life today. Goodness must have about it a dynamic quality of godliness if it is to meet the issues of our present age.

1. *The Positives of Holy Living* (15:1-2)

What are the positive characteristics of the citizen of Zion? Five are mentioned:

a. Abiding (15:1). To **abide** suggests permanence. It means to come to stay. Thus Jesus spoke of the Comforter who was to

---

[35]*Op. cit.,* p. 69.

come to His disciples at Pentecost: "He shall give you another Comforter, that he may abide with you for ever" (John 14:16). To **abide** in the **tabernacle** of the Lord means to establish one's life in God.

b. Dwelling (15:1). To **dwell** adds the idea of being at home, a member of the household, having permanent status in the family. No earthly or Satanic power can tear us away from our dwelling in God's holy hill if our hearts are set on Him. A Christian may leave home, but he never need fear that he will be kidnapped!

c. Walking uprightly (15:2). Walking describes a habitual course of life. **He that walketh uprightly** is the same language as used in Gen. 17:1, where God said to Abraham, "Walk before me, and be thou perfect." Kirkpatrick observes: "The word *tamim* means (1) *complete*, (2) *without blemish*, of sacrificial victims, (3) in a moral sense, *perfect, sincere, blameless*. It includes whole-hearted devotion to God, and complete integrity in dealing with men."[36] A good description of evangelical perfection as taught in the New Testament (Matt. 5:48; Heb. 6:1; I John 4:17-19)!

d. Working righteousness (15:2). Outward conduct must be right. **Righteousness** (*tsaddiq*) means "to be straight," according to rule.

e. Speaking truth (15:2). To speak **truth in his heart** means to live in absolute sincerity. Truth on the lips is important. Truth in the heart is all-important. The Psalmist's conviction for needed cleansing was based upon his realization that God "desirest truth in the inward parts" (Ps. 51:6-7).

2. *The Negatives of Holy Living* (15:3-5)

The negations of the life of holiness are next in view. They are eight in number:

a. No backbiting (15:3). **Backbiteth not with his tongue** is literally, "He has no slander on his tongue." Originating or passing on tales that are injurious to the reputations of others is a sin that has no place in the life of Zion's citizen.

b. No evildoing (15:3). The Hebrew (*ra*) is a generic term that includes all harm, evil, or sin. It is as broad as the English term "bad." The man approved of God does not harm his fellows.

[36]*Ibid.*, p. 70.

c. *No slander* (15:3). To take **up a reproach against his neighbour** may mean either to originate slander and ridicule or to pass on what otherwise might not be known. Or it may mean to add to another's misfortune by heaping reproach upon him. "Do you know what I heard?" is the prelude to many a murderous assault upon someone's good name.

d. *No condoning of sin* (15:4). **In whose eyes a vile person is contemned** is literally, "Despised in his eyes is a reprobate." The citizen of Zion does not rejoice in the record of iniquity. Neither does he condone sin and whitewash conduct that is in violation of God's law.

e. *No changing word* (15:4). "His word is as good as his bond." Promises made are to be kept unless there would be sin involved in the keeping. The mere fact that a promise turns out to be disadvantageous to its maker does not relieve him of the obligation to keep it.

f. *No usury* (15:5). **Usury** is sometimes defined as any kind of interest. But the Hebrew term comes from a root meaning "to strike with a sting" as a serpent, or "to oppress." Certainly by NT times commercial interest was recognized as legitimate (Matt. 25:27). So probably the meaning of the term should be understood as exorbitant or unreasonable interest—the meaning it most commonly has at present.

g. *No bribery* (15:5). **Nor taketh reward against the innocent** means "a bribe against a guiltless person." Always the curse of Oriental countries, bribery is forbidden in Exod. 23: 7-8; Deut. 16:19; 27:25, and is frequently condemned by the prophets.

h. *No vacillation* (15:5). As both a condition and a consequence, **He that doeth these things shall never be moved.** The literal rendering is, "Doing these things he shall not be moved forever." Such a man as described here will prove to be steadfast and dependable in the midst of changing conditions and circumstances (I Cor. 15:58).

Psalm 16: THE GOODLY HERITAGE OF THE GODLY, 16:1-11

This psalm is entitled "Michtam of David." T. H. Robinson writes: "Six psalms (16, 56—60) have the word 'Michtam' in the title. This is normally connected with a root meaning 'gold,' and these psalms (which are all of unusual beauty, even for the psalms) are regarded as 'jewel pieces.' The same word is used in the heading to the hymn ascribed to Hezekiah in Is. 38:9-20, and said to have been composed by that king on his recovery from sickness."[37] Other suggestions as to the meaning have been given, such as "a poem of epigrammatic character" (Delitzsch), an unpublished poem, and a psalm of hidden, mysterious meaning.[38]

From NT usage of v. 10 (Acts 2:25-28, 31; 13:35), Psalm 16 may properly be typed as Messianic (cf. introductory comments on Psalm 2). Its joyous faith and expression of praise are indeed typical of the Saviour. Trust may not solve all the problems of the mind, but it imparts confidence and peace to the heart which rests in the assurance that where God is the Guide all is well.

1. Prayer (16:1-4)

The psalm opens in the mood of prayer in which is expressed the Psalmist's loyalty to the Lord and His people. God is the Source of his preservation and safekeeping, based on a constant faith: **for in thee do I put my trust** (1). From the depths of his **soul,** the Psalmist cries out to the Lord, **Thou art my Lord** (2). Different Hebrew words are here translated **Lord,** as indicated by the capital letters used in printing the first "LORD" and the initial capital and small letters used in printing the second "Lord." The first Hebrew term is *Yahweh,* the personal name of the true and living God. The second is *Adonai,* which means "master, ruler, lord." We might translate it, "My soul said to Jehovah, Thou art my Master, my Ruler."

My goodness extendeth not to thee is better translated either, "I have no good beyond thee" (ASV), or, "My wellbeing depends entirely on you" (Harrison). Robertson Smith says, "Not merely is God the source of all his weal, but everything which he recognizes as a true good, God actually contains within Himself."[39]

The third verse is admittedly difficult in the Hebrew. It should probably be understood as a separate sentence and translated, "As for the saints and the excellent who are in the earth, my delight is all in them." *The Berkeley Version* renders it, "As for the godly that are in the land, they are the glorious in whom is all my delight"; and Harrison, "The saints who are on earth are indeed illustrious; I admire them greatly."

---

[37]*Op. cit.,* p. 116.   [38]Kirkpatrick, *op. cit.,* p. xviii.
[39]Quoted, *ibid.,* p. 74.

The Psalmist's happy lot is quite in contrast with the multiplied sorrows of those who exchange the Lord for another god. **Their drink offerings of blood** (4) may have reference to pagan libations made in blood, or it may mean that the libations (liquids poured out as religious sacrifices) of the idolaters were as abominable as if they had been made of blood. In any event, the Psalmist will not so much as **take up their names into his lips.**

2. *Praise* (16:5-8)

Four great verses of joyous praise make up this second stanza of the psalm. The Psalmist finds in the Lord himself his goodly heritage. He is filled with joy at the counsel and presence of God. **The portion of mine inheritance . . . my lot** (5) harks back to the distribution of the land by lot among the people of Israel (Josh. 13:7; 14:2). While others might rejoice in fertile fields, the Psalmist finds his inheritance in the Lord God. Moffatt translates: "Thou art what I obtain from life, O thou Eternal, thou thyself art my share." What more could one have?

Because this is true, **The lines** (as of the tribal portions) **are fallen unto me in pleasant places; yea, I have a goodly heritage** (6). The Lord himself, more than all His gifts, is the reward of those who really love Him. One cannot but admire the deep devotion expressed in words such as these. They represent a depth of piety reached by few even in this more favored Christian dispensation.

I will bless the Lord (7), that is, give praise and adoration to Him. **Given me counsel** means taught me to trust and follow Him. Regarding **my reins** (*kelayoth*) Smith notes, "Probably there is always a direct or indirect reference to God's searching of what *we* call the conscience."[40] **In the night seasons**—"In the quiet hours of the night God admonishes and instructs him through the voice of conscience. Cp. iv.4; xvii.3. *The reins* stand for the organs of emotion, the feelings and conscience. 'Heart and reins' denote the whole innermost self, thought and will (vii.9)."[41]

I have set the Lord always before me (8) indicates the "practice of the presence of God." The Psalmist is therefore confident that he **shall not be moved,** with the Lord at his **right hand** as a Warrior defending him against every enemy.

---

[40]*Op. cit.*, p. 23.   [41]Kirkpatrick, *op. cit.*, **p. 76.**

3. Prospect (16:9-11)

While admitting that these words may express the Psalmist's confidence that the strong arm of his God will deliver him from threatened death at that time, it is impossible to ignore the interpretation Peter places on these verses in Acts 2:25-28. In this psalm is seen a prophecy of the resurrection of Jesus. Christ brought "life and immortality to light through the gospel" (II Tim. 1:10), and His resurrection adds a new dimension to many OT passages, of which this is certainly one. Indeed, the clearest intimations of the blessed future life found in the OT were based on the very grounds here given: that is, not even death itself can rob the trusting soul of the presence and fellowship of his God.

My glory rejoiceth (9)—here, as in 7:5; 30:12; and 57:8, **my glory** means my soul. The soul, as the noblest part of man and the image of the divine, might well be called **my glory**. Now, in confidence of God's protection from the untimely death threatened, and in the prospect of a resurrection like that of Christ (Rom. 6:5), the Psalmist sings, **My flesh also shall rest in hope.** His faith affirms, **Thou wilt not leave my soul in hell** (10; *Sheol*), the realm of the dead. **Neither wilt thou suffer thine Holy One to see corruption** was used by Paul (Acts 13:35) as well as by Peter in reference to the resurrection of Jesus. The presence of God is the Psalmist's assurance of **the path of life . . . fulness of joy . . .** and **pleasures for evermore** (11). Here or hereafter, no real harm can befall the one who puts his trust in the Lord and who walks with Him.

Psalm 17: An Urgent Prayer for Protection, 17:1-15

Psalm 17 bears a title found in only two others 86, 142), "A Prayer of David." Again a single enemy seems to be the prime source of danger, and here the Psalmist speaks of his companions in danger (v. 11). It is possible that the background is David's flight from Saul in the wilderness of Maon: "For Saul and his men compassed David and his men round about to take them" (I Sam. 23:25-26). Only word of an invasion by the Philistines caused Saul to interrupt his pursuit (I Sam. 23:27-29).

Although closely related to Psalm 16 (cf. 16:7 and 17:3; 16:8 and 17:5; 16:1 and 17:6-7), the urgent sense of danger makes this psalm more characteristically a song of lament.

1. *Desire* (17:1-5)

The heart of David's petition is the desire expressed in these verses for vindication and justice in view of the threats made against his life. He appeals for a hearing: **Hear the right** (1; *tsaddiq*), "righteousness," "justice." **My cry** is literally a shrill, piercing cry, coming **not out of feigned** (deceitful) **lips,** but wrung from a sincere and honest heart. **Let my sentence**—literally, my judgment—**come forth from thy presence** (2). David found no justice at the hands of Saul. But he is confident that the Lord's **eyes behold the things that are equal,** or, with *The Berkeley Version,* "Thine eyes see what is equitable." "May your eyes gaze upon my integrity" (Anchor).

Thou hast proved (tested) **mine heart** (3): cf. 16:7 and comments. David protests his innocence of wrong purpose. Neither in thought nor in word had he transgressed. **Concerning the works of men** (4) refers to his conduct as a man among men. Guided by the Word of God, the Psalmist had kept himself **from the paths of the destroyer,** the men of violence. **Hold up my goings** (5) should probably be translated positively in keeping with the context, as, e.g., "My steps have followed your paths; my feet have not faltered" (Harrison).

2. *Danger* (17:6-12)

The Psalmist expresses his confidence in the Lord and spells out in detail the dangers that beset him and his companions. He prays with the assurance that he will be heard. **O God** (6; *El*) is a form of address rare in the Davidic psalms (cf. 16:1). **Loving-kindness** (7; *chesed*) is the characteristic term for the covenant love of God. It is variously translated "mercy," "stedfast love" (RSV), "unfailing love" (Berk.), or "lovingkindness." Its meaning comes very close to that of the NT term "grace" (cf. the discussion in BBC, Vol. V, "Hosea," Introduction). **Keep me** (8; preserve me)—the same word as in 16:1—**as the apple** (pupil) **of the eye.** This is a frequent expression in the OT for that which is dearest or most precious and therefore guarded with special care (Deut. 32:10; Prov. 7:2; Zech. 2:8). **Under the shadow of thy wings** is also used elsewhere for the sense of security of young birds under their mother's wings (Ruth 2:12; Ps. 36:7; 57:1; 61:4, etc.; cf. Matt. 23:37).

The Psalmist describes the **enemies** who beset him. They **oppress** him (9), "have maltreated me" (Berk.). They are **deadly**

—intent on his destruction. They **compass me about** (surround me). **They are inclosed in their own fat** (10)—either, They prosper and grow fat in their iniquity; or, as with the ASV, "Their heart have they shut up" against all influences for good or any compassion for those they persecute. They speak proudly, boasting of their successes in wickedness. They have succeeded in surrounding the Psalmist and his companions (11). **They have set their eyes bowing down to the earth** is literally, "Their eyes will they set to bend [us] to the earth," or, "They fix their eyes to cast us to the ground" (Berk.). The enemy is like a vicious older **lion** killing for very blood lust, and like a **young lion** lurking in ambush for the unwary (12).

3. *Deliverance* (17:13-14)

Although there is still the form of prayer in these verses, it is prayer infused with confident hope. Continuing the comparison of his enemy to a lion, the Psalmist calls upon the Lord to **disappoint him, cast him down** (13)—i.e., confront the beast and make him crouch in submission. **Deliver my soul from the wicked, which is thy sword: from men which are thy hand** (13*b*-14*a*) means either that the wicked unwittingly serve God's purposes, as Assyria was the rod of His anger to chasten Israel (Isa. 10:5), or as with ASV and Berk., "By Thy sword . . . by Thy hand."

Those who seek to harm the godly are **men of the world, which have their portion in this life** (14). All they have of satisfaction they get here and now (cf. Luke 16:25). On the contrary, those for whom the Lord is "their portion" (16:5) receive not only His blessing and help here but the prospect of greater things to come (15). **Whose belly thou fillest** means permitting them to satisfy their base desires and physical appetites (Phil. 3:19). **Full of children** would be letting them have the large families they desired, to whom they are able to leave the fortunes accumulated by injustice and dishonesty. This is a striking picture of the earth-centered lives of those who live without God.

4. *Destiny* (17:15)

This verse is important enough to set off by itself as the triumphant conclusion to the psalm. It has already been anticipated by the description of the ungodly as preoccupied with "this life" (14). Although many commentators interpret v. 15 as a

continuation of the contrast between the lower and higher goals
of life, Oesterley is almost certainly right when he remarks that
we have here "the beginnings of the apprehension of a fuller life
hereafter."[42] In another context, the same author states, "It is
difficult to understand these words in the sense of awakening
from natural sleep; the psalmist shows that he is in constant
communion with God, and experiences the unceasing nearness of
God; he never contemplates separation from God; why, then,
should he be satisfied with the divine appearance only on awaking
from natural sleep? . . . It can scarcely be doubted, therefore,
that the psalmist is here thinking of awaking from the sleep of
death, and thus expresses belief in the life hereafter."[43] *The
Berkeley Version* translates it: "As for me, with righteousness
shall I behold Thy face; I shall be satisfied, when I awake with
Thy likeness."

Psalm 18: A SONG OF VICTORY, 18:1-50

This is the longest psalm in Book I, and is practically identical
with II Samuel 22, where the historian presents it as an illustration of the best of David's psalm-writing. The few modifications
made here seem to be in the direction of adapting the psalm for
public use. It is almost pure praise. The long struggles are ended.
The flight from Saul's vengeance is past. The Psalmist glorifies
the God of his salvation.

The long title presents an interesting variation. In addition to
inscribing the piece "To the chief Musician" and identifying it
as "A Psalm of David, the servant of the Lord" (used also in the
title of Psalm 36), the title embodies II Sam. 22:1, which serves
as an introduction to the psalm and locates it as being composed
after danger from Saul had ceased. Verses 43-45 would indicate
a time at the height of David's dominion.

The psalm breathes the atmosphere of extemporaneous praise.
There is no tight-knit structure. One thought leads to another,
alternating between direct address to God and joyous exclama-
tions about His power and mercy.

[42]*Op. cit.,* p. 161.

[43]*Ibid.,* p. 90. Cf. Anchor translation, "At my vindication I will gaze
upon your face; at the resurrection I will be saturated with your being."
Cf. Dahood's comments, *op. cit.,* p. 99, relating this to the resurrection
passages in Isa. 26:19 and Dan. 12:2.

178

1. The All-sufficiency of Salvation (18:1-3)

David protests his love for the Lord, and in a series of striking metaphors describes the all-sufficiency of His salvation. **The Lord is** his **strength** (1), his **rock** (2), or stronghold, his **fortress, his deliverer.** The statement **my God, my strength, in whom I will trust,** is literally, "My God, my rock, I will flee to Him"; or, "My God is my rock in whom I take refuge" (Berk.). The Lord is his **buckler** (shield) and **the horn of** his **salvation.** The **horn,** as of a wild beast, indicates strength. God is his **high tower,** providing vision and protection. The Psalmist expresses his conviction that God will answer prayer. God, who has saved him, will continue to keep him safe (3).

2. The Psalmist's Peril (18:4-6)

David looks back at the extreme peril from which the Lord has delivered him. **The sorrows of death** (4) should probably be understood as II Sam. 22:5 reads, "The waves [breakers] of death," making it parallel with **the floods of ungodly men.** The original of the latter is literally, "The streams or torrents of wickedness and ungodliness [*belial*] made me afraid." **The sorrows** (lit., cords) **of hell** (*Sheol*) surrounded and **prevented** (came before) the threatened one (5). In such deep distress, David **cried** to **God** and was **heard** (6).

3. The Lord's Supernatural Power (18:7-15)

The intervention of the Lord to help the Psalmist is described in terms of earthquake and storm, the stern and awful aspects of nature symbolizing the wrath of God. The action of God in behalf of His people is often represented in Scripture as accompanied by such extraordinary natural phenomena as here described (Exod. 19:16-18; Judg. 5:4-5; Job 38:1; Isa. 29:6; etc.). Earthquake (7), lightning (8), gathering **darkness** (9), and the full fury of the tempest follow in rapid succession.

God is envisioned as riding **upon a cherub,** flying **upon the wings of the wind** (10). Cherubim (*im* constitutes the Heb. masculine plural) are specially connected in Scripture with the throne and sovereignty of the Lord. God marshals all the forces of nature to bring deliverance to His own. **The Highest** (13), literally, "the Most High" (*Elyon*), is God as the supreme Sovereign of the universe. **Hail stones and coals of fire** (12-13) are hail and lightning.

4. *God Vindicates His Own* (18:16-19)

David here returns to the theme of personal deliverance. He is as one drawn **out of many waters** (16), a Bible symbol of great trouble. He is **delivered** from foes **too strong** for him to defeat or escape (17). **They prevented me** (18), "encountered me," or "came upon me" (Berk.). **The Lord was my stay** (support), "my staff" (Anchor).

Deliverance is always **out of** (16) and **into** (19). From the experience of being hemmed in by peril, David is brought **into a large place** (19). The Lord **delivered** him because **he delighted in** him.

5. *The Psalmist's Innocence* (18:20-24)

David protests his innocence of any wrongdoing. That this is not a gospel of salvation by good works is seen in the section following, where the mercy of the Lord becomes the theme. But God has rescued His servant from peril because he is innocent of any wrongs for which he might justly be punished. A righteous character and a clean life (20) depend upon keeping **the ways of the Lord** (21) and not departing in wickedness **from** his **God.** David held God's **judgments** (22; *mishpat*, commandments, ordinances) **before** him, and **did not put away** (out of his mind) **the statutes** of the divine law (in order to engage in sin without compunction).

As a result, the poet is able to assert his integrity before the Lord. **I was also upright before him** (23; *tammim*, perfect), however faulty he may have appeared before his human persecutors. **I kept myself from mine iniquity**—"Having guarded myself against my sinfulness" (Berk.). **The Lord** (24) therefore had **recompensed** (restored) him.

6. *The Mercy of the Lord* (18:25-29)

These verses state the general law of God's moral government of the world. His attitude toward men is conditioned by their response to His law and to His grace. Implied also is the NT principle that God's attitude toward men is dependent upon their attitude toward their fellows. Only **the merciful** can expect mercy (25; cf. Matt. 5:7; 6:14-15; 18:23-25). Only **the upright** (again, as in 23, *tammim*, perfect) can experience the perfection of God. Only **the pure** in heart may behold a pure and holy God (26; cf. Matt. 5:8; I John 3:3). The converse is also true: **with** the froward (perverse) **thou wilt shew thyself froward** (at cross-purposes with his sinful plans).

As a result, the Lord will **save the afflicted** and **bring down high looks** (27), that is, abase the haughty and proud (Luke 18:14). David is confident that the Lord will **light** his **candle** (lamp), and bring light into the **darkness** (28). In the strength of the Lord he can defeat every enemy and surmount every obstacle (29).

7. God's Perfect Deliverance (18:30-45)

David turns again to the theme of divine deliverance. He extols the perfection of God's **way** and **word** (30). **The word of the Lord is tried** (proven). **He is a buckler** (shield) **to all those that trust in him.** There is no **God** except Jehovah. There is no sure refuge except the Lord (31). God is the Source of **strength** and guidance for a perfect **way** (32). **Like hinds' feet** (33)—the hart (male) and the hind (female) were animals like the gazelle or deer, swift and surefooted. When pursued by the hunter, the hart or hind would climb swiftly up the rocky crags **(my high places).**

Changing the metaphor, the Lord had taught the Psalmist **to war** and gave him strength so that **a bow of steel** (brass) **is broken by mine arms** (34). In Homer's *Odyssey*, Ulysses boasted a bow which only he could bend, let alone break. The Lord protected His warrior **with the shield of thy salvation** and supported him with His strong **right hand** (35). **Thy gentleness** ("condescension," Berk., marg.; "help," RSV) **hath made me great.** Perhaps in the Psalmist's mind is the thought that he was but a shepherd lad when the Lord chose him to be king of his people.

Thou hast enlarged my steps under me (36), by giving him room to move unhindered (cf. 19). Victory over his **enemies** was complete and their forces were destroyed (37-38). It is the Lord who has made this possible (39-40). **Thou hast also given me the necks of mine enemies** (40) is better translated, "Yea, mine enemies hast thou made to turn their backs unto me" (ASV). They fled before him in utter rout with **none to save them** (41), even though they belatedly cried **unto the Lord.** Those who refuse to hear the call of the Lord may be refused when they call upon Him (Prov. 1:24-33; Isa. 65:12-14; 66:4). The Psalmist's enemies were totally destroyed, pounded to **dust,** blown away by **the wind,** and tramped like the mud **in the streets** (42). The result is political dominance both within the nation **(the**

strivings of the people) and over **the heathen,** the surrounding peoples (43). So great was David's reputation that potential foes were awed into submission (44). **The strangers shall fade away, and be afraid out of their close places** (45); better, "Foreigners fear and come trembling from their strongholds" (Berk.).

8. *The Living God* (18:46-50)

David continues his praise of the living God, who is his **rock** (sure Refuge) and **the God of** his **salvation** (46). He rightly left vengeance to the Lord (47; cf. 94:1; Rom. 12:19). It was God's act that delivered him and lifted him **up above** his **enemies** (48). He will therefore **give thanks** to the Lord **among the heathen** (49; lit., the nations), **and sing praises** to His **name. Great deliverance giveth he** (50) is literally, "Great salvation (s) giveth He." "He bestows glorious conquests" (Harrison). David is confident that the **mercy** (*chesed,* loving-kindness, steadfast love) he had known as the Lord's **anointed** would be extended **to his seed for evermore,** a prospect abundantly fulfilled in "David's greater Son."

Psalm 19: GOD'S WORKS AND GOD'S WORD, 19:1-14

Psalm 19 is entitled "To the chief Musician, a Psalm of David." It is rightly acclaimed as one of the most magnificent of the psalms. C. S. Lewis says, "I take this to be the greatest poem in the Psalter and one of the greatest lyrics in the world."[44]

A rather sharp division between vv. 1-6 and 7-14 has led to the theory that the psalm is the combination of two poems that were originally independent. This, however, is not at all necessary. The two divisions are very logically related, as C. S. Lewis has pointed out in the comment, "The searching and cleansing sun becomes an image of the searching and cleansing law."[45]

1. *The Glory of God's Works* (19:1-6)

Rightly understood, all of nature bears witness to its divine Creator. The Bible does not attempt to prove the existence of God from the existence of the universe. It does point to the

---

[44]*Op. cit.,* p. 63.

[45]*Ibid.,* p. 81. On the basis of grammatical analysis, Dahood concludes, "The author of both parts of the psalm was the same poet" (*op. cit.,* p. 121).

universe as an evidence of the majesty and wisdom of God. **The heavens declare the glory of God** (1) is emphatic present, "The heavens are declaring the glory of God." Theirs is a continuing witness. The Creator is identified here as *El,* God of power and might. His glory is the sum of His perfections: His wisdom, His power, His omniscience, and His omnipresence. **The firmament sheweth his handywork:** the great sky above is the work of His hands who has flung the stars from His fingertips and lighted the suns with His word.

Day unto day and **night unto night** (2) the universe is a mute but eloquent witness to its Source. There is the thought that this has always been, and will continue to be as long as the earth shall last. No one can outrun or outlive the voice of God in nature. **There is no speech nor language, where their voice is not heard** (3) may mean either that the testimony of creation is as wide as the human race (Harrison) or that this testimony is a silent witness that does not depend on words to communicate its truth (Anchor). Kirkpatrick draws attention to Addison's beautiful poetic paraphrase:

> *What though in solemn silence all*
> *Move round the dark terrestrial ball?*
> *What though no real voice nor sound*
> *Amid their radiant orbs be found?*
> *In reason's ear they all rejoice,*
> *And utter forth a glorious voice,*
> *For ever singing, as they shine,*
> *"The hand that made us is divine."*[46]

The universality of this proclamation of God's glory is stressed. **Their line** (4) refers to the measuring line marking the limits of possession. **All the earth** is the Lord's. Paul (Rom. 10:18) quotes these words to show the universal diffusion of the gospel. God is interested in the whole race of men, not simply in a chosen few.

Verses 4-6 narrow the thought to the domain of the sun, the solar heavens. The sun is a symbol of God's beneficence which, as Jesus said, is made to shine "on the evil and on the good" (Matt. 5:45). The heavens are as **a tabernacle** (dwelling) **for the sun** (4), which each morning comes forth **as a bridegroom** in

---

[46]*Op. cit.,* p. 103.

youthful happiness and **as a strong man** (5) eager to prove himself. The recurrent blessings of the Lord are extended to all mankind. All the earth profits from the beneficent heat of the radiant sun (6).

2. The Glory of God's Word (19: 7-14)

As great as are God's works, God's Word is greater. Natural religion must be supplemented by revealed religion. **The law of the Lord** (7) is the specific subject of vv. 7-11. **Law** (*torah*) means more than commandment or legislation, although it includes these. It stands for the total teaching of the revealed will of God throughout Scripture (cf. comment on 1:2). Seven statements are made about the revealed will of God:

a. It is a perfect law (19: 7a). The teaching **of the Lord is perfect** in every respect, **converting** and restoring **the soul.** It is through the Word of God that we become children of the Most High (I Pet. 1:23), and through it we are sanctified (John 17:17).

b. It is a sure testimony (19: 7b). **Sure** means "definite, decided, certain." It is a **testimony** because it bears witness to God's will and man's duty. Its effect is to make **wise the simple,** the untrained and uneducated, or those needing spiritual guidance. As in Proverbs, the term **simple** here means the open-minded, the teachable person, who can be instructed in the ways of the Lord.

c. It contains right statutes (19: 8a). **Statutes** are "precepts, commands, directions." **The statutes of the Lord are** eminently **right,** being exact expressions of His own nature and will. There are no requirements in the Bible which are arbitrary, imposed on man apart from the considerations of his best good. Everything the Lord requires of us is an expression of His own holiness and is in harmony with the structure of the universe in which we live. The result of keeping God's right statutes is a joyous **heart.**

d. Its commandments are pure (19: 8b). God's **commandment . . . is pure** in nature, and it tends to purity in those who keep it. The result is light in the soul in place of the darkness of sin. The combination of light and purity is stressed in I John 1:7.

e. "The fear of the Lord is clean" (19: 9a). **The fear of the Lord** is never slavish dread as of a harsh and tyrannical master. It is rather the wholesome reverence or respect man owes to God. In this sense we may both fear and love the Lord at the same time. **The fear of the Lord** is practically synonymous with what we should call piety or true religion. Such fear **is** morally **clean,** contrasting the uncleanness of sin and immorality. It is not a passing mood or transient impulse, but endures **for ever.**

f. God's judgments are true and righteous (19:9b). God's **judgments** (decisions, ordinances) are both absolutely **true** and absolutely **righteous.** In their truth, they are doctrine. In their righteousness, they are the foundation for life. The Bible does more than teach abstract truth. It provides an impulse to right living (cf. 119:9, 11).

g. God's law is of infinite value (19:10-11). All aspects of the Word of God are **more to be desired . . . than gold, yea, than much fine gold** (10). **Fine gold** is highly refined and purified. The most precious metal known to David helps to measure the value of the law of the Lord. As gold was the most valuable substance known, **honey** was the sweetest. The Word of God was to His servant more desirable than pure **gold** and **sweeter also than honey.** This is because it provides warning against that which would displease God and promises **great reward** in its **keeping** (11). It is well to remember that the reward is not in the knowing but in the keeping of God's precepts (Jas. 1:22-25).

What the law means in life is expressed in the prayer of vv. 12-14. Five results are noted: (1) *Convicting, 12a.* **Who can understand his errors?** The question is rhetorical, and the answer implied is that he may understand them best who views them honestly in the light of the Word. (2) *Cleansing, 12b.* **Cleanse thou me from secret faults.** The word **faults** has no counterpart in the original Hebrew, as the KJV italics indicate. The secret or hidden defect of the heart may well imply what we would call inbred sin. The eye can see the sins of the life. The Psalmist is not satisfied with understanding his errors. He is also concerned with the secret sin of the heart. He here prays for divine cleansing, a petition enlarged and echoed in 51:6-7, where almost identical language is used. (3) *Curbing, 13a.* **Keep back thy servant also from presumptuous sins,** "sins with a high hand," deliberate violations against God's law. The Word of the Lord also has the effect of restraining and fortifying the soul in temptation. Sin is a taskmaster to be feared: **let them not have dominion over me.** (4) *Correcting, 13b.* **Then shall I be upright, and I shall be innocent from the great transgression.** The negative side is curbing presumptuous sins. The positive side is constructive guidance that results in uprightness or perfection. Life cannot

thrive on negatives alone. The empty house is soon filled with
demons more wicked than those at first cast out (Matt. 12:43-45).
(5) *Confirming,* 14. **Let the words of my mouth, and the meditation of my heart, be acceptable,** as a sacrifice would prove
acceptable (Lev. 1:3-4). Not only his words, but his thoughts
must be such as to pass the inspection of the **Lord,** his **strength**
and **redeemer.**

Psalm 20: PRAYER FOR VICTORY, 20:1-9

This psalm is one of those titled, "To the chief Musician, a
Psalm of David." It is in the form of a prayer for victory on the
eve of a battle, and is closely related to Psalm 21, which is a
song of thanksgiving. Both are royal psalms, concerned with the
king as representative of the people, and may be classified as
liturgical, that is, associated with worship. Although anticipating
danger, Psalm 20 breathes an atmosphere of confidence and trust.

1. *Blessing and Prayer* (20:1-5)

It would appear that, while the sacrifice was being offered,
the Levites uttered the blessing and prayer of vv. 1-5. The
blessing of the first four verses is addressed to the king as the
Lord's anointed. It expresses the desire that **the Lord** shall **hear
. . . in the day of trouble** (1). **The name of the God of Jacob** is
invoked as a sure defense. In OT thought the name is often
equated with the person himself. There may be a memory here
of Gen. 35:3, "God, who answered me in the day of my distress,"
accounting for the title **God of Jacob.** The **sanctuary** of **Zion** is
the visible symbol of God's presence with and on behalf of His
people (2). **Offerings** and **burnt sacrifice** were prescribed elements in the OT worship (3). The king's faithfulness in this
regard would not be forgotten. **Selah;** cf. comment on 3:2.

**Grant thee according to thine own heart, and fulfil all thy
counsel** (4) has been translated, "May He grant you what your
heart desires, and fulfill all your plans" (Berk.). All will join in
rejoicing in the Lord's **salvation,** and **will set up** (wave) their
banners when the victory is won (5).

2. *Faith Is the Victory* (20:6-8)

The sacrifices have been offered, the prayer has been uttered,
and faith takes as an accomplished fact what has been asked. **Now
know I** (6), would be the response of the king. The Lord will save

186

his anointed, and will intervene on his behalf **with the saving strength of his right hand.** While others **trust in chariots, and . . . in horses,** the people of God rely on **the name of the Lord** (7). Those who put their trust in earthly weapons **are brought down and fallen** (8). On the contrary, the army of the Lord will **stand upright.**

3. A Final Prayer by All (20:9)

The service concludes with a final prayer: **Save, Lord: let the king hear us when we call.** An alternate translation is suggested by the LXX, "O Lord, save the king; and answer us when we call." It is fitting, however, that the king and his people together recognize their dependence on the King of heaven, whose representative on earth Israel's king was known to be.

Psalm 21: PRAISE FOR VICTORY, 21:1-13

Carrying the same title as the preceding one, Psalm 21 is characterized by its rejoicing in the victory which has been won. It glories in the abundance of God's help, and recounts the destruction of the foe. The structure is similar to Psalm 20, with two main stanzas followed by a brief concluding prayer. Its setting is probably also within the liturgy of the tabernacle-temple.

1. The Goodness of God to His Own (21:1-7)

The people glory in the goodness of God to their king. The Lord has preserved him in **strength** and **salvation** (1). He had been given **his heart's desire;** his prayer had been answered (2). **Selah;** cf. comment on 3:2. **For thou preventest him** (3) is better, "You set before him the blessings of prosperity" (Anchor). **Thou settest a crown of pure gold on his head** suggests that the king's authority was a derived authority. It came from God and was dependent on His ultimate sovereignty. The Hebrew monarchy was never absolute in the sense of being independent and underived.

The king's desire for **life** was granted, and **length of days for ever and ever** (4), "life eternal" (Anchor). In the strictest sense, these words would have to apply to David's Son and our Saviour. However, it may represent a manner of speaking, as in the greeting, "Let the king live for ever" (I Kings 1:31; Neh. 2:3). And as Kirkpatrick indicates, it was also true that the king was regarded as living on in his descendants.[47] **Glory, honour, majesty,** blessing, and **exceeding** gladness are the king's because he **trusteth in the Lord** (5-7). **Through the mercy** (*chesed;* cf. comment on 17:7) **of the most High** (*Elyon,* God in His sovereignty and power) **he shall not be moved**—"never swerve" (Anchor).

2. The Wrath of God Against His Enemies (21:8-12)

The victory already won is seen as the basis of confidence in even greater victories to come. Working through His chosen king, the Lord will bring utter destruction to His enemies. **Shall find out** (8) means to seek out the enemy in his retreat to complete his destruction. The **fiery oven** and **the fire** (9) are familiar biblical symbols of the judgment and wrath of God (Mal. 4:1; Luke 16:24; Rev. 20:14). The wicked shall be destroyed as fuel in a furnace. One of the greatest disasters that could befall an ancient Oriental was the destruction of his **fruit** (10; posterity), thereby blotting out his name from the earth.

Even though they were not able to carry out their **intended evil** (11), the enemies are to be judged on the basis of their wicked purposes. Jesus made motive the key to moral conduct (Matt. 5:21-48). The eternal issues of life lie within the heart of man. As a result, the foes of God's people will **turn their back** to flee when faced with the God-empowered weapons of Israel (12).

3. The Praise of God's Power (21:13)

The concluding prayer exalts God in His **strength,** and rejoices in His **power.** "Be Thou exalted, O Lord, in Thy strength; we will sing and praise Thy power" (Berk.).

Psalm 22: Suffering and Song, 22:1-31

Psalm 22 is the first of a tremendous trilogy. The relationship between Psalms 22, 23, and 24 has long been noted. Morgan captions them respectively "The Saviour," "The Shepherd," and "The Sovereign."[48] Another identifies the three psalms respectively with the *Cross,* the *Crook,* and the *Crown.*

---

[7]*Ibid.,* p. 111.   [48]*Op. cit.,* p. 229.

For Christians, the Christological importance of Psalm 22 is inescapable. It is quoted in the NT seven times in relation to Jesus (v. 1 in Matt. 27:46; Mark 15:34; v. 18 in the Passion accounts in all four Gospels; and v. 22 in Heb. 2:12). While the psalms ordinarily emphasize the kingly nature of Messiah's office, Psalm 22 (with Psalm 69) is linked with Isaiah 53 in noting the suffering Messiah. Both crown and cross appear in the OT in relation to the coming Deliverer, although in popular thought among the Jews the cross was obscured by the crown. The political aspects of Messiah's reign overshadowed the redemptive ministry He was to have.

Commentators debate the Messianic consciousness of the author of the psalm, but Leslie M'Caw states the case well: "To Christians this Psalm is inseparably associated with the crucifixion (as also Ps. lxix), not only because the opening words were quoted by the Lord, but because the first part of the poem seems to describe His bodily condition and emotional experience. Yet the first meaning of the poem must be sought in the days of its composition, although the Spirit of God undoubtedly constrained the psalmist so to frame his expression that it immediately acquired a significance beyond the range of his own life (see Acts ii.30, 31a). In other words, the Christological intention of the poem has a basis of Davidic experience."[49] Morgan, likewise, comments: "Whatever may have been the local conditions creating this psalm, it has become so perfectly and properly associated with the one Son of God that it is almost impossible to read it any other way."[50]

The psalm divides naturally into two great movements. The first (vv. 1-21) centers around the theme of suffering. The second (vv. 22-31) breaks forth into a song of the joy of deliverance. "The first admits us, as far as that can be, to the lonely suffering of the One on the altar of sacrifice (verses 1-21). The second brings us into the presence of the joy of the Victor, as through the travail He saw the triumph (verses 22-31)."[51]

The title adds the terms *'al ayyeleth ha-shahar* to the common title of psalms of this section—"set to 'the hind of the morning,'" probably the name of a melody to which the song was to be sung.

---

[49]*Op. cit.*, p. 427.   [50]*Op. cit.*, p. 229.
[51]*Ibid.*

1. *Trial* (22:1-21)

The opening words of the psalm are forever memorialized by forming the "Cry of Dereliction" from the Cross (Matt. 27:46; Mark 15:34—"Eli" in Matthew is the Hebrew version as here; "Eloi" in Mark is the Aramaic equivalent). Faith is beset by despair as the Psalmist addresses his cry to his God, yet expresses his sense of forsakenness. God seems sometimes to hide His face from His children, to be far from helping. But faith presses its claim in the face of seeming inattention. **My roaring** (1) suggests groans and plaints like the roaring of a lion. Day and night the sufferer lifts his cry to his God. (2).

But thou art holy (3; *qadosh*), i.e., separate from all limitations and imperfection; pure, free from all possible defilement, and radiant in glory. The holiness of God is a major emphasis of the OT, as the love of God is a major emphasis of the NT. The God of the Bible is a God of holy love. Holiness is not a single quality or attribute of God. It is His essential nature, in Norman Snaith's terms, His "Jehovah-ness," that which is "most intimately divine."[52] God dwells in **the praises of Israel.** He is present where and when His people praise Him (Mal. 3:16-17), and their praise like a cloud of incense envelops His throne in the heavens.

The Psalmist appeals to the experience of the past in support of his embattled faith. The **fathers trusted in** the Lord and were delivered (4); **they cried . . . and were not confounded** (5), that is, ashamed or disappointed. But the Psalmist finds himself in a very different situation. He feels himself trodden underfoot as **a worm,** reproached, and **despised** (6). Those around **laugh** him **to scorn** (7) or mock him. **They shoot out the lip** is literally, "They open the mouth"; and **they shake the head**—gestures of derision and scorn. Their jeering words are recalled by Matthew (27:43) as descriptive of the attitude of the crowd around the Cross.

In the midst of his trial, the Psalmist remembers the happier circumstances of his infancy. God's hand had been upon him from the very beginning of his life (9-10). **Hope when I was upon my mother's breasts** (9) is translated "tranquil on my mother's breast" (Anchor). **My God from my mother's belly** (10) may be rendered, "Since my mother bore me, Thou hast been my God" (Berk.). The cry of v. 1 now becomes a pathos-filled

---

[52]*The Distinctive Ideas of the Old Testament* (Philadelphia: Westminster Press, 1946), pp. 100 ff.

prayer: **Be not far from me; for trouble is near; for there is none to help** (11).

The situation seems to worsen before it begins to grow better. The darkest part of the night is just before the dawn. The poet feels himself surrounded by angry **bulls,** ready to charge upon him with their horns (12). **Bashan** (see map 1) was the rich pastureland east of the Jordan and to the north of Jerusalem, famed for its cattle raising. A change of figure pictures the enemies of the Psalmist as lions with gaping **mouths,** roaring and ravenous (13). In such circumstances his life is **poured out like water; his bones are out of joint;** his heart melts **like wax . . . in the midst of my bowels** (14; within me). His **strength** dries **up like a potsherd** (15)—a broken and dried piece of pottery. His **tongue** sticks to his mouth. He is brought down **into the dust of death.** The parallel to the agonies of the Crucified is obvious.

His enemies attack him like a pack of pariah **dogs,** snarling and pitiless. **They pierced my hands and my feet (16)** was literally fulfilled in the crucifixion of Jesus. **I may tell** (count) **all my bones: they look and stare upon me. They part my garments . . . and cast lots upon my vesture** (17-18), is quoted or alluded to in all four Gospels (Matt. 27:35; Mark 15:24; Luke 23:34; John 19:24).

Plaint turns to prayer as again the poet petitions for the presence of God, **Haste thee to help me** (19). He pleads for deliverance **from the sword** (20). **My darling** is "my only one" (Heb.), "my lonely self" (Berk.). **The unicorns** (21) are wild oxen (Heb.). The tense of the verb has changed. Faith reaches its Object. **Thou hast heard** is the response of trust. Suffering turns to song, prayer turns to praise, trial becomes triumph.

2. *Triumph* (22:22-31)

I will declare thy name unto my brethren (22) is applied to Christ in connection with His sanctified people (Heb. 2:11-12). The Psalmist's prayer has been public. His praise must also be made known to all. **The congregation** (*qahal*) is the OT term for what in the NT is called the Church, as in Heb. 2:12. The worshipper's appeal to his brethren is to **fear the Lord, praise him,** and **glorify him** (23). Two Hebrew words are translated **fear.** *The Berkeley Version* shows the distinction: "Ye who revere the Lord, praise Him; all you sons of Jacob, glorify Him; and stand in awe of Him, all you sons of Israel." The basis of this call to worship is the poet's own experience (24).

191

Alternating address to God and to the people, the Psalmist affirms his intention of praising the Lord in **the great congregation** (25). The Hebrew is literally, "Of Thee my praise shall be." God is both the Object and the Source of His people's praise. **I will pay my vows** means offering the thank offerings promised in times of trouble and presented in the manner prescribed in Leviticus 3 (called peace offerings). **The meek shall eat** (26) recalls Lev. 3:17; 7:16; Num. 15:3, where the people shared in the joy of deliverance by partaking of the carcass of the sacrifice after the kidneys, fat, and gall had been taken away to be burned and the blood to be sprinkled at the altar. **Your heart shall live for ever,** or, "Let your heart live forever," is a blessing the host pronounces on the guests at his thanksgiving feast.

In the poet's deliverance, he sees a forecast of the redemption planned for all mankind (27; cf. 2:8). In the Messianic reign, all the kingdoms of the earth shall become "the kingdoms of our Lord, and of his Christ" (28; Rev. 11:15). Verse 29 is difficult, but may be translated, "All the prosperous of the earth shall eat and bow down; indeed all who go down to the dust shall bow before Him, even he who is unable to keep his soul alive" (Berk.). "Every knee shall bow," of living and dead, before the Lord of all (Phil. 2:5-11).

A seed shall serve him (30-31) may be a reference to the doctrine of the remnant as developed by Isaiah later, in which the hope of the nation was not in the masses of its people but in a faithful minority. Or it may be rendered as with *The Berkeley Version,* "Posterity shall serve Him; it shall be told of the Lord to the coming generation; they will come and they will tell of His righteousness to a people yet to be born, for He has performed it."

Psalm 23: SHEPHERD AND HOST, 23:1-6

For the relation of Psalm 23 to the preceding and the following, see the introductory comments on Psalm 22. No part of scripture with the possible exception of the Lord's Prayer is better known than "The Shepherd Psalm." Its literary beauty and spiritual insight are unexcelled. As Taylor notes: "In the course of the centuries this psalm has won for itself a supreme place in the religious literature of the world. All who read it, whatever their age, race, or circumstances, find in the quiet beauty of its thoughts a range and depth of spiritual insight that both satisfies and possesses their souls. It belongs to that class of psalms that breathe confidence and trust in the Lord. . . . Here the psalmist has no preface of complaints about the pains of sickness or the treachery of enemies, but begins, as he ends, only with words of grateful acknowledgments of the never-failing goodness of the Lord."[53]

Oesterley also writes: "This exquisite little psalm, probably the most familiar of all the psalms, tells of one whose sublime trust in God has brought him peace and contentment. The close relationship to God felt by the psalmist is expressed by the two pictures representing the protecting Shepherd and the loving Host. The brief reference to his enemies indicates that he had not been free from trouble by the malice of the evil-disposed among his people but the mention of them is cursory. Unlike so many other psalmists who are the victim of unscrupulous foes, and who pour out their grief in bitterness of spirit, this happy and loyal servant of God has only words of grateful recognition of the divine lovingkindness. The whole psalm breathes a spirit of calm, and peace, and contentment, brought about through faith in God, which makes it one of the most inspiring in the Psalter."[54]

It is possible to interpret the entire psalm in terms of the relationship of Shepherd and sheep. However the more natural division is suggested by the title "Shepherd and Host." As Leslie M'Caw comments: "This poem owes much of its charm to the skilful blending of contrasted imagery which covers the major aspects of human life, viz. outdoors (1, 2) and indoors (6b), pastoral peace (2) and pilgrimage through peril (4b), the possibility of evil (4b) and the prospect of good (5), times of invigoration of soul (3a) and times of ominous gloom (4a); the experience of following (1, 2) and a life of stable security (6b). Nevertheless, all the literary facets of this lyrical gem are seen in the light of the Lord whose tender care, ceaseless vigilance and perpetual presence impart to life all its colour and satisfaction. Indeed the sevenfold activity of the Lord described in verses 2-5 (He maketh, He leadeth, He restoreth, He guideth, Thou art with me, Thou preparest a table, Thou anointest my head) is framed within the name of the Lord (the first and final words of the poem)."[55]

[53]*Op. cit.*, 4:123.
[54]*Op. cit.*, pp. 182-83.
[55]*Op. cit.*, p. 429.

1. *Pilgrimage with the Shepherd* (23:1-4)

David could write from a wealth of personal experience with sheep, **The Lord is my shepherd; I shall not want** (1; i.e., lack anything needful). There are "seven sufficiencies" of the Shepherd for His sheep outlined here:

a. "I shall not want for complete satisfaction" (23:2a). **He maketh me to lie down in green pastures** speaks, literally, of pastures of young, tender grass. Sheep never lie down, we are told, until they are satisfied with their grazing. Every spiritual need is supplied. The picture is one of utter restfulness in the satisfaction afforded under the watchful care of the great Shepherd. What a contrast with the restless throngs of the world!

b. "I shall not want for guidance" (23:2b). **He leadeth me beside the still waters,** or "waters of rest." Continuing the idea of provision for the needs of the flock, the poet adds the thought of guidance. The Eastern shepherd does not drive, he always leads, his sheep. This thought is memorialized in the gospel song:

> *He leadeth me! Oh, blessed thought!*
> *Oh, words with heavenly comfort fraught!*
> *Whate'er I do, where'er I be,*
> *Still 'tis God's hand that leadeth me* (J. H. Gilmore).

c. "I shall not want for renewal" (23:3a). **He restoreth my soul,** i.e., He revives, renews, and refreshes me. This is a frequent NT theme: "The inward man is renewed day by day" (II Cor. 4:16); "Be renewed in the spirit of your mind" (Eph. 4:23); "And have put on the new man, which is renewed in knowledge" (Col. 3:10). Here is grace that sustains the soul.

d. "I shall not want for instruction in righteousness" (23:3b). **He leadeth me in the paths of righteousness for his name's sake. The paths of righteousness** are straight paths. One of the functions of Scripture is "instruction in righteousness" (II Tim. 3:16). God not only warns against evil; He guides us in the way of righteousness. This is **for his name's sake,** vindicating the kind of God He is. God, whose name is holy (111:9; Matt. 6:9), wills that His people shall also be holy (Lev. 19:2; I Pet. 1:14-16).

e. "I shall not want for courage in danger" (23:4a). **Yea, though I walk through the valley of the shadow** (Heb., deep or deadly gloom) **of death, I will fear no evil.** Here is assurance of help in the hardest of all life's hard places. Death is no mean adversary. It is our last great enemy (I Cor. 15:26). If God can give us courage then, as He has given to so many others, He can help us anywhere. **Evil** (*ra*) is the broad term for any kind of harm or danger that may come.

f. "I shall not want for the Divine Presence" (23:4b). **For thou art with me.** This is the sufficient ground for all the Psalmist's confidence. The Lord will not leave nor forsake His own (Exod. 33:14; Deut. 31:6-8; Josh. 1:5-9; etc.). In that Presence are strength, comfort, rest, and hope. At this significant point, the "he" (vv. 2-3) with which the poem begins turns to **thou** as description gives way to adoration.

g. "I shall not want for comfort in sorrow" (23:4c). **Thy rod and thy staff they comfort me.** The shepherd's crook serves two functions—it is a **rod** for protection and a **staff** upon which the shepherd leans, standing for the comfort of his presence. The "man of sorrows" knows best how to meet the need of the sorrowing heart.

2. *Provision by the Host* (23:5-6)

The idea of the complete supply of every need with which the psalm began continues to control its development, but the comparison changes from Shepherd to Host, from the field to the home. **A table before me in the presence of mine enemies** (5) pictures the mark of public favor which the Oriental king would show to one he purposed especially to honor. This is the only passing reference to the enemies who figure so largely in many other Davidic psalms. **Thou anointest my head with oil** is not the anointing oil by which a king or priest was inducted into office; another Hebrew term is used for that. This was the perfumed oil largely used in ancient Oriental banquets as a mark of hospitality and favor. The head anointed with oil is a familiar Bible figure for high joy. **My cup runneth over** symbolizes the abundant provision made by the generous Host.

Surely goodness and mercy (*chesed*, loving-kindness, covenant love, grace; cf. comment on 17:7) **shall follow me all the days of my life** (6). The term translated **surely** also means "only." The Psalmist is confident that nothing but goodness and steadfast love will be his. **I will dwell in the house of the Lord for ever,** or literally, "to length of days." But the inner meaning is more than a long life on this earth. **Goodness and mercy . . . all the days of my life** will be followed by an eternal home in the presence of God when this life is done (John 14:1-3).

Psalm 24: WORSHIPING THE KING OF GLORY, 24:1-10

For the relationship between this psalm and the two which precede it, see the introductory comment on Psalm 22. This beautiful little liturgical piece is entitled simply "A Psalm of David." It may have been written for the occasion when the ark of the Lord was brought to the tent prepared for it on Mount Zion (II Sam. 6:1-15). No other psalm seems to fit as well. Yet as M'Caw notes, "The Psalm was greater than the occasion, and has generally been interpreted as a prophetic expression of Christ's ascension after victory over death and sin (see verse 8 and cf. Col. ii.15; Heb. ii.14, 15) and of His ultimate sovereignty over all (see verse 10 and cf. Jas. ii.1; Rev. v.11-14, xvii.14)."[56]

Kirkpatrick has envisioned the liturgical use of the psalm as follows: "Vv. 1-6 were perhaps intended to be sung as the procession mounted the hill; vv. 1, 2 by the full choir, the question of v. 3 as a solo, the answer of vv. 4, 5 as another solo, the response of v. 6 in chorus. Vv. 7-10 may have been sung as the procession halted before the venerable gates of the citadel; the summons of v. 7 and v. 9 by a single voice (or possibly by the choir), the challenge of v. 8a and v. 10a by a voice as from the gates, the triumphant response of v. 8b and v. 10b by the full choir."[57]

1. *The Character of True Worship* (24:1-6)

The first major division of the psalm deals with the requirements of true worship, first as to its Object, and second as to those who worship.

a. *The One worshiped* (24:1-2). Identity of the Object of true worship is established with the claim to universal sovereignty for Israel's God. There are no limitations of the authority and dominion of God to special place or time. **The whole earth (1)** with its fullness; **the world,** and all those who dwell in it, belong to the Lord as His substance and His subjects. Foreshadowed here is the claim of the gospel upon every creature, everywhere and for all time. God's claim is based on His creation: **For he hath founded it upon the seas, and established it upon the floods (2).** To this powerful reason, the NT adds another. Not only has God made the earth and them that dwell therein, but He has redeemed it as well. It is His by double

---

[56]*Ibid.*   [57]*Op. cit.*, p. 128

right: by right of creation, and by right of redemption or purchase (Rom. 14:8-9; I Pet. 1:18-19).

b. The ones worshiping (24:3-6). In view of the sovereignty of God, what are the requirements made of those who would worship Him? The spiritual and moral qualifications of those who would approach God "in spirit and in truth" (John 4:24) are set forth. Perowne describes vv. 3-6 as listing "the moral conditions which are necessary for all true approach to God in His sanctuary. The Psalm passes as usual from the general to the particular, from God's relation to all mankind as their Creator, to His especial relation to His chosen people in the midst of whom He has manifested His presence. The *Almighty* God is also the *Holy* God. His people therefore must be holy."[58] Note the parallels in 15:1-5 and Isa. 33:14-17.

The question of v. 3 is given in poetic parallelism: **Who shall ascend into the hill of the Lord? or who shall stand in his holy place?** The threefold answer demands clean hands, a pure heart, and a straight life. **He that hath clean hands** (4) is unstained by guilt of committed sins. Pilate washed his hands in water to symbolize his claim to innocence in the death of our Lord. But water cannot wash clean the stained hands of sinful men. Only the fountain opened to the house of David for sin and uncleanness can afford cleansing from guilt (Zech. 13:1). The hands stand for what a person does, but **a pure heart** stands for what he is. Even the OT reflects the gospel standard of heart purity (51:7-10; cf. Jas. 4:8).

But forgiveness of sins and cleansing from inner impurity are gates that lead to the way. The life must conform to the initial experiences. He who stands in God's holy presence must be one **who hath not lifted up his soul unto vanity, nor sworn deceitfully.** The term **vanity,** as Kirkpatrick notes, stands for "what is transitory (Job xv.31), false and unreal (Ps. xii.2), or sinful (Isa. v.18), and may even designate false gods (Ps. xxxi. 6). It includes all that is unlike or opposed to the nature of God."[59] "It may be taken here in the widest sense of all that the human heart puts in the place of God."[60] To lift up the soul means to desire, to set the heart on (cf. I John 2:15-17). **Sworn deceitfully,**

---

[58]*The Book of Psalms,* I (Grand Rapids, Michigan: Zondervan Publishing House, 1966 [reprint]), 255.

[59]*Op. cit.,* p. 129.   [60]Perowne, *op. cit.,* I, 255.

that is, "sworn in order to deceive." The Lord is a God of truth, and seeks truth in those who would be His servants (51:6).

Such as this **shall receive the blessing from the Lord, and righteousness from the God of his salvation** (5). The expression **this is the generation** (6) indicates the kind of persons **that seek him, that seek thy face, O Jacob.** The LXX is probably correct in reading the last phrase, "That seek Thy face, O God of Jacob"; "who seek for the Presence of Jacob" (Anchor). *The Berkeley Version,* on the other hand, translates, "Who seek Thy face, like Jacob," recalling Jacob's wrestling with the Angel at Peniel: "For I have seen God face to face, and my life is preserved" (Gen. 32:22-30). **Selah;** cf. comment on 3:2.

2. The Crowning of the King (24:7-10)

The ascending company of worshipers has now reached the gates. There is a pause. Then the call rings out, **Lift up your heads, O ye gates** (7). The head is often used in Scripture for the self, as in 7:16, "His mischief shall return upon his own head." The gates are personified and called upon to open in dignity and reverence for the entrance of **the King of glory.** The expression **ye everlasting doors** is better "ye ancient doors" (Berk.). **The King of glory** is the King to whom all glory should be ascribed.

The call is followed by a challenge from the gates: **Who is this King of glory?** (8) The answer is, **The Lord strong and mighty, the Lord mighty in battle.** God had proved himself more than a match for any foe that might rise. Again the call is repeated with great rhetorical effect (9). The second challenge is answered with the words, **The Lord of hosts, he is the King of glory** (10). This is the first occurrence in the Psalms of a familiar and beautiful title for the true God. He is **the Lord of hosts** (*Yahweh Tsebaoth*), Captain both of the armies of Israel and of all the hosts of heaven, the supreme Ruler of the universe. **Selah,** cf. comment on 3:2.

Psalm 25: SONG OF PRAYER AND PRAISE, 25:1-22

This is one of nine acrostic psalms (cf. Psalms 9 and 10) in which each verse begins with a successive letter of the twenty-two-letter Hebrew alphabet. In this case there are minor modifications (*vau* and *qoph* are missing, two verses begin with *resh,* and the last verse is a second *pe*). A somewhat similar modification is found in Psalm 34, suggesting that there is a relation between the two. The Hebrew title is incomplete, reading simply, "Of David."

Psalm 25 may be classified as a wisdom psalm. As is true of most of the acrostic psalms, it consists of a series of largely self-contained sayings.[61] Of the three stanzas, the first is a prayer (1-7), the second proceeds to praise and contemplation of the goodness of God (8-15), and the third returns again to renewed petition (16-22).

1. *Prayer* (25:1-7)

As contrasted with one who had "lifted up his soul unto vanity" (24:4), the Psalmist affirms, **Unto thee, O Lord, do I lift up my soul** (1). His desire, thought, and intention are fixed on God (cf. 24:4, comment). Since his trust is in the true and living God, he pleads that he may **not be ashamed** (2), i.e., put to confusion and disappointed in the help he expected. What he asks for himself, he asks for all others who **wait on thee** (3). Shame and confusion belong rather to those who **transgress without cause**—literally, who are treacherous or disloyal without any grounds.

The prayer for deliverance *from* becomes a prayer for deliverance *to*. The poet prays, **Shew me thy ways, O Lord; teach me thy paths** (4; cf. Exod. 33:13). He voices his plea to **the God of** his **salvation** (5), on whom he constantly waits in prayer and trust. **Lead me in thy truth, and teach me.** Human life cannot be lived as a vacuum. The ways of evil can be displaced only as the ways of the Lord are embraced.

David appeals to the Lord to **remember** His own **tender mercies** and acts of loving-kindness (*chesed;* steadfast love, mercy, grace; cf. 17:7, comment) as **of old** (6); and to **remember not the sins of my youth, nor my transgressions** (7). The word **sins** (*chattah*) comes from a term which means to miss the mark or lose the way. "It denotes primarily the failures, errors, lapses, of frailty; and so is naturally applied to the thoughtless offences of youth."[62] **Transgressions** (*pesha*) "means literally *rebellions,* and denotes the deliberate offences of riper years."[63] The mercy and grace of God are sufficient for both! David prays, **Remember not the sins . . .** but **remember thou me.**

[61]Cf. Oesterley, *op. cit.*, p. 189.   [62]Kirkpatrick, *op. cit.*, p. 133.
[63]*Ibid.*

2. *Praise and Contemplation* (25:8-15)

As so often in the Psalms, prayer passes very naturally over into praise. Sometimes when we cannot "pray our way through" we may "praise our way through." **Good and upright is the Lord: therefore will he teach sinners** (those who lose the way, miss the mark) **in the way** (8; of truth and righteousness). **The meek** (9) are those who are teachable, humble-minded—contrasted with the proud, scornful oppressors of the good.

The paths of the Lord are mercy and truth (10). They are manifestations of His constant love and faithfulness to those who **keep his covenant and his testimonies.** The great covenant (*berith*) made at Sinai and God's continued revelation in the history of His dealings with His people witness to the faithfulness of God to His law. In view of such mercy and divine faithfulness, the poet is conscious again of the greatness of his **iniquity** and pleads for pardon **for thy name's sake** (11), i.e., on the basis of the kind of forgiving God the Lord had made himself known to be.

Four specific benefits are promised the man who **feareth the Lord** (12-14). First, he will be taught **in the way that he shall choose** (12). The Lord will guide him in his choices. Second, **his soul shall dwell at ease** (13). The term **soul** is frequently used simply to designate the individual. **At ease** is literally "in good," that is, in prosperity, the blessing of the OT. Third, **his seed shall inherit the earth.** To have sons and daughters who will in their turn flourish is a commonly cherished human goal throughout all time. Fourth, such a blessed man will enjoy the benefit of spiritual instruction: **The secret of the Lord is with them that fear him; and he will shew them his covenant** (14). The word **secret** is literally "secret counsel" and suggests the intimate self-communication of a close friendship. The ASV margin and RSV therefore properly and beautifully translate **secret** as "the friendship of the Lord." Jesus said, "Ye are my friends" (John 15:13-15). As a consequence of these blessings, David will keep his heart fixed on the Lord, who will **pluck** his **feet out of the net** (15)—save him from the snares of his enemies and the entanglements of circumstances.

3. *Petition Renewed* (25:16-22)

The psalm returns again to the mood of supplication. The poet begs the Lord, **Turn thee unto me** (16); literally, "Turn Thy face toward me." He feels **desolate and afflicted** (Heb., alone and poor). **The troubles of my heart are enlarged** (17). The translation is a bit uncertain here, but the KJV has probably caught the sense. The Anchor translation has it, "Anguish cramps my heart, of my distress relieve me."

In the face of multiplied troubles, David prays for deliverance. He calls on God to **look upon mine affliction and my pain** (18), that is, to behold with compassion his trouble. **Forgive all my sins** sounds the note of penitence so striking in this psalm. The poet senses a connection between the troubles he is enduring and the sins of which he had been guilty. He is beset by many **enemies** who hate him **with cruel hatred** (19), literally, "hatred of violence," venting itself in cruel and violent actions as well as antagonistic attitudes. In such peril, David pleads that the Lord will **keep** him, **deliver** him, and save him from shame and confusion because of his **trust** in God (20). His safety will be in **integrity and uprightness** (21) and in waiting on the Lord. " 'Integrity' is the virtue of the 'perfect' man . . . Job was 'perfect and upright' (ii.3)."[64]

The final petition is for the redemption of **Israel**, the nation, **out of all its troubles** (22). **Redeem** (*padhah*) means to deliver from danger, difficulty, or bondage at the cost of personal effort, and to bring into a new state of freedom and release. It is one of the most common OT terms for the action of God in behalf of His people.

Psalm 26: PROFESSION AND PRAYER, 26:1-12

This psalm, like the preceding and the two following, is titled simply "Of David." It resembles Psalm 25 in some ways, but the confessions of sin found in 25 are lacking here. Robinson sees in Psalm 26 the form of an "oath of purgation," in which one charged of wrongdoing would take a formal oath of innocence: "The speaker begins 'Judge me, O Yahweh, for I have walked in my perfection'—using a word which implies that he is nowhere open to a criminal charge. He is ready, even eager to have Yahweh test him, for he knows that the most searching examination will reveal nothing in him that ought not to be there. He protests that he has had no dealings with false men, and that he hates the company of evildoers. He has washed his hands in innocence—a metaphor for the upright life which we meet again

---

[64]*Ibid.,* p. 136.

in Ps. 73:13, where it looks like a recognized formula—and his only delight has been in the worship of Yahweh. He pleads that he may not be classed with offenders, and ends much as he began. We may well believe that he pauses at the end of his statement and waits for the result of his appeal. It is favourable, and the last verse reads like the response of a man who has been set free from suspicion."[65]

Oesterley points out that the profession of righteousness prominent here developed into the spiritual pride and hypocrisy of the Pharisees in NT times. Such is not the case with the Psalmist, however. As Oesterley says, "Spiritual pride, arising out of a sense of self-righteousness, is not a characteristic of the psalmist, because he imputes to God his rectitude of life, 'in thee have I trusted, I shall not slide', he says. This is a very different attitude from that of the Pharisee in the parable (Luke 18:11, 12, 14). For a man to recognize, in the spirit of true humility, that he is striving to live according to the will of God, need not generate spiritual pride, but should be a source of sanctified joy. While, on the one hand, to confess sin is a supreme duty for man, the recognition of his virtues, when rightly envisaged, is, on the other hand, to acknowledge the action of divine grace."[66]

1. *Profession of Integrity* (26:1-7)

Judge me, O Lord (1), is a cry for justice and protection. It is based on a manner of life—**I have walked in mine integrity;** and upon an attitude of heart—**I have trusted also in the Lord.** The term **integrity** (*tam*) is the general OT term for perfection, sincerity of purpose, and single-hearted devotion. It is the quality attributed to Job (Job 1:1, 8; 2:3, 9), and the subject of God's command to Abraham (Gen. 17:1). **Therefore I shall not slide** is literally "not wavering," and the latter part of the verse may be translated as by the RV, ASV, and *Berkeley Version,* "I have trusted without wavering" (cf. Jas. 1:6-7).

David opens his heart to the Lord without reservation: **Examine me, O Lord, and prove me** (2). The expression **my reins and my heart** means "the whole of my inner life, feelings, thought, and will." He has kept the **lovingkindness** of the Lord ever in

---

[65]*Op. cit.,* p. 135. Dahood includes Psalms 5, 16, and 139 in this category of "psalms of innocence" (*op. cit.,* p. xxxiii). Cf. also Job 31 for a classic example of the "oath of purgation" in the Bible.
[66]*Op. cit.,* pp. 193-94.

his mind, and has **walked in** the ways to which God's **truth** pointed (3). **I have not sat**—to take counsel of or have fellowship with—**vain persons** (4), literally, "men of vanity" in the sense of both worthless men and those who were idolaters. **Neither will I go in with dissemblers,** i.e., "fellowship with pretenders" (Amp. OT). He detested **the congregation of evildoers** (5), those who meet together for their own evil ends in contrast with those who meet to worship the Lord as in v. 12. He **will not sit with the wicked** in fellowship or in participation in their evil counsels.

I will wash mine hands in innocency (6) recalls the washings of the priests as they approached the altar to minister its sacrificial worship (Exod. 30:17-21). Washing the hands was also symbolic of protesting innocence, as in the case of Pilate (Matt. 27:24). **So will I compass thine altar, O Lord,** is either "join the company of worshipers around the altar" or, with *The Berkeley Version,* "go about Thy altar, O Lord." Always associated with divine worship is to **publish with the voice of thanksgiving, and tell of all thy wondrous works** (7). One translation is, "That I may make the voice of thanksgiving to be heard, and tell of all Your wondrous works" (Amp. OT).

2. *Prayer for Intervention* (26:8-12)

In vv. 8-11 the Psalmist makes a direct appeal to the Judge for intervention on his behalf against those who have falsely accused him. Separation *from* the society of wicked men in their evildoing is at the same time separation *to* the tabernacle of the Lord and those who worship there. Moffatt's translation of 8 is striking and beautiful: "I love the precincts of thy house, the mansion of thy majesty." **Honour** may also be "glory" (RSV).

Gather not my soul with sinners (9) should be, "Do not take away my soul or life with sinners." The wicked will be prematurely cut off by death. **Bloody men** are those who do not stop short of violent assault and murder. **Mischief** (10) is literally "a plot" in the sense of deliberately planned evil. **Their right hand is full of bribes,** either to buy off those in authority or, having accepted money, to turn their heads the other way while evil is committed. Bribery and corruption is one of the unceasing problems of the administration of justice and the carrying on of government.

Others have chosen to live in sin and rebellion, but David says, **As for me, I will walk in mine integrity** (11; cf. comment on

1). He therefore can pray in faith that the Lord will **redeem
. . . and be merciful unto** him. Verse 12 seems to indicate a
judgment of vindication. The charges are dismissed, and the
Psalmist's innocence is established (cf. intro. to this psalm).
My foot standeth in an even place or "on even ground" (Berk.).
Firm footing is essential to security—for the soul as well as for
the body. **In the congregations** (meeting from time to time to
worship the Lord) **will I bless** (praise and glorify) **the Lord.**

Psalm 27: SUNSHINE AND SHADOW, 27:1-14

Psalm 27 is composed of two contrasting movements expressing very different moods. So striking is the difference in tone
between vv. 1-6 and 7-14 that some have expressed the conviction that we have here the combination of two psalms either
written by different authors or written at very different periods
in the author's life. However, G. Campbell Morgan feels that
the difference is sufficiently accounted for by the fact that praise
should precede prayer in the order of worship.[67] Like the two
preceding and the one following, the title in the Hebrew text is
simply "Of David."

Although Oesterley believes we have here the combination
of two different psalms, he notes that "the central point in its
religious teaching is the same, though presented from different
points of view. In the former, faith in God, which has sustained
the sufferer through his trials and brought him triumphantly
through them, has thereby become deeper. In the latter the
victim, in a piteous state of despair, surrounded by dangers, and
plunged in sorrow, is borne up solely by his faith in God. Thus,
whether in joy or sorrow, in prosperity or adversity, it is the
certitude of God's presence and his love which dominates all
things."[68]

1. *Praise* (27:1-6)

The first verses of this psalm are familiar to many in the
beautiful musical setting of Frances Allitson: **The Lord is my
light and my salvation** (1). **Light** is one of the great symbols
for God through both the OT and the NT (4:6; Isa. 10:17; Mic.
7:8; John 1:4, 9; 8:12; I John 1:5). **The Lord** was to David as a
light shining in a dark place, dispelling the shadows, showing
all things in their true colors; bringing joy and cheer to the day,
and driving away the fears that lurk in the dark. **The Lord is**

---

[68]*Op. cit.*, p. 197.   [67]*Op. cit.*, p. 231.

the strength of my life is literally "the fortress of my life"—"the stronghold of my life" (Berk.; Amp. OT). Secure in God's care, the Psalmist need **be afraid** of no one.

Life had not been free of obstacles and opposition. But the assaults were now past—or if this be the praise in preparation to the petition of vv. 7-13, it is the confident expectation that it will soon come to pass. **To eat up my flesh (2)** means "to consume or destroy me." **Stumbled and fell** indicates that they were brought to confusion, and failed in their attacks. Even an army encamped in siege against the poet will not now bring **fear (3)** to his heart. **Though war should rise against me** has a first application to the threat of renewed attacks upon the poet. But in times of "wars and rumours of wars" these words carry comfort and confidence to the hearts of God's people everywhere.

One thing have I desired (4) indicates the spiritual priorities of the Psalmist's life. Seeking first the kingdom of God and His righteousness, all other needful things would be added (Matt. 5:33). To **dwell in the house of the Lord** and **to behold the beauty** ("goodness," Moffatt) **of the Lord, and to enquire in his temple** are the sum of David's desire. The royal Host provides for and protects those who are of His household. Even in the OT, God was Loveliness as well as Law, the Source of delight as well as duty. **To enquire** also means "to ponder, to meditate." Cf. the Berkeley translation, "to observe the Lord's loveliness, and to meditate in His temple."

The Psalmist is realistic enough to know that not all problems are solved nor all difficulties surmounted. **In the time of trouble he shall hide me in his pavilion** ("His shelter," Amp. OT): **in the secret of his tabernacle** (tent) **shall he hide me; he shall set me up upon a rock,** as one protected in an impregnable rock fortress (5). The cumulative idea is one of total security. Its NT counterpart is Rom. 8:31-38.

In whatever lingering threat there may be, total victory is in sight: **And now shall mine head be lifted up above mine enemies (6).** He shall be exalted while his foes are abased. **Therefore will he offer** in the Lord's **tabernacle sacrifices of joy** —not only sacrifices prescribed as the thank offerings for deliverance, but joy itself as an acceptable offering to the Lord.

2. Petition (27:7-12)

Abruptly the mood changes. Either circumstances have altered or the preparation in praise is complete and the Psalmist turns to the need of the moment (see intro. to this psalm). **Hear, O Lord . . . have mercy . . . answer me** (7), is his plaint. There is some question as to the exact translation of v. 8, but the KJV no doubt gives the sense: **When thou saidst, Seek ye my face; my heart said unto thee, Thy face, Lord, will I seek.** The Anchor Bible has it, "Come, said my heart, seek his face; your face, O Yahweh, will I seek." We come to God in prayer not unbidden but by His invitation. In view of obedience to the command to seek the Lord's face, the poet prays, **Hide not thy face . . . put not thy servant away** (turn not away as in rejecting the plea) **. . . leave me not, neither forsake me** (9). God was already his **help** and the **God of** his **salvation.** The Hebrew text puts the next statement in the past tense: "For my father and my mother forsook me, but the Lord will take me up" (10). Although he be as a deserted child, the Lord will adopt him and take care of him. Instruction, guidance, and protection are next sought from on high: **Teach me . . . lead me** (11) **. . . Deliver me not over** (12). **False witnesses** were spreading slander. They were such as **breathe out cruelty**—the cruelty of the cutting, lying word—a form of trial by no means unknown today.

3. *Patience* (27:13-14)

It is through faith and patience that God's people inherit the promise (Heb. 6:12). **I had fainted, unless I had believed to see** conveys well the idea of the steadying power of true faith (13). However, "I believe that I shall see" is closer to the original text. **The land of the living** is, as our common use of the expression indicates, this life as contrasted with *Sheol*, the realm of the dead. God's goodness is known both here and hereafter. However the Anchor translation views this as an explicit statement of faith in a future life: "In the Victor do I trust, to behold the beauty of Yahweh in the land of life eternal."

The closing injunction of the psalm is to **wait on the Lord** (14), both in the sense of continuing in prayer and in the sense of patiently holding on until the answer comes. **Be of good courage, and he shall strengthen thine heart** is literally, "Be strong and let your heart be strong" in the conviction that deliverance is at hand. **Wait, I say, on the Lord** is in the Hebrew, simply, "And wait for the Lord." His coming is never too late to those who wait for Him

Psalm 28: TROUBLE AND THANKSGIVING, 28:1-9

This is the last of four psalms titled simply, "Of David." It is chiefly in the form of a song of lament. The circumstances may have been David's flight from Absalom's army (II Sam. 15: 1—18:33), since treachery seems involved (3) and the concluding prayer for the people would be fitting for a king whose land was torn by civil war. But it is very relevant to any situation in which treachery brings strife and division. In this psalm the order of prayer and praise is reversed from that found in Psalm 27; here prayer (1-5) precedes praise (6-9).

1. *Prayer for Help* (28:1-5)

The Psalmist's situation is desperate. Unless God answers, he will be **like them that go down into the pit** (1); the grave or *Sheol* was always thought to be down or beneath. He will therefore **cry** (2), a stronger word than is used in v. 1. *The Berkeley Version* and the Anchor Bible make the distinction by translating the term in v. 1 as "call," using "cry" to translate the term in v. 2. The Hebrew word means an urgent cry for help. **When I lift up my hands** was an outward symbol of the uplifted heart. **Thy holy oracle** would be the holy of holies, where the ark of the covenant reposed, symbolizing the presence of God with His people. Although David in flight from Absalom had sent the priests with the ark back to its tabernacle (II Sam. 15:24-29), he would address his petition to the visible symbol of God's presence.

The workers of iniquity from which the Psalmist seeks deliverance were those who **speak peace to their neighbours** with their mouths, but who have **mischief** (*ra*, stark evil) **in their hearts** (3). The term **mischief** was a much stronger word in 1611 when the KJV was translated. It is far too weak now to describe the unmitigated evil intended by the original Hebrew. With sense of justice outraged, the Psalmist prays that those wicked persons may be given in judicial sentence what their works deserve (4). **According to** would be both in kind and in proportion. Great evil deserves great punishment. The God of justice cannot fail finally to punish wrong, though execution of His sentence be delayed. Godless men **regard not the works of the Lord, nor the operation of his hands** (5), denying both His creation and His providence. **He shall destroy them** is literally, "He will overthrow them,"

207

which fits better with the words that follow, **and not build them up.**

2. *Praise for the Answer* (28:6-9)

Either these words were added after deliverance had come or faith becomes so strong that it regards the promised future as if it were present fact. Such, indeed, is of the very nature of faith. "What things so ever ye desire, when ye pray, believe that ye receive them [lit., ye do now receive them], and ye shall have them" (Mark 11:24).

The Psalmist breaks out in adoration. **Blessed be the Lord** (6) is the form of doxology with which each of the first four books of the Psalms closes (41:13; 72:18-19; 89:52; and 106:48 —the whole of Psalm 150 serves as the doxology for Book V). **Blessed be** means, "Glory, praise, and adoration be given to." Such ought to be our response to answered prayer. The Lord had proved himself **strength** and **shield** (7). The Psalmist **trusted** and was **helped.** Great is his rejoicing as he sings his **song of praise. The Lord is** the **strength** (8) of those who trust Him. **He is the saving strength,** literally, "the stronghold of salvation," to **his anointed.**

The psalm closes with a final prayer for all the people; the Lord is asked to **save . . . bless . . . feed . . . and lift them up** (9). This is a summary petition for all that God's redemption provides, then and now.

Psalm 29: A Psalm for Pentecost, 29:1-11

Entitled "A Psalm of David," this is the psalm traditionally used in the synagogue on the first day of the Feast of Tabernacles, which is the Day of Pentecost. It is a psalm of adoration, in which God's power in nature as experienced in a great storm is the central theme. M'Caw entitles the psalm, "The Thunder of God," and describes it as the "song of a thunderstorm."[69] W. E. Barnes captions it, "The God of the Storm Is Also the God of Peace."[70]

M'Caw says, "Verses 3-9, the core of the poem, describe the passage of a storm from the waters of the western sea across the forested hills of northern Palestine, to the waste places of Kadesh [not Kadesh-Barnea in the south] in the uttermost borders of

---

[69]*Op. cit.*, p. 432.   [70]*Op. cit.*, I, 142.

Edom (Num. xx.16). This event is depicted not as a demonstration of natural power, but as a symphony of praise to the Creator who indeed joins in with a voice of thunder (cf. Ps. xviii.13)."[71]

Nature throughout the psalms is seen as providing insight into the divine power and glory. Thus M'Caw notes: "The focus of all action and thought is the Lord Himself eternally enthroned, and unwaveringly bestowing upon His people not merely the gift of strength but the blessing of *peace* (verses 10, 11). The poem skilfully fuses the natural and the spiritual, but with clear emphasis on the latter aspect. The first word *give* is a call to worship and the last word *peace* implies His will to bless. Divine power prompts the one and provides the other."[72]

Oesterley says, "This fine and ancient hymn of praise is unique in the Psalter. It was doubtless inspired, in the first instance, by the awesome descriptions of the theophany on Mount Sinai (Exod. 19:16-19), and the divine presence on Mount Horeb (I Kgs. 19:11-12). The psalmist's aim is to proclaim Yahweh's supremacy in the heavens and on earth. The heavenly powers are described as 'sons of gods', and subordinate to Yahweh; a witness to monotheistic belief in contrast to the polytheism of the nations which regarded the highest god as different in rank. but not in nature, from the rest of the gods."[73]

1. Call to Worship (29:1-2)

The psalm opens with a call to worship the true and living God **in the beauty of holiness** (2). The expression **O ye mighty** (1) is literally "ye sons of the mighty," or "ye sons of God." To **give** in this context is "to ascribe." **The beauty of holiness** (2) is quite literally its majesty. God's holiness is beautiful and majestic, and He shares it with those who "worship him in spirit and in truth" (John 4:24; cf. II Pet. 1:3-4).

2. The Coming of the Storm (29:3-9)

M'Caw sees the onset and passing of the storm as the core of the poem (cf. intro. to the psalm). Verses 3-4 deal with the approach of the storm. Verses 5-7 describe the onset of the storm. Verses 8-9 detail the passing of the storm.[74] The three

---

[71]*Loc. cit.*   [72]*Ibid.*

[73]*Op. cit.*, p. 199. For the view of Ginsburg, *et al.*, that this psalm is an adaptation of a Canaanite hymn to a storm-god, cf. Dahood, *op. cit.*, p. 175.

[74]*Op. cit.*, p. 432.

dispensational signs which appeared on the Day of Pentecost in Jerusalem (Acts 2:1-4) are also intimated: **the voice of the Lord** breaking **the cedars** (5) prefigures the sound of the rushing mighty wind; the dividing of **the flames of fire** (7) suggests the cloven tongues as of fire; and the universal speaking of the **glory of the Lord** (9) relates to the gift of unlearned languages in which were spoken "the wonderful works of God" (Acts 2:11).

The repeated reference to **the voice of the Lord** (3, 4, 5, 7, 8, 9) is a distinctive feature of this psalm. Immediately, this may refer to thunder and wind.[75] But it has wider meaning in the power of the living Word of God (Heb. 4:12). Modern neoorthodoxy has made us familiar with the "God Who Acts."[76] The Bible, however, introduces us to the God who not only acts but speaks, and who in many situations acts by speaking through His inspired and "inscripturated" Word.

God's **voice** is equated with **the God of glory** (3) and with **the Lord** himself. It **is powerful** and **full of majesty** (4). It breaks **the cedars of Lebanon** (5), most majestic of the trees and typical of the pride and magnificence of men (Isa. 2:13). To **skip like a calf** or **like a young unicorn** (6; wild ox) pictures the violent motion of the storm-broken trees and the shaking of mountains. **Lebanon** refers to the mountain range. The name means "white," from the snow-covered peaks. **Sirion** is an older name for Mount Hermon in the north of Palestine. **The voice of the Lord** also **divideth the flames of fire** (7), an allusion to the forked lightning accompanying such a storm. It shakes **the wilderness of Kadesh** (8). **Lebanon** and Hermon were in the north, **Kadesh** in the south. The whole land was affected by God's voice. God's voice makes **the hinds to calve** (9). The deer will give birth to their young prematurely through fear induced by the violence of the tempest. **Discovereth the forests** is literally "laid bare the forests." "Discover" is an old English form for "uncover" or "expose." Only in the temple of the Lord are peace and confidence. **In his temple doth every one speak of his glory** reads in the Hebrew text, "In his temple all are saying, 'Glory,' " ascribing to God the glory called for in vv. 1-2.

[75]Cf. the title for Psalm 29 suggested by Franz Delitzsch, "The Psalm of the Seven Thunders," *op. cit.*, I, 445.

[76]Title of a definitive volume by G. Ernest Wright (Chicago: Henry Regnery Co., 1952).

3. *The Concluding Peace* (29:10-11)

The psalm that opens with glory and power closes with peace. **The sovereign Lord sitteth upon** (is enthroned on) **the flood** (10) and rules as **King** over nature and history **for ever.** God gives His people **strength,** and blesses them **with peace** (11). Delitzsch comments, "This closing word *with peace* is like a rainbow arch over the Psalm. The beginning of the Psalm shows us heaven open, and the throne of God in the midst of the angelic songs of praise; while its close shows us His victorious people upon earth, blessed with peace in the midst of the terrible utterance of His wrath. *Gloria in excelsis* is the beginning, and *pax in terris* the end."[77]

Psalm 30: THANKSGIVING FOR GOD'S HEALING TOUCH, 30:1-12

Psalm 30 is a fervent expression of praise to God for deliverance from death, threatened through what was probably a very severe illness. Verses 9-12 are echoed in Hezekiah's prayer of thanksgiving following his healing (Isa. 38:18-20). The title indicates that the psalm was used at the dedication of "the house of David." It may have been used in dedicating the second Temple (Ezra 6:16), as it was later in connection with the Maccabean Feast of Dedication.[78] The use would be appropriate since the history of the nation followed the pattern of individual experience.

1. *Experience* (30:1-3)

The writer vividly relates his experience of restoration from the very brink of the grave. **I will extol thee** (1; lit., exalt Thee). Because the Lord raised him up, his enemies lost their expected rejoicing over what would have been the Psalmist's untimely death. Prayer has been answered, and the man of God had been **healed** (2). Divine healing became much more prominent in the NT but it is often referred to in the OT (Exod. 15:26; 23:25; Deut. 7:15; 32:39; II Kings 20:1-11; Job 5:18; Ps. 103:3; 107:20; Isa. 19:22; 30:26; 53:5; 57:18-19; Jer. 30:17; 33:6; Hos. 6:1; 11:13; cf. Asa's death because "in his disease he sought not to the Lord, but to the physicians," II Chron. 16:12). The Church has yet

---

[77]Quoted by Kirkpatrick, *op. cit.,* p. 151.

[78]The Talmudic *Sopherim,* cited *ibid.*

to recover the strong sense of close relationship between spiritual and physical health that pervades the Bible.

The seriousness of the Psalmist's plight is clear from the strength of his language. He had been **brought up . . . from the grave** (3), *Sheol*, the place of the dead. He had been **kept . . . alive**, that he **should not go down to the pit**, or better, "You restored me to life as I was descending the Pit" (Anchor). As good as dead already, the Lord had given him "a new lease on life." **The pit** (*bor*) is the literal word for *hole* or *pit*. It is, as here, a common synonym for *Sheol*, place of the dead.

2. *Expression* (30: 4-6)

Verses 4-6 give expression to the singer's gratitude for his experience of the divine touch. He calls on all God's **saints** (4), the godly among the people, to join him in **thanks at the remembrance of his holiness.** The **holiness** of God in the OT is in many ways a summary description of His nature. It would include the mercy and faithfulness of the Lord as well as His radiant purity. The Hebrew is literally "to (or for) the memorial of his holiness." The restored health of the poet was a monument to the goodness of God.

The lesson of it all is expressed in v. 5: **Weeping may endure for a night, but joy cometh in the morning.** God's **anger** at most is momentary, and caused only by sin; **in his favour is life**—He gives forgiveness and eternal life to the humble and penitent. Part of the Psalmist's problem may have been a sense of self-sufficiency: **In my prosperity I said, I shall never be moved** (6). Nothing sweeps away such an attitude faster than the stroke of sickness. How little money and friends can do for us when illness lays us low!

3. *Expostulation* (30: 7-9)

The Psalmist's prayer of expostulation reminds us of a similar expression of Job in the time of his affliction (Job 10:3). With God's **favour** the Psalmist had been **strong.** When the Lord hid His **face, he was troubled** (7). In his trouble, he **cried** to the **Lord** and **made supplication** (8). His reasoning is paralleled by Hezekiah in Isa. 38:18-19. There would be no **profit** to the Lord in His servant's death (9). Indeed, death would interrupt the poet's **praise** and his declaration of God's **truth** (9; cf. comment on 6:5).

4. *Expectation* (30:10-12)

As so often throughout the psalms, the poet moves from prayer and praise to expectation. His faith sweeps ahead to eternity. He will continue to pray for **mercy** and help (10). His **mourning** has been **turned . . . into dancing** (11), the almost universal expression of joy. He had exchanged the **sackcloth** of his sorrow for the girdle of **gladness, all to the end that my glory may sing praise to thee, and not be silent** (12). As in 16:9 (see comments) and elsewhere, **my glory** means "my soul," since the soul as the divine image was the noblest part of man's being. "So that my heart might sing to you" (Anchor). **O Lord my God, I will give thanks unto thee for ever**—since praise is one of the chief occupations of eternity (Rev. 7:9-13).

Psalm 31: Tested yet Trusting, 31:1-24

This psalm, dedicated to the chief musician and inscribed as a psalm of David in the title, is a striking alternation of lament and praise. Morgan describes it as a "great song of trust struggling through tears to triumph."[79] He divides the psalm into "the seasons of the soul." Autumn, "with its winds and gathering clouds, yet having sunlight and a golden fruitage even though the breath of death is everywhere," is represented in vv. 1-8. Winter, "chill and lifeless, full of sobs and sighing," is pictured in 9-13. Spring, "with its hope and expectation and its sweeping rains and bursting sun gleams," is found in 14-18. Summer, "glad and golden," is found in 19-24. "We need them all to complete our year."[80]

1. *Trust* (31:1-8)

The dominant note of the first division of our psalm is the twice-repeated affirmation of implicit **trust** (1, 6) in the Lord in spite of the threatening circumstances. Petition is mingled with praise and confidence. **Trust**, the usual OT word for faith, is literally to take refuge. **Be ashamed** means be put to shame. God's righteousness is man's hope of deliverance. **Bow down thine ear** (2) is a Hebraism for "hear," or "listen to." Deliverance will come as God again proves himself a **strong rock . . . an house of defence,** or fortress. Affirmation follows petition: **For thou art my rock and my fortress** (3), "i.e. prove Thyself to be

[79]*Op. cit.*, p. 232.   [80]*Ibid.*

what I know Thou art. 'It is the logic of every believing prayer.'
Delitzsch."[81] The figures of speech are drawn from the tactics
of guerilla warfare in a mountainous country where rocky crag
and stone fortress were an effective defense. Cf. the Syrian explanation of their defeat at the hand of the "God of the hills,"
who, as they thought, would not be effective in the valleys
(I Kings 20:28).

For thy name's sake indicates that God's honor is involved
in His servant's deliverance. Although his enemies had spread a
net (4) in which to entrap him, the Psalmist appeals to the
Lord, his **strength,** to **pull** him **out.** The expression **laid privily**
means laid secretly, with cunning. The climaxing expression of
trust is forever hallowed since it was quoted by our Lord as His
last word from the Cross, **Into thine hand I commit my spirit**
(5). The spirit, as his life, is the Psalmist's most precious possession, and he commits it to God with the confident faith, **Thou
hast redeemed me, O Lord God of truth.** To be redeemed means
to be delivered, and the content of the term varies with the source
of the oppression. The Psalmist was delivered from those seeking to ensnare him. The Christian is redeemed from the bondage
of sin. The Hebrew term translated **truth** (*emeth*) also means
trustworthiness or faithfulness, and it is so used here. Harrison
translates, "You are a faithful God."

Love for and trust in the true God leads to contempt for
those **that regard lying vanities** (idols). "Vanity" is a favorite
OT name for false gods. The Psalmist **will be glad and rejoice in**
the Lord's **mercy** (7), who **considered** (took knowledge of) his
trouble (affliction) and who had **known** his **soul in adversities,**
or better, had "taken knowledge of the distresses of my soul."[82]
In contrast to the confinement planned for him by his enemies,
the Lord has **set** his **feet in a large room** (8), a wide place "with
plenty of room to move" (Berk., fn.).

2. *Trouble* (31:9-13)

There is a sharp shift in tone with v. 9. We enter the winter
of the soul, "full of sobs and sighing."[83] **Trouble** (9) is the key-
note. Life can be harsh and burdensome even for the child of
God (I Pet. 1:5-9). For us, as for David, the happiness and
serenity reflected in 6-8 may suddenly be disturbed by illness,

---

[81]Kirkpatrick, *op. cit.*, p. 156.   [82]*Ibid.*, p. 157.
[83]Morgan, *loc. cit.*

bereavement, betrayal, or natural disaster. Eyes dimmed with tears, soul and body (better than **belly**) afflicted, the Psalmist pours out his **grief** to his God.

My strength faileth because of mine iniquity (10) would pinpoint a sense of guilt as contributing to the writer's distress of mind and body. The LXX, however, attributes the failure of strength to the poet's "misery." **My bones are consumed**, no longer able to support the labor demanded of them. **I was a reproach** (11), the object of scorn. **A fear to mine acquaintance**, a fearful sight from which those who beheld would turn away. Like one **dead** and **forgotten**, or like a worthless bit of **broken** pottery, the Psalmist felt himself unpitied and cast off (12). His woe was compounded when he became the butt of **slander**, surrounded by occasions for **fear**, and plotted against (13; cf. Jer. 20:10).

3. *Truth* (31:14-18)

Having complained of the slander to which he was subject, the Psalmist affirms again his confidence in the final vindication of truth. Troubled times should be trusting times for those who love the Lord (14). **My times are in thy hand** (15) is a clear recognition of God's providential control of all in life that affects His own. This is the source of the line in Robert Browning's familiar "Rabbi Ben Ezra";

> *Grow old along with me!*
> *The best is yet to be,*
> *The last of life for which the first was made.*
> *Our times are in his hand*
> *Who saith, "A whole I planned.*
> *Youth shows but half; trust God: see all, nor be afraid!"*

Times (*eth*) can mean ways, seasons, circumstances. Moffatt translates it "fate"; the Anchor Bible, "life-stages"; Harrison, "My destiny is under your control." The outcomes of life for us are not left to chance or blind fate, but are in a loving and just Hand.

Recognition of God's guiding hand encourages the Psalmist to pray again for favor and deliverance: **Make thy face to shine upon** me (16). Not the one who calls on the Lord in sincerity and truth, but the godless, shall come to shame (17; concerning the imprecatory tone of this verse, cf. Intro.). **Lying** and **slanderous lips** should **be put to silence** (18). **Speak grievous things proudly**

and contemptuously against the righteous may be "speak insolently against the righteous with pride and contempt" (Berk.).

4. *Triumph* (31:19-24)

The cycle of the seasons swings into summer, "glad and golden."[84] Here is pure praise, expressing the triumph that comes out of trouble through trust. Perhaps looking ahead by faith, or more probably after the storm has passed, the Psalmist glories in "the victory that overcometh" (I John 5:4). There is a shout in the words, **How great is thy goodness!** (19)—"What a wealth of kindness thou hast laid up for thy worshippers" (Moffatt). It is a public display of divine favor, "in the sight of the sons of men" (Anchor).

God himself is to His people a Refuge **from the pride** ("plots," RSV) **of man** (20), **a pavilion** (shelter) in which they will be out of reach of **the strife of tongues** ("the scourge of slander," Moffatt). The Lord has shown **his marvellous kindness in a strong city** (21), literally, "a city of siege"—"an entrenched city" (Berk.), fully fortified against the foe. The poet confesses the despair he had felt (22), and sees it as another expression of the goodness of God that his prayer should have been heard.

The psalm closes with a call to **his saints** (23) to **love the Lord** and to **be of good courage** (24). The reason is that the Lord preserves the trusting and obedient; **and plentifully rewardeth** ("fully repays," Berk.) **the proud doer** (23; "arrogant man," Moffatt). **Be of good courage** (24) is literally, "Be strong, and let your heart be valiant, all you who hope in the Lord." **Hope in** is used in the sense of confident waiting for. "Those who trust Him wholly find Him wholly true" (Frances Ridley Havergal).

Psalm 32: THE JOY OF SINS FORGIVEN, 32:1-11

Psalm 32 is the second of the seven "penitential" psalms (cf. Psalm 6, intro.). Many commentators relate it closely to Psalm 51. Kirkpatrick holds that 32 is later than 51, expressing the successful conclusion of the penitence and prayer described in 51.[85] It is identified in the title as a psalm of David, and is called *Maschil*, a term found in twelve other psalm titles (42, 44, 45,

---

[84]*Ibid.*   [85]*Op. cit.*, p. 161.

52—55, 74, 78, 88, 89, 142). It probably comes from a term meaning "to instruct, to make attentive, intelligent." It would then identify what we might call a didactic or teaching psalm, or a meditation designed to teach.

The theme of the psalm is the joy of the forgiven heart. If vv. 3-4 be interpreted as many do in the sense of a physical illness, then the joy of God's healing touch is also included. "Among the psalms there is none which touches deeper things in the life of the soul or more perfectly reveals the method of Jehovah in sin, sorrow, and guidance. He is ready to pardon, able to deliver, and willing to guide."[86]

1. Covering (32:1-2)

The happiness of **forgiven** transgressions and **covered** sins is joyfully proclaimed (1). **Blessed** (cf. comment on 1:1). **Transgression** (*pesha*) is the strongest and most serious OT term for personal evil. Its basic meaning is rebellion, high treason against the sovereign. **Sin** (*chattah*) means wandering from the way, missing the mark. **Iniquity** (2; *avon*) is depravity or moral distortion.[87]

When rebellion **is forgiven** (1; *nasa*, "lift off, take away"), the rebel is restored to his rightful place as an obedient subject of his heavenly Lord (Rom. 5:1). When **sin is covered** (*kacah*, conceal, hide by filling up a void), the failure and emptiness are supplied from the fullness of the Lord. **Imputeth not** (2) means "does not charge" to (Berk.) or "has absolved" (Moffatt). In both the OT and the NT, to impute never means "to imagine," but always "to take account of what is." When the Lord imputes righteousness (Gen. 15:6), it is because His grace imparts it. When the Lord does not impute iniquity, it is because His grace takes it away. Paul interprets these verses in the context of the Christian experience of justification and regeneration in Rom. 4:6-8. The thought here is that in the initial experience of salvation not only are our transgressions forgiven and our sins covered, but the original sinful nature from which both transgres-

---

[86]Morgan, *op. cit.*, p. 233.

[87]Kirkpatrick, *op. cit.*, p. 162; cf. C. Ryder Smith, *The Bible Doctrine of Sin* (London: The Epworth Press, 1953), p. 17; Hermann Schultz, *Old Testament Theology*, translated by J. A. Paterson (Edinburgh: T. and T. Clark, 1909), II, 281 ff., 306; Ludwig Köhler, *Old Testament Theology*, translated by A. S. Todd (Philadelphia: The Westminster Press, 1957), p. 170.

sions and sins sprang—while not yet fully cleansed—is still not charged against us. **In whose spirit there is no guile** suggests that "full confession" (Moffatt) has cleansed away deceit and hypocrisy. The greatest hypocrisy of all is denial of sin on the part of the unforgiven.

2. *Conviction* (32:3-4)

It is possible, as noted in the introduction, that the condition described in these verses was a serious physical illness, possibly a raging fever. But these words are also vividly descriptive of the sickness of the soul convicted by its own sense of guilt, the faithful preaching of God's messenger (II Sam. 12:7-14), and the Holy Spirit (John 16:7-11). **When I kept silence (3)** — unrepenting, refusing to confess—**my bones waxed old,** strength and soundness departed. **Through my roaring all the day long** indicates constant complaining, but not yet confessing. The **hand of God was heavy upon** him **day and night (4),** and his **moisture is turned into the drought of summer**—"My marrow dried up as in a summer drought" (Berk.). For **Selah,** cf. comment on 3:2. Its use here indicates that this psalm was used in public worship, leading the people in penitence and praise.

3. *Confession* (32:5)

The only sure cure for conviction is confession. In a very real sense, the "unpardonable sin" is the unconfessed sin. Lawrence E. Toombs writes, "Attempts to find a cure for this disease on the psychiatrist's couch may only conceal it under the cover of a 'well-adjusted personality,' schooled in self-justification. By this method, sin is not dealt with. It is disregarded. Nor can a cure be effected by parading one's sins before those whom the sinner has offended. To do this is to seek forgiveness from those who are unable meaningfully to forgive, and whose forgiveness or continued resentment makes no ultimate difference. The psalmist knows that he must go for forgiveness to him in whom alone cleansing and healing are genuinely to be found.

> *I acknowledged my sin to thee,*
> *and I did not hide my iniquity."*[88]

[88]*The Old Testament in Christian Preaching* (Philadelphia: The Westminster Press, 1961), p. 172.

4. Confidence (32: 6-7)

In a narrow sense, forgiveness relates to the past. But it also imparts confidence for the future. Hope as well as faith is the ground of our salvation (Rom. 8:24). **For this** (6) is better "Therefore" (RSV). God's past faithfulness justifies our confidence that He will be found when we call upon Him wholeheartedly (Deut. 4:29). **In the floods of great waters** the people of God will be safe, as those who stand on high ground. The Lord is a **hiding place** (7) in whom there is preservation **from trouble** —not in the sense that trouble does not come, but that God makes a way **of deliverance.** "Many are the afflictions of the righteous: but the Lord delivereth him out of them all" (34:19). **Compass me about** means "surround me."

5. Counsel (32: 8-11)

Some have supposed that the speaker in these verses is the Psalmist, who now assumes the role of teacher. It would seem better, in light of the last clause of 8, to read these lines as the Lord's reply to His servant's profession of trust. In any case, forgiveness and faith must lead to obedience and righteousness. The "believing side" of the gospel is to be followed by the "behaving side." **I will guide thee with mine eye** (8), as by a glance in the right direction; or, as recent versions, "I will guide thee with mine eye upon thee" (cf. 33:18; 34:15); "I will instruct you and show you the way you must go" (Anchor). In contrast to the willing obedience of the forgiven soul is **the horse** (9) or **mule,** whose obedience must be compelled **with bit and bridle.** The expression **lest they come near unto thee** is better, "Then you can approach him" (Anchor).

The **many sorrows** of **the wicked** (10) are contrasted with the **mercy** that surrounds **the righteous** (11), who are urged to **be glad,** to **rejoice,** and to **shout for joy.** As Edmund Jacob has written, "Important as fear is in Israelite religion, it does not occupy the central place, joy far outweighs it; joy belongs to God. A God who laughs, a God who indulges so largely in humour, is a joyous God: the morning stars (Job 28:7) and wisdom (Prov. 8:22-31) which utters cries of joy before him are a poetic personification of the feelings which animate God himself when he takes pleasure in his created works (cf. Gen. 1 and Ps. 104:31) . . . . 'There is no word,' writes L. Koehler, 'which is more central in the Old Testament than the word joy.' God gives man a considerable share in his joy (Eccl. 2:26; 8:15; 9:7; 11:9 ff.), joy forms the centre of the cult, which consists in rejoicing before Yahweh and in communion with him . . . and when the future kingdom arrives its advent will be marked by great joy (Isa. 9:2)."[89] "Old Testament piety is a living, spiritual, personal, joyful thing."[90]

Psalm 33: PRAISE FOR GOD'S GREAT ACTS, 33:1-22

Unlike the majority of the psalms in Book I, this one is without a title in the Hebrew text (cf. 1, 2, and 10). It is a hymn of praise and adoration stressing the sovereign power of God's word and His works. It is a fitting answer to the call for joyous praise given in the last verse of the preceding psalm and echoed in the opening verses of this.[91] The psalm falls into three major divisions: praise to God for His word and works (*a*) in creation, vv. 1-9; (*b*) in history, 10-17; and (*c*) in redemption, 18-22.

1. *God in Creation* (33:1-9)

The first three verses are an enlarged call to praise and worship, addressed to the **righteous** and **the upright** (1; cf. 32:11). **Praise is comely**, i.e., "praise becomes" God's people (Berk.). **The psaltery and an instrument of ten strings** (2) is literally "a lyre ten-stringed." The **harp** and **the psaltery** (lyre) were both stringed instruments, differing only in form. The **harp** (*kinnor*—used here for the first time in the Psalms) is one of the oldest musical instruments known (Gen. 4:21). It was apparently small enough to be readily carried (I Sam. 10:5). David was famous for his skill with the harp (I Sam. 16:23), the strings of which he apparently plucked with his fingers. It is variously thought to have had eight or ten strings, stretched across a wooden frame. **The psaltery** (*nebel*) or lyre is first mentioned in I Sam. 10:5, and from that fact is thought to have been of Phoenician origin. It may have been larger than the harp to supply bass notes in the music. **A new song** (3) would be in recognition of the new blessings God daily bestows. **Play skilfully with a loud noise** is literally, "Be skillful to play with shouting" (cf. comment on 32:11).

[89]*Op. cit.*, p. 175.   [90]Vriezen, *op. cit.*, p. 302.

[91]Dahood, *op. cit.*, p. xxxi, points out the grammatical continuity between 32:11 and 33:1 as evidence that these two psalms actually belong together as one composition.

The call to praise is followed by a vivid description of the creative word and works of God in the universe. The Creator is One whose **word is right** (4; *yashar*, upright), whose **works are done in truth** (*emunah*, faithfulness), and who loves **righteousness and judgment** (5). "*Righteousness* is the principle of justice; *judgment* the application of it in act."[92] **The earth is full of the goodness** (*chesed*, loving-kindness, steadfast love) **of the Lord** (cf. comment on 17:9 and BBC, Vol. V, "Hosea," Introduction).

By the word of the Lord were the heavens made (6) is an expression of the omnipotent power which had but to will and to speak and it was done. The NT parallel, with its profound personalization of the Word that was with God and was God, is found in John 1:3. **The host of them** is reminiscent of Gen. 2:1, and refers to the ordered array of the stars and the heavenly bodies. The Psalmist had no idea of the vast numbers of stars modern astronomy has discovered, but he knew whence they had all come.

The gathering of **the waters** and the laying up of the deep (7) hark back to the separation of land and sea in the original creative acts of God (Gen. 1:9-10). The use of the present tense suggests a continuous action in maintaining the universe ("upholding all things by the word of his power," Heb. 1:3). Moffatt translates 7:

> *He holds the seas as in a water-skin,*
> *and stores up the abysses of the deep.*

In view of such majestic might, **Let all the earth fear the Lord** (8). The meaning is clearly stated in the parallel second line of this verse, **stand in awe of him.**

> *For he it was who spoke—and earth existed,*
> *'twas at his bidding it appeared* (9, Moffatt).

2. God in History (33:10-17)

Turning from God's power in creation to His sovereignty in history, the Psalmist notes that **the Lord bringeth the counsel of the heathen** (*goyyim*, the nations, Gentiles) **to nought** (10). "Man proposes, but God disposes." **Devices** are purposes or plans. In contrast with the purposes of the heathen and the plans

---

[92]Kirkpatrick, *op. cit.*, p. 166.

of the people are set the purposes **of the Lord** (11) and **the
thoughts of his heart.** Because they are "on the Lord's side,"
happy **is the nation whose God is the Lord** (12). Words that
had special meaning for the **people whom he hath chosen** have
even more meaning for those who in Christ are "a chosen generation, a royal priesthood, an holy nation, a peculiar [special]
people" (I Pet. 2:9).

God maintains oversight of **all the sons of men** (13). Because **he fashioneth their hearts alike** (15), He can know and
justly evaluate all human works.

> *He who alone made their minds,*
> *he notes all they do* (Moffatt).

Rampant militarism receives a just rebuke in 16-17. Large
armies, military might, huge armaments, and great strength are
insufficient to guarantee the safety of a nation now as well as in
the Psalmist's day. The prophetic words of Rudyard Kipling's
"Recessional," written on the occasion of Queen Victoria's Dia-
mond Jubilee, June, 1897, are a valid modern application:

> *Far-called, our navies melt away;*
> *On dune and headland sinks the fire—*
> *Lo, all our pomp of yesterday*
> *Is one with Nineveh and Tyre!*
> *Judge of the Nations, spare us yet,*
> *Lest we forget—lest we forget!*
>
> . . . .
>
> *For heathen heart that puts her trust*
> *In reeking tube and iron shard—*
> *All valiant dust that builds on dust,*
> *And guarding, calls not Thee to guard—*
> *For frantic boast and foolish word,*
> *Thy mercy on Thy people, Lord!*
> *Amen.*

3. God in Redemption (33:18-22)

The God of creation and the Lord of history is known to His
own as their Redeemer. **The eye of the Lord** (18), undimmed,
ever-wakeful, **is upon them that fear him** and **that hope in his
mercy**—"rest their hopes upon his kindness" (Moffatt). He

delivers **their soul from death** (19) as by pestilence or drought, and keeps **them alive in famine.** In quiet confidence His people wait **for the Lord** (20), who is both **help** and **shield** to those who trust **in his holy name** (21). The rejoicing of **hope** (22) is expressed in Paul's description of the "grace wherein we stand, and rejoice in hope of the glory of God" (Rom. 5:2).

Psalm 34: A PSALM OF DELIVERANCE, 34:1-22

Psalm 34 is universally loved, and is one of the most beautiful in the Psalter. It is properly a song of deliverance from fear, danger, trouble, and affliction (vv. 4, 7, 17, 19). The title inscribes it to "David, when he changed his behaviour before Abimelech, who drove him away, and he departed." This is a reference to I Sam. 21:10-13, possibly as an example of the kind of deliverance in mind here. The psalm is alphabetical or acrostic in that each successive verse begins with a different letter of the Hebrew alphabet (except that *vau,* the sixth letter, has been dropped, and an extra *pe,* the seventeenth letter, has been added at the end; cf. also Psalms 9, 10, 25).

1. *Praise* (34:1-6)

The poet proclaims his purpose to praise **the Lord at all times** (1). The term **bless** (*barak*) is derived from a root meaning to kneel to or before; hence, to acknowledge, to worship, to praise, to thank. **Make her boast** (2) is literally "glory in." Hearing what God has done, **the humble** will **be glad. To magnify the Lord** (3) would be to make God great in the eyes of others by telling of His greatness. God's **name** is exalted as His saving power is made known abroad.

The exhortation to praise is reinforced by personal testimony to deliverance **from all my fears** (4). Fear and an attitude of faith in the goodness of God are contradictory moods. "The fear of the Lord" destroys all unnatural fears and anxieties. All who, like the Psalmist, **looked unto him . . . were lightened** (5). A striking translation of this line is, "They looked unto Him and were radiant" (cf. ASV, RSV, Berk.). Moffatt translates, "Look to him, and you shall beam with joy." This is the radiance and winsomeness of the Christlike personality. Again, the personal note is sounded—God had delivered His praying servant **out of all his troubles** (6); not that he would not encounter troubles, but he would be **saved . . . out of** them.

2. *Provision* (34:7-10)

God's provision for legitimate human needs is complete and surpasses anything that is found in nature. **The angel of the Lord** (7) is mentioned here for the first time in the Psalms (cf. 35:5-6). This is not just any angel, but is the characteristic OT phrase for that Divine Presence which is at once identified with God and distinguished from Him (cf. Gen. 16:7, 13; Judg. 13:21-22; Hos. 12:4-5). Many rightly see in **the angel of the Lord** a preincarnate appearance of the Second Person of the Trinity.[93] On **encampeth round about**, cf. 125:2. **O taste and see** (8) is the biblical appeal to personal experience. If you will taste, you will see. If you do not taste, you cannot see that the Lord is good. "Tasting stands before seeing; for spiritual experience leads to spiritual knowledge and not conversely. David desires that others likewise may experience what he has experienced, in order to know what he has known; the goodness of God."[94]

Nothing in the natural order can equal the security of God's people. **No want** (9) means no deficiency, need, or impoverishment. A different form of the same root is found in 10 and in 23:1. It is not "want" in the sense of desire but "want" in the sense of deficiency that is supplied by the Father's provident hand. Even though **the young lions** at the height of their powers to capture prey **do lack, and suffer hunger . . . they that seek the Lord shall not want any good thing** (10).

3. *Practice* (34:11-14)

The last half of the psalm is devoted to ethical instruction, and in the manner of the wisdom writers is addressed, **Come, my children, hearken unto me** (11; cf. Prov. 1:8; 2:1; 3:1, 11; etc.). **The fear of the Lord** is the OT term for true religion. It is the central motif of the Book of Proverbs. Here, as there, "by *fear of the Lord* we should understand all that piety, i.e. a right relationship with God, means. It is the nearest approach in Hebrew thought to what we mean when we speak of 'religion.' The term

---

[93]Cf. A. B. Davidson, *The Theology of the Old Testament* (Edinburgh: T. and T. Clark, 1904), pp. 291-300; Schultz, *op. cit.*, II, 214-37; Gustave F. Oehler, *Theology of the Old Testament*, translated by George E. Day (Grand Rapids, Michigan: Zondervan Publishing House [reprint]), paragraphs 59-60.

[94]Delitzsch, *op. cit., ad loc.*

carries the meaning of a right attitude to God and the practical expression of this attitude in a man's life day by day."[95]

What man is he that desireth life? (12) is a rhetorical question with the sense of "everyone who desires life and good." The directions are explicit: **tongue** and **lips** (13) are to be kept from **evil** and **speaking guile** (insincerity, hypocrisy). The life is to be free from **evil** and full of **good** (14). God's man was to pursue **peace** (*shalom*, including also the ideas of well-being, health, wholeness, soundness, perfection—cf. Heb. 12:14). More than the legalism of later Judaism, this was the inspired pattern for the good life in the OT.

4. *Protection* (34:15-22)

The constant recurrence throughout the Psalms of the promise of protection from the perils of life is a reminder of the insecurity of man's existence apart from his faith in God. **The eyes of the Lord** (15; His watchful care) and His willingness to hear **the cry** of the **righteous** are emphasized. Conversely, God's judgment is expressed **against them that do evil** (16). For v. 17, cf. comment on 6.

The Lord is near the sorrowing and the humbly penitent (18), a thought reechoed throughout the Psalms (cf., esp., 51:17). **The Lord** delivers **the righteous** out of his many **afflictions** (19). One commented, "I'd rather have a thousand afflictions and be delivered out of them all, than have half a dozen and get stuck in the midst of them!" The **bones** (20) are the structural framework of the physical body. Hence, **keepeth all his bones** stands for the strength of the whole man. **Evil shall slay the wicked** (21); their own sins bring with them the wages of death (Rom. 6:23). **Be desolate** is literally "be guilty" (*asham*). Hatred and animosity, as well as the violent deeds to which these emotions lead, are under the judgment of God (Matt. 5:21-22; I John 2:9-11; 3:15). **The Lord redeemeth** (22) is present tense, "is redeeming." Salvation is continuous as well as instantaneous. **Desolate,** as in 21, is *asham* (guilty).

Psalm 35: PRAYER IN PERSONAL PERIL, 35:1-28

This is the first of the imprecatory psalms (see Intro., "Classification of the Psalms") to be found in Book I. It gets this

---

[95]Edgar Jones, *Proverbs and Ecclesiastes* ("Torch Bible Commentaries"; New York: The Macmillan Co., 1961), p. 58.

classification chiefly from vv. 3-8, 25-26. Yet the major emphasis is upon the Psalmist's lament in his trouble, and his strong cry for divine help. Morgan comments, "There is agony in this song. The singer is sore beset with enemies. They are striving with him, fighting against him. They are plotting against him, treacherously spreading a net for his feet. . . . Before we criticize the singer for his attitude toward his foes, let us imagine ourselves in his place. In no sense is the level of spiritual realization in this psalm equal to that in many others. One of the greatest values in the collection is its revelation of how, under all circumstances, the soul may turn to God."[96]

Yet Oesterley's point is well made: "In spite of grievous wrong suffered by the psalmist, he nowhere expresses the intention, or even the wish, of taking personal revenge upon his enemies and traducers; that he should desire their punishment is natural enough; but this is left wholly in the hands of the Almighty; we recall Rom. 12:19: 'Vengeance is mine, saith the Lord, I will repay,' cp. Deut. 32:35. This wholehearted placing of his cause in the care of the all-knowing God witnesses to a true sincerity of religious belief."[97]

The psalm divides into three major divisions, each of which ends with a vow of thanksgiving (1-10, 11-18, 19-28). Its Hebrew title is simply, "A psalm of David."

1. Plea (35:1-10)

The Psalmist lays his case before the Lord in an eloquent plea for vindication. He is the object of strife and opposition, and earnestly calls upon God to take his side against his foes. The imagery of 1-3 is that of the battlefield: **strive . . . fight . . . shield and buckler . . . spear.** The **shield** was a small arm-shield, and the **buckler** a larger one to cover the entire body.

Draw out (3) suggests securing weapons as from an armory or storehouse. **Stop the way against them** is understood by some to call for the use of a weapon not otherwise named, perhaps a javelin (so RSV) or battle-axe (so Moffatt). However, *The Berkeley Version* makes good sense of this difficult Hebrew construction: "Step in to encounter my pursuers." "Ready the spear and the javelin to confront my pursuers" (Anchor). **Salvation** as here used is an example of the breadth of the term.

---

[96]*Op. cit.*, pp. 233-34.   [97]*Op. cit.*, pp. 218-19.

Cf. comment on 3:8. **Confounded** (confused, perplexed) **and put to shame (4) . . . turned back and brought to confusion** continue the picture of a battlefield. **As chaff before the wind (5)**, driven along a **dark and slippery** way **(6)** by **the angel of the Lord** (cf. comment on 34:7), the enemy should be routed.

In v. 7 the metaphor changes to hunter and hunted—**net . . . pit . . . digged.** With no provocation on his part, David's foes (Saul and his supporters may well be in mind here) hunted him with all the secrecy and skill of a trapper. But evil is self-destructive, and the hidden **net** will snare the hunter himself **(8).** In the phrase **at unawares,** Moffatt sees the meaning, Let him be "surprised by ruin!" **Into that very destruction let him fall** has been interpreted, "With destruction let him fall into it" (Berk.).

The section closes with a vow of thanksgiving typical of the closing of most psalms of lament. The Psalmist expects a divine intervention so that his **soul shall be joyful in the Lord (9)**, rejoicing **in his salvation.** His **bones** (cf. comment, 34:20) **shall say, Lord, who is like unto thee,** delivering **the poor** from his **strong** despoilers **(10)**?

2. Peril (35:11-18)

David returns to the recital of his peril. He was the object of lying slander **(11)**; his good was repaid with evil **to the spoiling (12)**—literally, "bereaving, stripping or impoverishing"—**of my soul.** Nor was the attitude of his enemies in any way a reflection of his own. **When they** had been **sick (13)**, he had worn **sackcloth** —traditional symbol of mourning—and had fasted and prayed for them. **My prayer returned into mine own bosom** may be interpreted either as one with head deeply bowed on his bosom in prayer or as one who recognizes that his prayers had not reached the Lord because of the rebellion of those for whom he prayed Kirkpatrick, probably better, suggests that, though the prayers had not benefited those for whom they were offered, they had returned in a measure of blessing to the one who prayed.[98] David's whole conduct had been that of **friend** and **brother (14)**; he had been as concerned **as one that mourneth for his mother.**

Yet these very people **rejoiced** in the Psalmist's **adversity** when conditions were reversed **(15). The abjects gathered**

[98]*Op. cit.,* p. 180.

themselves together is a phrase that has baffled the translators. **Abjects** is an obsolete English term for outcasts. Various suggestions have been made. ASV marg. and Anchor give "smiters"; RSV is "cripples"; Berk. renders it "slanderers." The general sense is clear. Innocent of wrongdoing, the poet is betrayed by those whom he deemed his friends, who turned on him with slanderous lies. **Gnashed upon** (16) is a figure of speech. Harrison interprets it, "Tearing my reputation to shreds incessantly."

This section also closes with prayer and promise. **Lord, how long?** (17) is the cry of a soul beset with trouble. God seems to be but an onlooker. **Rescue . . . my darling** is literally "my only one," in the sense of his life. **The lions** represent his savage opponents. The vow, on condition of deliverance, is for **thanks in the great congregation** (18) and **praise . . . among much people.** The term **great congregation** means the multitude of worshipers. **Much people** is literally "a mighty nation."

3. *Prospect* (35:19-28)

Although the Psalmist returns to his plaint and prayer, it is in somewhat calmer tone. He is concerned lest his enemies **wrongfully** (falsely) **rejoice over** his misfortunes (19), and **wink with the eye** in satisfaction with their causeless malice. The general conduct of these foes is to **devise deceitful matters against them that are quiet in the land** (20); they hatch "crafty plots against the peaceable" (Moffatt). In scorn, **they opened their mouth wide** (21), exclaiming with satisfaction, **Our eye hath seen** the fall of the object of our envy.

David appeals to the Lord to render **judgment in righteousness** (22-24). He is concerned that the evil designs against him do not succeed (25), but that his enemies be **brought to confusion** (26). On the other hand, he desires that those who **favour my righteous cause** (27) may rejoice at the evidence that **the Lord . . . hath pleasure in the prosperity of his servant.** The customary vow of thanksgiving concludes the psalm (28).

Psalm 36: WICKEDNESS AND WISDOM, 36:1-12

Psalm 36 is one of the wisdom psalms, with a characteristic portrayal of the two contrasting ways of life, the way of wickedness and the way of wisdom. The title dedicates the psalm "to the chief Musician" and identifies it as "a psalm of David the servant of the Lord," as in the introductory note to Psalm 18.

1. *The Corruption of the Godless* (36:1-4)

Verses 1-4 portray the character of the godless man who makes evil his deliberate choice. **The transgression of the wicked saith** (1) is described by Oesterley: "The personification of Transgression, as here set forth, is unique in the *Psalms*. It is represented as a demon who whispers temptation into the heart of him who is prepared to listen, i.e., the sinner. The reference here is not to atheism, as in Ps. 53:1: 'The fool hath said in his heart, There is no God' (Ps. 14:1); it is even worse, for while the existence of God is acknowledged, disregard for his own honour is imputed to him."[99] **Within my heart** should probably be read as with the LXX, "within his heart." The self-satisfaction of the wicked man is reflected in **flattereth himself** (2). **Until his iniquity be found to be hateful** may be understood either, as with the KJV and Berk., that the wicked person's complacency will be shattered when the results of his sins come back upon him; or, as with RSV and Moffatt, that the wicked person deceives himself with the thought that his iniquity will never be found out. The total depravity of the soul sold out to sin is described in vivid terms: **The words of his mouth are iniquity and deceit** (3) . . . **left off to be wise, and to do good. . . . deviseth mischief** (*avon,* iniquity, corruption) **upon his bed** (4) . . . **setteth himself in a way** (takes a course) **that is not good** . . . **abhorreth not** (in the sense of actually delighting in) **evil.** "Evil he never shuns" (Anchor).

2. *The Character of God* (36:5-9)

From evil men, the thought of the Psalmist turns to the adorable character of the Lord. God's **mercy, faithfulness** (5), **righteousness,** and **judgments** (6; *mishpat,* decisions, ordinances) are the basis of the grace that **preservest man and beast.** Because of the excellence of God's **lovingkindness** (7; *chesed*— mercy, enduring or steadfast love, grace; cf. 17:7, comment), **men put their trust under the shadow of** His **wings.** Here is a familiar and beautiful metaphor of protection and care (91:4; Matt. 23:37). Abundant satisfaction is assured those who partake of the

[99]*Op. cit.,* p. 219.

good things God provides, and who learn to enjoy what is pleasing to Him (8). **Fatness** here means "abundance" (RSV).

> *For life's own fountain is within thy presence,*
> *and in thy smile we have the light of life* (9, Moffatt).

3. *Continuance in Grace* (36:10-12)

The psalm concludes with a prayer for continuance in **lovingkindness** (10; *chesed,* as in 7) and **righteousness** to those who **know** the Lord and are **upright in heart.** The Psalmist prays, **Let not the foot of pride** (the insolent) **come against me** (11), in the sense of trampling him down. But **the workers of iniquity** (12) shall be **cast down** never more **to rise.**

Psalm 37: THE RIGHTEOUS AND THE WICKED, 37:1-40

Psalm 37 is another wisdom psalm (cf. intro. to Psalm 36). Titled simply "A psalm of David," it is one of three (cf. 49, 73) dealing with the ever-perplexing problem of the prosperity of the wicked. Much of the wisdom literature (in particular, the Book of Job) is given to pondering this theme. Here the suggestion is made that the prosperity of the wicked is but temporary. The key to the psalm is its opening injunction, "Fret not."

This is another alphabetical or acrostic psalm, with the added feature that each successive letter of the Hebrew alphabet begins alternate lines, resulting in two lines under each letter. Most of the pairs of verses throughout are complete and self-contained, much like the individual proverbs in Prov. 10:1—22:16. While no completely satisfactory outline is possible, four major divisions may be noted and described as: Commitment (1-11); Catastrophe (12-22); Confidence (23-31); and Contrast (32-40).

1. *Commitment* (37:1-11)

The Psalmist throughout this section addresses himself to the righteous soul perplexed by the inequities of life (cf. 7). His key thought is that commitment to God contributes to contentment and serenity even in the face of the contradictions of experience. The faithful are not to **fret** over or be **envious** of **evildoers** or **the workers of iniquity** (1). These **shall soon be cut down** to **wither** like **the** grass or **the green herb** (2; plant). Lodging and food are sure to those who **trust in the Lord, and do good** (3).

Those **who delight . . . in the Lord** (4) shall have **the desires** of their hearts—a promise as sweeping as John 14:13 and 15:7, and based on the fact that those whose delight is in the Lord will desire His will above all else. The committed way (5), the vindication of God's leadings (6), a calm **rest in the Lord** (7), and a refusal to seek self-vindication (8) are the essentials of a godly life. **Commit thy way** (5) is literally, "Roll thy way upon the Lord." **Righteousness as the light** (6) suggests that, as the sun grows brighter through the day, the righteous cause of God's people will be more and more vindicated as time goes by. **Fret not thyself in any wise to do evil** (8) should be read with Moffatt, "Fret not—it only leads to evil." The Anchor Bible renders it, "Be not wrought up, it only brings harm." Fretfulness, impatience, and envy are snares of the devil.

The solution of the Psalmist to the problem of evil men prospering while the righteous suffer is indicated again in 9-10, as it was in 2. The disparities of life are but temporary. Evil will soon receive its just reward. In contrast, **those that wait upon the Lord** (9), and **the meek** (11) **shall inherit the earth** (cf. Matt. 5:5). They shall live **in the abundance of peace.**

2. Catastrophe (37:12-22)

In all but two verses of this section, the disasters awaiting evil men are described. **The wicked** plot **against the just** and rage against them (12); but **the Lord shall laugh at** them (13), for their judgment **day is coming. The sword** of the wicked, **drawn** (14) against the godly, **shall enter into their own heart** (15) and their weapons will be shattered. **Upright conversation** (14) means upright conduct. The **righteous man** may have but **little** (16), yet this **is better than** all the wealth of the **wicked** put together. **The arms** (a metaphor for "strength") **of the wicked shall be broken** (17); **but the Lord** supports the righteous. Moffatt translates v. 18, "The fortunes of the upright are the Eternal's care, and their possessions last for ever." In hard times, God will supply their need (19; cf. Phil. 4:19), the best security earth or heaven can know. **The wicked** are as transient as **the fat of lambs** (20), i.e., the smoke of a burning sacrifice. They prosper through dishonest business, while **the righteous** (21) deem it "more blessed to give than to receive" (cf. Acts 20:35). The final outcomes of life depend upon man's relationship with

231

his Maker and whether one **be blessed of him** or **cursed of him** (22).

3. *Confidence* (37:23-31)

As the preceding section was preoccupied with the catastrophe awaiting the wicked, the present section gives major attention to the confident assurance of the righteous. The wicked are mentioned but once (28). **The steps of a good man are ordered by the Lord** (23). George Muller of Bristol used to say that this also means "the *stops* of a good man"—those unexplained providences that may lay the best of men "on the shelf" for a time. Verse 24 is strikingly translated by Moffatt, "He may fall, but he never falls down, for the Eternal holds him by the hand." The Psalmist is personal witness to the unfailing providences of God (25). **His seed** (25, 26, 28) would be his children. Through all the vicissitudes and changes of life, it shall be well with God's people (28-30). The righteous man is **merciful,** he is liberal (26), and he lives right (27). His very conversation is wise and just (30). The secret is, **The law of his God is in his heart** (31; cf. Jer. 31:33; Heb. 10:16); **none of his steps shall slide** (i.e., "His feet never slip," Anchor).

4. *Contrast* (37:32-40)

The stark contrast between the present attitudes and future destinies of the righteous and the wicked has run throughout the psalm. The contrast is climaxed in this concluding section. **The wicked** oppose **the righteous** at every turn (32), but **the Lord** rescues His own and does not **condemn** His saints when they are wrongly **judged** by men (33). God's faithful servants are encouraged to **wait on the Lord, and keep his way** (34). They will yet see the justice of the Lord. As the Psalmist drew on his own past experience to confirm God's providential care for His people (25), he now draws on his observation to illustrate the passing of the temporary power of the wicked (35-36). One historian summarized "the evolution of a dictator" in three words: Hero, Nero, Zero. **Green bay tree** (35) is interpreted by several modern translations as a "cedar of Lebanon." The contrasting outcomes of life for the righteous and the wicked are given in 37-38 (cf. Rom. 6:23). The Lord is to His people (1) **salvation;** (2) **strength in the time of trouble;** (3) **help** and deliverance—**because they trust in him** (39-40).

Psalm 38: THE PRAYER OF THE PENITENT, 38:1-22

Psalm 38 is the third penitential psalm (cf. 6, 32). It is entitled "A psalm of David, to bring to remembrance" or "for memorial," a phrase found again in the title of Psalm 70. Its theme is the intolerable burden of sin and guilt. Along with Psalms 6, 51, and 32, it is traditionally related to the sin of David with Bath-sheba. Delitzsch suggests that the chronological order of the four psalms so related would be 6, 38, 51, and 32.[100] Morgan comments, "The circumstances of the singer were most distressing. He was suffering from some terrible physical malady, deserted by his friends, and persecuted by his enemies. The deepest bitterness of his soul was caused by his overwhelming sense of his moral pollution. He recognized that all his sufferings were the rebukes and chastisements of Jehovah for his sin. This sense of sin crushed him and in his distress he cried out to Jehovah."[101]

1. Punished for His Sin (38:1-8)

The Psalmist is sick in soul and body. Both kinds of sickness he sees as the direct result of his sin. Particularly does he feel his illness as the Lord's wrathful rebuke and chastening (1-3). That sickness by no means always results from personal wrongdoing we know from Job 2:7-10. That it sometimes does, we know from I Cor. 11:30 and Jas. 5:15. **Mine iniquities are gone over mine head** (4), or, "My iniquities are overwhelming me" (Moffatt). The load was **too heavy** to carry. **My wounds stink and are corrupt** (5)—cf. Isa. 1:5-6. Deeply **troubled, mourning** (6), **feeble and sore broken** (8), he cries out in his agony. The language here expresses in vivid metaphor the corruption of sin. **I have roared by reason of the disquietness of my heart** has been translated, "I groan because of the tumult of my heart" (RSV).

2. Forsaken by His Friends (38:9-14)

Adding to the penitent's distress is the fact that his friends and relatives forsook him, and his enemies rallied to take advantage of his condition. He addresses his **desire** and his **groaning** directly to the **Lord** (9). **My heart panteth** (10)—"throbbeth" (ASV), "beats fast" (Berk.). The Psalmist feels forsaken by

---

[100]Cf. quotation to this effect in Kirkpatrick, *op. cit.*, p. 198.
[101]*Op. cit.*, p. 235.

lovers ("loved ones," Berk.) and **friends (11)** and beset by foes
(12). Because of his sense of guilt he is as one who cannot hear
and he cannot speak out in his own defense **(13-14).**

3. *Pleading for Salvation* (38:15-22)

"Man's extremity is God's opportunity." At the end of himself, David cries, "I am ready to fall" (17, RSV). Beyond the
help of others, he turns with his whole heart to the Lord. He
will no longer hold back from expressing penitent sorrow for sin:
I will declare mine iniquity (18). Although he had sinned, he
had not cut himself off from return to God. Like the prodigal son
in Luke 15:11-24, the Psalmist had lost his way, but he had not
forgotten his address: **I follow the thing that good is (20).** He
closes on the urgent note of petition: **Make haste to help me, O
Lord my salvation (22).**

Psalm 39: ANOTHER PENITENTIAL PRAYER, 39:1-13

Psalm 39 is properly a sequel to 38, although not technically
classified as a penitential psalm. William Taylor speculates that
39 is not included among the penitentials because the Psalmist's
sense of personal sin seems less prominent than his feeling of the
pathos of human life. "His sin he acknowledges, but he sees it
in relation to the unutterable tragedy of man's brief and shadowy
existence, a passing phenomenon in the world. Short as his poem
is, he has the skill to reveal, or to suggest, the variety of moods
which his reflections invoke—faith, rebellion, despair, penitence,
resignation, and trust.[102]

The title dedicates the psalm to "the chief musician Jeduthun," whose name also occurs in the titles of 62 and 77. Jeduthun is found along with Heman and Asaph as one of the directors
of the Temple music (I Chron. 16:41; 25:1; etc.). The psalm is
credited to David.

1. *Silence and Speech* (39:1-5)

Possibly convicted in his own heart of speaking against God,
the Psalmist held himself to suffering in silence **(1-2).** But **the
fire** of his strong emotion was too fierce to be restrained **(3).**
He therefore addresses his desire to the Lord, that He may **make
him know** his **end, and the measure of his days (4)—how frail I**

---

[102]*Op. cit.,* 4:204.

am. His days were but **as an handbreadth** (5), as nothing in the sight of God. **Verily every man at his best state is altogether vanity** is translated by Berk., "Surely, all mankind, so self-confident, is as a breath." **Selah**—cf. comment on 3:2.

2. *Surrender* (39:6-11)

The struggle to amass **riches** is sheer folly—a **vain shew** (6). The Psalmist sees his hope as surrender to the deeper purposes of his affliction (7-11). He connects deliverance from his transgressions with removal of the physical illness he had suffered.

> *Thou chastenest mortal man, in punishing his guilt,*
> *eating away his comeliness like a moth—*
> > *man is no better than an empty breath!* (11, Moffatt)

Selah—cf. comment on 3:2.

3. *Supplication* (39:12-13)

The last two verses are strong supplication that God will hear His servant's **prayer,** his **cry,** and be moved by his **tears** (12); there is an ascending intensity in petition. **Stranger and sojourner** were technical terms for what we would call "resident aliens," enjoying the hospitality of the land without ownership (Exod. 22:21). The idea seems to be that David and his forebears were the guests of God and, according to Eastern custom, entitled to His protection and provision. Feeling the urgency of his need, he prayed, **O spare me, that I may recover strength, before I go hence, and be no more** (13). For the OT concept of life after death, cf. comments on 6:5; 11:7.

Psalm 40: The Nature of True Worship, 40:1-17

Psalm 40 appears to be a combination of two independent songs, since vv. 13-17 are practically identical with Psalm 70. Both are ascribed to David and dedicated to the chief musician. Because of the NT use of vv. 6-8 (Heb. 10:5-9), the psalm may be typed as Messianic; that is, referring at least in part to Christ. For this reason, it is commonly used in liturgical churches in the readings for Good Friday.

1. *Song* (40:1-5)

The first section of the psalm is a song of praise to God for answered prayer. David recalls his patient waiting **for the Lord**

(1) and God's answer. The Lord's saving act for the Psalmist lifted him **out of an horrible pit** (2; lit., a roaring pit), the bottom of which was **miry clay** (a quagmire, or even quicksand), and put his **feet upon a rock.** Such deliverance called for a **new song** (3) of **praise unto our God.** These verses are the basis of H. J. Zelley's well-known gospel song "He Brought Me Out." Happy is the man who makes **the Lord his trust** (4). **Respecteth not** is literally "has not turned to." The song of praise merges into a hymn of adoration in praise of the **wonderful works** (5) of God and His **thoughts** (benevolent purposes) for His people. Some have amended the Hebrew text of **they cannot be reckoned up in order** to read, "There is none like thee" (cf. RSV). However, as it stands, it suggests that the number and wonder of God's purposes for His people are so great that no human mind can "set them in order," or figure up the total—**they are more than can be numbered.**

2. *Submission* (40:6-12)

In its original context, this is a noble expression of the prophetic insight that God was more concerned with obedience and submission to His will for all of life than He was with the sacrifices and offerings prescribed in the OT cult. Many have read into these and similar statements in the prophets (e.g., Isa. 1:11-15; Mic. 6:6-8) a rejection of the divinely ordered Temple worship. But such was not the case. The objection was to sacrifice without sincerity, ritual without real righteousness.

However, to Christians, these words will always have a Messianic meaning (Heb. 10:5-7). Their final fulfillment is in David's Greater Son, excepting only v. 12 (*q.v.*). **Mine ears hast thou opened** (6)—for the variation in Hebrews, cf. BBC, Vol. IX, p. 118. **In the volume of the book** (7) is literally "in the roll of the book," ancient books being made in the form of rolls or scrolls. The speaker delights in the will of God, and declares His **righteousness** and grace abroad (9-10). In view of this, he asks continual preservation through God's **lovingkindness and . . . truth** (11). **Innumerable evils** (*raoth;* 12) is the broadest term in Hebrew for the bad, hard, or harmful in life. **Mine iniquities** —literally in the case of the Psalmist; figuratively in the case of the Saviour, who "bare our sins in his own body on the tree" (I Pet. 2:24).

3. *Supplication* (40:13-17)

These verses, with minor changes, comprise Psalm 70. The Psalmist prays for deliverance, **help** (13), vindication in the face of scorn (14-15), and blessing for the people of God (16). **Confounded** (14) is "confused" or "baffled." On **Aha, aha** (15), cf. comment on 35:21. **Desolate for a reward of their shame** (15) means desolate as a recompense for their shameful behavior. In spite of his poverty and need, he can say, **The Lord thinketh upon me** (17)—designs good for me; for God is both **help** and **deliverer. Make no tarrying,** as in 13, means, "Make haste."

Psalm 41: BENEVOLENCE AND BETRAYAL, 41:1-13

As with seventeen other psalms of Book I, Psalm 41 is dedicated "to the chief Musician." It is also titled, "A psalm of David." The psalm is in main a song of lament, but actually deals with such varied subjects as the value of charity, penitence for sin, oppression from enemies, betrayal by friends, and prayer for healing. It is no wonder that some have questioned the unity of the psalm. However, as Oesterley observes, "The absence of a strictly logical sequence of thought, noticeable in some other psalms of similar nature, is a mark of realism, and shows how very human the psalmists were."[103]

1. *Compassion* (41:1-3)

These verses describe the blessedness of those who have compassion on and consideration for **the poor.** While the language is general, David probably is reflecting his own attitude toward those who were in need of his help. Deliverance (1), preservation, blessing (2), and strength (3) are among the rewards for benevolence. Concern for the poor is one of the consistent notes in the OT (e.g., Lev. 19:9-10; 23:22; Deut. 24:19; etc.). **Thou wilt make all his bed in his sickness** is literally, "Thou wilt turn his bed in his sickness," i.e., turn his sickbed into one of health and restoring rest.

2. *Contrast* (41:4-9)

There are two stanzas in this section, each of which contrasts the treatment the Psalmist received in his hour of need with that which he had given to others. Verses 4-6 recount a time of sickness, with prayer for healing, and confession of sin (4). As before, his **enemies** gloated in his illness, and awaited with antici-

[103]*Op. cit.,* p. 238.

pation his death (5). Even those who came to see him, in pretense of concern, spoke **vanity** (6), that is, falsehood, in a hypocritical profession of their desire for his recovery.

The second stanza is particularly pathetic in its recital of betrayal. A "whispering campaign" was started against him. **They devise my hurt** (7); i.e., they were plotting evil. **Cleaveth fast unto him** (8) has been interpreted, "courses in his veins" (Moffatt). **Mine own familiar friend** (9) was perhaps, as M'Caw supposes, Ahithophel (II Sam. 15:12, 31).[104] **Did eat of my bread** expresses the obligation that custom placed upon a guest who accepted Oriental hospitality. **Lifted up his heel against,** perhaps in the sense of using his nearness to trip him (so Moffatt translated, "trips me up heavily"). The verse is quoted in John 13:18 in reference to the betrayal of Jesus by Judas.

3. Cry and Confidence (41:10-13)

A closing prayer and an expression of faith conclude the psalm. The Psalmist prays for healing, **that I may requite them** (10). This is not the usual way of expressing a desire for the punishment of evildoers. Usually, vengeance is left to God. However, if the background of this psalm be Absalom's insurrection, David, as king, could well feel it his duty to administer justice to those who betrayed him. Even survival, under the circumstances, was a hint of divine favor (11). In God's smile was his strength (12). **Settest me before thy face for ever** has been rendered "settling me for ever in thy presence" (Moffatt).

Verse 13 is a doxology added to close Book I, as in the case of each of the other books except Book V, for which Psalm 150 serves as the doxology. Snaith suggests that it "may well have been used, though at a later period, at the conclusion of each psalm, and is probably the ultimate origin of the present-day custom of concluding with the *"Gloria."*[105] God's blessedness is **from everlasting, and to everlasting**—from eternity past to eternity future, without beginning and without end. **Amen, and amen,** is the response of the congregation, "So is it," or, "So let it be"—intensified by being repeated. **Amen** is derived from a Hebrew term meaning "true, faithful." It was carried over directly into the Greek of the NT, where it is sometimes translated into English by "verily" or "truly." Usually it is not translated, but comes into our English by simple transliteration from both the Hebrew of the OT and the Greek of the NT.

---

[104]*Op. cit.,* p. 441.   [105]*Hymns of the Temple,* p. 14.

Section **II** *Book Two: Psalms of the Temple*

Book II of the Psalms includes 42—72. Of the thirty-one psalms it contains, only eighteen are attributed to David—contrasting with Book I, in which David is the only author named (cf. Intro.). Book II is part of what is known as the "Elohistic psalter," since the consistent name for the Deity is *Elohim,* "God," rather than *Yahweh,* "the Lord" or Jehovah (cf. Intro.). A major subgrouping is 42—49, inscribed "to [or for] the sons of Korah." Norman Snaith has made the intriguing suggestion that this group may have become dislocated when the collection was finally made. If Psalms 42—50 are lifted out and placed between Psalms 72 and 73, all of the "Psalms of Asaph" (cf. introductions to Psalm 50 and to Book III) are brought together, and follow immediately after the "Psalms of the Sons of Korah."[1]

Psalms 42—43: The Deep Longings of the Soul, 42: 1—43: 5

There is virtually unanimous opinion among commentators that originally Psalms 42 and 43 were one poem. Several existing Hebrew manuscripts combine them, and Psalm 43 is the only psalm in Book II which does not have a title. The total poem was a psalm of lament, and 42:5, 11 and 43:5 are identical verses which serve as a sort of refrain throughout the whole. Similar ideas run throughout, and the phrase, "Why go I mourning because of the oppression of the enemy?" (42:9) is repeated in 43:2. We shall consider them as a single production.

The title of Psalm 42 contains the familiar phrase, "To the chief Musician." It also describes the psalm as "Maschil" (cf. intro. to Psalm 32), "for the sons of Korah," who appear in I Chron. 9:19; 26:1, 19 as composing a guild of Temple servants. Heman, one of the Korahites (I Chron. 6:33-38), was the ancestor of a group of Temple singers organized by David (I Chron. 15:17; 16:41-42; 25:4-5). In all, eleven psalms contain reference in their superscriptions to "the sons of Korah" (in addition to those of this immediate group, cf. 84, 85, 87, 88).

[1]*Op. cit.,* pp. 14-17.

Morgan writes of Psalm 42: "This is the song of an exile and, moreover, of an exile among enemies who have no sympathy for his religious convictions. He cries out after God with all the intensity of one who knows God and cares supremely for the honor of God's name. His greatest grief is their mocking inquiry after his God. By contrast he remembers being in the midst of worshiping multitudes, their leader and companion."[2]

Psalms 42—43 divide into three sections, each closing with the same refrain.

1. *Separation* (42:1-5)

The longing of the poet's soul for communion with God is so keen that it is described as the thirst of **the hart** (1; deer) for a refreshing drink from a mountain stream.

> *Like as the hart, athirst in desert dreary,*
> *Pants for the brooklet and the soft green sod,*
> *So doth my soul, with toil and sorrow weary,*
> *Yearn for the presence of the living God.*[3]

Norman Snaith comments: "The psalmist is speaking of the anxious craving for fellowship with God of the man who once has known that fellowship. Here his craving is directly associated with the worship of God in His sanctuary. Those people, then or now, who are lackadaisical about attendance at church have never known what it really means to worship God. The man who knows in his own personal experience something of the joy of fellowship with God is not lackadaisical about any opportunity of renewing that fellowship, whether it be in private devotions or in public worship. In the last resort no enticement to be present in church is of avail other than that soul-hunger which can be fed only with the Bread of Heaven. Such a man cannot keep away. His own soul-hunger will drive him thither."[4]

The living God (2) appears for the first time here in the Psalms. The phrase is most descriptive of the OT concept of the true God. It is used in natural contrast with idols, who were vain and empty beings, "dead" in every sense of the word. **Come**

---

[2]*Op. cit.,* p. 236.

[3]J. Lewis Milligan, "Where Is Thy God?" *Masterpieces of Religious Verse,* ed. James Dalton Morrison (New York: Harper and Brothers, Publishers, 1948), p. 141. Used by permission.

[4]*Op. cit.,* pp. 33-34.

and appear before God refers to the Temple, the place designated as His abode. There is no explanation why the poet should
have been exiled, apparently to Mount Mizar, within sight of the
peaks of Hermon (see map 1), on the east side of the Jordan (6).
This was the area to which David fled during the rebellion of
Absalom. The reason may be the accusations of deceitful and
unjust men (43:1).

Tears have been my meat (3), means, "Instead of eating I
have wept." **Day and night** is the common expression for constantly or continually. Among his burdens were the taunts and
accusations of those around him, **Where is thy God?** To all appearances, God himself had forsaken His servant. The recollection of better days was also a burden to bear. **Pour out my soul
in me** has been interpreted, "My soul is melting with secret
sorrow" (Moffatt). The refrain, repeated in 11 and 43:5, expresses the hope and conviction that a reversal of his fortune will
come through **the help of his countenance** (5), i.e., God's face
turned in favor toward His own.

2. *Condemnation* (42:6-11)

The Psalmist returns to his lament, with greater emphasis
upon the fact that his enemies had unjustly condemned him. For
Hermonites and **hill Mizar** (6), cf. comment on v. 2. **Deep calleth
unto deep at the noise of thy waterspouts** (7) means either, "Soul
wants to commune with soul, spirit with spirit" (Berk., fn.); or,
as Moffatt, "Flood follows flood, as thy cataracts thunder, thy
breakers and billows are surging over me." The latter fits best
in the context. In his desperate straits, the exile sees a ray of
light (8) and determines to press his prayer before **God,** his **rock**
(9), his Refuge and Strength. **As with a sword in my bones** (10)
is literally "with a shattering in my bones," crippling him and
threatening his life. **While they say** (10), cf. v. 3. For 11, cf. 5.
Note that "the help of his countenance" (5) becomes **the health
of my countenance, and my God** (11).

3. *Restoration* (43:1-5)

Through a continued note of lament, the strain of hope grows
stronger. The Psalmist calls upon the Lord to **judge** (with the
sense of vindicating) him, and to take up his **cause against an
ungodly nation** (1). The expression **deceitful and unjust man**
is probably to be understood as a generalized statement of the

source of his trouble, rather than the specific indictment of a particular individual enemy. For v. 2, cf. 42:9. Verse 3, **O send out thy light and thy truth: let them lead me,** is remembered for its musical setting by Charles Gounod. **Thy holy hill** is literally "the mountain of thy holiness"; **thy tabernacles** would be "thy dwelling places." When vindication comes, the Psalmist anticipates first returning to **the altar of God** (4) in the Temple. **God my exceeding joy** is rendered by Moffatt "my joy and delight." For **harp** (*kinnor*) cf. comment on 33:2. For 5, cf. comments on 42:5 and 11.

Psalm 44: FAITH AND FACT, 44:1-26

Oesterley describes this psalm as the lament of one caught "between his theology and the facts of life."[5] Like Psalm 42, it bears a superscription dedicating it "to the chief Musician for the sons of Korah" and identifying it as a *Maschil* (cf. intro. to 42). The time was a period of national defeat and distress. Verse 11, if taken literally, would indicate a postexilic date, that is, some time after 586 B.C. If this be the case, it would represent the reflections of a soul still baffled by the paradox of God's chosen people afflicted and dispersed by heathen powers. The disaster which had come seems national rather than individual. It may well be the reaction of one innocent of personal wrongdoing who suffers with the guilty.

1. *The Past* (44:1-3)

The psalm begins with a retrospect, reviewing the wonderful works of God in behalf of the fathers. The poet speaks for people with a goodly heritage. What they had is clearly seen to be, not the result of their own efforts or what they deserved, but the unmerited favor of God.

> *For the land was not won by the sword of our fathers,*
> *nor the victory gained by their arm;*
> *thine was the hand and the arm,*
> *thine was the favour that smiled on them* (3, Moffatt).

2. *The Present* (44:4-8)

The Psalmist turns to the present with a strong statement of his faith in God. Past deliverance will not suffice for the present.

[5]*Op. cit.*, p. 250.

Jacob (4) is a poetic name for the entire nation of Israel. Neither **bow** nor **sword** (6) can save. Only God is sufficient. **Put them to shame** (7) means humbled or abased them. **In God we boast** (8) may be translated, "Of God we boast" (Moffatt). **Selah;** cf. comment on 3:2.

3. *The Problem* (44:9-14)

When the writer takes the measure of his people's circumstances, faith seems contradicted by hard fact. **But thou hast cast off** (9) represents an abrupt transition from history to present reality. The strong complaint of these verses reminds us of a Job or a Jeremiah. **They which hate us spoil for themselves** (10) has been rendered, "They who hated us take plunder for themselves" (Berk.). **Thou sellest thy people for nought** (12), i.e., surrender them into the hands of their enemies. **A reproach to our neighbours** (13) is rather "the taunt of our neighbors" (Amp. OT), the object of their scorn and derision. **A byword among the heathen** (14) is a phrase from the Hebrew of Deut. 28:37, included as one of the results of disobedience which would come upon the nation. Moffatt understands **a shaking of the head** as "jeered at by the nations."

4. *The Persecutors* (44:15-21)

In face of bitter persecution, the Psalmist urges innocence of wrongdoing. This is the heart of his problem, as it was with Job. God seems to have permitted persecution to come without cause. **Confusion** (15) is literally "dishonor," "disgrace" (Anchor). The **covenant** (17; *berith*) was the basis of the Hebrew faith, executed at Sinai and embracing the law as its condition from the human side. The writer claims for himself and his fellows not to have **dealt falsely with thy covenant;** i.e., they had given complete conformity to God's law, both outward and inward (18). **Sore broken us in the place of dragons** (19) is literally "crushed us in the place of jackals." This may refer either to the location of a decisive defeat, in the wilderness far from the haunts of men;[6] or the meaning may be figurative, "Thou hast crushed us and made us to dwell in wasted or waste places, which are the haunts of jackals."[7] **Covered us with the shadow of death** is literally "covered us over with a deadly

---

[6]Delitzsch, *op. cit.*, II, 83.   [7]Taylor, *op. cit.*, 4:232.

shade" or "deep darkness" (RSV). The light in which they had walked had given way to darkness and gloom. Since God knows **the secrets of the heart** (21), "the dark corners of the heart" (Anchor), He is challenged—again in the mood of Job—to indicate where even in heart or hidden purpose the people have sinned.

5. *The Petition* (44:22-26)

Using words taken by Paul to show the universality of persecution (22; cf. Rom. 8:36), the poet calls upon God to vindicate His people. God has seemed asleep (23); He has hidden His **face** and forgotten the plight of His people (24). As Norman Snaith explains, "The idea of forgetting is one of the figures of speech adopted by the psalmist in order to express the 'delayed action' of God. . . . God's remembrance therefore means that God is taking action. . . . Remembrance did not mean 'take note of and file away for reference for future action.' It means remember and take action now."[8] **Our belly** (body) **cleaveth unto the earth** (25); death itself is near. **Thy mercies' sake** (26) is on the ground of Thy faithful love (*chesed;* cf. comment on 17:7).

Psalm 45: The Bridegroom and His Bride, 45:1-17

This is one of the royal or kingly psalms with a strong Messianic meaning. It may be interpreted on two levels. There was an immediate and local application to the wedding of one of Israel's kings, much in the manner of the Song of Solomon. But there is a higher and universal application to the King of Kings and His spiritual bride, as is attested by the NT use of vv. 6-7 (Heb. 1:8-9).

The superscription includes five items. It dedicates the psalm "to the chief Musician upon Shoshannim," or "set to 'The Lilies,'" evidently a tune title which also occurs in the title of Psalm 69. The song is "for the sons of Korah," and is a *Maschil* or teaching poem (cf. intro. to Psalm 32). It is also identified as "a song of loves," or "a love song" (Moffatt, Smith-Goodspeed, RSV), a phrase not found elsewhere in the titles of the Psalms but descriptive of the character of this poem.

[8]*Op. cit.,* pp. 65-67.

1. *The Royal Bridegroom* (45:1-9)

The psalm opens with an introductory statement by the author concerning the inspiration for the poem which follows. **My heart is inditing** (1) means "my heart overflows with" (Berk.). **I speak of the things which I have made touching the king** is correctly understood as, "I address my verses to the king" (RSV). **Tongue is the pen of a ready writer** indicates "a skillful scribe," fluent and accurate.

The king is addressed and described in eulogy in vv. 2-9, all of which is most appropriate in relation to Christ (cf. intro. to the psalm). He is **fairer than the children of men** (2); **grace** (graciousness) marks His speech; He is **blessed by God . . . for ever;** He is **mighty,** with **glory** and **majesty** (3); His conquests are made with **truth and meekness and righteousness** (4); He is a conquering Warrior (5); His **throne** is eternal and His **sceptre** is righteousness (6); because He loves **righteousness** and hates **wickedness,** He is **anointed . . . with the oil of gladness** more than any other; His **garments** are fragrant as He comes from **the ivory palaces** (8); His retinue is composed of princesses, and His **queen** is arrayed **in gold of Ophir** (9). **Ride prosperously** (4), or triumphantly. **Thy right hand shall teach thee terrible things** is better, "Let Your right hand guide You to tremendous things" (Amp. OT). **Thy throne, O God** (6), understood in connection with the local application (see intro. to the psalm), is interpreted as "Your divine throne" (RSV), or, "God is thy throne."[9] The Messianic application in Heb. 1:8-9 makes this an unqualified statement of the deity of Christ. **A right sceptre** would be just and fair rule. **God . . . hath anointed thee** (7) to be King. **Anointed** is the term from which *Messiah* is derived. "Christ" is the Greek equivalent of *Messiah,* and also means **anointed. Myrrh . . . aloes, and cassia** (8) were all sources of fragrant perfumes in ancient times. **Whereby they have made thee glad** is literally, "Stringed instruments have gladdened thee." **Ophir** (9) was a noted source of gold, in either south Arabia or east Africa (cf. I Kings 9:26-28; Job 22:24).

2. *The Royal Bride* (45:10-15)

The Psalmist next addresses (vv. 10-12) and describes (13-15) the royal bride and her retinue. She is called upon to **forget her own people** and her **father's house** (10). **The king** will **desire**

---

[9]Barnes, *op. cit.,* II, 224.

her **beauty** and she will **worship** him (11). Others will bring gifts
and her **favour** will be sought (12). The twofold application
(cf. intro. to the psalm) is apparent here, as a princess becomes
a type of the Church. **The daughter of Tyre** has led to the highly
improbable identification of the king with Ahab, and his bride
with Jezebel![10] Tyre, the noted center for merchandise in the
ancient world, is to be the source of the gifts brought to honor
Israel's king and his bride.

The king's daughter is all glorious within (13) is probably
to be understood as, "All glorious is the king's daughter within
(the palace)" (Berk.). She is clothed in beautiful garments and
accompanied by her maids (14). **Gladness and rejoicing** mark
the entrance of the wedding party **into the king's palace** (15),
typical of the joy of the "marriage of the Lamb" (Rev. 19:7).

3. *The Royal Blessing* (45:16-17)

The concluding verses picture the blessedness of the royal
union. The future belongs to the **children** (16) of the king and
his bride. His **name** shall **be remembered in all generations** (17)
and be the object of **praise . . . for ever and ever**—words again
most fitting when applied to King Messiah.

Psalm 46: THE STRONG REFUGE, 46:1-11

Psalm 46 is the first of three poems with a common theme,
the greatness and adequacy of God now and for the future. Kirkpatrick calls the three "a trilogy of praise."[11] The present psalm
bears the familiar title, "To the chief Musician for the sons of
Korah," and in addition is labeled, "A Song upon Alamoth."
This designation is found only here in the psalms (although cf.
I Chron. 15:20), and possibly means "for soprano voices."[12] It
has come to be known as "Luther's Psalm," as the probable inspiration for his great hymn "A Mighty Fortress Is Our God."[13]
Oesterley and others think of this as an apocalyptic or eschatological psalm, representing "the destruction of the earth at the

---

[10]Oesterley, *op. cit.*, pp. 250-54; *et al.*   [11]*Op. cit.*, II, 253.

[12]*Ibid.*, p. xxv.

[13]Edwin McNeill Poteat, "Psalms 42—89" (Exposition), *The Interpreter's
Bible,* ed. George A. Buttrick, *et al.*, IV (New York: Abingdon Press, 1955),
240.

end of the present world-order."[14] The essence of apocalyptic is a fundamental belief in the final victory of God and the subjection of all nations to Him in acknowledgment of His sovereignty.

The psalm divides into three rather well-marked stanzas, each ending with *Selah.* A sort of refrain occurs in verses 7 and 11: "The Lord of hosts is with us; the God of Jacob is our refuge."

1. *The Protection of God* (46:1-3)

God's protecting presence and power are the source of His people's courage. **Though the earth be removed (2)** or "changed" (Heb.), and **the mountains be carried into the midst of the seas,** may either represent the apocalyptic destruction and renovation of the earth (cf. II Pet. 3:10-13) or may be a hypothetical statement of the most terrible disasters that could be imagined. In either case, people who find in God their **refuge and strength (1) will not . . . fear (2). Selah (3),** cf. comment on 3:2. The refrain of 7 and 11 may have been dropped from 3 in copying.[15]

2. *The Presence of God* (46:4-7)

God's presence **in the midst (5)** is assurance of safety. **A river, the streams whereof shall make glad (4),** cf. Ezek. 47:1-12; Rev. 22:1-2. **And that right early (5)** is literally "at the appearing of the morning." The morning of God's eternal day will see the final vindication of His people. On **The heathen raged (6),** cf. comment on 2:1. **The earth melted;** cf. II Pet. 3:10-12. **God . . . our refuge (7)** is in the Hebrew, "God . . . our high place." **Selah;** cf. comment on 3:2.

3. *The Power of God* (46:8-11)

Men are challenged to look upon **the works of the Lord (8).** In the last days, **wars shall cease (9;** cf. Isa. 2:2-4; Hos. 2:18; Mic. 4:1-3). In view of this, man's response is to **be still, and know (10)** that the Lord **is God** and **will be exalted among the heathen** and **in the earth.** For v. 11, cf. comment on 7.

Psalm 47: The Lord Is King of All, 47:1-9

Second of a "triology of praise" (cf. intro. to Psalm 46), this psalm is entitled simply, "To the chief Musician, A Psalm for the

---

[14]Oesterley, *op. cit.,* p. 254.   [15]Taylor, *op. cit.,* 4:241.

sons of Korah." Its theme is the sovereignty of God. As M'Caw states, "This festive hymn elaborates the words, 'I will be exalted in the earth,' which occur at the end of the previous Psalm. The main concept is that God, having come down from heaven in power and great might to deliver His people, is now returning to His throne. . . . The poem, therefore, has two themes closely interwoven. The first is a call to the peoples of the earth, regarded as assembled to acclaim Jehovah as king, to clap hands and shout (1). . . . The second theme is a description of the majesty of God."[16] Oesterley describes it as "the culminating act of the eschatological drama."[17]

1. *The Sovereign* (47:1-4)

All . . . people (1) are summoned to praise **the Lord most high** (2) who **is terrible** ("excites terror, awe and dread," Amp. OT), and **a great king over all the earth.** That God is King is a familiar OT theme (44:4; 48:2; 74:12; I Sam. 12:12; Isa. 41:21; 52:7-10). A number of commentators follow the lead of Sigmund Mowinckel[18] in identifying this psalm (together with 93, 96—99) as an "Enthronement Psalm." It is supposed that in postexilic times when they had no earthly king, the Jews observed their New Year's Day as a celebration of the Lord's enthronement to rule the nations for the coming year, a practice patterned after Babylonian New Year ceremonies in honor of their god Marduk. It must be noted, however, that there is no trace of such a ceremony either in the Bible or in other Jewish sources. That a psalm such as this would have particular appeal to a people who had lost their sovereignty may well be admitted. God was their **King,** and not only theirs but King of **the nations** as well (3).

He shall choose our inheritance for us, the excellency of Jacob whom he loved (4), may be translated, "He selects for us our inheritance, the pride of Jacob, whom He loves" (Berk.). **Selah;** cf. comment on 3:2.

2. *The Song* (47:5-9)

The fivefold repetition of **Sing praises** (6-7) is the key to this section of the psalm. The Lord has ascended **with a shout, and with the sound of a trumpet** (5). He is **the King of all the**

---

[16]*Op. cit.,* p. 445.   [17]*Op. cit.,* p. 258.
[18]Cited by Taylor, *op. cit.,* 4:245. Cf. Barnes, *op. cit.,* II, 233, *contra.*

earth (7), reigning **over the heathen** (8), sitting **upon the throne
of his holiness.** In v. 9 **the shields of the earth belong unto God**
is better "for the world's warriors belong to God" (Moffatt).

Psalm 48: GOD'S HOLY CITY, 48:1-14

The praise of Zion as the Lord's holy mount is the theme of
the third of the "triology of praise" (cf. intro. to Psalm 46). It is
called in the superscription, "A Song and Psalm for the sons of
Korah." Two major lines of interpretation have been given
the psalm. It has been understood in the context of some historical event such as the deliverance of Jerusalem from the
Assyrian assault of Sennacherib recorded in II Kings 18—19 and
Isaiah 36—37. Since Zion is presented as "the joy of the whole
earth" (2), the psalm has also been given an eschatological interpretation, as indicating Zion's place in the future kingdom of
the Messiah. Oesterley suggests that both may be accepted: "An
actual historical event forms the basis, and this is idealized and
presented as a picture of what will take place at the final consummation."[19]

In a Christian frame of reference, Zion stands as a type of
the Church, the "city of God" (cf. Heb. 12:18-24). What is said
about Zion as the site of Israel's Temple is true of the spiritual
temple which is the Church (Eph. 2:20-22; I Pet. 2:5-8).

1. *The Lord's Protection of His Own* (48:1-8)

God's greatness is a fit subject for His people's praise. **The
mountain of his holiness** (1; Zion) is beautifully situated. **On
the sides of the north** (2) is translated "high and fair on the
northern slope" (Moffatt). She is **the city of the great King.
God is known in her** as a **refuge** (3). Verses 4-6 may represent
the historical setting in which foreign kings planned assault but
were driven off in fear (cf. II Kings 19:35-36). God's control of
natural forces is such that He breaks **the ships of Tarshish with
an east wind** (7; cf. I Kings 22:48; Jonah 1:3-16). **Ships of
Tarshish,** literally, "refinery ships," were the largest and most
seaworthy vessels of OT times, and were engaged in trade with
Tarshish (Tartessus) in Spain. History and the teaching of the
fathers will be confirmed in experience: **God will establish** His
city **for ever** (8). **Selah,** cf. comment on 3:2.

[19]*Op. cit.,* p. 261

2. The Lessons to Be Learned (48:9-14)

God's protection of His city arouses thoughts of His **loving-kindness** (9). The statement, **According to thy name, O God, so is thy praise** (10), declares that the greatness of God's name and nature should encourage the highest of praise. **Zion** and her inhabitants should **rejoice** and **be glad, because of thy judgments (11)** executed against the enemy. The readers are called upon to **tell** (12; note well) the beauty and strength of Zion, that they **may tell it to the generation following (13)**. **Towers** (12) are vantage points for vision; **bulwarks** (13) are fortifications for defense; **palaces** are symbolic of the authority of the king and his decrees. **Our guide even unto death** (14) is a phrase subject to some textual problems in the original. The LXX reads "unto eternity," hence "evermore" (Moffatt) and "for ever" (RSV). In any case, the assurance is complete. There is no failure on the part of our heavenly Guide (cf. 23:2-6). "Our eternal and everlasting God—he will guide us eternally" (Anchor).

Psalms 49: DEATH THE GREAT LEVELLER, 49:1-20

The poem is a wisdom psalm concerned with the problem of the wicked who prosper and the righteous who are poor and afflicted. It is closely related in theme with Psalms 37 and 73. Psalm 37 had found a solution to this age-old puzzle in the conviction that the prospering of the wicked was only temporary. The author of this Psalm 49 carries it a step farther. The inequities of life may never be corrected here in this world. But death equalizes all. Rich and poor, high and low, prince and pauper, all come to the same end. When men once grasp the fact that riches hold no assurance for eternity, much of the problem disappears. "The fundamental idea is, that the pious have no ground to fear under such circumstances in this transitory world, because the rich man cannot with all his gold purchase exemption from death, but by his vanity and folly becomes more and more like mere brutes that perish."[20] "The money of the rich, before whom men are awed, can buy all that the world has to offer, but it cannot buy off death. They can offer no ransom great enough to extricate themselves from the common lot of men."[21] "It pro-

[20]John Forsyth, "Psalms XLII—L," *A Commentary on the Holy Scriptures,* ed. John Peter Lange (Grand Rapids: Zondervan Publishing House [reprint], n.d.), p. 312.

[21]Taylor, *op. cit.,* 4:255.

claims a very necessary truth which is more pointedly set forth in the Parable of the Rich Fool (Lk. 12:16-21)."[22]

1. Call to Consider (49:1-4)

The introduction is the familiar call of the wisdom writers for a hearing on the part of those they address (cf. Prov. 1:8; 2:1; etc.). **All** are called upon to **give** attention (1-2). **Wisdom** and **understanding** (3) are the concern of the writer as he speaks of **a parable** (4; *mashal,* also translated "proverb" or "wise saying, instruction") and explains his **dark saying** to the accompaniment **of the harp.** The expression **dark saying** "denotes (1) an enigma or riddle; (2) a parable or simile; (3) any profound or obscure utterance, a problem. . . . The prosperity of the godless was one of the great 'enigmas of life' to the pious Israelite, demanding a solution which could only be partially given before the fuller revelation of Christ 'brought life and immortality to light.' What he has learned on this perplexing question he will set forth in a poem accompanied by music."[23]

2. The Folly of Trusting Wealth (49:5-13)

The "riddle" is indicated in the question, **Wherefore should I fear in the days of evil?** (5) Much of the source of the puzzling inequities of life was the unscrupulous conduct of ungodly men. **When the iniquity of my heels shall compass me about** is better "when the iniquity of those who would supplant me surrounds me on every side" (Amp. OT). The answer is given in the Psalmist's recognition of the futility of placing confidence in **wealth** and **the multitude of . . . riches** (6). Money cannot **redeem his brother** (7) nor enable the rich man to **live for ever** (9). The parenthesis of 8 should be translated as by *The Berkeley Version,* "For such redemption of their life is costly and [money] can never suffice." Nothing less than the sacrifice of God's own Son could redeem the soul and give eternal life (I Pet. 1:17-21). All alike die, and all alike leave behind whatever they might have possessed (10; cf. Eccles. 2:18-19). Man's ultimate **folly** is to seek any kind of immortality in earthly things (11-13), such as naming his lands after himself. Moffatt's translation of 13 is helpful: "Such is the fate of the self-satisfied, the end of all whose faith is in themselves." **Selah;** cf. comment on 3:2.

---

[22]Oesterley, *op. cit.,* p. 267.   [23]Kirkpatrick, *op. cit., ad loc.*

3. *The Contrasting Hope of the Righteous* (49:14-15)

Death brings all man's glory to the dust (14). The righteous are assured of triumph **in the morning** of God's coming day. The hope of the righteous is redemption **from the power of the grave** (*Sheol,* the abode of the dead): for God **shall receive me** (15). This is one of the strong intimations of immortality in the Psalms. As Harold H. Rowley has commented, "What the psalmist is saying is that the inequalities of this life will be rectified in the next. The wicked may have good fortune here, but the miseries of Sheol are all that he can look forward to; whereas the righteous may have suffering here, but hereafter he will have bliss, for God will take him to himself. C. F. Burney says, 'The more I examine this psalm the more does the conviction force itself upon me that the writer has in view something more than the mere temporary recompense of the righteous during this earthly life.' With this view I find myself in the fullest agreement."[24]

4. *The False Value of Riches* (49:16-20)

There may be a temporary advantage in wealth, but it is not enough to cause one to devote the whole of life to its pursuit. **Be not thou afraid** (16), in the sense of fearing that ungodliness will really prove more profitable than piety. **His glory shall not descend** (17), since *Sheol,* the afterlife or place of the dead, was always thought of as being "down." The Hebrew term is probably derived from a root meaning "pit, hole, cavern," just as "hell" is derived from *holle,* "hole." **He blessed his soul** (18), the same fatal mistake of the rich fool (Luke 12:16-21), who supposed that his "much goods laid up for many years" could satisfy his soul. **Men will praise thee, when thou doest well to thyself,** better, "Praising himself for his prosperity" (Moffatt). **They shall never see light** (19), since *Sheol* was also thought of as a place of shadow and darkness.

> *Man with all his pomp but without insight*
> *is like the animals that perish* (20, Berk.) —

not that he has no existence beyond the time of death, but that he has no hope. The OT never thinks of death as an end of human existence. It is, however, an end of all that makes existence tolerable for the ungodly.

[24]*Op. cit.,* p. 171.

Psalm 50: GOD THE JUDGE OF ALL, 50:1-23

Psalm 50 is the first of twelve each entitled "A Psalm of Asaph," "to Asaph," or "for Asaph." The other eleven are grouped as Psalms 73—83 (cf. intro. to Book II for suggestion as to probable original placement of Psalm 50). Asaph is known from the historical books as the chief Temple musician under David (I Chron. 15:17-19; 16:4-5) and as an author of psalms (II Chron. 29:30). Leslie M'Caw notes: "Some of these cannot have been written by a man of David's time, e.g., Pss. lxxiv and lxxix are associated with the destruction of Jerusalem by the Babylonians. Hence the phrase 'to (of, or for) Asaph' is unlikely to refer to his authorship so much as to a certain style or school of psalmody."[25]

Scholars have noted in Psalm 50 the emphasis that became prominent in the prophetic writings of the OT on the inwardness of true religion and the futility of sacrifices without obedience and faith.[26] Vriezen says, "In Ps. 50 we meet with a singular case: the testimony of a poet who knows that the congregation in Israel lives by those sacrificial practices while he himself is convinced that God cannot be honoured with offerings but only with praise and thanks (verses 14-21). In this psalm we have apparently a clear echo of the prophetic teaching. The poet does not simply reject the offerings, but is conscious of something surpassing them. He stands in the transitional phase between the old and the new appreciation of the offerings and attempts to reconcile the two views."[27]

Morgan summarizes the lesson of this wisdom psalm: "Forgetfulness of God issues in gravest peril, while the remembrance which worships ensures the blessing of salvation . . . The wicked can have no part in such manifestation of God, and therein lie their chief sin and failure. This is a thought of most searching power. Our most heinous sin is not the act of wrong done, but the fact that such wrong incapacitates us from fulfilling our highest function of glorifying God, and showing forth His praise."[28]

---

[25]*Op. cit.*, p. 447.

[26]Cf. Taylor, *op. cit.*, 4:260-61; Oesterley, *op. cit.*, p. 267; Vriezen, *op. cit.*, p. 306.

[27]*Op. cit.*, p. 306.   [28]*Op. cit.*, p. 239.

1. Call (50:1-6)

The psalm opens with a call to recognize that God is Judge of all. **The mighty God** (1) is literally "the God of gods." **Called the earth** (*eretz*) in the sense of the inhabitants of the entire earth, as in Gen. 6:11; 9:13; Deut. 32:1; I Chron. 16:31; etc. (cf. also Luke 2:1). God's power and glory are manifest from **Zion** (2) in symbols of **fire** and **storm** (3). The call of God is to **judge his people** (4), in the sense of both condemning their evil and vindicating their faithfulness. **Gather my saints** (5) is "My faithful and holy ones," those who are in a **covenant** relationship with the Lord. God's declared **righteousness** (6) is His supreme qualification to be **judge himself.** For **Selah,** cf. comment on 3:2.

2. Correction (50:7-15)

The Lord's complaint against His people is not their failure to perform the ritual of the OT cult. Their **sacrifices** and **burnt offerings** (8) had been scrupulously given. **To have been continually before me** is better "are continuously before me" (RSV). God was not seeking their bullocks or their **goats** (9). **For,** He says, **every beast of the forest is mine, and the cattle upon a thousand hills** (10). The birds and the **beasts** of mountain and field belong to the Lord (11). He is not a beggar, to satisfy His "hunger" with **the flesh of bulls** or **the blood of goats** (12-13). The offering **God** desires is **thanksgiving** (14) and obedience **(pay thy vows),** prayer and to be glorified by His own (15). To recognize this, Jesus said, is to be "not far from the kingdom of God" (Mark 12:33-34).

3. Contrast (50:16-23)

The last section of the psalm is a stinging indictment of **the wicked** (16). **What hast thou to do to declare my statutes?** is more simply, "What right have you to report my laws?" (Moffatt) Such piety as they might profess was only in word, not in obedience to God's instruction and His words (17). They are condemned not only for the wrong they themselves do, but for a permissive attitude toward others who do evil (18; cf. Rom. 1:32). They are deceitful and slanderous in speech (19-20). Because God **kept silence** (21), i.e., did not immediately punish them, they impugned His character in their minds; cf. Eccles. 8:11. **Set them in order** would be to state the case against them. God challenges them, **Now consider this, ye that forget God, lest I tear you in pieces, and there be none to deliver** (22). There is still time to "remember . . . and repent" (Rev. 2:5). Those who offer **praise** (23) glorify God, and **salvation** is promised to those who live aright. **His conversation** means his whole way of life.

Psalm 51: PRAYER FOR PARDON AND PURITY, 51:1-19

Psalm 51 is the fourth of the "penitential psalms" (cf. Intro.), and in it the OT comes to its truest view of sin and its remedy.[29] As Perowne incisively says, "It is a prayer, first, for forgiveness, with a humble confession of sinful deeds springing from a sinful nature as their bitter root; and then for renewal and sanctification through the Holy Ghost."[30] The title indicates the Davidic authorship of the psalm, and relates it to his confession of his sin with Bath-sheba (cf. intro. to Psalm 32). This tragic episode in David's life seems to have given him a deep apprehension of the true nature of evil. Lying behind the guilt of his transgression he finds the deeper stain of a sinful nature with which he was born (5). Hence he utters this double prayer for a double cure.

The psalm is entirely addressed to God. Morgan writes: "The penitent soul cried for forgiveness on the basis of confession. Suddenly the intensity of conviction deepens as the act of sin is traced back to its reason in the pollution of the nature. This leads to a deeper cry. As the first was for pardon, the second is for purity, for cleansing of heart, and renewal of spirit. The prayer goes on to seek for the things which follow such cleansing, maintenance of fellowship, and consciousness of joy. Looking on in hope, the song anticipates that service of thanksgiving and praise which will issue from such pardon and purity."[31] Oesterley calls it "the most heart-searching of all the penitential psalms" and states, "For the realization of the sense of sin, set forth with unflinching candor, it has no equal in the Psalter."[32]

1. Pardon (51:1-4)

This psalm is not a studied theological treatise, but an impassioned cry from a deeply troubled heart. There is therefore

---

[29]Cf. C. Ryder Smith, *The Bible Doctrine of Salvation* (London: The Epworth Press, 1946), p. 62.

[30]*Op. cit.*, I, 411.   [31]*Op. cit.*, pp. 239-40.

[32]*Op. cit.*, pp. 270-71.

no careful analysis of the differences between sinful acts and the sinful nature, between the need for pardon and the call for purity. Yet there is a natural movement of thought from the cry for pardon, through insight into the deeper problem, on to prayer for purity and promise of praise and service. The **lovingkindness** and **tender mercies** (1) of **God** are the basis for the cry, **Blot out my transgressions.** David felt deeply the guilt of his conniving, lying, adultery, and finally murder. Behind these transgressions, he catches sight of their root and cause and prays for the Lord to **wash** him **throughly** (thoroughly) from his **iniquity** and to **cleanse** him from his **sin** (2). There is no masking or excusing the depth of his need (3). Although others had been greatly wronged, essentially all sin is seen to be against God, and God will be its Judge. The last part of 4 is better, "Yes, thou art just in thy charge, justified in thy sentence" (Moffatt).

2. Problem (51:5-9)

Conviction deepens to include not only what the Psalmist had done, but what he was by nature: **shapen in iniquity,** conceived **in sin** (5). Sinful tendencies and dispositions go back to a racial pollution, part of man's liability as springing from a fallen race. God desires **truth** (6; *emeth*, truthfulness, faithfulness, soundness, integrity) **in the inward parts** ("the inner self," Berk.). **In the hidden part thou shalt make me to know wisdom** has been translated, "Therefore teach me wisdom in my secret heart" (RSV).

Such insight leads to renewed prayer for purging and washing. **Hyssop** (7) was the sprig of desert shrub used to sprinkle the blood upon a leper for his cleansing and healing (Lev. 14:4; cf. Heb. 9:13-14; I John 1:7). **Wash me** is a striking expression in the original. Lawrence Toombs explains, "The Hebrew language has two words for 'wash.' The first is applied to washing the body, kitchen utensils, and, in general, any object that can be dipped in water or have water poured over it. The second is almost a specific word for washing garments by beating them with a stick or pounding them on a flat rock submerged in water. The psalmist deliberately chooses the second word, rejecting by implication the metaphor of the warm shower and the mild soap pleasantly rinsing away the dirt while the bather luxuriates. He knows that sin is so deeply entrenched in his nature that God

may literally have to beat it out of him."[33] **Whiter than snow,**
without even minute particles of dust or soot in the snowflakes
(cf. Isa. 1:18).

So bitter was the conviction of sin, it was like the pain of
bones . . . broken (8). Perowne writes, "As constituting the
strength and framework of the body, the crushing of the bones
[is] a very strong figure, denoting the most complete prostration,
mental and bodily."[34] God's intervention and action are the
Psalmist's only hope (9).

3. *Purity* (51:10-13)

The results of the sought-for purging and washing will be
the creation of **a clean heart** and the renewal of **a right spirit**
(10). **Create** "is used of the creative operation of God, bringing
into being what did not exist before. . . . It is not the restoration
of what was there before that he desires, but a radical change of
heart and spirit."[35] **Right spirit** is properly a "steadfast spirit"
(Berk.), "fixed and resolute in its allegiance to God, unmoved by
the assaults of temptation. Such a clean heart and steadfast
spirit, the condition of fellowship with God, the spring of a holy
life, can only come from the creative, life-giving power of God."[36]

Such a cleansing will assure God's **presence** and the abiding
fulness of His **holy spirit** (11). This is one of three times the OT
speaks of the Holy Spirit in that exact phraseology. The other
two are found in a similar context in Isa. 63:10-11. Purity will
also result in **the joy of thy salvation,** and the support of **thy free
spirit** (12), literally, "a willing spirit." A further result will be
the teaching of God's **ways** to **transgressors** and the conversion
of **sinners** (13; cf. John 16:7-11; Acts 1:8).

4. *Promise* (51:14-19)

The psalm concludes, as the penitentials customarily do, with
a promise of praise and thanksgiving. As in 50:7-15, the note of
the prophets is also sounded here. God cannot be appeased with
sacrifice and **burnt offering** (16). His **sacrifices . . . are a broken
spirit: a broken and a contrite heart** He will **not despise** (17).
At v. 18 the interest broadens to encompass **Zion** and **Jerusalem.**
Verse 19 shows that it was not ritual as such that was offensive
to God, but ritual without **righteousness.** God will be pleased

---

[33]*Op. cit.,* p. 178.   [34]*Op. cit.,* I, 420.
[35]Kirkpatrick, *op. cit., ad loc.*   [36]*Ibid.*

with the **burnt offering** and the sacrifice of **bullocks** when the ritual comes from right motives and is the expression of a loving and obedient heart.

Someone has said that the melody of this prayer hymn is dominated by five notes. (1) The mournful note of *sin*, 1-2. (2) The serious note of *responsibility*. David put no blame on anyone else, not even Bath-sheba. The abundant personal pronouns in the prayer indicate David's full honesty in the confession. (3) The decisive note of *repentance*. David renounced sin forever. (4) The glad note of *forgiveness and cleansing*, 7-14. (5) The certain note of *testimony*, 12-13, 15. God's grace can make out of the vilest sinner a flaming witness for Him (Earl C. Wolf).

Psalm 52: The Contrast of Sinner and Saint, 52:1-9

This is a wisdom psalm reminiscent in some ways of Psalm 1 in the sharp contrast into which it throws the wicked and the righteous. Its tone, however, is much sharper than Psalm 1, expressing as it does the resentment felt by the godly against those who have no fear of God, and giving expression to the doctrine of divine retribution.

Its title identifies it as a *maschil* (cf. intro. to Psalm 32), and associates it with the disastrous report of Doeg to Saul when David fled to the temporary sanctuary of Ahimelech in Nob (cf. I Sam. 21:1—22:19).

1. The Character and Fate of the Ungodly (52:1-5)

The psalm opens with a challenge to the **mighty man** (1) in his wickedness. **Mischief** is much too weak to convey the meaning of the Hebrew *ra*, a generic term for evil. Cf. Harrison, "Why do you boast of evil, you wicked tyrant?" **Deviseth mischiefs** (2) is a different word than in 1, meaning "destruction, ruin." The tongue of the evil man is like a **razor, working deceitfully.** For **Selah,** cf. comment on 3:2. Retribution is certain—the evil man shall be destroyed, plucked out, rooted **out of the land of the living** (5).

2. The Contrast of the Righteous (52:6-9)

The righteous . . . shall see (6) the disaster that falls upon the wicked, and shall be filled with awe. They will **laugh,** and utter a taunt with regard to **the man that made not God his**

strength; but trusted in the abundance of his riches (7). The righteous man will be like a green olive tree (8), flourishing and fruitful (cf. 1:3), trusting the eternal mercy of God, and praising Him (9). Moffatt renders it is good before thy saints as, "I will declare how good thou art, in [the] presence of thy followers."

Psalm 53: The Danger of Practical Atheism, 53:1-6

Psalm 53 is a revision of Psalm 14, and is practically identical with it, with the major exception that it substitutes "God" (*Elohim*) for "the Lord" (*Yahweh*—cf. Intro.). See comments on Psalm 14. Another significant difference is found in v. 5, where instead of "God is in the generation of the righteous. Ye have shamed the counsel of the poor, because the Lord is his refuge" (14:6), we have, For God hath scattered the bones of him that encampeth against thee: thou hast put them to shame, because God hath despised them. The language in 53:5 is much more concrete and specific, and may have in mind an assault against the righteous which had been beaten off with great loss to the attackers. The title of 53 adds the type of psalm (*maschil*, cf. intro. to Psalm 32) and what is probably the name of a tune to which it could be sung (*Mahalath*—the meaning of which is unknown to us).

Psalm 54: A Cry for Help, 54:1-7

This is a short psalm of lament. It is dedicated in its superscription "to the chief Musician on *Neginoth*" (stringed instruments; cf. intro. to Psalm 4). It is further identified as a *maschil* (cf. intro. to Psalm 32), and is related to the betrayal of David by the men of Ziph (I Sam. 23:19-26; 26:1-4).

1. *Cry* (54:1-3)

The first stanza of the psalm voices David's cry to God for help in his hour of danger. In the OT a person's name (1) often stands for the person himself. Judge me is used in the sense of "Vindicate me." Those who rose against him had not set God before them (3), i.e., had no regard for the Lord. Selah; cf. comment on 3:2.

2. *Confidence* (54:4-7)

Although still endangered, the Psalmist expresses his confidence that God will deliver him. Morgan comments, "Already, though perhaps yet in the midst of the peril, he sings the song of deliverance, as though it were already realized. The central sentence of the song is, 'God is my Helper.' Wherever man is conscious of this fact he is superior to all the opposition of his enemies, and so is able, in the midst of the most difficult circumstances. to sing the song of deliverance."[37]

Reward evil (5) may be understood as "return the damage upon" (Berk.). **Mine eye hath seen his desire upon mine enemies** (7) means, "My eye has looked (in triumph) on my enemies" (Amp. OT).

Psalm 55: A BALLAD OF BETRAYAL, 55:1-23

This is another *maschil* (cf. intro. to Psalm 32), a psalm of David dedicated in its title to "the chief Musician on *Neginoth*" (cf. intro. to Psalm 4). It is a psalm of betrayal, in which the pain of adversity is increased a thousandfold by the fact that a trusted friend has turned against the Psalmist. Oesterley says, "Here is a man living in a world of violence and treachery which threaten to overwhelm him, longing to escape from it all, and yet confident in the God to whom he has committed himself. . . . Though he would shelter from the storm, and cannot, yet the temple of his life is founded on a rock, the rock of his faith."[38]

Morgan finds three movements in the psalm which he titles: *Fear* (1-8), *Fury* (9-15), and *Faith* (16-23). He says, "Fear leads only to desire to flee. Fury only emphasizes the consciousness of wrong. Faith alone creates courage."[39]

1. *Fear* (55:1-8)

The Psalmist prays aloud and in agony for God's help (1-2). **Because of the voice of the enemy** (3), their threatenings against him, his **heart is sore pained** ("throbbing in my breast," Moffatt), **and the terrors of death** have **fallen upon** him (4). **Cast iniquity upon me** (3) has been interpreted, "Bring trouble upon me" (RSV). **Fearfulness . . . trembling . . . and horror** are his lot (5). He longs to **fly away on wings like a dove** (6) and find refuge in the peace of **the wilderness** (7). **Selah**; cf. comment on 3:2. Thus would he **escape from the windy storm and tempest** (8).

---

[37]*Op. cit.*, pp. 240-41   [38]*Op. cit.*, p. 286.
[39]*Op. cit.*, p. 241.

2. *Fury* (55:9-15)

Those who were the occasion of the Psalmist's fear are referred to God to be objects of His wrath. **Destroy . . . and divide their tongues (9)**, i.e., set them one against another instead of against the innocent. **In the city** from which he would flee, he sees only **violence and strife, mischief** (evil) **and sorrow (10), wickedness . . . deceit and guile (11)**, a description that would fit all too many cities today. **Magnify himself against me (12)** is to deal insolently with me.

The most poignant note in the psalm is the identification of the leader of the opposition—not an announced enemy, but **thou, a man mine equal, my guide, and mine acquaintance (13)**, with whom he had **walked unto the house of God (14)**. There is no pain so great as the pain of betrayal by a trusted friend or loved one. Such treason can deserve only **death,** a quick plunge into *Sheol* **(15)**, in this instance rightly translated **hell,** since it would be an expression of God's wrath.

3. *Faith* (55:16-23)

Faith, while not free as yet from preoccupation with the encircling enemy, begins its ascent to the throne of God. **Evening, morning, and at noon (17)** the Psalmist will **pray;** and deliverance is so certain that he can speak of it as already won. **With me (18)** means "against me" (RSV). **Selah (19;** cf. comment on 3:2). **Because they have no changes** is better, "Because in them there has been no change" (Berk.), **therefore they fear not God.**

The note of betrayal and treachery comes in again (20-21), but faith reaches its pinnacle: **Cast thy burden upon the Lord, and he shall sustain thee: he shall never suffer** (permit) **the righteous to be moved (22)**, or, "He will never allow the righteous to be pushed over" (Berk.). The wicked will be brought **down into the pit of destruction (23),** and **shall not live out half their days.** But the poet says, **I will trust in thee.**

Psalm 56: Trouble and Trust, 56:1-13

This psalm, like several of Book II, is related to an episode in David's life. According to the title, it grows out of David's flight to Achish, king of the Philistine city of Gath, when the fugitive saved his life by pretending insanity (I Sam. 21:10-15). It is dedicated to the chief musician, and *Jonath-elem-rechokim,* "dove of the distant terebinths," or "A Silent Dove among Strangers" (Berk.), probably the name of the tune. It is a *michtam* (cf. intro. to Psalm 16).

The psalm is a cry of suffering, rising into the serenity of trust, "another testimony to the firm belief of the pious Israelite in the justice, mercy, and love of God."[40] It divides into two almost equal parts, with a sort of refrain occurring in 4 and again in 10-11. Because of its repeated emphasis on the word of God, Barnes describes it as a psalm which expresses "the mind of a prophet."[41]

1. *Trouble* (56:1-7)

As typical of psalms of lament, the poem opens with an appeal to God for mercy. **Swallow me up** (1-2) means devouring or trampling upon him constantly, "oppressing me continually" (Harrison). Fear finds its antidote in faith (3), for **in God I have put my trust; I will not fear what flesh can do unto me** (4; cf. 11). The source of courage is God's **word.** Evil men **wrest** (twist) David's **words** (5). They secretly **mark** (6; watch) his every move, hoping to trap him. **Shall they escape by iniquity?** (7) is, "They think to escape with iniquity" (Amp. OT), i.e., to "get away with" their evil.

2. *Trust* (56:8-13)

From the men who would entrap and defeat him, the Psalmist's face is turned toward God, in whom he put his trust. **Thou tellest my wanderings** (8), or, "You number *and* record my wanderings" (Amp. OT). **Put thou my tears into thy bottle,** possibly in the sense that the prayers of the saints are preserved in golden vials (Rev. 5:8), certainly as taking note of the Psalmist's deep distress. **This I know; for God is for me** (9) is better, "This I know, that God is with me" (RSV). Such is indeed our "Blessed Assurance." **In God will I praise ...** (10-11), as RSV:

> In God, whose word I praise,
>   in the Lord, whose word I praise,
> in God I trust without a fear.
>   What can man do to me?

Cf. v. 4 for a parallel. Nothing can defeat a man with faith such as this.

---

⁴⁰Oesterley, *op. cit.,* p. 289.   ⁴¹*Op. cit.,* II. 269.

Thy vows are upon me (12) is better understood as, "I am under vows to thee" (Moffatt); they were vows to **render praises** for the Lord's deliverance. **Thou hast delivered my soul from death . . . my feet from falling** (13) is found again in 116:8. **In the light of the living** is rendered "in the sunshine of life" (Moffatt). Light is associated with life, darkness with death, throughout the Scriptures.

Psalm 57: Peril and Prayer, 57:1-11

This is another psalm of lament and includes in its title a dedication "to the chief Musician" and an identification as a *"Michtam* of David" (cf. intro. to Psalm 16). *Altaschith* in the title is found in the superscriptions to three other psalms (58, 59, 75). A literal translation is, "Destroy not." It is probably a reference to a melody to be used with the psalm. A historical note in the title relates the psalm to David's flight from Saul "in the cave of Adullam" (cf. I Sam. 22:1; or possibly 24:3-8, the Psalmist's near capture by Saul).

Since vv. 7-11 are identical with 108:1-5, it has been supposed that this psalm is a combination of two other psalms or sections of psalms. However it is more likely that Psalm 108 (*q.v.*) is the combination, having borrowed from 57. A refrain, "Be thou exalted, O God," occurs in vv. 5 and 11.

The psalm contains no new truths. Oesterley comments, "We have, once more, the familiar truths that God hears prayer, that he punishes the wicked, and that he justifies the righteous."[42] Morgan summarizes the teaching of the psalm: "Faith does not free us from trial, but it does enable us to triumph over it. Moreover, faith lifts us high above the purely personal sense of pain, and creates a passion for the exaltation of God among the nations. The heart at leisure from itself is always the heart fixed in God."[43]

1. Plea for Protection (57:1-5)

The Psalmist finds himself in peril from **calamities** (1) brought about by those who **would swallow** him **up** (3), raging like **lions** (4) and aflame with hatred and animosity toward him. His plea is for protection **in the shadow of thy wings** (1; cf. comment on 36:7). **Calamities be overpast** is "deadly danger

⁴²*Op. cit.*, p. 291   ⁴³*Op. cit.*, p. 241.

passes" (Moffatt). **Swallow me up** (3) is "trample me down" (Moffatt; cf. 56:1-2). **Selah;** cf. comment on 3:2. **My soul is among lions** (4) compares his enemies with hungry beasts of prey **whose teeth** are actually their **spears and arrows** and whose **tongue** is a **sharp sword.** The prayer, **Be thou exalted, O God, above the heavens; let thy glory be above all the earth** (5), is the refrain (cf. 11). God is over everything **in the heavens** or on **earth.** His **glory** is His own presence.

2. *Promise of Praise* (57:6-11)

The peril is still present, but confidence of deliverance grows. **Prepared a net** (6) and **digged a pit** are references to methods used by hunters to take game. Yet evil is self-destructive, and the wicked fall into their own traps. In contrast, the Psalmist proclaims, **My heart is fixed** (7), literally, "steadfast" (Perowne); "ready" (Moffatt); "confident" (Berk.), "resolute" (Harrison). The Psalmist cries, **Awake up, my glory** (8). Since man's soul is the image of God, it is man's **glory;** thus, "Awake, my glory—my inner self" (Amp. OT) or, "Awake, my soul" (Moffatt; RSV). **Psaltery and harp** are "harp and lyre" (cf. comment on 33:2). The great **mercy** of God and His high **truth** (faithfulness) are the reason for praise **among the people** and **the nations** (9-10) For v. 11, cf. comment on 5.

Psalm 58: The Doom of the Godless, 58:1-11

Psalm 58 is classed among the imprecatory psalms (cf. Intro.), chiefly because of the sevenfold curse in vv. 6-9. In this, as in the consideration of other imprecatory psalms, the caution of Morgan is well taken: "The whole psalm will be misunderstood save as we carefully note its opening questions. The reason of the judgment is not personal wrong. It is rather the failure of the rulers to administer justice. They are silent when they should speak. Their judgments are not upright. Evil in heart, they lie in word, and poison like serpents, and no charming wins them."[44] This is a call for the public vindication of God's righteous judgment. A holy God cannot tolerate evil. This truth must be so clearly proved that none can doubt. It is to this end that David pleads for justice.

For the superscription, cf. introduction to Psalm 57.

[44]*Op. cit.,* p. 242.

1. The Description of Evil (58:1-5)

The psalm opens with a vivid description of rampant evil. **O congregation** (1) should be understood as "O you judges" (Berk.) or "O you mighty ones" (Amp. OT). "You gods" (RSV) is misleading. The address is not to divinities but to men charged with responsibility to administer justice ("sovereign rulers," Harrison), yet corrupt in spite of their protestations of righteousness. **Ye weigh the violence of your hands** (2) means, "You weigh out" oppression and injustice instead of righteousness and equity. Justice, from time immemorial, has been pictured as a scales, balancing evidence and impartially weighing both sides.

A vivid statement of the innate depravity of the soul is given in 3. Evil is not learned. It comes as a natural expression of man's fallen state. The godless are like **the deaf adder** (4; a poisonous snake), that cannot be brought under control by the enchanter's art (5; cf. similar references in Eccles. 10:11 and Jer. 8:17).

2. The Divine Vengeance (58:6-11)

The sevenfold curse of vv. 6-9 describes the retribution which will come from the hand of God against such evil. **Break their teeth** (6), is a prayer in figurative language asking God to render them powerless to harm others. On **break out the great teeth of the young lions,** cf. 17:12; 34:10; 35:17; 57:4. **Let them melt away as waters** (7), leaving the stream bed empty and dry. **Let them be as cut in pieces,** and thereby utterly destroyed. **As a snail which melteth, let every one of them pass away** (8), killed by exposure to a merciless sun. **Like the untimely birth of a woman,** a miscarriage disposed of in silence and sorrow. **He shall take them away as with a whirlwind** (9), striking so suddenly that the **pots** set over a fire of **thorns** (a quick, hot flame) would not even be warm.

The reaction of **the righteous** will be to **rejoice** (10-11). If this seems less than Christian, let it be acknowledged. But also let it be remembered that the wrath of God is strongly pictured in the NT as well as in the Old, and the rejoicing is more over the public vindication of divine justice than over the fate of the people involved.

Psalm 59: PRAYER FOR PROTECTION IN THE NIGHT, 59:1-17

This is a psalm of lament with a title identical to those of Psalms 57 (q.v.) and 58, except that a historical note is added

relating it to the attempt of Saul's retainers to capture or kill
David when he fled to his own house from the king's court (I Sam.
19:10-17). A sort of refrain in vv. 6 and 14 suggests the dangers
that lurk in the darkness. A second refrain, "God is my defence"
(vv. 9, 17), summarizes the positive faith that overcomes fear.

1. *Danger* (59:1-5)

The danger so keenly felt by the Psalmist is here, as so
often elsewhere, the presence of malignant foes about him. They
are described as **them that rise up against** (1) him, **workers of
iniquity** (2), **bloody men,** men lying **in wait** (3), **the mighty . . .
gathered against** him. **My soul** is here "my life" (RSV). While
the Psalmist was often imperilled by men of his own nation, v. 5
may suggest that **the heathen**—foes from outside Israel—were
the source of his present threat (cf. also 8, 13). At any rate,
they were **wicked transgressors**—men "who treacherously plot
evil" (Berk.)—and this in spite of the fact that the Psalmist was
not guilty of any wrongdoing against them (3-4). Moffatt interprets the last clause of 5, "Spare not one vile traitor." **Selah;**
cf. comment on 3:2.

2. *Deliverance* (59:6-13)

The refrain (6, 14) speaks of the enemies lurking in the
darkness, snarling **like a dog,** prowling around **the city.** Savage
packs of dogs are still the scourge of the East. Moffatt translates
They belch out with their mouth (7), "There they are, bluster-
ing, arrogant, insults on their lips!" **For whom, say they, doth
hear?** indicates their unbelief, imagining that God does not know
of their secret and evil purposes. For v. 8, cf. Prov. 1:24-33.

For **Because of his strength** (9), read with *The Berkeley
Version,* "O my Strength, I will wait on Thee, for God is my
stronghold." **Defence** is literally "high tower." Morgan notes:
"There is perhaps no more beautiful description of what God is
to His tried people [than indicated in this theme, God is my High
Tower]. The phrase suggests at once strength and peace. A
tower against which all the might of the foe hurls itself in vain.
A high tower so that the soul taking refuge in it is lifted far above
the turmoil and the strife, and enabled to view from a vantage
ground of perfect safety the violence which is futile and the
victory of God."[45] Cf. repetition in 17.

[45] *Ibid.*

God of my mercy shall prevent (go before) **me** (10). God's enabling grace will be sufficient for any possible need. Scattered, but not slain, the foe will be a constant reminder to God's people of His power and justice (11). For **O Lord our shield** cf. comment on 5:12. **Be taken in their pride** (12) is translated, "Let their own pride trap them" (Moffatt). **God ruleth in Jacob unto the ends of the earth** (13) reveals that, although especially the God of Israel, the Lord is sovereign over all the earth. Israel was to be the "home base" from which the justice and righteousness of God would reach to all mankind.

3. *Defense* (59:14-17)

For the refrain in 14, cf. comment on 6. Half-wild dogs are insatiable; **and grudge if they be not satisfied** (15) is better "growling if they miss it" (Moffatt). But secure in his **defence and refuge** (high tower and fortress), the poet wakes **in the morning** to **sing** of God's **power** (16). Though **the day** of his **trouble** be not yet passed, he still sings praise to the source of his **strength**. For v. 17, cf. comment on 9.

Psalm 60: A PSALM IN DEFEAT, 60:1-12

This is another lament, apparently occasioned by a defeat of Israel's army in battle. The long superscription contains the familiar dedication "to the chief Musician," and a probable tune-title, *Shushan-eduth,* literally, "the lily of testimony." It is a *michtam* (cf. intro. to Psalm 16) of David, "to teach," and is related to David's Syrian wars (II Sam. 8:3-5; 10:16-19; I Chron. 18:3-12). Apparently a defeat had occurred in the early stages of the conflict, although it is not mentioned in the highly condensed accounts in II Samuel and I Chronicles. Abishai (I Chron. 18:12) seems to have acted in behalf of his brother Joab in the defeat of the Edomites in the Valley of Salt.

Verses 6-12 are found also in 108:6-13.

1. *Defeat* (60:1-5)

The psalm opens with a recognition that the defeat suffered had been due to God's withdrawal of help, but no reason is given for His withdrawal. There is no confession of sin, or indication as to why God may have been displeased (1). **The earth** (2) should be translated "the land." Israel's security was shaken. **The wine of astonishment** (3) is a figure of speech. "wine that

makes us reel" (Berk.). Yet the Lord had given them a banner
(4) around which to rally in defense of His truth. For Selah, cf.
comment on 3:2. Confident of the enduring love of God, the poet
pleads with God to save with thy right hand (5).

2. Declaration (60:6-8)

These verses are a divine oracle, declaring God's intention
with regard to the nations involved in the conflict: God hath
spoken in his holiness (6; sanctuary). Shechem (see map 1)
was west of the Jordan; and while the valley of Succoth cannot
be identified with certainty, there was a city of Succoth east of
the Jordan (Judg. 8:4-5). The meaning of the verse may be,
"I will divide up the whole land both east and west of the Jordan
River."[46] Gilead . . . Manasseh . . . Ephraim . . . Judah (7) are
the areas that together made up the kingdom of Israel. Each is
assured of divine possession, with Ephraim as a "helmet" (RSV)
and Judah as the lawgiver—leader, governor. Moab . . . Edom
. . . Philistia (8) were neighboring nations all hostile to Israel.
My washpot, in which the feet were washed—therefore a symbol
of humiliation. Cast out my shoe is a figure meaning to be
treated as a slave (e.g., Matt. 3:11). Moffatt interprets, "Edom
I claim as subject." Triumph thou because of me may be
translated, "Over Philistia I shout in triumph" (Berk.). The
defeat and humiliation of the enemy will be complete.

3. Deliverance (60:9-12)

The Psalmist resumes his prayer, asking who will be the
leader of the Lord's host (9). It will be God who had cast them
off, and who had not previously gone out with their armies (10).
He is the only help in trouble: for vain is the help of man (11).
It is through God we shall do valiantly (12)—he it is that shall
tread down our enemies. What was true of Israel in its military
conflicts with its neighbors is abundantly true in the Christian's
warfare against "principalities and powers" (II Cor. 10:3-5; Eph.
6:11-20).

Psalm 61: PRAYER OF AN EXILE, 61:1-8

This brief lament is titled "A Psalm of David" and dedicated "to the chief Musician upon *Neginah*," a singular form of

---

[46]Barnes, *op. cit.*, II, 287.

neginoth, stringed instruments (cf. intro. to Psalm 4). It would seem to be the prayer of one exiled from home (2), longing for access to the tabernacle of the Lord (4). There is here the normal pattern of psalms of lament: the plea, the plight, the petition, and the promise.

1. *Prayer* (61:1-4)

In spite of his distance from the familiar place of divine worship, the Psalmist will address his prayer to God. **Lead me to the rock that is higher than I** (2), is a petition that has found its way into the song and devotion of God's people through the ages. **Higher than I** is literally "too high for me." The meaning is clear: God has resources far beyond man's puny power. "Set me upon a towering crag" (Harrison). Instead of **a shelter for me** (3), read "a refuge for me" (Amp. OT). **A strong tower** was the most effective type of protection in ancient warfare (cf. comment on 59:9). The Psalmist's determination is to **abide** in God's **tabernacle for ever,** trusting **in the covert** (covering; therefore, shelter) **of** His **wings** (4; cf. comment on 17:8).

2. *Praise and Promise* (61:5-8)

The poet is confident that God has **heard** his **vows** (5). **Those that fear thy name** is better "those who revere Thy name" (Berk.). The land of Canaan was the heritage of God's people Israel. The Lord himself is the Heritage of His new Israel. **Long life** for the king (6) and that he **may abide before God for ever** (7) are the Psalmist's petitions. **Mercy and truth,** i.e., God's unchanging faithfulness, will **preserve him.**

> And I will ever sing thy praise,
>   paying my vows through all my days (8, Moffatt).

Psalm 62: God Alone Is a Sure Defense, 62:1-12

Psalm 62 is also identified as "A Psalm of David" in its title, and is dedicated "to the chief Musician, to Jeduthun" (cf. I Chron. 16:41). It repeats the refrain of 59:9, 17, "He is my defence [high tower]," in vv. 2 and 6. There is the same background of conflict we find in a number of the psalms, yet a strong note of confidence prevails. This is depicted in Moffatt's paraphrase of v. 1, "Leave it all quietly to God, my soul."

1. *The Enemy* (62:1-4)

My soul waiteth upon God (1) is literally, "My soul is silent before God." This silence in the presence of God is sometimes the most eloquent form of prayer. "Salvation is of the Lord," then and always. For **he only is my rock and my salvation** (2; cf. comment on 27:5). **My defence** is literally "high tower"; cf. comment on 59:9. In stark contrast with the Psalmist's confidence in God are the character and conduct of his foes. **Imagine mischief against** (3) is literally "rush upon," attack or assault. The strong tone of the verse is captured by Moffatt:

> *How long will you be threatening a man,*
>   *you murderers all,*
> *as if he were a shaky fence,*
>   *a tottering wall?*

In lying deceit, his foes **consult** against him (4). **Selah**; cf. comment on 3:2.

2. *The Expectation* (62:5-8)

Verse 5 parallels v. 1, and 6 repeats 2. **My expectation** (5) is the deliverance for which he prays. The last clause of 6, **I shall not be moved,** is even stronger than the last clause of 2, "I shall not be greatly moved"; viz., Harrison, "I shall not be dispossessed" (2), "I shall not be overthrown" (6). For 6-7, cf. comments on 2. All **people** are encouraged to **trust** God **at all times** (8). **Pour out your heart before him,** in prayer and supplication, for **God is a refuge for us.**

3. *The Evaluation* (62:9-12)

Prayer and faith have given the Psalmist a correct evaluation of the status and wealth in pursuit of which the irreligious spend their lives. **Low degree** and **high degree** (9) are alike **vanity** ("a breath," Eccles. 1:2) and **a lie** (lit., "a disappointment"). Status promises much but usually disappoints those who seek it. In their context, these words may mean that men of high rank had proved a disappointment to the Psalmist. Weighed **in the balance,** all human distinctions of rank and importance **are altogether lighter than vanity**—they do not even weigh as much as a breath!

Wealth gained at the cost of honesty is bought at too high a price (10). **If riches increase,** as they may for the godly, **set**

not your heart upon them. In an age that almost universally looked upon prosperity as a mark of divine favor (cf. the problem discussed in Psalms 37 and 49), this is a high note indeed (cf. also 73:3-5, in addition to 37:16 and 49:16-18). **God hath spoken once; twice have I heard this** (11) indicates that "a divine revelation given more than once has special weight. The content of this revelation therefore is not two separate things but one: God's omnipotence and kindness together work to the end that every man, good or evil, receives his just recompense."[47] **Power belongeth unto God.** So also does **mercy** (12; *chesed*), the constant, dependable love of the Lord for His own. (Cf. comment on 17:7.)

Psalm 63: God Is All in All, 63:1-11

This is a psalm of trust and confidence in God's continual help. Unlike others of the kind (e.g., 23, 27), it is a hymn-type poem, its words addressed entirely to and not about God. It reaches a peak of spiritual devotion. "The earnest yearning for God, and the insight into communion with him on the part of a truly good man, as these are set forth in this psalm, are unrivalled in the Psalter."[48] Morgan sees in this psalm the consummate expression of the confidence expressed in the two preceding psalms. He finds two things necessary for such a victorious faith as this. "These are indicated in the opening words of the psalm. First, there must be the consciousness of personal relationship, 'O God, Thou art my God'; and, second, there must be earnest seeking after God: 'Early will I seek thee.' Relationship must be established. Fellowship must be cultivated."[49]

The title relates the psalm to David's flight from Saul during the period he spent in the wilderness of Judah (I Sam. 23:14—26:25).

1. The Fellowship of God (63:1-8)

This is OT religion at its best. **Morning** (1) and **night** (6) the Psalmist centers his thought and desire upon the Lord. **My soul thirsteth** (1; cf. comment on 42:2). As **in a dry and thirsty land,** David longs for **the sanctuary** of the Lord, where he had

---

[47]Taylor, *op. cit.*, 4:326.   [48]Oesterley, *op. cit.*, p. 307.
[49]*Op. cit.*, p. 244.

seen the **power and the glory** of God (2). **Thy lovingkindness**
(*chesed,* constant, enduring, covenant love; cf. comment on
17:7) **is better than life** (3), and life would be all but intolerable without it. **My soul shall be satisfied as with marrow and
fatness** (5), "richly fed" (Moffatt). Sleepless hours at night turn
to joy **when I remember thee upon my bed, and meditate on
thee in the night watches** (6). Past help engenders present joy
in the shadow of His **wings** (7; cf. comments on 17:8 and 61:4).

2. *The Fate of the Godless* (63:9-11)

The thought of the Psalmist's oppressors is a passing shadow.
Those who **seek to destroy** his life **shall go into the lower parts
of the earth** (9), to *Sheol,* the place of the dead. **A portion for
foxes** (10), i.e., the scavenging jackals of the wilderness will feed
on their unburied bodies. **Every one that sweareth by him** (11)
would be everyone "who binds himself by God's authority,
acknowledging His supremacy, and devoting himself to His glory
and service alone" (Amp. OT). All such persons **shall glory.**
Instead of **but the mouth,** read "for the mouth" (Perowne).

Psalm 64: THE FOLLY AND FATE OF THE FOE, 64:1-10

This psalm is a typical psalm of lament, following the familiar pattern of plea, plight, petition, and promise. Its preoccupation is with the "workers of iniquity" (2) who beset its
author. The form of opposition seems to be malicious slander.
Yet the distress of the Psalmist is not despair, for he sees the
defeat of evil counsel by the working of God.

The title inscribes the poem "to the chief Musician" and
identifies it as "A Psalm of David."

1. *The Slander* (64:1-6)

The plea is, **Hear my voice . . . preserve my life** (1). The
unchanged method of the purveyors of slander is vividly described: **secret counsel** (2) . . . **insurrection** ("conspiracy," Amp.
OT) . . . **tongue like a sword** (3) . . . **arrows, even bitter words**
. . . **shoot in secret** (4) . . . **laying snares** (5). **Whet their tongue**
(3) is to sharpen it like a sword is sharpened. **The perfect** (4;
tammim) are those who are whole, sound, complete. Men of low
character are rarely the objects of slander. **Encourage themselves in an evil matter** (5) is rendered "confirm for themselves
an evil agreement" (Berk.). Secure in the thought that their evil

will never be found out, **they commune of laying snares privily**
(secretly). For 6, read with *The Berkeley Version:*

> *They work out wicked schemes;*
> *they are ready with a well-conceived plan;*
> *for the inner man and the heart are fathomless.*

2. *The Settlement* (64:7-10)

But the issues of life are never left to the designs of the
wicked. The Psalmist loses his "fear of the enemy" (1) in the
thought that **God shall shoot at them with an arrow** (7), as they
have shot at and wounded the righteous. **Their own tongue** (8)
will **fall upon** (bear witness against) **themselves.** Those who look
on will **flee away,** or as the Hebrew may be translated, "shake
their heads." The outcome will be the final vindication of God's
justice before the eyes of all. **The righteous** will **be glad,** and
will have their **trust** confirmed (10). Victims of lying tongues
may not find it easy to wait. But the settlement, though slow,
is sure to come.

Psalm 65: A Song of Worship, 65:1-13

Psalm 65 is a psalm of adoration, perhaps at the harvest
festival or on the occasion of an especially bountiful harvest. It
centers around the duty and privilege of worship, and stresses
the glory of God in His temple, among the nations, and in the
fruitfulness of nature. It is addressed by title "to the chief Musician," and is "A Psalm and Song of David." The words have
only a slight difference; "psalm" probably indicates an instrumental accompaniment.

1. *The Glory of God in His House* (65:1-4)

The nature and joy of divine worship are the opening theme
of the psalm. **Praise** (1), **prayer** (2), the purging of sin (3),
and worshipful adoration (4) are the elements of true worship.
The emphasis is upon public worship—**in Sion** (1; a variant spelling of *Zion,* the hill on which the Temple was built), and God's
house, even . . . the **holy temple** (4). **All flesh** (2), i.e., all people. On **Iniquities prevail against me** (3), cf. Moffatt, "Though
our sins be too much for us, 'tis thine to cancel our transgressions." The man chosen **to approach** God and **dwell in** His
courts is **blessed** indeed (4).

2. *The Glory of God Among the Nations* (65:5-8)

The author speaks of God's sovereign power in all the earth. **By terrible things in righteousness wilt thou answer us** (5) may be read, "By dread deeds thou dost answer us with deliverance" (RSV). God is the **confidence** of men to **the ends of the earth and afar off upon the sea.** His power is seen in the forces of nature (6-7) and as He quiets **the tumult of the people** ("the clamor of the nations," Berk.). **Thy tokens** (8) are the irresistible forces of nature. The **outgoings of the morning and evening** are the east and west, places of sunrise and sunset. God's universal sovereignty is proclaimed in these vivid and concrete images.

3. *The Glory of God in the Harvest* (65:9-13)

This last division, which some have thought to be a separate psalm, gives glory to God for the bounty of the harvest and beauty of the countryside. Palestine depended entirely on rainfall for its fruitfulness. Water was both a gift of God's bounty and a symbol of His presence: **Thou visitest the earth, and waterest it** (9). **River of God** refers to "God's store of water in the clouds and atmosphere, which he can.at any time retain or let loose."[50] **Thou preparest them corn** (grain); God's provision, not man's industry, supplied the need. The rain and the fruitfulness of "the good earth" crowned **the year with** God's **goodness** (11). The countryside seems to **rejoice** (12) when **the pastures are clothed with flocks** (13) and **the valleys also are covered over with corn.**

Psalm 66: A Psalm of Deliverance, 66:1-20

This psalm of adoration is addressed "to the chief Musician," and is titled "A Song or Psalm" (cf. intro. to Psalm 65) without the name of David. It clearly divides into two major sections, marked at v. 13 by a change of pronoun from plural to singular. M'Caw identifies vv. 1-12 with corporate worship and 13-20 with personal worship.[51]

---

[50]George Rawlinson, "The Book of Psalms" (Exposition), *The Pulpit Commentary*, ed. H. D. M. Spence and Joseph S. Exell (Grand Rapids, Michigan: Wm. B. Eerdmans Publishing Company, 1950 [reprint]), II, 30.

[51]*Op. cit.*, pp. 456-57.

1. *Public Praise* (66:1-12)

This is a call for all to praise God because of His mighty works both at the Exodus and in more recent providences.

a. *"All the earth shall worship thee"* (66:1-4). **All . . . lands** are called upon to **make a joyful noise unto God**, singing **the honour of his name** and making **his praise glorious** (1-2). **A joyful noise** is a shout of joy (cf. 81:1; 95:1; 98:4; 100:1). **How terrible art thou in thy works!** (3) has been translated, "How awesome *and* fearfully glorious are Your works!" (Amp. OT) **All . . . shall worship thee, and . . . sing to thy name** (4). **Selah;** cf. comment on 3:2.

b. *"He turned the sea into dry land"* (66:5-7). There is a dual reference to the Exodus and the crossing of the Jordan (Exod. 14:21; Josh. 3:14-17). For **terrible** (5) read "awesome." The Exodus in particular became for Israel the central fact of faith.

c. *"Thou broughtest us out"* (66:8-12). The mercies of God did not stop with the notable deliverances of the past. In the trials of history and in some new and recent peril, the Lord again had made known His power. **Holdeth our soul in life** (9) may be read "keeps our soul in life" (Berk.). **Thou, O God, hast proved** (tested) **us** (10). For **loins** (11) read "hips"; carrying loads on the hip was customary (Berk., fn.). Like **silver** (10) through the refining fire, the people had been **through fire and through water** (12); but the Lord had brought them **out into a wealthy place**—"a rich relief, setting us free in liberty" (Moffatt).

2. *Personal Devotion* (66:13-20)

The change from plural to singular personal pronouns at this point marks a different emphasis in the psalm. It is the expression of one coming to God's **house** to worship **with burnt offerings** (13) and to **pay . . . vows** made while **in trouble** (14). **Fatlings** (fat, healthy lambs), **rams, bullocks,** and **goats** (15) were all acceptable for "peace offerings," that is, those expressing thanksgiving and love for God, or in the payment of vows (Lev. 3:1-17).

With the offering was a public testimony to what God **hath done for my soul** (16). There may have been a detailed statement of particulars, but all is summarized in praise for answered prayer (17-20). **If I regard** (cherish) **iniquity in my heart, the**

275

Lord will not hear me (18), is a truth stated in a number of
ways elsewhere in Scripture (e.g., Job 27:9; 31:27; Prov. 15:29;
28:9; Isa. 1:15; Zech. 7:13; John 9:31; etc.). Insincerity or secret
sin shuts the channels of prayer.

Psalm 67: A Hymn of Praise, 67:1-7

This is a psalm of adoration and praise, dedicated "to the
chief Musician on *Neginoth*," or stringed instruments (cf. intro.
to Psalm 4), and titled "A Psalm or Song" (cf. intro. to Psalm 65).
The first line of v. 6 has led to the classification of the psalm as a
harvest festival song, but its immediate occasion is overshadowed
by a much wider outlook. If it were a harvest hymn, it would
have probably been used at the Feast of Tabernacles.

1. *The Reason for Praise* (67:1-4)

God's righteous providence is the basis for the adoration expressed in the psalm. The first verse is in the nature of a note
of petition. Oesterley points out that such is not out of place,
for "when a divine blessing has been granted, one of the first
emotions in a man, like our psalmist, of real religious insight,
is a sense of unworthiness; and this is followed by the spontaneous and ardent wish that the blessing may be used aright;
this can be the case only if God's graciousness continues to be
accorded; hence the cry: 'O God,—may he be gracious.' "[52]

Cause his face to shine upon us (1) means to "look upon
us with His favor and approval." **Selah;** cf. comment on 3:2. **Thy
saving health** (2) is, in Hebrew, "thy salvation"; cf. RSV, "thy
saving power." **Thou shalt judge the people righteously** (4),
condemning the evil and vindicating the righteous. **Govern the
nations upon earth** is literally "lead the peoples of the earth."
God's sovereignty is universal.

2. *The Result of Praise* (67:5-7).

When **all the people praise** (5) the Lord, three results follow: (*a*) **Then shall the earth yield her increase** (6) in bountiful
harvests; (*b*) **God shall bless us** (7) spiritually as well as materially; and (*c*) **All the ends of the earth shall fear him,** look to
Him with reverence and awe.

---

[52]*Op. cit.,* p. 319.

Psalm 68: God and His Worshiping Host, 68:1-35

This long psalm is dedicated "to the chief Musician" and is identified in its superscription as "A Psalm or Song of David" (cf. intro. to Psalm 65). It has proved difficult for the scholars to classify, since it treats of a number of subjects. Oesterley believed it to be a collection of shorter pieces,[53] and Taylor describes it as a processional hymn used by a company of priests and worshipers on the way to the sanctuary (vv. 24-25), entitling it "A Libretto of Songs for the Sanctuary."[54] There is a strong Messianic note in v. 18 (cf. Eph. 4:8).

1. *Praise* (68:1-6)

The opening section of the psalm declares the praise of the Lord on earth and in the heavens. None who **hate him** (1) can stand. **As wax melteth before the fire, so let the wicked perish at the presence of God** (2)—His very presence is intolerable to the wicked. **But . . . the righteous shall be glad** (3) and **exceedingly rejoice,** singing **praises to his name** (4). **Extol him that rideth upon the heavens** is a possible translation of a difficult Hebrew construction. Alternate translations are, "Cast up a high way for him that rideth through the deserts" (ASV; Amp. OT); "Raise a highway for Him who rides through the wilderness" (Berk.); "Lift up a song to him who rides upon the clouds" (RSV); and, "Give glory to Him who rides upon the storm clouds" (Harrison). **His name JAH,** or *Yah,* is an alternate or contracted form of *Yahweh,* the personal name of the true God, translated "Jehovah" (ASV), "the Eternal" (Moffatt), and "the Lord" (LXX, KJV, Smith-Goodspeed, RSV, Berk., Amp. OT). Use of "the Lord" has the support of NT usage, since the Hebrew *Yahweh* is consistently translated *ho Kyrios* (the Lord) in quotations from the OT. *JAH* is found in the Hebrew text of Exod. 15:2; 17:16; Ps. 68:18; 89:8; and Isa. 12:2; but Psalm 68 is the only place in the KJV where it is transliterated into the English form. It is frequent in compound names in the OT, coming into English as *-iah* as in Jeremiah (appointed by *JAH*), Isaiah (salvation of *JAH*), Zechariah (*JAH* has remembered), and the like. Cf. "Hallelujah" (*Hallelu-Yah*), "praise be to *JAH.*"

God is **a father of the fatherless, and a judge of the widows** (5). Special protection was given in Bible times to persons who would otherwise be defenseless. **Judge of** means Defender

---

[53]*Ibid.*, p. 320.   [54]*Op. cit.*, 4:353-54.

and Vindicator of the rights of (cf. Luke 18:1-7). **Setteth the solitary in families (6)** has been rendered "brings the lonely home" (Moffatt) and "gives the desolate a home to live in" (RSV). A **dry land** would be a parched, desert waste.

2. Past (68:7-14)

These verses comprise a distinct division in the psalm, and review the events surrounding and following the Exodus, showing the favor of the Lord toward His people. **God . . . wentest forth before (7)** in the pillar of cloud and fire (cf. Exod. 13:21-22; 33:14-15). **Selah;** cf. comment on 3:2. On **The earth shook . . . even Sinai itself (8)** see Exod. 19:16-19. **A plentiful rain (9)** probably refers to "a rain of gracious gifts," the quail and the manna, as well as literal rain upon **thine inheritance**—land and people. **Thy congregation hath dwelt therein (10)** has been translated, "Thy flock found a dwelling in it" (RSV). The reference is to Canaan, the land of His people's inheritance.

The Lord gave the word (11), i.e., the decisive command; and **great was the company of those that published it,** in the sense of spreading the tidings that **kings of armies did flee apace (12)**. The last part of 12 may be read, "The women at home divided the booty" (Berk.). **Though ye have lien among the pots (13)** is a difficult Hebrew construction, variously translated, "Lie among the sheepfolds" (ASV), or "camp among the sheepfolds" (Berk.). The thought probably relates to v. 12, the meaning being that the women divided the spoil even though they stayed near the sheepfolds at home. **As the wings of a dove covered with silver, and her feathers with yellow gold** is a picture of Israel, the dove, returning from the battle won by the power of God, laden with the spoils of war in silver and gold. **Salmon (14)** was a hill in central Palestine, exact location not now known. The meaning is probably that the defeat of the kings at the hand of God and His people was as effortless as the fall of **snow** on a hillside.

3. Present (68:15-23)

God's presence and power are more than historical fact. They are present reality. These verses sound the glory of God in the blessings He gives day by day. For **The hill of God is as the hill of Bashan (15)**, read, "A mountain of God is the mountain of Bashan" (Berk.). Bashan was the mountainous district northeast of Galilee. Although it was at the border of the land, it was the Lord's possession, but is pictured as envious of Mount Zion in Jerusalem. Verse 16 should be read as with Moffatt:

> But what is your grudge, O range of peaks,
> at the hill that God loves for his home,
> where the Eternal dwells for evermore?

Even thousands of angels (17) is literally "thousands upon thousands." The hosts of God cannot be numbered.

God as a victorious King has **ascended on high** (18), "with captives in thy train" (Moffatt), receiving tribute from men—which He then distributes to His own (cf. the application by Paul in Eph. 4:8). God's beneficent purpose includes **the rebellious also.** The summary of the section is in 19: **Blessed be the Lord, who daily loadeth us with benefits, even the God of our salvation.** The expression **daily loadeth** us is also translated "daily bears us up" (RSV) or "day by day He carries us" (Berk.).

Unto God the Lord belong the issues from death (20) has been interpreted, "Unto God, the Lord, belong the exits to death" (Smith-Goodspeed). The issues of life and death are in the hand of God. There is a terrible fate awaiting the **enemies of** the Lord (21-23), such as persist in their **trespasses.** The odd term **hairy scalp** (21) is an allusion to the custom of soldiers letting their hair grow until the successful conclusion of the war, when it was shaved off upon their return home. **From Bashan ... from the depths of the sea** (22) may mean "from the heights [cf. 15] to the depths."

4. Procession (68:24-29)

These verses may be a clue to the purpose and use of the psalm (cf. intro.). They picture **the goings of . . . God**—the Lord leading the way into **the sanctuary** (24), **the singers** next, followed by **players on instruments** (25), with **damsels** (maidens) **playing with timbrels** (tambourines). The song is, **Bless ye God in the congregations, even the Lord, from the fountain of Israel** (26). The ASV has "ye that are of the fountain of Israel," that is, the descendants of Jacob. In the procession are the leaders of **little Benjamin . . . Judah . . . Zebulun, and . . . Naphtali** (27), two southern and two northern tribes, representing all of Israel. God's **strength** and power are manifest in and through His **temple at Jerusalem** (28-29).

5. *Prospect* (68:30-35)

Victories of the past and present lead onward to confidence for the future. The Lord will shatter all opposition. For the **company of spearmen** (30) read "the beasts of the reeds" (Berk.); thus crocodiles, **bulls,** and **calves** represent the enemies of the righteous. **Princes shall come out of Egypt** (31) to worship the Lord, and **Ethiopia shall soon stretch out her hands** in submission and adoration. The **kingdoms of the earth** (32) will **sing unto God,** who **rideth upon the heavens of heavens** (33), or the highest heavens. God's **strength** is exalted (34). **O God, thou art terrible out of thy holy place** (35) is better, "Awe-inspiring art Thou, O God, from Thy sanctuary" (Berk.).

Psalm 69: DESPAIR AND DESIRE, 69:1-36

This is a song in minor key with a strong note of imprecation (vv. 22-28, cf. Intro.) and some Messianic overtones (vv. 9, 21). The title "Upon *Shoshannim*" means "set to The Lilies," and is probably a tune title (cf. intro. to Psalm 45). The singer's agony of spirit was deep and intense. He was beset by enemies, troubled by sickness, and all but overwhelmed by the sense of despair. Morgan comments, "Perhaps in no psalm in the whole psalter is the sense of sorrow profounder or more intense than in this. The soul of the singer pours itself out in unrestrained abandonment to the overwhelming and terrible grief which consumes it."[55]

1. *A Time of Extreme Need* (69:1-5)

The Psalmist's situation is stated in vivid figures of speech. **The waters are come in unto my soul** (1; "up to my lips," Berk.). He finds himself sinking **in deep mire** (2) with no place to stand. **I am weary of my crying** (3) suggests, "I have cried until I am exhausted" (Berk.). The Psalmist was hated **without a cause** (4), his **enemies wrongfully** opposing him, so that he is forced to restore what he had not taken away. Yet he had not been without his **foolishness** (5; folly). This is an OT synonym for wrongdoing, and he confesses his **sins to God.**

2. *Distress for the Lord's Sake* (69:6-13)

As is usual in the psalms, the basis of the opposition was religious. Verse 6 is the noble prayer of a man whose concern is

[55]*Op. cit.,* p. 246.

not only for himself but also for the faithful who might be damaged by any failure on his part. For the Lord's **sake . . . shame** had been poured upon him (7) and he had become as a **stranger** and **an alien** among his own (8). Verse 9 is memorable for its use in reference to the cleansing of the Temple by Jesus (John 2:17), and the latter part of the verse is quoted by Paul as illustrated in the example of our Lord in bearing the burdens of the weak (Rom. 15:3).

When I wept . . . that was to my reproach (10) is better read with Moffatt: "When I chastened my soul with fasting, men jeered at me." **Sackcloth** (11) was the traditional symbol of deep mourning. **Became a proverb** (byword) **to them** means that his name was used as an expression of contempt. **They that sit in the gate** (12) were the elders of the city (Ruth 4:1; Job 29: 7-8). **The song of the drunkards** indicates that the low as well as the high conspired to pour contempt upon him. The Psalmist's sole hope was that God would hear. Punctuate v. 13 as with *The Berkeley Version:*

> But as for me, my prayer is to Thee, Lord;
> at an opportune moment, O God, in Thy plenteous grace,
> answer me with the truth of Thy salvation.

3. The Hope of Answered Prayer (69:14-20)

Prayer is the only hope in such a situation. The Psalmist returns to the despairing picture of 2, feeling himself to be sinking in **the mire** and **the deep waters** (14), with **the pit** of death about to close over him (15). God is reminded of His **lovingkindness** and **the multitude of thy tender mercies** (16). All the poet's misery is laid out before the Lord: **I am in trouble** (17); **. . . my reproach, and my shame, and my dishonour** (19) **. . . hath broken my heart . . . I am full of heaviness** (20). There were none **to take pity** or be his **comforters.**

4. Malediction upon the Enemies (69:21-28)

These verses are one of the strongest imprecatory passages in the Psalms (cf. Intro.). The **gall** and **vinegar** of 21 are strikingly paralleled at the crucifixion of Jesus (Matt. 27:34). In its OT context, the meaning is probably a complaint that the Psalmist's food and drink were bitter and unpalatable. There is a **sevenfold curse** upon these wicked men: (1) upon their food

(22); (2) upon **their eyes** (23); (3) upon their bodies (23*b*); (4) the outpoured wrath of God (24); (5) upon their dwellings (25); (6) the sum of their guilt increased (27); (7) their names **blotted out of the book** of life (28). **Talk to the grief** (26) may be "gossip of the pain" (Berk.); following the LXX, the RSV renders it, "They afflict still more."

5. *A Note of Hope* (69:29-36)

As so often throughout the psalms, the poet rises through the gloom to a glimpse of hope. When God's **salvation** shall **set him up on high** (29), he **will praise the name of God with a song and with thanksgiving** (30), which is better in God's sight than an animal sacrifice (31). His vindication will make **the humble . . . glad** (32). He declares, **Your heart shall live that seek God. For the Lord heareth the poor** (33) and does not despise **his prisoners**—His people who have been afflicted or exiled. **Heaven and earth . . . the seas . . . and every thing that moveth therein** (34) should praise God. **God will save Zion, and will build the cities of Judah** (35), and His people shall possess it as their inheritance (36).

Psalm 70: AN URGENT CRY FOR HELP, 70:1-5

This psalm is identical with 40:13-17. An added note is found in the title, "to bring to remembrance," perhaps indicating its use as a memorial of some particular time of need. Morgan comments: "This short psalm is a rushing sob of anxious solicitude. There is little restfulness in it. Enemies are engaged in cruel persecution and mockery. It seems as though the singer felt that the strain was becoming too much for him, and in fear lest he should be overcome he cries aloud for God to hasten his deliverance. The faith of the singer is evident in that he cries to God, and evidently has no room in his heart to question God's ability to keep him. The only question is whether help will arrive in time."[56] For comments, refer to 40:13-17. The major differences in the two versions are the substitution of **Make haste** (1) for "Be pleased" (40:13) and its addition in 5; in 4 there is the substitution of **God** for "The Lord" (40:16); and the contrasting substitution of **O Lord** (5) for "O my God" (40:17). None of these changes alter the sense.

---

[56]*Ibid.*, pp. 246-47.

Psalm 71: "E'EN DOWN TO OLD AGE," 71:1-24

With the exception of Psalm 43, which was probably originally part of 42, this is the only psalm in Book II without a title. It is the prayer and testimony of an aged man (9, 18). As M'Caw observes, "There is a mellowness and serenity about it which is characteristic of a long life spent in reliance upon God (cf. 5, 17)."[57] "For its deep piety and religious spirit it stands among some of the most beautiful productions in the Psalter."[58] "What is particularly noteworthy, and almost unique in the Psalter, is the beautiful picture of one, now well advanced in years, who can look back upon his past life in the happy conviction that he has done his duty to God; and that, in spite of troubles, God has been with him and upheld him."[59]

1. A Strong Refuge for All of Life (71:1-8)

Still beset by dangers, the Psalmist is cheered by grateful remembrance of God's past deliverances. He affirms his **trust** in the **Lord** (1), and prays that he **never be put to confusion** but delivered in the Lord's **righteousness** and enabled **to escape** (2). He asks that the Lord will be the **strong habitation**, the **rock** and **fortress** to which he **may continually resort** (3). Deliverance from **the unrighteous and cruel man** (4) must come from the **Lord God,** who had been his **hope** and his **trust from** his **youth** (5). From birth, God had been his Support (6). **I am as a wonder unto many** (7) may also be understood as "a sign, or portent" of the faithfulness of God.

2. The Perils of Advancing Years (71:9-16)

Old age with its failing strength (9) had been wrongly understood by his **enemies** (10) as an indication that **God had forsaken him** (11) and that there would be **none to deliver him.** But such is not the case, and the poet prays for the nearness of his **God** (12) and the confusion of his enemies (13). In spite of pressures without and within, the Psalmist will not give up **hope** (14) but **will yet praise** the Lord **more and more,** telling of His **righteousness** and His **salvation all the day** (15). The expression **for I know not the numbers thereof** shows that God's mercies are beyond all counting; Moffatt translates, "Never can I

[57]*Op. cit.,* p. 461.   [58]Oesterley, *op. cit.,* p. 333.
[59]*Ibid.,* p. 336.

tell it to the full." With his own strength failing markedly, he **will go in the strength of the Lord God** (16); cf. Paul's parallel in II Cor. 12:9.

3. The Hope of Old Age (71:17-24)

Taught by the Lord **from** his **youth** (17), now **old and grey-headed,** our poet prays, **O God, forsake me not** (18). None is like the Lord in **righteousness** and power (19). Having been through **great and sore troubles** (20), the Lord who had revived him before will **quicken** him again. **Thou shalt increase my greatness** (21) is better, add to "my honor" (RSV). For **psaltery** and **harp** (22) cf. comment on 33:2. **Holy One of Israel** is one of the most striking titles for the true God, found here for the first time in the Psalms (cf. also 78:41). It was Isaiah's favorite title for the Lord (Isa. 1:4; 5:19, 24; 10:17, 20, and throughout). The Psalmist will **talk of** God's **righteousness all the day long** (24); **righteousness** in the sense of His saving act of deliverance. For his enemies **are confounded** and **brought unto shame** (24), "daunted and disgraced" (Moffatt).

Psalm 72: THE IDEAL KING, 72:1-20

This poem is titled "A Psalm for Solomon." Psalm 127 bears a similar title. It has been interpreted both in relation to an earthly king and in reference to the Messiah. Certainly the character and rule of the king here described have never yet been realized on this earth, and will not be short of the everlasting kingdom of our Lord. Morgan writes: "This is the Kingdom for which the world still waits. It is a perfect order which has never yet been established, because the ultimate rule of God has never yet been recognized and obeyed. This was surely all in the view of Jesus when He taught us to pray for the coming of the Kingdom. The One King has come, and men would not have Him to reign. Therefore, notwithstanding all the best and highest efforts of man without Him, the needy are still oppressed, and peace and prosperity are postponed. To us the song of this psalm is a prophecy of hope. We have seen the King, and we know the perfect Kingdom must come, for God cannot be defeated."[60] And Leslie M'Caw observes, "The conditions of social righteousness, stability, prosperity and peace which the Psalm

---

[60]*Op. cit.,* p. 247.

depicts are not merely ideals; their actual and ultimate fulfilment is fully implied because of the messianic hope."[61]

1. The King's Righteousness (72:1-6)

The righteousness of the king and his consequent justice are
the theme of the opening stanza of the song. God's **judgments**
(*mishpat*, ordinance, statute, law) and His **righteousness** (1;
tsedeqah, justice, integrity, rightness) are besought on behalf
of **the king,** who was the son of royalty. Having received this
divine endowment, the ruler would then exercise his office
aright (2), bringing **peace to the people** "from the very hills and
mountains" (3, Moffatt). Special concern is given to **the poor**
and **the needy** (4), and their oppressor shall be destroyed. The
Messianic dimension in the psalm is seen in 5-6. The kingly
Messiah will be reverenced **as long as the sun and moon endure**
(5). His blessings shall be **like rain upon the mown grass: as
showers that water the earth** (6).

2. The King's Rule (72:7-11)

The extent of the ideal King's dominion is stated. **In his days**
(7), when His reign is established fully, **the righteous** shall
flourish in an abundance of peace. His kingdom shall extend
from sea to sea, and from the river unto the ends of the earth (8)
—expressions of universality. His rule will be absolute (9), and
kings from **Tarshish** (in Spain) and **the isles** (10; the west) to
Sheba and Seba (the east and south) **shall offer gifts.** Before
Him **all kings shall fall down** and **all nations shall serve him**
(11; cf. Phil. 2:5-11).

3. The King's Redemption (72:12-14)

The King is a Redeemer-King, for **he shall deliver the needy,**
the **poor,** and the helpless (12). He shall **save the souls of the
needy** (13), and **shall redeem their soul from deceit and violence**
(14). **Precious shall their blood be in his sight,** setting such
value upon them that He will not permit them to be oppressed
(cf. I Sam. 26:21; II Kings 1:14; Ps. 116:15).

4. The King's Recognition (72:15-17)

The King will be recognized and honored by all. **And he
shall live** (15) refers to the poor and needy one who has been

[61]*Op. cit.,* p. 462.

redeemed. In his gratitude for his deliverance, he shall give his King **the gold of Sheba,** a country famous for its fine gold. **Prayer also shall be made for him continually**—for the earthly king whose limited reign was to be patterned after the ideal, and for the extension of the heavenly King's dominion. **An handful of corn (16)** is better translated "an abundance of grain." **Shake like Lebanon** means the harvest will be so abundant that the breeze through its ripening fields will sway the grain like the cedars of Lebanon move in the wind from the sea. Verse 17 is clearly Messianic in its fullest application. The King's **name** is eternal; **men shall be blessed in him, and all nations shall call him blessed.**

5. Doxology (72:18-19)

Each of the books of the Psalter ends with a doxology (cf. Intro.). These verses comprise the doxology for Book II. **The Lord God of Israel** is the only Source of the **wondrous things** done in behalf of His people **(18).** Through all time and over all the **earth** His **glory** and **his glorious name** shall be known **(19).** For **Amen, and Amen,** cf. comments on 41:13.

6. Editorial Note (72:20)

The note, **The prayers of David the son of Jesse are ended,** is one of the indications that our total Book of Psalms is composed of other smaller collections (see Intro.). It does not mean that all the Davidic psalms are included in the two books preceding, since 86, 101, 103, 108—10, 122, 124, 131, 133, 139—45 are identified by title with Israel's great psalmist-king. It would most naturally mark the end of an earlier collection of David's psalms, now, of course, part of the larger whole. A similar editorial note is found in Prov. 25:1, identifying a group of "proverbs of Solomon, which the men of Hezekiah king of Judah copied out."

Psalms 73—89

Book III consists of seventeen psalms. All have titles indicating personal names: eleven, Asaph; three, Korah; and one each, David, Heman, and Ethan. Each major psalm type is represented except penitential (cf. Intro.): six psalms of lament, five of adoration, worship, praise, and thanksgiving; three wisdom psalms; and one each of the imprecatory, liturgical, and Messianic psalms. Some of the finest and most dearly loved pieces in the Psalter are found in this section.

Psalm 73: THE PROBLEM OF THE WICKED WHO PROSPER, 73:1-28

Typed as wisdom literature, Psalm 73 is the first of a group of eleven associated with Asaph by title or superscription (cf. intro. to Psalm 50). It deals with the same problem that had been the theme of Psalms 37 and 49, why a just God would permit the wicked to prosper and the righteous to suffer and be oppressed. Much of the wisdom literature in the OT is given to pondering this question. The proverbs assert the blessedness of the righteous and the misery of transgressors. Job examines this thesis from the point of view of a righteous man who suffered much. Ecclesiastes looks at it from the side of a somewhat vain and cynical man who was not "righteous overmuch" (Eccles. 7:16) and yet who "had everything" in the way of wealth, culture, pleasure, and luxury.

Many have commented on the resemblance between Psalm 73 and the Book of Job. Robinson says, "The writer of Ps. 73, for example, like the great poet whose work is enshrined for us in the Book of Job, had faced the question of suffering and its distribution, and takes us through his own spiritual battle."[1] Oesterley comments: "In a sense, this psalm is an epitome of the book of Job . . . it deals with the same problem, follows the same line of thought, and offers one of the few Old Testament

---

[1]*Op. cit.*, p. 124.

adumbrations of a genuine doctrine of immortality. . . . A problem in religious thought, as in science, is created by an apparent clash between theory and fact. Either the theory must be abandoned, or further truth must be elucidated which will bring the discordant fact into the universal scheme. The theory here is the character of God, as revealed through the great prophets; the conflicting fact is the seeming injustice and inequality of divine retribution."[2]

1. *The Problem of the Righteous* (73:1-3)

The first three verses tersely tell the Psalmist's spiritual problem. His faith asserts the fact that **God is good to Israel . . . to such as are of a clean heart** (1). The pure in heart are blessed indeed (Matt. 5:8). From this faith the Psalmist starts, and to this faith he returns. But first certain facts must be brought into focus. He found his spiritual footing threatened (2), and says, "For I was envious of the arrogant, when I saw the prosperity of the wicked" (3, Berk.). Men will always be driven to grapple with the problems posed by the apparent success and prosperity of ungodly and unscrupulous men, and the suffering and hardships borne by those "of whom the world was not worthy" (Heb. 11:38). Many allow their questions to fester into damaging doubt of the justice and goodness of God.

2. *The Prosperity of the Wicked* (73:4-12)

The wealth, pride, and prosperity of the godless are sketched in vivid terms. That such is not the case with all the unrighteous does not obscure the fact that it is true of many. **There are no bands in their death: but their strength is firm** (4) is better, "They suffer no violent pain; their body is well nourished" (Berk.). They seem free from **trouble** (5), secure in their **pride** and unchecked in their **violence** or unscrupulous conduct (6). Among an ancient people always on the edge of starvation, they are fat and **have more than heart could wish** (7). Their speech is cynical and wicked, boastful and blasphemous (8-9). Verses 10-11 are clearer as Moffatt translates: "So people turn to follow them, and see no wrong in them, thinking, 'What does God care? How can the Almighty heed?' " since these **ungodly** folk **prosper in the world** and **increase in riches** (12).

[2]*Op. cit.*, p. 345.

3. *Progress Toward the Solution* (73:13-20)

In the light of what he had observed, the Psalmist was driven to wonder if he had **cleansed** his **heart in vain, and washed** his **hands in innocency** to no effect (13). If the wicked "get ahead," why trouble to be good? In fact, actual suffering and affliction had been his lot (14). Verse 15 means that, even though he had thought such things, he had not breathed his doubts aloud—for to have done so would have been to "have played false to Thy children" (Berk.). He had kept his doubts to himself. Yet his pondering was painful—"Sorely did it trouble me" (16, Moffatt).

Light broke in at last when he went **into the sanctuary of God** (17). Then he saw that the Lord does not immediately settle all accounts. Suddenly he understood that the prosperous wicked whom he had foolishly envied were **set . . . in slippery places** (18) and destined for **destruction. Desolation** and **terrors** would be theirs (19). As everything in **a dream** (20) changes with the moment of awakening, so when God should awake to judgment, everything would be reversed, as for the rich man and Lazarus (cf. Luke 16:19-31). **Thou shalt despise their image** ("imaginings," Berk.).

Lawrence Toombs has eloquently stated this sudden insight: "Not infrequently, as in the case of the psalmist, the situation is seen in a different light in the sanctuary from that in which it appears in the world. The psalmist felt that the difficulty was in his surroundings. In the sanctuary he learned that it was in himself. . . . In the sanctuary the center of the psalmist's life was changed from self to God. . . . The change of center made possible a startling revelation. In his poverty and oppression, he neverthless possessed the only thing in the world worth having: the presence of God in his life (v. 23). To be with God, to have his guidance and counsel, and to be the heir of his promises (v. 24) is a treasure beside which the possessions of the worldly are shoddy trinkets. . . . The prosperity of the wicked was a dream, the presence of God was the reality."[3]

4. *The Prospect for Eternity* (73:21-28)

The new insight brought an immediate and humble confession (21-22; cf. Job 42:3-6). **Reins** (21) would be feelings or conscience. So often when new light comes, we wonder, Why

---

[3]*Op. cit.*, pp. 183-84.

didn't I see that before? God's continual presence was the great-est treasure life could hold (23). Guidance here and glory here-after are the certainty of the saints (24). Who could wish for more? **In heaven or upon earth,** nothing could be better than the Lord himself (25). Though the body grow weak and finally fail, God will be his **portion for ever** (26). Commentators dis-agree as to how clearly the Psalmist envisioned a glory beyond the grave. Certainly what Oesterley notes is true: "Here again the primary condition of belief in a future life is expressed: com-munion with God; but in this psalm what that communion finally results in is more fully realized. Union with the eternal, un-changing God cannot be interrupted by death. As in life on this earth God is with his servant, so in the world to come God will be with him. In the presence of God there is life."[4]

Verses 27-28 give in vivid summary the contrasting ultimate destinies of the wicked and the righteous: **They . . . shall perish . . . destroyed all** (27); **But it is good for me to draw near to God: I have put my trust in the Lord God, that I may declare all thy works** (28). The expression **go a whoring from thee** (27) describes spiritual infidelity against the Lover of their souls.

Psalm 74: LAMENT FOR THE DESOLATION OF THE CITY, 74:1-23

This pitiful poem in the mood of Jeremiah's Lamentations is entitled "Maschil of Asaph" (cf. intro. to Psalms 32 and 50). With one gleam of light in the retrospect of vv. 12-17, it is almost pure dirge, written in a sad minor key. However, that it should be uttered in a prayer to God is in itself an expression of a deep and abiding faith in the face of almost overwhelming tragedy. Commentators differ in assigning dates to the psalm and in iden-tifying the cause of the grief expressed. It has been related to the destruction of Jerusalem in 586 B.C., and again to the Macca-bean period. But the language is sufficiently indefinite to make any dogmatism unadvisable.

1. *The Tragedy of the Present* (74:1-11)

In the tragedy of the times, the poet cries out, **O God, why . . . ?** (1) Ruin, he sees, has fallen upon the land because of divine wrath. **Thine anger smoke**—God's wrath is often associ-ated with burning in the OT. It is "kindled" (e.g., Num. 11:33;

---

[4]*Op. cit.,* p. 91.

Deut. 11:17; II Kings 22:13, 17; Ps. 106:40; etc.). Deut. 29:20 employs the same expression as is found here. The Lord, in wrath, is a "consuming fire" (Deut. 4:24; Heb. 12:29). God is called upon to **remember** His **congregation . . . purchased** and **redeemed,** and **mount Zion,** the place of His dwelling (2). **The rod of thine inheritance** is better "the tribe of thine inheritance" (ASV). **Lift up thy feet unto** (3)—"Turn thy steps toward" (Moffatt)—in order to inflict retribution on the enemy and bring restoration to His house. The foe had invaded **the sanctuary** itself, setting **up their ensigns for signs** (4) and therefore defiling the sacred place. Some have related this to "the abomination that maketh desolate" of Dan. 11:31 and 12:11, but the language does not seem sufficiently strong to warrant such an identification.[5]

Verses 5-6 are difficult in the Hebrew text, but may plausibly be translated, "It looks as if one had brought down the axe on brushwood; all its carved work, too, they have broken down with axe and hammer" (Berk.). The beautiful, carved, wood panelling of the Temple had been smashed and set afire (7). The burning of the Temple is mentioned only on the occasion of Nebuchadnezzar's destruction of Jerusalem in 586 B.C. (II Kings 25:9). **The synagogues of God** (8) in the Hebrew means "meeting places" or "holy places." If **synagogues** is a proper translation, the psalm would be very late, since synagogues came into common use only after the Exile, and are not mentioned anywhere else in the OT.

We see not our signs (9) is the same word as in 4. "We do not see the evidences of God's blessing, only the signs of our enemy's triumph." **No more any prophet** would mean no one to speak with authority for the true God; and none can discern **how long** the ruin will prevail. **O God, why?** (1) is followed by **O God, how long?** (10) How long shall this go on? Will God submit to blasphemy **for ever?** God seems to stand by as with folded hands, doing nothing (11). **Pluck it out of thy bosom** is interpreted by Moffatt, "Stretch out thy right hand and strike!"

2. *The Testimony of the Past* (74:12-17)

The one ray of light in the darkness is the memory of what the Lord had done in the past. "God my King is from old" (12, RSV) recalls the God of the fathers, whose saving power was

---

[5]Cf. Barnes, *op. cit.,* II, 357.

attested in the history of His people. **Divide the sea** (13); cf. Exod. 14:21. **The heads of the dragons in the waters and leviathan** (14) are biblical symbolism for Egypt. Cf. comments on Job 41:1. **Cleave the fountain and the flood** (15) is interpreted as, "Open springs and torrents" (Moffatt)—cf. Exod. 17:6; Num. 20:11. **Driedst up mighty rivers** refers to Israel crossing the Jordan (cf. Josh. 3:15-16).

The day is thine, the night also is thine (16), both literally and figuratively. God is Lord of the deepest night as well as of the brightest day. "Standing somewhere in the shadows you will find Him." God is the sovereign Lord of nature (17). Certainly He can help His brokenhearted people.

3. The Thought of the Prospect (74:18-23)

Deliverance is not yet, but faith begins to rise. More than God's people, the **Lord** himself has been **blasphemed** (18). **Foolish people** are "impious people" (Moffatt, RSV). In the OT, "fools" and the "foolish" are not the silly or the thoughtless, but the evil and the godless. **Turtledove** (19) or dove is a symbol of Israel in its defenselessness. **The congregation of thy poor** is better "the life of Thy afflicted ones" (Berk.). Israel's only hope is that God will keep His side of **the covenant** although the nation had broken its side shamelessly by disobedience and idolatry (20). Verse 20 suggests that even **the dark places** (caves) had not been a refuge from the violence and cruelty of the invader. **Let not the oppressed return ashamed** (21) means, Let them not be turned away from the presence of the Lord with their petitions denied. **The foolish man** (22); cf. comment on 18. The **voice** of His **enemies** (23) in their boasting and blasphemy should arouse the Lord to judgment. The answer tarried long, but it came in God's appointed time, not a day too early and not a moment too late (cf. Ezra 1:1-6).

Psalm 75: A LITURGY OF PRAISE, 75:1-10

This hymn of thanksgiving is in happy contrast to the gloom of Psalm 74. It bears in its superscription the identification "of Asaph" (cf. intro. to Psalm 50), common to the psalms of this group. In addition it is inscribed to "the chief Musician" and described by the word *Altaschith* (cf. intro. to Psalm 57). Morgan conceives of the psalm as a dramatic poem: "It opens with a chorus which is an ascription of praise (verse 1). This is answered directly by God himself. He declares that in the set time He judges. All the appearances of the hour may be perplexing, but the heart may know that He knows, and awaits only the right moment to act. Chaos may characterize the outlook, but order enwraps it all, for God has set up the pillars (verses 2, 3). Then the solo of the confident soul breaks forth, and, addressing the wicked, charges them not to be confident because God is the judge."[6]

1. *Recognition* (75:1)

An invocation recognizes the nearness of **God** in His **wondrous works,** and the propriety of praise and thanksgiving to Him. **Thy name is near**—God, as here, is often identified with His name (cf. Isa. 30:27). This very presence is cause for praise.

2. *Response* (75:2-3)

God speaks, in this section and the next, declaring His sovereignty and His justice. **When I shall receive the congregation** (2) is better, "At the time which I have appointed I will render fair judgments" (Berk.). "The Judge of all sets His own time" (Berk., fn.). The Amp. OT clarifies 3: "When the earth totters, and all the inhabitants of it, it is I who will poise *and* keep steady its pillars." **Selah;** cf. comment on 3:2.

3. *Retribution* (75:4-8)

In God's good time, accounts will be balanced and retribution will be visited upon those who persist in their sinful ways. **For unto the fools** (4), cf. comment on 74:18. **Lift not up the horn** (5) is clarified by Moffatt: "Do not flaunt your power." **A stiff neck,** either in stubbornness and pride, refusing to bow the head, or "with full throat"—that is, loud and boastful. **Promotion cometh neither from the east** (6); not chance but justice controls the ultimate outcomes of life. "Whosoever exalteth himself shall be abased; and he that humbleth himself shall be exalted" (Luke 14:11). **God is the judge** (7) is a fact His people seem to have trouble keeping in mind. He does not give the right of judgment to any other. This truth is the terror of the godless. **In the hand of the Lord there is a cup** (8), filled with red wine (lit., "foaming," dangerously fermented), which the wicked shall drink to the last bitter drop of **the dregs thereof.**

---

[6]*Op. cit., ad loc.*

4. *Rejoicing* (75: 9-10)

In sharp contrast, the righteous, represented by the Psalmist, will **declare** God's goodness **for ever** and **sing praises to the God of Jacob** (9; Israel). **The horns** (10) stands for the power **of the wicked** and **of the righteous.** The power **of the wicked** will be **cut off,** but the power **of the righteous shall be exalted.**

Psalm 76: A Song of Celebration, 76: 1-12

This is another psalm in major key, rejoicing in the celebration of a great victory and redundant with praise to the power of God. For *Neginoth* in the superscription, cf. introduction to Psalm 4; for "Asaph," cf. introduction to Psalm 50. In style and mood, this hymn is related to Psalms 46 and 48, both of which also exalt the Lord as the Deliverer of Zion. No certain historical identification of the deliverance is possible, although many commentators take their clue from an addition of the words, "With reference to the Assyrian" in the title in the LXX. They then refer it to the deliverance of Jerusalem from Sennacherib in 701 B.C. (II Kings 19: 35-37; Isa. 37: 36-38).

1. *Defense* (76: 1-3)

God as the Defense of His people is the theme of the first stanza. The Lord is the **God** of **Judah** in particular and all **Israel** in general (1). **Salem** (2) is a short form for Jerusalem (Gen. 14: 18; Heb. 7: 1-2). **His tabernacle** (Heb., "pavilion") is not the term used for the Tabernacle constructed by Moses in the wilderness and which served until the construction of the Temple by Solomon. It is a general term suggesting a temporary abode. The source of the great victory (3) was the presence of God "in the camp." **Selah;** cf. comment on 3: 2.

2. *Defeat of the Foe* (76: 4-6)

These verses lend credence to the LXX addition to the title (cf. intro. to the psalm). The Lord has defeated Israel's enemy, and **sleep** (death) is twice mentioned as associated with the defeat. Verse 4 has given the translators considerable difficulty. *The Berkeley Version* follows KJV, "Glorious Thou art, more glorious and more excellent than the mountains of prey." But Moffatt follows a LXX variant reading, "Thou didst strike terror from the hills eternal." He also renders the first part of 5, "The valiant fell a prey to thee and slept their last." **None of the men** of might have found their hands (5) is better, "None of the men of might could raise their hands" (Amp. OT).

3. Danger in God's Terrible Wrath (76:7-9)

The wicked are exposed to the searing fire of the wrath of God. Neither here nor elsewhere in the Bible is the anger of the Lord to be thought of as comparable to the carnal rage of human frustration. It is always the necessary reaction of the supremely Holy One against the evil that would destroy the objects of His love. Even the earth (8) may be said to stand in awe at the revelation of divine judgment. The two-sidedness of judgment is seen here also. It is condemnation on the rebellious but vindication to the meek (9), the godly and oppressed.

4. Dedication (76:10-12)

In view of God's mighty acts, the faithful are called upon to make their vows and bring their gifts in worship to the Lord their God. Surely the wrath of man shall praise thee (10) declares that a sovereign God brings even man's evil wrath and its works around to work His glory (cf. Exod. 9:16; Isa. 45:24). "We know that in everything God works for good with those who love him, who are called according to his purpose" (Rom. 8:28, RSV). The remainder of wrath shalt thou restrain, or as Perowne translates, "With the remainder of wrath Thou girdest Thyself." "With the remainder of man's wrath, his last impotent efforts to assert his own power, God girds Himself, puts it on, so to speak, as an ornament—clothes Himself therewith to His own glory."[7]

Vow, and pay (11), since the vow without the payment is mockery (Eccles. 5:4-5). Let all that be round about him shows the Lord as the rallying point and true center of His people. Cut off the spirit of princes (12) may mean, as suggested by The Berkeley Version, snuff out their lives; or "cut off the spirit (of pride and fury) of princes." (Amp. OT). Moffatt interprets the last part of 12, He "terrifies a tyrant."

Psalm 77: Song Instead of Sorrow, 77:1-20

This psalm is a lament that like so many of its kind begins in the shadow of sorrow and rises to the sunshine of song. For

---

[7]Perowne, op. cit., II, 44.

terms in the superscription see as follows: "Jeduthun," introduction to Psalm 39; "Asaph," introduction to Psalm 50. Morgan's characterization of the psalm is significant:

> Verse 10 is the pivot on which the psalm turns, from a description of an experience of darkness and sorrow to one of gladness and praise. The first part tells of sorrow overwhelming the soul. The second gives a song which is the outcome of a vision that has robbed sorrow of its sting. In the first part, a great infirmity overshadows the sky, and there is no song. In the second, a great song pours itself out, and sorrow is forgotten. The difference is that between a man brooding over trouble and a man seeing high above it the enthroned God. In the first half, self is predominant. In the second, God is seen in His glory. A very simple method with the psalm makes this perfectly clear. In verses 1 to 9 the first personal pronoun occurs twenty-two times, and there are eleven references to God by name, title, and pronoun. In the second, there are only three personal references and twenty-four mentions of God.
>
> The message of the psalm is that to brood on sorrow is to be broken and disheartened, while to see God is to sing on the darkest day. Once we come to know that our years are of His right hand, there is light everywhere, and the song ascends.[8]

Since the psalm is chiefly a personal lament, no historical occasion can be found. A possible indication of date of composition is the similarity between vv. 16-20 and Hab. 3:10-15. Although scholarly opinion differs, the priority of the psalm seems most likely. In such an event, it would be dated before 600 B.C.[9] Others see in the reference to "Jacob and Joseph" (15) an indication that the Northern Kingdom (Joseph) was still in existence and prefer a date earlier than 722 B.C.[10]

1. Sorrow (77:1-3)

Day and night the Psalmist sought the Lord in earnest prayer. He was deeply troubled. The KJV rendering, **My sore ran in the night** (2), suggests a physical illness as the source of or as compounding the sorrow. However, the Hebrew text more naturally reads, "My hand was stretched out in the night and failed not," indicating the outstretched hands of supplication. Whatever the cause of his deep grief, his **soul refused to be com-**

---

[8]*Op. cit.,* p. 249.   [9]Perowne, *op. cit.,* II, 47.

[10]W. Stewart McCullough, "Psalms 72—92, 94, 97—99, 101—19, 139" (Exegesis), *The Interpreter's Bible,* ed. George A. Buttrick, *et al.,* IV (New York: Abingdon Press, 1955), 409.

forted, as, in Gen. 37:35, Jacob refused to be comforted when brought word of Joseph's supposed death. Read v. 3, more correctly: "When I was moaning, I thought of God; when my spirit was faint, I pondered" (Berk.). **Selah** (3); cf. comment on 3:2.

2. *Searching* (77:4-9)

In the hour of his extremity, the Psalmist commences his search for God. He remembers former blessings, and his soul breaks out in an agony of questioning. The memory of better days past adds poignancy to the pains of the present. Sleep fled from his eyes, and his sorrow sank into wordlessness (4). **The years of ancient times** (5) would be "the years of ages (past)."[11] The misery of the moment brought to mind earlier times when he had a **song in the night** (6; cf. 42:8; Job 35:10). **My spirit made diligent search** for some ray of light in the darkness.

The direction of the Psalmist's search is shown in the six questions that tumble from his lips. These are genuine heart cries, and yet rhetorical in that they clearly demand negative answers. God has not **cast off for ever** (7); He will not fail **to be favourable** again; **his mercy** is not **clean gone** (ceased) **for ever** (8); **his promise** does not **fail;** He has not **forgotten to be gracious** (9); He has not **in anger shut up** (stopped) **his tender mercies.**

3. *Surrender* (77:10-15)

The questions are followed by a series of commitments indicated by the repeated **I will** of surrender (10-12). The Psalmist begins to turn from self to the Saviour, and finds in the memory of past faithfulness faith for future fulfilment. **This is my infirmity** (10) probably means, "This is my trial, that God seems to have cast me aside." The latter part of the verse is difficult, and has been understood in various ways: "This is my grief, that the Most High no longer has the strength he had" (Moffatt); "This is my sorrow, that the right hand of the Highest has changed"[12]; "This grieves me; the right hand of the Most High changes" (Berk.). Here is the low point. The only direction from the bottom is up, and from these depths of doubt the Psalmist begins his ascent (cf. intro. to the psalm).

---

[11]Perowne, *op. cit.*, II, 47.   [12]*Ibid.*, p. 50.

Memory of **the works of the Lord** (11), **God's wonders of old, His work** (12), **His doings,** and **His way** (13) compel the conclusion implied in another rhetorical question, **Who is so great a God as our God? Thy way . . . is in the sanctuary** has been variously translated: "Thy dealings were divine" (Moffatt); "Thy way . . . is holy" (Berk., RSV); "Thy way is in holiness" (Smith-Goodspeed). All emphasize the purity and rightness of God's ways. **Thou hast declared thy strength** (14) is better "made known Thy strength" by demonstration as well as declaration. **Thou hast with thine arm redeemed thy people** (15) is a typical OT description for the display of God's mighty power at the Exodus (cf. Exod. 15:16; Isa. 63:12).

4. *Sovereignty* (77:16-20)

The supremacy of God in both nature and history is carolled in the closing section of the psalm. Verse 16 is similar to 114:3, where both the Red Sea and the Jordan are mentioned. In both instances, God's power over the floods was evident: **they were afraid.** Cloudburst, **thunder,** lightning (17), and earthquake (18) have all given evidence of the power of the Creator-God. He who fashioned the earth also controls it. **Thy way is in the sea, and thy path in the great waters, and thy footsteps are not known** (19)—as Perowne quotes, "We know not, they knew not, by what precise means the deliverance was wrought . . . and we need not know; the obscurity, the mystery here, as elsewhere, was part of the lesson. . . . All that we see distinctly is, that through this dark and terrible night, with the enemy pressing close behind, and the driving sea on either side, He led His people like sheep by the hand of Moses and Aaron."[13] Through the terror and mystery of the crossing of the Red Sea shines the wonder of God's care for His people like a shepherd for his **flock.** Even though it was **by the hand of Moses and Aaron** (20), it was the Lord who led.

Psalm 78: THE HAND OF GOD IN HISTORY, 78:1-72

This is the longest of what are sometimes called "historical psalms" (including 105, 106, 114, and 136). Its dominant theme is the central fact of Israel's history, the deliverance from Egypt. It has been called a "didactic ballad,"[14] and opens much like

---

[13]*Ibid.,* pp. 52-53.   [14]McCullough, *op. cit.,* 4:414.

some of the chapters in the Book of Proverbs, actually using the word *mashal* (v. 2, parable), which is the ordinary term for "proverb." Robinson describes the psalm as "a poetic summary of Israel's history down to the establishment of the monarchy, described in order to illustrate the dangers of forgetting the 'instruction' which people like the Psalmist could give."[15] For "Maschil" in the title, cf. introduction to Psalm 32; for "Asaph," cf. introduction to Psalm 50.

It has been noted that the Psalmist appears more favorable to Judah[16] and most critical of Ephraim, the northern kingdom.[17] This would almost certainly imply a date following the division of Solomon's kingdom under Rehoboam and the rebellion and apostasy of the northern tribes under Jeroboam. The author shows acquaintance with the Pentateuch, and particularly the Book of Deuteronomy. As Snaith notes, the charge against the people "is not that they were more irreligious than their neighbors. The charge is that they were indistinguishable from them. It was but a small minority who were different and were faithful to Jehovah alone."[18]

1. The Purpose of History (78:1-8)

The psalm opens with a section showing its didactic or instructional purpose. History is "His-story," the recital of God's wonderful works designed to impress upon the minds of the young the inescapable conviction that disobedience always leads to disaster. The people are called upon to **give ear** (obedient attention) ... **to my law** (1), literally "my *torah*," teaching, guidance, instruction. The Psalmist speaks as God's representative. **Parable** (2, *mashal*) is literally "a comparison," whether in likeness or contrast. **Dark sayings** comes from a term meaning either a pointed, sharp saying or a riddle, the meaning of which may not be at first apparent. This verse is cited in Matt. 13:34-35 in reference to Christ's use of parables, where **dark sayings of old** is given as "things which have been kept secret from the foundation of the world," following the LXX. It is the moral lesson of history that the Psalmist has in mind. What is to be recited and taught to the generations to come has been received from **our fathers** (3). The instruction to be passed along to succeed-

[15]*Op. cit.*, p. 144.
[17]Perowne, *op. cit.*, II, 56-58.
[16]Oesterley, *op. cit.*, pp. 368-69.
[18]*Op. cit.*, II, 52.

ing generations concerns **the praises of the Lord, and his strength, and his wonderful works that he hath done (4)**.

God has **established a testimony . . . and appointed a law (5)** for His people. The tablets of stone upon which the Ten Commandments were written are called "the testimony" (Exod. 25:16, 21). This law was to be faithfully transmitted to **the children (6)**—our charter for Christian education (cf. Deut. 4:9-10; 6:6-7; 11:18-19; etc.). The purpose of such instruction was the practical one, **That they might set their hope in God, and . . . keep his commandments (7)**. In such obedience they would differ from their fathers, who were **a stubborn and rebellious generation . . . that set not their heart aright, and whose spirit was not stedfast with God (8)**.

2. *Ephraim's Rebellious Spirit* (78:9-16)

The reason for selecting **Ephraim (9)** for special rebuke appears in vv. 67-68. **Ephraim** was the younger son of Joseph, and was blessed before his older brother, Manasseh (Gen. 48:8-20). After the tribe of Levi was selected as the priestly tribe, the descendants of each of Joseph's sons were designated as separate tribes. Because the tribe of Ephraim became the leading tribe of the northern group, the Northern Kingdom was frequently called Ephraim. Within the borders of the tribe were located both Shiloh, the religious capital of the nation before David, and Shechem (see map 1), the historic gathering place of the tribes (Josh. 24:1; Judg. 9:2; I Kings 12:1). After the revolt of the ten northern tribes, Ephraim led the apostasy that resulted in the final destruction of the Northern Kingdom as a political entity in 722 B.C. Like cowardly though well-armed soldiers, they **turned back in the day of battle (9), kept not the covenant of God (10), refused to walk in his law**, and forgot **his works, and his wonders that he had shewed them (11)**.

In rapid recital, the Psalmist recounts **the marvellous things (12)** the Lord wrought **in the sight of their fathers, in the land of Egypt, in the field of Zoan**, or Tanis, near the eastern border of lower Egypt (see map 2). Its mention here seems to identify it as the residence of the Pharaoh with whom Moses and Aaron dealt (Exod. 5:1—12:31). **The field of Zoan** was probably the rich alluvial plain surrounding that delta city. The plagues inflicted upon the Egyptians are described in some detail in 43-51. Here there is mention simply of the division of **the sea** at the time of the Exodus (13; Exod. 14:15-22) and the pillar of **cloud** and **of fire** (14; Exod. 13:21-22). Noted also was the provision of water **in the wilderness** (15:16; Exod. 17:1-6; Num. 20:7-11).

3. *Rebellion in the Wilderness* (78:17-39)

In a long passage, the poet gives instance after instance of the faithless and vacillating conduct of the people during their sojourn in the wilderness between Egypt and Canaan. The fearful unbelief of the tribes in the face of possible famine was answered both by the manna (24; Exod. 16:14) and by the flight of quails (27; Num. 11:31). **They tempted** (tested) **God in their heart** (18) by demanding special manifestations of His supernatural power—a sin the Saviour refused in His wilderness experience (Matt. 4:5-7; Luke 4:9-12). They asked **meat for their lust** (inordinate appetite). Despite the miraculous provision of water, the people questioned God's power to provide **bread** and **flesh** (20). Cynical unbelief brought the wrath of God upon them (21-22). The **manna** is described as **the corn of heaven** (24) and **angels' food** (25), literally, "bread of the mighty." No very convincing natural explanation has been suggested for the occurrence of the manna, at least in sufficient quantities to feed the numbers of Israelites involved. On the other hand, **the south** and the **east wind** is described as bringing the vast numbers of birds (quail, Num. 11:31-32); they were migratory fowl flying from southern Egypt up into Arabia. Even in this abundant provision, **they were not estranged from their lust** (30). They were filled, but not satisfied, as so many are today in the multitude of the things they possess. The result was **wrath** and judgment (31-33; cf. Num. 11:33). **The fattest** (31) would be the most haughty. **Vanity** (33) here means frustration or futility. **Their years in trouble** is literally "years in terror."

Divine judgment brought temporary but apparently insincere repentance (34-36). **When he slew them** (34) is better "When he smote them" (Smith-Goodspeed). If the "goodness of God" does not lead "to repentance" (Rom. 2:4), He may have to employ severity. But so often "deathbed repentance"—if the subject recovers—does not prove to be genuine. The problem was a **heart** that **was not right** (37), and a temporizing attitude toward **his covenant**. Yet the **compassion** and mercy of God were seen over and over again, in that His justice did not exact all its due (38). **He remembered** the weakness and transiency of the people He sought to lead (39). In v. 38, Oesterley **sees** the suggestion of an idea that "lies at the heart of the Christian Gospel. The breach between God and man, cleft by human sin, must be bridged by 'atonement.' This is true of all religions, and the almost universal theory is that this atonement must be made from the human side. In his ascription of the initiative to God, the psalmist seems unconsciously to foreshadow the great truth whose full expression is that 'God was in Christ reconciling the world unto himself.' "[19]

4. *The Signs in Egypt and Israel's Failure* (78:40-64)

The Psalmist returns again to the events surrounding the Exodus with the design of reinforcing his argument that the unbelief and disobedience of the nation were inexcusable in the light of what God had done for them. The history in this section is carried down to the desolation of Shiloh and the establishment of Zion. The nation provoked ("rebelled against," RSV) and grieved the Lord (40). **They turned back,** tested and **limited** (dishonored) Him (41). The reason was their forgetfulness of the events surrounding the Exodus (42-43). For **field of Zoan,** cf. comment on v. 12. **His hand** (42) is better "His power."

Most of the plagues inflicted on the Egyptians are recalled: the turning of the water into **blood** (44; the first plague, Exod. 7:20); the **flies** (45; the fourth plague, Exod. 8:21-24); the **frogs** (45; the second plague, Exod. 8:2-13); the locusts (46; the eighth plague, Exod. 10:4-15; **the caterpiller** represents the larva stage of the locust); **the hail** (47-48; the seventh plague, Exod. 9:18-33); **frost** (47) would be sleet or hailstones; and the **death** of **the firstborn** (49-51; the last plague, Exod. 12:29-30). **Evil angels** (49), or messengers of evil ("the destroyer" of Exod. 12:13, 23), resulted in **the pestilence** (50). **He made a way to his anger** (50) is better, "He made a path for his anger" (RSV). **The tabernacles of Ham** (51) is a reference to the "Table of the Nations" in which the descendants of Ham, second son of Noah, settled in the area which later became Egypt (Gen. 10:6-20; cf. 105:23, 27; 106:22).

Contrasting the progressive judgments against the people of Egypt and their false gods, the people of Israel were led **forth like sheep** (52), **like a flock,** and in safety from **their enemies** (53). **His sanctuary, even . . . this mountain** (54), was Mount Zion, where the Temple was built. **His right hand** had **purchased** it by giving supernatural aid in driving out the pagan occupants (55). **Divided them an inheritance by line** is literally "allotted them their inheritance"—an allusion to the casting of lots in apportioning the land of Canaan among the tribes (Josh. 14:1 ff.).

Despite the repeated manifestations of God's power, the people **tempted** (tested) **and provoked the most high God, and kept not his testimonies** (56), or laws (cf. comment, v. 5). The generations living after the possession and partition of the Promised Land were as faithless as **their fathers** in the wilderness (57). **A deceitful bow** is "one which disappoints the archer, by not sending the arrow straight to the mark."[20] **Their high places** (58) were shrines dedicated to idol worship. **Moved him to jealousy** is a common OT expression to describe God's claim to exclusive loyalty from the people He had redeemed. **Graven images** were idols. **When God heard this** (59), i.e., took note of it, He **greatly abhorred Israel,** or as the Hebrew literally reads, "He rejected Israel utterly." God rejects those who reject Him (cf. I Sam. 15:23; Hos. 4:6).

He forsook the tabernacle of Shiloh (60). The Tabernacle constructed in the wilderness (Exodus 25—40) was at Shiloh (in the territory allotted the tribe of Ephraim, about thirty-five miles north northeast of Jerusalem) during the entire period of the judges (Josh. 18:10; Judg. 18:31; I Sam. 4:3). God forsook it when the ark was captured by the Philistines (I Samuel 4), for the ark was never brought back to Shiloh. The Tabernacle itself was first moved to Nob (I Samuel 21), and later to Gibeon (I Kings 3:4). The ark of the covenant is called **his strength . . . and his glory** (61; cf. I Sam. 4:3, 21; 132:8). The people, described as God's **inheritance** (62), were given into the hands of bitter enemies who ruthlessly destroyed both **young men** (63) and **priests** (64). The utter desolation of the land is seen in its silence. Neither the joyous songs of **marriage** (63) nor the **lamentation** of the bereaved (64) is to be heard.

5. *God's Purpose Fulfilled in Zion* (78:65-72)

These verses describe the renewal of Israel's fortunes, with probable reference to the long series of victories won by Samuel, Saul, and David over the Philistines (I Samuel 7 and throughout). **The Lord awaked** (65) is the poet's familiar description of

[20]Perowne, *op. cit.,* II, 70.

divine intervention on behalf of His people (cf. 7:7; 44:24). **A mighty man that shouteth by reason of wine;** cf. Isa. 42:13. Explosive, exuberant power **smote his enemies** (66). **Perpetual reproach**—as the term "Philistine" actually is to this day. Long before the final rebellion and destruction of the northern tribes headed by **Ephraim,** God's choice of **Judah** and **mount Zion** was indicated (67-68). The Temple had by this time been built by Solomon (69), the son of David whom the Lord **chose** to lead **his people** (70-71). The establishment of the kingdom with its capital in Jerusalem, where Zion was located, was a tribute to the statesmanship of David (72).

Psalm 79: "The Funeral Anthem of a Nation,"[21] 79:1-13

This psalm of lament, bearing an inscription to Asaph (cf. intro. to Psalm 50), was composed on the occasion of a great national catastrophe, probably the same one mourned with similar pathos in Psalm 74. Here, as there, opinions differ as to the historical occasion, varying from the desolation of Jerusalem in 586 B.C. to the conquest of the city by Antiochus Epiphanes in the much later Maccabean period. There seems no way to fix the date with certainty. This, of course, does not in any sense alter its value in expressing deep personal and national grief in times of disaster.

1. *Complaint* (79:1-4)

Characteristic of psalms of lament is the utterance of the poet's distress in the face of the circumstances by which he is confronted. **The heathen** (literally, *goyyim,* the nations) **are come into thine inheritance** (1), defiling the **temple** and desolating the city. Great numbers of the people had been slain (4), **and there was none to bury them** (3). **Become a reproach** (4), the butt of **scorn and derision.**

2. *Cry for Vengeance* (79:5-12)

The major portion of the poem is the Psalmist's impassioned plea for vengeance to be visited upon those who had caused the calamity. **How long?** (5) is the instinctive question of any heart in the time of oppression. On **thy jealousy** see comment on 78:58. God had allowed other nations to become "the rod of his

---

²¹*Ibid.,* II, 74.

anger" (cf. Isa. 10:5) in bringing judgment to disobedient Israel. But certainly His justice would visit the sins of **the heathen** upon them (6). Verse 8 is a plea for mercy and forgiveness. **Prevent us** is, in the Hebrew, "come to meet us," in the gracious manner of the father with the prodigal (Luke 15:20). The Lord is the **God of our salvation** (9), who acts **for the glory of His name.** Here is a striking prayer for atonement, since the term translated **purge away** is literally "make atonement for" (cf. comment on 78:39).

Those who ask, **Where is their God?** (10) may see Him in His acts of judgment against those who had shed **the blood of His servants.** God should be moved to pity by **the sighing of the prisoner** (11). **Preserve thou those that are appointed to die** is, literally, "Spare the sons of death." **Sevenfold into their bosom** (12) suggests a perfect and complete retribution as indicated by the number seven.

3. *Commitment to Praise* (79:13)

The typical vow of thanksgiving that characterizes psalms of lament is very brief but very expressive: **So we thy people and sheep of thy pasture will give thee thanks for ever: we will shew forth thy praise to all generations.**

Psalm 80: A CRY FOR RESTORATION, 80:1-19

This is another psalm of lament, differing from the majority of the type in that it focuses its attention more exclusively on God than on circumstances. Oesterley comments: "The psalmist is convinced of Yahweh's special relation to Israel, and of his care manifested in the past. He cannot believe in the final desertion of the people, and pleads that the power of Yahweh, which he does not for an instant doubt, will be once more revealed in the restoration of his chosen race. It is true that calamity has befallen the nation. . . . But this poet . . . unlike so many of the Psalmists . . . can simply turn back to the Shepherd of Israel with his faith unshaken, and be sure that in the end all will be well."[22]

The psalm is noteworthy also for a refrain, "Turn us again . . . cause thy face to shine; and we shall be saved" (3, 7, 19), with an increasing intensity in the divine appellation: "O God"

[22]*Op. cit.*, p. 369.

(3); "O God of hosts" (7); "O Lord God of hosts" (19). For the terms in the title, see introductions to Psalms 50 and 60.

1. *The Lord as Shepherd* (80:1-3)

God is designated as the **Shepherd of Israel** (1), one of the most beautiful metaphors in the Bible (cf. Psalm 23; Isa. 40:11; etc.). **Leadest Joseph** indicates a rather obvious preoccupation with the northern tribes (cf. comment on 2), leading to the speculation that the poet may have been a native of the Northern Kingdom. **Dwellest between the cherubims** is literally "sitting above" or "enthroned above" the cherubim over the ark of the covenant in the holy of holies, the special location of God's throne on earth (cf. I Chron. 13:6; Ps. 99:1; Isa. 6:1). The combination of these names **Ephraim and Benjamin and Manasseh** (2) has intrigued the commentators. Benjamin remained with Judah after the division of the tribes, although its proximity to Ephraim and Manasseh may have led many of its inhabitants to defect to the north. It has been noted that Ephraim and Manasseh were the sons of Joseph, and Joseph and Benjamin were the sons of Jacob's best-loved wife, Rachel. It is also interesting to note that these three tribes were placed together in the order of march in the wilderness, immediately following the ark (Num. 2:17-24), a circumstance which may well account for their conjunction here in connection with the obvious reference to the ark in v. 1.

The refrain (cf. intro.) occurs first in v. 3, at the close of the section. **Cause thy face to shine** means, "Look upon us favorably." **We shall be saved,** i.e., delivered from our enemies, our calamities, and more basically, the sins that brought disaster upon us. The first refrain is addressed simply *Elohim,* **O God.**

2. *The Lord as Judge* (80:4-7)

The verses down to the second refrain reflect the judgments of God against the evils of the people. The cry of the Psalmist is to the **Lord God of hosts** (4), a term for the sovereign control by God of "armies" both of angels and of men. **Against the prayer of thy people** is better translated "against Thy people who pray." The object of God's wrath was not the prayers but the pray-ers. **Bread of tears** and **tears to drink** (5) indicated that tears had been their portion day and night. **A strife unto**

(6), in the sense of being the object of attack by the smaller nearby nations. **Our enemies laugh** in scorn and evil satisfaction at the distress of the Israelites. For the refrain in 7, cf. comment on 3. The address here is to the **God of hosts,** *Elohim Sabaoth,* "God of armies, of heavenly and earthly powers."

3. *The Lord as Husbandman* (80:8-19)

The balance of the psalm is built around the familiar biblical comparison of the husbandman and the vine. In the OT, Israel is compared with vine and vineyard in Isa. 5:1-7; 27:2-6; Jer. 2:21; 12:10; Ezek. 17:5-10. God brought His **vine out of Egypt** (8). He **cast out the heathen** (from Canaan), cleared the ground, **and planted it.** It took **deep root,** and **filled the land** (9). It flourished until its **shadow** covered **the hills,** and the branches **were like the goodly cedars** (10), literally, "cedars of God." Its **boughs** extended from **the sea** to **the river** (11), from the Mediterranean to the Euphrates (cf. Gen. 28:14; Deut. 11:24; Josh. 1:4; I Kings 4:24). All of this is a vivid description of the flourishing kingdom of David and Solomon.

In striking contrast to the prosperity of the past was the misery of the moment. The Psalmist, now, does not seek the moral and spiritual causes of Israel's defeats. His **Why?** (12) is rhetorical as he seeks to contrast the present with the past. His hope, soon to be expressed in prayer, is that the mercy of God may restore the blessings of days gone by. But at the present the choice vine of God's planting is unprotected by the **hedges** (walls or fences) He had built, and is prey for every passerby. Wild animals desolate it without hindrance (13).

Complaint gives way to petition as the **God of hosts** (14) is besought to **return,** and **visit** (with deliverance and restoration) His **vine . . . vineyard** (15) and **branch. Thy right hand** would be God's purpose and power. **Seared with fire** and **cut down** (16), it is ready to **perish at the rebuke of thy countenance.** The statement, **Let thy hand be upon the man of thy right hand, upon the son of man whom thou madest strong for thyself** (17), has been variously interpreted as referring to the Messiah or to the nation of Israel. The context would seem to tip the scales in favor of understanding these words as a poetic description of the nation. The prophets not uncommonly speak of Israel as God's son (cf. Exod. 4:22; Isa. 1:2; 63:16; 64:8; Jer. 31:9; Hos. 11:1; Mal. 1:6).

The vow of obedience or thanksgiving that customarily closes psalms of lament is found in 18: **So will not we go back from thee.** Here is an admission that the cause of the disaster Israel had suffered is the fact that the people had turned away from the Lord. **Quicken us** is, literally, "Keep us alive." For the refrain of 19, cf. comment on 3. The address is to *Yahweh Elohim Sabaoth,* **Lord God of hosts** (cf. comment on 7).

Psalm 81: The Meaning of Religious Ritual, 81:1-16

Psalm 81 is a psalm of adoration intended apparently to be used at the Feast of Trumpets in connection with *Yom Kippur,* the Day of Atonement, and the Feast of Tabernacles. These were fall festivals, occurring in late September and early October by our calendar, and they marked the beginning of the civil new year. More than all the annual religious festivals of the OT, these were marked with joyous celebration of the goodness of God.

The purpose of the psalm seems to be to interpret to the people the meaning and the practical lessons of their ceremonial observances. One of the major problems of the religious life is the loss of meaning for ritual that becomes more or less a matter of mechanical repetition. Perowne comments, "There could be no grander conception of the true significance of the religious feasts of the nation than this. They are so many memorials of God's love and power, so many monuments set up to testify at once of His goodness, and of Israel's ingratitude and perverseness, so many solemn occasions on which He comes as King and Father to visit them, to rekindle anew their loyalty and their affection, and to scatter amongst them the treasures of His bounty. To give this interpretation to the Festivals, to put in its true light the national joy at their celebration, appears to have been the object of the Psalmist."[23]

Oesterley also states, from a slightly different point of view, that the psalm has a single lesson: "Absolute and unwavering fidelity and consecration to the one living and true God is the indispensable condition of success and prosperity. While human experience belies the doctrine on the lower planes, in the highest sense it still remains, and ever must remain, profoundly true."[24]

For the terms in the superscription, cf. introductions to Psalms 8 and 50.

---

[23]*Op. cit.,* II, 94.　　　　　　　[24]*Op. cit.,* p. 373.

1. The Summons to Song (81:1-5)

The first division of the psalm is in the poet's own words. It is his call to the people to join in the joy and worship of the festival. Joyous music, both in song and with instruments, is to characterize the worship of the Lord. The blessing and joy that mark OT piety at its best are here clearly seen. **Sing aloud unto God our strength** (1), is the summons, making **a joyful noise unto the God of Jacob.** The phrase **Take a psalm** (2) is literally, "Bring a melody," or, "Raise a song." For **timbrel** (tambourine) **... harp ... psaltery,** cf. comments on 33:2. **Blow up the trumpet** (3) is better, "Blow the trumpet." The *shophar* or ram's horn is still used in the synagogue at this particular festival as per Num. 29:1. **In the new moon, in the time appointed,** is literally "in the new moon, at the full moon," recognizing that the festivals in question begin on the first day of the month and conclude after the fifteenth day. The reason for these observances is the **statute** (4) and **law ... ordained ... for a testimony** (5) at the time of the Exodus from Egypt. **Where I heard a language that I understood not** is thought by some to be the Egyptian language, but more probably the voice of God, since what follows is an oracle in which the Lord himself speaks to the people. The RSV translates, "I hear a voice I had not known." Delitzsch comments: "It was the language of a known, and yet unknown, God, which Israel heard from Sinai. God, in fact, now revealed Himself to Israel in a new character, not only as the Redeemer and Saviour of His people from their Egyptian bondage, but also as their King, giving them a law which bound them together as a people, and was the basis of their national existence."[25]

2. The Sovereign Speaks (81:6-16)

The balance of the psalm is in the form of an oracle, in which the Psalmist utters the words of the Lord in the first person. It falls into two distinct divisions:

a. The meaning of the Exodus (81:6-10). The Lord recounts the deliverance of the people from their bondage in Egypt. It was a deliverance from grinding labor. **I removed his shoulder from the burden: his hands were delivered from the pots** (6), is a probable reference to the type of labor in which the Israelites were employed in Egypt (Exod. 1:11, 13-14; 5:6-10). **Pots** is translated "heavy hod" (Moffatt) and "freight basket" (Berk.).

[25]*Op. cit., ad loc.*

In the deliverance, **God answered . . . in the secret place of thunder** (7), perhaps the cloud of Exod. 14:19 or at Sinai (Exod. 19: 16-25). **I proved thee** (tested you) **at the waters of Meribah** (Exod. 17:1-7). **Selah;** cf. comment on 3:2.

In view of His goodness to them, God calls for the loyalty of His people. **I will testify unto thee** (8) reads in the Hebrew, "I will testify against thee." The major issue at stake throughout the history of Israel down to the Exile was the worship of idols: **Neither shalt thou worship any strange** (foreign) **god** (9). The Lord claimed the exclusive loyalty of His people. The first commandment is: "Thou shalt have no other gods before [besides] me" (Exod. 20:3), and the reason is the same as is cited here: "I am the Lord thy God, which have brought thee out of the land of Egypt, out of the house of bondage" (Exod. 20:2). The limitless power of the Lord gives encouragement to ask largely: **Open thy mouth wide, and I will fill it** (10; cf. John 16:24).

b. The rebellion of the people (81:11-16). In an abrupt change of tone, God speaks of disobedience and faithlessness. **My people would not hearken** (in obedient faith) **to my voice; and Israel would none of me** (11); or as Perowne translates, "was not willing to obey Me."[26] The terrible result of rebellion was that God **gave them up unto their own hearts' lust: and they walked in their own counsels** (12). Their sin became their greatest punishment, as Paul states it in Rom. 1:24, "Wherefore God also gave them up to uncleanness through the lusts of their own hearts, to dishonour their own bodies between themselves."

How different the history of Israel might have been is indicated in 13-14. Had His people **hearkened** and **walked in** His **ways** (13), God would quickly **have subdued their enemies** (14). Even these Israelitish **haters of the Lord** (15) would have been conquered by Him, and would not have been destroyed—**their time should have endured for ever.** The Lord would **have fed them also with the finest of the wheat** (16), and would **have satisfied** them **with honey out of the rock.** There is infinite pathos in the contrast between what was and what might have been. The difference was all in the issue of obedience.

Psalm 82: A VISION OF JUDGMENT, 82:1-8

This is a wisdom psalm characterized by Morgan as "a cry for justice, born of a sense of the maladministration of those in

[26]*Op. cit.,* II, 99.

authority. It first announces that God is the supreme Judge. This is a recognition of the perfect equity of the standard of justice. The judges in mind have erred in that they have shown respect for the persons of the wicked, and thus departed from the strict justice which ever characterizes the dealings of the God to whom they are all responsible."[27]

Commentators have disagreed sharply on the meaning of v. 1, and thus as to the application of the psalm. "The gods" have been taken to mean subordinate deities (Oesterley), or angels (Hupfeld). However, the context and our Lord's use of v. 6 in John 10:34 make it virtually certain that the Psalmist has in mind human kings and magistrates who have been guilty of using their office for selfish ends.

For "Asaph" in the title, cf. introduction to Psalm 50.

1. *Judge of the Judges* (82:1-2)

Verse 1 would be literally translated, "God [*Elohim*] is standing in the congregation of God [*El*]; in the midst of the gods [*elohim*] will He judge." The same language is used in v. 6, "I have said, Ye are gods [*elohim*]." It should be observed that *elohim*, a plural noun ordinarily translated God or gods, is also used for supernatural beings such as angels, and for men of high rank and supreme authority.[28] The best understanding of the verse would therefore indicate "God as the supreme judge in the midst of Israel's corrupt rulers and judges in order to rebuke and condemn them."[29] The point on which the judges are being called into court is indicated in 2, **How long will ye judge unjustly, and accept the persons of the wicked?**—that is, judge with partiality. Such a complaint was nothing new (cf. I Sam. 8:3; Isa. 1:17; 3:13-15; Jer. 21:12; Amos 5:12, 15; Mic. 7:3; Zech. 8:9-10). **Selah**; cf. comment on 3:2.

2. *The Trust and Its Betrayal* (82:3-7)

The particular obligation of the judges was to champion the cause of **the poor and fatherless** (3), **the afflicted and needy,** protecting them against the oppression **of the wicked** (4) **Rid them** is better "rescue them" (Berk.). The difficulty the defense-

[27]*Op. cit.*, p. 252.
[28]Cf. the discussion in McCullough, *op. cit.*, 4:444.
[29]M'Caw, *op. cit.*, p. 470.

less had in getting a hearing before corrupt magistrates is illustrated in Luke 18:1-6. In contrast to what they should be, these men **know (care) not** (5), closing their eyes to a proper understanding of their duty. **They walk on in darkness** and self-will until **all the foundations of the earth are out of course**—the whole structure of society is disordered and corrupted.

God had endowed the rulers with dignity and authority. On **Ye are gods** (6), cf. comment on v. 1, and the application Jesus makes of this in John 10:34. They were **children of the most High** in respect to the power and responsibility given to them. Paul describes human magistrates, in the exercise of their function, as keepers of the peace, as "powers . . . ordained of God" and "God's ministers," whom to resist is to resist the power of God (Rom. 13:1-6). Because of their flagrant betrayal of trust, these corrupt officials are told, **Ye shall die like other men, and fall like one of the princes** (7). Their office and rank will not save them from doom.

3. *Judge of All* (82:8)

The Judge of the judges is also the Judge of all the earth, who claims all nations for His own inheritance or possession. The psalm closes with the poet's own petition: **Arise, O God, judge the earth: for thou shalt inherit all nations.**

Psalm 83: PRAYER IN A TIME OF NATIONAL PERIL, 83:1-18

The nation was threatened by a vast coalition of evil forces, arrayed with overwhelming odds against the people of God. Various conjectures as to the exact historical occasion have been offered, ranging from the confederacy that threatened Israel in the period of the judges (Judges 7—8) to the forces arrayed against Jehoshaphat in II Chronicles 20. Verse 8 would seem to indicate a time before the emergence of Assyria as a dominant power, since "Assur" is listed as one of the minor confederates. While we may not speak with certainty as to the occasion of its composition, the psalm is appropriate for many periods in the history of God's beleaguered people.

There is a natural division between vv. 8 and 9. The first half describes the situation. The second half is almost exclusively imprecatory, and for this reason the psalm is usually classified as one of the imprecatory psalms (cf. Intro.). For "Asaph" in the superscription, cf. introduction to Psalm 50.

1. Description (83:1-8)

God is implored to intervene on behalf of His defenseless people: **Keep not thou silence, O God: hold not thy peace, and be not still, O God** (1). The occasion is an uprising of those who are God's enemies and those **that hate** Him (2), plotting **against His people . . . against thy hidden ones** (3), or "treasured ones," held as in "the hollow of His hand." The aim of the enemy is the extermination of Israel as **a nation** (4)—still, incidentally, the avowed goal of the Arab states in the Near East. **The tabernacles** (6, tents) would be either the tents of these peoples at home or the tents of their armies. The federation consisted of many of the longtime hereditary enemies of Israel (see map 1): the Edomites, **the Ishmaelites**, the Moabites (6), the Ammonites, the Amalekites, **the Philistines** (7), with the Assyrians (**Assur**, 8) as a minor ally. **The Hagarenes** (6) are less well known. They were a people living in the territory of Gilead, east of the Jordan, and were driven out by the tribe of Reuben in the time of Saul (I Chron. 5:10, 18-20). **Gebal** (7), mentioned in I Kings 5:18 and Ezek. 27:9, apparently applied to the territory south of the Dead Sea, in the neighborhood of Petra. It is still known by the Arabic name *Dgebel*. **The inhabitants of Tyre** were also on occasion arrayed against the Israelites and condemned by the prophets (cf. Jer. 25:15-22; Ezek. 26:2—28:26; Amos 1:9-10; Zech. 9:2-4). **Assur** (8) was Assyria. **The children of Lot** were the Moabites and Ammonites. **Selah;** cf. comment on 3:2.

2. Imprecation (83:9-18)

This passage is filled with reminiscences of two great former deliverances of Israel by the power of God from the oppression of formidable foes. Concerning its vindictiveness, Perowne writes: "He prays that it may be with them as with the other enemies of Israel, with Jabin and Sisera, in days of old. But he prays for more than deliverance or victory. He prays that the Name of Jehovah may be magnified, and that all may seek that Name. Two expressions, in fact, give the key to the Psalm —show us the attitude of the Poet in presence of the danger: ver. 5, 'They are confederate against *Thee;*' ver. 18, 'Let them know that *Thou* art most high over all the earth.' "[30]

Both deliverances are mentioned together in 9, although the victory over the hosts of **Midian** is not enlarged upon until 11-12.

[30]*Op. cit.*, II, 110.

The victory of Deborah and Barak over **Sisera** and **Jabin** (9) is described in Judg. 4:1—5:31. The location of the major action was at the river **Kison** or Kishon (Judg. 4:7, 13; 5:21). Here a sudden cloudburst immobilized the chariots of the enemy and swept away his army. **Jabin** was king of the Canaanites at Hazor in northern Palestine, and **Sisera** was the general in command of his army. **En-dor** (10) is not named in the account in Judges, but was traditionally associated with the deaths of the two Canaanite leaders. It was about forty miles south of Hazor. **Oreb, Zeeb, Zebah,** and **Zalmunna** (11) are named in connection with Gideon's smashing defeat of the Midianites, described in Judg. 7:1—8:13 and mentioned in Isa. 10:26 as an example of great slaughter. **Oreb** and **Zeeb** are described as **princes** both in 11 and in Judg. 7:25; they appear to have been the field generals in charge of the battle. **Zebah** and **Zalmunna** are identified as "kings of Midian" in Judg. 8:5. Their boastful pride is indicated in their purpose, **Let us take to ourselves the houses** (literally, habitations; or pastures—RSV, Berk.) **of God in possession** (12).

The Psalmist prays that his enemies (and the Lord's) may be made **like a wheel** (13)—better, as the Hebrew, "whirling dust"—and **as the stubble before the wind,** both pictures of helplessness and futility. They are to be as a storm-driven forest fire which appears to set **the mountains on fire** (14). **Persecute** (15) is better "pursue." Yet the object of the divine wrath is to be ultimately redemptive. The bitterness of the imprecation is relieved somewhat by the purpose of the judgments: **That they may seek thy name, O Lord** (16); and, **That men may know that thou, whose name alone is JEHOVAH, art the most high over all the earth** (18). Only here in the Psalms, and three other times in the OT, is the sacred name *Yahweh* translated **Jehovah** in the KJV. In all other instances of its use (more than 6,000 in all), "The Lord" is the translation given.

There is much in this, as in the other imprecatory psalms, which does not appeal to Christians who live in the light of the Sermon on the Mount (specifically, Matt. 5:43-48). The Psalmist was one of "them of old time" (Matt. 5:21, 27, 33) whose teachings Jesus "fulfilled" by amending them and giving them different direction. Yet we should recognize even in such psalms as these that it is the Lord's enemies who are the objects of anger (Ps. 83:2). Also there is the expressed desire that at least some may be brought to seek the Lord through recognition of the connection between their sins and the divine judgments brought upon them. There is nothing arbitrary about the wrath and judgments of God. Men are tragically slow to learn that one can't go against the grain of the universe without getting festering sores from the splinters.

Psalm 84: HUNGER FOR THE HOUSE OF GOD, 84:1-12

There are few poems in the Bible or out of it that can equal Psalm 84 in depth of feeling or beauty of expression. It is closely akin to the thought of Psalms 42—43, so much so that many commentators (e.g., Ewald, Perowne, McCullough) attribute them to a common authorship. For the terms in the title or superscription, cf. the introductions to Psalms 8 and 42.

The psalm has long been associated with the Feast of Tabernacles in the fall, and, as Oesterley surmises, may well have been the song of pilgrims coming for the autumn festival after a long and dry summer.[31] "Our conception of religion, its methods and its purposes, has grown during the centuries. Material prosperity is no longer the sole test of divine favour, nor do we think of the welfare of the community as summed up in the life of its individual head. But it is still true that the highest blessing known to the human spirit is the sense of communion with God, and that in the 'fellowship of the Holy Spirit' we most certainly have an experience of that which is unseen and eternal."[32]

1. *Longing for the Lord's House* (84:1-4)

How amiable are thy tabernacles (1), or as we would now say, "How lovely is thy dwelling place" (RSV). The Hebrew in both 1 and 2 is plural—"dwelling places" and **courts**. This may represent the various parts of the entire sanctuary, or more probably may simply reflect the Hebrew practice of using the plural to intensify the meaning of a word, the so-called "plural of majesty." **Soul, heart,** and **flesh** (2) all yearn for the presence of **the living God**—this latter phrase being found in the Psalms only here and in 42:2 (cf. comment there).

The reference to **the sparrow** and **the swallow** (3) has been understood either as an expression of desire for what the birds have so freely, access to the vicinity of the house of God (Perowne, McCullough), or as Moffatt suggests, the Psalmist compares his own spirit with the nesting birds who find a home in

---

[31]*Op. cit.*, p. 378.   [32]*Ibid.*, p. 381.

and near the sanctuary. "At thy altars" (RSV) is preferable to **even thine altars,** since birds might nest near the altar in the open courtyard of the Temple and even near the incense altar in the sanctuary but scarcely upon the altars themselves. Nothing can equal the blessedness of those who **dwell in thy house** (4). The expression **will be still praising thee** is rendered, "They shall ever sing Thy praise" (Berk.). **Selah;** cf. comment on 3:2.

2. The Triumph of Trust (84:5-8)

Although still not present in the sanctuary, the poet envisions the pilgrimage as terminating in Zion in the house of the Lord. Perowne indicates the relation of this stanza with the preceding, and shows its meaning in the words: "But not only blessed are they who dwell in the holy place in God's city, and near to His house; blessed are they who can visit it, with the caravan of pilgrims at the great national festivals. They cherish the remembrance of such seasons. Every spot of the familiar road, every station at which they have rested, lives in their heart. The path may be dry and dusty, through a lonely and sorrowful valley, but nevertheless they love it. The pilgrim band, rich in hope, forget the trials and difficulties of the way: hope changes the rugged and stony waste into living fountains. The vale blossoms as if the sweet rain of heaven had covered it with blessings. Hope sustains them at every step; from station to station they renew their strength as they draw nearer to the end of their journey, till at last they appear before God, present themselves as His worshipers, in His sanctuary in Zion."[33]

In whose heart are the ways (5) may be understood either in the sense that they cherish God's ways in their hearts (Berk.) or that they love every part of the way to Zion (RSV). **Of them** may be omitted; note italics in KJV. **Valley of Baca** (6) means "valley of weeping." For **well** read "a spring." "The meaning of the verse is, that the faith and hope and joy of the pilgrims make the sandy waste a place of fountains, and then (this is the Divine side of the picture) God from heaven sends down the rain of His grace. The word [lit., the early rain] denotes the soft, gentle autumnal rain (Joel ii.23) which fell after the crops were sown. Thus the Vale of Weeping becomes a Vale of Joy."[34]

---

[33]*Op. cit.,* II, 119.   [34]*Ibid.,* p. 120.

They go from strength to strength (7), renewing their energies after each day's toilsome journey (cf. Isa. 40:31). They appear **before God** for worship and for His examination and blessing. Having pictured in his mind the blessings of those who dwell in God's house and of those who journey toward it, the poet pours out his **prayer** that he may soon share the same blessing (8).

3. The Reward of God's Own Presence (84:9-12)

The blessings of God's house are surpassed only by the blessing of His own presence. For **God our shield** (9) cf. comment on 3:3. **Thine anointed** is the typical expression for the king, leading to the view that the psalm may have been composed by one of Israel's kings. However, the context would seem to favor the idea that the prayer is uttered in behalf of the king—or that the poet spiritualized the anointing, and thinks of himself as the Lord's anointed.

So great is the Psalmist's devotion to God that **a single day** in the house of God seems to him **better than a thousand** elsewhere (10). Moffatt brings out the contrast of the latter part of the verse:

I would rather sit at the threshold of God's house
than live inside the tents of worldly men.

The Lord God (11) is *Yahweh Elohim,* used only here in the Psalms but most characteristic of Gen. 2:14—3:24. (Psalms 68:18 and 85:8 employ a briefer form, *Yah Elohim.*) Usually where the KJV has "the Lord God," the Hebrew is *Adonai Yahweh* or *Adonai Elohim.* This is the only place where God is directly called **a sun,** although cf. "Sun of righteousness" in Mal. 4:2. For **shield,** cf. comment on 3:3. **Grace and glory** must come in that order. Grace precedes the glory, but the glory follows the grace. We need both.

No good thing means, first, "all things that pertain unto life and godliness" (II Pet. 1:3), and then the supply of other needs according to His will (Matt. 6:33; Phil. 4:19). **That walk uprightly** is, literally, "in perfectness" (*tammim,* perfect, entire, whole, in integrity). "And the Psalmist rises at last to the joyful conviction, not only that they are blessed who dwell in God's house (ver. 4), or they who swell the festal throng on their way to that house (ver. 5), but they who, whether they worship in it

317

or not, are one with Him by faith: 'Blessed is the man that *trusteth* in Thee.' "[35]

Psalm 85: PRAISE, PRAYER, AND PROSPECT, 85:1-13

This psalm of adoration was apparently written after the return of the exiles from the Babylonian captivity, and in this is very comparable with Psalm 126.[36] Yet there is in it also earnest prayer for revival and continued mercy. The whole tenor of the poem fits well with the circumstances described in Neh. 1:3 or Hag. 1:6-11; 2:15-19. Certainly, in any case, there are both rejoicing in the mercies of the past and clear recognition of dependence upon continued mercies for the future. For "sons of Korah" in the title, cf. introduction to Psalm 42.

1. *Praise* (85:1-3)

God's grace had marvellously restored His people. He had **been favourable unto** His **land** and had **brought back the captivity of Jacob** (1). These words would most naturally fit the restoration from Babylonian captivity. But those who argue for an earlier date for the psalm point out that any restored fortunes might thus be described (so RSV translates, "Thou didst restore the fortunes of Jacob"—as also Moffatt and Smith-Goodspeed). At any point in a life-history, God's people can rejoice in His graciousness and goodness. The **iniquity** of the people had been **forgiven,** and **their sin** was **covered** (2); therefore God's **wrath** had been removed and **the fierceness** of His **anger** abated (3). The connection is clear between the people's sin and the wrath of God. The one must be dealt with conclusively before the other could be turned aside. **Selah** (2); cf. comment on 3:2.

2. *Prayer* (85:4-7)

At v. 4 there is an abrupt transition from praise to prayer, from thanksgiving to petition (cf. Phil. 4:6). But the order is correct. Praise and thanksgiving for blessings already received should precede prayer for further help. The task is unfinished. If, as M'Caw suggests, these are the thoughts of godly men faced with the toil of reconstruction after the Exile in the face of poverty and desolation,[37] then there were indeed great chal-

---

[35]*Ibid.*, p. 122.   [36]*Contra*, cf. McCullough, *op. cit.*, 4:458.
[37]*Op. cit.*, p. 472.

lenges before the Psalmist and his companions. The privations of the present were in a real sense the consequence of God's prior judgments (4-5). **Turn us** (4; "deliver us again," Moffatt). God's favor was not a guarantee of immunity from trouble, and the Psalmist's prayer is for adequacy in trouble.

Wilt thou not revive us again? (6) is a great and valid revival text. The emphasis in the Hebrew is on the pronoun **thou**, "for God alone can thus revive the sad hearts and broken hopes of His people."[38] The result would be that **thy people may rejoice in thee**—not in the material blessings they receive, but in the Giver of all good and perfect gifts. **Thy mercy** (7, *chesed*) would be loving-kindness, steadfast love, the covenant faithfulness of God to His promises (cf. comment on 17:7).

3. *Prospect* (85:8-13)

Like Habakkuk mounting his watchtower to hear what the Lord would say (Hab. 2:1), the poet pauses to listen (8). The balance of the psalm is the substance of the divine reassurance, promise for the future. **The Lord will speak . . . peace unto his people, and to his saints** ("devout men," Moffatt)—provided, of course, that they do not turn again to folly. The LXX follows a different rendering, "to those who turn their hearts to Him." But the Hebrew is probably to be preferred. **Folly**, as elsewhere throughout the Bible, does not mean simply foolishness, but stark evil. The term in the OT often meant idolatry, a pointed statement here if this be indeed a postexilic psalm. The Exile was caused by idolatry and, as far as the Hebrew people were concerned, pretty well cured it.

God's deliverance is **nigh them that fear him** (9); it is never far from the honest and seeking soul. **Glory** is the manifest presence of God with and among His people. Thus, Moffatt, "till his Great Presence dwells within our land." Perowne observes, "This hope was destined to have its fulfilment, but in a better and a higher sense, when He who was the brightness of the Father's glory tabernacled in human flesh, and men 'beheld His glory, the glory as of the only-begotten of the Father.' "[39]

Mercy and truth are met together (10) is translated by Moffatt, "Kindness and faithfulness unite," in God's dealings with His own. **Righteousness and peace** may be understood as "victory and peace" (Moffatt). **Have kissed each other** is

---

[38]Perowne, *op. cit.*, II, 125.   [39]*Ibid.*, p. 126.

parallel in meaning to **are met together**. These four attributes
of God and virtues of men are also central in the NT. **Truth**
(faithfulness in this context) **shall spring out of the earth; and
righteousness shall look down from heaven** (11). God's gift of
righteousness answers man's faithfulness in meeting its conditions in obedience and faith.

The psalm closes with two verses of assurance. Perowne
says, "The present misery is forgotten in the dawning of a glorious future. The prayer has been uttered; the storm of the soul
is hushed."[40]

> *Yes, the Lord will give what is good,*
> *and our land will yield its produce.*
> *Righteousness will go before Him*
> *and make His footsteps into a way* (12-13, Berk.).

Psalm 86: PRAYING THE PRAYER OF FAITH, 86:1-17

This is another psalm of lament, attributed by title to David;
the only one in Book III which is so inscribed. There is no ready
explanation for the inclusion of this psalm with the psalms of the
sons of Korah. It is also unique in its use of the divine name
Adonai in preference to *Yahweh*. *Adonai* occurs seven times
here, and is identified in the KJV by setting the type in lower
case, "the Lord." *Yahweh*, in the original, is printed in capital
letters as "the LORD."

The psalm divides into four sections, each of which ends
with an affirmation about God: "Thou . . . art good, and ready
to forgive" (5); "Thou art great . . . God alone" (10); "Thou . . .
art . . . full of compassion, and gracious" (15); and, "Thou, Lord,
hast holpen me, and comforted me" (17).

1. *The Goodness of God* (86:1-5)

From the depths of his trouble, the poet reaches out to the
goodness of God. He lays before the Lord the wretchedness of
his condition: **I am poor and needy** (1), "weak and wretched"
(Moffatt). **Poor** (*ani*) does not refer to economic poverty as
much as to distress and oppression. It is the sense of need that
drives men to God. **I am holy** (2, *chasid*) is not a self-righteous
boast. The term has been variously translated "one whom thou
lovest" (Perowne), "true to thee" (Moffatt), "godly" (RSV,

[40]*Ibid.*, p. 124.

Smith-Goodspeed), and "dedicated" (Berk.). In this light, the assertion is "the language of honest straightforward simplicity."[41] The poet's prayer is a **daily** petition (3). For **Rejoice the soul** (4), we would say today, "Gladden the soul," or, "Gladden the heart." The goodness of God, His readiness **to forgive,** and His abundant **mercy** are given to **all them that call upon** Him (5).

2. The Greatness of God (86:6-10)

The Psalmist presses his plaint with the quickening confidence that the greatness of God guarantees relief. With **prayer and supplications** (6) he **will call upon** the Lord (7), confident that **among the gods there is none like unto** Him (8), nor **any works like His works.** Reference to **the gods** is not to be taken as an indication of polytheism or henotheism (worship of a tribal god along with the recognition of existence of others). **Thou art God alone** (10) reveals the writer's monotheism. What are called gods are in fact no gods at all. A similar statement is made by Paul, "For though there be that are called gods, whether in heaven or in earth, (as there be gods many, and lords many,) but to us there is but one God, the Father, of whom are all things" (I Cor. 8:5-6).

Since God is Creator of all, the Psalmist foresees the day when **all nations whom thou hast made shall come and worship before thee** (9; cf. Phil. 2:5-11). **For thou art great** (10), able to answer the cry of His people. "There are two kinds of doubt which are wont in the house of temptation to assail the soul; the doubt as to God's *willingness,* and the doubt as to God's *power,* to succor. The first of these the Psalmist has already put from him: he now shows that he has overcome the second. God is able as well as willing to help."[42]

3. The Grace of God (86:11-15)

God is good, great, and gracious—i.e., kindly disposed toward those who seek Him. Verse 11 is a notable prayer for guidance and integrity, and a pledge to walk in faithfulness and truth. Moffatt renders it, "Teach me what is thy way, O thou Eternal, how to live loyal to thee." **Unite my heart to fear thy name** has been interpreted, "Suffer it no more to scatter itself upon a multiplicity of objects, to be drawn hither and thither by a

---

[41]*Ibid.,* p. 129.   [42]*Ibid.*

thousand different aims, but to turn all its powers, all its affections in one direction, collect them in one focus, make them all
one in Thee."[43] "To be pure in heart is to will one thing" (cf.
Hos. 10:2; Phil. 3:13). Such a unified heart is necessary if one is
to praise the Lord with all his heart (12). **Thou hast delivered
my soul from the lowest hell** (13), literally, "from Sheol," "the
unseen world beneath" (Perowne), "the very depths of death"
(Moffatt), "the lower world beyond" (Berk.). **The proud** and
violent men who forsake the ways of the Lord (14) have **risen
against** him. **But thou, O Lord, art a God full of compassion,
and gracious, longsuffering, and plenteous in mercy and truth**
(15). The word **truth** is here "faithfulness" (RSV) or "fidelity"
(Smith-Goodspeed).

4. *The Gifts of God* (86:16-17)

The gifts the Psalmist seeks are **mercy, strength,** and salvation (16). He asks for **a token for good** (17; i.e., "a sign
of thy favor," RSV) which will confound his foes. Past help
will guarantee future favors: **because thou, Lord, hast holpen**
(helped) **me, and comforted me.** "These verses (16-17) supply
the traditional ending to a prayer of petition. The situation the
petitioner has described, compounded of a threat of immediate
peril from men and a long and incessant hope in God, creates a
burden of necessity he cannot bear alone. What sort of support
he needs he states very simply: he needs pity, strength, rescue,
and a portent of the divine favor. Such a demonstration would
not only serve to imbue him with confidence; conversely, it
would shame those who hated him, because they would see in
his deliverance the stout aid of the Lord."[44]

Psalm 87: THE GLORIES OF ZION, 87:1-7

This song of adoration, like others of the group, bears the
inscription "to" or "for the sons of Korah" (cf. intro. to Psalm
42). It is a beautiful gem in praise of Zion envisioned spiritually,
not necessarily geographically. The mention of Babylon in 4
would probably date the song as postexilic.[45] It is one of those
striking passages in the OT where the particularism of the Jew
is transcended and the universality of the divine purpose shows

---

[43]*Ibid.*, p. 130.   [44]Poteat, *op. cit.*, 4:466.

[45]Although see Perowne, *op. cit.*, II, 135, for a date in Hezekiah's reign.

through. Perowne observes: "Foreign nations are here described, not as captives or tributaries, not even as doing voluntary homage to the greatness and glory of Zion, but as actually incorporated and enrolled, by a new birth, among her sons. Even the worst enemies of their race, the tyrants and oppressors of the Jews, Egypt and Babylon, are threatened with no curse, no shout of joy is raised in the prospect of their overthrow, but the privileges of citizenship are extended to them, and they are welcomed as brothers."[46] Other OT passages (e.g., Isa. 2:2-4; 19:22-25) speak of the offer of salvation to the Gentiles, but this psalm "stands alone amongst the writings of the Old Testament, in representing this union of nations as a new birth into the city of God. This idea gives it a singular interest, and clearly stamps it as Messianic."[47] Oesterley comments, "The psalmist, with his sublime outlook, envisages a time in world-history when, irrespective of nationality, men will come to themselves, and therefore to God. It is an ideal; but, with divine optimism, the psalmist portrays its superb realization as taking place within time-space. The when is not his concern; he is content with framing the beautiful ideal."[48]

1. The City of Zion (87:1-3)

The affection for and delight in the holy city are reminiscent of Psalm 48. The antecedent of **His** (1) is made clear in Perowne's translation: "His foundation upon the holy mountains doth Jehovah love." **Foundation** is used in the sense of "the founded (or established) city." **The gates of Zion** (2) are both its fortification and its place of gathering, and are more precious to the Lord than any or all other places of Israel's habitation. **Glorious things are spoken of thee** (3) does not refer to earthly glories but to the gathering of the nations within the Lord's spiritual fold as in the following verses. The glory of Zion is her concern for the "other sheep . . . which are not of this fold" (John 10:16). **Selah;** cf. comment on 3:2.

2. The Citizens of Zion (87:4-6)

I will make mention of Rahab and Babylon to them that know me (4) is better, "I will mention Rahab and Babylon as included among those acquainted with me" (Harrison). **Rahab**

---

[46]*Ibid.*, p. 133.   [47]*Loc. cit.*
[48]*Op. cit.*, p. 392.

is a poetical name for Egypt (cf. Isa. 30:7). The word originally meant "pride" or "ferocity." It also stood for a sea monster, and for the crocodile—which may explain its application to Egypt. **Philistia** (see map 1), along the Mediterranean west of Israel; **Tyre,** just north of Philistia; and **Ethiopia,** in Africa just south of Egypt, will all contribute to the citizenry of the spiritual Zion. **This man was born there** (4) is made clearer by Moffatt, who translates the verse: "Egypt and Babylon, Philistia, Tyre, and Ethiopia, I count them as mine, for there this follower and that was born." "This is Gospel; all those Gentiles who know Him are being divinely registered as natives of the Kingdom of God" (Berk., fn.). **This and that man was born in her** (5) suggests, "One after another is born in her" (Perowne). "It is remarkable that the figure of a new birth is used to express the admission of the different nations to the rights of citizenship in Zion."[49] **The Lord shall count, when he writeth up the people, that this man was born there** (6); i.e., each one whose name is inscribed in the Lamb's book of life is accounted as born in Zion.

3. Conclusion (87:7)

Singers and players on instruments will welcome the new citizens of the spiritual Kingdom. **Players on instruments** has been otherwise translated, "they that dance" (Perowne), "dancers" (RSV), or "in processionals" (Berk.). The difficulty of the Hebrew text accounts for the varied translations. But the thought is obviously the joy there is over repenting sinners. **All my springs are in thee** reflects the fact that the ultimate source of joy and blessing is in the Lord and the spiritual city He establishes (cf. 5).

Psalm 88: "The Dark Night of the Soul," 88:1-18

This song of lament has been called the darkest, saddest psalm in the entire Psalter.[50] Perowne says, "It is one wail of sorrow from beginning to end. It is the only Psalm in which the expression of feeling, the pouring out of the burdened heart before God, fails to bring relief and consolation."[51] Oesterley says, "This psalm is unique. It is a desperate cry of suffering, unre-

---

[49]Perowne, *op. cit.,* II, 137.   [50]*Ibid.,* p. 140.
[51]*Loc. cit.*

lieved by a single ray of comfort or of hope. . . . There are good grounds for supposing that the author was acquainted with the book of *Job*, and may himself also have been a leper."[52]

McCullough notes that "the psalmist appears to have some wasting disease with which he has been afflicted from his youth (perhaps leprosy or palsy). It has cost him his friends who can no longer bear the sight of him, and now he is on the point of death. He complains of no attacks by enemies and he has no sins to confess; yet he looks upon his prolonged experience of suffering as due in some measure to the Lord's wrath. It is therefore to the Lord that his plea is directed. But—and this is what makes it the most somber lament in the Psalter—when the psalm is finished there is no answering voice nor any mitigation of the speaker's plight, and as has often been noticed, the last word in the poem is darkness."[53]

For *Mahalath* in the superscription, cf. introduction to Psalm 53. *Leannoth* probably means "for singing," or as *The Berkeley Version* translates, "to chant mournfully." "Heman the Ezrahite" was a noted wise man mentioned in I Kings 4:31. For *Maschil* cf. introduction to Psalm 32.

1. *Failing* (88:1-7)

The first stanza of the poem seems to recognize the approach of death. The single ray of light in the entire lament is the glimmer of faith that addresses the **Lord** as **God of my salvation (1)**. He prays from the very brink of **the grave (3,** *Sheol*), the place of the dead. His companions have already **counted** him as being as one going **down into the pit (4,** *bor*), literally, a cistern, narrow at the top but deep and spacious at the bottom; a synonym for the grave, or *Sheol.* The Hebrew of **free among the dead (5)** means separation from one's fellows; hence the more recent translations, "cast off" (ASV), "forsaken" (RSV). Harrison, catching the sense while preserving the idea of **free,** translates: "released from life's violence." **Whom thou rememberest no more . . . cut off from thy hand** is a reflection of a view of *Sheol* and the afterlife without the light that shines from the empty grave of Christ (II Tim. 1:10). **The lowest pit . . . darkness** and **the deeps (6)** reflect additional elements of the view of death then current. **Thy waves (7)** are waves of wrath and judgment. The writer

[52]*Op. cit.*, p. 393.   [53]*Op. cit.*, 4:473.

does not say and may not know the reason why he felt himself to have come under the wrath of God. **Selah:** cf. comment on 3:2.

2. *Friendless* (88:8-10)

Not least among the afflictions the Psalmist suffered was the bitterness of being forsaken by his friends, a source of intense grief to Job also (Job 2:9-10; 12:4; 16:1-4). He felt his **acquaintance far from** him (8). He had become **an abomination** ("object of loathing," Berk.) **unto them.** He lamented, **I am shut up, and I cannot come forth,** i.e., "I am hemmed in so that I cannot escape" (Harrison). The **Lord** is the only One to whom he can turn (9). Even in prayer his questions, **Wilt thou shew wonders to the dead?** (10) "Shall the shades below arise and give Thee thanks?" (Perowne), receive no affirmative answer. On **Shall the dead arise and praise thee?** Barnes writes, "One of the disabilities of the dead according to Hebrew thought is that they cannot worship God (cf. cxv. 17, 18)."[54]

3. *Forsaken* (88:11-18)

Verses 11 and 12 continue the thought of 10. The afterlife is called variously **the grave** (11), **destruction** (*Abaddon,* used in Job 26:6 as another synonym for *Sheol*), **the dark** (12), **the land of forgetfulness.** Here God's **lovingkindness** and His **faithfulness** (11) cannot **be declared,** nor His **wonders** or His **righteousness** made **known.**

The Psalmist makes a renewed appeal **in the morning** (13). **Prevent thee** is better "comes before Thee" (Berk.). Yet God still seems to cast him off and to hide His **face** from him (14). From his **youth** he had suffered, his life imperiled, **distracted** ("crushed," Moffatt) by God's **terrors** (15). God's **fierce wrath** and His **terrors** (16) surround him **daily like water** (17). **Darkness** (18) here may mean obscurity. Not only God but man had forsaken him:

You have made admirer and friend alike stand aloof from me; obscurity is my only companion (18, Harrison).

Psalm 89: The Faithfulness of God, 89:1-52

The last psalm of Book III is in striking contrast to the one just preceding, although attributed in its title to the brother of

---

[54]*Op. cit.,* II, 422.

the composer of Psalm 88, "Ethan the Ezrahite" (cf. I Kings 4:31; I Chron. 6:44; 15:17, 19). Its use in the NT in reference to Christ justifies inclusion among the Messianic psalms. The varying subject matter of the psalm has led some (e.g., Oesterley) to surmise that it is a combination of three originally independent pieces. This supposition is by no means necessary, however, since it is possible to follow a developing theme throughout. The Psalmist is "by prayer and supplication with thanksgiving" letting his "requests be made known unto God" (Phil. 4:6).

Scholarly views as to date and occasion vary widely, from the Northern Kingdom under Jeroboam II (Gunkel); the reign of Jehoiachin (Perowne); to the late Maccabean period, 88 B.C. (Duhm). The content of the psalm would seem to fit better with a period such as that of Jehoiachin, when the Davidic monarchy was threatened but not extinct. Oesterley says, "The psalm teaches . . . that there is an intimate relationship between the destiny of the nation and the divine purpose concerning it. God, all-powerful in heaven and earth, ordained the kingship for his people as a means of social well-being among them, and chose the Davidic line. But the divine plan was thwarted by the sinful will of men, as the psalmist seems to be beginning to realize, though he did not see the final end of the monarchy which was at hand . . . God is the God of history; and though men, being free agents by God's will, blight his purposes, yet in his mercy he overrules their folly."[55] For *Maschil* in the title, cf. introduction to Psalm 32.

1. *Praise* (89:1-4)

The psalm opens with the poet's praise (1-2) and the Lord's response (3-4). **The mercies** (*chesed,* loving-kindness, steadfast love; cf. comment on 17:7) **of the Lord** (1) and His **faithfulness** are the Psalmist's theme. **Be built up** (2), "like some stately palace, rising ever greater and fairer, stone by stone, before the wondering eyes of men, knowing no decay, never destined to fall into ruin."[56]

Verses 3-4 are applied to Christ in Acts 2:30, and with v. 20 give a Messianic character to the psalm. God had indeed **made a covenant with . . . David** (3) that his **seed** should be established **for ever** and his **throne to all generations** (4). This promise has

[55]*Op. cit.,* p. 403.   [56]Perowne, *op. cit.,* II, 147-48.

been fulfilled in David's greater Son (Matt. 1:1, etc.). **Selah;**
cf. comment on 3:2.

2. *Past* (89:5-12)

Having expressed his faith and received God's answer, the
Psalmist now turns to a recital of the wonders of God's power in
creation and history which betoken the fulfillment of His promises
to David. The Lord has not only the desire but the ability to do
what He has promised. First, God's power in creation and in
nature is described. **The heavens** sing the **praise** of God's **wonders** (5; cf. 19:1-6). His **faithfulness** is extolled **in the congregation of the saints**—probably a reference to the angelic assembly, from the parallel with **the sons of the mighty** (6), although
certainly the saints on earth have no higher theme. **The Lord is**
the Incomparable One, **greatly to be feared** (7) with the reverent
awe which is "the fear of the Lord" in both OT and NT. **Strong
Lord** (8) means the sovereign Ruler of the universe. Even **the
raging of the sea** (9) is subject to His will: **when the waves
thereof arise, thou stillest them** (cf. Matt. 8:23-27; Mark 4:36-41;
Luke 8:22-25). **Rahab** (10), possibly symbolic of Egypt as in
87:4, but from the context more likely the fierce and awesome
powers of the raging deep, as a sea monster. **The heavens and
the earth . . . the world and the fulness thereof** (11) are God's
by creative act, both **north** and **south** (12). **Tabor and Hermon**
are thought by some to represent east and west in contrast with
the **north** and **south,** but are more probably cited as conspicuous
and upstanding mountains in a mountainous country (see map 1).

3. *Present* (89:13-18)

The Lord of nature, who "created the heaven and the
earth" (Gen. 1:1), is also and even more significantly the God
of His people. His **arm** is **mighty** and His **right hand** is **high** (13).
"The *arm* and the *hand* suggest power which is active, not merely
latent. Literally, *an arm with might,* another rugged construction
used by this Psalmist."[57] **Justice** (righteousness) **and judgment
. . . mercy and truth** (14) are the basis of God's sovereign rule
over His universe.

The blessedness of God's people is described in 15-18 in
majestic terms. These verses are part of the synagogue ritual for

---

[57]Barnes, *op. cit.,* II, 428.

the observance of the Jewish New Year, and are recited immediately following the sounding of the trumpet. *The Berkeley Version* has captured much of the beauty of the original:

> *Blessed are the people that recognize the festal call.*
> *They walk, O Lord, in the light of Thy countenance;*
> *in Thy name they rejoice all day long,*
> *and through Thy righteousness they are exalted.*
> *For the glory of their strength art Thou,*
> *and through Thy favor shall our horn be raised high.*
> *For our shield is of the Lord,*
> *and our king of the Holy One of Israel.*

Joyful sound (15) is better "trumpet sound," or call to the festival. **Walk . . . in the light of thy countenance** has been translated, "go about radiant with Your presence" (Harrison). **Our horn shall be exalted** (17) means, "Our power is increased" (Harrison)—the horn of the ram or the ox symbolized strength.

4. *Promise* (89:19-37)

This long passage is devoted to the promise of God to **David** (20) and **his seed** (29). As Peter set vv. 3-4 in a Messianic setting (Acts 2:30), so Paul used v. 20 in his synagogue address at Antioch in Pisidia in reference to Christ (Acts 13:22-23). Its limited application is to David and his earthly successors. Its ultimate application is to Jesus, the Messiah. **Thy holy one** (19) is better "thy trusted seer" (Moffatt). David was helped, **chosen, anointed** (20), **established** (21), and strengthened. Therefore **the enemy shall not exact upon** ("assail," Harrison) **him** (22); **but God will beat down his foes . . . and plague them that hate him** (23). **His horn be exalted** (24)—cf. comment on 17.

I will set his hand also in the sea, and his right hand in the rivers (25) is better, "I will extend his power to the sea, and his authority far as the Euphrates" (Moffatt); cf. 72:8; Zech. 9:10. The king (both human and divine) shall recognize **God** as his **father** (26) and in return shall be proclaimed the Lord's **firstborn** (27), a term which in its strictest application belongs to Christ alone (John 1:14; Rom. 8:29). God's covenant with David and **his seed** is eternal (28-29). The disobedience of the king's **children** will result in their own punishment, but will not set at nought the longer purposes of God (30-34). God's covenant oath was based on His **holiness** (35), i.e., His own nature (cf.

60:6; Heb. 6:13-20). **Established for ever as the moon (37)** has been translated, "It shall be permanently established like the moon, and be as enduring as the skies" (Harrison).

5. Prospect (39:38-45)

There is, to be sure, a tragic contrast between the promise and the immediate prospect. In part, the Psalmist's problem was that of the disciples of Jesus much later when they expected the Lord to "restore again the kingdom to Israel" (Acts 1:6). God's purpose has not been the restoration of the old, but the realization of the new. The old had to pass before the new could appear. These verses reflect a low state in the affairs of Israel's kingdom. It appears that God has **cast off and abhorred** His **anointed (38)**. **The covenant** seems to have been **made void,** the king's **crown . . . profaned** by being cast to the ground **(39)**. **All his hedges (40)** would be "all his defences" (Harrison). **All that pass by the way spoil him (41)** means, "All who pass on the road plunder him" (Berk.). **A reproach to his neighbours** may be "the joke of the neighborhood" (Harrison).

As the king grew weak, **his enemies** grew strong **(42)**. Defeat in **battle (43)** and the humiliation of **his throne (44)** had been the lot of the youthful monarch **(45)**. As a result, the king had been **covered . . . with shame.**

6. Petition (89:46-51)

Under circumstances such as this the heart's cry is, **How long, Lord? (46)** A series of rhetorical questions expresses the desire that God will soon turn again to His beleaguered representative. "The pleading consists of two parts, each comprised in three verses. The argument of the first is the shortness of human life; that of the second, the dishonour cast upon God by the triumph of His enemies."[58] The urgency of the petition is based upon the shortness of life and the certainty of **death (47-48)**.

God's honor is the next basis upon which the Psalmist presses his plea. The Lord is reminded of His **former mercies,** and His oath to **David (49)**. He is called upon to **remember . . . the reproach (50,** "disgrace," Harrison) **of** His **servants,** "and how

---

[58]Perowne, *op. cit.,* II, 154.

I bear within myself the abuse of many nations" (Harrison). Those who thus oppose the speaker are the **enemies** of the **Lord** (51).

7. Doxology (89:52)

The last verse is generally conceded to be no part of the original psalm; it is, rather, the doxology added to all of the psalms of Book III. **Amen, and Amen** is repetition intensifying the meaning of "May it be so," or "So let it be." Cf. the doxologies which close the other books (41:13; 72:18-19; 106:48; and comment on Psalm 150).

Section **IV** *Book Four: Miscellaneous Psalms*

Psalms 90—106

Book IV is the shortest of the five books identified within the Psalms. Of its seventeen psalms, titles are appended to seven. It contains a group known as "The Sabbath Psalms" (90—99) from their use in the synagogue, and "one for an ordinary day" (100). Psalms 105 and 106 are important historical psalms. Most of the varied psalm types are included with a strong leaning toward psalms of adoration and of worship.

Psalm 90: MORTAL MAN AND ETERNAL GOD, 90:1-17

This psalm has been described as "one of the most precious gems in the Psalter."[1] Kittel called it "an impressive song of almost unique elevation and power."[2] Isaac Taylor cited Psalm 90 "as perhaps the most sublime of human compositions, the deepest in feeling, the loftiest in theological conception, the most magnificent in its imagery."[3] Its emphasis on the shortness of human life accounts for its inclusion in many funeral services.

The title identifies the psalm as "A prayer of Moses the man of God." Since the titles are not part of the inspired text, even evangelical scholars point out that the total thrust of the poem would be much more appropriate to a later time. Verses 13-17 seem to indicate a duration of history longer than would have been the case in the wilderness.[4] However, since Moses was recognized as the great lawgiver of the OT, it is a tribute to the quality of the psalm that it should have been ascribed or dedicated to him.

1. *The Sovereignty of God* (90:1-6)

The first stanza recognized the sovereign God as Israel's **Refuge in all generations** (1). The **Lord** is God **from everlasting to everlasting** (2), "from the infinite past to the infinite future."[5] The entire **earth** is His creation. **Thou turnest man to destruction** (3) is better, "Thou turnest mortal man back to dust"

---

[1]McCullough, *op. cit.*, 4:487.   [2]Quoted, *loc. cit.*
[3]Quoted, Perowne, *op. cit.*, II, 161.   [4]Cf. Kirkpatrick, *op. cit.*, pp. 547-48.
[5]*Ibid.*, p. 549.

(Berk.), as in Gen. 3:19. **Return, ye children of men** is given two different interpretations. Most versions and commentators regard this as an explanation of the line preceding, that man is bidden to return to the dust, from whence his body came. Some, however, regard this as an injunction to return to God in repentance: "You bring mankind to a state of contrition, saying, 'Repent, offspring of man' " (Harrison).

Time is no limitation with God. **A thousand years in thy sight are but as yesterday when it is past, and as a watch in the night (4)**—cf. 102:24, 27; II Pet. 3:8. A **watch** in the OT was approximately four hours. The idea is probably that a millennium is no longer to the Lord than a watch in the night seems to a sleeping man. The comparatively brief and tentative existence of man is described in striking metaphors: like a building swept **away . . . with a** sudden **flood (5)**; like the hours of a dreamless **sleep**; like the **grass** that grows up quickly, flourishes, and is as quickly **cut down, and withereth (6)**.

2. The Shortness of Life (90:7-12)

The theme introduced in the first stanza is pursued in the second. The brevity of life is accentuated by the fact that sin has brought it under the cloud of God's wrath. **Iniquities** and **secret sins** had brought the consuming **anger** and troubling **wrath** of a holy God (7-8). There is no word corresponding to **sins** in the Hebrew of v. 8. *"Our secret (sin)* is rather the inward sin of the heart unseen by man but known to God."[6] God not only knows the iniquities of men's lives, but the hidden principle of sin within the soul. **Our days are passed away in thy wrath (9)** is better, "Our days pass away under thy wrath" (RSV). **Our years as a tale that is told** has been translated "our years as a sighing" (Berk.). The Hebrew here is literally "as a breathing," or "as a murmur." **Tale that is told** in the KJV does not mean "story that is related" but rather "number that is counted," since the old English meaning of **tale** is a counting or enumeration as in "the tale of the bricks" of Exod. 5:8.

Threescore years and ten or **fourscore (10)**, i.e., seventy or eighty years, may constitute our days on earth; and the extension of life beyond this may be but **labour and sorrow**. However many the years, they are **soon** gone and **we fly away** (cf. Job 20:8). In such a situation we need to recognize **the power** of God's **anger**

[6]*Ibid.*, p. 551.

(11) and **number our days** (12), counting each of value, so **that we may apply our hearts unto wisdom**—"acquire discerning minds" (Berk.). Kirkpatrick interprets v. 11 as, "Who understands or lays to heart the intensity of God's wrath against sin so as to fear Him duly with that reverence which is man's safeguard against offending Him?"[7]

3. The Supplication for God's Favor (90:13-17)

The psalm ends with a prayer of supplication typical of the psalms of lament. In view of God's eternity and man's short and sin-stained life, the poet pleads for God's gracious favor. The connection with the preceding sections of the psalm is natural. Contemplation turns to supplication. As in 6:3, the sentence, **Return, O Lord, how long?** is not completed. The meaning is, "How long wilt Thou delay in turning again to be merciful to us?" **Let it repent thee** is a common form of the plea that God will change His manner of dealing with His now repentant people. The Lord "is not a man, that he should repent" (I Sam. 15:29) as a human being would need to repent of evil intended or done. But God's dealings with His people are conditioned by their obedience to His law. For Him to **repent** would mean simply to turn from wrath to mercy.

Satisfy us early (14) is literally "in the morning." The night is dark; may the dawn soon come. The context suggests that God satisfy us early in life in order **that we may . . . be glad all our days.** The expression **glad according to the days** (15) indicates a newborn joy commensurate with the sorrows of the past. Both God's judgments and His saving acts are described by the term here translated **work** (16). God's glory will be seen in every aspect of His work of salvation so ardently desired. The term translated **beauty** (17) is sweetness, pleasantness, and is variously rendered "graciousness" (Perowne, Berk.), "loving favour" (Moffatt), or simply "favor" (RSV, Harrison). **Establish thou the work of our hands upon us** means, "Prosper all the work we undertake" (Moffatt).

Psalm 91: THE SECURITY OF THE TRUSTING HEART, 91:1-16

This song of adoration, together with the wisdom psalm which follows, is often joined with the preceding in a sort of trilogy of trust. Several links of thought and expression serve to

---

[7]*Ibid.*, p. 552.

tie them together. Psalm 90 represents the plea for deliverance; Psalm 92 rejoices in its accomplishment; and the present psalm links prayer and its answer together in an almost unequalled expression of trust.

Commentators have been reminded of Rom. 8:31 by the theme of this psalm. "It is St. Paul's fervid exclamation, 'If God be for us, who can be against us?' expressed in rich and varied poetry."[8] Cf. also McCullough.[9]

Some have wondered about the alternation of first and second person pronouns (I, me; thee, thou). But the Psalmist simply professes his own faith, and on the basis of that faith addresses words of comfort to his people.

1. *Trust* (91:1-8)

The first alternation of first and second persons is in 1-8. In 1-2, the poet expresses his confidence in the security afforded by **the secret place of** the **most High** (1), who is his **refuge** and his **fortress** (2). In 3-8, he addresses words of confidence and comfort to his hearers or readers. **The secret place** (1) is the covert or hiding place provided by God's sheltering care; **the shadow** is God's protection—possibly a hint of the metaphor of the eagle's wings to follow in v. 4. The titles **most High** and **Almighty** are allusions to the sovereign power of God to protect and provide for His own. In the Lord God the Psalmist finds his **refuge** and his **fortress** (cf. comment on 18:2; 31:3; and 71:3).

The poet now turns to his companions with an expression of the conviction that God will **deliver** them **from the snare of the fowler** (3), the almost invisible net of the bird catchers. **The noisome** (deadly or destroying) **pestilence,** possibly referred to again in 6-7, may indicate an epidemic raging at the time.[10] God himself will be their Shelter, as the eagle protects its young (4; cf. Deut. 32:11, with a slightly different application). **His truth** (faithfulness) . . . **thy shield and buckler** is better, "His fidelity is your assurance of security" (Harrison).

Verses 5-6 provide a double parallelism: **the terror by night** and **the arrow** . . . **by day** (5); **the pestilence** . . . **in darkness, the destruction** . . . **at noonday** (6). **The terror by night** is prob-

[8]Perowne, op. cit., II, 172.   [9]Op. cit., 4:493.
[10]Ibid., 4:494-95.

ably the swift night attack common to the warfare of the times; so 5 would represent dangers from men and 6 dangers from disease, epidemic, or plague. Harrison translates 6: "Neither the plague that stalks at dead of night, nor the epidemic which devastates at midday." Multitudes of others (the wicked) shall be cut down, but the righteous shall be spared (7-8). The Psalmist knew, of course, that rewards do not always measure out in strict justice in this life. What he speaks of is the conviction that, in a moral universe governed by a holy God, it must finally be well with the righteous and ill with the wicked. The problems arising from a temporary disparity in rewards and punishment are treated in Job and in Psalms 37, 49, and 73 (q.v.).

2. Triumph (91:9-13)

Another expression of personal faith, and its application to Israel, characterizes this division of the psalm. The Hebrew of v. 9 is admittedly difficult, and many modern translations emend the text to avoid the first person. *The Berkeley Version* best adheres to the Hebrew while giving a smooth English translation: "For Thou, O Lord, art my refuge. Since you too have established the Most High as your shelter, no harm shall befall you . . ." Evil and plague will be kept away (10). The promise of 11-12, out of context, was quoted by Satan in the wilderness temptation of Jesus (Matt. 4:6; Luke 4:10-11). Lion . . . adder . . . young lion and dragon (13) vividly symbolize the destructive and poisonous powers of evil over which the Lord causes His people to triumph.

3. Troth (91:14-16)

God himself speaks in the last three verses, and adds His pledge to the assurances of the poet. The condition upon which all depends is simple: Because he hath set his love upon me (14). The expression means to cleave to God in complete devotion. Obedience and faith are both the natural outflow of the love shed abroad in human hearts by the Holy Spirit (Rom. 5:5; cf. John 14:15; I John 4:18). Known by name means more than information about the name of the true God. It implies a personal acquaintance with the God whose nature is revealed in His name. The results that follow such love and acquaintance are deliverance, exaltation, answered prayer (15), His presence in trouble, honor, long life (16), and salvation.

Psalm 92: God's Sovereign Justice, 92:1-15

This is a wisdom psalm which deals in broad terms with the problems raised in the Book of Job and Psalms 37, 49, and 73. Our psalmist here, however, has no doubt about the solution. Although the wicked may seem to prosper, it is only to the end that they may be brought down and destroyed forever. The ultimate and certain triumph of justice is cause for unceasing praise. Oesterley comments, "This psalm sets forth very beautifully the truth that temporal benefits are the gifts of God, and that gratitude for these must be expressed in praise to the Almighty. It is not too much to say that these things are but too often taken for granted, or ascribed to personal prowess and industry; of course these have their part to play, the divine gift of free-will is accorded to every man; but it must not be forgotten that all things are in the hand of God."[11]

Psalm 92 is titled "A Psalm or Song for the sabbath day." The Jewish *Mishnah* indicates that it was used in the Temple at the time of the morning sacrifice on the Sabbath. Verse 2 refers to prayer both morning and evening. The poem is difficult to divide, and several different outlines have been suggested. The most natural would recognize two main divisions.

1. Praise for Present Confidence (92:1-8)

Verses 1-3 emphasize the blessing and duty of praise, and the balance of the section sets forth the bounty for which God is to be glorified. **To give thanks** and **to sing praises** to **the Lord,** the **most High**, is **a good thing** (1). **Morning** and evening God's **lovingkindness** and **faithfulness** are to be declared (2). Lovingkindness is *chesed* (mercy, stedfast love; cf. comment on 17:7). The precise nature of the musical instruments here named is difficult to determine, but they all appear to have been stringed instruments of various sizes. **An instrument of ten strings** (3) was probably a lute; **the psaltery** would be a harp or lyre (cf. comment on 33:2).

The special cause for praise is the demonstration of God's justice and sovereignty. The Lord has blessed and **made** His servant **glad** (4). God's **works** are **great**, and His **thoughts** are **deep** (5) or profound. The **brutish man** (6) is the one who is stupid or dull, not comprehending the principles of divine equity. The **fool** here, as in the Proverbs and elsewhere in Scripture, is

[11]*Op. cit.,* p. 414.

not the mentally incompetent but the morally perverse. Such persons see the temporary prosperity of the wicked, and do not understand the outcome of such a life—that **they shall be destroyed for ever** (7), "whereas You, Lord, remain supreme forever" (8, Harrison).

2. Proofs of Perfect Equity (92:9-15)

In the manner of Psalm 1, the differing fate of the wicked and the righteous is indicated. God's **enemies shall perish,** and **the workers of iniquity shall be scattered** (9), literally, "shall scatter themselves." "The seemingly solid phalanx of antagonism breaks up and disperses, disintegrated from within."[12] So it always has been, and so it always shall be. In contrast, the Psalmist's **horn** shall be exalted **like the horn of an unicorn** (10). The **horn** represents the power or strength of the wild ox, an animal whose ferocity and strength are described in Job 39:9-12. The Hebrew of 10*b* is uncertain; it is interpreted, "I am anointed with invigorating oil" (Berk.) and, "Thou dost revive my failing strength" (Moffatt). **The righteous** will **flourish like the palm tree** (12) and **like a cedar in Lebanon.** The date palm was prized for both its beauty and its fruit (Song of Sol. 7:7). While cedars grew throughout Palestine, they flourished best in the mountains of Lebanon, from whence their timbers were often imported into Israel. The people of God are envisioned as having their roots **in the house of the Lord** (13), where even down to **old age** they continue to be fruitful (14). **Fat** would mean "full of sap and green" (Perowne). The effect of this good providence is to demonstrate the righteousness of God in governing the world. **My rock** (15) is a figure for a firm and unshakable foundation.

Psalm 93: THE GOD OF HOLINESS REIGNS, 93:1-5

This psalm is one of several (47, 96—99) which are marked by the repeated words, "The Lord reigneth," or, "The Lord is King." Some have viewed these as "enthronement psalms," and have supposed that they were used during a New Year's ceremony of enthronement for the Lord as King over the earth and its peoples. While traces of such ceremonies have been found in other ancient oriental religions, there is no reference to an observance like this in Israel. It is probably better to recognize in

---

[12]Kirkpatrick, *op. cit.,* p. 561.

these psalms the conviction of God's eternal sovereignty over nature and man.

M'Caw points out "the development of the thought, from the first creep of these flood-waters, through the increasing swirl of their currents and the deepening roar of their destructive efforts, even to their final manifestation as broad waters whipped in tumult, thundering menaces ('voices') and crashing as breakers of a sea. Yet is the Lord on high unmoved and unperturbed, ever glorious in power."[13]

1. The Strength of the Lord (93:1-2)

Clothed with majesty and **strength, the Lord** reigns (1). God has **girded himself,** which speaks of an act, not merely a fact. At a time when men and nations looked upon His cause as languishing in defeat through the Exile, the Lord asserted His power to bring a remnant back to their promised land again. **The world also is stablished**—"The moral order of the world which seemed tottering to its fall is reestablished."[14] The Psalmist worships in awe and adoration: **Thy throne is established of old: thou art from everlasting** (2).

2. The Sovereignty of the Lord (93:3-5)

The floods (3) represent all the forces arrayed against the righteous rule of the Lord—nations such as Egypt, Assyria, Babylon; and the unseen hosts of evil that compose the kingdom of darkness, the "principalities and powers" of which the NT speaks (Rom. 8:38; Eph. 1:21; 6:12; Col. 2:15). The Psalmist views their threat as more noise than power. They **have lifted up their voice, but the Lord on high is mightier than the noise of many waters** (4). **Thy testimonies** (5), that is, the law which bears witness to God's will and man's duty, "are firmly established" (Harrison). **Holiness becometh thine house, O Lord, for ever** suggests both separating God's house from the secular and profane and characterizing the people who worship there. This is rightly made the motto of many churches which purpose to preach a gospel bigger than the deepest needs of the human heart.

Psalm 94: GOD ALONE IS OUR HELP, 94:1-23

Psalm 94 is a wisdom psalm which seeks to reconcile the inequities of life with the goodness and power of God. Other

---

[13]Op. cit., p. 479.   [14]Kirkpatrick, op. cit., p. 564.

psalms dealing with the same problem are 37, 49, and 73 (*q.v.*). The source of the problem is the existence of men who persecute those who serve the Lord. It is, as M'Caw says, "a reminder of the anomaly of man's deviltry within the moral order established by God."[15] The Psalmist finds the answer in the sufficiency of God's grace. "Whether external troubles assail, or perplexities of mind cause worry and anxiety, he who brings them in trustful faith before God knows that, in the beautiful words of the psalmist, His love upholds, His comforts refresh."[16]

It has been noted[17] that vv. 1-15 deal chiefly with the nation in an appeal to God for help, whereas vv. 16-23 are oriented about the individual appeal for help.

1. *Complaint* (94:1-7)

The first stanza is a direct appeal to God to intervene in behalf of those victimized by workers of iniquity. The **Lord God** is the One **to whom vengeance belongeth** (1), a thought drawn from Deut. 32:35 and emphasized in Rom. 12:19. Dr. H. Orton Wiley used to comment, "Vengeance belongs to God alone, and He never gives it to anyone else." As **judge of the earth** (2), God is implored to show His just reward for evil. Three rhetorical questions show that **the wicked triumph** (3), **they utter and speak hard** (arrogant) **things** (4), and they **boast themselves** ("exult," RSV). These godless persecutors **break in pieces** (crush) God's **people** (5). They **afflict His heritage,** those the Lord has chosen for himself. Their crimes are particularly directed against those who have no defense against them: **the widow** (6), **the stranger** (sojourner, or what we would call a resident alien), and **the fatherless.** In all this, their boast is that **the Lord** will pay no attention (7).

2. *Correction* (94:8-11)

Against the assumption that God does not heed the evils thus wrought, the Psalmist addresses a ringing corrective. **Brutish among the people** (8), "dull-witted people" (Harrison). **Fools,** "dolts" (Harrison). Cf. comment on 92:6. How ridiculous to suppose that the Creator of **the ear** is deaf, and that He who

[15]*Op. cit.*, p. 479.   [16]Oesterley, *op. cit.*, p. 419.
[17]McCullough, *op. cit.*, 4:507

designed the eye is blind (9)! "Can he not punish men, he who is training them? Has he no knowledge, he who teaches men?" (10, Moffatt) Indeed, The Lord knoweth the thoughts of man, that they are vanity (11), or "futile" (Berk.). God's wisdom and power will bring all man's scheming to nought.

3. Chastening (94:12-15)

There is infinite consolation in the thought that the adversities of life may be the chastening of the Lord. Chastening as in 12 and Heb. 12:5-11 does not mean punishment for wrongdoing, although it may include this. It stands for the whole process of child training, the disciplines of life that lead to maturity. Here it is placed in parallel construction with teachest him out of thy law. To rest from the days of adversity (13) means that the mercy of God will alleviate the suffering of the righteous even before the judgment of the wicked is accomplished. God will never forsake his own (14), but "goodness shall have justice done to it—the future is with men of upright mind" (15, Moffatt).

4. Cry (94:16-21)

From his defense of others, the Psalmist turns to plead for his own cause: Who will rise up ("take his stand," Harrison) for me against the evildoers? (16) "If the Lord had not been my help, my soul would soon have dwelt in the land of silence" (17, RSV). God had answered His servant's cry for help with a sustaining arm (18). The consolations of the Lord were his delight (19). The throne of iniquity (20; "wicked sovereign," Harrison) can have no fellowship with God, for the godless ruler uses the very law itself to work his evil ends. Such evil princes band together against the righteous. and condemn the innocent blood (21), i.e., "condemn the innocent to death" (Harrison).

5. Confidence (94:22-23)

The psalm closes with a reiteration of the poet's confidence in the Lord, who was his defence . . . the rock of his refuge (22). The justice of the Lord will bring upon evildoers their own iniquity (23). There is a sense in which sin is its own punishment, and men are doomed to reap what they sow (Gal. 6:7-8). The righteousness of God guarantees the working of a moral law which is built into the very fiber of the universe.

Psalm 95: PRAISE AND PATIENCE, 95:1-11

Psalms 95—100 comprise one of three groups of liturgical psalms characteristic of Books IV and V of the Psalter. The other groupings are Psalms 113—18 and 146—50. A common theme in the present group is the joyous praise of the Lord as the Ruler of all creation as well as the covenant God of Israel. They thus represent the same emphasis found in the prophecies of Isaiah and Jonah upon the universal reign of Israel's Lord. Morgan entitles them, "Songs of the King."[18]

Psalm 95 is traditionally used among the Jews as one of the special psalms for morning prayer on the Sabbath. Oesterley writes, "Especially to be noticed here is the way in which the joy in worship is emphasized; this is engendered by the conviction of the divine presence. The true worship of him who is all-powerful and all-loving will of necessity inspire happiness. On the other hand, the psalm contains a warning for every age; mere external acts of worship, without sincerity of heart, become a mockery. The true rest of God can be the lot of those only who worship him 'in spirit and in truth.' "[19]

1. *Worship* (95:1-7a)

The psalm naturally divides into two sections in the middle of v. 7. The first half is a call to worship. Many of the terms and phrases have already been encountered in the Psalms, and are also found in the latter part of Isaiah. God's people are called to **sing** and **make a joyful noise** unto **the Lord** (1), **coming before his presence with thanksgiving, and . . . with psalms** (2). He **is a great God** and **King above all gods** (3). The latter term is not a concession to polytheism, but a recognition that God is supreme over every power and person in the universe. God's greatness is seen in His sovereign control of the earth (4) and **the sea** (5).

In the presence of such a God, one can only **worship** and adore (6). **For he is our God; and we are the people of his pasture, and the sheep of his hand** (7a).

2. *Warning* (95:7b-11)

The balance of the psalm is a warning against unfaithfulness, based on the rebellion of the fathers in the wilderness. It is extensively quoted in Heb. 3:7-11, 15; 4:7, where it is applied

---

[18]*Op. cit.*, p. 257.   [19]*Op. cit.*, p. 422.

to Christians who fail to go on into the "rest of faith" provided for them in the sanctifying purpose of God. Warnings from the failure of Israel to go on into Canaan immediately after the Exodus are significantly applied in the NT to Christians in relation to God's call to holiness (Hebrews 3—4; Jude 5).

To day if ye will hear his voice (7b) is better, "O that today you would hearken to his voice" (RSV). Disobedience and unbelief result in the hardening of the heart. **The provocation** (8; "Meribah") and **temptation** ("Massah") are described in Exod. 17:1-7 with a parallel occurrence in Num. 20:1-13. "Your forebears doubted Me, putting Me to the test, though they had witnessed My doings" (9, Harrison). **A people that do err in their heart** (10) has been interpreted "a people whose heart strays" (Berk.). **Unto whom I sware in my wrath that they should not enter into my rest** (11) shows that there are some choices that cannot be changed. Those who made their decision to stay in the wilderness spent the rest of their lives in the wilderness, even though later they would have reversed themselves.

Psalm 96: "SING . . . A NEW SONG," 96:1-13

Psalm 96 is found practically word for word in I Chron. 16:23-33, where it is part of a longer composition attributed to David. As with others of this group (cf. intro. to Psalms 95), its emphasis is upon the universal sovereignty of God. "Ps. 96 is an appeal to all nations to recognize that it is Yahweh alone who is their God. The reasons given in this piece are not elaborated; Yahweh is great and praise-worthy, and will eventually judge the whole earth."[20]

1. *The Glory of the One God* (96:1-6)

The phrase, **O sing unto the Lord a new song** (1), is echoed in 33:3; 98:1; 149:1; and Isa. 42:10. The fresh blessings of the Lord require a new song of praise for **his salvation** (2). The **glory** of the Lord and **his wonders** (3) are to be made known to **all people. The Lord is great** (4), **to be feared above all gods** (cf. comment on 95:3). **All the gods of the nations are idols** (5), literally, "things of nought," or "nothings" (cf. 115:4-8). Isa. 40:18-23 and 44:9-20 are scathing indictments of the folly of idol worship in which this point is made with great force. In total contrast to the idols of the nations, **the Lord made the**

---

[20]Robinson, *op. cit.*, p. 126.

heavens. Therefore **honour and majesty are before him: strength and beauty are in his sanctuary** (6).

2. *The Duty of Man to Worship* (96:7-13)

The similarity of these verses to 29:1-2 is apparent (cf. comments there). **Kindreds of the people** (7) is better "families of the peoples" (RSV). All nations of earth are called to the worship of the true God in consecration (7-8) and **the beauty of holiness** (9). Harrison translates, "Worship the Lord with a sanctified spirit." The sovereignty of the Lord must be acknowledged **among the heathen** (10). **Heavens** and **earth** and nature itself are all called upon to **rejoice before the Lord** (11-13). The psalm closes with the apocalyptic note that **the Lord . . . cometh to judge the earth . . . with righteousness, and the people with his truth** (13). The basis of divine judgment is the truth of God's Word and the person of God's Son (Acts 17:31; Rev. 20:11-12).

Psalm 97: GOD OF JUDGMENT AND GRACE, 97:1-12

There is a striking prophetic note in Psalm 97 picturing the awesomeness of God's judgment throne. Morgan says, "The reign of Jehovah, while wholly beneficent in purpose and in ultimate issue, is yet full of terror and of judgment in its process toward the issue. This is also cause for rejoicing. The method of God's judgments is described . . . the effects of His judgments are declared. . . . The vision of the certainty, method, and victory of the judgments of the King gives rise to the sense of their underlying reason. He is the Holy One, and all wickedness is hateful to Him, because of the harm it works among His people, for the fierceness of God's holiness is ever His love. Therefore let His saints learn the lesson, and 'hate evil.' The promise to those who obey is very full of beauty, 'light is sown . . . and gladness.' It is a figure of the dawn, shedding its light. To walk in light is to be able to discover the true pathway leading toward the desired consummation. To walk in that pathway is to have gladness in the heart indeed."[21]

1. *The Awesome Judgments of the Lord* (97:1-7)

The psalm opens with the characteristic refrain of the group, **The Lord reigneth** (1; cf. intro. to Psalm 95). This is cause for

---

[21]*Op. cit.*, pp. 257-58.

rejoicing on the part of **the earth** and **the multitude of isles.
Judgment** (2) means "justice." God's throne and His appearance
are described in terms drawn from the account of the giving of
the law at Sinai (cf. Exod. 19:9, 16; 20:21; Deut. 4:11; 5:23).
Clouds ... darkness ... fire, i.e., storms, earthquake, and lightning characterize **the presence of the Lord** (2-5). In 4, **enlightened** means "lighted up." Not even **hills** and mountains can
stand before **the Lord of the whole earth** (5). For 6, cf. 19:1-9.
Confounded (7) means "ashamed" (Berk.) or "disgraced" (Harrison). **Worship him, all ye gods** has been interpreted, "All
gods lay prostrate at his feet" (Moffatt); cf. comment on 95:3.

2. *The Joy of the Righteous* (97:8-12)

Zion heard (8) of the Lord's mighty acts, **and the daughters**
("cities," Berk.) **of Judah rejoiced because of His judgments,**
i.e., "God's vindication of himself and of his people in the events
of history."[22] **Thou, Lord, art high** (9)—the Hebrew reads "Most
High." For **above all gods** cf. comment on 95:3. To **love the
Lord** is to **hate evil** (10). Christians must never lose a capacity
for righteous anger in the face of stark evil. **Light is sown** (11)
is rendered, "Light dawns" (RSV). The people of God are
assured of preservation, deliverance, **light,** and **gladness.** Therefore they should **rejoice in the Lord** (12), **and give thanks at
the remembrance of his holiness**—or, as the Hebrew is better
translated, "Give thanks to His holy Name" (Perowne).

Psalm 98: THE WHY AND HOW OF WORSHIP, 98:1-9

As Psalm 97 emphasizes the righteous judgments of the
Lord, Psalm 98 stresses His mercy and His salvation. Again the
elements of nature are called upon to glorify God. Morgan points
out a pattern similar to that of other psalms, with widening
circles of praise and sovereignty: Israel, vv. 1-3; the whole earth,
vv. 4-6; and all nature, vv. 7-8.[23] The psalm begins and ends with
the same phrases as found at the beginning and ending of Psalm
96. It bears the simple Hebrew title, *mizmor,* "A Psalm." This
comes from a term which seems originally to have meant "to
make music," and should probably be understood as indicating a
song with instrumental accompaniment.[24]

[22]McCullough, *op. cit.,* 4:524. [23]*Op. cit.,* p. 258.
[24]Kirkpatrick, *op. cit.,* p. xix.

1. *The Reasons for Divine Worship* (98:1-3)

The psalm opens with a call for **a new song** (cf. comment on 96:1), in recognition that the Lord **hath done marvellous things** (1). **His right hand** and **his holy arm** are expressions for God's power; manifested in behalf of His people they have **gotten him the victory. Salvation . . . righteousness** (2), **mercy and . . . truth** (3) have been openly manifested both to **the house of Israel** and **in the sight of the heathen** (2). **All the ends of the earth have seen the salvation of our God** (3). It is probably correct to regard these expressions as instances of the use of what has been called "the prophetic perfect" tense. One of the most famous uses of this prophetic perfect is found in Isa. 9:6, where the coming of Christ seven centuries later is spoken of as having already occurred: "Unto us a child is born, unto us a son is given." So sure was the predicted event in the mind of the writer that it could be spoken of as having already happened. The gospel is yet to be preached to the very **ends of the earth;** yet so sure is God's purpose that it is proper to say, **All the ends of the earth have seen the salvation of our God.**

2. *The Means of Divine Worship* (98:4-9)

God is to be worshiped with **a joyful noise** (4), with rejoicing, **praise**, singing, **with the harp, and the voice of a psalm** (5; Heb., "melody"); **with trumpets and sound of cornet** (6). In view of frequent references such as this and in Psalm 150, can any reasonably forbid the use of instrumental music in the sanctuary? Not only man and his instruments of music, but **the sea . . . the world** (7), **the floods . . . the hills** (8)—all nature is called upon to rejoice **before the Lord** (9). Cf. comment on 96:13. **The fulness thereof** (7), i.e., "all within it" (Moffatt).

Psalm 99: THE GOD OF HOLINESS, 99:1-9

McCullough describes this as "a hymn to the God of holiness."[25] Each of the three sections of the psalm ends with a similar refrain: "It is holy" (3), "He is holy" (5), and, "Our God is holy" (9). Morgan makes the interesting suggestion that "in the fuller light of the Christian revelation we see the threefold fact in the life of God suggested. The Father enthroned, the Son administering His Kingdom, the Spirit interpreting His will

[25]*Op. cit.*, p. 528.

through leaders and circumstances, through pity and through punishment."[26]

1. Holy in Power (99:1-3)

The psalm opens with the familiar proclamation of God's sovereign reign (1). **He sitteth between the cherubims** is a reference to the belief that God's throne on earth was above the mercy seat of the ark of the covenant between the two winged creatures known as cherubim (Exod. 25:18-22; 37:7-9). The ark was in the holy of holies—first in the Tabernacle, and later in the Temple. The greatness and exalted majesty of **the Lord** (2) is cause for praise to His **great and terrible name; for it is holy** (3; Heb., "He is holy").

2. Holy in Justice (99:4-5)

The king's strength also loveth judgment (4) is variously translated: "Thou art a King, in love with justice" (Moffatt); "The King's energy is keenly set on justice" (Berk.). The thought is that God's might is pledged to the vindication of His justice, as King of the universe. He establishes **equity,** and executes **judgment** (justice) **and righteousness.** Therefore He is to be exalted and His people are called to **worship at his footstool; for he is holy** (5).

3. Holy in Mercy (99:6-9)

Moses and Aaron . . . and Samuel (6) are named as exemplars of those whose prayers the Lord had answered. **The cloudy pillar** (7) applies particularly to **Moses and Aaron** and refers to the means of God's appearance and guidance in the wilderness (cf. Exod. 14:19-20; Num. 12:5). Moses and Samuel are cited as men of powerful intercession in Jer. 15:1. **Thou wast a God that forgavest them** (8) is a reference, not to the three named, but to the whole nation. **Though thou tookest vengeance of their inventions** is better, "Thou didst make them pay for their evil practices" (Berk.). While God pardons, "He must still vindicate His holiness by chastisement, lest men should imagine that He makes light of sin. See Ex. xxxiv.7; Num. xiv.20 ff.; and the prophet's touching identification of himself with the guilty people in Mic. vii.9 ff."[27] In view of God's mercies, His people are

[26]*Op. cit.,* p. 258.   [27]Kirkpatrick, *op. cit.,* p. 587.

347

called to **worship at his holy hill** (Zion); **for the Lord our God is holy** (9).

Psalm 100: THE LORD IS THE TRUE GOD, 100:1-5

This brief song is similar to Psalm 95, and would appear to have been sung by the procession of worshippers as they approached the Temple with their thank offerings. Perowne would regard it as a doxology of the group of psalms beginning with 95. He quotes Delitzsch, "Among the Psalms of triumph and thanksgiving this stands preeminent, as rising to the highest point of joy and grandeur."[28]

1. The Works of the Lord (100:1-3)

God is to be glorified for His creative works with **a joyful noise** (1), **with gladness** and **with singing** (2). The obligation to praise is universal—**all ye lands** (1). What identifies **the Lord** of Israel as the true **God** is that He has **made us, and not we ourselves** (3). There are in reality no "self-made" men. Verse 3 parallels 95:6-7 (q.v.).

2. The Worship of the Lord (100:4-5)

The **gates** and the **courts** (4) of the Lord refer to His house, the place of public worship. An essential part of worship is **thanksgiving**, perhaps a thank offering (so the Amp. OT), and **praise**. The highest point of worship is not recognition of God as Creator, but that **the Lord is good; his mercy is everlasting; and his truth endureth to all generations** (5). **Truth**, here as frequently in the psalms, carries the thought of faithfulness, dependability.

Psalm 101: THE KING'S NOBLE PURPOSE, 101:1-8

Entitled "A Psalm of David," this poem is described by M'Caw as "the Davidic ideal," "the principles upon which he intended to act during his reign in Zion, the city of the Lord."[29] Kirkpatrick would associate it with the restoration of the ark to Jerusalem (II Sam. 6:12-19).[30] J. A. Alexander views it as David's guidance for his successors, and believes that this accounts for the correspondence between the psalm and the teach-

[28]Op. cit., II, 210.   [29]Op. cit., p. 482.
[30]Op. cit., pp. 589-90.

ings of the Book of Proverbs with regard to the conduct of the kingly office.[31] Certainly, it aptly applies to all who hold authority over others under the providence of God, whether they be civil or church leaders.

1. The King's Purpose for Himself (101:1-4)

The first part of the psalm has more direct bearing on the personal life and conduct of the king. His song, addressed to the **Lord,** will be **of mercy and judgment** (1). He has himself been the object of God's mercy and righteous judgment, and must in his turn minister the same to those for whom he is responsible. Therefore will he **behave** himself **wisely in a perfect way** (2). Kirkpatrick interprets thus: "I will give heed unto the way of integrity, deliberately and of set purpose make whole-hearted devotion to God and perfect uprightness towards men the rule of my conduct."[32] The Hebrew terms translated **perfect** twice in this verse are *tammim* and *tam* and mean "without a blemish or defect," "blameless."[33] "The term is used of Jehovah's character and conduct about the same number of times as of man's, suggesting the possibility of man resembling his God."[34]

Involved in such perfection is the rejection of every **wicked thing** (3; lit., "a thing of Belial," worthless, base) and **the work of them that turn aside.** Moffatt renders it, "Apostates and their practices I hate." **It shall not cleave to me,** i.e., "It shall not gain a hold on me" (Harrison). A **froward heart** (4) indicates "a perverse nature" (Berk.) or "an evil mind" (Harrison). **I will not know a wicked person** means, "I disown evil men" (Moffatt).

2. The King's Purpose for His Court (101:5-8)

The king's purpose with regard to those he associates with himself is set forth in the last half of the psalm. "I will destroy the man who maligns his friend secretly. I cannot tolerate the supercilious and haughty person" (5, Harrison). The talebearer and the conceited quickly work havoc in any organization. In contrast, those who are **faithful** and who walk **in a perfect way**

---

[31]*The Psalms Translated and Explained* (Grand Rapids, Michigan: Zondervan Publishing House [reprint], n.d.), pp. 406-7.

[32]*Op. cit.,* p. 591.

[33]George Allen Turner, *The Vision Which Transforms* (Kansas City, Mo.: Beacon Hill Press, 1964), pp. 42-43.

[34]*Ibid.,* p. 43.

(6) **shall serve** the king and his nation. For **perfect** (Heb., *tammim*), cf. comment on 2. Deceitful and lying persons will not be tolerated (7), and the king's power and authority will be directed against **the wicked** and **wicked doers** (8). As Perowne observes, "Day by day will he exercise his work of righteous judgment, purging out all ungodliness from the Holy City. . . . It is a hope which finds its accomplishment in the Apocalyptic vision, in that new Jerusalem into which 'there shall in no wise enter any thing that defileth, or worketh abomination, or maketh a lie.' (Rev. xxi.27.)"[35]

Psalm 102: A PRAYER OF THE AFFLICTED, 102:1-28

The superscription of the psalm is translated by Moffatt, "The prayer of an unhappy soul who is overwhelmed and pours out his plaint before the Eternal." This is the only title of this sort in the book, since it gives no musical instruction or indication of authorship or dedication. Verses 13-16, 20, and 22 seem quite clearly to place the time of composition in the Exile period. Perowne's description of the different moods reflected in the psalm is helpful: "In mournful strains he described his bitter lot. Sorrow and pain had been very busy with him. His very heart was smitten within him, as the grass is withered in the hot eye of the sun. . . . But when he has time to look away from his sorrow, a prospect so bright and so glorious opens before him, that in the thought of it all else is swallowed up and forgotten. Zion's deliverance is at hand. Her God has not forsaken her."[36]

Although listed as one of the seven penitential psalms (cf. 6; 32; 38; 41; 130; 143), the element of penitence is not to be found in it. The Psalmist does not trace his miseries to his sin, but to his circumstances and his own physical weakness.

1. *The Plea for Help* (102:1-11)

The opening prayer is similar to the pleas found elsewhere quite frequently in the psalms (18:6; 39:12; 59:16; 69:17; etc.). The poet calls on the Lord to **hear,** to let his cry come up before Him (1), to **hide not** His **face from** him (2), to **incline** His **ear** and to **answer . . . speedily.** Unless God intervenes quickly, it will be too late, **For my days are consumed like smoke, and my**

---

[35]*Op. cit.*, II, 216.   [36]*Ibid.*, II, 217.

bones are burned as an hearth (3). *The Berkeley Version* translates, "For my days go up in smoke; my bones are inflamed as a bonfire." His physical afflictions had **withered** his **heart** (4), and due to his **groaning** (5; **troubles**) he finds himself reduced to "skin and bones." **I am like a pelican . . . an owl,** (6), **a sparrow alone** (7), are symbols of utter loneliness and desolation. **They that are mad against me are sworn against me** (8) means, "They that are angry with me use my name for a curse" (Amp. OT). "I eat ashes with my food, tears fall into my drink" (9, Moffatt). While no reason is given for God's **indignation and . . . wrath** (10), the Psalmist feels that he is an object of divine displeasure. He is **lifted . . . up** only to be **cast . . . down** again. His **days are like a shadow that declineth** (11), as at the evening time. Death is near. **I am,** he says, **withered like grass.**

2. *The Purpose of the Lord* (102: 12-22)

The mood changes. In contrast to the Psalmist's misery stands God's eternal purpose. The difference is expressed in the simple adversative, **But thou, O Lord** (12). God's eternity is assured: He will **endure for ever,** and His **remembrance unto all generations.** The Lord will **arise, and have mercy upon Zion** (13). The **set time** is generally conceded to be the end of the predicted seventy years of exile in Babylonia (cf. Jer. 29:10; Dan. 9:2). Even the **stones** and **the dust** of Zion (14) were precious to the people of God. The rebuilding of Jerusalem would give cause to **the heathen** to **fear the name of the Lord** (15). The full scope of the poet's vision—**all the kings of the earth** recognizing the **glory** of the Lord—would, of course, have to await the long-range fulfillment of God's purpose in Christ. But the building of **Zion** would glorify the Lord (16) and would constitute His answer to **the prayer of the destitute** (17) people of Israel.

This shall be written for the generation to come (18) is better, "Let this be recorded for future ages" (Harrison). One of the great incentives to faith is the record of fulfilled prophecy. **The people which shall be created,** or "a people yet to be born" (Berk.), **shall praise the Lord.** The reason is that God **looked down from the height of his sanctuary** (19), that is, from heaven, to bring the expected deliverance. **Appointed to death** (20), literally, "sons of death," means "doomed unto death" (Perowne). The eschatological note is again sounded in 22, **When the people**

are gathered together, and the kingdoms, to serve the Lord
(cf. Isa. 2:2-4; Mic. 4:1-2).

3. The Passing and the Permanent (102:23-28)

For the moment, the vision fades and the Psalmist's own
personal predicament comes back into focus. The weakness he
feels (23) and the shortness of his life cause him to cry out that
the Lord will not take him away in the midst of his days (24).
But the timelessness of the eternal God again comes to mind.
Thy years is better "Your existence" (Harrison). God created
the heavens and the earth (25) as a changing order (26), but He
is ever the same (27). Verses 25-27 are cited in Heb. 1:10-12,
and there applied to the Christ, who is "the same yesterday, and
to day, and for ever" (Heb. 13:8). Henry Lyte's touching lines
are based on these passages:

> Swift to its close ebbs out life's little day.
> Earth's joys grow dim; its glories pass away.
> Change and decay in all around I see;
> O Thou who changest not, abide with me!

In this abiding Presence is the security of God's people (28).

Psalm 103: THE SONG OF A FULL HEART, 103:1-22

This is a psalm of adoration attributed by title to David. It is
a hymn of pure praise whose beauties have been universally
recognized. Kirkpatrick says, "The Psalm is one of singular
beauty. Its tenderness, its trustfulness, its hopefulness, anticipate
the spirit of the N.T. It does not contain one jarring note, and
it furnishes fit language of thanksgiving for the greater blessings
of a more marvellous redemption than that of Israel from Babylon."[37] Oesterley writes, "In words as beautiful as any in the
Psalter, the psalmist tells of the love of God towards those who
fear him."[38] And McCullough states, "This psalm, as the place
it has won in the devotional life of the church testifies, is one of
the noblest hymns in the O.T. It appears to have had its genesis
in an individual's deep sense of gratitude to God for sins forgiven
and for recovery from a desperate illness. . . . Heinrich Herkenne
rightly remarks that 'scarcely any other part of the O.T. lets us
perceive the truth "God is love" so intimately as Ps. 103.' "[39]

[37]Op. cit., p. 600.   [38]Op. cit., p. 437.
[39]Op. cit., 4:544.

1. Personal Testimony (103:1-5)

The poet calls upon **all that is within** him (1), all his powers and faculties, to unite in praise to God for **all his benefits** (2). Pardon, power for healing, protection of life, provision of every need, and promise for the future are all included in these benefits. Forgiveness is properly mentioned first (3), as the greatest of God's blessings to the sinful soul. Healing of **all thy diseases,** addressed as it is to the soul, may well represent all spiritual diseases. But there is also included healing for the body. Augustine's comment on these words is memorable: "Even when sin is forgiven, thou still carriest about with thee an infirm body. . . . Death is not yet swallowed up in victory, this corruptible hath not yet put on incorruption, still the soul herself is shaken by passions and temptations. . . . [But] thy sicknesses shall all be healed, doubt it not. They are great, thou wilt say; but the physician is greater. To an Omnipotent Physician no sickness is incurable; only suffer thyself to be healed, thrust not away His hand; He knoweth what He doeth. . . . A human physician is mistaken sometimes; why? Because he did not make that which he undertakes to heal. God made thy body. God made thy soul; He knoweth how to re-form that which He formed; only be thou still under the hands of the Physician . . . suffer thou His hands, O soul that blesseth Him, forgetting not all His benefits; for He healeth all thy sicknesses."[40]

The Lord **redeemeth thy life from destruction** (4), literally, "the pit." Salvation not only redeems the soul, but saves the life from the destructive forces of sin that operate in human relationships and which even bring physical sickness and premature death. Perowne comments on the phrase **who crowneth thee:** "The love of God not only delivers from sin, disease, and death. He makes His children kings, and weaves their crown out of His own glorious attributes of loving-kindness and tender mercies."[41] **Who satisfieth thy mouth with good things** (5) has been interpreted, "He satisfies your desire for good things" (Harrison). Regarding the statement, **Thy youth is renewed like the eagle's,** Perowne[42] and Kirkpatrick[43] both reject any allusion to the fable that the eagle renews its youth by soaring up toward the sun and then plunging into the sea. McCullough

[40]Quoted by Perowne, *op. cit.*, II, 226-27.　[41]*Ibid.*, p. 237.
[42]*Ibid.*
[43]*Op. cit.*, p. 601.

suggests that "the size, strength, and comparative longevity of the eagle explain the simile. Possibly there is a reference to the bird's annual molting, though some detect an allusion to the phoenix legend (cf. Job 29:18; 33:25; Isa. 40:31)."[44]

2. Past Blessings (103:6-12)

The personal experience of the poet is further confirmed by his recollection of God's mercies as revealed in history. The Lord is the Guarantor of **righteousness and judgment** (justice) **for all that are oppressed** (6). The history of Israel reveals that He **is merciful and gracious, slow to anger, and plenteous in mercy** (7-8). **He will not always chide; neither will he keep his anger for ever** (9) does not mean, "He will not restrain His anger," but rather, "He will not retain His anger." To **chide**, as used here, is literally "to contend." Harrison translates, "He will not reprimand continually." His forgiveness means that He does not exact the penalty our sins would have merited (10). **His mercy** is as great as the distance between **earth** and **heaven** (11), and He **has removed our transgressions from us—as far as the east is from the west** (12). Modern astronomy, with its measures of stellar distances into millions of light-years (the light-year representing the distance a ray of light, at the rate of 186,342 miles per second, would travel in a year), has vastly increased our wonder and awe at the majesty of God's redeeming grace. He casts our "sins into the depths of the sea" (Mic. 7:19).

3. Present Help (103:13-18)

God's faithfulness to His covenant and His present help in time of need are seen in contrast to man's immaturity and weakness. "As a father has compassion for his children, so the Lord tenderly sympathizes with those who revere Him" (13, Berk.). Man's days are as fleeting and insubstantial as the **grass** or the **wild flower of the field,** so quickly gone (15-16; cf. comment on 90:5-6). In contrast, God's **mercy** (*chesed,* steadfast or covenant love; cf. comment on 17:7) is eternal to those who serve Him with **fear** (17; reverent awe), and His righteous help avails to all generations that **keep his covenant** and obey **his commandments** (18).

---

[44]*Op. cit.,* 4:547. The "phoenix legend" concerned a bird whose life was renewed by fire, rising from the ashes to live again.

4. Praise for the Sovereign Lord (103:19-22)

The psalm begins and ends with a call for praise to the Lord. The sovereign Lord **ruleth over all** (19). His mighty **angels** (20), "who constitute his armies" (21, Harrison) and who minister as His servants, are called upon to **bless the Lord. All his works** are to give the Lord adoration. And last, as well as first, the poet's own soul, is to give praise to the God of all **dominion** (22). "What a transformation there would be in this generation if the church could so recapture this spirit that men and women would go forth from their sanctuaries with a song like that in their hearts!"[45]

Psalm 104: THE GLORY OF OUR GREAT GOD, 104:1-35

Psalm 104 is often paired off with 103 as a companion piece. It does indeed share the same almost breathless sense of adoration. There is one significant difference, however, in that the entire psalm with the exception of the first sentence and the last five verses is addressed directly to God as a magnificent hymn. Its central theme is the majesty of God in creation, and M'Caw states, "The Psalm may be regarded as a poetical commentary upon the first chapter of Genesis."[46]

Oesterley comments, "It is impossible to read this glorious psalm without feeling the triumphant joy that pulsates throughout. It reflects, as undoubtedly the psalmist intended that it should, the solemn happiness of the Creator in the beneficent work he has wrought; in his loving forethought in providing all living beings with what they need; he has brought satisfaction, gratitude, joy to all. Should not that happiness granted by a loving Creator to all his creatures give happiness to him too? It could not be otherwise. We must, therefore, discern in this psalm the thought, unexpressed but none the less present and real, of the happiness of God—a thought as beautiful as it is true."[47]

To those who would find extensive borrowings in this psalm from an Egyptian "Hymn to the Sun" composed by Pharaoh Amenophis IV,[48] it should be pointed out with McCullough that

---

[45]Frank H. Ballard, "Psalms 90—150" (Exposition), *The Interpreter's Bible*, ed. George A. Buttrick, *et al.*, IV (New York: Abingdon Press, 1955), 549.

[46]*Op. cit.*, p. 485.   [47]*Op. cit.*, p. 455.

[48]For example, Oesterley, *op. cit.*, pp. 440-44.

"the differences between the poems are actually more notable than the similarities, not the least of the former being that in the Egyptian hymn the sun is the creator, whereas in the Hebrew psalm the sun is but a part of the handiwork of the Lord."[49]

1. God's Glory in Creation (104:1-23)

The major section of the psalm is given to the present magnificence of the creative acts described in Genesis 1. The order of topics follows that of the original creation account, beginning with light and concluding with man. The psalm begins and ends with the same call for praise that opens and closes Psalm 103, **Bless the Lord, O my soul** (1). Immediately, then, the poet turns his face toward God and worships Him in His greatness, **honour and majesty.** God clothes himself **with light** (2), a familiar biblical symbol for Deity (cf. Isa. 60:19; I Tim. 6:16; I John 1:5). **The heavens** are prepared first (2-4), then **the foundations of the earth** (5-6a), and **the waters** (6b-13), which have special significance to those who dwell in a semiarid land. In sparkling symbolism the poet envisions God's hand stretching **out the heavens like a curtain** (2) and laying the foundation **beams of His dwelling in the waters** "above the firmament" (3; Gen. 1:7). This is perhaps a parallelism to riding on **the clouds,** and walking on the winds. Verse 4 is cited in Heb. 1:7, where the point is the subservience of angels to Christ. **Angels** may be translated "messengers"; **spirits** and "winds" is the same word in Hebrew. *The Berkeley Version* translates 4: "Making the spirits His messengers, flames of fire His servants." The declaration that **the foundations of the earth . . . should not be removed for ever** (5) would not contradict II Pet. 3:10, but would be understood in the light of II Pet. 3:13.

Verses 6-9 refer most naturally to the creative work of the first part of the third day (Gen. 1:9-10). **The waters** are envisioned as covering even **the mountains,** but in obedience to the Creator's **voice** they were gathered into oceans, and the permanent dry lands were called forth. "The mountains rose, the valleys sank down to the positions which You had planned for them" (8, Harrison). Although the bounds of the waters were removed during the Flood, they are permanently set in the purpose of God (9). The earth is made fruitful by its **springs** (10-12) and the rain which is pictured as coming from the **chambers**

(13) of God. The earth brings forth bountifully, **wine** to gladden **the heart, oil** to anoint the skin, and **bread** to strengthen the body (14-15). Nature provides a habitat for the creatures God has formed (16-18). **Conies** are marmots (Moffatt) or rock-badgers (Berk.). The alternation of night and day provides a rhythm of life for both animals and men (19-23).

2. God's Glory in Conservation (104:24-30)

One of the striking features of this psalm is its emphasis on the continuing activity of God in nature. This truth is also taught elsewhere in the Scripture: "My Father worketh hitherto, and I work" (John 5:17); "By him all things consist" ("exist and hold together," Norlie) (Col. 1:17); "Upholding all things by the word of his power" (Heb. 1:3). Most of the verbs in 10-23 are in the present tense, but the point comes to sharp focus in this second section. The whole economy of nature shows the **wisdom** of the Lord (24)—**The earth is full of thy riches.** The teeming life of the sea depends upon the Lord to **give . . . meat in due season** (25-27). **Leviathan** (26) would refer to some kind of sea-creature, perhaps dolphins or whales.[50] The expression, **These wait all** (27), Moffatt reasonably takes to include all living creatures referred to in the psalm, not only sea life. All creatures depend upon God's daily bounty (28), living by His favor and dying when He withdraws **their breath** (29). Each life is the product of God's creating and renewing Spirit (30).

3. God's Glory in Correction (104:31-35)

The last stanza of the poem continues the adoration of God's glory in creation and conservation, but contains the solemn note that correction of evil among men is necessary. God's **glory . . . shall endure for ever** (31). The Lord himself takes joy **in his works** (e.g., Gen. 1:31). **The earth** trembles at His look; the mountains **smoke** at His touch (32). Therefore will His servant **sing** unto Him **as long as he lives** (33). Most modern translations render **My meditation of him shall be sweet** (34) as a prayer: "May these my thoughts please him" (Moffatt); "Let my meditation be sweet unto Him" (Perowne); "May my meditation please Him" (Berk.). It is true that meditation about such a God is sweet to the soul. It is more important that our meditations be such as are pleasing in His sight (cf. 19:14).

---

[50] Cf. M'Caw, *op. cit.*, p. 485.

In all the symphony of nature there is but one discordant note and the Psalmist yearns for the removal of the disharmony. Among men there are **sinners** and **the wicked** (35). Reginald Heber's "Missionary Hymn" echoes this thought:

> *What tho' the spicy breezes*
> *Blow soft o'er Ceylon's isle,*
> *Tho' every prospect pleases,*
> *And only man is vile?*
> *In vain with lavish kindness*
> *The gifts of God are strown;*
> *The heathen in his blindness*
> *Bows down to wood and stone.*

As it began, so this magnificent hymn ends: **Bless thou the Lord, O my soul.** The exhortation **Praise ye the Lord** is (Heb., *Hallelu-Yah*), "Hallelujah!" Many modern versions leave it untranslated (e.g., Perowne, Moffatt, Berk.). This is the first occurrence of *Hallelu-Yah* in the Psalter, although it occurs frequently from here on (e.g., 105:45; 106:1, 48; 112:1; 113:1; etc.).

Psalm 105: God's Wondrous Works, 105:1-45

Book IV of the Psalms closes with a pair of magnificent historical psalms in which the lessons of the past are used to correct and encourage the people of God. Psalms 78, 107, 114, and 136 also illustrate this type. The connection between Psalms 105 and 106 is God's power and faithfulness in contrast with the people's failure. Ps. 105:1-15 is found in I Chron. 16:8-22, where it is attributed to David on the occasion of the bringing of the ark of the covenant to Jerusalem.

"Joy in worship" and "the divine guidance in history" are the important emphases of the psalm according to Oesterley.[51] Morgan notes, "The master word in the psalm is the pronoun 'He.' In constant repetition it shows the one thought uppermost in the mind of the singer. It is the thought of the perpetual activity of God in all those experiences through which His people have passed."[52]

1. *Glory in God's Holy Name* (105:1-6)

The opening stanza is a call to worship summoning the people to praise and prayer based on the memory of God's won-

---

[51]*Op. cit.*, p. 448.   [52]*Op. cit.*, pp. 260-61.

drous works. The commands are: **Give thanks** (1); **call upon
his name: make known his deeds . . . Sing** (2), **talk . . . Glory
ye in** (3), **rejoice . . . Seek** (4); **Remember** (5). The reasons
for praise are the Lord's **deeds** (1); **his wonderous works** (2);
his marvellous works (5), **his wonders,** and the **judgments of
his mouth.** The descendants of **Abraham his servant** and of
Jacob his chosen (6) are addressed.

2. God of the Patriarchs (105:7-22)

The poet traces the history of his people back to Abraham
and the age of the patriarchs. While the Lord's **judgments** (sovereignty or rule) **are in all the earth** (7), He is specifically the
covenant God of His chosen people **for ever** (8). The expression
a thousand generations comes from Deut. 7:9, where it is specifically related to the elective love of God for Israel. The parallelism of this verse makes it clear that it is intended as a synonym
of **for ever.** The **covenant** has been **made with Abraham . . .
Isaac** (9), and with **Jacob** and his descendants (10). Included in
the covenant was the promise of a possession in **Canaan as a lot**
(portion) for their **inheritance** (11). Whether the covenant is to
be regarded as conditional or unconditional, as promise or
prophecy, has divided interpreters into two rather distinct camps.
Eminent names may be cited in support of each position. The
NT lends strong weight to the view that ultimately the covenant
with Israel is fulfilled in the new covenant through Christ (cf.
Acts 13:16-34; Rom. 2:28-29; 4:12-17, 22-25; Gal. 3:7, 28; 4:28-29;
Heb. 10:15-22).

The writer stresses God's protection for the patriarchs while
they were **strangers** in the land that had been promised to them
(12-15). **He reproved kings for their sakes** (14); cf. Gen. 12:
14-20; 20:1-16; 26:6-11. **Mine anointed** (15) indicates one set
apart and consecrated with oil, as in the case of kings and priests.
My prophets is here a broad use of the term, in the sense that
God spoke to and through the patriarchs.

Verse 16 marks a transition from the patriarchal period to
the sojourn of Israel in Egypt. The historical narrative is found
in Genesis 37; 39—47. The last part of the verse is interpreted
by Moffatt as "destroying all the Egyptians' sustenance." Perowne comments, "The famine in Canaan was no chance occurrence; God called for it. (Comp. 2 Kings viii.1; Am. v. 8; Hag.
i.11.) Joseph's position in Egypt was no accident; God had sent

him thither; so he himself traces the hand of God, Gen. xlv.5, 1.20."[53] **The word of the Lord tried him** (19) refers to the contrast between his servile status in Potiphar's house and the prison, and the promises conveyed by the dreams recorded in Gen. 37: 5-11. Faith may be tried in the waiting period between the assurance and the actual possession of what is promised. The picture of Joseph's exaltation is drawn in striking terms (20-22). To **teach his senators** (Heb., elders) **wisdom** (22) recalls Joseph's prudent example in storing up food during the years of plenty (Gen. 41: 46-49).

3. *God and the Egyptians* (105: 23-36)

These verses describe the Israelites' history in Egypt from the coming of Jacob to the Exodus. The amazing growth of the people is described as God's work (23-24). **Land of Ham** (23), as in 78:51, is a poetical description of Egypt (cf. Gen. 10:6). **He turned their heart to hate his people** (25) should be understood in the same light as the hardening of Pharaoh's heart, which was the result of Pharaoh hardening his own heart (Exod. 8:15, 32; 9:34). Moffatt translates 24-25, "God multiplied his people greatly till they outnumbered the Egyptians, who turned to hate his people, to handle his servants craftily." The plagues are described, as in Psalm 78, without regard to the order of their occurrence in Exodus 7—12. It has been conjectured that the ninth plague is placed first (**darkness,** 28) because it was the one which finally brought conviction to the minds of the Egyptians at large, although the death of the firstborn was needed finally to convince Pharaoh.[54] The last part of 28, **They rebelled not against his word,** would seem to bear this out. **Their coasts** (31, 33) would be their borders or their land. **Flaming fire in their land** (32) is better "lightning that flamed on their land" (Berk.). Moffatt interprets **the chief of all their strength** (36) as "each oldest male child." The rebellion of the Egyptians was broken. The cumulative effect of all the plagues was to demonstrate the superiority of Israel's God over the gods of Egypt.

4. *God and the Exodus* (105: 37-45)

The Exodus from Egypt is described in 37-39, with little attention to the events of the wilderness period (40-51). **Not one feeble person** (37) has been interpreted, "There was no straggler

---

[53]*Op. cit.,* II, 252.   [54]Cf. Kirkpatrick, *op. cit.,* p. 621.

in their ranks" (Smith-Goodspeed). No mention of the sinful rebellion of Israel is made here. The fulfillment of God's **promise to Abraham** in Israel's possession of the Promised Land climaxes the psalm (42-45). **Praise ye the Lord** (45) is "Hallelujah" (Heb., *Hallelu-Yah*). Whatever might seem one-sided about this ignoring of the unfavorable elements in the history is balanced out in Psalm 106.

Psalm 106: SIN AND SALVATION, 106:1-48

The closing psalm of Book IV is another historical psalm, the special emphasis of which is the continued mercy of the Lord in the face of Israel's continual lapses into sin and unbelief (cf. Psalm 105, intro.). The psalm is a monument to the utter realism of the Bible. As M'Caw notes, it is a rare thing to find a national hymn commemorating the sins of the people![55] Verse 47 would seem to indicate a date of composition during the Exile.

1. *A Prayer of Confession* (106:1-6)

Thanksgiving and confession mingle in the opening stanza of the poem. In the light of God's great goodness, the failures of the people are glaring indeed. **Praise ye the Lord** (1) is "Hallelujah " (Heb., *Hallelu-Yah*). The enduring **mercy of the Lord** is a recurrent note in the psalms (cf. 107:1; and especially Psalm 136). **The mighty acts** of God are beyond the powers of description (2). There is special blessing for those who **keep judgment** (3; "observe justice," RSV) and do **righteousness at all times.** The Psalmist's personal prayer is to be included within the covenant provisions, that he may **see the good** (5; "prosperity," RSV), **rejoice in the gladness,** and **glory with** the Lord's **inheritance.** The obstacle to God's blessing is confessed: **We have sinned with our fathers** (6), that is, in the same manner as our fathers; **we have committed iniquity, we have done wickedly.**

2. *The Seven Sins of Israel in the Wilderness* (106:7-33)

The major portion of the psalm is given to this detailing of the sins of the Israelites in the wilderness. Seven instances of disobedience and unbelief are described.

a. Murmuring at the Red Sea (106:7-12). Even with the **wonders in Egypt** (7) fresh in their minds, the people **provoked**

---

[55]*Op. cit.*, p. 487.

(lit., rebelled against) the Lord **at the Red sea** (Exod. 14:10-12). In spite of this, God's mercy endured, and He delivered His people **for his name's sake** (8), dividing the waters of the sea, and destroying **their enemies** in its depths (9-11). **Then, for a brief time, believed they his words; they sang his praise** (12). See Exod. 14:13—15:22.

b. *Faithless impatience* (106:13-15). **They soon forgat . . . they waited not for his counsel** (13; "advice," Smith-Goodspeed; "purposes," Moffatt). Impatiently, they complained and expressed their doubts. Desire for water and food, both of which God would have provided, led them to the verge of outright rebellion (Exod. 15:23—17:7). **Lusted exceedingly** (14) is "had a wanton craving" (RSV). **He gave them their request; but sent leanness into their soul** (15). Here is the potential tragedy of prayer without the footnote, "Nevertheless, not as I will, but as thou wilt" (Matt. 26:39). While the immediate reference may be to the nausea and death experienced by the Israelites (Num. 11:20, 33), Perowne suggests the appropriateness of a figurative sense: "The very heart and spirit of a man, when bent only or supremely on the satisfaction of its earthly desires and appetites, is always dried up and withered. It becomes a lean, shrunk, miserable thing, always craving more food, yet drawing thence no nourishment."[56]

c. *Jealousy of the authority of Moses and Aaron* (106:16-18; cf. Numbers 16). Insurrection against God-appointed leaders constituted the third sin here listed. **Aaron the saint of the Lord** (16; "the holy one of Yahweh") was so constituted by his office, not his personal character. **Dathan** and **Abiram**, together with **Korah**, who is not mentioned by the Psalmist, were the leaders of the jealous revolt. Num. 16:27 and 26:11 seem to imply that **Dathan** and **Abiram** were the leaders of the opposition (cf. Deut. 11:6). The opposition to Moses and Aaron is bluntly laid to envy or jealousy.

d. *Worship of the golden calf* (106:19-23; cf. Exodus 32; Deut. 9:8-29). **Horeb** (19) is the name for Sinai used most by Moses in Deuteronomy. **Their glory** (20) would be their God. The scorn visited upon idolatry is clearly seen (cf. Isa. 40:19-20). **The land of Ham** (22) was Egypt. Only the intercession of **Moses** (Exod. 32:31-35) saved the nation from destruction (23). **In the breach**—"The intercession of Moses is compared to the act of a

[56]*Op. cit.*, II, 261.

brave leader, covering with his body the breach made in the walls of his fortress."[57] See Exod. 32:30.

e. *Disobedience at Kadesh-barnea* (106:24-27; cf. Num. 13: 1—14:45). The tragic loss of faith at Kadesh is next described. Believing the majority report of the men sent to "spy out the land," the Israelites "regarded the pleasant land with contempt" (24, Harrison). **The pleasant land** is an apt description of Canaan; "Surely it floweth with milk and honey" (Num. 13:27). Yet unbelief barred their entrance more effectively than any possible enemy in the land (Heb. 3:7-19). Bible scholars have seen here quite correctly an OT picture of the "second rest" provided for the people of God (Hebrews 3—4). *Kadesh* is the KJV spelling of *Qodesh,* a Hebrew term that means "consecration" or "holiness." An entire generation died in the wilderness because they lacked faith at the point of consecration and holiness. **He lifted up his hand against them** (26), in the gesture customary when taking an oath.

f. *Idolatry at Baal-peor* (106:28-31; Num. 25:1-18). **Baal** is the generic name for any Canaanite fertility god; **peor** (28; cf. Num. 23:28) appears to have been the name of a hill or mountain where one of the Moabite fertility shrines was located. Canaanite baal worship involved cultic prostitution. Union with the shrine prostitute was supposed to constitute union with the god; hence the expression **joined themselves also unto** (cf. I Cor. 6:13-20). **Ate the sacrifices of the dead** means either, as Berk., "ate the sacrifices to lifeless idols" in contrast with "the living God"; or, as Moffatt, "ate food offered to the dead," i.e., in some kind of necromancy or seeking to consult the dead (cf. Deut. 18:11; Isa. 8:19). The result of such flagrant sin was a deadly **plague** (29), halted only by the decisive act of **judgment** performed by **Phinehas** (30; cf. Num. 25:6-9). **Inventions** (29) is better "doings" (RSV). Verse 31 apparently refers to the promise made to Phinehas in Num. 25:12-13.

g. *Unbelief at Meribah* (106:32-33; Num. 20:1-13). Although not last in the chronological order of Numbers, the sin at Meribah is probably placed in a climactic last position here because it involved Moses in an impatient command that cost him the privilege of leading the nation into Canaan.[58] **Waters of strife** (32), Hebrew, waters of *Meribah.* The apparent relative

---

[57]*Ibid.,* p. 263.   [58]Cf. Kirkpatrick, *loc. cit.*

severity of God's dealings with Moses vividly illustrates the fact that much light implies great responsibility.

3. Disobedience in Canaan (106:34-39)

Even possession of the Promised Land did not end the sorry tale of disobedience and unbelief. The Israelites did not destroy the heathen tribes of Canaan as they had been commanded to do, but instead **were mingled among** them, and **learned their works** (ways, 35). Idolatry was the curse and **snare** (36) of the Israelites from the Exodus to the Exile. It was cured only by the rigorous fires of the Babylonian captivity. At its extreme, such pagan worship involved human sacrifice (37-38; cf. Deut. 12:31; 18:9-10; II Chron. 33:5-6; Ezek. 16:20-21; 20:31). **Sacrificed . . . unto devils** (37) and **the idols of Canaan** (38) shows that the "gods" of the Canaanites were actually demons in the estimation of the Psalmist. "They were defiled by what they did; they were immoral in their practices" (39, Berk.).

4. God's Repeated Judgments and Mercies (106:40-46)

There is a primary reference here to the cycles of oppression, repentance, and deliverance described throughout the Book of Judges. Yet the same picture prevailed throughout most of Israel's history from the time of Solomon on. Sin brought **wrath** and judgment (40) through the domination of foreign oppressors (41-42). Yet **many times** God **delivered** the nation (43-44). **Their counsel** (43) is better "their purposes" (RSV). **He . . . repented according to the multitude of his mercies** (45; cf. comment on 90:13). "He made them objects of sympathy on the part of their captors" (46, Harrison; cf. I Kings 8:50, and instances in Neh. 1:11; Dan. 1:9).

5. The Closing Prayer and Doxology (106:47-48)

The closing prayer of the poet, which seems to date the psalm in the dispersion period, is that the Lord will **gather** His people **from among the heathen** (47), in order that they may **give thanks unto** His **holy name, and** may **triumph in** His **praise.** The doxology of 48 closes Book IV of the psalms. **Praise ye the Lord** is "Hallelujah" (Heb., *Hallelu-Yah*). It is noteworthy that a psalm so preoccupied with sin and judgment closes on a note that presupposes forgiveness and grace. As Frank Ballard comments, "Sin has caused almost unparalleled suffering. It has frustrated the dreams of generations, made havoc of schemes for a better order, and brought the world to the edge of despair. Yet there remains forever a way of hope. It is no new way. It is suggested in this psalm, developed by prophet and evangelist, and attested by multitudes of the faithful: it is the way of repentance and forgiveness. There is truth in the grim doctrine of retribution which has been dwelt on so insistently, especially by the novelist and playwright. But there is greater truth in the gospel of grace, truth which has been illustrated and justified in countless men who have rejoiced in the experience of redemption."[59]

[59]*Op. cit.*, 4: 570

Section V Book Five: Psalms for Worship

The last book within the Psalter is the longest both in terms of content and in the number of psalms it contains. Most of the psalms in Book V are oriented toward public worship. Few of them have titles, and most of the titles refer only to authorship or dedication (of or to David, 13: of or for Solomon, 1) or to liturgical use (e.g., the "songs of degrees," 120—34).

Four minor collections have been noted within Book V. The first is "The Egyptian Hallel," Psalms 113—18. The second is the collection of "Songs of Degrees, or Ascents," Psalms 120—34. The third, 138—45, is called "A Little Davidic Collection," since each of this group contains the name of David in the title. The last is known as "The Great Hallel," Psalms 146—50 (cf. intro. to Psalm 136).

Psalm 107: SONG OF THE REDEEMED, 107:1-43

This psalm of adoration has close connections with the two which precede it. Psalms 105—7 have, in fact, many times been regarded as a trilogy, probably from the hand of one author. Psalm 107, however, is not historical. Its descriptions of the varied circumstances of human life are not related to specific episodes in the story of Israel. They are rather generalized observations of the many ways in which God's deliverances are seen.

Perowne says, "There can be no doubt as to the great lesson which it inculcates. It teaches us not only that God's providence watches over men, but that His ear is open to their prayers. It teaches us that prayer may be put up for temporal deliverance, and that such prayer is answered. It teaches us that it is right to acknowledge with thanksgiving such answers to our petitions. This was the simple faith of the Hebrew Poet."[1] Oesterley notes, "Probably in no other psalm is the belief in the divine intervention in the ordinary affairs of men expressed in more detail than here. The intense conviction that, when in need or stress, men

[1] *Op. cit.*, II, 273.

seek help from God, that help is forthcoming, is also a striking characteristic of the psalm."[2]

Another noteworthy feature is the refrain that occurs in 8, 15, 21, 31. Each division of the psalm calls for praise to the Lord for some great aspect of His ways with men.

1. Praise for Restoration from Afar (107:1-7)

With the exception of the initial *Hallelu-Yah,* the first verse is identical with 106:1. God's goodness and eternal **mercy are the basis for a call to praise. Let the redeemed of the Lord say so (2)** means that the redeemed of the Lord are to say that **he is good: for his mercy endureth for ever (1).** The redemption in question is from the hand of the enemy, gathering **them out of the lands, from the east, and from the west, from the north, and from the south (3),** an evident allusion to the return from Babylonian exile.

Something of the restlessness of the exiles is reflected in vv. 4-5. Although physical conditions were not unbearable in Babylon and many became so well satisfied with their life abroad that they never returned to Palestine, yet to the truly devout it was like a homeless pilgrimage in the desert. When the heart turns to **the Lord in ... trouble (6),** His deliverance is at hand. The way God leads is always **the right way (7). A city of habitation** is "a city where they might establish their homes" (Amp. OT).

2. Praise for Renewal of Hope and Joy (107:8-14)

Verse 8 establishes a refrain repeated in 15, 21, and 31. In the original, it is much more like v. 1 than the KJV suggests. Perowne translates it, "Let them give thanks to Jehovah for His loving-kindness, and for His wonders to the children of men." In the Lord is satisfaction for **the longing soul (9).** Since **hungry soul** probably refers to literal hunger, **goodness** is here better translated "good things" (RSV). Verse 10 is reminiscent of Isa. 9:2 as cited in Matt. 4:15-16. **Darkness** and bondage were the result of rebellion **against the words of God (11). Contemned** means "had contempt for," or despised. Sin burdens the **heart with labour (12)** and robs man of his only source of **help.** For v. 13, cf. comment on 6. The stanza begins with darkness, the shadow of death, and bonds of affliction; it ends with deliverance

---

[2]*Op. cit.,* p. 456.

from **darkness and the shadow of death** (14), and the breaking
of **their bands in sunder,** "snapping their bands apart" (Berk.).

3. *Praise the Lord for Revelation of Power* (107:15-20)

For v. 15, cf. comment on 8. God's power breaks **gates of
brass** (16) and cuts **bars of iron,** fulfilling the promise of Isa.
45:2. No might of man can stand against the power of God. **Fools**
(17) are not those who are ignorant or thoughtless, but those
who are morally perverse. So the term is commonly used in
Proverbs (7:22; 10:8, 10, 18, 23; 11:29; etc.), and in the Gospels
(Matt. 7:26; 25:2). *"Folly* denotes moral perversity, not mere
weakness or ignorance; it leads to ruin. It is the opposite of
wisdom, which leads to life."[3] Verse 18 is related to 17; **because
of . . . transgression** "they loathed any kind of food, and they
drew near to the gates of death" (RSV). Sin robs the soul of
satisfaction and pays off in the coinage of **death** (cf. Rom. 6:23).
Yet there is hope. When **trouble** turns the heart to the Lord,
deliverance comes (19; cf. 6, 13). The power of God is through
his word (20) and brings healing and deliverance. Not unrea-
sonably, Perowne connects this idea with 147:15, 18; and calls
attention to 105:19 and Isa. 9:8; 55:11. He then says, "We detect
in such passages the first glimmering of St. John's doctrine of the
agency of the personal Word. The Word by which the heavens
were made (xxxiii.6) is seen to be not merely the expression of
God's will, but His messenger mediating between Himself and
His creatures."[4] **Their destructions** is, literally, pits; i.e., the
graves to which they were so close.

4. *Praise for Rescue from Physical Peril* (107:21-30)

Instead of giving an immediate reason why men should
praise the Lord, as in 8-9 and 15-16, the poet here enlarges on
the call for praise and suggests **the sacrifices of thanksgiving**
(22). "Thank offerings were a division of the peace offerings
(Lev. 7:11-15; 22:29-30)."[5] The balance of the stanza is a remarkable description of God's power over the elemental forces
of the sea. The expression **down to the sea in ships** (23) reflects
the fact that the ocean lies lower than the land. **Wind** and **waves**
are subject to God's will (25). **Their soul is melted** (26) means,
"In their danger their courage melted away" (Harrison). **At their**

---

[3]Kirkpatrick, *op. cit.,* p. 642.   [4]*Op. cit.,* II, 279.
[5]McCullough, *op. cit.,* 4:575.

wit's end (27) has become a proverbial expression for coming to the end of man's ingenuity and resourcefulness. The Hebrew reads, "All their wisdom swallows itself up." For v. 28, note the corresponding verses in the earlier stanzas, 6, 13, 19. The Lord **stills the storm,** and brings the mariners **unto their desired haven** (29-30).

5. Praise for Righteous Judgments (107:31-43)

The development of the refrain in 31-32 is comparable to that in 21-22. The note of public worship—**congregation and assembly**—is clear and strong. The barrenness and fruitfulness of the land itself are related to judgment and reward. The wickedness of man causes the Lord to turn **rivers into a wilderness** (33), **watersprings into dry ground,** and the **fruitful land into barrenness** (34)—"a productive area becomes a salt marsh" (Harrison). Conversely, the desert is made the scene of **vineyards** and **fields** (35-37), the implied condition being the obedience and righteousness of the people. Population grows or declines under much the same condition (38-39). **Suffereth** (38) is "permits." **Minished** (39) is better "become few" (Berk.). Verse 40a appears to be a quotation from Job 12:21. No one, whatever his rank, is exempt from God's judgments on sin. The high are brought low, and the humble are exalted (41; cf. Prov. 3:34; Jas. 4:6). This is cause for the rejoicing of **the righteous** (42). The statement **all iniquity shall stop her mouth** means "wrongdoers are silenced" (Moffatt). **Whoso is wise, and will observe these things, even they shall understand the lovingkindness of the Lord** (43). The verse expresses the truth Jesus stated, "If any man will do his will, he shall know of the doctrine, whether it be of God, or whether I speak of myself" (John 7:17). The statement often attributed to Augustine is, "The Word of God belongs to those who obey it." Only in the faith of commitment and obedience is there real knowledge of spiritual truth.

Psalm 108: A MEDLEY OF PRAISE, 108:1-13

Identified by title as "A Song or Psalm of David," this poem is unique in the Psalter in that it is entirely composed of excerpts from two earlier psalms, also attributed to David. It is repetitions such as these that provide the strongest evidence that portions of our Book of Psalms were originally separate collections (cf. Intro.).

1. *Adoration* (108:1-5)

This poem is practically identical with Ps. 57: 7-11. The differences are even fewer in the original than in the translations. The most significant change is the alteration of *Adonai* (Lord) in 57:9 to *Yahweh* (LORD) in 108:3. See the comments on 57: 7-11.

2. *Appeal* (108:6-13)

This material is taken from Ps. 60:5-12, where the comments may be consulted.

Morgan describes the attitude of mind that led to the putting together of these two particular portions of other psalms: "The circumstances of the writer (or compiler) would seem to be very similar to those obtaining in the earlier psalms. They are only hinted at in passing. The soul's fixity of heart enables the singer to rejoice from beginning to end. Relation to God affects all the relationships. To be homed in His will and submissive to His throne is to be triumphant under all circumstances. Triumph in the very hour of defeat is the finest, but it is possible only when the heart is fixed in God."[6]

Psalm 109: A CRY FOR VINDICATION AND JUSTICE, 109:1-31

This is the last of the "imprecatory psalms" (cf. Intro.), and one of the strongest. Some have urged that the imprecations are quotations from the Psalmist's enemies, and were curses that had been directed against the writer himself.[7] However, it is probably sufficient to recall that the Psalmist looks upon those who had made themselves his enemies as chiefly the enemies of God. Divine justice would require the vindication of the righteous in judgment against the wicked.

For the terms in the inscription, cf. introduction to Psalms 3 and 4.

---

[6]*Op. cit.*, p. 262.

[7]Cf. *The Holy Scriptures* (Philadelphia: The Jewish Publication Society of America, 1958), *ad loc.*, where the verses are placed in quotation marks. Cf. also Morgan, *op. cit.*, pp. 262-63.

1. The Psalmist's Enemies (109:1-5)

The poet first utters his complaint against the whole company of **the wicked** (2), **the deceitful** who had **spoken against him with a lying tongue.** He had been the object of totally unjustified slander. There was no justification for the opposition raised against him (3). **For my love they are my adversaries** (4) is better, "They repay my love with enmity" (Harrison). **I give myself unto prayer** means, "For my part I pray for them" (Harrison). As opposed to the sentiments of 6-19, this verse breathes the spirit of Christ in the Sermon on the Mount (Matt. 5:43-48). In spite of all he can do, the Psalmist finds his **good** returned by **evil,** and his **love** requited by **hatred** (5).

2. The Leader (109:6-20)

Those who take this passage to be what was spoken about the Psalmist and not by him (cf. intro. to psalm) point out the change in pronoun from the plural "they" to the singular "his" and "him." The change may be accounted for, on the other hand, by a shift of attention from the whole group of the poet's enemies to the one who is their leader or who personifies their opposition. The enemy is to be ruled by **a wicked man** (6) who is to have **Satan stand at his right hand,** the position occupied by a trusted adviser. The Hebrew reads literally, "Let a satan stand at his right hand." Since *satan* (Heb.) literally means "adversary," many recent versions translate the term "accuser" (RSV, Moffatt), "perverse accuser" (Berk.), or "adversary" (Perowne, Harrison). It is, of course, Satan's function to lead astray, and to be an accuser (Rev. 12:10) and adversary (I Pet. 5:8) to the people of God.

The maledictions continue. This wicked one is to **be judged** without mercy, and even **his prayer** is to be counted a **sin** (7). He is to be prematurely cut off, and **his office** (place) filled by **another** (8)—a verse cited with respect to Judas in Acts 1:20. **His children** are to be **fatherless . . . vagabonds and his wife a widow** (9-10). **Let them seek their bread also out of their desolate places** means "dispossessed from their hovels" (Harrison). **Let the extortioner catch all that he hath** (11) is interpreted, "May creditors seize all that he has" (Moffatt). **Strangers spoil his labour** is better, "Strangers plunder the fruit of his toil" (Berk.). Not only should the enemy himself be without **mercy,** but the same fate should fall upon his children (12) and his line of descent become extinct (13). This was one of the greatest tragedies that could happen to a man of the ancient East. Upon him should be visited **the iniquity of his** ancestors (14-15), and all this because the man himself was merciless (16; cf. Jas. 2:13). The sins in which he has **delighted** will become his punishment (17-18), as inescapable as the clothes he wears (19). The RSV renders v. 18: "He clothed himself with cursing as his coat, may it soak into his body like water, like oil into his bones." Harrison gives the summary in v. 20, "May this be the way in which the Lord will reward my accusers, and those who malign me."

3. *The Psalmist's Sad State* (109:21-25)

The poet looks away from the heartlessness of his enemies to the goodness of God. He pleads for God's intervention in his defense. **Do thou for me** (21) is better, "Act on my behalf" (Moffatt). He lays his pitiful state out before the Lord: **I am poor and needy, and my heart is wounded within me** (22); **gone like the shadow when it declineth** (23) at eventide. To be **tossed up and down as the locust** means driven away as helplessly as an insect in the wind. His **knees were weak, his flesh failed** (24). He had become **a reproach** (25), "an object of scorn" (RSV), to those who "nod their heads" (Harrison) in approval as they look at his painful condition.

4. *His Hope of Vindication* (109:26-31)

The psalm closes with a strong plea for and expression of confidence in the poet's vindication at the hand of the Lord. He turns to the **Lord his God** with the prayer to be saved **according to** divine **mercy** (26), to the end that all may witness what God has done (27). His enemies may **curse,** but God will **bless;** the shame of the adversaries will be contrasted with the rejoicing of the righteous (28). It is as God's **servant** that he prays. The **shame** and **confusion** with which his foes will **be clothed** is the fabric of their own weaving (29). Perowne, ASV (marg.), and Kirkpatrick,[8] on grammatical grounds, translate 28 and 29 in the indicative rather than optative mood—that is, as a prediction rather than a prayer. E.g., Perowne's rendering:

[8]*Op. cit.,* p. 660.

Though they curse, yet Thou blessest;
They arose and were put to shame,
But Thy servant rejoiceth.
Mine adversaries are clothed with confusion;
They cover themselves with their own shame (as with)
a mantle.[9]

As is usual in psalms of lament, the poem closes with a vow: **I will greatly praise the Lord with my mouth; yea, I will praise him among the multitude** (30). It is God who stands **at the right hand of the poor** (31), as the great Defender, **to save him from those that condemn** (or, better, "judge") **his soul.**

Psalm 110: SONG OF THE SOVEREIGN LORD, 110: 1-7

This jewel among the psalms is one of the outstanding Messianic passages in the OT. It has the distinction of being quoted a total of twenty-one times in the NT in relation to Christ and His kingdom, and most notably by Jesus himself. Morgan states, "This psalm is purely Messianic, and was always considered to be so. When Jesus quoted it in His conversation with the rulers it is perfectly evident that they looked on it in that light. It is equally certain that He made use of it in that sense."[10]

This contention does not go unchallenged, mainly in the direction of claiming for the psalm some immediate and local application. But such may be granted if it be recognized that the whole meaning is not exhausted in the local occasion and that its larger application is to be made to Christ. Both the Jews of Christ's day and the Early Church viewed it as Messianic in meaning.[11]

1. *The Divinely Ordained King* (110:1-3)

Verse 1 is cited in Matt. 22:44; 26:64; Mark 12:36; 14:62; 16:19; Luke 20:42-43; 22:69; Acts 2:34; I Cor. 15:25; Eph. 1:20; Col. 3:1; Heb. 1:3, 13; 10:12-13; 12:2. In addition there are numerous "echoes" in other portions of the NT. The Psalmist's **Lord** (*Adonai*) is told by the **Lord** (*Yahweh*) to **sit at His right hand, until** all **enemies** be made a **footstool** (1), "until I subdue your enemies completely" (Harrison). **The rod of thy strength**

---

[9]*Op. cit.,* II, 293.   [10]*Op. cit.,* p. 263.
[11]Cf. Kirkpatrick, *op. cit.,* pp. 660-65; McCullough, *op. cit.,* 4:588.

(2) is translated "your mighty scepter" (RSV). **Rule thou in the midst of thine enemies** indicates that Christ's sovereignty does not await the submission of all to His authority. Christ is even now Lord of all, though the masses be in revolt against His rule.

Christ's kingdom is destined to be a Kingdom of glory (Phil. 2:5-11) even as it is a Kingdom of grace. **Thy people shall be willing** (3) is better "offer themselves willingly." Consecration is always the act of a freely surrendered will. Reluctant service, while better than none at all, can never fully satisfy the requirements of the divine holiness. The translators differ in their applications of the second clause of the verse, but the majority attach it to the Lord who is the subject of the stanza. Thus Perowne, "In holy attire; as from the womb of the morning, Thou hast the dew of Thy youth."

2. *The Divinely Ordained Priest* (110:4)

The kingly and priestly functions are combined in the Psalmist's **Lord.** This verse is quoted six times in Hebrews (5:6, 10; 6:20; 7:11, 15, 21), where it provides the writer's thought that the priesthood of Christ is of an order different from and superior to that of Aaron, namely, a priesthood **after the order of Melchizedek.** As such, it does not depend upon human lineage (Heb. 7:3). It was antecedent to and better than the priesthood of the sons of Levi (7:4-10). It betokens a change in the law (7:11-12). It explains how Jesus, of the tribe of Judah rather than of Levi, can properly be a Priest (7:13-14). It was a priesthood certified by and grounded in God's oath (7:20-22). And because it is eternal, not subject to a changing human succession of high priests, it is the ground of our full and unending salvation (7:23-28).

Even the name **Melchizedek** is significant, a point which made the Psalmist's terminology especially important. Melchizedek means "king of righteousness." He was identified in Gen. 14:18-20 as "king of Salem," which means "king of peace." He was spoken of as "the priest of the most high God" seven hundred years before the Levitical priesthood was instituted. In the kingly priest of righteousness and peace we have a fitting type of Christ, who unites in himself the OT functions of prophet, priest, and king.

3. The Assurance of Triumph (110: 5-7)

The last stanza of this magnificent psalm returns to the military tone of v. 2 and assumes the character of a hymn addressed directly to the Lord (*Yahweh*) God. **The Lord at thy right hand (5)** is the *Adonai* to whom the invitation of 1 is addressed, that is, the Messiah. He **shall strike through kings** is better "crush" (Harrison) or "shatter kings" (Berk.) **in the day of his wrath** (cf. Rev. 6: 15-17; 17: 14; 19: 11-21). In fulfillment of the foregoing, the Priest-King shall become the Judge. Moffatt translates 7, "He drinks from any stream he has to cross, then charges forward triumphing." Perowne's comment on 5-7 is: "The victorious leader, who has made so terrible a slaughter that the field of battle is covered with corpses, is now seen pursuing his enemies. Wearied with the battle and the pursuit, he stops for a moment on his way to refresh himself by drinking of the torrent rushing by, and then 'lifts up his head,' derives new vigour to continue the pursuit."[12]

Psalm 111: THE TRUSTWORTHINESS OF THE LORD, 111: 1-10

By general consensus, Psalms 111 and 112 are seen as a pair. Each consists of ten verses. Each psalm contains twenty-two lines or phrases each beginning with a successive letter of the Hebrew alphabet. In the original, most of the lines contain exactly three words. The themes are parallel. Psalm 111 deals with the character of the Lord God. Psalm 112 deals with the character of the godly man. The acrostic or alphabetical pattern identifies these as wisdom psalms. M'Caw suggests the possibility that Psalms 111 and 112 may be intended as a prelude to the Egyptian Hallel (Psalms 113—18), which immediately follows.[13] Psalms 111—19 are without titles or superscriptions.

1. God's Righteous Works (111: 1-5)

The logical connection of lines within an alphabetical psalm is almost necessarily somewhat limited. However, the first half of the song (letters *Aleph* through *Yod*, the first eleven letters of the Heb. alphabet) is in praise of God's mighty works of righteousness. **Praise ye the lord (1)** (Heb., *Hallelu-Yah*) is "Hallelujah!" Wholehearted **praise to the Lord** will be offered **in the assembly of the upright, and in the congregation**—"in gather-

¹²*Op. cit.*, II, 310.   ¹³*Op. cit.*, p. 492.

ings of good men for fellowship" (Moffatt). God's great **works are sought out of all them that have pleasure therein** (2). His work is "splendid and glorious" (3, Moffatt), evidence of his **righteousness that endureth for ever.** God's **wonderful works** are memorable, for He is **full of** grace and **compassion** (4). The Lord gives **meat** (5, lit., food) to those who revere Him with holy awe, and **he will ever be mindful of his covenant.**

2. The Trustworthiness of the Lord (111:6-10)

The last line of the preceding stanza introduces the thought of this second one. God's works are indisputable proof that His covenant is trustworthy. **The heritage of the heathen** (6) that God has given to His people refers specifically, of course, to the possession of the Promised Land. **Verity and judgment** (7) is better "truth and justice" (Harrison). **All his commandments are sure** means, "All His decrees are trustworthy" (Berk.). Moffatt translates 8, "His orders are enacted for all time, issued in faithfulness and justice." **Holy and reverend is his name** (9) is better as in *The Berkeley Version,* "Holy and awe-inspiring is His name!" The **reverend** in the KJV has nothing whatever to do with the courtesy title given to ministers in our day. **The fear of the Lord is the beginning of wisdom** (10) is the "golden text" of the wisdom movement (cf. Job 28:28; Prov. 1:7). True wisdom is a proper reverence for the Lord. "The first thing in knowledge is reverence for the Eternal" (Moffatt). **A good understanding** ("sound sense," Moffatt) **have all they that do his commandments**—obedience to God's law both proves and increases the understanding of those who follow His precepts.

Psalm 112: THE TRUSTFULNESS OF THE GODLY, 112:1-10

The introduction to Psalm 111 should be consulted. Psalm 112, dealing with the character of God's people, also divides into two equal stanzas.

1. The Character of the Godly (112:1-5)

Praise ye the Lord (1) is "Hallelujah" (Heb., *Hallelu-Yah*). **Blessed** (*asher*) means "happy" (cf. 1:1). To **fear the Lord** and to **delight greatly in his commandments** are parallel expressions descriptive of the godly. "His offspring shall be the mighty in the land; a blessing shall attend the race of the upright" (2, Berk.). **Wealth and riches shall be in his house** (3) expresses the general position of the wisdom writers in the OT with regard to the fact that righteousness and rewards go together. That there are exceptions has already been seen in the Book of Job and in Psalms 37, 49, and 73. **The upright,** however, enjoy **light in the darkness** (4); they are **gracious, and full of compassion, and rightetous.** **A good man** is disposed to be helpful, and strives to **guide his affairs with discretion** (5).

2. The Trustfulness of the Servant of God (112:6-10)

As the character of the godly reflects the grace streaming from the righteous works of the Lord in 111:1-5, so the trustfulness of the servant of God described in 6-10 answers to the trustworthiness of the Lord (111:6-10). Immovable in devotion to the right (6), and kept forever in God's **remembrance,** the man of God need **not be afraid of evil tidings** (7). All that comes he will view in the light of God's sovereignty and grace. His **heart is fixed,** confidently **trusting in the Lord.** "His heart is firm and fearless, certain that he will see his foes collapse" (8, Moffatt). **He hath dispersed** (9), in "the free and active exercise of charity. This verse is quoted by St. Paul when exhorting the Corinthians to liberal contributions on behalf of the poor, 2 Cor. ix. 9."[14] **His horn** is a frequent OT metaphor for strength or power. Seeing the reward of the righteous, **the wicked** "become irritated" (10, Harrison). Moffatt translates the balance of the verse, "They gnash their teeth and—disappear; the ungodly's hope will come to nothing."

"This then is the good life as it is sketched by the Hebrew poet. It is not a finished portrait. Nor is it a perfect picture. For perfection, let it be said again, we must pass beyond O.T. pages to the strong Son of God, who gave his life a ransom for many. There we find forgiveness without self-righteousness, mercy and magnanimity without condescension or condoning, love that knew no limits, yet never descended to sentimentality."[15]

Psalm 113: "Praise Ye the Lord," 113:1-9

Psalms 113—18 constitute a liturgical group commonly called "The Egyptian Hallel" from the reference to the Exodus in 114:1. This is sometimes known popularly as "the great Hallel," but the latter title is more properly reserved for Psalm 136, or 146—50.

---

[14]Perowne, op. cit., II, 321.   [15]Ballard, op. cit., 4:599.

These were the special psalms used in the synagogue during the festivals of Passover, Tabernacles, and Pentecost, as well as *Hanukkah,* the later Feast of Dedication. This is almost certainly the hymn sung by Jesus and His disciples before going out into the Garden of Gethsemane (Matt. 26:30).

Of Psalm 113, McCullough says, "This simple but pleasing hymn of praise contains in its few verses some of the basic theological ideas of the O.T. The opening verse, addressed to the servants of the Lord, may have been spoken to a choir or choirs by an officiating priest in the temple."[16] Oesterley notes, "The ancient way of reciting this [the Hallel] was for the leader to begin with 'Hallelujah,' which was repeated by the congregation; then after each half-verse the congregation fell in with 'Hallelujah,' which was thus said 123 times."[17]

1. God Alone Is Worthy (113:1-3)

The psalm opens with the Hebrew term *Hallelu-Yah*—Hallelujah! **Praise ye the Lord** (1). The **servants of the Lord** are called to **praise His name,** a thought repeated in each of the three verses. Oesterley suggests that the emphasis upon **the name of the Lord** is reminiscent of the phrase in the Lord's Prayer, "Hallowed be thy name."[18] The identification of the name with the personality of its bearer is common in ancient times and is often noted in the OT. God revealed His name to Israel (Exod. 3:13-14; 6:2-3) in order that it might be made known to the nations. Low moral conduct had the effect of profaning His name. If His character and demands were rightly represented, the result was to hallow that name.[19] Therefore praising the name of the Lord (1-2) **from the rising of the sun unto the going down of the same** (3) meant praising God himself wherever the sun should shine, and all the day.

2. The Greatness of Our God (113:4-6)

The reason for praise is the exaltation, glory, and greatness of our God. He is **high above all nations, and his glory** transcends **the heavens** (4). There is none like the Lord, dwelling **on high** (5), and condescending to take notice of things **in heaven, and in the earth!** (6) The point is, God does concern himself with the affairs of men.

[16]*Op. cit.,* 4:599.   [17]*Op. cit.,* p. 100.
[18]*Ibid.,* pp. 468-70.   [19]*Ibid.*

3. The Mercy of the Lord (113: 7-9)

The poet gives some examples of the love and grace of God. Verses 7-8a are taken from the song of Hannah in I Sam. 2: 8. God lifts **the poor** and **the needy** out of the lowest depths ("from utter degradation," 7, Harrison) and sets them **with princes** (8). In 9 the allusion to Hannah made earlier may suggest the thought that finds expression here. A wider application would be a reference to Zion's children, as for example, in Isa. 54: 1 and 66: 8. The first part of 9 is better, "He gives the barren woman a home" (RSV). The psalm ends as it begins, with "Hallelujah" (*Hallelu-Yah*).

Psalm 114: THE GREAT DELIVERANCE, 114: 1-8

In the reference to Egypt in the first verse of this psalm we have the source of the usual name attached to this group, the "Egyptian Hallel" (cf. intro. to Psalm 113). Two great acts of deliverance on the part of God underlie the psalm, the crossing of the Red Sea, and the later crossing of the Jordan into the Promised Land. McCullough comments, "This, the second of the Hallel group, is one of the most original of all the psalms. It refrains from the conventional language of the hymn, and yet it extols the power of Israel's God in an artistic little poem that is a model of concise and vivid description. The psalmist uses as illustrative material some of the great moments of the past, and in his appeal to God's hand in history (contrast the mythology of Egypt and Mesopotamia) we see one of the sources of the strength of Israel's faith."[20]

1. The Miracle of Redemption (114: 1-4)

The OT throughout views the Exodus as the ground of Israel's faith in the redemptive power of God. It is the theme that unifies the OT, and is picked up in the NT concept of the resurrection of Christ, giving unity to the entire Bible.[21] **When Israel** was led **out of Egypt** (1), the nation became the Lord's **sanctuary** ("his own," Moffatt) and **dominion** (2; "domain," Smith-Goodspeed). No distinction is intended here between **Israel** and **Jacob**, or between **Judah** and **Israel** in 2. The names are used as syn-

---

[20]*Op. cit.*, 4: 603.

[21]Cf. H. H. Rowley, *The Unity of the Bible* (Philadelphia: The Westminster Press, 1953), where this idea is developed throughout.

onyms in poetic parallelism. The Red **sea** (3), the river **Jordan,** the **mountains** (4), and the **hills** are personified. Nature itself is subject to God's commands, and rejoices in His wonderful works.

2. The Source of Redemption (114:5-8)

A series of rhetorical questions leads up to the climactic announcement of the identity of Israel's Redeemer. The sea, Jordan, mountains, little hills—indeed, earth itself should tremble . . . at the presence of the Lord (5-7), the God of Jacob. He it is who turned the rock into a standing (pool of) water, the flint into "a gushing spring" (Harrison). The reference is, of course, to the miraculous provision of water in the desert (Exod. 17:6; Num. 20:8-11). "The reader is left to draw for himself the natural and obvious conclusion, that the God, who thus drew water from a flinty rock for the supply of Israel, can still educe the richest blessings from what seem to be the hardest and most inauspicious situations. When this thought is supplied, the psalm no longer seems unfinished or abrupt in its conclusion."[22]

Psalm 115: OUR GOD IS FAR ABOVE IDOLS, 115:1-18

The last four psalms of the Hallel (115—18) were sung after the Passover meal was finished. This would therefore begin the particular portion identified in Matt. 26:30. Morgan comments, "This third psalm in the Hallel is born of passion for the glory of the name of Jehovah. . . . Not first for the welfare of the people does he care, but for the vindication of his God. This is a deep note, and all too rare in our music. We are ever in danger of putting the welfare of man before the glory of God."[23]

1. The Scoffing of Unbelievers (115:1-3)

The **glory** of **the Lord,** not the honor of His people alone, is at stake in the scoffing of **the heathen** who say, **Where is now their God?** (1-2) Because God could not be seen and handled, idolatrous nations would raise such a question. The answer is given immediately: **Our God is in the heavens** (3). **He hath done whatsoever he hath pleased;** His will is sovereign, and is "good, and acceptable, and perfect" (Rom. 12:2). God's power is never used arbitrarily. What He pleases is always good. **Mercy**

---

[22]Alexander, *op. cit.,* p. 468.   [23]*Op. cit.,* p. 265.

and truth (1) may be understood as "kindness" and "faithfulness" (Smith-Goodspeed).

2. The Emptiness of Idolatry (115:4-8)

These penetrating words of satire regarding idolatry are repeated in 135:15-18. **Their idols are silver and gold** (4). Barnes notes, "The scorn intended by these words is brought out in the words which follow, *The work of men's hands.* A *stone* idol might be meteoric and unshapen by human hands; it might be regarded as having fallen down from heaven (Acts xix.35); a *wooden* idol might be a rough-hewn post, and hardly to be distinguished from a natural object, but where silver and gold were used, the craftsman's hand would be conspicuous on the figure of the god: Jer. x.8, 9)."[24] Fashioned in the form of man or beast, the idols **have mouths, eyes, ears, noses, hands, feet,** throats—and yet are dumb, blind, deaf, without ability to smell, unable to handle anything, immobile, quite without utterance (5-7). Some have suspected an interpolation of either the first or the last of these characterizations, since both have to do with speech. But this repetition is better seen as part of the poet's emphasis: first and last, these are dumb idols that have no word to speak to men. The contrast with the living, speaking God is complete.

They that make them are like unto them (8)—the amazing thing is that those who make and those who worship such gods become like the idols themselves. The heathen fashion their gods in their own image, and then become like them! Such is the effect upon us of what we worship. Our idols today may be money, power, pleasure, or anything else to which we might give our hearts. But if we worship anything other than God, we become mercenary and hard, or trifling and shallow.

3. Trust God Supremely (115:9-13)

With a thrice-repeated refrain, **He is their help and their shield** (9, 10, 11), **Israel, the house of Aaron,** and **all that fear the Lord** are urged to **trust** only in Him. **House of Aaron** refers to the priests. Those who **fear the Lord** may include Gentile proselytes, since three specific classes (the people of Israel, the priests, and the God-fearers) seem to be in mind and are mentioned again in vv. 12-13; 118:2-4; and 135:19-20. **Help** and **shield** may suggest power and safety. Harrison translates, "Their help

[24]*Op. cit.,* II, 548-49.

and their protection." Such trust is justified because the Lord
had **been mindful** of His people (12); He had remembered His
own and will continue to **bless them** . . . **both small and great**
(13)—"one and all without distinction of rank or condition."[25]

4. *The Promised Blessing* (115:14-18)

The expected blessing includes an **increase** . . . **more and
more, you and your children** (14). This promise of enlarged
numbers would be particularly encouraging to a small and
struggling band of returning exiles. It is an encouragement to
any Christian group today neither to despise the day of small
things nor to rest content with it. The God of the trusting heart
is **the Lord which made heaven and earth** (15) and who is therefore abundantly able to do what He has promised.

Moffatt views 16 as an explanation of the last clause of 15.
The Lord made heaven and earth, and reserves **the heavens** for
himself (cf. I Kings 8:27) but places **the earth** under the control
of **the children of men**, a Hebraism for the whole human race
(cf. Gen. 1:28-30; Ps. 8:6). Harrison renders it, "The heavens
are the Lord's own, but He has allotted the earth for human
society."

**The dead praise not the Lord, neither any that go down
into silence** (17) reflects the partial light of the OT on the final
destiny of the soul. *Sheol*, the place of the dead, is translated
generally either "hell" or "the grave" by the KJV. It was regarded as a place of silence and gloom, a shadowy underworld.
While there are clear intimations in the OT of an afterlife for
the righteous in the fellowship of God, it must be remembered
that "life and immortality" were brought to light only through
Christ and the gospel (II Tim. 1:10). One such intimation of
redemption from the gloom and loss of Sheol is found in 18,
where the righteous express determination to praise **the Lord
from this time forth and for evermore. Praise the Lord** is "Hallelujah" (*Hallelu-Yah*).

Psalm 116: A Song of Personal Testimony, 116:1-19

The intensely personal nature of this psalm is indicated by
the exclusive use of the first person pronouns *I, my,* and *me.* Its
inclusion in a group of what are primarily psalms of public

---

[25]Kirkpatrick, *op. cit.*, p. 686.

worship testifies to the truth that any congregation, whether large or small, is finally made up of individuals who lift their own hearts to God in prayer and praise. The references in 17-18 to "the sacrifice of thanksgiving" and the payment of vows would indicate the setting as the giving of a thank offering for deliverance from the affliction related in the early part of the psalm. To scholars who would rearrange the verses of the psalm to achieve a more logical progression of thought, Barnes answers, "A strictly logical sequence is not to be expected in the prayer of a struggling saint. Such an one will certainly mingle petition with thanksgiving. Delivered to-day he faces fresh conflicts tomorrow."[26] This "ebb and flow of feeling under the storms of life"[27] is found in other psalms, and reflects the experience of the devout throughout the ages.

1. Praise for Answered Prayer (116:1-4)

The poet affirms his **love** for **the Lord,** specifically because he has been the recipient of answered prayer (1). **Voice** and **supplications** should not be distinguished, but understood as a slight variation from the usual phrase, "the voice of my supplications" (cf. 28:2, 6; 31:22; 130:2; 140:6)—or, with Harrison, "my supplicating voice." Answers to prayer already received encourage continued prayer (2). The Psalmist had been at the very point of **death** (3), its **sorrows** (Heb., cords) already surrounding him and **the pains of hell** (*Sheol*) already pressing in upon him; **trouble and sorrow** were his unwanted companions. In that extremity, he **called . . . upon the name of the Lord** (4) for deliverance, and was heard.

2. Praise for Deliverance from Death (116:5-9)

The Lord is **gracious, righteous** (just), and **merciful** (5; compassionate). **Preserveth the simple** (6) is better "protects the innocent" (Harrison). **Brought low** and at the point of death, the poet found help from above. His **soul** found **rest** in the Lord's bountiful dealing with him (7). Verses 8-9 are practically identical with 56:13. Here **land of the living** is substituted for "light of the living." God's threefold deliverance is one that the Christian may cherish: the deliverance of the **soul from death,** the **eyes from tears,** and the **feet from falling.**

---

[26]*Op. cit.,* II, 551.   [27]*Ibid.*

3. Faith Shaken but Steadfast (116:10-14)

The victory had not been won without battle. Verse 10 is better translated, "I kept my faith, even when I said, 'I am greatly afflicted'" (RSV); or, "I clung to my faith, even when I said, 'I am sorely afflicted'" (Berk.). Such was the Psalmist's distress that he cried out in alarm (rather than **haste**), **All men are liars** (11). The Hebrew is literally "a lie." The thought is that all human help is "a resource which fails";[28] Harrison translates, "Everyone is unreliable."

Blessing brings obligation. Prayer and supplication must be offered with thanksgiving (Phil. 4:6). In return **for all God's benefits** (12), the poet determines to **take the cup of salvation** (13). This probably refers to the drink offering of wine to be poured into a bowl by the altar as one of the aspects of a thank-offering sacrifice (cf. Exod. 29:40; Lev. 33:37; Deut. 32:38; Ezek. 20:28).[29] This was a public rendition of praise and thanksgiving **in the presence of all his people** (14).

4. The Sacrifice of Thanksgiving (116:15-19)

In its context, 15 does not mean that the death of the Lord's saints is agreeable or pleasing to Him. It rather means, "The death of His saints is of great concern to Him; He does not lightly permit it."[30] Having been delivered from imminent death, the poet determines to devote his renewed strength and extended life to the service of his Lord (16), the reasonable obligation of all who receive God's healing touch. **The son of thine hand-maid** is simply a reinforcement of **I am thy servant**; he served God as his parents had before him. Verses 17-18 parallel 13-14 and identify the "cup of salvation" as part of the **sacrifice of thanksgiving.** The place of the sacrifice is made explicit: **in the courts of the Lord's house, in the midst of . . . Jerusalem** (19). The closing exclamation is the familiar **Praise ye the Lord,** "Hallelujah" (*Hallelu-Yah*). Morgan says, "Whatever the local circumstances which give rise to this song, it is evident that all its rich meaning was fulfilled, when in the midst of that little company of perplexed souls the shadows of the One Death already upon Him, Jesus sang this song of prophetic triumph over the darkness of the hour of passion to which He was passing. He has made it over to all His own as their triumph song over death."[31]

---

[28]Barnes, *op. cit.*, I, lxviii.
[30]*Berkeley Version, in loc.*, marg.
[29]McCullough, *op. cit.*, 4:613.
[31]*Op. cit.*, p. 265.

Psalm 117: Doxology, 117:1-2

This psalm of pure doxology is the shortest in the Psalter, leading some scholars to conclude that it is a fragment detached from its original context. It stands better alone, however, than when attached to either the preceding or the following psalm. Kirkpatrick says, "It is in the truest sense a Messianic Psalm, and is quoted by St. Paul in Rom. xv.11 as one of the Scriptures which foretold the extension of God's mercy to the Gentiles in Christ."[32]

All . . . nations (the same word translated "Gentiles" in many passages) are to **praise the Lord** (1) and **all . . . people** are to laud or extol Him (a different Heb. term is used in the second exhortation to praise); "Praise the Lord, all ye Gentiles; and laud him, all ye people" (Rom. 15:11).

His merciful kindness is *chesed,* "steadfast love" (RSV), or grace (cf. comment on 17:7). **The truth** (faithfulness or fidelity) **of the Lord endureth for ever. Praise ye the Lord** is "Hallelujah" (*Hallelu-Yah*).

Psalm 118: Strength, Song, and Salvation, 118:1-29

The last of the psalms in this "Hallel" group (cf. Psalm 113, intro.) is one of the most magnificent in the book. Text and outline, if one may call it such, are found in v. 14 of this remarkable psalm: "The Lord is my strength and song, and is become my salvation." McCullough describes it as "a litany of thanksgiving."[33] He remarks, "It is in truth one of the great hymns of the Psalter. It was a favorite psalm of Luther, who said of it: 'This is the psalm that I love . . . for it has often served me well and has helped me out of grave troubles, when neither emperors, kings, wise men, clever men, nor saints could have helped me.' "[34]

A unique feature is the use of a double refrain: "His mercy endureth for ever" (1-4, 29), and, "In the name of the Lord will I destroy them" (10-12)—rather clear evidence of the use of the hymn in the Temple worship. Ezra 3:11, where "together by course" is literally "one to another," indicates the probable use of such psalms in worship. A soloist would chant the first line of a verse and the choir would chant the second; or

[32]*Op. cit.,* pp. 691-92.   [33]*Op. cit.,* 4:616.
[34]Quoted by McCullough, *ibid.*

one choir would sound the first line and a second choir respond with the second.

1. *"The Lord Is My Strength"* (118:1-14)

The Lord's enduring **mercy** (*chesed*) is "steadfast" or covenant love, grace; cf. comment on 17:7. This is the theme of 1-4. After a general call to **give thanks unto the Lord** (1), each of the three groups listed in 115:9-11 (cf. comments there) are bidden to sound the refrain: the people of **Israel** in general (2), the priests or **house of Aaron** (3), and all who **fear the Lord** (4), devout men everywhere.

Verses 5-13 give the poet's testimony to the ways in which God had proved to be his Strength and the Strength of his people. **In distress**, he had **called upon the Lord** and had been **answered** and **set . . . in a large place** (5), i.e., "set . . . free" (Moffatt), "liberated" (Harrison). With **the Lord** on his **side**, he **will not fear** (6). Nothing **man** can do will permanently harm him. **The Lord taketh my part with them that help me** (7) is a difficult construction. The meaning is that the Lord is chief among those who stand with the Psalmist to help him. *The Berkeley Version* translates it, "The Lord is for me; He is my help, and I look in triumph on them that hate me."

Trust in the Lord is **better** than **confidence in man** (8) or even **in princes** (9). Elsewhere the Psalmist writes, "Give us help from trouble: for vain is the help of man" (60:11). The meaning and verb tenses of 10 are not clear. The **me** and **I** of 10-12 are personifications of the nation. The Hebrew verb translated, **I will destroy them** (10, 11, 12), is in a "graphic imperfect" form, and can mean either present or future. From 5 and 13, it would appear that the crisis has already passed and therefore the translation of almost all recent versions is justified: "In the name of the Lord, I beat them down" (Berk.), or, "I routed them, relying on the Eternal" (Moffatt). **Compassed me about** (10-12) means "surrounded me." The figure **like bees** (12) suggests that the enemies were aroused and angry. **Quenched as the fire of thorns** refers to a fire that burns hot but quickly dies. **Thou hast thrust sore at me** (13) is addressed to the poet's foes. The Lord's help saved him from falling before the enemy. **The Lord is my strength and song, and is become my salvation** (14) comes from the "Song of Moses" in Exod. 15:2 and is used again in Isa. 12:2. Moffatt renders it, "The Eternal is my strength, of him I sing, he has delivered me indeed." God's people find it so in every age. **The Lord** himself is our **salvation**: "Of him are ye in Christ Jesus, who of God is made unto us wisdom, and righteousness, and sanctification, and redemption" (I Cor. 1:30). Not in what He gives but in himself we find our strength, song, and salvation.

2. The Lord Is "My ... Song" (118:15-20)

The voice of rejoicing and salvation (15) is the theme of this stanza of the poem. **The tabernacles of the righteous** are "where the upright are living" (Harrison). **The right hand of the Lord doeth valiantly** (16) is the theme of the song, the **right hand** being an expression for the power or might of the person concerned.

The poem again reverts to the first person in 17-19, and the singular form, "I, me," is again a personification for the entire people. Israel would **not die, but live to declare the works of the Lord** (17), though **chastened . . . sore** through exile and dispersion. **The gates of righteousness** (19) and **this gate of the Lord** (20) are the Temple gates, through which the people of the Lord enter to praise Him. Moffatt regards 19 as the call of the approaching pilgrims before the gates of the Temple, and 20 as the reply from within:

> Open to me the gates of Victory,
>   that I may enter in to thank the Eternal.
> "Here is the Eternal's gate;
>   the just alone can enter."

3. The Lord Is "My Salvation" (118:21-29)

Beyond the limitations of the day and the political and military victories celebrated in this poem is the strong Messianic note of the last stanza. The poet now addresses the Lord, **I will praise thee: for thou . . . art become my salvation** (21). Verses 22-23 are cited four times in the NT in relation to Christ's rejection by His generation and to His subsequent exaltation (Matt. 21:42; Mark 12:10-11; Luke 20:17; I Pet. 2:7). Moffatt has caught rhyme as well as rhythm in his translation of 22:

> The stone the builders cast aside
>   is now the building's strength and pride.

God alone, in the marvellous workings of His providence, can bring victory out of defeat, life out of death, resurrection out of a cross, and turn the wrath of man into His glory (23). The Messianic overtones of the passage suggest that **the day which the Lord hath made** (24) is the day of salvation, Christ's day, in which His people are to **rejoice and be glad.** There is, however, a general application. Each day comes to us fresh from the hand of God, and is for us a day of rejoicing and gladness. With such a faith, no child of God need fear the dawning of a new day.

Prayer, blessing, praise, and promise blend in the last five verses. The Psalmist prays for deliverance and **prosperity** ("success," Harrison; 25) and pronounces a blessing on those who come to **the house of the Lord** in His **name** (26). **God . . . the Lord** is the Source of **light** (27). The exact meaning of the latter part of 27 is obscure. The KJV is a literal translation of the Hebrew. **The horns of the altar** were upturned extensions of the corners of the Temple altar, and were regarded as most sacred. The sacrificial blood was sprinkled there (Lev. 4: 7; 8:15; 9:9) and there one whose life was imperilled might find refuge (I Kings 1:50). The OT never refers to a practice of tying sacrificial victims there. Of the various suggestions that have been offered, that of the *Amplified Bible* is one of the most reasonable: "Decorate the festival with leafy boughs *and* bind the sacrifices to be offered with thick cords [all over the priest's court, right up] to the horns of the altar" (cf. also RSV, Moffatt).

The poet promises his praise and exaltation to God, and closes with the same note with which he began, a call to **give thanks unto the Lord** (29) for His goodness and enduring **mercy.** "In these words we are brought back to the point from which we started, and the circle of praise returns into itself."[35]

Psalm 119: WHOLEHEARTED LOVE FOR THE LAW, 119:1-176

This is the longest and most carefully worked out of the alphabetical or acrostic wisdom psalms. The KJV and other English translations have preserved a sense of the alphabetical feature by printing the Hebrew letters at the head of each section. The psalm is divided into twenty-two sections, one for each letter of the Hebrew alphabet. Each section is composed of eight verses. Each verse in the Hebrew begins with a word the initial letter of which is the letter heading the division. Thus, vv. 1-8

---

[35]Alexander, *op. cit.*, p. 481.

each start with words beginning with *aleph*, vv. 9-16 with words beginning with *beth*, vv. 17-24 with *gimel*, etc.

The theme of the psalm is the glorious law of the Lord, and the wholehearted observance of that law (cf. 2, 10, 34, 58, 69, 145). The basic word translated law is *torah*, a term much broader in meaning than our English word "law" would suggest. *Torah* is, in fact, the will of God as made known to Israel. It carries with it the idea of guidance, and its basic meaning is teaching or instruction.

M'Caw notes that the major feature of Psalm 119 is "the melodious repetition of eight synonyms of the will of God, viz. *law*, the *torah*; *testimonies*, the general principles of action; *precepts* (*piqqudim*), particularly rules of conduct; *statutes* (*huqqim*), social regulations; *commandments* (*mitzvah*), religious principles; *ordinances* (*mishpattim*), the right judgments which should operate in human relations; *word* (*dabhar*), the declared will of God, His promises, decrees, etc.; *word* (*imra*), the word or speech of God as it is brought to light among men. A frequent variant of the usual eight synonyms is *way* (*derek*). There can be little doubt that these were largely derived from Ps. 19:7-9. One or other of these terms occurs in every verse of the Psalm, except verse 122; but they have no methodical sequence from stanza to stanza."[36]

Morgan refers to the same terms: "A careful consideration of them will reveal one underlying conception. It is the conception of the will of God as that will has been made known to man. Every word reveals some aspect of the will in itself, of the method of its revelation, and its value in human life."[37] Oesterley writes, "The law is the expression of the divine will . . . he loves the law because it tells of God's will; and he loves it because he loves God first. Unless this fact is recognized all through, we shall neither do justice to the writer, nor apprehend the deeply religious character of the whole psalm."[38]

1. Aleph: The Blessedness of Keeping the Law (119:1-8)

The opening verse sets the tone of the entire poem. **Happy are the undefiled** (1; *tammim*), "the perfect, upright, blameless," **who walk in the law** (*torah*, cf. intro.) **of the Lord.** Those who follow the principles of action His Word sets forth and who **seek**

[36]*Op. cit.*, p. 496.   [37]*Op. cit.*, p. 266.
[38]*Op. cit.*, p. 499.

389

him with the whole heart (2) are blessed indeed. Wholehearted devotion to the will of God is pretty close to "the Christian's secret of a happy life." Negatively, such persons **do no iniquity** (3). Positively, **they walk in his ways.** The balance of the stanza is prayer, praise, and promise addressed directly to God. He has **commanded us to keep** His **precepts** (4; particular rules of conduct) carefully. The Psalmist desires that his **ways be directed to keep** the Lord's **statutes** (5). **Not be ashamed** (6) means "not endure humiliation" (Harrison). **Have respect unto** is to "heed" (Moffatt). The RSV translates it, "Having my eyes fixed on all thy commandments." The poet has set his soul to learn and to **keep** God's **judgments** and **statutes** (7-8). **O forsake me not utterly** does not express fear but faith. The Psalmist asks what he is confident God will do.

2. Beth: The Cleansing Word (119:9-16)

It has been concluded from v. 9 that the author of the psalm was a young man. It may, however, reflect the interest of the wisdom teachers in the welfare of the youth of the nation. **Young** or old, our **way** is cleansed **by taking heed thereto according to** God's **word** and by hiding it in our hearts (11). Moffatt translates clearly and forcefully, "By keeping to thy word." **Let me not wander** (10) means, "Let me not err through ignorance or inadvertence (verse 67; xix.12). My intention is good, but my knowledge is imperfect and my strength is small. 'The self-mistrust of the second clause is a proof of the reality of the first' (Aglen)."[39]

The will and Word of God are not only cleansing for the way; they are joy for the heart. The **statutes** (12), **judgments** (commandments; 13), **testimonies** (14), **precepts . . . ways** (15), and **word** (16) of the Lord are a joy and delight to the heart of God's servant.

3. Gimel: The Aim of Life (119:17-24)

"The knowledge and observance of God's law (is) the aim of life, a strength and comfort in time of contempt and persecution."[40] The Word of God is a source of life (17), vision (18), guidance (19), and aspiration (20). Love such as this for the will of God is a mark of the deepest piety. **Bountifully** (17) is better "kindly" or "generously" (cf. Moffatt, Berk.). **Stranger**

---

[39]Kirkpatrick, *op. cit.*, p. 707.   [40]*Ibid.*, p. 708.

(19) indicates "having no experience or knowledge of the world; hence, in special need of divine guidance" (Berk., fn.). **The proud,** on the contrary, **err from** ("swerve from," Moffatt) God's **commandments** (21) and are rebuked and cursed. God's law is a defense against **reproach and contempt** (22) and false speaking (23). There are joy and guidance in the **testimonies** of the Lord (24).

Verse 18 was the inspiration for Charles H. Scott's prayer-hymn,

> *Open mine eyes, that I may see*
> *Glimpses of truth Thou hast for me;*
> *Place in my hands the wonderful key*
> *That shall unclasp and set me free.*

4. Daleth: The Great Choice (119:25-32)

In distress of spirit, the poet cries for revival (25). "I lie prone in the dust; revive me according to Your promise" (Harrison). He had hidden nothing from the Lord (26). Learning God's **statutes** and **precepts,** he would **talk of the Lord's wondrous works** (27). **My soul melteth for heaviness** (28) is better, "I am weeping in my sorrow" (Harrison). **Remove from me the way of lying** (29) does not refer to falsehood in the ordinary sense, but unfaithfulness to the truth of God. Moffatt catches this, "Keep me from being false to thee." The Psalmist's determination is strong. He has made his choice (30). "Thy demands are my desire" (Moffatt). **I have stuck unto** (31) is better, "I cling to" (Berk.). **Enlarge my heart** (32) means to expand it in understanding, joy, and trust. "When his heart is set free from the cramping constraint of trouble and anxiety, the Psalmist will use his liberty for more energetic service"[41]; that is, he will run and not merely walk.

5. He: Prayer for Establishment (119:33-40)

This stanza is made up of a series of petitions centering around the Psalmist's desire for instruction and understanding, and God's help in fulfilling the requirements of His law. **Teach me** (33; *torehni*), the verb from which *torah* comes. Deeper than information is understanding, which alone leads to a whole-hearted keeping of the law (34). The Lord's **commandments** are

[41]*Ibid.,* p. 710.

His followers' delight (35). As against the unjust gain of **cov-etousness** and the attraction of the unreal and passing **vanity** (36-37), the poet seeks God's **testimonies** and His **way. Stablish thy word** (38) means, "Confirm Your promise" (Harrison). **Turn away my reproach** (39) is rendered, "Remove the insults" (Moffatt).

6. *Vau: Unashamed of the Word* (119:41-48)

The sixth stanza continues with expressions of longing and desire for the help and guidance that come through the Word of the Lord. God's **mercies** ("steadfast love," RSV) and **salvation** ("daily deliverance from the power of sin," Berk., fn.) are chan-nelled through His **word** (41). Moffatt renders 42, "Then can I face my revilers, relying on thy promise." **I have hoped in** (43) is better, "I have waited for" (Perowne) **thy judgments** (instructions). With the teaching (*torah*) of the Lord as his guide continually (44), the Psalmist **will walk at liberty** (45), or "walk with freedom" (Berk.), literally, "in a broad place." Even **before kings,** he **will not be ashamed** of the Lord's **testi-monies** (46). The **commandments,** which he loves, will be a source of **delight** (47). **My hands also will I lift up unto thy commandments** (48) as an act of prayer and devotion.

7. *Zain: The Life-giving Word* (119:49-56)

In the midst of trouble, the Psalmist finds **hope** (49) and **comfort** (50) in the **word** of God. "Thy promise puts life into me" (50*b*, Moffatt). In spite of the **derision of the proud** (51), the poet had **not declined** from God's **law**—"I have not deviated from Thy law" (Berk.). The memory of God's **judgments** in other days **comforted** him (52). **Horror hath taken hold** (53) is better, as with *The Berkeley Version,* "Burning indignation has seized me." There is a place for righteous anger on the part of God's people in the face of rampant evil. **Thy statutes have been my songs** (54) means, "God's statutes form the theme of his songs; they calm his mind and refresh his spirit in this transitory life of trial . . . as songs beguile the night (Job xxxv.10), or cheer the traveller on his journey."[42] The writer had the memory of God's **name** (and nature, as the **name** suggests) **in the night** because he **kept** the **precepts** of the Word (55-56).

---

[42]*Ibid.,* p. 714.

8. Cheth: The Company of the Committed (119: 57-64)

God and His Word are the Psalmist's chief treasure, and have brought him into a companionship with the God-fearing of his people. His purpose is to keep, in heart and life, the words God spoke (57). Wholehearted prayer (58), thoughtful reflection on his ways (59), and urgency of spirit (60) had brought him into harmony with the testimonies and commandments of the Lord. The bands of the wicked (61) is literally "the cords of the wicked," a figure of speech taken from the practice of snaring or catching game in a noose. Although threatened by such snares, his soul had escaped because he had not forgotten God's law. In the midnight hour his praise will rise to God (62). He had found fellowship with all who fear the Lord and keep His precepts (63). The abundance of God's mercies created a desire to know more about his Lord (64).

9. Teth: The Value of Affliction (119: 65-72)

The writer had learned the disciplinary value of affliction. The chastening that had been hard to bear had yielded its "peaceable fruit of righteousness" (Heb. 12:11) and he could now say, Thou hast dealt well with thy servant, O Lord (65). Affliction had taught him obedience (67). The proud ("godless," RSV) have forged a lie (69), i.e., "patched up, fabricated a lie" (Berk., fn.). As fat as grease (70) is a vivid metaphor for "stupid" (Harrison) or "dull" (Moffatt)—as unfeeling and insensible as so much lard! As in 67, verse 71 reinforces the good effects of affliction. E. Stanley Jones writes, *The way to meet unmerited suffering and injustice is not to bear them, but to use them. When I saw that possibility years ago . . . an entirely new world opened before me. I had been trying to explain suffering, and now I saw that we are not to explain it, but to use it."*[43] Better . . . than thousands of gold and silver (72) means that the truth of God is beyond the possibility of economic measurement (cf. 19:10; Job 28:15-28).

10. Jod: The Cry for Soundness of Soul (119: 73-80)

The ways of the Lord with His people are both encouragement for the righteous and confusion to the ungodly. The

---

[43]*Growing Spiritually* (New York: Abingdon Press, 1953), p. 355 (italics in original).

Psalmist knows himself to be the beneficiary of God's good providence (73); it is God who **made** him, and he therefore desires to be taught of Him. Thus taught, he is sure he will be an inspiration to those who **fear** the Lord (74). Though God permits or sends affliction, it is always for our good (75; cf. Rom. 8:28). **Comfort** (76), life (77), and joy are found in the divine Word. Harrison translates 78, "Let the arrogant be humiliated because they have behaved deceitfully towards me." In the support and confidence of those of like mind (79), the poet pleads, **Let my heart be sound in thy statutes** (80)—"Let my obedience to thee be perfect" (Moffatt); "Let my heart be healthy in Thy statutes" (Berk.); "May I adhere wholeheartedly to Your precepts" (Harrison).

11. *Caph: Support Under Pressure* (119:81-88)

The Psalmist is in deep trouble, possibly both through illness and through active persecution from those who were the enemies of righteousness. His **soul** was faint (81) and longed for God's **salvation** (saving aid). His **eyes** failing (82) is perhaps a metaphor from the idea of searching the horizon for signs of divine deliverance. **Like a bottle in the smoke** (83), or, since glass bottles were unknown in Bible times, "like a wineskin in the smoke," blackened and wrinkled and almost unrecognizable. Some have seen here a trace of the practice of putting a wineskin in the smoke of a fire to hasten the mellowing of the wine. But the more probable interpretation is a reference to the premature aging brought about by what the poet had suffered. He longs for a speedy vindication (84), because **the proud** (85; godless) had attempted to trap him like an animal caught in a camouflaged pit. Persecuted **wrongfully** (86) and **almost** destroyed (87), he still clings to the support of God's promise. He prays, "As thou art loving, revive me, and I will do thy bidding" (88, Moffatt).

12. *Lamed: God's Established Word* (119:89-96)

While the circumstances and the sciences of men are changing and impermanent, **For ever, O Lord, thy word is settled in heaven** (89). It is "firmly fixed in the heavens" (RSV), "stands fast" (Moffatt), "is established permanently" (Harrison). Even the abiding **earth** (90) with its Gibraltars and its Alps owes its degree of permanence to the ordaining will of God. **For all are thy servants** (91) is better, "Everything is subservient to You"

(Harrison). Only delight in the counsels of God delivered the poet from perishing in his **affliction** (92) and brought him renewed life (93). **I have seen an end of all perfection: but thy commandment is exceeding broad** (96) means, "I have seen that there is a limit to everything which is counted perfect by mankind, but there is no limit to the greatness of Jehovah's Law."[44]

13. Mem: Wisdom Through the Word (119:97-104)

The value of the law of the Lord in imparting wisdom and understanding to the obedient is the theme of this stanza. By meditating on the teachings of God's Word, the Psalmist had gained wisdom greater than his **enemies** (97-98). Verse 98 reflects the importance of continued exposure to the Scriptures. RSV translates it, "Thy commandment makes me wiser . . . for it is ever with me." There is more **understanding** of spiritual things through the Scriptures than through the instruction of **teachers** who gain their insights from other sources, be they ancient or modern (99-100). Perhaps John Wesley's word of caution is in order here, however: "So you ascribe all the knowledge you have to God; and in this respect you are humble. But if you think you have more than you really have; or if you think you are so taught of God, as no longer to need man's teaching; pride lieth at the door. . . . Always remember, much grace does not imply much light. These do not always go together. As there may be much light where there is but little love, so there may be much love where there is little light. The heart has more heat than the eye; yet it cannot see. . . . To imagine none can teach you, but those who are themselves saved from sin, is a very great and dangerous mistake. Give not place to it for a moment; it would lead you into a thousand other mistakes, and that irrecoverably. . . . Know their place and your own; always remembering, much love does not imply much light."[45]

Keeping God's Word keeps the **feet from . . . evil ways** (101), and the converse is also true—following evil ways will keep one from the Word of God. Both instruction (102) and delight

[44]Barnes, op. cit., p. 581.

[45]A Plain Account of Christian Perfection (Kansas City, Mo.: Beacon Hill Press of Kansas City, 1966 [reprint]), pp. 95-96, Section 25, Question 32.

(103) are in the law of the Lord (cf. 19:10; Prov. 16:24). Love for the **precepts** of the Lord leads to hatred of **every false way** (104). Moffatt translates the verse, "I learn sense from thy behests, learn to hate the godless ways."

14. *Nun: The Light of Life* (119:105-12)

The **word** of God gives light for guidance, both step by step and along the **path** (105). Here we have both specific guidance —a **lamp unto my feet**—and general guidance for the whole course of life—a **light unto my path.** The Psalmist has registered his oath of obedience (106), and in the midst of much affliction prays, **Quicken** (revive) **me . . . according** to Your promise (107). **The freewill offerings of my mouth** (108) would be "the sacrifice of prayer and praise (Heb. xiii.15); voluntary vows of devotion to the law. Cp. xix.14."[46] **My soul is continually in my hand** (109) is, as we would say, taking our lives in our hands, that is, placing them in jeopardy. Moffatt translates, "My life is ever in danger." The Psalmist is still surrounded by his foes, who lay traps for his feet as hunters spread snares for their game (110). Yet the Psalmist makes God's **testimonies** his treasure, and rejoices in them (111). **I have inclined my heart** (112) may be, "I have set myself" (Harrison). Right down to **the end,** the writer purposes to perform the requirements of the Lord's way.

15. *Samech: Way of Life and Way of Death* (119:113-20)

I hate vain (literally, doubtful) **thoughts** (113) is clearer in some of the modern versions: "I hate double-minded men" (RSV), "I hate men who are half and half" (Moffatt), or, "I detest people of uncertain allegiance" (Harrison). In the Lord, the poet finds safety and protection (114) from the continual attacks of **evildoers** (115). Hope (116) and safety (117) for him are found only in the Lord. In contrast, "All who swerve from thy will, thou spurnest; their notions end in nothing" (118, Moffatt). The wicked are **trodden down** is literally "set at nought," "come to nothing." They are **like dross** (119), the worthless residue of the refining process. The **fear** of God (120) reminds us that there is always a place in the minds of God's people for reverent awe in the face of the majesty and holiness

---

[46]Kirkpatrick, *op. cit.*, p. 722.

of God. "The fear of the Lord is the beginning of wisdom" (111: 10; Prov. 1:7).

16. *Ain: Tribulation and Testimony* (119:121-28)

In the midst of oppression and tribulation, the Psalmist testifies to his loyalty to the law of God and prays for continued support. Those who oppose him do so without basis of wrongdoing on his part (121). RSV translates, "I have done what is just and right." **Be surety for thy servant for good** (122) is better, "Give your servant comforting assurance" (Harrison). **For mine eyes fail** (123), cf. comment on 82. Confident of God's mercy, the writer prays for continued instruction and **understanding** (124-25). The time has come for the Lord to vindicate His justice and punish those who **make void** His **law** (126) by violating its requirements. The Word of God was more to him than **gold. Fine gold** (127) is gold highly refined and therefore more valuable—as we should say, "twenty-four-karat gold," absolutely pure (cf. 19:10). In all things God's **precepts** prove **to be right,** and love for the **right** way leads to **hate** for **every false way** (128).

17. *Pe: Freedom in the Light of the Law* (119:129-36)

The poet finds the testimonies of the Lord **wonderful** ("marvelous," Berk.) and **therefore** determines to **keep them.** In v. 130, **The entrance of thy words** is literally, "The opening of Thy words," that is, their unfolding or exposition. In OT terminology, **the simple** are not the foolish or simpleminded, but those who are easily led, still open to instruction, teachable. They have committed themselves as yet neither to righteousness nor to evil. In 131, desire for the Word of God is as keen and urgent as the eager panting for air on the part of the breathless. **As thou usest to do** (132) is God's customary provision for **those** who **love** His **name.** This encourages the poet to expect God's favor. **Order my steps** (133) means, "Direct my behavior" (Harrison). **˙**A life according to God's pattern will be free from the dominion of any form of **iniquity** (cf. Rom. 6:14). Here is an OT prayer for NT perfection. There is also freedom **from the oppression of man** and the continued favor of God in keeping His **precepts** (134-35). Verse 136 is noteworthy. The psalmists were capable of great indignation toward those who despise God's law. Yet they could also be deeply compassionate and weep over the sins of the people (cf. Jer. 9:1). Harrison translates: "My eyes are streaming with tears, because people do not observe Your law."

18. *Tzaddi: God's Everlasting Righteousness* (119:137-44)

"The righteousness, purity, and truth of God's law command the Psalmist's deepest love and reverence."[47] The Lord is **righteous, upright,** and **faithful** in His **judgments** (expressions of His will) and **testimonies** (137-38). The writer is **consumed** with **zeal** ("My enthusiasm devours me," Harrison) when he is confronted with the waywardness of his **enemies. Thy word is very pure** (lit., refined; 140), Moffatt translates, "Thy promises are tried and true"; cf. comment on 127. Harrison renders 141, "I am lowly, and regarded with contempt; yet I have not forgotten Your precepts." God's **righteousness** is **everlasting** (142, 144), and the poet finds delight in it in spite of the **trouble** into which he has fallen (143). **Understanding** of the things of God is the basis of his very life (144).

19. *Koph: Truth Helps Overcome Trouble* (119:145-52)

Deeply troubled, the poet promises obedience to God's Word, and pleads for help (145-46). **I prevented the dawning of the morning** (147) is better, "I was up before dawn" (Berk.). Here and in 148 **prevent** is used in the old English sense of "come before." **Mine eyes prevent the night watches** would be, "My eyes are awake before the watches of the night" (RSV). Early in the morning and through the night hours, prayer and meditation occupy his mind. **Quicken me** (149), i.e., "Revive me." Verse 150 is rendered, "My pursuers draw near in malice, far away from thy law" (Moffatt). In the nearness of God (151) and in the assurance of the everlasting truth of His Word, the writer finds hope (152).

20. *Resh: Prayer for Revival and Deliverance* (119:153-60)

The petition, **Quicken me,** repeated three times (154, 156, 159), dominates this cry for deliverance from persecutors. To **quicken** is to "make alive." Most recent translations render it, "Revive me" (Moffatt, Berk., Harrison), although cf. RSV, "Give me life." The Psalmist is in **affliction** (153), embattled (154), and persecuted by **enemies** (157), yet he holds fast his loyalty to the law of the Lord. **According to thy judgments** (156) is "according to Thy wisdom and choice." **Do I not decline** (157)

---

[47] Ibid., p. 726.

is better, "I have not deviated" (Berk.). For 158, cf. comment on 136. God's **word is true from the beginning** (160) and for ever.

21. Schin: Persecuted, yet in Peace (119:161-68)

The Psalmist experiences the paradox of peace in the midst of persecution with all the turmoil it brings. **Princes** (161) "are probably . . . Israelite nobles, who exercised judicial and administrative functions."[48] **As one that findeth great spoil** (162) is better "like one who discovers a hoard of treasure" (Harrison; cf. Matt. 13:44). **Seven times a day** (164) would be a way of saying "constantly and repeatedly." **Great peace have they which love thy law** (165) is a cherished verse, full of great meaning to the people of God. **Nothing shall offend them** is literally, "There is not for them a stumbling block," or, "No obstacle can cause them to stumble" (Harrison). **I have hoped for** (166) is, "I am looking for" (Berk.). The verse clearly reflects the twofold formula for a godly life—trust and obey. As the poet has walked in the **testimonies** and **precepts** of the Lord, **all** his **ways** are an open book **before** God (167-68).

22. Tau: A Prayer for Help and Guidance (119:169-76)

In prayer and supplication, the Psalmist stands upon the **word** of the Lord (169-70). His **lips** and his **tongue** shall be placed at the service of the Word (171-72). He has **chosen God's precepts** (173), has **longed for** His **salvation,** and has made the divine **law** his **delight** (174). Life and help are sought from above (175). It appears strange that one who had professed such loyalty to God's commandments should describe himself as **a lost sheep** (176) even at the moment he claims to remember the commandments. Kirkpatrick makes a helpful suggestion: "It seems however more in accordance with the general spirit of the Psalm to suppose that the Psalmist is describing his outward circumstances rather than his spiritual state, the helplessness of his condition rather than his moral failures. He is a wanderer in the wilderness of the world; like a sheep that has been separated from the flock he is exposed to constant dangers, and therefore he beseeches God not to leave him to wander alone, but in accordance with His promise (Ezek. xxxiv.11 ff.) to seek for him, for amid all these dangers he does not forget God's law."[49]

[48]*Ibid.*, p. 730.   [49]*Ibid.*, p. 733.

Psalm 120: THE LAMENT OF AN EXILE, 120:1-7

Psalm 120 is the first of fifteen songs each bearing the title *Shir ha-maaloth*, literally, "A song of the goings-up." *Maaloth* is a term used in I Kings 10:19-20 of the steps leading to Solomon's throne. There is much disagreement as to the meaning of the title. It has been conjectured from a statement in the Jewish *Mishnah* that the reference is to a liturgy connected with the fifteen steps between the two courts of the Temple.[50] This would be the basis for the KJV translation, "A Song of degrees." *Maaloth* is more commonly taken to mean "the going up" from Babylonian captivity, or in fact any "going up" to Jerusalem on an annual pilgrimage. Thus Moffatt translates the phrase, "A pilgrim song"; RSV and *The Berkeley Version* use, "A song of ascents."

The common title identifies the songs as a collection within the larger collection. M'Caw calls it a sort of "miniature Psalter" divided into five groups of three psalms each.[51] Duhm writes: "These pilgrim songs are as a collection the most valuable of all the small booklets from which the Psalter was composed. . . . These Psalms form a true People's Song Book speaking the language of the people and revealing their feelings and sentiments; it introduces us to their religion, and also to their civil life, their family life, their day's work—such things indeed as the people themselves tell in a natural and naive manner. Only two or three of these Psalms are pilgrim-songs in the strict sense of the term, but they may have all been sung on pilgrimages."[52]

Barnes sees a unity of theme within each of the five groupings which he calls trilogies.[53] The first trilogy, Psalms 120—22, traces the Psalmist's "ascent" from exile in a hostile environment, to a vision of Jerusalem, to the actual joy of presence in the Lord's house. In Psalm 120 the Psalmist expresses the restless longing of one living in an unfriendly community.

1. *Prayer for Deliverance* (120:1-2)

Verse 1 is generally translated as in the KJV as an expression of previously answered prayer. God's help in the past encourages prayer and faith for the future. The RSV however, not impossibly, translates the entire psalm in the form of a lament,

---

[50]Barnes, *op. cit.*, p. 590.   [51]*Op. cit.*, p. 498.
[52]Quoted by Barnes, *op. cit.*, p. 591, from *Psalmen*, p. 428.
[53]*Ibid.*, pp. 591-622.

"In my distress I cry to the Lord, that he may answer me." In either case, the pressure of the present moment arises **from lying lips, and from a deceitful tongue** (2), slander and deception on the part of those about. There is little distress as great as that of one who is falsely accused and who cannot count on the truthfulness and honor of those with whom he must live.

2. *Warning of Retribution* (120:3-4)

Addressing his enemies, the writer asks, "What will you get from Him, O crafty tongue, what punishment in full?" (Moffatt). The answer is, **Sharp arrows as mighty** warriors use, **with coals of juniper** (4). The **juniper** is "the white broom (*Retama roetam*) which is in the Near East the most popular of the thorny brushwoods collected for burning because it ensures a long, hot fire."[54] While literal arrows and fire may be intended, it is quite likely that the Psalmist views the arrows and the coals as representing the tongues and the lies that had been directed against him returning in retribution upon those who had slandered him. Those who had lied about him will in their turn be lied about. Those who had trafficked in slander will be slandered (cf. Matt. 7:1-2; Gal. 6:7).

3. *Longing for Peace* (120:5-7)

Longing for the peaceful environs of the Holy City, the Psalmist sees it only **woe** that he is forced to dwell in **Mesech . . . in the tents of Kedar** (5). **Mesech** (Meshech) may have meant either the territory far to the east mentioned in Gen. 10:2 and Ezek. 32:26-27,[55] or a tribe of Arabs in Syria.[56] **Kedar** was one of the descendants of Ishmael, and so the name of an Arabian tribe (cf. Gen. 25:13; I Chron. 1:29). Although a peaceful man, the Psalmist was forced to live among quarrelsome and warlike people (6-7). The conflict of "doves" and "hawks" is not at all new.

Psalm 121: The Traveler's Psalm, 121:1-8

This much-loved piece is commonly known as the traveler's psalm. It depicts the journey toward the beloved city. The poem breathes the atmosphere of deep and steady trust in the faithful-

---

[54]Taylor, *op. cit.*, 4:642.   [55]*Ibid.*, 4:643.
[56]Barnes, *op. cit.*, p. 594.

ness of the Lord. Perowne comments, "This beautiful Psalm is the trustful expression of a heart rejoicing in its own safety under the watchful eye of Him who is both the Maker of heaven and earth, and the Keeper of Israel. . . . The one ever-recurring thought, the one characteristic word of the Psalm, is this word *keep.* Six times it is repeated in the last five verses of this one short ode. The beauty of this repetition is unfortunately destroyed in the Authorized Version by the substitution in the last three instances, in verses 7 and 8, of the verb 'preserve' for the word 'keep.' . . . The use of the same word in the original is evidently designed,—designed to mark by this emphasis of iteration the truth of God's loving care for the individual, and so to banish all shadow of doubt, fear, anxiety, lest in the vast sum the unit should be forgotten."[57]

1. *The Lord Will Help* (121:1-4)

Verses 1-2 become more meaningful when the second clause of 1 is translated as a question: "From whence cometh my help?" Morgan writes, "In Jehovah's keeping, even though far from the center of external worship, the pilgrim realizes his safety. He lifts his longing eyes toward the mountains of Zion, where stands the house of his God, and asks:

> From whence shall my help come?

Not from those mountains, precious as they are, but from Jehovah, who is with him even in the valley of distance."[58]

He will not suffer thy foot to be moved (3) is better, "He will not allow your foot to slip" (Berk.). This is not to engender a false security but to encourage a steady trust in the faithfulness of God. No inadvertent misstep or overwhelming temptation can destroy the trusting and obedient soul (cf. I Cor. 10:13). The Lord who keeps His people is never "off guard" (3-4).

2. *The Lord Will Keep* (121:5-8)

God's presence is protection and shelter for His people against any natural forces that might threaten—**the sun . . . by day** and **the moon by night** (5-6). The peril of sunstroke in the desert is well-known. It is not necessary to suppose that the Psalmist refers to the suspicion that exposure to the moon causes lunacy, as the term suggests (*luna,* "moon"). The thought simply is that

---

[57]*Op. cit.,* II, 373.   [58]*Op. cit.,* p. 267.

by day and by night God would guard and guide. **Shall preserve**
(7) is the same word translated "keep" in 3-4. There is no failure on the part of God. He is "able to keep you from falling, and
to preserve you faultless before the presence of his glory with
exceeding joy" (Jude 24; cf. Rom. 8:31-39). The other side of
"perseverance" is "preservation." **Preserve thy going out and
thy coming in** (8) is "a phrase denoting the whole life and occupations of a man. . . . The three-fold expression, 'shall keep *thee*
. . . *thy soul* . . . *thy going out* and *thy coming in*' marks the completeness of the protection vouchsafed, extending to all that the
man is and that he does."[59] This completeness is expressed by
Paul, "And the very God of peace sanctify you wholly; and I pray
God your whole spirit and soul and body be preserved blameless
unto the coming of our Lord Jesus Christ" (I Thess. 5:23).

Psalm 122: "Jerusalem the Golden," 122:1-9

This psalm completes the first trilogy in the "songs of degrees, or ascents." Its theme is the "golden" city of Jerusalem,
the pride and joy of the Psalmist and the goal of his aspirations.
He has left his foreign habitation, and has taken his successful
journey. Now he rejoices in the goal attained. Frank Ballard
writes: "Of all the pilgrim psalms this is the one that makes us
most conscious of the visits to Jerusalem paid on stated occasions
by pious and patriotic Jews. It is easy to imagine the prepara-
tions that were made in anticipation, the dangers and delights of
the journey, the thrill as swelling processions pressed upon the
Holy City and the temple itself, and then when the festivities
were over, the leave-taking, the return home, and the restarting
of old duties."[60]

1. *The Pilgrim's Joy* (122:1-2)

There are few more eloquent expressions of deep love for
the worship of the Lord than the opening sentence of this psalm:
**I was glad when they said unto me, Let us go into the house of
the Lord** (1). The Hebrew verb in 2 should be either "do stand"
or "have stood," and so the more recent versions translate it.
The KJV translators understood v. 2 as part of the statement of
the pilgrim's fellows, and thus as still future. But the grammatically correct sense is that the trip has been made, the goal

---

[59]Perowne, *op. cit.*, II, 376.   [60]*Op. cit.*, 4:649.

has been reached, and the joy of anticipation has become the added joy of realization.

2. The Pilgrim's Estimate of Jerusalem (122:3-5)

Having reached the city of his dreams, the pilgrim finds it even better than he had anticipated. He describes it in glowing terms. **Jerusalem is builded** (or "rebuilt," as the Heb. word may be translated). It is **a city that is compact together** (3), i.e., "a city solid and unbroken" (Moffatt). Here is the rendezvous of **the tribes of the Lord** (4), the people of Israel, who **go up . . . unto the testimony of Israel;** that is, in obedience to the law of the Lord—"as enjoined upon Israel" (Berk.). The purpose of their going is **to give thanks unto the name of the Lord.** In v. 5, **thrones of judgment, the thrones of the house of David** refers to Jerusalem as the seat of justice and the administration of justice as well as the center of worship. The administration of **David** and his descendants was looked upon as a time when justice prevailed. The implication is strong that the psalm belongs to a later period in the history of Israel than David's time, although the title of the piece relates it to David.

3. The Pilgrim's Prayer (122:6-9)

The sacred associations of Jerusalem make the city a proper subject for prayer. All the poet's readers are urged to **pray for the peace of Jerusalem** (6). The term **peace** (*shalom*) means "peace, prosperity, perfection, health." The well-being of the sacred city is uppermost in the Psalmist's mind. **They shall prosper** could be a petition, "May they prosper," since the grammatical form may mean either. Addressing the city in v. 7 as in 2, the writer prays, "May peace reside within your walls, and prosperity in your palaces" (Harrison). The prayer includes recognition of the needs of **brethren and companions** (8), and relates to the fact that Jerusalem is the site **of the house of the Lord** (9). The keenest delight in worship and the most ardent love for the things of God breathe all through the psalm.

Psalm 123: LAMENT UNDER THE LASH OF SCORN, 123:1-4

This is the first psalm of the second trilogy, three psalms that Barnes entitles "The Rising Tide of Faith."[61] Its tone and psy-

---

[61]*Op. cit.,* II, 598.

chological setting parallel the first psalm of the first trilogy (cf. intro. to Psalm 120). It is a cry from the depths of scorn and depression. The geographical ascent of the first trilogy is matched by the spiritual ascent of the second.

1. *Uplifted Eyes* (123:1-2)

The Psalmist looks with "The Eye of Hope"[62] to his God in **the heavens** (1), **as the eyes of servants** (2) are fixed upon the hands of their masters or mistresses, seeking to anticipate the meaning of every gesture. Perowne comments, "As *the eyes of slaves,* watching anxiously the least movement, the smallest sign of their master's will. The image expresses complete and absolute dependence . . . the eye which waits, and hopes, and is patient, looking only to Him and none other for help."[63]

2. *A Cry for Mercy* (123:3-4)

We are exceedingly filled with contempt (3) does not mean that the Psalmist has contempt for others. The particular trial from which deliverance is sought is **the contempt of the proud** (4), the bitter disdain and scorn to which the people of God are sometimes subject. It is as difficult for sensitive souls to bear scorn as to endure outright physical persecution. Writers have frequently noted that there is nothing of a retaliatory spirit here, no prayer for the punishment of the scornful. "The psalm witnesses to what was best in the Jewish religion."[64] **Exceedingly filled with** (3) could be "swamped with" (Harrison). "We have had our fill, and more, of scorn and sneers" (Moffatt). Yet faith enables the poet to endure without descending to the level of those whose ridicule and contempt he felt so keenly. Oesterley comments, "Religion plays an important *role* here in preserving the spirit of men from falling into servile attitudes to those who have a present advantage over them. One can humble oneself before God without losing one's self-respect; but one cannot do so before human pride and power."[65]

Psalm 124: DELIVERANCE FROM DESPAIR, 124:1-8

From the depths described in Psalm 124, the soul of the Psalmist begins to rise. As in Psalm 121, the second psalm of the

---

[62]Perowne, *op. cit.*, II, 382.   [63]*Ibid.*, p. 333.
[64]Oesterley, *op. cit.*, p. 509.   [65]*Ibid.*

first trilogy (cf. intro. to Psalm 120), the present poem finds in the Lord the only Source of help in the dark hour.

1. *The Lord on Our Side* (124: 1-5)

Disaster would have overwhelmed the people **if it had not been the Lord who was on our side** (1-2). Without God on their side **when men rose up against** them, they would have been **swallowed . . . up quick** (3), literally, "swallowed us up alive," like a monster would swallow its helpless victim or like the earth swallowed the rebels against Moses (Num. 16: 31-34). Without God they would have been washed away as by **the waters** of a flood (4-5). **Proud waters** is better "wild waves" (Moffatt). These verses recall the lines from Luther's famous hymn:

> *A mighty fortress is our God,*
> *A bulwark never failing:*
> *Our helper He amid the flood*
> *Of mortal ills prevailing.*

2. *The Way of Escape* (124: 6-8)

The safety of God's people is due to the mercy of the Lord. **A prey to their teeth** (6) is better "prey for them to devour" (Harrison), as a wild beast devours its helpless victim. **As a bird out of the snare of the fowlers** (bird hunters; 7) is a striking figure for the deliverance of the weak from the mighty or crafty (91: 3; Prov. 6: 5). Birds were most commonly caught in nets or snares. Harrison translates 8, "We are helped by the power of the Lord, who made heaven and earth."

Psalm 125: THE SECURITY OF THE TRUSTING HEART, 125: 1-5

The last member of the second trilogy (cf. intro. to Psalms 120, 123) brings the Psalmist again to the heights of security and trust in Mount Zion and in Jerusalem as typifying the refuge of his soul. The danger has not disappeared (cf. vv. 3, 5), but serenity has come to the trusting heart. Not without reason, some commentators see in this and the preceding psalm the conditions in Nehemiah's day (cf. Nehemiah 6).[66] Deservedly, this piece is a favorite of many Christians.

---

[66]Cf. Perowne, *op. cit.,* II, 388: Kirkpatrick, *op. cit.,* p. 746.

1. The Encircling Mountains (125:1-3)

Trust in the Lord (1) renders the soul as unshakable as **mount Zion**—like Gibraltar for us—the symbol of stability and strength for the people of the OT. **The mountains are round about Jerusalem** (2), not as encircled with mountainous peaks, but set in the midst of mountainous terrain. *The Berkeley Version* translates v. 2, "As there are mountains around Jerusalem, so the Lord is around His people from this time forth and for evermore." Since this is true, **the rod of the wicked shall not rest upon the lot of the righteous** (3), that is, wicked men will not be permitted to rule over the portion allotted to the righteous. The concern of the Psalmist is the danger that the righteous may turn aside into iniquity. "Prolonged oppression might tempt Israelites in despair to deny their allegiance to Jehovah and their duty to their country, and make common cause with the enemies of their religion and nation."[67]

2. The Contrasting Ways (125:4-5)

The Lord is besought to **do good** to **those that be good** (4), to those who are upright in their hearts. In contrast, those who **turn aside unto their crooked ways** (5)—"who become attracted to dishonest enterprises" (Harrison)—shall be led forth to judgment. **But peace shall be upon Israel.**

Psalm 126: THE SONG OF A FULL HEART, 126:1-6

This is the first psalm of the third trilogy (cf. intro. to Psalm 120), a group Barnes entitles "Return and Restoration." He interprets them as dealing with three subjects, the return from Babylonian captivity (126), the rebuilding (127), and the repeopling (128) of Jerusalem.[68] The reversal of Israel's fortunes after seventy years in exile filled the hearts of the people with great joy. This joy is the theme of the present poem.

1. The Wonder of the Return (126:1-3)

It was the Lord who **turned again the captivity of Zion** (1), that is, "brought the exiles back to Sion" (Moffatt). The return of the Jews from Babylonia occurred after the decree of Cyrus made it possible (cf. Ezra 1:1-3), just as the inhumane policy of Nebuchadnezzar had created the conditions of the Exile in the

---

[67]Kirkpatrick, *op. cit.*, p. 747.   [68]*Op. cit.*, II, 602.

first place (II Chron. 36:6-21). But the inspired writers never gave credit or blame to either Cyrus or Nebuchadnezzar in themselves. They regarded the history of their people as shaping up under the hand of God as He punished their sins and carried out His purposes. For them, as it should be more often for us, history was "His story." The news of the return was so wonderful that those who heard it **were like them that dream**—scarcely able to believe it, for the joy they felt. Joyous **laughter** and happy **singing** (2) were their understandable reaction. Moffatt interprets the last part of 2, "The very heathen said, 'The Eternal has done great things for them.' "—a theme the people gladly echoed in v. 3.

2. *The Wish for Revival* (126:4-6)

The wonder at what God had already wrought incited the wish that He might continue to work in their behalf. Recent translations properly render the first half of v. 4, "Restore our fortunes" (Smith-Goodspeed, RSV, Berk.), although Moffatt holds to the context with his translation of the entire verse, "Bring back now the rest of our exiles, to fill us up, like streams in the dry south." Those who had returned were but a scant trickle such as would be found in the watercourses of the Negeb (the southern desert region of Palestine). The prayer is for all of the exiles, whose return would be like the full flash floods of the rainy season.

There is universal meaning in the promise, **They that sow in tears shall reap in joy** (5). The "sowing" or "seedtime" period in any enterprise is a time of toil and anxiety, but a bountiful harvest makes up for all the labor that has gone before. Christians will always read v. 6 with the parable of the sower in mind (Matt. 13:1-15; Mark 4:1-12; Luke 8:4-10). "The seed is the word"; and while the sower knows that some will fall on the path, among the thorns, or on the rock, he also knows that some will fall on good ground and bring forth fruit unto salvation, some thirty, some sixty, and some a hundred fold. Verses 5-6 were the inspiration for Knowles Shaw's well-known gospel song "Bringing in the Sheaves."

Psalm 127: A Secure Habitation, 127:1-5

The association of this psalm with Solomon in its title or superscription, and its concern with the issues of practical daily life, identify it as a wisdom psalm. For its relation to 126 and 128, cf. the introduction to 126. The subject matter of the psalm is admittedly different from that of the typical pilgrim psalm. Barnes explains this difference on the basis of its concern with the settling of the people in Jerusalem after their return from exile, rebuilding their homes and reestablishing their lives.[69] Taylor relates it more directly to the wisdom literature: "The wisdom writers are concerned with teaching some of the principles and practices the observance of which yields the largest dividends of happiness in this life. Their point of view is secular rather than priestly; they orient themselves to the laity rather than to the cult. Our psalm is in this respect no exception. . . . The presence of the psalm in the pilgrim collection is probably due to the human touch and the freshness and charm of literary expression which it shares with others of the group."[70]

1. God Our Only Safety (127:1-2)

Totally in vain are all efforts toward security outside the will and working of God. Whether it be **house** or **city**, the labor of the builder and the vigilance of the watchmen are worthless without the overriding providence of **the Lord** (1). Early or late hours, long days of toil and anxious care, are without value apart from the divine provision. **Eat the bread of sorrows** (2) is better "gaining your bread with anxious toil" (Moffatt). Most commentators understand **he giveth his beloved sleep** to mean that God gives to His beloved the necessities of life in sleep, or while they sleep. However it is possible that the Psalmist views sleep as evidence of the trustful attitude that banishes anxiety. The thought is that expressed by Jesus in Matt. 6:25-34. The servant of the Lord is still required to labor at the tasks that are his. But his labor is not fretful and anxious. He can lie down in restful sleep at night in the confident faith that God will take the best he has been able to do and make it sufficient for the need.

2. The Blessings of Family Life (127:3-5)

Children are an heritage of the Lord (3) has been translated, "Sons are a gift of the Eternal, and children are a boon from him" (Moffatt). Particularly valuable are **children of the youth** (4), children born while their father is himself relatively young. They will be his strength in his old age, **as arrows are in the hand of a mighty man**, a defense against his foes. Some

⁶⁹*Ibid.*   ⁷⁰*Op. cit.*, 4:667-68.

interpret **speak with the enemies in the gate** (5) to indicate
defense against false accusation in court, since the gate of the
city was where the elders assembled to adjudicate disputes.
Harrison renders it, "They will not feel humiliated when they
dispute with their enemies in court." Others interpret the expression as having to do with defending the city against attacking
foes, since the gate was where the assault was usually launched.
"He need not fear to face a hostile band" (Moffatt). In either
case, a man's numerous sons would be his strength and security,
a source of satisfaction and joy to him.

Psalm 128: THE BLESSEDNESS OF THOSE WHO FEAR GOD, 128:1-6

This is the concluding piece in the third trilogy of songs
"of degrees" or pilgrim songs (cf. intro. to Psalms 120, 126). It
continues the thought of the last part of 127, and concerns the
blessedness of the one who fears the Lord. His many children
will add to the population and thus to the prosperity of Jerusalem.

1. Blessed with a Happy Home (128:1-3)

The **fear of the Lord** is the characteristic description of OT
religion. The attitude of the true follower of God was an attitude
of reverent awe that led him to walk in the **ways** outlined in the
law (1). To **eat the labour of thine hands** (2) was to enjoy a
peaceable life, with no marauder to carry off the harvest, and
no drouth or blight to cause famine. The **wife** would be **a fruitful
vine** (3), with numerous **children**. Taylor comments on v. 3, "As
her husband looks on his sons while they gather about his table,
he is reminded of the numerous seedlings that shoot up under
a cultivated olive tree."[71]

2. Blessed with a Long Life (128:4-6)

The blessings promised the God-fearer are reiterated. **The
good of Jerusalem** (5) would be "the welfare of Jerusalem"
(Smith-Goodspeed). The godly man will live to see his grandchildren, and the blessing of **peace** upon his people (6). Long life
was one of the blessings most coveted by the people of the OT,
in times when premature death often came (cf. 91:8). Without
the arts of medical science, death usually came when the physi-

---

[71]*Ibid.,* pp. 672-73.

cal organism was depleted. The tragedies of today's world are not only the tragedy of dying too soon but also the tragedy of living too long. It is difficult to assess the value of prolonging life beyond its normal span.

Psalm 129: PRESERVATION AND PRAYER, 129:1-8

This is the first of what Barnes calls "The Fourth Trilogy" of the pilgrim songs, and which he describes as "a trilogy of hope and waiting."[72] The psalm speaks in the first person, but the poet represents his nation and describes the long history of opposition and oppression to which it was subjected.

1. *The Sorrows of Israel's Past* (129:1-4)

Many a time (1) would better be translated "much," or "greatly." Israel's history had been turbulent from **youth** (the very beginning), yet the enemies of God's people had never prevailed against them. **Plowed upon my back** (3), perhaps as the slave driver's lash would bite into the backs of his victims. Yet a just God had preserved His people, and **cut asunder the cords** (bondage, oppression) **of the wicked** (4), breaking the bonds that held Israel in slavery. The survival of Israel not only in Bible times but throughout the centuries since is a miracle of history.

2. *A Prayer for Vindication* (129:5-8)

The prayer of the Psalmist is that those who **hate Zion** (5), as representative of the nation, may **be confounded and turned back** ("disgraced and dispersed," Harrison). They are to **be as the grass upon the house tops** (6), springing up in the shallow soil that would gather on the flat roof of an Oriental house, only to die in the heat of the sun. The last two verses amplify the sad end of the housetop plants. They will never be useful to the harvester (7); because they offer no promise of food, they will not be blessed by those who pass by (8). In typical "wisdom" fashion, the godly are to be blessed, and the wicked are to perish. This is not only wish but prediction. It cannot be otherwise, at least in the long run, in a universe governed by a holy and just God.

---

[72]*Op. cit.,* II, 607.

Psalm 130: PENITENCE AND PARDON, 130:1-8

This psalm is one of the seven penitential psalms (cf. Intro.) and expresses a sense of sin and penitence as deep and sincere as anywhere in the OT. With the cry "out of the depths" is combined the assurance of forgiveness. Morgan says, "The deepest note in all true worship is this sense of 'plenteous redemption,' and the perfection of Jehovah's love as thus manifested. To mark iniquities would be to fill us with despair. To redeem from all iniquities is to inspire us with hope."[73] The psalm has been called *De Profundis* from its opening words in the Vulgate, "Out of the depths."

1. *The Cry of Penitence* (130:1-4)

The poet utters a deep cry of penitence in which he voices not only his personal sense of sin but his lament for the sins of his people. Kirkpatrick notes that the psalm "may best be understood as the prayer of a representative godly Israelite, such as Nehemiah" and that there are resemblances between the psalm and the prayer of Nehemiah in Neh. 1:4-11.[74] **Out of the depths** (1) is a figure of deep waters that so often describe the distress and danger of the soul. In the depths one can only look up.

If the **Lord** were to keep the record of **iniquities** without blotting them out in His forgiveness and mercy, **who** indeed would be able to **stand?** (3) But God is a forgiving God, to be served with reverent awe (4). In these verses there is none of the idea of religion as perpetual forgiveness for perpetual sinning. God's forgiveness is granted that those who receive it may reverence and serve Him. "The fear of the Lord" is the beginning of that wisdom which turns away from folly and sin, and dedicates itself to obedient walking in His ways.

2. *The Hope of Pardon* (130:5-8)

The forgiveness promised is now claimed. The poet expresses his determination to **wait for the Lord** (5), to place such confidence in God that he rests his case with the mercy of the Lord. The basis of this confidence is God's own **word** of promise. But waiting is not passive. It is as expectant as the watchman who scans the skies for the earliest light of the dawn. Harrison's

[73]*Op. cit.*, p. 271.   [74]*Op. cit.*, p. 758.

translation suggests the great confidence of the poet: "I have greater hope in the Lord than the watchmen who wait for the dawn; more than the sentry who expects the morning light" (6). He calls upon all to join him in his hope, for **with him** (God) **is plenteous redemption** (7; "a wealth of saving power," Moffatt). **He shall redeem** (8) in the Hebrew reads, "It is He himself who will redeem." "The stress is on the pronoun: Jehovah Himself will provide the fine or ransom . . ."[75] Here, as in Matt. 1:21, redemption is from all his iniquities, not "in" them as some seem to suggest. The Hebrew construction is literally, "It is He who will redeem Israel *out of all* his iniquities."

Psalm 131: THE CONFESSION OF CHILDLIKE TRUST, 131:1-3

This little gem is quite unique in the Psalter. Oesterley says of it: "The writer, in repudiating the spirit of presumptuous knowledge, implies that at one time this had been his attitude of mind; but now he has come to his better self, and has quieted the restless turbulence of his thoughts. In sweet humility he compares his trustful rest in the Lord with that of a little child lying in blissful repose on its mother's breast. Like other psalmists, what he has gained he wishes others to share, and his yearning is that they should experience the happy calm which he enjoys; so he ends with an exhortation to his people to 'wait for Yahweh from henceforth and for ever.' "[76]

1. *The Renunciation of Pride* (131:1)

One of the most subtle and pervasive of human sins is the sin of pride. The Psalmist renounces a **heart** that is **haughty** and **eyes** that are **lofty** (disdainful; 1). He will not concern himself with **great matters, or in things too high for him.** This may be understood either in the practical sense, "I have not aimed at a position above me, involving duties and responsibilities too heavy for me";[77] or in a theoretical way, attempting to solve the problems and mysteries of theology in areas where God has not revealed the answers. The Lord has not chosen to answer all our questions, and there are times when we must bow to the silence of the Scriptures and not speculate where we cannot know.

[75]Barnes, *op. cit.*, II, 611.   [76]*Op. cit.*, pp. 527-28.
[77]Perowne, *op. cit.*, II, 407.

2. The Serene Faith of a Child (131:2-3)

Interpretations of these verses differ. Most commentators follow the KJV translation, and apply the reference to a weaned child who after the struggles incident to weaning rests on his mother's bosom. Taylor, however, states with good reason: "The translation **weaned** is due to a misunderstanding of the context. The word so rendered means, literally, 'finished' or 'completed' and may imply either weaned or 'nursed.' But a weaned child is not *ipso facto* a tranquil child. The figure is that of a child which after being suckled is composed."[78] Therefore the RSV here reads, "But I have calmed and quieted my soul, like a child quieted at its mother's breast; like a child that is quieted is my soul." In either case, of course, the picture is one of quiet trust and confident serenity. **All Israel** is called upon to **hope in the Lord from henceforth** (now) **and for ever** (3) in just such serene faith.

Psalm 132: A PRAYER FOR THE HOUSE OF GOD, 132:1-18

This is the longest of the "songs of degrees" or pilgrim psalms, and first of the fifth and last trilogy (cf. intro. to 120). Barnes identifies the subject of the final three pilgrim songs as the Temple and the Lord's blessing that radiates from it.[79] A portion of the psalm is quoted in Solomon's prayer of dedication for the Temple (cf. vv. 8-9 and II Chron. 6:41-42). Verse 11 is cited in Acts 2:30 with reference to Christ reigning on David's throne. Oesterley comments on the meaning of the psalm in its historical context: "It witnesses to the innate religious instinct of ancient Israel in every sphere . . . the principle of the union which should subsist between religion and the State. The basic purpose of the psalm is to glorify the Sanctuary together with the kingship, which are inextricably bound together."[80]

1. Determination to Build the House (132:1-7)

The Psalmist recalls the eagerness of **David** to make provision for the ark of the Lord (I Chron. 28:2-6). **All his afflictions** (1) refers to the struggle for the kingship against the jealousy and constant pursuit of King Saul, and in establishing Jerusalem as a place where the ark might be sheltered and the

---

[78]*Op. cit.*, 4:683-84.   [79]*Op. cit.*, II, 612.
[80]*Op. cit.*, p. 533.

Temple might be built. **The mighty God of Jacob** (2) is a phrase drawn from Gen. 49:24 and used again only once in v. 5. It is literally "the mighty One of Jacob."

David's concern for the sanctuary of the Lord was shown at two stages: in the bringing of the ark of the covenant from the house of Abinadab to the specially prepared Tabernacle set up for it in Jerusalem (II Sam. 6:1-19); and in his purpose to build a permanent Temple for the ark (II Sam. 7:1-29), a purpose he was not permitted to carry out. The vow described in vv. 3-5 would probably be related to the bringing of the ark to Zion, since the purpose appears to have been realized.

The people join their king in his concern for the symbol of God's presence: **We heard of it at Ephratah: we found it in the fields of the wood** (6). This verse has puzzled the commentators. **Ephratah** is usually referred to the town of Bethlehem (see map 3). Here it appears to have been used as a name for the entire district in which Kirjath-jearim was located ("the city of forests"), near which the ark had remained for many years (cf. I Sam. 7:1-2). It refers to the ark. **Worship at his footstool** (7) would mean to worship before the ark, since the throne of God was above it.

2. Dedication of the House of God (132:8-12)

The first three verses of this stanza are a prayer addressed directly to God and are quoted with minor variations at (or from) the conclusion of Solomon's prayer at the dedication of the Temple. Their appropriateness for the dedication is apparent. **The ark of thy strength** (8) is mentioned here for the first time, although it is implied in the verses preceding. In the Psalms, this is the only reference to the ark by name. Perowne sees in the wording of the verse an allusion to Num. 10:33-36, in which the "ark of the covenant of the Lord went before them in the three days' journey, to search out a resting place for them" and in which Moses said, "Rise up, Lord, and let thine enemies be scattered."[81] The **rest** would be the rest the Lord gave His people when they were victorious in battle.

Both priests and people are subjects of the petition of 9, the **priests** to **be clothed with righteousness,** and the **saints** to **shout for joy.** The thought is repeated in 16 in the form of a promise. Righteousness in the pulpit and rejoicing in the pew

[81]*Op. cit.*, II, 415.

combine to make a victorious church anytime. **Turn not away the face of thine anointed** (10), that is, by refusing to hear his prayer. Moffatt interprets it, "Reject not thine own king." God's promise to **David** of posterity **upon his throne** (11), together with the reference to the **anointed** (10; *meshiach,* messiah, or Gr., *Christos*), is cited by Peter in his Pentecost day sermon (Acts 2:30). Promises of the perpetuity of the throne of David found throughout the OT are fulfilled in Christ. These promises are conditioned upon obedience (12)—the obedience of the literal descendants of David in the first instance and of the Church in the second.

3. *Divine Blessing on the House* (132:13-18)

The final stanza of the song is God's response to the prayer and act of dedication. It is introduced with the assurance that **the Lord hath chosen Zion; he hath desired it for his habitation** (13). **Zion**—Jerusalem in that day and the Church in ours—is to be God's **rest for ever** (14) and His dwelling place. He will **bless** and prosper her "in basket and in store" (15; cf. Deut. 28: 1-14). He will answer the prayer for **priests** and people (16; cf. 9). **Make the horn of David to bud** (17) is better "make the power of David flourish" (Harrison)—"giving ever new strength to his house and victory over all all enemies."[82] **Ordained a lamp for mine anointed**—cf. I Kings 11:36, "And unto his son will I give one tribe, that David my servant may have a lamp always before me in Jerusalem, the city which I have chosen me to put my name there." The Messianic meaning is Christ, "the light of the world" (John 8:12). David's (and Christ's) **enemies** will be clothed **with shame** (18), "but his own crown shall sparkle" (Moffatt).

Psalm 133: THE BLESSINGS OF BRETHREN UNITED, 133:1-3

This little gem is a brief song in praise of the joys of union among brethren, both in the sense of the natural family and of God's spiritual family. Oesterley[83] and Taylor[84] both take the psalm as referring to the levirate arrangement of family life wherein married brothers continue to live in the same household. Barnes views it as the dwelling together of Jews coming to Jerusalem for the annual feasts.[85] However, it has a broader

---

[82]*Ibid.*, p. 416.   [83]*Op. cit.*, pp. 534-36.
[84]*Op. cit.*, 4:688-89.   [85]*Op. cit.*, II, 616.

meaning in relation to the household of faith. There is a spiritual unity among the children of God that transcends even denominational barriers. As the old saying has it, "You don't see the fences when the grain is high."

1. "Good and Pleasant" (133:1)

The unity of the brethren is **good and . . . pleasant** (1), "rare" and "lovely" (Moffatt). Harrison renders the verse, "What a wonderful thing it is when brothers live together in harmony." There is an ecumenism that is not organizational and imposed from without, but that grows out of a community of spirit and faith. It is (or ought to be) a distinctive mark of holiness people (John 17:17-23). It was in the thought of P. F. Bresee when he said of his small band in the beginning days of the Church of the Nazarene, "We are blood brothers of every Blood-bought and Blood-washed soul in the universe."

2. "Like the Precious Ointment" (133:2)

There is reference here to the anointing oil placed upon Aaron at his consecration (Exod. 30:22-30). The olive oil was made fragrant with the addition of spices and aromatic herbs such as myrrh, cinnamon, calamus (possibly the high-scented sweet sedge), and cassia (a species of fragrant wood). In its deeper symbolism it stands for the fragrant blessings of the Holy Spirit crowning the gathering of brethren in true spiritual oneness.

3. "As the Dew of Hermon" (133:3)

The loveliness of spiritual unity is compared with **the dew of Hermon, and as the dew that descended upon the mountains of Zion.** The italicized words in the KJV, **and as the dew,** were added to account for the fact that the dew of **Hermon,** far to the north (see map 3), did not fall upon the mountains around Jerusalem. But this is perhaps to take the poetic figure too literally. What is intended is obviously an emphasis on the freshness and refreshing quality of God's blessings falling upon His people. Barnes says, "In a parched country dew is an apt emblem of the blessing of God: Gen. xxvii.28; Hosea xiv.5, 'I will be as the dew unto Israel.' "[86] Harrison translates the last part

[86]*Ibid.*

417

of v. 3, "The Lord appointed in that place the blessing of life eternal." Eternal **life,** for themselves and for others, comes out of the unity of the brethren: "that they may be made perfect in one; and that the world may know that thou hast sent me" (John 17:23).

Psalm 134: MINISTERING IN THE HOUSE OF THE LORD, 134:1-3

This is the last of the pilgrim psalms (cf. intro. to Psalm 120), and brings us into the very sanctuary of the house of the Lord. Oesterley places it totally within a priestly context. He understands vv. 1-2 to have been chanted by the high priest, with v. 3 as the response of the priestly choir. "We have here a very instructive indication of the preparation for divine service on the part of God's ordained ministers. They upon whom devolved the high privilege of blessing the worshippers, utter a preparatory mutual blessing upon each other, and are thus endowed with spiritual power. Strengthened by the knowledge of this power having been conferred upon them, they can undertake their sacred duties in the sanctuary in the conviction that they are acting under divine guidance, and imparting to others the blessing of which they themselves have been recipients."[87]

1. *"Bless Ye the Lord"* (134:1)

Behold is better, "Come" (Moffatt, RSV, Berk.), **all ye servants of the Lord, which by night stand in the house of the Lord.** The expression **by night** refers to the "night watch" of priests, standing to minister before the altar of the Lord. Taylor notes, "It is probable that the psalm belonged to the liturgy of the feast of Tabernacles, since the implication of vs. 1c is that the priestly ministrants were on duty in the temple not for one night, as would have been the case on the eve of Passover, but for several nights, and since the presence of the congregation in the temple at night would not accord with the regulation for the observance of the eve of Passover by families in their homes or places of sojourn (cf. Exod. 12:18-20)."[88]

2. *"Lift Up Your Hands"* (134:2)

The customary posture for prayer included uplifted **hands** (cf. 28:2; 141:2; Lam. 2:19; I Tim. 2:8). This may also repre-

[87]*Op. cit.,* pp. 537-38.   [88]*Op. cit.,* 4:691.

sent the gesture of the priests in pronouncing a blessing upon the people. **In the sanctuary** is in KJV, marg., "in holiness." It parallels the thought of Paul in I Tim. 2: 8, "I will therefore that men pray every where, lifting up holy hands, without wrath and doubting." To **bless the Lord** is here, as always throughout the Psalms, to magnify and praise God.

3. "The Lord . . . Bless Thee" (134: 3)

This is in the form of a response to the words that have preceded. It is either addressed to the high priest (cf. intro.) or spoken by the priests in conveying a benediction to the people (cf. Num. 6: 24-26 for the full form of the "Levitical benediction"). Since God **made heaven and earth,** He is well able to **bless** His people **out of** (from) **Zion,** the symbol of His abiding presence with them.

Psalm 135: THE GREATNESS OF OUR GOD, 135: 1-21

This, although not included with others of its kind, is one of the "Hallelujah Psalms." It is so designated from its opening and closing words, **Praise ye the Lord**—"Hallelujah" (*Hallelu-Yah*). Its free use of thoughts and phrases from other portions of Scripture led Delitzsch to describe it as a species of mosaic.[89] The most prominent parallels are seen in comparing v. 1 with 134: 1; v. 3 with 147: 1; vv. 6, 15-20 with Psalm 95; v. 7 with Jer. 10: 13; v. 14 with Deut. 32: 36; and vv. 8-12 with 136: 10-22. A recognition of its "mosaic" character, however, should not be allowed to obscure the progress of the thought, which is consistent and logical. The greatness of God is introduced (1-5) as seen in His creative power (5-7), His sovereignty in history (8-12), and the fact that all the gods of the heathen are nothing (13-18). Therefore all should praise and bless His name (19-21).

1. The Lord Is to Be Praised (135: 1-12)

The first three verses present the call to worship. **Praise ye the Lord** (1) is "Hallelujah" (*Hallelu-Yah*)! The call is addressed initially to the **servants of the Lord,** who stand **in the house of the Lord** (2; cf. 134: 1). The latter phrase describes the service of the priests in the Temple. Since the Temple proper consisted only of the building housing the holy place and the holy of holies,

---

[89]Quoted by Perowne, *op. cit.,* p. 423.

most of the functions of service and worship were carried on in **the courts of the house of our God** (cf. the Temple plan in BBC, 6:622). **The Lord** and **his name** are to be praised, **for the Lord is good** (3) and **his name . . . is pleasant** ("sweet," Berk.; "gracious," Moffatt).

Three special reasons are given for praising the Lord:

a. His elective love (4). The Lord chose the descendants of **Jacob** for **himself, and Israel for his peculiar treasure** ("prized possession," Moffatt). This thought runs through the OT and indeed all through the life of "the chosen people." What the Israelites often forgot was the purpose for which they were chosen —that through them all nations of the earth might be blessed (Gen. 12:3; 18:18; 22:18; 26:4; etc.). Israel's election (as ours) was an election to responsibility more than to privilege.

b. His creative power (5-7). The greatness and preeminence of God (5) are seen in His power in nature (6-7). The universe as it exists is the expression of His good pleasure (6), and He is continually active in its ongoing. Verse 7 is taken almost word for word from Jer. 10:13 and 51:16. The OT writers never argue from the existence of the universe to the existence of God (the so-called "cosmological argument" of theology and philosophy). They do reason from the majestic span of the universe with its awesome powers to the greatness and majesty of its Creator.

c. His sovereignty in history (8-12). Next to God's power in creation the OT places God's power in history. History is indeed and in fact *His story,* and God speaks through its events. Isaiah had declared that even Assyria was only the rod of God's anger (10:5) and Cyrus, though he knew it not, was actually the Lord's servant (44:28). This sovereign power in history was seen preeminently in **Egypt** and at the Exodus (8-9), in the wilderness (10-11*a*), and in the possession of the promised **land** (11*b*-12).

2. The Lord Alone Is God (135:13-18)

The poet-author of this psalm is a monotheist of the purest kind. Israel's Lord alone is God. His **name,** as His **memorial** (fame, renown), **endureth for ever** (13). **The Lord will judge his people** (14) in the sense of vindicating them in the face of their enemies. **He will repent himself,** i.e., He will change His manner of dealing with **his servants.** *The Berkeley Version* translates v. 14, "For the Lord will vindicate the cause of His people, and will have compassion on His servants."

The eternity and compassion of the Lord are in complete contrast with the emptiness of the idols that pagan nations worship. **The idols of the heathen** are objects of **silver and gold, and are the work of men's hands** (15). Formed with **mouths, eyes,** and **ears,** they are yet silent, blind, deaf, and without **breath** (*ruach*, "spirit"; 16-17). Worse yet, those who **make** and trust in **them are like . . . them,** without real life or spirit (18; cf. Isa. 44:9). The tendency is for men to become like their gods. They create their idol-gods in their own image and then worship their own magnified weakness and vice. Greater foolishness is hard for the OT writers to imagine.

3. A Call to Praise the Lord (135:19-21)

The call to praise with which the psalm began is now broadened to include all the **house of Israel** (19) as well as the **house of Aaron** (the priests) and the **house of Levi** (20; the Temple workers, Levites not of the priestly family of Aaron). All God-fearers are included (cf. comment on 115:9-11). For v. 21, cf. comment on 134:3. Verse 21 is clearer as, "The Lord be blessed from Zion, He who dwells at Jerusalem!" (Berk.) **Praise ye the Lord** is "Hallelujah" (*Hallelu-Yah*)!

Psalm 136: GOD'S ENDURING MERCY, 136:1-26

The form of this psalm is quite unique. The last half of each verse consists of the same phrase, "For his mercy endureth for ever," just three words in the Hebrew. It was apparently chanted responsively with the first half of each verse sung by one of the priests or by the Levitical choir, and the rhythmic response given by the congregation (cf. II Chron. 7:3, 6; Neh. 12:40). Apparently, also, the response was added after the composition was written, since it interrupts the thought in several instances (e.g., vv. 7-9, 10-12, 13-15, 17-22, 23-25). The order of topics is similar to 135:6-12, and identical phrases occur.

In Jewish writings Psalm 136 was known as "The Great Hallel" from its often repeated praise of God's enduring mercy, although this title has also been given to the entire group of "hallelujah psalms" from 113 to 118;[90] and by others to Psalms 146—50. Its theme is "the God of gods" (2) and "the Lord of

[90]Delitzsch; quoted by Kirkpatrick, *op. cit.*, p. 776.

lords" (3), and following the course of Psalm 135, it glorifies first the Creator God and then the Redeemer God.

1. The Creator God (136:1-9)

The goodness of God, as often, is offered as the basis for thanksgiving (1). **For his mercy endureth for ever** is literally "because forever is His mercy." **Mercy** (*chesed*) is grace, loving-kindness, "steadfast love" (RSV), "covenant love" (Berk.); cf. comment on 17:7; "He is eternally constant" (Harrison). The refrain is repeated twenty-six times (cf. intro.). **The God of gods** (2) and **the Lord of lords** (3) are from Deut. 10:17, a clear and forceful statement of the preeminence of Israel's Lord and the God of the Bible. The expressions are typical Hebrew superlatives, and do not hint at the real existence of other gods or lords. God is further identified as the One **who alone doeth great wonders** (4), who **by wisdom made the heavens** (5) and **stretched out the earth above the waters** (6), a reference to Gen. 1:2, 7-10. God also created **great lights** (7), **the sun . . . by day** (8), **the moon and stars . . . by night** (9). This again is in direct reference to the language of Gen. 1:14-18.

2. The Redeemer God (136:10-26)

Verses 10-22 are a very close paraphrase of 135:8-12, with the insertion of the refrain after each line. God is to be praised for His deliverance of His people from **Egypt** and from **the Red sea (10-15).** A **strong hand** and **stretched out arm** (12) would be God's manifest power. He **led his people through the wilderness,** overthrowing the tribal **kings** who attempted to interfere (16-20), giving their territories to His people as their **heritage** (21-22). **In our low estate** (23) is better "when we were humiliated" (Harrison). God's creative and redemptive acts in the past are supplemented by His providential provisions in the present: **He giveth food to all flesh** (25). He is **the God of heaven** (26), a phrase that occurs only here in the Psalms, but often in the later books of the OT (e.g., II Chron. 36:23; Ezra 1:2; 5:11-12; 6:9; etc.; Neh. 1:4-5; 2:4; Dan. 2:18, 44; 5:23; Jonah 1:9).

Psalm 137: THE LAMENT OF AN EXILE, 137:1-9

This psalm has proved to be one of the most controversial in the Psalter by reason of the bitterly strong and quite unrelieved imprecatory note at the end. Without attempting to gloss over the pre-Christian character of this vindictive element, there is wisdom in Morgan's comment: "The prayer for vengeance must be interpreted by the first part of the song, with its revelation of the treatment they received. It must, of course, be interpreted by the times in which they lived. Our times are different. We have more light. And yet it is well to remember that the deepest sense of justice still makes punishment a necessary part of the economy of God. That conception of God which denies the equity of retribution is false."[91]

Oesterley states: "The clash of emotions expressed in the psalm reveals human nature at its best and at its worst. Sorrow at the thought of being hindered from singing the praises of God in the sanctuary where his presence rested was the outcome of deep devotion to him, and reveals a heart imbued with all that is best.... The dominant note ... of the psalm is a truly religious one, and witnesses to the loyalty of those who, in the land of their captivity, were surrounded by subtle temptations, but who withstood them in the strength of that loyalty."[92]

1. Yearning for Jerusalem (137:1-6)

Far from his beloved homeland, the exile **wept** over his memories of **Zion**, city of his God (1). On **the rivers of Babylon,** Kirkpatrick comments: "Characteristically a land of streams, as Palestine was a land of hills; it was the feature of the country which would impress itself upon the mind of the exiles. Cp. Jer. li. 13. They may have resorted to the banks of the rivers and canals to mourn; partly for the sake of the shade of the trees which grew there, partly because such places were suitable to melancholy meditation."[93] They hung their **harps upon the willows** (2; the branches of the trees) there because all joyful song was gone.

The bitterness of exile was increased by the scorn of the Babylonians with their taunting demand for **one of the songs of Zion** (3). The issue was not just one of simulating mirth in the midst of sorrow, but of amusing their pagan neighbors with **the Lord's song** (4), the Temple hymns that would be profaned if sung in a strange land. Should Jerusalem ever dim in his affections, the exiled singer invokes dire consequences upon himself— his **right hand** to **forget her cunning** (5) and his **tongue** to **cleave to the roof of** his **mouth** (6). These would be calamities indeed

[91]Op. cit., p. 273.   [92]Op. cit., pp. 548-49.
[93]Op. cit., p. 781.

for the musician who plucks the strings of his lyre and sings to the glory of God.

2. The Doom of Zion's Foes (137:7-9)

Against the background of longing for Zion, the exile lapses into bitter condemnation of Zion's foes. "The new law, 'Thou shalt love thine enemy,' had not yet taken the place of the old maxim, 'Thou shalt love thy neighbour and hate thine enemy.' The law of stern retribution for cruel wrong seems to the Psalmist only just, and the peculiarly barbarous form in which he expresses his desire for the extermination of the destroyer of his country is only such as was familiar to his age."[94]

Verse 7 has historical reference to the fall **of Jerusalem.** Although the Edomites had taken no active part in the destruction of the city, they had rejoiced in it and had urged the enemy to complete its ruin (cf. Obad. 10-16). **Rase it, rase it** is literally, "Lay it bare," tear it down right to the foundations.

The chief imprecation is reserved for the Babylonians, whose destruction is predicted (8). The enemy will reap as he has sown. The OT and ancient history are replete with illustrations of the utter disregard for human life practiced in ancient warfare where extermination of the entire enemy people was the goal. Neither women nor children were spared. What Babylon had done to Jerusalem was to be done to her. Cf. introduction to this psalm and discussion of the imprecatory psalms in the introduction to the book. While these imprecatory elements occur in the Psalms, let it be recorded to the credit of the Jewish rabbis that they never included these passages in their synagogue ritual.

Psalm 138: A PSALM OF THANKSGIVING, 138:1-8

This is the first of a series of eight psalms whose titles or superscriptions refer them to David. Although generally considered postexilic in date, there is really no compelling reason why Alexander's judgment should not be accepted that these psalms are "probably the last composed by David, a kind of commentary on the great Messianic promise in 2 Sam. vii."[95] The present psalm is one of pure thanksgiving, and expresses the poet's thanks for God's promise (2), His pity (3a), His power (3b), His protection (7), and His persistence (8).[96]

---

[94]*Ibid.*, pp. 779-80.   [95]*Op. cit.*, p. 536.
[96]Suggested by Carl N. Hall.

1. Praise for God's Word and Name (138:1-3)

The Psalmist determines to utter God's **praise** with his **whole heart** (1). There are no limitations or qualifications in his mind with regard to the worthiness of his Lord. **Before the gods** is not a concession to polytheism (the worship of many gods), but a literal translation of a Hebrew word that may apply to any supernatural beings or even to men of exalted rank or power (cf. comment on 82:1). No company is too exalted to hear the poet's song of praise. **Worship toward thy holy temple** (2) was a Jewish custom indicated in Solomon's prayer of dedication (II Chron. 6:20) and was the practice of Daniel (Dan. 6:10). The Temple was the visible representation of God's presence among His people, and as such received special respect from the devout.

Thou hast magnified thy word above all thy name translates a somewhat ambiguous Hebrew word order which is literally, "Thou hast magnified above all thy name thy word." Feeling a difficulty in asserting that anything should be exalted above the name of the Lord, which ordinarily denotes His nature, several translate the words, "Thou hast magnified thy name and thy word above all things" (English Prayer Book Version); "Thou hast exalted above everything thy name and thy word" (RSV); "You have exalted Your name and Your word above all else" (Harrison). To relate the Word with the name of the Lord is to pay it the highest possible tribute. The Psalmist rejoices in the immediate answer the Lord gives. Whatever the outward circumstances might be, God gives **strength in** the **soul** (3; cf. Eph. 3:16).

2. Praise for God's Sovereign Rule (138:4-6)

The Lord is King of Kings and Lord of Lords (cf. Rev. 17:14; 19:16), and when they learn of His wondrous works toward His people, **all the kings of the earth shall praise** Him (4). **Sing in the ways of the Lord** (5) is better "sing of the ways of the Lord" (RSV). God's exalted majesty does not prevent Him from having **respect unto the lowly** (6), that is, concern for the humble. **The proud he knoweth** (sees their nature) **afar off—** they cannot escape His all-knowing eye.

3. Praise for God's Help in Trouble (138:7-8)

The closing verses are the Psalmist's personal conviction that the Lord will see him through trouble and opposition. Walking **in the midst of trouble** (7), he finds the Lord with him to **revive** him—to give him renewed life, or as *The Berkeley Version,* "Thou bringest me through alive." God will defend him against all his enemies. **The Lord will perfect that which concerneth me** (8) is better "will accomplish His promises and purposes for me."[97] **Forsake not the works of thine own hands,** i.e., works begun in behalf of the Psalmist and his people. What God has begun He will complete.

Psalm 139: THE WONDER OF THE LORD, 139:1-24

Psalm 139, deservedly, has been highly praised. Rabbi Aben Ezra is reported to have acclaimed it "The Crown of all the Psalms." M'Caw says, "This is one of the finest poems in the Psalter; it is outstanding both theologically and psychologically."[98] Oesterley writes, "For the conceptions regarding the Divine Nature, the omniscience, and the omnipresence of God, this psalm stands out as the greatest gem in the Psalter. Parallels to it have been thought to exist in Babylonian and other sacred writings of the past; but in the religious literature of the ancient world it is unique."[99] McCullough states, "This poem is not only one of the chief glories of the Psalter, but in its religious insight and devotional warmth it is conspicuous among the great passages of the OT. As a psalm, it is difficult to classify. It has some of the qualities of a hymn and of a psalm of trust, but it is perhaps best considered as a personal prayer. . . . The psalmist is deeply impressed with the omniscience and omnipresence of the Lord, not however as formal attributes of a sovereign God, but as what he has found to be true in his own experience."[100]

1. *God's Omniscience* (139:1-6)

The Psalmist stands in manifest wonder at the fact that God knows all that concerns him. God had **searched** him (1), looked him through and examined his motives. **Downsitting and . . . uprising** (2), that is, his whole life, whether in rest and relaxation or in activity. **My thought afar off,** Harrison suggests, means "my thoughts when scarcely formulated." **Thou compassest my path and my lying down** (3) is better, "Walking or resting, I am scanned by thee" (Moffatt). Kirkpatrick comments

---

[97]Kirkpatrick, *op. cit.,* p. 785. [98]*Op. cit.,* p. 506.
[99]*Op. cit.,* p. 553. [100]*Op. cit.,* 4:712.

on **there is not a word . . . but . . . thou knowest it altogether**
(4): "God knows not merely the spoken word which men can
hear, but its true meaning, and the secret thoughts which prompt
its utterance."[101] **Beset** (5) is the word used of besieging a city.
The Psalmist sees himself surrounded, "hemmed in," by God.
Moffatt translates, "Thou art on every side, behind me and before, laying thy hand on me." **Knowledge** such as this is far
beyond the attainment and even the comprehension of man (6).

2. God's Omnipresence (139: 7-12)

The all-knowing God is ever and everywhere present. There
is no successful flight from Him. His **spirit** and His **presence** are
all-pervading (7). Neither **heaven** above nor **hell** (*Sheol*, the
place of the dead) are "off limits" to the Lord (8). Neither **the
wings of the morning** nor **the uttermost parts of the sea** (9) can
carry one beyond or be out of reach of God's **right hand** to **lead**
and to **hold** (10).

> *I know not where His islands lift*
> *Their fronded palms in air;*
> *I only know I cannot drift*
> *Beyond His love and care.*[102]

Darkness itself is no **cover,** for **even the night shall be light
about me** (11) and **darkness and light are both alike** to God
(12). The omnipresence of God is one of the clearly defined
doctrines of systematic theology. "By omnipresence we mean
that God is not excluded from anything on the one hand, or
included in anything on the other."[103] Wiley quotes Thomas
Aquinas, "God is in all things, not indeed as a part of their
essence, nor as an accident, but as an agent is present to that
upon which it works," and adds, "God is present wherever there
is a manifestation of His power."[104]

3. God's Personal Concern (139: 13-16)

The all-knowing and all-present God is personally concerned
with every detail of the Psalmist's life. God knows him in every

---

[101]*Op. cit.,* p. 787.

[102]John Greenleaf Whittier, from "The Eternal Goodness."

[103]H. Orton Wiley, *Christian Theology* (Kansas City, Mo.: Beacon Hill
Press, 1940), I, 345.

[104]*Ibid.,* pp. 346-47.

aspect of his being, for it was the Lord who **possessed** his **reins** (13; "form my being," Moffatt), and **covered** him, i.e., watched over his development even in his **mother's womb.** The expression **fearfully and wonderfully made (14)** is a judgment that modern man, with all his scientific knowledge of human anatomy, cannot surpass. **Curiously wrought (15)** is from an old English usage derived from the Latin *curiosus,* "wrought with care." **In the lower parts of the earth** would be "in the womb, as dark and mysterious as the nether world. The formation of the body is meant, and there is no reference to the doctrine of the preexistence of souls."[105]

In thy book all my members were written, which in continuance were fashioned (16) has been difficult to translate and interpret, as is seen in the variety of versions. "All the days of my life were foreseen by thee, set down within thy book" (Moffatt). "In thy book were written, every one of them, the days that were formed for me" (RSV). "In Thy book all was recorded and prepared day by day" (Berk.). "In Your record were assessed the days that were intended for me" (Harrison).

The analytical modern mind has some difficulty reconciling God's foreknowledge of life with the real freedom of choice left to man, but the biblical writers felt no such difficulty. With them, it was sufficient to proclaim that God knows the end from the beginning without thereby predetermining that end. Yet even modern man, fully convinced of freedom of choice, can find comfort in the truth that nothing takes God by surprise. He knows the future unknown to us, and can therefore guide us through its trackless ways if we are responsive to His leadership.

4. *God's Providential Control* (139:17-22)

Conscious of the all-pervading will of God, the Psalmist was also persuaded that God's will is "good, and acceptable, and perfect" (Rom. 12:2). God's **thoughts** toward him are **precious** to him (17), and **more in number than the sand (18).** **When I awake, I am still with thee** may be understood either, as Moffatt, "I wake from my reverie, and I am still lost in thee"; or, as Harrison and RSV, marg., "If I came to the end, I would still be with You." Neither reverie, sleep, nor death itself can separate the trusting soul from the Lord.

[105]Kirkpatrick, *op. cit.,* p. 789.

The obverse side of God's love and care for the righteous is never very far from the poet's mind. The providence that protects the righteous condemns and ultimately destroys **the wicked** (19). A high sense of the holiness of God results in a deep conviction of the awfulness of sin. **Bloody men** are men of violence and murder. The Psalmist strongly affirms his **hatred** of evildoers and their ways (21-22). Caution must be exercised at this point, to be sure, lest hatred of evil be subtly transformed into hatred of the persons of the evildoers rather than of the evil that they do. Yet it remains that to love righteousness is to hate evil. Christians, no less than OT men, must not lose a capacity for holy anger in the face of stark evil.

5. *A Concluding Prayer* (139: 23-24)

The prayer with which the psalm concludes is one of the most beautiful and meaningful in the entire Psalter. As if aware of the danger that his hatred or evil might unconsciously slip over into an attitude in itself displeasing to God, the Psalmist bares his heart to the Lord. **Try me, and know my thoughts** (23) is better, "Ascertain my motives" (Harrison). **See if there be any wicked way in me** (24) is literally "any way of grief," or "any hurtful way," "any way that would become hateful or grievous."[106] It is not that our writer suspects the presence within him of actual wickedness. His fear is that in weakness or by carelessness he may grieve God. Safeguarded from the wicked way, he aspires to be led in **the way everlasting**. A worthy prayer expresses the three petitions here made: (1) **Search me;** (2) **Try me;** (3) **Lead me.**

> Search me, O God, and know my heart today;
> Try me, O Saviour, know my thoughts, I pray;
> See if there be some wicked way in me:
> Cleanse me from every sin, and set me free.[107]

Psalm 140: A Prayer for Deliverance, 140: 1-13

Psalm 140 is another of a rather substantial number of psalms which reflect the existence within Israel of some very bitter cross-currents of antagonism and persecution. Some of the enemies to which the psalms refer were Gentiles. Most of them were fellow Jews whose apostasy took the form not only of re-

---

[106]M'Caw, *op. cit.*, p. 508.   [107]J. Edwin Orr in "Cleanse Me."

jecting the exclusive lordship of Jehovah but also of persecuting those who were true to Him.

Oesterley writes: "It would be unreasonable to expect to find in the *Psalms* the Christian ideal of a man's attitude toward his enemies: 'Love your enemies, and pray for them that persecute you' (Matt. 5:44); but in this psalm we have the next best thing to it; for there is no hint of the desire of any personal retaliation against the vindictive enemies of the psalmist; all is left in the hands of God. That there should be some words of bitterness is natural enough; but the passive attitude of the victim of oppression himself reveals a spirit of true godliness."[108]

1. The Violence of the Wicked (140:1-3)

The poet prays for deliverance and protection against **evil** and **violent** men (1). **Imagine mischiefs in their heart** (2) is better "scheme evil in their minds" (Harrison). **Gathered together for war** may be translated, "All the day they stir up wars" (Perowne), or "constantly stir up warfare" (Berk.). The poisoned words of his detractors remind the poet of the sharp tongue of **a serpent** and the **poison** of an adder (3). **Selah;** cf. comment on 3:2.

2. Prayer for Preservation (140:4-5)

In circumstances like these the Psalmist wisely puts himself and his reputation in the hands of God. He prays to be preserved from those who **have purposed to overthrow** his **goings** (4), or "plotted to trip my feet" (Berk.). Evil men are consistently identified in the psalms as **the proud** (5). Some professing Christians have argued that "a little sin keeps men humble," but the biblical writers were wiser than they. They saw that sin in its essence is pride, the manifestation of arrogant independence from God. **Snare . . . cords . . . net . . . gins** are all descriptive of the equipment of the trapper or hunter.

3. In God Is Salvation (140:6-8)

The Psalmist recounts his commitment to **the Lord** as his **God** and asks a hearing for his petitions (6). **O GOD the Lord** (7; *Yahweh Adonai*) is an unusual phrase in the Hebrew. It occurs elsewhere only in 68:20; 109:21; 141:8; and Hab. 3:19. Both *Yahweh* and *Adonai* are regularly translated "Lord" in most

---

[108]*Op. cit.,* pp. 560-61.

English versions, capital letters being used to indicate the Hebrew Yahweh. When both occur together as in thes'e instances, either "Jehovah Lord" (Berk.) or "Lord, my Lord" (RSV) would be better. **Covered my head in the day of battle** means "afforded me protection in time of conflict" (Harrison). God is implored not to allow success to **the desires** and devices **of the wicked** (8).

4. The Wicked and the Righteous (140:9-13)

The respective destinies of the evil and the righteous are contrasted in the last stanza. The general principle of retribution for the wicked is that their wickedness returns to curse them, and their sin becomes its own punishment. **The mischief of their own lips shall cover them** ("overwhelm them," RSV; 9). **Let burning coals fall upon them** (10) refers to "the fate of Sodom."[109] **Cast into the fire; into deep pits** is an uncertain Hebrew construction, but obviously indicating total and utter calamity for which there is no remedy. **Let not an evil speaker be established** (11) means that he shall not prosper or flourish. Rather his own **evil,** devised for others, will **hunt** him down and **overthrow him.**

The poem closes on a positive note. The doom of the wicked is the dark background against which the blessedness of the righteous is painted. God's justice certifies that, whatever the vicissitudes of the present, in the end it will be well with those who put their trust in Him. **The Lord will maintain the cause** (12) is better "champions the rights of" (Moffatt). **The afflicted** and **the poor** have always been objects of God's special care, a fact reflected over and over throughout the Psalms (cf. 9:18; 10:2; 18:27; 22:24; 35:10; etc.). **The righteous** will have occasion to **give thanks,** and **the upright** are assured that they **shall dwell** in God's **presence** (13).

Psalm 141: Deliverance from Sin and Wicked Men, 141:1-10

This is a psalm of lament with a strong penitential element in it, although it is not listed among the penitential psalms as such (cf. Intro.). It is the prayer of one who recognizes that his only hope of survival in the face of bitter assault lies in keeping himself free from sin. It has some direct points of affinity

[109]Kirkpatrick, op. cit., p. 795.

with Psalm 140 (e.g., vv. 9-10 in relation to 140:5). **The general framework and setting are the same.**

1. *Preservation from Evil* (141:1-4)

The first stanza of the poem is a prayer for preservation from evil. The Psalmist desires a quick response to his **cry** (1), and would have his **prayer . . . set forth before** the Lord **as incense** (2). The words **set forth** mean "prepared" or "set in order" as **the evening sacrifice** was prepared and offered with incense (cf. Exod. 30:7-8; Lev. 2:2). **The lifting up of . . . hands** was the customary attitude of prayer (28:2; 63:4; I Tim. 2:8). Of particular concern to the Psalmist is grace to resist temptation to sin whether in word or in work. He prays for a guard on his **lips** (3). The prayer, **Incline not my heart to any evil thing** (4), would better be translated, "Let not my heart incline to evil" (Berk.). The inclination of the heart toward evil would not be God's act. His grace is needed to overcome that inclination, a grace described particularly in the NT as sanctification (I Thess. 4:7-8; 5:23-24). **Wicked works** involve and grow out of association **with men that work iniquity. To eat of their dainties** would be "to sample their pleasures" (Harrison).

2. *The Fellowship of the Righteous* (141:5-8)

In place of association with the wicked, the poet would substitute the fellowship of **the righteous.** Should they **smite** him by deserved reproof, it would **be a kindness** (5). **An excellent oil, which shall not break my head** means that their reproof would be healing, rather than wounding in any adverse sense. **Yet my prayer also shall be in their calamities** is a rendition of a sentence in the Hebrew text most difficult to understand, as the variety of the versions illustrates. Moffatt's suggestion is most plausible, "I would pray ever to have their goodwill." Verses 6-7 are hard to relate to the balance of the poem. Probably the best paraphrase would recognize a transition to discussion of the wicked again, and indicate that **when their judges** (leaders of the enemies) are destroyed, the truth of the Psalmist's **words** will be recognized (6). The connection of 7 is not clear, but it would seem to picture temporary desolation of the righteous. Even so, in all the circumstances of life, the poet puts his **trust in the Lord** and is confident that he will not be left desolate (8).

3. Peril from Evildoers (141:9-10)

The concluding verses are a prayer for deliverance from the subtle traps set for the righteous by those who are workers of iniquity. **Gins (9)** is an obsolete term for traps. **The wicked will fall into their own nets** (traps) while the man of God will **escape** them (10).

Psalm 142: FROM TROUBLE TO TRIUMPH, 142:1-7

This is another psalm of lament in which the Psalmist pours out his heart in prayer to the Lord. The title identifies it as a "maschil of David" (cf. intro. to Psalm 32) when "he was in the cave," a reference similar to the title of Psalm 57 (q.v.). He feels his situation to be desperate, yet the very act of praying turns his thought toward the deliverance so keenly desired. "Notable is the fact that in spite of his sufferings, the psalmist utters no vindictive cry for vengeance, an attitude not infrequently found in other psalms."[110]

1. The Psalmist's Problem (142:1-2)

In deep trouble, the poet cried aloud to the Lord. Two references are made specifically to the fact that this was a verbalized prayer (1). Oesterley comments, "The uttering of private prayer aloud, as here taught, is something worth thinking about. . . . The fact cannot be denied that the sound of one's own voice in prayer tends to realism and sincerity. It helps to envisage the nearness of God, the apprehension of which must be the yearning of every true believer. . . . One other thing which this beautiful little psalm teaches is the blessedness and comfort of telling one's troubles to God; a fearless, intimate intercourse with God is a means of union with him, which sanctifies a life and all life's activities."[111] **I poured out my complaint before him** (2)—the proper place to bring most of our "complaints."

2. The Psalmist's Prayer (142:3-5)

The content of the prayer is given in words addressed directly to the Lord. At the time of his deepest distress, God knew his **path** (3). That the Lord knows does not mean simply

---

[110]Oesterley, op. cit., p. 564.   [111]Ibid., p. 565.

that He takes cognizance of or is informed about, but that He
cares and is concerned. **Privily laid a snare,** i.e., "hidden a
snare" (Perowne). All human reliance had failed. **I looked on
my right hand** (4), where a counsellor or defender would stand,
but there was no one there. **No man that would know me** means
that none would acknowledge acquaintance with him. He stood
absolutely alone. **No man cared for my soul** is a tragically
pathetic plaint. Christians, burdened for the salvation of loved
ones or neighbors, might well determine within themselves that
no one within their sphere of influence shall honestly echo these
words. In his desolation, the Psalmist turned to the Lord. Forsaken by all others, he could still testify, **Thou art my refuge and
my portion in the land of the living** (5); Moffatt renders it,
"Thou art my help, I have thee as my very own, in the land of
the living."

3. *The Psalmist's Prospect* (142:6-7)

The prayer takes on added urgency, and rises to specific
requests for the future. It closes with an expression of faith.
From the depths, the poet pleads for deliverance from powerful
persecutors (6). **Bring my soul out of prison** (7) has been
thought by some to represent an actual imprisonment such as
suffered by Jeremiah for his faith. It may just as well be used
figuratively for relief from extreme distress. Isolated from his
companions as he had been, the writer looks forward in expectation to the time when the **righteous shall compass** him **about,**
that is, surround him. He is confident that the Lord will **deal
bountifully** (generously or kindly) **with** him.

Psalm 143: LONGING AND LIVING FOR THE LORD, 143:1-12

This psalm is the last of the seven "penitential" psalms (cf.
Intro.). It expresses the plea of the penitent that "judgment may
be tempered with mercy." The desolation of the Psalmist's spirit
is coupled with determination to do the will of God as the Lord
may enable him so to do. From the fact that the psalm borrows
many thoughts and phrases from earlier psalms, Perowne concludes that the title is to be understood as representing the spirit
and mood of the Davidic psalms rather than his immediate
authorship. He adds, "It is a witness to us of the depth and
reality also of the religious life in the later history of the nation,
and an evidence also of the way in which that life was upheld and

cherished by the inspired words of David and other Psalmists and prophets of old."[112]

1. Longing for the Lord (143:1-6)

The poem opens with a plea for audience with the Lord and for an answer in God's **faithfulness** and **righteousness** (1). Convicted of his guilt, the Psalmist prays that God will not **enter . . . into judgment with** him (2); Harrison interprets it, "Do not summon Your servant for sentence." **In thy sight shall no man living be justified**—this is basic to the theology of both the OT and the NT. "All have sinned, and come short of the glory of God" (Rom. 3:23); "God hath concluded them all in unbelief, that he might have mercy upon all" (Rom. 11:32); "If we say that we have not sinned, we make him a liar, and his word is not in us" (I John 1:10). On the other hand, these words must not be taken to deny the triumph of grace in human life and to argue for a religion of perpetual sinning and perpetual forgiveness. They mean what they say; they do not mean more than they say.

The poet sees in the oppression of his enemies an added burden, and possibly one permitted because of his own spiritual failures (3). **Smitten my life down to the ground** is better "trampled me to the ground" (Harrison). **To dwell in darkness, as those that have been long dead** reflects the prevailing view of *Sheol*, the place of the dead, as a realm of shades and darkness. Even in life, the poet tastes the bitterness and deprivation of death. His **spirit**, therefore, is **overwhelmed** (4), literally, has fainted; and his **heart . . . is desolate**, "grows numb within" him (Moffatt).

In this extremity, he remembers better **days** (5). He meditates on the **works** of the Lord, and stretches forth his **hands** to God (6) in prayer and as a gesture of desire. His thirst for the Lord is like the thirst of desert **land** for refreshing rain and springs of water. **Selah;** cf. comment on 3:2.

2. Living for the Lord (143:7-12)

The penitential character of the psalm is seen not only in the sense of spiritual desolation and thirsting for God. It also appears in the sincere prayer for grace to live in ways pleasing to the Lord. There is no genuine penitence without a purpose for

[112]*Op. cit.*, II, 459.

the amendment of life. Sorrow for past sins may be no more than "the sorrow of the world" if it is lacking in a genuine desire to do differently in the future (II Cor. 7:10). The Psalmist sees clearly that unless help comes **speedily** (7), he will **be like unto them that go down into the pit**—words borrowed from 28:1. **The pit** is a synonym for *Sheol*, the place of the dead, which was always thought of as down, located beneath the surface of the earth.

Verse 8 petitions for the revelation of God's **lovingkindness in the morning**, and for knowledge of **the way wherein he should walk.** The answers are sought on the basis of faith and continuing prayer: **In thee do I trust . . . I lift up my soul unto thee.** **Lovingkindness** (*chesed*) means mercy, grace, covenant love, or "steadfast love" (RSV); cf. comment on 17:7. **In the morning** speaks of the light that is to follow the dark night of despair, in whose darkest moments the poet was even then living. Deliverance and refuge are both to be found in God alone (9).

Teach me to do thy will (10), is a worthy prayer for every devout soul. Alignment with the will of God is the greatest good the soul can know. The fact that the Lord is **God** makes His will both duty and delight to His people. **Thy spirit is good; lead me . . .** would better be translated, "May Thy good Spirit lead me on level ground" (Berk.). "As many as are led by the Spirit of God, they are the sons of God" (Rom. 8:14). **Land of uprightness** is literally "land of the plain." **Quicken me** (11) means to "revive" or "give me life." A "new lease on life" and deliverance out of trouble are both for the sake of God's name and righteousness. Oesterley comments on **cut off mine enemies** (12): "The edifying character of the psalm is somewhat marred by the bitter spirit evinced in the concluding verse; the cruel treatment he is suffering from his enemies (see v. 3) must be pleaded in extenuation."[113]

Psalm 144: NATIONAL BLESSINGS, 144:1-15

This psalm is often classified as a "royal" or kingly psalm and deals as others of its type with some of the issues of national life. The title or superscription relates it to David, possibly from its resemblance to Psalm 18 and from the use of David's name in v. 10. It is a poem that has much for our day, since it expresses some of the moral and spiritual conditions upon which the true well-being of men and nations rests.

[113]*Op. cit.*, p. 566.

1. *The Lord Our Strength* (144:1-2)

The Lord is hailed as the Psalmist's **strength** (1; Heb., "rock"), his **goodness** (2), his **fortress**, his **high tower**, his **deliverer**, his **shield**, the object of his **trust**, and the One who gives him the loyalty of his **people**. These are all elements drawn from 18:1-2, 34, 47. They are the natural expressions of one accustomed to warfare in a rocky and mountainous land. The Psalmist attributes his military skills to the instruction of the Lord. Although intended, no doubt, quite literally, these ideas have applications to the Christian's warfare (cf. II Cor. 10:3-5; Eph. 6:10-17).

2. *The Weakness and Wickedness of Man* (144:3-8)

Verse 3 bears an obvious relation to 8:4, but is designed here chiefly to emphasize the fragile and transitory nature of life. **Like to vanity** (4) is literally, "a breath"; Harrison, "a puff of wind"; as insubstantial **as a shadow that passeth away.** In contrast to man's weakness is God's power manifest in nature. **Bow thy heavens** (5) probably refers to the lowering skies before a storm. Other awesome manifestations of power recalled are the volcanic eruption of **mountains** and **lightning** (6) bolts that flash as the **arrows** of divine wrath to **destroy** man and his works.

Man's weakness is matched only by his wickedness, from which the Psalmist prays for deliverance. **Thine hand** (7) would be God's power. **Great waters** is a figure for a flood of troubles. **Strange children** means strangers, foreigners, aliens. Men's mouths speak **vanity,** and even their oaths are not to be counted on (8). **Right hand is a right hand of falsehood** refers to the hand raised in the taking of a false oath; or, as Harrison, "whose hands transact treachery." Instead of a man's word being as good as his bond, neither his word nor his bond is dependable!

3. *A New Song* (144:9-10)

So confidently is victory over every foe anticipated that the poet pledges to **sing a new song unto** the Lord (9) accompanied on **a psaltery and an instrument of ten strings,** literally, "a harp with ten strings" (cf. comment on 32:2). The extent to which instrumental as well as vocal music is featured in the OT is seen most clearly in 150:3-5. God gives **salvation** (here, victory) and delivers **his servant from the hurtful sword** (10), "sword of evil" (Berk.), "cruel sword" (Harrison). A *Berkeley Version* footnote recalls that this has been understood by some as a reference to the sword of Goliath.[114] It represents, even more broadly, any sword or any military power in the service of evil.

4. A Happy Nation (144: 11-15)

Verse 11 is joined with the preceding stanza by many commentators and in most modern versions. As the KJV presents it, it is the precondition for the well-being of the nation, and so we consider it here. It is a repetition of the content of vv. 7-8 (cf. comments there). The blessings of national life are related directly to the welfare of **sons** and **daughters** (12) and temporal prosperity (13-14). **Sons . . . as plants grown up in their youth** (12) may mean either "straight and strong like saplings" (Moffatt) or "plants which develop quickly in their early stages." **Daughters . . . as corner stones** certainly means young women as beautiful as the ornaments **of a palace,** possibly in the sense of "tall and stately." "The psalmist's first consideration in an ideal society is for people. Then he turns to speak of full granaries and fields covered with flocks."[115]

The scene painted in 13-14 is natural to a rural people whose wealth consisted in fields and flocks and herds. **In our streets** (14) is better "in our pastures" (Berk.). Full **garners** (13), growing flocks of **sheep,** and strong **oxen** (14) represent a prosperous economy, an affluent society. Yet even so, peace is necessary, and the moral underpinnings are vitally important. **That there be no breaking in, nor going out** means "no hostile invasions of the country: or, no breach in the city walls by which the enemy may enter (Neh. vi.1). . . . No *going forth* to surrender to the enemy (Am. iv.3; 2 Kings xxiv.12), or into captivity (Jer. xxix.16): or no *sallying forth* to repel an attacking force."[116] **That there be no complaining in our streets** has been rendered, "May there be no disturbances in our city streets" (Harrison).

Such is the OT understanding of "the great society." **Happy is that people . . . in such a case** (15). But happiness is the lot only of **that people, whose God is the Lord.** More important than the blessings of affluence and a stable society are the blessings of loyalty to the true and living God. The foundations upon which

[114]*Ad loc.*   [115]Taylor, *op. cit.,* 4: 739.
[116]Kirkpatrick, *op. cit.,* p. 812.

the whole structure of national life must rest are laid deep on the solid rock of God's holy law. It is still true that "righteousness exalteth a nation: but sin is a reproach to any people" (Prov. 14:34).

Psalms 145: "GREAT IS THE LORD," 145:1-21

Psalm 145 is the last of the acrostic or alphabetical psalms. Each of the verses begins with a successive letter of the Hebrew alphabet, with the exception of the letter *nun*, which should come between vv. 13 and 14 but is missing. It is interesting to note that the LXX has an additional verse at this point that reads, "The Lord is faithful in his words, and holy in all his works." The Hebrew version of these words would begin with *nun*, and in all probability stood in the copy of the Hebrew text the LXX translators worked from.[117] The title of the psalm is the only one of its kind, using the word *tehillah*, "praise," or "hymn"; the plural (*tehillim*) is the Hebrew title for the entire Psalter.

In the Jewish liturgy, Psalm 145 is used in the daily prayers of the religious year. Simpson remarks, "It is easy to understand why this particular psalm should have come to occupy so important a place in the Jewish liturgy. Day in, day out, it is read twice in the morning and once in the afternoon service. The greatness of God, and his constant love for all who reverence him, are its recurrent themes. Its climax is reached in the affirmation that not only Israel ('my mouth') but the whole family of mankind ('all flesh') 'shall bless his holy Name for ever.' "[118] Oesterley says, "As a hymn of praise to God this psalm stands out as one of the most beautiful in the Psalter. What must particularly demand our sympathetic attention is the earnest attempt to depict the glory of God."[119]

1. A Hymn of Praise (145:1-7)

The first stanza is in direct address as a hymn of praise to God as **king** (1). Praise in the **name** of the Lord is fitting **every day . . . for ever and ever** (2). God's greatness is unsearchable (3), "limitless" (Harrison). **One generation** is to **praise** God's **works to another,** declaring His **mighty acts** (4)—here is another

---

[117]Barnes, *op. cit.,* II, 659. Perowne, on the other hand, believes the LXX translators intercalated the verse (*op. cit.,* II, 469).

[118]*Op. cit.,* p. 60.   [119]*Op. cit.,* p. 575.

charter verse for Christian education. The poet speaks of **the glorious honour** ("splendor," Berk.) **of** God's **majesty (5)**. The statement, **Men shall speak of the might of thy terrible acts (6)**, is better, "They will discuss the power which underlies Your miracles" (Harrison). God's acts inspire terror in the hearts of the godless, and wonder in the minds of His people. The **great goodness (7)** of God will be recalled, and men **shall sing of** His **righteousness.**

2. The Goodness and Grace of God (145:8-9)

These are words about the Lord, as compared with the direct address to Him in the first stanza. This magnificent description of the loving mercy and grace of God is drawn largely from the self-revelation of the Lord to Moses recorded in Exod. 34:6-7. **The Lord is gracious (8)** is literally kind, favorable, **and full of compassion,** "sympathetic" (Harrison). He is **slow to anger, and of great mercy** ("very kind," Moffatt). **The Lord is good to all (9)** in His provision for their needs, since **his tender mercies** ("compassion," RSV) **are over all his works.**

3. God's People Declare His Glory (145:10-16)

God's **works** and His **saints** ("faithful followers," Moffatt) join in declaring the praises of God (10). Especially is the **kingdom** of God magnified: its **glory** and **power (11)**, its **majesty (12)**, and its **everlasting . . . dominion (13)**. All are to be made **known to the sons of men (12)**, i.e., all mankind. With reference to 14, Perowne wrote, "The glory, the majesty, the eternity of God's kingdom, of which so much has been said—how are they manifested? Where is the conspicuous excellence of that kingdom seen? Not in symbols of earthly pride and power, but in gracious condescension to the fallen and the crushed, in the gracious care which provides for the wants of every living thing."[120]

> All thy creatures look to thee,
>   for their food in season due,
>   and from thine open hand
>   they feast upon thy favour (15-16, Moffatt).

The Psalmist was very conscious that "every good gift and every perfect gift is from above, and cometh down from the Father of

[120]*Op. cit.,* p. 511.

lights, with whom is no variableness, neither shadow of turning" (Jas. 1:17). He would keep all mindful that the good things they have are the gifts of God.

4. The Availability of God's Help (145:17-21)

The poet does not stop with God's provision in nature for the needs of all. He turns to the availability of God's help in the moral needs and crises of life. The righteousness and holiness of God (17) are both the standard and the hope of man. God is **near to all** (18) who **call upon him in truth** ("sincerely," Harrison). The only qualification is an earnest need and an honest heart. When the Psalmist wrote, **He will fulfil the desire of them that fear him** (19), he was of course aware of the fact that not all prayer is answered affirmatively or immediately. Yet those who truly fear Him seek constantly to bring their desires into harmony with God's will. It is no lack of faith that prays, "Nevertheless not as I will, but as thou wilt" (Matt. 26:39). The Lord **will hear their cry, and will save them** by the kind of deliverance appropriate to their immediate need. Preservation is the reward of those who **love** God, and destruction is the fate of **the wicked** (20). The Psalmist himself will **praise . . . the Lord** aloud, and he calls on **all flesh**—everything living—to **bless his holy name for ever and ever** (21).

Psalm 146: God Is Our Help, 146:1-10

This is the first of the "Hallelujah Psalms," 146—50, so-called because each of the five begins and concludes with the Hebrew *Hallelu-Yah*, "Praise ye the Lord!" All five have been used daily in the morning synagogue service from very early times. M'Caw writes, "The songs cxlvi-cl form an elaborate and comprehensive doxology to the whole Psalter. The element of petition and personal need disappears entirely; the historical factor in the nation's experience is reduced to a minor role. These Psalms are essentially 'praise-hymns,' and this characteristic is plainly indicated in the 'Hallelujah' which is both prologue and epilogue to each song in the group. In each case it is the Lord who is praised, but the divine attributes and activities which evoke this sustained adoration vary from one poem to another."[121]

At several points, Psalm 146 resembles 145. The most important of these are in v. 2 (145:2); vv. 5, 7 (145:15); v. 8 (145:

---

[121]*Op. cit.*, p. 511.

14); and v. 10 (145:13). It has been argued that vv. 3-4 picture conditions in the time of Nehemiah and later. However, one of Israel's constant temptations from the time of Solomon on was to put reliance on man and on foreign alliances rather than to trust in the Lord. It is, incidentally, a temptation not unknown in our day.

1. Our Only Help (146:1-4)

The psalm, as noted in the introduction, opens with the word Hallelu-Yah, **Praise ye Yah,** a frequent contraction of Yahweh, the personal name of the true and living God. This word (it was always written as one word by the Massoretes or scribes who copied the Scriptures) occurs in the OT only in the Psalms, and first in 104:35. It has come over into English as a Christian ejaculation of praise, "Hallelujah!" The Psalmist vows his constant **praise** to **God** as long as he has **being** (2). Neither **princes, nor . . . the son of man** are able to help in life's greatest crises. **The son of man** would be "mere mortals" (Moffatt). All, nobility and commoner alike, are destined to return to **his earth** (4), i.e., "to dust" (Harrison). It is true that the light of immortality was dim in OT times. However, **in that very day his thoughts perish** does not mean that he becomes extinct or devoid of consciousness. Rather, it means that his purposes or schemings come to nought.

2. God Is Able (146:5-10)

In contrast with the weakness and mortality of man are the greatness and eternity of God. **Happy** (5) indeed is the one who has **the God of Jacob for his help** ("to help him," Harrison). His **hope is** not in the puny might of men but **in the Lord his God,** Creator of the universe **and all that** is in it (6). **Keepeth truth for ever** is better "keeps faith forever" (Berk.). "This word emeth (truth) is closely related to the word for 'faithfulness' (emunah) and here connotes promise keeping and covenant faithfulness in His providential sustaining of the created universe."[122]

God's faithfulness is witnessed in that he **executeth judgment for** (vindicates) **the oppressed** (7); He supplies **food to the hungry,** liberates the captives, opens **the eyes of the blind** (8), and raises those who **are bowed down** in grief or despair.

[122]Berkeley Version, fn., ad loc.

The parallel with Isa. 61:1 and the miracles of Jesus is quite apparent. The Lord especially loves **the righteous.** He **preserveth the strangers** ("poor foreigners," Moffatt; 9); and "sustains the orphan and widow" (Harrison). **But the way of the wicked he turneth upside down,** frustrating their evil designs and bringing upon their own heads the mischief they plan for others. The eternal sovereignty of Zion's God is the guarantee that He is able to do as He has promised (10). Particularly impressive in these verses is the sixfold repetition of the name of *Yahweh,* "the Lord." **Praise ye the Lord,** *Hallelu-Yah,* Hallelujah!

Psalm 147: MEASURELESS POWER AND MATCHLESS GRACE, 147:1-20

Psalm 147 appears as two poems in the Greek OT (LXX), dividing between 11 and 12. There is, however, no more difference between the last stanza and the preceding two than is found in many of the psalms not so divided. The wide range of God's beneficent acts is the theme of the entire poem. Oesterley says, "The outpouring of a heart so full of gratitude for the marks of divine solicitude manifest in all around, must endear this psalm to all who, like this psalmist, look beneath the surface of things which happen in the world, whether in Nature or among men, and discern in them workings, infinitesimal as they may appear individually, of a divine plan of action."[123]

1. *God's Power in Redemption* (147:1-6)

Praise ye the Lord is *Hallelu-Yah,* Hallelujah! (Cf. comment on 146:1.) The construction differs here in that **Praise ye the Lord** (*Hallelu-Yah*) does not stand by itself as a call to praise, as it does in the other psalms of this group, but appears as part of the first sentence. **It is good** (the right thing to do) **and pleasant** (a source of joy) **to sing** God's **praises.** Such **praise is comely,** i.e., fitting and proper.

The varied dimensions of God's works are listed: He builds up **His holy city,** and **gathers Israel's** exiles together (2). He **heals the broken** hearted and **binds up their wounds** (3). **He telleth** (ascertains or determines) **the number of the stars** (4), and gives each its name. **His power is great** and **his understanding is infinite** (5). Harrison translates the verse, "Our Lord is

[123]*Op. cit.,* p. 578.

great, abounding in power, limitless in His wisdom." He lifts **the meek (6)**, literally, "the humble," but casts **the wicked down to the ground.**

2. *God's Power in Nature* (147:7-11)

The second stanza deals chiefly with God's power as manifest in the phenomena of nature. The stanza opens with another call to **sing unto the Lord with thanksgiving (7)**. To **sing praise upon the harp** means to sing to the accompaniment of the harp (*kinnor*), a small stringed instrument, the earliest and most common mentioned in the Bible. God is to be praised for giving **rain,** making **grass to grow (8)**, and providing **food** for beasts and birds **(9)**. Yet the Lord's delight is **not in the strength of the horse (10)** nor **in the legs** (athletic prowess) **of a man,** but in those who **fear him** and **hope in his mercy (11)**. All that nature offers is to the end that man may worship and trust his Creator.

3. *God's Power in History and Providence* (147:12-20)

Several different phases of God's action are cited as reasons why **Jerusalem** and **Zion** should **praise the Lord (12)**. He **strengthened the bars of thy gates (13;** the city's defenses) and **blessed** its inhabitants. He gave **peace** and provided **the finest of the wheat (14)**. For man's moral guidance and health, God sends **forth his commandment** and utters His swift-running **word (15)**. *The Berkeley Version* translates it, "His word speeds swiftly on its way." **Snow, hoarfrost (16),** ice, and **cold (17)** are subject to His will **(18)**. Man cannot cope with the bitter cold but God merely says the **word** and the ice **melteth.** But best of all, the Lord has made **his word** known **unto Jacob, his statutes and his judgments unto Israel (19)**. Hamilton interprets the verse, "He declared His promises to Jacob, His enactments and decrees to Israel." **He hath not dealt so with any nation (20)** means no other nation has been so favored. Israel was prone to forget, however, that much light means much responsibility, and that God's election was to service more than to privilege. For **praise ye the Lord** (*Hallelu-Yah*), cf. comment on 146:1.

Psalm 148: "HALLELUJAH, PRAISE JEHOVAH!" 148:1-14

This beautiful piece is notable for its orderly structure, and for its insight into the worship of God by the angelic hosts. It has become a biblical basis for the gospel song set to music by William J. Kirkpatrick.[124] In general, it proceeds from the heavens to the earth and calls upon all to "praise ye the Lord."

1. Praise to God from the Heavens (148:1-6)

Praise ye the Lord means "Hallelujah!" Cf. comment on 146:1. There is a series of *hallelu's* (**praise ye**) in vv. 1-4, calling for God's praise **from the heavens** and **in the heights** (of heaven) **by all his angels** and **all his hosts** (2), the **sun, moon,** and **stars** (3), the **heavens of heavens** (the highest heavens), and the **waters that be above the heavens** (4; the clouds), as per Gen. 1:6-7, the source of the beneficent rain.

> *Hallelujah, praise Jehovah!*
> *From the heavens praise His name.*
> *Praise Jehovah in the highest;*
> *All His angels, praise proclaim.*
> *All His hosts, together praise Him—*
> *Sun, and moon, and stars on high.*
> *Praise Him, O ye heav'n of heavens,*
> *And ye floods above the sky.*[125]

The claim to praise is based on the fact of God's creative work—**He commanded, and they were created** (5). Throughout Scripture, it is God's spoken word that calls into being the finite universe ("And God said"—Gen. 1:1, 6, 9, 11, etc.; Heb. 1:3; 11:3).

> *Let them praises give Jehovah;*
> *They were made at His command.*
> *Them forever He established;*
> *His decree shall ever stand.*[126]

2. Praise to God from the Earth (148:7-14)

The poet turns to the earth and calls on the **dragons** (7)— "sea monsters" (Berk.), "denizens of the deep" (Harrison)—and the ocean depths to join in praise to God. **Fire, and hail; snow, and vapours** (fog); and **stormy wind** are called to praise God by **fulfilling his word** (8). Inanimate (9) and animate nature (10),

---

[124]*Praise and Worship*, hymnal (Kansas City, Mo.: Lillenas Publishing Co., n.d.), No. 373.

[125]*Ibid.*   [126]*Ibid.*

together with all classes and ages of men (11-12), are summoned
to praise the Lord.

> *From the earth, oh, praise Jehovah,*
> *All ye floods, ye dragons all;*
> *Fire, and hail, and snow, and vapors,*
> *Stormy winds that hear Him call.*

> *All ye fruitful trees and cedars,*
> *All ye hills and mountains high,*
> *Creeping things and beasts and cattle,*
> *Birds that in the heavens fly;*
> *Kings of earth and all ye people,*
> *Princes great, earth's judges all;*
> *Praise His name, young men and maidens,*
> *Aged men, and children small.*[127]

God's **name**, the symbol of His nature, is to be praised, **for
his name alone is excellent** (13)—"His name alone is exalted
and supreme!" (Amp. Bible) **Exalteth the horn of his people**
(14) means increases their strength or raises their power. **His
saints** and **a people near unto him** are in parallel construction;
i.e., there is a sense in which the saints may be defined as the
people near the Lord. For **Praise ye the Lord** (*Hallelu-Yah*),
cf. comment on 146:1.

> *Let them praises give Jehovah,*
> *For His name alone is high,*
> *And His glory is exalted . . .*
> *Far above the earth and sky.*[128]

Psalm 149: PRAISE FOR SALVATION AND VINDICATION, 149:1-9

This short psalm presents sharply contrasting moods in its
two stanzas. In the first four verses we have a beautiful call to
worship. In the last five, there is a strong note of judgment
against the enemies of the people. While there is nothing in the
poem itself to indicate an occasion in the history of Israel, it is
thought by some that the psalm may have been composed to
celebrate a notable victory.[129] Taylor, on the other hand, inter-

---

[127]*Ibid.*   [128]*Ibid.*
[129]E.g., Oesterley, *op. cit.*, pp. 584-87.

prets the victory as that which saves the people from some kind of distress, not a military conquest.[130]

1. Praise to God for Salvation (149:1-4)

For **Praise ye the Lord** (1; *Hallelu-Yah*) cf. comment on 146:1. The song of the Lord is to be **a new song** (cf. 144:9; Isa. 42:10), not to make the old obsolete but to celebrate the fresh and up-to-date blessings of salvation. **The congregation of the saints** is the OT equivalent of the Church in the NT. God is to be worshipped as Creator and as **King** (2). The religious **dance** (3)—certainly not to be confused with the so-called "modern dance"—and joyous music are to be used in praise to God. The **timbrel** was "a kind of tambourine held and struck with the hand. It was used as an accompaniment to singing and dancing (Ex. xv. 20). It is always associated in the Old Testament with joy and gladness."[131] For **harp** cf. comment on 33:2. The reason for such praise is stated in a verse of rare charm: **For the Lord taketh pleasure in his people: he will beautify the meek with salvation** (4). In the immediate context, these words have been taken to refer to the victory alluded to in the next stanza. Thus RSV translates, "He adorns the humble with victory"; and Harrison renders the line, "He adorns the humble with triumph." Yet **salvation** in its full biblical meaning is a "beauty treatment" for the character, if not for the face and figure.

2. Praise to God for Vindication (149:5-9)

The saints are to be **joyful in glory** (5), or as Moffatt translates it, "exult over their triumph," praising God for the salvation and deliverance of the preceding verse. **Sing aloud upon their beds,** that is, "on the same beds on which they had wept out their laments during their days of oppression."[132] They are to have **the high praises of God . . . in their mouth, and a twoedged sword in their hand** (6). Readers of the NT will remember the reference to the Word of God as a "twoedged sword" (Heb. 4:12) and "the sword of the Spirit, which is the word of God" (Eph. 6:17). The fate of the enemies of the Lord is to be **vengeance**

---

[130]*Op. cit.,* 4:758-59.

[131]D. G. Stradling, "Music and Musical Instruments," *The New Bible Dictionary,* ed. J. D. Douglas, *et al.* (Grand Rapids, Michigan: Wm. B. Eerdmans Publishing Co., 1962), p. 856.

[132]*Berkeley Version,* fn., *ad loc.*

. . . **punishments** (7), binding **with chains and fetters of iron** (8), and the execution of **judgment** (9). **This honour have all his saints** is better, "He (the Lord) is the honor of all His saints" (Amp. Bible). For **Praise ye the Lord** (*Hallelu-Yah*), cf. comment on 146:1.

Psalm 150: DOXOLOGY: "PRAISE YE THE LORD," 150:1-6

The last psalm in the Book of Psalms is a fitting doxology to the whole. It is very probable that it was composed for just that purpose. Morgan calls it "the most comprehensive and illuminate illustration of perfect praise in the whole Psalter."[133] Oesterley wrote, "The triumphant strains resounding in this Hallelujah finale make a noble and fitting conclusion to the Psalms, the grandest symphony of praise to God ever composed on earth."[134] It is incidental but clear evidence of the abundant use of music and musical instruments in the Temple.

1. *Call to Praise* (150:1-2)

Praise ye the Lord (1; *Hallelu-Yah*) is Hallelujah! Cf. comment on 146:1. God is to be praised both **in his sanctuary** and **in the firmament of his power** ("in His majestic heaven," Harrison). He is to be praised **for his mighty acts** and for **his excellent greatness** (2); i.e., for "his mighty deeds" and "his sovereign strength" (Moffatt).

2. *The Instruments of Praise* (150:3-6)

Three types of instruments of music are to be employed in praise to God, wind, stringed, and percussion. Wind instruments include **the trumpet** (3), and **organs** (4) or pipes. Stringed instruments are **the psaltery and harp** (3). Percussion instruments include **the timbrel** (4), and **the loud** and **high sounding cymbals** of 5. **The trumpet** (*shophar*), "a long horn with a turned-up end, was the national trumpet of the Israelites. It was used on military and religious occasions to summon the people."[135] **The psaltery** (Heb., *nebel*) "was a kind of harp, as it is rendered in RSV, although its exact description is uncertain."[136] For **harp** cf. comment on 33:2. For **timbrel and dance** see comment on 149:3. **Organs** (*ugab*) were instruments of uncertain nature,

[133]*Op. cit.*, p. 277.   [134]*Op. cit.*, p. 587.
[135]Stradling, *op. cit.*, p. 855.   [136]*Ibid.*, p. 853.

but probably "some form of pipe or possibly a group of pipes."[137]
Cymbals (5; *tseltselim*) were "two shallow metal plates held one
in each hand and struck together."[138] The word is used twice
with different adjectives—**loud,** "resounding" (Moffatt), and
high sounding, "loud clanging" (Berk.). Not only instruments,
but voice is to be used in praising God by all **that hath breath**
(6). **Praise ye the Lord** (Hallelu-Yah), "Hallelujah!" Cf. comment on 146:1.

Kirkpatrick quotes Maclaren: "This noble close of the Psalter
rings out one clear note of praise, and is the end of all the many
moods and experiences recorded in its wonderful sighs and songs.
Tears, groans, wailings for sin, meditations on the dark depths
of Providence, fainting faith and foiled aspirations, all lead up to
this. The Psalm is more than an artistic close of the Psalter; it
is a prophecy of the last result of the devout life, and in its un-
clouded sunniness as well as in its universality, it proclaims the
certain end of the weary years for the individual and the world.
'Everything that hath breath' shall yet praise Jehovah."[139]

---

[137]*Ibid.*, p. 855.   [138]*Ibid.*
[139]*Op. cit.*, pp. 831-32.

Bibliography

I. COMMENTARIES

ALEXANDER, JOSEPH ADDISON. *The Psalms Translated and Explained.* Grand Rapids, Michigan: Zondervan Publishing House, n.d. (reprint).

BALLARD, FRANK H. "Psalms 90—150" (Exposition). *The Interpreter's Bible.* Edited by GEORGE A. BUTTRICK, et al., Vol. IV. New York: Abingdon Press, 1955.

BARNES, W. E. *The Psalms: With Introduction and Notes.* New York: E. P. Dutton and Company, Inc., n.d. Two volumes.

BRIGGS, CHARLES AUGUSTUS. *A Critical and Exegetical Commentary on the Book of Psalms.* "International Critical Commentaries." New York: Charles Scribner's Sons, 1906. Two volumes.

BUTTENWIESER, MOSES. *The Psalms: Chronologically Treated with a New Translation.* Chicago: University of Chicago Press, 1938.

DAHOOD, MITCHELL. *Psalms I (1—50).* "The Anchor Bible," edited by WILLIAM FOXWELL ALBRIGHT and DAVID NOEL FREEDMAN. Garden City, New York: Doubleday and Company, Inc., 1966.

DELITZSCH, FRANZ. *A Commentary on the Book of Psalms.* Translated by EATON and DUGUID. New York: Funk and Wagnalls, n.d. Three volumes.

EISELEN, FREDERICK C. *The Psalms and Other Sacred Writings.* New York: Methodist Book Concern, 1918.

FORSYTH, JOHN. "Psalms XLII—L." *A Commentary on the Holy Scriptures.* Edited by JOHN PETER LANGE. Grand Rapids: Zondervan Publishing House, n.d. (reprint).

KIRKPATRICK, A. F. *The Book of Psalms.* "The Cambridge Bible for Schools and Colleges." Cambridge: University Press, 1894.

LESLIE, ELMER. *The Psalms.* New York: Abingdon-Cokesbury Press, 1949.

M'CAW, LESLIE. "Psalms." *The New Bible Commentary.* Edited by FRANCIS DAVIDSON, et al. Grand Rapids, Michigan: Wm. B. Eerdmans Publishing Company, 1956.

MORGAN, G. CAMPBELL. *An Exposition of the Whole Bible.* Westwood, New Jersey: Fleming H. Revell Company, 1954.

McCULLOUGH, W. STEWART. "The Book of Psalms" (Introduction). *The Interpreter's Bible.* Edited by GEORGE A. BUTTRICK, et al., Vol. IV. New York: Abingdon Press, 1955.

————. "Psalms 72—92, 94, 97—99, 101—19, 139" (Exegesis). *The Interpreter's Bible.* Edited by GEORGE A. BUTTRICK, et al., Vol. IV. New York: Abingdon Press, 1955.

OESTERLEY, W. O. E. *The Psalms:* translated with text-critical and exegetical notes. London: S. P. C. K., 1953.

PEROWNE, J. J. STEWART. *The Book of Psalms.* Grand Rapids, Michigan: Zondervan Publishing House, 1966 (reprint). Two volumes.

POTEAT, EDWIN MCNEILL. "Psalms 42—89" (Exposition). *The Interpreter's Bible.* Edited by GEORGE A. BUTTRICK, et al., Vol. IV. New York: Abingdon Press, 1955.

RAPPOPORT, A. S. *The Psalms*. London: The Centenary Press, 1935.

RAWLINSON, GEORGE. "The Book of Psalms" (Exposition). *The Pulpit Commentary*. Edited by H. D. M. SPENCE and JOSEPH S. EXELL. Grand Rapids, Michigan: Wm. B. Eerdmans Publishing Company, 1950 (reprint). Two volumes.

SNAITH, NORMAN. *Hymns of the Temple*. London: SCM Press, Ltd., 1951.

TAYLOR, WILLIAM R. "Psalms 1—71, 93, 95—96, 100, 120—28, 140—50" (Exegesis). *The Interpreter's Bible*. Edited by GEORGE A. BUTTRICK, *et al.*, Vol. IV. New York: Abingdon Press, 1955.

TERRIEN, SAMUEL. *The Psalms and Their Meaning for Today*. New York: Bobbs-Merrill Co., 1952.

II. OTHER BOOKS

CARTLEDGE, SAMUEL A. *A Conservative Introduction to the Old Testament*. Second edition. Atlanta: University of Georgia Press, 1944.

CHASE, MARY ELLEN. *The Psalms for the Common Reader*. New York: W. W. Norton and Company, Inc., 1962.

DAVIDSON, A. B. *The Theology of the Old Testament*. Edinburgh: T. and T. Clark, 1904.

Holy Scriptures, The. Philadelphia: The Jewish Publication Society of America, 1958.

JACOB, EDMOND. *Theology of the Old Testament*. New York: Harper and Brothers, 1958.

JONES, EDGAR. *Proverbs and Ecclesiastes*. "Torch Bible Commentaries." New York: The Macmillan Company, 1961.

JONES, E. STANLEY. *Growing Spiritually*. Nashville: Abingdon Press, 1953.

KANT, IMMANUEL. *Critique of Practical Reason and Other Writings in Moral Philosophy*. Translated by LOUIS WHITE BECK. Chicago: University of Chicago Press, 1949.

KOHLER, LUDWIG. *Old Testament Theology*. Translated by A. S. TODD. Philadelphia: The Westminster Press, 1961.

LEWIS, CLIVE STAPLES. *Reflections on the Psalms*. New York: Harcourt, Brace and Company, 1958.

MOWINCKEL, SIGMUND. *The Psalms in Israel's Worship*. Translated by D. R. AP-THOMAS. New York: Abingdon Press, 1962. Two volumes.

OEHLER, GUSTAVE F. *Theology of the Old Testament*. Translated by GEORGE E. DAY. Grand Rapids, Michigan: Zondervan Publishing House (reprint).

PATERSON, JOHN. *The Praises of Israel*. New York: Charles Scribner's Sons, 1950.

Praise and Worship. Hymnal. Kansas City, Mo.: Lillenas Publishing Co., n.d.

PROTHERO, ROWLAND E. *The Psalms in Human Life*. New York: E. P. Dutton and Co., 1905.

RHODES, ARNOLD B. *Layman's Bible Commentary*. Edited by BALMER H. KELLY, *et al.* Richmond, Va.: John Knox Press, 1959.

ROBERTSON, JAMES. *Poetry and Religion of the Psalms*. London: William Blackwood and Sons, 1898.

ROBINSON, THEODORE H. *The Poetry of the Old Testament*. London: Gerald Duckworth and Co., Ltd., 1947.

ROWLEY, HAROLD H. *The Faith of Israel: Aspects of Old Testament Thought.* Philadelphia: The Westminister Press, 1956.

――. *The Unity of the Bible.* Philadelphia: The Westminster Press, 1953.

SCHULTZ, HERMANN. *Old Testament Theology.* Translated by J. A. PATERSON. Edinburgh: T. and T. Clark, 1909.

SIMPSON, WILLIAM W. *Jewish Prayer and Worship.* Naperville, Ill.: SCM Book Club, 1965.

SMITH, C. RYDER. *The Bible Doctrine of Man.* London: The Epworth Press, 1951.

――. *The Bible Doctrine of Salvation.* London: The Epworth Press, 1946.

――. *The Bible Doctrine of Sin.* London: The Epworth Press, 1953.

SNAITH, NORMAN. *The Distinctive Ideas of the Old Testament.* Philadelphia: The Westminster Press, 1946.

TOOMBS, LAWRENCE. *The Old Testament in Christian Preaching.* Philadelphia: The Westminster Press, 1961.

TURNER, GEORGE ALLEN. *The Vision Which Transforms.* Kansas City, Mo.: Beacon Hill Press of Kansas City, 1964.

VRIEZEN, TH. C. *An Outline of Old Testament Theology.* Boston, Mass.: Charles T. Branford Company, 1958.

WESLEY, JOHN. *A Plain Account of Christian Perfection.* Kansas City, Mo.: Beacon Hill Press of Kansas City, 1966 (reprint).

WILEY, H. ORTON. *Christian Theology.* Kansas City, Mo.: Beacon Hill Press, 1940. Three volumes.

WRIGHT, G. ERNEST. *God Who Acts: Biblical Theology as Recital.* Chicago: Henry Regnery Co., 1952.

YATES, KYLE M. *Preaching from the Psalms.* New York: Harper and Brothers, 1948.

――. *Studies in the Psalms.* Nashville: Broadman Press, 1953.

III. ARTICLES

STRADLING, D. G. "Music and Musical Instruments." *The New Bible Dictionary.* Edited by J. D. DOUGLAS, et al. Grand Rapids, Michigan: Wm. B. Eerdmans Publishing Co., 1962.

THOMPSON, J. G. S. S. "Psalms." *The New Bible Dictionary.* Edited by J. D. DOUGLAS, et al. Grand Rapids, Michigan: Wm. B. Eerdmans Publishing Co., 1962.

The Book of

PROVERBS

Earl C. Wolf

Introduction

The Book of Proverbs is an inspired anthology of Hebrew wisdom. This wisdom, however, is not merely intellectual or secular. It is mainly the application of the tenets of a revealed faith to the tasks of everyday living. In the Psalms we have the Hebrew's hymnbook; in Proverbs we have his manual for daily righteousness. In the latter we find practical and ethical guidelines for pure and undefiled religion. Jones and Walls say: "The proverbs in this book are not so much popular sayings as the distillation of the wisdom of teachers who knew the law of God and were applying its principles to the whole of life. . . . These are the words by the way for wayfaring men who are seeking to tread the way of holiness."[1]

A. AUTHORSHIP AND DATE

The Hebrew tradition ascribed the Book of Proverbs to Solomon just as it ascribed the Psalms to David. Israel thought of King Solomon as her sage *par excellence*. And there is sound justification for this acclaim. Solomon's forty-year reign in Israel was most brilliant. Granted these years were not without their mistakes. Solomon's multiple marriages were not to his credit (I Kings 11:1-9). In the latter portion of his reign he set the stage for the dissolution of his great empire (I Kings 12:10). Nevertheless, he reigned well in Israel's golden age of prosperity and power. Archaeology testifies to his skill in architecture and engineering, his competence in administration, and his ability as an industrialist.[2]

The sacred historian of I Kings tells us that Solomon loved the Lord (3:3); he prayed for an understanding heart (3:3-14); he demonstrated wisdom in the practical matters of administration (3:16-28); his wisdom was God-given (4:29); he was known for his superior wisdom by surrounding nations (4:29-34); he

[1]"The Proverbs," *The New Bible Commentary*, ed. F. Davidson (Grand Rapids: Wm. B. Eerdmans Publishing Co., 1953), p. 516.

[2]See Madeline S. and J. Lane Miller, *Harper's Bible Dictionary* (New York: Harper and Brothers, 1956), art. "Solomon," pp. 692-94; art. "Eziongeber," p. 182; art. "Gezer," pp. 223-25; art. "Hiram," p. 262; art. "Megiddo," pp. 434-36; art. "Millo," pp. 445-46; J. A. Thompson, *The Bible and Archaeology* (Grand Rapids: Wm. B. Eerdmans Publishing Co., 1962), pp. 100-107.

composed 3,000 proverbs and more than a thousand songs (4:32); and he was competent to handle the more difficult questions of the queen of Sheba (10:1-10).

Just as not all of the psalms, however, were written by David, so not all of the Book of Proverbs was the work of Solomon. A portion of the book is designated as "the words of the wise" (22:17—24:34). The last two chapters of the book contain the works of Agur, the son of Jakeh (30:1-33), and of Lemuel, king of Massa (31:1-9). The beautiful acrostic poem on the perfect wife and mother (31:10-31) was composed by an unknown writer. Conservative scholarship accepts the Solomonic authorship of the major portions of the Book of Proverbs and its inclusion as a whole into the Old Testament canon.

Critical scholarship, however, tends to reject the traditional ascription of a major portion of the Book of Proverbs to Solomon. W. O. E. Oesterley says: "Most modern critics reject entirely the tradition that Solomon composed a number of proverbs."[3] S. H. Blank comments: "It is not necessary to take seriously the attribution of Proverbs to Solomon in 1:1; 10:1; 25:1. . . . The canonical Proverbs of Solomon need have no more claim to genuine Solomonic authorship than the apocryphal Wisdom of Solomon."[4] Yet this same writer recognizes the growing tendency to accept the validity of the Jewish tradition. He says: "The possibility cannot be denied, and recent scholarly opinion inclines to the view that Solomon at best cultivated the proverbial art and was responsible for the kernel of the book ascribed to him."[5]

While major portions of the Book of Proverbs derive from the time of Solomon, in the tenth century B.C., the completion of the work cannot be dated earlier than 700 B.C., about two hundred fifty years after his reign. One section (25:1—29:27) contains the collection of proverbs which Hezekiah's scribes copied from earlier works of Solomon. Some scholars place the final editing of Proverbs still later but prior to the close of the Old Testament period—400 B.C. Others place it even in the intertestamental period. Reference to the Book of Proverbs in

---

[3]*The Book of Proverbs*, "Westminster Commentaries," editors, Walter Lock and D. C. Simpson (London: Methuen and Co., 1929), pp. xxi-xxii.

[4]"Book of Proverbs," *The Interpreter's Dictionary of the Bible*, Vol. K-G, ed. George A. Buttrick, et al. (New York and Nashville: Abingdon Press, 1962), p. 938.

[5]*Ibid.*, p. 939.

the apocryphal book, "The Wisdom of Jesus Son of Sirach" (Ecclesiasticus), written about 180 b.c., indicates that by this time Proverbs was widely accepted as a part of Israel's religious and literary tradition.

B. Definition and Literary Form

The word proverb in our day means a short, pithy saying expressing a valid or homely observation regarding human experience—for example, "A stitch in time saves nine." Benjamin Franklin's *Poor Richard's Almanac* is a representative collection of modern proverbs. To the ancient Hebrew, however, the word proverb (*mashal*) had a much wider meaning. It was used not merely to express a maxim but to interpret the ethical teachings of the faith of Israel. It is derived from a verb which means "to be like or to compare." Hence in the Book of Proverbs we find a variety of similes, contrasts, and parallelisms. The two-line parallelism is the predominant form found in Proverbs. Within this mode of expression is amazing variety. There are the antithetical parallelism (10:1), the synonymous parallelism (22:1), and the progressive parallelism (11:22). Such parallelism is found also in other portions of the Old Testament scriptures, notably in the Psalms.

In some portions of the Old Testament the *mashal* has still broader usages. In Judges it is used to describe a fable (9:7-21) and as a term for a riddle (14:12). In II Sam. 12:1-6 and Ezek. 17:2-10 it refers to a parable or allegory. In Jer. 24:9 it identifies a byword. In Isaiah it characterizes a taunt (14:4), and in Micah a lament (2:4).

The Book of Proverbs is cast in poetic form, the sayings appearing usually in couplets. Many of the modern-language translations and versions follow the poetic pattern of the original Hebrew. Outlining of the major sections of the book is not difficult (see outline). The contents, however, within these sections often defy orderly arrangement. Many times there is no logical connection between one proverb and those adjacent to it.

C. Proverbs and Other Wisdom Literature

The wisdom literature of the Old Testament includes the Book of Job, Ecclesiastes, and the Song of Solomon, as well as Proverbs. That this Hebrew wisdom had its antecedents in more primitive cultures and its counterparts among neighboring nations cannot be denied. Israel was situated "at the cultural crossroads of the Fertile Crescent."[6] Solomon and Hezekiah and the wise men of their day were in touch with their times and were no doubt aware of the extant wisdom literature.

Archaeology has given us a number of collections from ancient Egypt and Mesopotamia. Two of these are particularly significant—"The Words of Ahiqar" and "The Instruction of Amen-em-opet [Amenemope]." Because of the similarities of thought and structure between these writings and the Book of Proverbs critical scholars have inclined toward the opinion of direct or indirect dependence of the Hebrews upon this wisdom literature. These scholars call special attention to the similarities between Prov. 22:17—23:14 and "The Instruction of Amen-em-opet [Amenemope]."[7] Fritsch reminds us, however, that "we must not overlook the possibility that Prov. 22:17—23:14 as a unit was in existence long before its incorporation in the present book, and that it might have actually influenced the Egyptian scribe."[8]

Conservative scholarship rejects the view of the dependence of the Hebrew writers on the Egyptian literature on the basis that there are contrasts as well as similarities and certainly major theological differences. Kitchen says: "The total disagreement in order of topics and clear theological differences between Proverbs 22:1—24:22 and Amenemope preclude direct copying either way."[9] Edward J. Young believes that the polytheism of Amenemope would have been repulsive to the monotheistic Hebrew and would thus have precluded dependence on this Egyptian literature.[10]

D. RELEVANT MESSAGE

The message of the Book of Proverbs is ever relevant. Its teachings "sweep the whole horizon of practical everyday in-

[6]Bernhard W. Anderson, *Understanding the Old Testament* (Englewood Cliffs, N.J.: Prentice-Hall, 1957), p. 465.

[7]See John A. Wilson, trans., "Egyptian Instructions," *Ancient Near Eastern Texts Relating to the Old Testament*, ed. James B. Pritchard (Princeton: Princeton University Press, 1950), pp. 421-24; H. L. Ginsberg, trans., "Aramaic Proverbs and Precepts," pp. 427-30.

[8]"Proverbs" (Introduction), *The Interpreter's Bible*, ed. George A. Buttrick, *et al.*, IV (New York: Abingdon Press, 1955), 769.

[9]"Proverbs," *The Biblical Expositor*, II, consulting editor, Carl F. H. Henry (Philadelphia: A. J. Holman, 1960), 73.

[10]*An Introduction to the Old Testament* (Grand Rapids: Wm. B. Eerdmans Publishing Co., 1950), pp. 303-4.

terests, touching upon every facet of man's existence. Man is taught to be honest, industrious, self-reliant, a good neighbor, an ideal citizen, and a model husband and father. Above all, the wise man is to walk uprightly before the Lord."[11]

The wisdom of Proverbs puts God at the center of man's life. This wisdom, expressed by Solomon of the Old Testament, was to find its fuller revelation in Jesus Christ in the day of the new covenant. Said Jesus, "The queen of the south shall rise up in the judgment with the men of this generation, and condemn them: for she came from the uttermost parts of the earth to hear the wisdom of Solomon; and, behold, a greater than Solomon is here" (Matt. 12:42; Luke 11:31). Paul spoke of Christ as "the wisdom of God" (I Cor. 1:24; Col. 2:3). Kidner says that wisdom in the Book of Proverbs "is God-centered, and even when it is most down-to-earth it consists in the shrewd and sound handling of one's affairs in God's world, in submission to His will."[12] Wisdom is finding God's grace and living daily in harmony with His redemptive purposes for us.

[11]W. T. Purkiser, et al., Exploring the Old Testament (Kansas City: Beacon Hill Press, 1955), p. 255.

[12]The Proverbs (An Introduction and Commentary) (London: The Tyndale Press, 1964), pp. 13-14; see also pp. 31-35.

Outline

I. A Tribute to Wisdom, Proverbs 1:1—9:18
   A. Title and Purpose, 1:1-6
   B. The Major Theme, 1:7
   C. Warnings Against Violence, 1:8-19
   D. Warnings Against Neglecting Wisdom, 1:20-33
   E. Rewards of Heeding Wisdom, 2:1-22
   F. Blessings of Wisdom, 3:1-35
   G. The Primacy of Wisdom, 4:1-27
   H. Instruction on Marriage, 5:1-23
   I. A Group of Warnings, 6:1-19
   J. Wisdom and Adultery, 6:20—7:27
   K. Wisdom's Fame and Excellence, 8:1-36
   L. Wisdom and Folly Contrasted, 9:1-18

II. The Proverbs of Solomon, 10:1—22:16
   A. Proverbs of Contrast, 10:1—15:33
   B. Proverbs Largely Parallel, 16:1—22:16

III. The Words of the Wise, 22:17—24:34
   A. Introduction, 22:17-21
   B. First Collection, 22:22—23:14
   C. Second Group, 23:15—24:22
   D. Additional Admonitions, 24:23-34

IV. The Hezekiah Collection of Solomon's Proverbs, 25:1—29:27
   A. First Collection, 25:1—27:27
   B. Second Collection, 28:1—29:27

V. The Words of Agur, 30:1-33
   A. Personal Observations, 30:1-9
   B. Numerical Proverbs, 30:10-33

VI. The Words of Lemuel, 31:1-9
   A. Title, 31:1
   B. Warnings Against Lust and Strong Drink, 31:2-7
   C. Rule in Righteousness, 31:8-9

VII. The Virtuous Wife and Mother, 31:10-31
   A. Crowning Characteristics, 31:10-29
   B. A Concluding Tribute, 31:30-31

Section I A Tribute to Wisdom

Proverbs 1:1—9:18

The Book of Proverbs is a book for every age. The people of Israel cherished it as a part of their religious heritage. The people of the New Testament era have loved it as a part of God's message to them. The New Testament writers were influenced by it (cf. 3:7 and Rom. 12:16; 3:11-12 and Heb. 12:5-6; 3:34 and Jas. 4:6 and I Pet. 5:5). We find it echoed in the teachings of Jesus (cf. 14:11 and Matt. 7:24-27; 25:6-7 and Luke 14:7-11; 27:1 and Luke 12:13-21). The Hebrew word for proverb (*mashal*) is best rendered in the Greek as parable (*parabole*). The parabolic method so characteristic of Proverbs was a technique that Jesus used frequently in His teaching.

A. TITLE AND PURPOSE, 1:1-6

When the Hebrew people thought of the law, their minds turned inevitably to Moses. When they expressed themselves in song, they used the compositions of David. And when they recalled their proverbial sayings, they thought of Solomon.

1. The Significance of the Title (1:1)

Verse 1 probably gives us the editorial title for the entire book as well as the caption for the first section of it. This ascription does not mean that all that is contained in the book originated with Solomon. It does recognize him as the author of the major sections of Proverbs and also pays tribute to him as Israel's peerless sage. See the introduction for a fuller discussion of the authorship of Proverbs.

For the meaning of **proverbs** (*mashal*) see the introduction. The expression **the son of David** restates explicitly the lineage of Solomon (I Kings 11:12). Of this statement Matthew Henry says: "Christ is often called *the Son of David,* and Solomon was a type of him in this, as in other things, that he *opened his mouth in parables or proverbs.*"[1]

2. The Purpose of the Book (1:2-6)

Much of Proverbs has universal application. Its basic purpose, however, is religious. Solomon sought to do more than

---

[1]*Commentary on the Whole Bible* (New York: Fleming H. Revell Co., n.d.), VIII, 791.

share his knowledge; he endeavored to show Israel the way of holiness. The three words **to know wisdom** give us in capsule form the purpose of the entire book. Edgar Jones says that the Hebrew term **to know** "carries a sense of personal encounter and fellowship that goes beyond merely intellectual curiosity. . . . The purpose of the book is to gain the allegiance of young people to the moral law of God. Beyond curiosity there is committal."[2]

Proverbs is beamed first of all to **the young** (4) and inexperienced, but is for all ages and stages of life. The **wise man** —the older and experienced person—may **increase** his **learning** (5). The Hebrew word for **the simple** (4) "designates the opposite of a moral man. It does not mean a simpleton in our sense of the term, but a sinner, a rascal. Proverbs has a message of morality for the wicked."[3] This message, however, is expressed somewhat indirectly by **dark sayings** (6), riddles or other proverbial forms requiring some interpretation, rather than by the more direct method of the forthright prophetic utterances of Israel's prophets.

B. THE MAJOR THEME, 1:7

After the remarkably clear statement of purpose (1:2-6), the writer expresses the major theme of Proverbs and the fundamental principle of revealed religion in v. 7. This is the key verse and contains the key word of the entire book—**wisdom. The fear of the Lord** is a common expression in the Scriptures, particularly in Psalms and Proverbs. This fear is not the slavish fear of torment but rather the fear of reverence and awe. It is a "reverent and worshipful fear" (Amp. OT). Rylaarsdam says: "To fear God is not to be afraid of him but to stand in awe of him, because the meaning of everything and the destiny of every person are determined by what God is and does."[4]

[2]*Proverbs and Ecclesiastes,* "Torch Bible Commentaries" (New York: The Macmillan Co., 1961), pp. 55-56.

[3]R. Laird Harris, "Proverbs," *The Wycliffe Bible Commentary,* eds. Charles F. Pfeiffer and Everett F. Harrison (Chicago: Moody Press, 1962), p. 558.

[4]*The Proverbs, Ecclesiastes, The Song of Solomon,* "The Layman's Bible Commentary," ed. Balmer H. Kelley, *et al.* (Richmond: John Knox Press, 1964), X, 16.

Of a similar expression in Ps. 111:10, Davies says: *"The fear of the Lord* in Scripture signifies not only that pious passion or filial reverence of our adorable Father who is in heaven, but it is frequently put for the whole of practical religion . . . [it] implies all the graces and all the virtues of Christianity; in short, all that holiness of heart and life which is necessary to the enjoyment of everlasting happiness."[5]

The word **Lord** is significant in this key verse. It is the English translation of the Hebrew name for God that was revealed to the people of Israel (Exod. 3:13-15). This name was composed of four consonants, *YHWH*, and probably pronounced *Yahweh*. This was the God who had revealed himself to His people Israel and gave to them a special sense of destiny among the nations of earth.

The beginning, "starting point" or "chief part," suggests more than a chronological position. It is "the principal and choice part of knowledge—that is, its starting point and its essence" (Amp. OT). Kidner says, *"The beginning* (i.e. the first and controlling principle, rather than a stage which one leaves behind; cf. Ec. 12:13) is not merely a right method of thought but a right relation; a worshipping submission *(fear)* of the God of the covenant, who has revealed Himself."[6]

Fools despise wisdom. Such **fools** are those who reject the divine directives for life and walk in the way of ungodliness. Their stubborn way is the opposite to that of the man of wisdom or godliness. The fool, in the sense used in Proverbs, is not just a simpleton. "Fools make a mock at sin" (Prov. 14:9). The fool is spiritually rebellious, indifferent to divine counsel, and rejects the fear of the Lord.[7] Jesus portrayed this type of person when He termed a man foolish who heeded not His teachings (Matt. 7:26-27).

In this key verse may be found "God's Requirements for Holy Living." There must be (1) a right relationship with God—**the fear of the Lord;** (2) a continuing discipleship—**the beginning of knowledge;** and (3) a respect for divine guidance—only **fools despise wisdom and instruction.** There must be the initia-

[5]C. H. Spurgeon, in *The Treasury of David* (London: Passmore and Alabaster, 1881), V, 219-20.

[6]*Op. cit.,* p. 59.

[7]For a more complete discussion of the word *fool* see Kidner, *op. cit.,* pp. 39-41.

tion of our walk with God, the continuation of the redemptive fellowship, and the application of our hearts to the discipline of divine instruction.

C. WARNINGS AGAINST VIOLENCE, 1:8-19

1. *The Way of Wisdom* (1:8-9)

The wise man now moves to a practical application of wisdom to temptation and conduct. He urges the young man to be obedient to God and respectful to parents. In this approach youth will find the best safeguard against evil. This way—although not so alluring and glamorous as sin's enticements—is his best way in life. **My son** (8) is an endearing term of the teacher for his pupil and is frequently used in Proverbs. **Hear** might better be translated "obey" or "heed" (Berk.). **The instruction** (training or discipline) **of thy father** suggests the primary place of the father in the Jewish home (Exod. 12:26-28; Deut. 6:6-7). But the writer adds, **And forsake not,** or "reject not" (RSV), **the law,** "teachings" (Berk.) or "directions" (Moffatt), **of thy mother.** Such teachings were significant also and were not considered inferior to those of the father. No book in the Bible exceeds Proverbs in its encouragement to love and respect for mother. Parents are the first teachers of religion, and Hebrew children first learned the way of wisdom from them.

The heeding of parental instruction was not to be without its reward. Such conduct would decorate the young man's life with honor. He would have **an ornament of grace** (9; "a graceful garland," Moffatt) on his **head, and chains** ("adornments," Berk.) for his **neck.** These were decorations like those worn by kings (Gen. 41:42; Dan. 5:29).

2. *The Way of Sinners* (1:10-19)

This passage might be entitled "Yield Not to Temptation." In it we see that: (1) Evil is alluring. The desperado or racketeer[8] says, **Come with us** (11). Here is an appeal to man's instinct to belong—"Be one of the gang." The gangster further promises material abundance (13-14)—an appeal to man's desire to acquire. (2) Evil is assailing. It is an aggressor and spares

---

[8]See F. C. Cook, *The Bible Commentary: Proverbs—Ezekiel,* abridged and edited by J. M. Fuller (Grand Rapids, Michigan: Baker Book House, 1953), p. 16; J. Coert Rylaarsdam, *op. cit.,* pp. 16-17.

no one. It is as ruthless as death. **Let us swallow them up alive as the grave** (12). (3) Evil is afflicting. It is hurtful to others. The desperado makes **haste to shed blood** (16). Evil also traps and destroys the sinner himself (17-19). "Even a silly bird knows better than to approach a trap he sees being set; yet these sinners set a trap and fall in it themselves."[9] Those who are **greedy of gain** (19) find that sin always boomerangs. Centuries later Jesus asked, "What is a man profited, if he shall gain the whole world, and lose his own soul?" (Matt. 16:26)

D. WARNINGS AGAINST NEGLECTING WISDOM, 1:20-33

In this passage wisdom is personified for the first of many times in the Book of Proverbs. **Wisdom** goes in the role of a prophet of God with an urgent message, which is proclaimed **in the streets** (20), **the chief place of concourse**, and **the gates** (21). Here "where cross the crowded ways of life" wisdom makes her impassioned appeal. In v. 22 she uses three terms to describe those who reject the divine revelation. They are the **simple ones** (morally neutral), **the scorners** (defiant), and the **fools** (spiritually obstinate).

Turn you (23) is a prophetic call of repentance (cf. Jer. 3:12-14, 22; 4:1). To reject this call is tragic indeed. For those who do, wisdom says, **I also will laugh at your calamity** (26). These words Kidner says are "not an expression of personal heartlessness, but of the absurdity of choosing folly, the complete vindication of wisdom, and the incontestable fitness of disaster."[10]

The judgment that shall come upon the rejecters of God will be as sudden **as a whirlwind** (27). This calamity shall be **the fruit of their own way** (31). They shall reap what they have sown (cf. Gal. 6:7-8). The **turning away** (32; "backsliding," Amp. OT; or "waywardness," Berk.) **of the simple** and **the prosperity** ("the careless ease," Amp. OT; or "the self-assurance," Berk.) **of fools** shall be their undoing. Those who listen to wisdom, however, need have no fear of the disastrous calamities that come as the consequence of sinful folly (33).

E. REWARDS OF HEEDING WISDOM, 2:1-22

In this chapter the teacher speaks in the name of wisdom just as the prophets spoke in the name of God. This Hebrew

[9] Berk., fn., *loc. cit.*   [10] *Op. cit.*, p. 60.

poem falls into six divisions. The opening lines (1-4), or protasis, contain an urgent plea for the pupil to heed wisdom's call. Then follows the outcome, or apodosis, which describes five results or fruits of knowing God (5-22).

1. *The Urgency of Wisdom's Plea* (2:1-4)

The urgency of the wise man's appeal is indicated by four sets of parallel clauses—one set in each of the verses of this section. In v. 1 the condition is, **If thou wilt receive** (lit., take or accept) . . . **and hide** ("treasure up," RSV). **Incline thine ear** (make "your ear attentive," RSV) . . . **and apply thine heart** (let "your heart reach out," Berk.) are found in v. 2. **If thou criest after** ("if you beseech," Berk.) . . . **and liftest up thy voice** are conditions of v. 3. In 4 we read, **If thou seekest her as silver, and searchest** (dig) **for her as for hid treasures.** Only such singleness of heart as the teacher pleads for in these verses will result in the pupil's knowledge of God's holy will. Paul's declaration in Phil. 3:13-14 is a New Testament illustration of this intensity of purpose.

The word **heart** (Heb., *leb*) in v. 2 is particularly significant. It has a much broader meaning in the Hebrew than in English, including intellectual and moral sensibilities as well as emotional. It is the center of man's being from which self-decision springs. The Bible never speaks of the brain as the location of man's intellect. **Apply thine heart** (2) implies real earnestness. The teacher is pleading with his pupil to seek wisdom with his whole being—his reason, his emotions, his will—so that there would be no dilution of purpose.[11]

2. *The Five Fruits of Wisdom* (2:5-22)

The teacher's urgent plea for an all-out response to wisdom's call is followed by the assuring promises that his pupil's efforts would not be in vain.

a. The seeker shall find God (2:5-8). The spiritual quest brings one into fellowship with God. **Then**—after diligent search —the seeker shall **understand the fear of the Lord** (5; see comment on 1:7). Personal religion begins with the revelation of God to one's heart. This is the supreme reward of the pupil's

---

[11]See E. C. Blackman, art. "Mind, Heart," *A Theological Word Book of the Bible,* ed. Alan Richardson (New York: The Macmillan Co., paperback edition, 1962), pp. 144-46.

search (cf. John 17:3). What the seeker finds is God's gift to him—**For the Lord giveth wisdom** (6). The pupil discovers all that is essential for righteous living—**sound,** or practical, **wisdom,** and protection (7). **The Lord is a buckler** or shield (Gen. 15:1; Ps. 59:11; 84:11) **to them that walk uprightly** ("to those walking in integrity," Berk.). Such protection is for **his saints** (8); literally, "devoted ones" (cf. Ps. 12:1; 30:4; 31:23).

b. *Wisdom gives understanding and freedom* (2:9-11). God's gift of himself and the insights into His purposes for our lives bring us the power and principles for right conduct. Such divine bestowments are **pleasant** (10), protecting and guarding (11). Strength within is the best answer to the evil without. The saint—the person devoted to God—finds a rich life and freedom to walk life's way with assurance of victory over evil. To know God and do His will makes a man free (John 8:32).

c. *God's man is delivered from the evil way* (2:12-15). This blessing and the two that follow are corollaries of the first two fruits of wisdom. They may be considered as resulting from finding God (5-8) and from God-given understanding (9-11). In this passage the teacher speaks of evil in general. **The way of the evil man** (12) is the opposite of the way of righteousness. These contrasting ways are often depicted in the Scriptures (Psalms 1; Isa. 59:8; Matt. 7:13-14, 24-27). **The evil man** is a slave to the way of sinful folly. But the man of wisdom walks another way. His choice of God gives him power to refuse the enticements of the road to ruin and eternal death.

The character of **the evil man** is described in this passage. He is a man **that speaketh froward things** (12). His speech is twisted ("perverted," Berk). Moffatt says his speech is "self-willed"—suggesting the rejection of God's will for his own. He walks **in the ways of darkness** (13; cf. Deut. 28:29; Ps. 82:5; Prov. 4:19; Isa. 59:9). Furthermore, he rejoices in **evil** and delights to see others take this same perverse path (14). His **ways are crooked** (15), i.e., contrary to that which is true and morally straight.

d. *He is saved from the unchaste woman* (2:16-19). The man of God is not only delivered from the evil way in general but from the **strange woman** (16) in particular. Prostitution was not uncommon in ancient Israel. Adultery, as well as idolatry, was one of her common sins (cf. Jer. 23:10, 14; Hos. 4:14). Proverbs devotes considerable space to the lewd or seductive woman (5:1-23; 6:20-35; 7:1-27; 9:13-18). **The strange** ("loose," RSV) **woman** personifies the way that is opposite to wisdom and the path that ends in **death** instead of life (18-19). "The wages of sin is death" (Rom. 6:23).

The Berkeley Version translates the words **strange** and **stranger** (16) as "alien" and "foreigner." The reason for the use of these terms is given in a footnote. "Such a woman had forfeited the right to be called an Israelite."[12] Toy says that "the general character of the descriptions here and in chs. 5, 7, 9:13-18, and the contrast expressed in 5:19, 20, make it almost certain that the writer has in mind dissolute women without regard to nationality, and that the *strange woman* is one who is not bound to the man by legal ties, who is outside the circle of his proper relations, that is, a harlot or an adulteress."[13] This profligate is a married woman who has forsaken both the **guide** ("companion," RSV, or "husband," Berk.) **of her youth** and also **the covenant of her God** (17). A relationship to God and a commitment to His will give one strength to reject the temptations of such a person. Centuries later Paul said to the Galatians, "This I say then, Walk in the Spirit, and ye shall not fulfil the lust of the flesh" (5:16).

e. He will have a special inheritance (2:20-22). Those who take **the way of good men** (20) **shall dwell in the land** (21). The primary reference here is to the land of Canaan, which was promised to God's people (Exod. 20:12; Lev. 25:18-24; Ps. 37: 9-11). To dwell in Canaan was to enjoy God's favor and blessing. To be exiled from this land was an indication of disobedience and of divine disfavor. Jesus expressed a similar truth when He said, "Blessed are the meek: for they shall inherit the earth" (Matt. 5:5). God's possessions are shared with His children. **But the wicked** (22) are not so blessed. They shall be **cut off** and **rooted out** (Deut. 28:63) of the land of their fathers. The retribution for rejecting God's way is sure and tragic.

F. THE BLESSINGS OF WISDOM, 3:1-35

This section continues the emphasis of the previous chapter on the blessings of wisdom. In c. 2 moral stability was the main

---

[12]Fn., p. 643.

[13]*The Book of Proverbs*, "The International Critical Commentary," ed. Charles A. Briggs, Samuel R. Driver, Alfred Plummer (New York: Charles Scribner's Sons, 1904), p. 46.

fruit of wisdom. Here happiness and security are the primary and positive rewards. The chapter consists of three distinct discourses, each beginning with the expression "My son." The first (1-10) is a call to complete commitment. The second (11-20) speaks of the happiness of trust in God. The final division (21-35) stresses the security in walking with God.

1. A Call to Complete Commitment (3:1-10)

The main thrust of the teacher in this section is for commitment to God's will. He pleads kindly and earnestly for obedience to the divine directives for life. **My son, forget not my law** (1). Fritsch says: "One of the golden words of religion is 'remember.' There is no spiritual life or growth apart from the great spiritual heritage of the past. No religion recognized this truth more clearly than Judaism, with its strong emphasis on the teaching of its youth concerning the great facts and truths of its holy history (Exod. 12:26-27; Deut. 6)."[14] A strong faith is based on sound teaching rooted in a rich religious tradition. In today's Church, evangelism and Christian education must go hand in hand.

Let thine heart keep my commandments. In other words, commit yourself to God. Maclaren says: "The mother of all graces of conduct is the bowing of the will to divine authority. The will is the man, and where it ceases to lift itself up in self-sacrificing and self-determining rebellion, and dissolves into running waters of submission, these will flow through the life and make it pure."[15] One of the rewards for a committed life is **length of days** (2). Here is a concept found often in the Scriptures (cf. Gen. 25:8; Exod. 20:12; Deut. 5:16; 22:7; Prov. 2:21; 4:10). Paul wrote: "Godliness is profitable unto all things, having promise of the life that now is, and of that which is to come" (I Tim. 4:8).

Another reward of godliness is that of **peace.** Here the Hebrew word is *shalom*, which means wholeness or completeness. A right relationship with God and a right regard for one's fellowman make life truly complete and worth living.

Of the words, **Let not mercy and truth forsake thee** (3), Jones and Walls say: *"Mercy (hesedh)* is a word which is hard

---

[14]*Op. cit.,* IB, 4:797.

[15]*Expositions of Holy Scripture* (II Kings, c. VIII—Ecclesiastes) (Grand Rapids, Michigan: Wm. B. Eerdmans Publishing Co., 1938), pp. 84-85.

to understand apart from the idea of *covenant*. It represents *covenant*-love, and the full range of what that means we see from the Great Commandment and the one like unto it (Dt. vi. 5 and Lv. xix. 18). **Truth** (Heb. *'emeth*) means 'firmness' and hence 'trustworthiness', 'stability', 'faithfulness', and eventually what faithfulness demands—reality and truth."[16] The terms **mercy** and **truth** are often linked together in the Old Testament. They speak of God's faithfulness to His promises. As applied to men, they describe integrity in its broadest sense.

Judaism took the expressions **bind them** and **write them** literally. Phylacteries containing portions of Scripture were worn on the head and on the hand (Exod. 13:9; Deut. 6:8-9; 11:18). In their deepest significance **mercy** ("lovingkindness," Berk.) and **truth** ("faithfulness," RSV) are principles to meditate upon and to live by.

In vv. 5 and 6 we have choice words that reflect the tenor of the entire Book of Proverbs. **Trust in the Lord . . . lean not unto thine own understanding** (5). Human wisdom is inadequate, but divine wisdom is sufficient guidance for life. The assurance is that God will **direct** (6) our lives and enable us to reach our destination. Moffatt says: "He will clear the road for you." The reference is to removing the obstacles in laying a highway (Isa. 40:3; 45:13).

The writer says, **Be not wise in thine own eyes** (7), or, "Never pride yourself in your own wisdom" (Moffatt). Here is essentially a repetition of the plea of vv. 5-6 to put one's trust in the Lord. Here we are urged not to take ourselves too seriously, but to reverence God. Such reverence will result in "healing to your body and nourishment to your bones" (8, Berk.). The **navel** and **bones** are used as symbols for the entire body. A knowledge of God that leads to spiritual well-being has its effects on the psychological and physical aspects of human personality.

In vv. 9-10 we have a plea for the proper use of material possessions. Man is, after all, a steward and everything he has belongs to God (Psalms 50). When he honors God with a portion of his increase, he will be blessed materially—**So shall thy barns be filled** (10). Here we have a principle of stewardship and not a guarantee of material riches. We can trust God with our gifts and for our material needs (Matt. 6:33). The Christian steward

---

[16]*Op. cit.*, p. 520.

need never fear that he will be the loser by giving to God (Mal. 3:8-10). No man loses by faith or by obedience. The man of God is not a reluctant but a glad and responsible steward.

2. The Happiness of Trust in God (3:11-20)

The problem of human suffering, which is the theme of the Book of Job, is introduced here in vv. 11 and 12. At first this emphasis seems to be a digression in a treatise on the blessings of godliness. Often good people are not blessed with riches or strong bodies, and the wicked are not always poor and miserable. In v. 12 the teacher gives a solution to this perplexing problem. He says that the **chastening** (11; "discipline," Berk.) and the **correction** ("reproof," RSV) are indications of a loving Father's continuing concern for the welfare of His child (cf. Heb. 12:5-11). In adversity or prosperity, God's children are never separated from His love (Rom. 8:38-39). Whether or not we understand fully our disciplines and reproofs, we can know God's love is ours and that our lives are in His hands.

Adversity does not destroy the lasting happiness of the man of God. The way of wisdom, though costly, is rewarding. The word **happy** (13) here is the "blessed" used in the Beatitudes of the Sermon on the Mount. It is found frequently in the Psalms (1:1; 112:1; 119:1) and in Proverbs (8:34; 16:20; 20:7; 28:14). While all around are engaged in the pursuit of earthly riches, the man of wisdom has discovered treasures superior to **silver** and **gold** (14). His treasures are even **more precious than rubies** (15)—gems, or red corals (Job 28:18; Lam. 4:7). Earthly treasures cannot give **length of days** (16) or **peace** of heart and mind (17). Wisdom is **a tree of life** (18), which symbolizes the life-giving power of God.[17]

In vv. 19-20 we see creation as an expression of the **wisdom** of God—the same wisdom that He shares with His children. Edgar Jones says: "As Wisdom changes human life from chaos to order so Wisdom functioned in the beginning."[18] How could the man of God be other than blessed!

3. Security in Walking with God (3:21-35)

The final division of this chapter begins with v. 21. The teacher tells his pupil that **wisdom** is doubly rewarding. It will

---

[17]For a fuller discussion of the meaningful symbol of the tree of life, see Kidner, *op. cit.*, p. 54, and Rylaarsdam, *op. cit.*, p. 25.

[18]*Op. cit.*, pp. 72-73.

bring life unto his **soul, and grace to** his **neck** (22). Such wisdom gives resources for the inner man and makes gracious his outward appearance. The teacher makes it plain that wisdom means walking with God (23). Such a walk brings a sense of security and delivers one from tormenting fears (24). Reliance upon God gives one a rewarding **confidence** (26).

The man who places his trust in God (3:1-10) and walks happily with Him (3:11-20) will manifest his faith in social relationships. No man can have rich fellowship with God without a right relationship to his fellowman. In vv. 27-30 there are four prohibitions dealing with man's responsibility to others. First of all, the godly man must be kind and just—**withhold not good** (27)—to those to whom some payment **is due** or to whom some favor should be shown. He should not delay but give promptly (28) wages due or help needed (cf. Jas. 2:16). He must **devise not** (29; "plot no evil," Smith-Goodspeed) **against** his **neighbour.** Finally, he must not be contentious (30).

In vv. 31-35 we have a series of contrasts between the destinies of the man of wisdom and the man of wickedness. The wicked man is not to be envied because of his apparent success. He is an **abomination to the Lord** (32), but the **righteous** enjoy God's **secret,** "intimate counsel" (Berk.) or "confidence" (Smith-Goodspeed). Only the man of wisdom is honored by God (33-35).

G. THE PRIMACY OF WISDOM, 4:1-27

In this section we have a choice portrayal of the primacy of wisdom. The chapter contains three distinct discourses. In the first (1-9) a father seeks to transmit his love for wisdom to his son; in the second (10-19) the choice between life's contrasting ways is emphasized; and in the final section (20-27) we find a plea for purity of heart and life.

1. *A Father's Love for Wisdom* (4:1-9)

Hear, ye children, the instruction of a father (1). The teacher here either assumes the role of a father or, as a father, recalls his own valuable religious heritage. The latter seems more likely in view of the autobiographical statements in vv. 3-4. Certainly ancient Israel believed that religion should be *taught* as well as *caught.* Precept and practice were both important in

472

the propagation of the faith. In line with this heritage Christianity is justifiably a teaching religion.

The teacher speaks beautifully of his own Jewish home. When he was **tender** (3; young in years), his father and mother both shared in his education. A devotion to the highest values in life is transmitted by the personal impact of devout parents on the lives of their children, and teachers on the lives of pupils. Edgar Jones reminds us that "the relationship between the teacher and the taught is personal, not perfunctory. Within this relationship of mutual trust real education is possible."[19]

Get wisdom, get understanding (5). The repetition of the verb **get** is significant. It is not enough to be taught, important as that is. One must acquire wisdom for himself. Kidner thinks that the teacher's expression here "is a blunt way of saying: 'What it takes is not brains or opportunity, but decision. Do you want it? Come and get it.' "[20] The New Testament parables of the hidden treasure and the pearl of great price (Matt. 13:44-46) are illustrative of the truth the father was seeking to communicate.

The primacy of wisdom is underscored again in vv. 6-9. The son is to **love** wisdom as he would love his bride (6). Such love brings its rich rewards (cf. Ps. 45:13; Prov. 1:9; Isa. 61:10). Paul said, "Godliness with contentment is great gain" (I Tim. 6:6). A knowledge of God is worth more than all it costs to obtain it.

2. *A Choice of Two Ways* (4:10-19)

The teacher sets forth in sharp contrast in vv. 10-19 the two paths of life (see comment on 2:12-15). **The way of wisdom** (11) is depicted in vv. 10-13. This way is the better route for life's pilgrimage. It is **not . . . straitened** (12)—that is, free from stumbling blocks (cf. Jude 24a). The admonitions of 13 challenge the man of God to urgent faithfulness. The way of the wicked is portrayed quite differently in 14-17. The wicked are zealous in their evil doings. **They sleep not** (16). That is, they delight in doing wrong (Eph. 4:19). Their food and drink are acquired by wicked means (17).

The two ways are summarized in 18-19. **The path of the just is as a shining light** (18), or "the light of dawn" (RSV), that

---

[19]*Op. cit.*, p. 76.   [20]*Op. cit.*, p. 67.

increases in brilliance **unto the perfect day,** or "to the full light of day" (Moffatt). But **the way of the wicked is as darkness** ("deep darkness," Berk.), and **they know not at what they stumble** (19). Schloerb says: "They cannot diagnose their plight; they go on tripping over the same obstacle again and again."[21]

3. A Plea for Purity of Heart and Life (4:20-27)

The secret of a holy life is given in 20-27. It is, first of all, trust in God that enables one to walk the way of righteousness. **My son, attend to my word** (20) with all your human personality —ear (20); eyes (21, 25); heart (21, 23); flesh (22); mouth . . . lips (24); hands and feet (27). Secondly, the **heart** must be guarded **with all diligence; for out of it are the issues of life** (23); from it "flow the springs of life" (Amp. OT). Horton says: "All conduct is the outcome of hidden fountains. All words are the expression of thoughts. The first thing and the main thing is that the hidden fountains of thought and feeling are pure. The source of all our trouble is the bitterness of heart, the envious feeling, the sudden outbreak of corrupt desire. A merely outward salvation will be of no avail; a change of place, a magic formula, a conventional pardon, could not touch the root of the mischief. 'I wish you would change my heart,' said the chief Sekomi to Livingstone. 'Give me medicine to change it, for it is proud, proud and angry, angry always.' He would not hear of the New Testament way of changing the heart; he wanted an outward, mechanical way—and that way was not to be found."[22]

In the teacher's plea for purity, deep in the revelation of the Old Testament, is found the concept that Jesus emphasized more fully in the New. He spoke of the necessity of soul purity when He showed that the heart of man was the source of evil thoughts and deeds (Matt. 15:18-19; Mark 7:20-23). He proclaimed heart purity as one of the "blesseds" of the new covenant (Matt. 5:8).

H. INSTRUCTION ON MARRIAGE, 5:1-23

In c. 5 we have the application of wisdom to the relationship between the sexes. After an introductory plea for strict atten-

---

[21]"Proverbs" (Exposition), *The Interpreter's Bible*, ed. George A. Buttrick, *et al.*, IV (New York: Abingdon Press, 1955), 810.

[22]*The Book of Proverbs*, "The Expositor's Bible," ed. W. Robertson Nicoll (New York: A. C. Armstrong and Son, 1903), p. 58.

tion to teaching (1-2), there is a strong warning against the fascinations of sin (3-6). Then follows a sharp admonition to shun infidelity (7-14). The final section contains an urgent plea for marital faithfulness (15-23).

1. *Avoid the Fascinations of Sin* (5:1-6)

The teacher pleads for attention to his words, **Bow thine ear to my understanding** (1). Hearing precedes believing. A person must know the alternatives in order to make a responsible choice (cf. Rom. 10:14-17). One must accept God for himself and walk discreetly. For proper conduct there must be sound judgment and spiritual discernment. One must even guard his speech by **knowledge** (2). Greenstone aptly comments: "Be guided in your speech by knowledge and not by the impulse of the moment."[23]

The reason for the teacher's strong appeal is evident in v. 3. One will either be the servant of God or the slave of sin; he will either choose the chains of divine discipline or the fetters of evil. **For** (3) there is the **strange woman**, the adulteress, who will present her temptations.

She is representative of the allurements of sin—of self-will as opposed to God's will. She is the wife of another man (see comment on 2:16-19). **Her lips ... drop as an honeycomb** ("drop honeyed words," Berk.), **and her mouth is smoother than oil.** That is, her speech is flattering and seductive. An example of such is given in 7:13-21.

The outcome, however, of involvement with the adulteress is just the opposite of the promises she makes to the object of her scarlet designs. **Her end is bitter as wormwood** (4). The word **end** (Heb. *'aharith*) is often used to express the idea of final judgment (cf. 5:11; 14:12-13; 16:25; 19:20; 20:21; 23:18; 24:14; 25:8; 29:21). Instead of the sweetness of honey and the smoothness of oil there comes bitterness. **Wormwood** (4) is a bitter-tasting plant that is used often in the Bible to describe the tragic results of sin (Deut. 29:18; Jer. 9:15; Lam. 3:19; Amos 5:7; 6:12). The **twoedged sword** suggests the devouring nature of sin (Jer. 46:10; Nah. 2:13). In v. 5 the words **death and hell** (Heb., *Sheol*) are virtually synonymous. *Sheol* means the place

---

[23]*Proverbs with Commentary* (Philadelphia: The Jewish Publication Society of America, 1950), p. 46.

of departed spirits. Here death is spoken of as an outcome of the way of sin.[24]

The profligate woman is further described in 6. The word translated **thou** from the Hebrew text is uncertain. It more likely should be rendered "she," referring to the adulteress. Moffatt translates the first line: "The high road of Life is not for her." *The Berkeley Version* reads: "The path of life she does not consider." Her ways are **moveable,** or "shifty and slippery" (Moffatt). Thus God's Word underscores the destructiveness of sin. Rylaarsdam says: "The wise men and prophets did a profound thing when they chose harlotry as the metaphor for idolatry; both express unfaithfulness because both are motivated by self-centeredness and irresponsibility. But just because of this both are self-destructive, for 'whoever would save his life will lose it' (Matt. 16: 25)."[25]

2. The High Cost of Infidelity (5: 7-14)

In these verses the destructiveness of immorality is graphically sketched. First, the teacher warns again that the adulteress should be shunned. **Remove thy way far from her** (8)—"Keep clear of her" (Moffatt). In today's language we might say, "Don't play with fire unless you want to get burned." The teacher tells us that the self-indulgent comes to the end of his days with his heart remorseful and his physical energies dissipated (9-11). Too late he sees the error of his way. He says, **How have I hated instruction** (12), literally, "How could I have been so foolish as to refuse to follow guidance?"

The dissolute man is foolish not only before God but also in the sight of men. **I was almost in all evil in the midst of the congregation** (14) means, "I was nearly sentenced to death by the congregation" (Moffatt), or, "I was at the point of utter ruin" (RSV). The words of 14 could mean that this adulterer nearly came to public trial and conviction that could have meant severe punishment and death (Lev. 20:10; Deut. 22:22; Ezek. 16:40). The words could also mean that sin brought this man to public disgrace even though he was a member of the congregation of Israel.

---

[24]For a fuller discussion of the words **death** and **hell** in v. 5 see Kidner, *op. cit.,* pp. 53-56; R. Laird Harris, *op. cit.,* pp. 559-60.

[25]*Op. cit.,* p. 32.

3. *A Plea for Faithfulness* (5:15-23)

After the strong condemnation of sexual promiscuity of the previous section, the writer now moves to a masterful plea for marital faithfulness. While extramarital relations are contrary to God's will, the sexual relationship in marriage has divine approval. An honorable and happy marriage, described in 15-20, is seen as a safeguard against unfaithfulness.

In the typical imagery of the ancient East the writer uses water, cistern, well, and fountain as metaphors to describe a man's wife (Song of Sol. 4:12, 15). The phrases **thine own cistern** and **thine own well** (15) stress fidelity in marriage. In 15 we have a reflection of the seventh commandment: "Thou shalt not commit adultery" (Exod. 20:14). A knowledge of God and obedience to His moral demands are combined in this chapter. Proverbs thus echoes the supreme contribution of Israel to the world—the law revealed through Moses and personalized religion through the prophets.

In 16 the Hebrew is difficult to interpret. We have either a reference to bringing up children within the sacred marriage relationship or to the wastefulness of promiscuity. Some scholars prefer the first view, and the structure of the sentence tends to support them. Others make a question of the verse, "Should your springs [offspring] be dispersed abroad, your courses of water [children] in the streets?" (Berk.) Either interpretation stresses the importance of fidelity in the marriage relationship.

The writer speaks in v. 17 of a monogamous relationship. He talks in 18 of enjoying **the wife of thy youth.** In 19 he uses the frank imagery of the Song of Solomon (4:5) to speak of the appeal the husband should allow his wife to have for him. He urges the husband (19-20) to keep romance in his marriage. The word **ravished** in 19-20, rendered "infatuated" in some translations, would be better translated as "lost in" or "intoxicated with."

In 21-23 the teacher stresses again the fate of evildoers. He says that all conduct is **before the eyes of the Lord** (21). Greenstone comments: "Man's ways are open before God; even the acts done in strictest secrecy are perceived by God, and this should be an additional deterrent against indulging in unseemly acts."[26] True morality is a reflection of the holiness of God. The writer makes it clear that the sinner forges the chains **of his**

[26]*Op. cit.*, p. 53.

sins that bind him (22) and that his plight is due to his failure
to obey the laws of God (23).

Alexander Maclaren's treatment of v. 22 is entitled "The
Cords of Sin." He suggests that: (1) Our evil deeds become evil
habits; (2) Our evil deeds imprison us; (3) Our evil deeds
work their own punishment; and (4) The cords can be loosened.

I. A GROUP OF WARNINGS, 6:1-19

Proverbs is full of warning signals, flashing red lights to
alert one of danger and disaster ahead. In this section we have
four such flashing red lights. These warnings remind us again
of the relevance of the message of Proverbs. In a day of moral
revolt and ethical relativism it is well to read often the forthright words of Israel's wise men "who spoke unashamedly of the
evils of their day and pointed young men to the way of wisdom
which is the way of God."[27]

1. *Against Suretyship* (6:1-5)

The wise man's warning here is not to be understood as an
outright prohibition against all suretyship—the assumption of
the obligation of another. In ancient Israel charity toward a
brother in the Hebrew community was frequently urged and
usury (interest on loans) condemned (Exod. 22:25-26; Lev. 25:
36-37; Deut. 23:19-20; Ps. 15:5; Ezek. 18:8, 13, 17). There were
also certain obligations regarding the debts of one's relatives
(Ruth 4:1-6).

In this Proverbs passage, however, the writer is dealing in a
practical manner with the impulsive assumption of the debts of
other people—the **friend** or **stranger** (1). Similar warnings
against such suretyship appear in other places in Proverbs (11:
15; 17:18; 22:26-27). The counsel is not against thoughtful
generosity. Kidner states it well: "It does not banish generosity;
it is nearer to banishing gambling."[28] The rash, too-easy assumption of the debts of others will result, like gambling, in hardship to
both the impulsive person and his family.

If thou hast stricken thy hand simply means, "If you have
made a pledge or agreement." In such case one is **snared** (2;

[27]Charles T. Fritsch, art. "The Gospel in the Book of Proverbs," *Theology Today,* VII, April, 1950—January, 1951, ed. John A. Mackay (Princeton, N.J.), 170-71.

[28]*Op. cit.,* p. 71.

"trapped," Moffatt) by his own **words.** The solution to this problem is at any cost to cancel his pledge immediately—**Do this now** (3). One is to "importune" the stranger to secure release (cf. Luke 18:1-8). He is to **deliver** (5) himself from the involvements of his impulsive agreement. He is to be free like the **roe** ("gazelle," Berk.) that has escaped **the hunter** and the bird that has eluded **the fowler.**

2. Against Indolence (6:6-11)

The second warning deals with the virtues of diligence and industry. Warnings against indolence appear frequently in Proverbs (10:26; 13:4; 19:15; 24:30-34). The teacher believed that laziness militated against prosperity (10:4; 12:11; 20:13; 23:21; 24:33-34; 28:19). Solomon here turned to nature to provide an example of diligence (cf. I Kings 4:33). **The ant** (6), mentioned only here and in 30:25, can teach us some lessons about industry and foresight. It labors diligently and voluntarily (7) to provide its food in the **harvest** season for the winter ahead (8).

The threefold appearance of the word **little** (10) underscores the fact that minor neglects result in major deficiencies. Today another little "drink for the road" can result in a major highway tragedy. As the result of repeated indolence, the wise man warns that "poverty will pounce upon you" and "want will overpower you" (11, Moffatt).

3. Against Sowing Discord (6:12-15)

The third warning deals with the characteristics of a perverse man. He is **a naughty person** (12; Heb., "a man of Belial"). The word "Belial" is used later in the New Testament as a designation of Satan (II Cor. 6:15). Wickedness as well as worthlessness is implied here. While a number of translations term this person "worthless" (Berk., RSV), Moffatt calls him "a rascal." Greenstone says: "The rabbis understand by it one without a yoke, who has thrown off the yoke of moral and religious responsibility, a person depraved."[29] This man's speech is **froward** (12); literally, "crooked or twisted." His winking indicates insincerity and maliciousness; the gestures of his feet and hands are typical of a wicked man.

This perverse person **soweth discord** (14), or literally, "lets loose strife." Moffatt says, "He is always sowing discord." Such

[29]*Op. cit.,* p. 60.

a man was particularly troublesome in a primitive society. But he is the bane of any society. Horton says: "It is this kind of man that is the leaven of hypocrisy and malice in the Christian Church; he intrigues and cabals. He sets the people against the minister and stirs up the minister to suspect his people. He undertakes religious work, because it is in that capacity he can do most mischief. He is never better pleased than when he can pose as a champion of orthodoxy, because then he seems to be sheltered and approved by the banner which he is defending."[30]

4. Against Seven Sins (6:16-19)

In this fourth warning the writer makes it clear that sin is not only disastrous to man but distasteful to God. A holy God abhors evil. The listing of the sins the young man should avoid is expressed by a Hebrew idiomatic expression—these six things . . . yea, seven (16). The poetic parallelism should not be thought of as limiting evil to seven sins, nor of making a meaningful distinction between the first six and the seventh sin. For similar parallel expressions see Job 5:19; Prov. 30:18, 21, 29; Eccles. 11:2; Amos 1:2—2:8. The detestable sins so offensive to God are listed in 17-19.

J. WISDOM AND ADULTERY, 6:20—7:27

After the interlude composed of four brief warnings, the writer returns to the peril of adultery in a fashion similar to that of 2:16-19; 5:3-11; 9:13-18. Following an introductory paragraph on the importance of obedience to parental authority (20-23), the teacher points out the peril of adultery (24-35). Chapter 7 is a continuation of 6:20-35. This further discourse contains an additional warning on the folly of yielding to a harlot. It also highlights wisdom as the answer to temptation and as the only safe guide in the struggles of life. This entire section (6:20—7:27) is the longest discourse in Proverbs dealing with the sin of adultery.

1. A Plea for Obedience (6:20-23)

In these verses the writer points out again the value of parental instruction (see comments on 1:8 and 4:1-9). For an

---

[30]Op. cit., p. 87.

explanation of the expressions **bind them** and **tie them** (21) see comment on 1:8 and 3:3. In 22 we have a beautiful tribute to the faithfulness of the divine directives to bless one's life. These directives of the law (*Torah*) were taught the young student by his parents (Deut. 6:6-7). Two significant statements occur in 23. **The commandment is a lamp** to shed light on life's treacherous way (Ps. 19:8; 119:105). As the source of parental teachings, **the law is light;** therefore, "he who disregards these commandments is as if his candle was quenched."[31]

2. *The Peril of Adultery* (6:24-35)

The heeding of parental instruction will **keep** (24), or "preserve" (RSV), the young man from the snares of the seductive woman. The expression **strange woman** (24) "always means one that is not a man's own; and sometimes it may also imply a *foreign harlot,* one who is also a *stranger* to the God of Israel."[32] It is significant that the Hebrew word for **lust not** (25) used here is the same as that used in the tenth commandment (Exod. 20:17; Deut. 5:21). The teacher warns that the adulteress will especially hunt for **the precious life** (26), i.e., the young, inexperienced person.

With two rhetorical questions in 27-28, the writer seeks to show the deadly risk involved in adultery. The answer to the questions about **fire** (27) and **hot coals** (28) is an emphatic "No." The adulterer is embracing fire, and the damaging outcome of such action is inescapable. He shall **not be innocent** (29); literally, "He shall be punished."

The teacher underscores his lesson in 30-35 by the implement of comparison. A thief may be motivated by mitigating circumstances, such as physical hunger. For his theft he can make restitution, even if it takes all his possessions. **Sevenfold** (31) does not necessarily mean seven times the amount stolen but a full and complete restitution. The adulterer, however, cannot so readily make amends. His sin starts a chain of disastrous consequences. He takes the risk of destroying himself—**his own soul** (32). For no restitution, even **many gifts** (35), will satisfy the offended husband, who will insist on the death pen-

[31]Greenstone, *op. cit.,* p. 64.

[32]Adam Clarke, *The Holy Bible with a Commentary and Critical Notes,* III (New York and Nashville: Abingdon-Cokesbury Press, n.d.), 717.

alty (Lev. 20:10; Deut. 22:22-24). Rylaarsdam says: "In Israelite psychology the adulterer is literally a murderer and is worthy of a murderer's fate."[33]

3. An Introductory Appeal (7:1-5)

In the first five verses of this chapter we have a strong appeal for the young man to take the way of wisdom, which is the way of the Lord. The synonyms for wisdom in 1-4 make this clear: **words** (1), **commandments** (1-2), **law** (2), and **understanding** (4). More is needed than good advice to fortify one against temptation. It is faith in God and the application of that faith to daily living that provide the best safeguards against evil. By taking God's way one is truly wise and finds the secret of victorious living.

Keep . . . my law as the apple of thine eye (2). One's concern for the way of the Lord should be as sensitive as the care of the pupil of one's eye. **The apple of thine eye** is a proverbial expression for something most precious, requiring scrupulous care (cf. Deut. 32:10; Ps. 17:8). Thus should we cherish the will of God. Such positive singleness of purpose is the best protection against sin of any kind.

Bind them . . . write them (3) are expressions of deep religious significance (see comment on 3:3). More is intended here than an exhortation to the literal practice of attaching the phylacteries to the person or the inscribing of the law on the doorposts and gates of the house (Deut. 6:8-9). Edgar Jones sees here "an inwardness . . . enjoined that goes far beyond merely external rites. May we not see an echo of Jeremiah 31 with his teaching of the Inner Covenant?"[34]

The appeal of the teacher reaches a climax in v. 4. The term **my sister** is a designation given to a bride or a wife (Song of Sol. 4:9; 5:1-2). One is to cherish wisdom as he would his bride. "Say to Wisdom, 'You are my darling' " (Moffatt). **Call understanding thy kinswoman** ("intimate friend," RSV). A kinsman (cf. Ruth 2:1; 3:2) is a relative on whose protection one may rightfully depend. So the thrust of 4 is simply that **wisdom** and **understanding,** like a good marriage and a "close friend" (Berk.), are the best safeguards against **the strange woman** (5).

---

[33]*Op. cit.*, p. 37.   [34]*Op. cit.*, p. 91.

4. The Seductive Art of the Temptress (7:6-23)

In this passage the sage depicts in graphic detail the story of a young man who was the object of the evil designs of an adulteress. He relates the tragic outcome of the young man's yielding to the seductive strategy of this profligate woman.

a. The object of evil design (7:6-9). The writer here presents in realistic and vivid detail the snare of the adulteress. He tells of looking through the casement (6; "lattice," Berk.) of his Oriental house and observing the young man who was the object of evil intention. Toy says, "The windows of Oriental houses (like those of Europe some centuries ago) are not enclosed with glass, but have trellis-work of wood or metal, through which a person standing within may see the street without being seen from without; the window was a favorite place of observation."[35]

The object of the adulteress was a young man from among the simple ones (7), or from among "the empty-headed and empty-hearted" group (Amp. OT). This young man was void of understanding. The RSV calls him "a young man without sense." Kidner describes him as "young, inexperienced, feather-brained."[36] The young man was lacking in a grasp of moral principles, but he was not just a simpleton (see comment on 1:4).

This young man was strolling aimlessly along the street. He seemed not only aimless but unaware of the dangers involved in loitering near (8) the house of the temptress. He thus placed himself in a position advantageous to her. He began his stroll at twilight (9), but soon came night and the darkness. Cook comments: "There is a certain symbolic meaning in the picture of the gathering gloom . . . Night is falling over the young man's life as the shadows deepen."[37]

b. The strategy of the seductive (7:10-20). The adulteress was not aimless like the young man. Her designs were definite. She was shameless in her scheming. While she had a husband (19-20), she presents herself in the attire of an harlot (10; cf. Gen. 38:14-15). The young man need have no fear of the law in becoming involved with her, since there is no reprisal from a husband in the case of the professional harlot. This temptress is subtil of heart (10), hard and unyielding in her evil purpose. She is loud and stubborn (11; "turbulent and wilful," Amp. OT).

---

[35]Op. cit., p. 146.   [36]Op. cit., p. 75.
[37]Op. cit., p. 28.

Her "rebellion is obviously a refusal of God's law and the obligations of morality."[38] She is a frequent transgressor, for **her feet abide not in her house. She lieth in wait** ("sets her ambush," Berk.) **at every corner** (12).

The allurements of the adulteress come in rapid succession. She boldly embraces the young man and speaks to him **with an impudent face** (13); literally, she "put on a bold face" (cf. Jer. 3:3). Toy says: "This expression . . . does not intimate that the woman assumes an attitude not natural to her, but simply describes her meretricious boldness."[39]

The adulteress continues her enticements by telling the young man that "her refrigerator is full, as we would say."[40] **I have peace offerings** (14). The flesh of the sacrificial animals was to be eaten the day of the sacrifice, or the day following. That which was not consumed had to be burned the third day (Lev. 7:16-18). The temptress tells the young victim that her sacrifices have been offered and that there is plenty of meat in her house. They will have a feast together. Strange, isn't it, that a person who has been faithful in keeping her religious vows and in observing the sacrificial rituals would fail to see the contradiction between these things and her sinful designs (cf. Isa. 1:11-15)!

The temptress now turns to flattery. She tells the young man he was the very one she had in mind for the festive occasion. Now **I have found thee** (15). He's her "tall, dark, and handsome" dream man. She descends to the level of the sensuous for her next appeal (16-18). Her victim is then assured that her husband has gone on an extensive trip and will not return until **the day appointed** (20); literally, "after many days."

c. *The tragic outcome* (7:21-23). The allurements are effective. The young man yields to temptation. He follows the temptress **as an ox goeth to the slaughter,** as a criminal in chains to his punishment, or as **a bird . . . to the snare** set for it (22-23). But his sin will cost him **his life** (23). This expression depicts moral corruption with its guilt and misery as well as suggesting the tragic consequences that may result when the husband of the adulteress discovers the illicit love affair (see comment on 6:30-35).

---

[38]R. Laird Harris, *op. cit.*, p. 563.   [39]*Op. cit.*, p. 151.
[40]R. Laird Harris, *op. cit.*, p. 563.

5. *A Concluding Exhortation* (7: 24-27)

With the example of the young victim before them, the teacher pleads in solemn tones with his pupils to guard against such temptations. First of all, they were to heed his **words** (24). Wisdom is their only sure protection. Secondly, they were to guard their hearts against the **ways** (25) of the temptress (see comment on 4: 23). Thirdly, they were to keep their distance literally from **her paths.** Finally, they were not to forget that the casualties of sin are numerous—**She hath cast down many—** and that the outcome of sin is the destruction of body and soul (26-27). Fritsch comments: "In the book's descriptions of doom and punishment which the sinner suffers there is a note of finality and hopelessness which makes the Christian shudder. The law instructs the soul in the right way and warns against the calamities that will befall if its precepts are not followed."[41] The adulteress is, therefore, a symbol of the denial of God's rule and the rejection of God always has far-reaching and tragic consequences.

K. WISDOM'S FAME AND EXCELLENCE, 8: 1-36

In the previous chapter we had a revolting portrayal of seduction and sin. In this we have a superb portrait of wisdom. The contrast is like moving from the marshy lowlands of sin's degradation to the highlands of godliness, where the air is fresh and the vision clear. In c. 8 the Hebrew concept of wisdom reaches its zenith of expression in the Old Testament. Greenstone well says of the chapter: "This is not a series of discourses on the beauty of family life, nor even in praise of chastity, but an appeal to the young student to devote himself assiduously to the pursuit of wisdom which offers the safest guide to life."[42]

1. *The Invitation of Wisdom* (8: 1-21)

In this section and throughout c. 8 wisdom is again personified. As in 1: 20-33, she is a prophetic preacher. Here she is also an evangelist, a herald of the good tidings of God's love and concern for all men.

a. *The universal call of wisdom* (8: 1-5). Here the evange-

list proclaims the good news. She gives her message in the most
public and conspicuous places possible (2-3). Horton aptly says:

> Wisdom, unlike the vicious woman who lurks in the twilight
> at the corner of the street which contains her lair, stands in the
> open places; she makes herself as manifest as may be by occupy-
> ing some elevated position, from which her ringing voice may be
> heard down the streets and up the crossways, and may attract the
> attention of those who are entering the city gates or the doors of
> the houses. As her voice is strong and clear, so her words are full
> and rounded; there is no whispering, no muttering, no dark hint, no
> subtle incitement to secret pleasures; her tone is breezy and stir-
> ring as the dawn; there is something about it which makes one
> involuntarily think of the open air, and the wide sky, and the
> great works of God.[43]

The urgent message of wisdom "is as relevant to the shop-
ping-centre (2, 3) as to heaven itself (22)."[44] Furthermore, it is
universal in its offerings. The words **men** and **sons of man** (4)
suggest all classes of mankind, the Gentiles as well as the Jews.
There is nothing exclusive nor provincial about wisdom's invitation. Even the **simple** (5; "heedless," Moffatt) and the **fools,** or
spiritually obstinate, can come, if they will (cf. Matt. 7:7-8).

b. *The character and worth of wisdom* (8:6-16). The message of wisdom is characterized by truth and righteousness (6-9).
There is **nothing froward or perverse** (8; "twisted or crooked,"
Berk.) in the preacher's words. What's more, her proclamations
**are all plain to him that understandeth, and right to them that
find knowledge** (9). Here "a fundamental principle is affirmed.
Those who are willing to commit themselves to receive Wisdom
will be able to understand more fully its nature."[45] In the words
of Jesus, "If any man will do his will, he shall know of the
doctrine, whether it be of God" (John 7:17), we have a New
Testament equivalent of what the preacher was saying in v. 9
(cf. John 8:31-32).

The worth of wisdom is stressed again (see comment on
3:13-17). It is more valuable than such precious things as **silver,
choice gold,** or **rubies** (10-11). All the **things that may be desired
are not to be compared to it.** Moffatt says, "No treasure is equal
to her" (11). Certainly God's seeking love and redemptive provisions are incomparable (cf. Job 28:15, 18; Ps. 19:10; 119:127).

---

[43]*Op. cit.,* p. 107.   [44]"Kidner, *op. cit.,* pp. 76-77.
[45]Edgar Jones, *op. cit.,* p. 97.

Here wisdom stresses the truth that more important than earthly riches are heavenly treasures (Matt. 6: 19-21). Wisdom describes additional virtues in 12-16. She is practical and resourceful—**I . . . find out knowledge** (12). She identifies herself with **the fear of the Lord** (13; see comment on 1: 7). She hates evil of every kind. Harris says that "true godliness is not all positive. The teaching that sin is hateful is a wonderful and vital truth."[46] She is able—**I have strength** (14)—to put wisdom into practice. True statesmanship comes through her guidance (15-16). Solomon found her help for his reign (I Kings 3: 5-12).

c. *The rewards of wisdom* (8: 17-21). In this passage wisdom offers many rewards to those who respond affirmatively to the prophetic challenge. All those who **love God—those that seek Him early** (17; "diligently," RSV)—**shall find** Him (cf. Matt. 5: 6). Material prosperity is included (18, 21), but the favor and friendship of God are the supreme blessings of wisdom's way (19).

2. *The Eternity and Creativity of Wisdom* (8: 22-31)

This section has been called "the greatest passage in the Book of Proverbs."[47] Fritsch sees here "one of the most perfect pictures of Christ to be found in the Old Testament."[48] This magnificent section anticipates such significant New Testament passages as John 1: 1-14; I Cor. 1: 24, 30; Col. 1: 15-18; and Heb. 1: 1-4. Greenstone denies any connection between this sublime personification of wisdom and the concept of the Logos.[49] Yet Deane and Taylor-Taswell say: "There is . . . nothing forced or incongruous in seeing in this episode a portraiture of the Second Person of the blessed Trinity, the essential Wisdom of God personified, the Logos of later books, and of the gospel."[50] Fritsch says that the early Church Fathers "used this passage to formulate their ideas about the Second Person of the Trinity."[51] Athanasius and other leaders met one of the great doctrinal crises of

[46]*Op. cit.,* p. 564.   [47]Edgar Jones, *op. cit.,* p. 100.
[48]*Op. cit., Theology Today,* VII, 181.
[49]*Op. cit.,* p. 84.
[50]"Proverbs" (Exposition), *The Pulpit Commentary,* ed. H. D. M. Spence and Joseph S. Exell (London and New York: Funk and Wagnalls Co., 1913), p. 164.
[51]*Op. cit., Theology Today,* VII, 170.

the Christian Church with their Nicene Christology that drew from this deep well of the Old Testament revelation as it did from the fountains of the inspired New Testament record.

a. *The timelessness of wisdom* (8:22-23). In 22 we have one of the most discussed passages in the Old Testament. The word rendered **possessed me** (Heb., *qanah*) is somewhat ambiguous and has therefore been translated in several ways. Its most common meaning is "to buy," "acquire," or "possess." The word is used in this way in at least a dozen other passages in Proverbs. Its less usual meaning is "to create" (cf. Deut. 32:6; Ps. 139:13). So it has been translated "formed me" (Smith-Goodspeed, Moffatt), "made me" (Berk.), or "created me" (RSV, LXX, Targum). The heretical Arians used 22 as a basis for their thesis that Christ was a created being, subordinate to God. He was, therefore, neither divine nor eternal. Athanasius, however, translated this difficult phrase: "constituted [appointed] me [Christ] as head of creation."

Both the more common meaning of the Hebrew *qanah* and the general tenor of the entire passage (22-31) suggest that wisdom existed before God created the world and that it was active in the creative process (cf. 3:19). Kidner keenly observes: "Goods are possessed by purchase, children by birth . . . wisdom —for mortals—by learning. And wisdom for God? To say at first He lacked it and had to create or learn it, is both alien to this passage and absurd."[52]

Of vv. 22-23, Maclaren comments: "The personified Wisdom of Proverbs is the personal Word of John's prologue. John almost quotes the former when he says 'the same was in the beginning with God,' for his word recalls the grand declaration, 'The Lord possessed me in the beginning of His way . . . I was set up in the beginning or ever the earth was.' Then there are two beginnings, one lost in the depths of timeless being, one, the commencement of creative activity, and the Word was with God in the remotest, as in the nearer, beginning."[53]

b. *The primacy of wisdom* (8:24-26). These three verses constitute a beautiful poetic proclamation of the eternity of wisdom. Before any of the physical universe came into being, wisdom was in existence (cf. John 1:1). The Psalmist wrote a similar declaration of God: "Before the mountains were brought

[52]*Op. cit.*, p. 80.   [53]*Op. cit.*, p. 140.

forth, or ever thou hadst formed the earth and the world, even from everlasting to everlasting, thou art God" (90:2).

c. The role of wisdom in creation (8:27-31). This passage sets forth wisdom's role in the creation of the world. By doing so, it undergirds the unity of the Godhead in the creative venture. The key verse in this section is 30: **Then I was by him;** literally, "beside him." These words tie together God the Redeemer and God the Creator (cf. John 1:1-4).

As one brought up with him is another expression with varying interpretations. The difficulty is due to the words **brought up** (Heb., *amon*), which mean either "master workman, craftsman" or "little child, ward." Wisdom was alongside God "as a master and director of the work" (Amp. OT). Wisdom was "a master workman" (RSV), or "a master builder" (Berk.). A child or ward, however, is one who is constantly with his parents or guardians. Therefore wisdom was "a ward of his" (Smith-Goodspeed) or "his foster-child" (Moffatt). Both interpretations of *amon* make wisdom a part of the creative venture. The first, however, makes wisdom active in creation. This seems to be the more satisfactory view, since it fits into the total context better and is more in harmony with the later Christology of the New Testament. In v. 31 we learn that the outcome of the creative activity was delightful to wisdom (cf. Ps. 16:3).

The theme of vv. 22-31 is "Christ—Wisdom Incarnate." We see: (1) His eternity or preexistence, 22-26; (2) His primal blessedness, 30; (3) His active role in creation, 27-30; and (4) His delight in mankind, 31.

3. The Climactic Appeal of Wisdom (8:32-36)

Here is the sermon's challenging conclusion. And **now** (32) —in the light of all that the preacher has said—the pupils are to make their decision. They are not deciding on an incidental matter. The ultimate consequences are again stated. Great blessings are in store for those who heed wisdom's words (32, 34-35). Great tragedy will result from rejecting them. **All that hate me love death** (36)—spiritual death (cf. Deut. 11:26-28; 30:19-20).

L. WISDOM AND FOLLY CONTRASTED, 9:1-18

This concluding chapter of the first section of Proverbs presents the alternatives of life in the two contrasting invitations of wisdom (1-6) and folly (13-18). Both are personified as rival hostesses who offer their respective feasts to all. Their invitations are separated by an interesting interlude (7-12). Some scholars see this interlude as belonging to the next section of Proverbs and placed here by mistake. Moffatt places this passage at the end of the chapter. Kidner, however, sees its inclusion here as significant. He says: "Its position allows the chapter (and section of the book) to end on a shattering climax (18); its content corrects the impression that men are saved or lost merely through an isolated, impulsive decision. The choice is seen ripening into character and so into destiny."[54]

1. The Invitation of Wisdom (9:1-6)

Previously we have seen wisdom personified as a prophetic preacher (1:20-33; 8:1-21). In this passage we see her as a gracious hostess. She has built a house with **seven pillars** (1). This phrase may simply mean many pillars or it could be a reference to the number of pillars supporting a large Eastern house. The allegorical interpretations of the expression are numerous.[55] Wisdom prepared her lavish feast. She even **mingled** (mixed) **her wine** (2). The mixing was the addition of spices to make the wine more tasty. The real feast of this passage is, of course, a spiritual one and intended to help those invited to make their decision to take the right way in the midst of life's alternatives (see comment on 4:10-19).

The invitation to the feast is heralded to all—even to the **simple** and the man that **wanteth understanding** (4). Says Edgar Jones: "The simple are the uncommitted section of the people, especially youths who are subject to so many influences and pressures but have not as yet made irrevocable decisions."[56] The one who **wanteth understanding**, literally "heart," is he who needs spiritual strength. The scene anticipates the marriage feast in the parable of Jesus (Matt. 22:2-10). The invitation: **Come, eat . . . and drink** (5), reminds one of the evangelical call of Isa. 55:1-5 and of John 6:35. The hour of decision is here. **Forsake the foolish, and live** (6). Renounce the way of folly and sin and take the way of life.

---

[54]*Op. cit.,* p. 82.

[55]See Greenstone, *op. cit.,* p. 90; Edgar Jones, *op. cit.,* pp. 103-4; Kidner, *op. cit.,* p. 32.

[56]*Op. cit.,* p. 105

2. The Interesting Interlude (9:7-12)

In vv. 7-9 the writer treats the problem of dealing with those who reject the way of wisdom, i.e., the way of God. Because one may suffer **shame** (7; "abuse," RSV), he is not free from his obligation to rebuke his neighbor for his transgressions. This passage recognizes realistically the reactions of the wicked. The **wise man**, however, appreciates correction (9). Those who **fear ... the Lord** are teachable (10).

The concept of individual responsibility is underscored in 12. Kidner observes: "This is perhaps the strongest expression of individualism in the Bible."[57] Similar expressions of this truth are found in Deut. 24:16; Jer. 31:30; and Ezek. 18:4. Character is the outcome of a man's personal choices, and for his ultimate destiny he must bear full responsibility. This truth is fittingly placed here between the two invitations of this chapter.

3. The Invitation of the Woman of Folly (9:13-18)

In contrast to the invitation to the banquet of life we now have the invitation to the feast of folly. The **foolish woman is clamorous** (13; "loud and alluring," Moffatt). She **knoweth nothing,** or has "no sense of shame" (Moffatt) in her efforts to seduce men. She has no respect for eternal values. Her invitation has been compared to the serpent's appeal in Eden (Gen. 3:4). In the expression, **Stolen waters are sweet** (17; cf. 20:17; Isa. 5:20), Rylaarsdam says we have "an intimation of adultery (see 5:15), though that particular sin is symbolic of all evil and, more to the point, of the satanic invitation to evil which is everywhere contending the call of God in Wisdom."[58]

The foolish or sinful appear to be enjoying life (17), but the outcome of their way is death (18). Thus the first major section of Proverbs closes with a dramatic appeal, reminding us that the only satisfying and fully adequate choice is to take God's way. The alternative is ultimately disappointing—ever the way of death.

⁵⁷*Op. cit..* p. 83   ⁵⁸*Op. cit.,* p. 47.

Section **II** *The Proverbs of Solomon*

Proverbs 10:1—22:16

We come now to the main section of Proverbs. We find here no lengthy discourses such as we encountered in the first nine chapters. This section consists of 375 aphoristic, two-line couplets. They are brief, complete in themselves, and independent of one another. They almost defy any logical arrangement or grouping. They comprise a somewhat patternless mosaic. Because of this fact exposition is difficult. Here and there a few couplets seem to be related. In 10:1—15:33 the couplets are predominantly antithetic, or proverbs of contrast. In 16:1—22:16 the couplets are largely parallel. Fritsch points out the fact that only 33 out of the 191 of these couplets are expressed in contrasting lines.[1] In most of the couplets of this latter section we find a synonymous parallelism, where the second line simply repeats in different words the first line.

The topical headings in the commentary on this central section of Proverbs seek to provide some general structure and aim to highlight a dominant theme that appears in a group or in a chapter. The biblical text, however, is such that the topical arrangements suggested are neither fully definitive nor fully adequate. Despite problems of arrangement, the overall purpose of this central section of Proverbs is clear. Wisdom is challenging the uncommitted to take the way of the Lord. Harris aptly says: "Again we must insist that this is not a *Poor Richard's Almanac* of pithy, common sense sayings bearing on life's problems; this is a divine collection of sayings pointing out the way of holiness."[2]

A. Proverbs of Contrast, 10:1—15:33

1. *The Righteous and the Wicked* (10:1-22)

In v. 1 we have the second of three occasions where Solomonic authorship is indicated (cf. 1:1; 25:1). In this collection Solomon begins with a proverb on the home, so significant in teaching the way of God (cf. 13:1). Greenstone says that the terms **wise** and **foolish** in 1, as elsewhere in Proverbs, "are not to be taken in the intellectual but in the moral sense. The wise

[1]*Op. cit.*, IB, 4:775.   [2]*Op. cit.*, p. 566.

is he who follows the path of wisdom which is the path of right conduct, while the foolish is the wicked, perverse and immoral."[3] In 9:12 we had the emphasis on individual responsibility. In v. 1 we have the principle of social obligation. Holiness of heart and life is always both personal and social.

Treasures of wickedness (2; "ill-gotten gains," Moffatt) will profit us nothing in the hour of judgment. This expression anticipates the words of Jesus: "For what is a man profited, if he shall gain the whole world, and lose his own soul? or what shall a man give in exchange for his soul?" (Matt. 16:26) Righteousness, however, is man's best security and will be to his advantage in the day of judgment.

The words **righteousness** (2) and **righteous** (3), so prominent in this chapter, are key words in Proverbs. They describe the opposites of *wickedness* and *wicked*. The **righteous** man will not suffer hunger (3; cf. Ps. 37:25). His labor is attended by God's blessing (4-5, 16; see comments on 6:6-11). He is blessed and his good name and influence live on (6-7). He continues to learn (8) and he has nothing to hide (9). **The mouth of the righteous is a well** ("fountain," Berk.) **of life** (11). "The talk of good men is a life-giving fountain" (Moffatt). God himself is the Source of this life (Ps. 36:9; Jer. 2:13). Jesus used similar language to describe the gift of the Spirit (John 4:14; 7:38-39). The righteous man is guided by **wisdom** (13) and his speech is disciplined (14). He remains teachable (17). His speech is worth hearing (20). His words are a blessing to others (21). His wealth is the superior riches that God alone can give (22). Throughout this picture the way of the wicked is presented by the antithesis of the proverbs.

2. *Outcomes of Right and Wrong Living* (10:23-32)

The wicked find pleasure in evil, but the righteous man finds his delight in doing God's will (23). The wicked fears the consequences of his deeds, but the righteous desires only what is in God's will for him, and what is **granted** to him (24). **The wicked** soon passes away as in a **whirlwind** (25), but **the righteous** has a **foundation** that will last forever (cf. 1:27; Matt. 7:24-27). In 26 the wise man says that **the sluggard** is as irritating as **vinegar** and **smoke.**

[3]*Op. cit.,* p. 98.

In v. 27 **the fear of the Lord** brings length of **days, but the life of the wicked shall be shortened** (cf. 2:18; 3:2). The glad **hope of the righteous** (28) and the despair of **the wicked** are compared. The righteous find **strength** ("a stronghold," Berk.) in God, but the same power brings **destruction** to the wicked (29). **The righteous shall never be removed** from his land (see comment on 2:21-22), **but the wicked** shall not be so blessed (30). The characters of the righteous and the wicked are revealed by their speech (31). **The righteous** knows **what is acceptable** to God and edifying to his neighbor, but **the wicked speaketh frowardness** (32), or "what is obstinately willful and contrary" (Amp. OT). Clarke says: "As the love of God is not in his heart; so the law of kindness is not on his lips."[4]

3. The Upright and the Godless (11:1-11)

The first couplet in this chapter relates honesty to the will of **the Lord.** "A false balance is loathsome to the Eternal" (1, Moffatt). The law prohibited the use of false weights and measures (Lev. 19:35-36; Deut. 25:13-15). The prophets warned against dishonesty in business (Ezek. 45:10; Amos 8:5; Mic. 6:11). The wise men of Israel thus reflected the teachings of the law and the prophets (cf. 11:1; 16:11; 20:10, 23). **A just weight** is literally "a full or complete stone." It was easy to grind off or chip away a portion of the stone that was used in that day as a standard of weight, and thus the balance would give the customer a short amount. **Pride** or arrogance is contrasted with humility (2). **The lowly** (Heb., *tsenium*) means "humble" or "modest." It occurs only here and in Mic. 6:8.

In vv. 3-9 righteousness is contrasted with wickedness and the effects of each way of life are stressed. **Integrity . . . shall guide** (3) the upright. This **integrity** is moral perfectness or completeness. The verb **guide** "is used of a shepherd guiding a lamb in a dangerous place."[5] While material wealth is not bad in itself, it will not suffice **in the day of wrath,** or in the day of judgment (cf. Zeph. 1:15-18), or even in the hour of **death** (4). The **wicked man** is spiritually bankrupt (7). **The righteous** may be exposed to **trouble** (8) but he is vindicated. The wicked get into the kinds of trouble that the righteous escape. **Through** his **knowledge** of the Lord **the just** will be saved (9). In vv. 10-11 we have the impact of **the righteous** on society. Whether or not the world seems to appreciate righteousness, it is a blessing to society (cf. Matt. 5:13-14). In contrast, the wicked are damaging in their influence on others.

4. The Trustworthy and the Talebearer (11:12-23)

The person who lacks **wisdom** (12; "good sense," Berk.) **despiseth** ("belittles," RSV) **his neighbour.** Kidner says: "The most misleading way to feel wise is to feel superior (14:21 goes further: it is sin), for one is denying that God is the only competent judge of human worth."[6] The man who speaks contemptuously of others is also **a talebearer** (13); literally, "a slanderer" (Heb., *rakil*).[7] In contrast to him is the man of **a faithful spirit**— "a steadfast or trustworthy" person.

In v. 14 wisdom is related to sound statesmanship. **Where no counsel is** ("where there is no guidance," RSV), **people** suffer. The word "guidance" is that used for steering a ship. So "the ship of state" needs much "leadership" (Berk.) to give it proper direction. In 15 we have another warning against **suretiship** (see comment on 6:1-5). In v. 16 the noble traits of **a gracious woman** —literally, "a woman of grace"—are compared to the get-rich-quick schemes of evil men. Moffatt catches the significance of this verse in these words: "A charming woman wins respect: high-handed men win only wealth."

In vv. 17-21 we have more couplets describing the consequences of good and evil. **Though hand join in hand** (21) is a rather difficult expression. The Hebrew is literally "hand to hand," probably referring to the custom of shaking hands on a promise (Job 17:3). The writer is saying, "Be assured" (RSV) that no wicked person shall escape retribution. In 22 the wise man says that beauty without character is worthless. The **woman ... without discretion** ("good taste," Berk.) is one without moral discrimination. In v. 23 the outcome of a man's life is related to his **desire**, or to that which motivates his life and character.

5. The Rewards and Punishments (11:24-31)

In vv. 24-29 the generous man and the miser are compared. **The liberal soul shall be made fat** (25; "enriched," Berk.). Jesus said: "Give, and it shall be given unto you" (Luke 6:38). The

---

[6]*Op. cit.,* p. 91.

[7]See the excellent discussion on the biblical concept of the nature of speech by Rylaarsdam, *op. cit.,* pp. 51-53.

miserly person **withholdeth corn** (26) when **the people** need it. Today we would think of this man as engaged in the black market. A person gets what he goes after in life (27). The error of the miserly, however, is not in having **riches** but in trusting in them (28). The miser creates disturbance in his own home and may be reduced to slavery (29).

The expression **a tree of life** (30) means that the righteous man not only takes the way of life but he also has a life-giving influence on others. **He that winneth souls** is literally "one who taketh or acquireth souls." The idea is that of capturing others with ideas or influences. Jesus told His disciples that they were to "catch men" (Luke 5:10). Jones and Walls say: "The meaning is surely that the wise man by his example gains the lives of other men, so that his righteousness is *a tree of life* to others as well as himself."[8] Neither **the righteous** nor **the wicked** shall sin with impunity (31; cf. Jer. 25:29; Ezek. 18:24; I Pet. 4:12-19).

6. The Way of Discipline (12:1-8)

Men react differently to moral and religious **instruction** (1; "discipline," RSV). The sincere seeker after knowledge will accept correction and profit from it. But the person who resents discipline is "like a brute beast, stupid and indiscriminating" (Amp. OT). Toy says: "The proverb may allude to all sorts of teaching (by parents, friends, priests, lawyers), but probably contemplates especially the schools or writings of sages, in which were given rules for the conduct of life."[9]

In vv. 2-3 the fortunes of good and evil men are contrasted. **A good man** finds favor in God's sight but an evil man He pronounces guilty. **Wickedness** (3) provides no adequate basis for a man's life, but righteousness brings a desired permanency (cf. 7, 12, 19; Ps. 1:3-4). In v. 4 we have a capsule description of a good wife. A detailed presentation is given in 31:10-31. The word **virtuous** (Heb., *hayil*) means power in both body and mind. So a good wife is one of strong character. Such a woman is her husband's **crown** (cf. Job 19:9; Lam. 5:16); she is "his glory and joy, bringing him happiness at home and honor abroad by her household arrangements, and the respect which her character commands."[10] The woman who **maketh ashamed** ("acts

---

[8]*Op. cit.*, pp. 528-29.   [9]*Op. cit.*, p. 242.
[10]*Ibid.*, p. 243.

disgracefully," Berk.) is like a disease in a man's **bones,** taking his strength and destroying his happiness (cf. 31:23; I Cor. 11:7). In 5-6 man's basic intentions are compared. The **thoughts** (5), designs or plans, **of the righteous** are compared to the deceptive **counsels of the wicked.** A New Testament equivalent of this verse is, "By their fruits ye shall know them" (Matt. 7:20). **The words of the wicked** (6) are like assassins, lying in wait to destroy their victims. But the speech **of the upright** is his best defense against slander. In 7 we have the impermanence of evil in contrast to the prosperity of **the righteous** (cf. Matt. 7:24-27). In 8 the respected man of **wisdom** is compared to the despised man **of a perverse heart.**

7. The Way of Diligence (12:9-14)

In v. 9 we have a protest against ostentation. Edgar Jones says that this verse points out "the fallacy of the social facade."[11] The contrast is between the humble man who can afford only one **servant** and the man who puts on airs but does not have enough to eat. The usual price of a slave was about eighteen dollars (thirty shekels; Exod. 21:32). The **righteous man** is considerate of animals (9; cf. Exod. 23:12; Deut. 25:4). In v. 11 the diligent man will "have plenty of food" (Moffatt), but "he who follows worthless pursuits" (Amp. OT) doesn't have much sense.

The Hebrew in 12 is obscure. **The wicked desireth the net of evil men,** i.e., what their net yields. Greenstone says: "The wicked covet the produce normal to men of their type, the easy way of acquiring wealth by taking away the gains that others accumulated through hard toil."[12] The **fruit,** however, of a righteous man's labor will be more permanent. In vv. 13-14 we have underlined the truth that a man's words and deeds will have their reward (cf. Matt. 12:36-37; II Cor. 5:10). We might say: "Chickens come home to roost." For a New Testament expression of this truth see Gal. 6:7.

8. The Wise and the Foolish (12:15-28)

A **fool** is self-opinionated, but a **wise** man is teachable (15). A fool gives way to his self-destroying emotions, but a wise man has self-control, even when he is insulted (16). "The prudent man ignores an insult" (Moffatt). In 17-19 we have three

---

[11]*Op. cit.*, p. 123.   [12]*Op. cit.*, p. 130.

contrasting proverbs on speech. Many of the proverbs in the latter portion of this chapter deal with the use of the tongue.[13] Fritsch says that more than one hundred verses in Proverbs deal with the tongue.[14] Verse 17 makes it clear that a man's words reveal his character. A fool is hurtful with his words, but a wise man's speech is healing (18). **Truth** is permanent, but falsehood is **only for a moment.**

The wicked not only tell falsehoods, but they are false **in the heart** (20). In v. 21 the fates of **the just** and **the wicked** are compared (cf. Ps. 91:10; Rom. 8:28). In 22-23 are two more contrasts of speech. The Lord hates **lying lips** but delights in the truth (cf. 6:17; 11:20; Rev. 22:15). Toy sees 23 as "wise reticence and foolish babbling."[15]

Diligence is rewarding, but laziness is costly (24). **The slothful shall be under tribute,** or "put to forced labor" (Amp. OT). **Heaviness** (25; "worry," Moffatt) is hard on a man's spirit, **but a good word** "cheers him up" (Moffatt). In 26 the Hebrew of the first line is difficult, but the meaning of the verse is that **the righteous** are helpful and **the wicked** hurtful. In v. 27 the lazy person is described as too indolent even to roast what he has caught. In v. 28 the two ultimate sanctions are again expressed—**life** and **death.**

9. *The Way of True Riches* (13:1-11)

In v. 1 the **wise son** and the **cynic** are compared in their attitude to paternal discipline. The verb **heareth** in the first portion, missing in the Hebrew text, is supplied in harmony with the second line of the parallelism. In 2 we have the outcome of conduct. A good man enjoys the fruits of righteousness (cf. 12:14), but the **transgressors** ("faithless," Smith-Goodspeed) shall feed on **violence.** Some scholars see retribution in the second line. Moffatt translates it: "But evil souls come to an untimely end." Verse 3 gives a warning against rash speaking (cf. 10:19; 21:23; Ps. 39:1; Jas. 1:26). In 4 we see that diligence is superior to dreaming about work and its rewards. To be made **fat** means to prosper. While a good man hates **lying . . . a wicked man is loathsome;** literally, "causeth a stench" (5). The outcomes of right and wrong living are compared in 6 (cf. 11:3-9).

---

[13]For a helpful study on words as used in Proverbs see Kidner, *op. cit.*, pp. 46-49.

[14]*Op. cit.*, IB, 4:853-54.   [15]*Op. cit.*, p. 255.

In vv. 7-8 riches and poverty are compared. Verse 7 can be understood in two ways. First is as the pretense of the spendthrift or social climber and the cover-up of the miser (RSV, ASV, et al.). A second interpretation sees here a comparison between true and false riches (cf. Luke 12:21, 23; II Cor. 8:9). In 8 we see both the advantage and disadvantage of wealth. While **riches** serve as a protection from danger, they also expose the wealthy man to robbery and extortion. **The poor heareth not rebuke;** rather, "heareth no threatening." The poor are not so apt to be the object of robbery or blackmail. In 9 the happiness of **the righteous** is compared with the plight of **the wicked**. On the symbolism of **light** and **lamp** here see Esther 8:16; Job 18:5-6; Ps. 27:1. In v. 10 **pride** is compared with the humility of the person who fears God. In 11 we have contrasted results of the two ways of gaining **wealth**—by fraudulent means or by industry and thrift.

10. The Source of True Hope (13:12-25)

Delay in the fulfillment of one's hopes is the basis for disappointment, if not despondency (12). The **heart** here, as elsewhere in Proverbs, means the total personality. However, to realize one's **desire** (hopes or longings) brings joy. The **tree of life** is an expression of fulfillment and happiness (cf. 3:18; 11:30). In v. 13 we have a warning regarding the importance of obeying the Word of God. Kidner says: "*Word* and *commandment* are a reminder that *revealed* religion is presupposed in Proverbs."[16] On 14, **The law** (teachings) **of the wise is a fountain of life**, see comment on 10:11. The obedient are saved from many dangers (I Tim. 6:9; II Tim. 2:25-26).

The expression **good understanding** (15) has been variously translated. Moffatt terms this person "a man of tact." Smith-Goodspeed likely comes nearer the original intent by translating it "good conduct." **Understanding** (Heb., *sekel*) and **favour** (*hen*) Harris thinks "are here so clearly moral terms, coming as the result of God's commandments, that it is difficult to see how Delitzsch can call *sekel* 'fine culture.'"[17] The comparison is likely that of goodness with transgressions in the second line. **The way of transgressors is hard** ("rugged," Berk.), "like the barren, dry soil or the impassable swamp" (Amp. OT).

[16]*Op. cit.*, p. 103.   [17]*Op. cit.*, p. 569.

The **prudent man** (16) is in contrast to the **fool** who **layeth open** (displays) **his folly.** In v. 17 **wicked** and **faithful** messengers are compared. Fritsch says: "In the ancient days the nature and results of a message depended to a great extent upon the character of the messenger."[18] The sage next says that the teachable are successful but those who reject **instruction** shall come to **poverty and shame** (18; cf. 1:20-33). Fulfillment of **desire** is **sweet to the soul** (19), but a fool will not give up his evil way even for this rightful sense of fulfillment. In 20 we are reminded that a man's wisdom is affected by the company he keeps.

The fates of the righteous and the wicked are contrasted in 21-22 (cf. 25). Even **the wealth of the sinner,** if not dissipated in his lifetime, becomes the inheritance of the righteous. While 23 is difficult to translate, Kidner says: "The point of this terse proverb seems to be that the size of your resources matters less than the judgment with which you handle them."[19] In v. 24 we have a familiar proverb that underscores again the seriousness with which the Hebrew parents faced the discipline of their children (cf. Eph. 6:4; Heb. 12:5-11). In v. 25 the truth of 21-22 is again expressed.

11. *Wisdom and Folly* (14:1-19)

In v. 1 the constructive nature of wisdom is placed alongside the destructive powers of folly. Here wisdom is personified as a **woman** (cf. RSV), and this verse reflects the invitations of wisdom and folly in 9:1-6 and 9:13-18. In v. 2 we are told that the ways of the upright and the **perverse** are determined by one's regard for God and His will. Verse 3 is another proverb that stresses the importance of restraint in speech. The word rendered **rod** is "sprig" and occurs only here and in Isa. 11:1. *The Berkeley Version* translates it, "In the mouth of the foolish man lies a rod for his pride." Jones and Walls say: "The point behind verse 4 is probably, 'No oxen, no stable-cleaning; but also no ploughing, and therefore no corn.' "[20] In 5 **true** and **false** witnesses are contrasted. Perjury in court is frequently condemned in Proverbs (6:9; 12:17; 14:25; 19:5, 9; 21:28; *et al.*).

The sage reminds us that **the scorner** (6; scoffer) has disqualified himself in his search for wisdom because he does not

---

[18]*Op. cit.,* IB, 4:859.　　　　　　　[19]*Op. cit.,* p. 105.

[20]*Op. cit.,* p. 530.

fear the Lord (cf. 1:7). Association with the **foolish man** (7) is not rewarding, for "you will not find a word of sense in him" (Moffatt). **Wisdom** helps a man to rightly assess his conduct, **but the folly of fools** (8) "is deceiving" (RSV), both to themselves and to others. Scholars have difficulty in interpreting 9. The word **sin** (Heb., *asham*) is frequently translated "sin offering." So "a sin offering mocks fools." Some interpreters see in this the emptiness of the sinner's ceremonial observances. Others see here the sinner's insolence in making fun of sin and thus incurring guilt—"Guilt has its home among fools" (Smith-Goodspeed). The RSV translates 9*b*, "The upright enjoy his [God's] favor." In v. 10 we have a statement of rare beauty that emphasizes the solitariness of sorrow and joy. Only God and close human friends can share a man's experiences of these emotions.

In v. 11 the fates of the righteous and wicked are compared The **house of the wicked** will not endure, but **the tabernacle** (tent) of the righteous shall not only last, but prosper. **There is a way which seemeth right** (12; lit., "straight") but its outcome is most tragic. It ends in "the depths of hell" (LXX). This verse is repeated in 16:25. In v. 13 the writer says that **laughter** often covers inner pain, and that joy is followed by grief. Here is no expression of pessimism, but of realism regarding life's changing moods. Verse 14 has been interpreted, "He whose heart is turned away will have the reward of his ways in full measure; but a good man will have the reward of his doings" (BB).

In vv. 15-16 the care and caution of the **wise** are set in contrast to the gullibility and overconfidence of **the fool.** In vv. 17-18 the impulsive anger and the deliberate evil of the fool are in contrast to the patience of the wise man whose life is crowned with knowledge. In v. 19 we have the vindication of goodness.

12. *The Rich and the Poor* (14:20-35)

In vv. 20-21 we have parallelisms on the rich and the poor. While poverty often brings loneliness and wealth attracts **many friends** (20), **he that hath mercy on the poor** will find happiness (21). This proverb anticipates the almsgiving of New Testament times (cf. Matt. 6:1). In the first line of 22 there is a rhetorical question used to underscore the certainty of the issue. It might be translated, "They certainly do **err** who **devise evil.**" The word **err** means to "go astray" and is a figure of speech borrowed from travel. Toy says: "The bad man wanders hopelessly."[21] In 23 industry is seen as valuable to all, but idle talk is denounced as conducive to poverty.

The wise man (24) is adorned by his "wealth of wisdom" (Amp. OT), but "the garland of fools is folly" (Smith-Goodspeed). Verse 25 declares that the faithful **witness** saves lives, while a false testimony causes the innocent to suffer (cf. 6:19; 12:16; 19:28; 25:18). Moreover, the faithful witness fears **the Lord** and gives **his children** the security of faith (26-27). In v. 28 some scholars see a purely secular description of a king and his power. But Greenstone says: "Some of the Jewish commentators connect this with the previous verse and obtain the meaning that the God-fearing man is more secure than the king with his armies."[22]

In v. 29 we see the patience of wisdom in contrast to the rashness of folly (cf. 16:32; Jas. 1:19). Verse 30 teaches us that "a tranquil mind gives life to the flesh" (RSV) but jealousy, resentment, and other unwholesome mental attitudes are injurious to one's health. Those who oppress **the poor** are offensive to God (31; cf. 17:5; Matt. 25:40, 45). In 32 the fate of the wicked is contrasted to the hope of the righteous regarding death. In 33 we are reminded that "wisdom has her resting place in the mind of the wise, but she is not seen among the foolish" (BB). In v. 34 a nation's strength is measured by its relationship to the law of God. In 35 **the king's favour** (recognition) is seen as based on a man's own character and deeds.

13. The Tongue of the Wise (15:1-20)

In v. 1 we have one of the best known of the proverbs on the power of gentle speech (cf. 18). In 2 there is a reminder of the kind of talk that comes from **the wise** and from **fools** (cf. 7). In v. 3 we see God's concern for all His created children—both **the evil and the good.** Here Israel's personal name for God (*Yahweh*) appears again.[23] Words are life-giving or damaging to man's **spirit** (4). A wise man accepts **instruction** and correction (5). Godliness is rewarded by **much treasure** (6; "ample wealth," Smith-Goodspeed), but the ill-gotten gain of **the wicked** will eventually be lost. A wise man loves to share knowledge, but a fool is indifferent to it (7; cf. 2).

[21]*Op. cit.*, p. 295.   [22]*Op. cit.*, p. 157.

[23]See Rylaarsdam's discussion of the use of the name LORD in Proverbs, *op. cit.*, pp. 59-61

In vv. 8-9, God does not condemn the sacrificial system as such, but stresses the necessity of right attitudes and conduct to give validity to man's approach to Him (cf. I Sam. 15:22; Isa. 1:11; Jer. 7:22; Amos 5:21-24). In v. 10 the importance of continued right choice is emphasized again. Toy says: "Life is represented as a discipline—woe to him who fails to profit thereby."[24] In 11 hell (Heb., *Sheol*) and destruction (Heb., *Abaddon*) are synonyms. Edgar Jones captures the thought of this verse: "If God knows the hidden mysteries of Sheol and Abaddon then how much more the shiftings and evasions of the human mind and heart."[25] A scorner (12; conceited, proud man) is fixed in his rejection of wisdom. Joy is contagious, but sorrow is depressing both to oneself and to others (13). The wise feed on knowledge; the fools, on folly (14). Affliction is depressing, but the man of inner gladness has a continuing banquet (15).

In v. 16 the sage stresses the superiority of riches of the spirit—the fear of the Lord. A sumptuous feast is not satisfying when love is missing. A vegetable platter in an atmosphere of love is better than a juicy steak in the midst of hatred (17). A wrathful man ("hot-tempered," Berk.) causes strife, but a disciplined man eases tension (18; cf. 1). The path of the indolent is an hedge of thorns ("overgrown with thorns," Amp. OT), but the way of the righteous is free of obstacles (19; cf. Isa. 57:14; Jer. 18:15). For v. 20 see note on 10:1.

14. The Secrets of a Cheerful Heart (15:21-33)

The fool delights in his folly and does not seem to comprehend the outcome of his immoral deeds. Kidner calls him "the playboy."[26] But the man of God walketh uprightly (21). For v. 22 see comment on 11:14. An apt reply brings joy to a man, and particularly when this fitting word is appropriately timed (23). "The path of life leads upward for the wise, that he may avoid Sheol below" (24, Berk.). In 25 we are told that God is opposed to exploitation, especially of the widow. Verse 26 reminds us that God hates the thoughts of the wicked. He that is greedy of gain ("plunders for profit," Berk.) brings trouble on himself and his family, but he that refuses bribes shall live (27; cf. Isa. 5:8; Jer. 17:11).

[24]*Op. cit.*, p. 307.   [25]*Op. cit.*, pp. 142-43.
[26]*Op. cit.*, p. 116.

503

In v. 28 we have a contrast between deliberate speech and a deluge of thoughtless words (cf. I Pet. 3:15). Wickedness puts distance between God and the sinner (Exod. 33:3). But God is near **the righteous** and hears their **prayer** (29; cf. 8-9). There is a **light of the eyes** in the bearer of good news and such cheerfulness builds a man's morale (30). **The ear** (31) stands for the whole man. The person who listens to **reproof** has a permanence to his life. Verse 32 stresses the rewards of teachability (cf. 10, 12). **The fear of the Lord** (33) is not only the beginning of wisdom (1:7) but also its continuance. Those who have the **humility** to accept God and His guidance shall be honored of Him.

B. PROVERBS LARGELY PARALLEL, 16:1—22:16

1. *The Lord of Life* (16:1-11)

It is significant that in each of vv. 1-7 Israel's personal name for God (*Yahweh*) appears. This section stresses God's activity in the affairs of men. In 1 the sage says that both man's plans and their expression are subject to divine control. The KJV is preferred here to the ASV and RSV. The words in 2—**All the ways of a man are clean in his own eyes**—Maclaren says describe "our strange power of blinding ourselves."[27] A man may be satisfied with his life, but it needs the scrutiny of the Lord and His holy law (cf. 12:15; 21:2), for God **weigheth the spirits**; He goes behind the actions and evaluates a person's motives. In v. 3 the writer gives us a prescription for anxiety. He says **commit thy works**—place your works in the hands of God (cf. Ps. 37:5; 90:17; I Pet. 5:7). Verse 4 stresses God's purpose in all things. He made men to serve Him, though some have rebelled against Him. Even the consequences of sin will serve as a lesson to others. This verse, however, should neither be misconstrued to teach the predestination of the evil nor to make God the Author of moral wrong (cf. Jas. 1:13).[28]

God despises the attitude of arrogance (5). For the meaning of **though hand join in hand** see comment on 11:21. **Mercy and truth** (6; "love and faithfulness," Berk.) are necessary fruits in the life of the man who by grace walks with God in **the fear of the Lord**. In v. 7 there is a word of encouragement for the man of God (cf. Jer. 39:12). In 8 we have a plea for integrity

---

[27]*Op. cit.*, p. 196.
[28]See comment on this verse by R. Laird Harris, *op. cit.*, p. 570.

similar to that expressed in 15:16. In v. 9 God's sovereignty is stressed (cf. 1; Jer. 10:23). In v. 10 we have a proverb on the responsibility of a **king** to be faithful in his judgments. For v. 11 see comment on 11:1.

2. Wisdom as the Fountain of Life (16:12-24)

In vv. 12-15 we have sayings dealing with the responsibilities of kingship. Jones and Walls say: "How far short of this ideal the actual royal house fell is revealed in history. But the portrait remained, to be drawn more clearly by the prophets and fulfilled in the Kingship of Christ."[29] A familiar truth in Proverbs is expressed in v. 16 (see comments on 3:13-18 and 8:10-11, 19). **The highway of the upright** (17) is not only free from obstacles that would defeat one (15:19), but also it continues to avoid moral **evil** (cf. Isa. 35:8). Both the wise men and the prophets of Israel indicted pride (18; cf. Isa. 2:11-17; Jer. 13:15). In v. 19 a metaphor from military life is used: "It is better to be humble in spirit among the poor, than to divide the plunder with the proud" (Berk.).

Even in the ordinary affairs of life one needs the support of faith (20). Verse 21 extols courteous speech and points out its persuasiveness—"His friendly words add to his influence" (Moffatt). In 22 wisdom is seen as a **wellspring of life** (see comments on 10:11). Verse 23 is similar to 21. Kind words are like a **honeycomb** (24; cf. Ps. 19:10).

3. Man's Evil Designs (16:25-33)

Verse 25 is identical with 14:12 (see comment there). In 26 the wise man tells us that hard work is necessary for physical existence: "A worker's appetite works for him, for his mouth urges him on" (Berk.). In 27-30 we have four descriptions of ungodly men. In v. 27 the **ungodly man** (lit., the "man of Belial"; see comments on 6:12) is malicious and his words "scorch like fire" (Moffatt). In 28 a **froward** (perverse) **man** (see comment on 2:12) sows dissension and damages friendships. In 29 **a violent man,** "a man of immoral or criminal methods,"[30] leads others astray. In v. 30 we are reminded that much mischief can be done through a simple movement of the **eyes** and the expression of the **lips.**

[29]*Op. cit.,* p. 531.   [30]Toy, *op. cit.,* p. 332.

The glory of old age is righteousness (31). In v. 32 the man
of patience and self-control is honored above the hero of the
battlefield. In the first line of 33 there is reference to the casting
of lots (cf. Num. 34:13; I Sam. 14:41-42; Jonah 1:7; Acts 1:26).
But the second line makes it clear that in the moral realm there
is no place for chance. Maclaren says: "Nothing happens by accident. Man's little province is bounded on all sides by God's, and
the two touch. There is no neutral territory between, where
godless chance rules."[31] So c. 16 closes on the same note as it
opened—the controlling hand of God in the affairs of men.

4. God Refines Man's Character (17:1-12)

The harmony of a household is treated in v. 1. The dry
morsel, or meagre meal, eaten in contentment is better than an
elaborate dinner in an atmosphere of strife (see comment on
15:17). Sacrifices with strife (lit., "strife-offerings") are in
contrast to the peace offerings of an Israelite family (cf. Deut.
12:15; I Sam. 20:6). In v. 2 a faithful servant replaces an unworthy son in his father's pleasure and inheritance. A historical
fulfillment of this proverb is seen in the lives of Jeroboam and
Rehoboam (I Kings 11:26—12:19). The fining pot (3; "smelter,"
Moffatt) is used to refine silver as the furnace is for gold. Likewise God uses trials to refine man's character (cf. Mal. 3:3).
Verse 4 speaks of the responsibility of the listener, a stewardship
often forgotten. In 5, Israel's sage warns those who are heartless
—devoid of compassion (cf. 14:31).

The significance of the family in the Hebrew tradition is set
forth in v. 6. Grandchildren are a special boon to the aged, and
a good father is the glory of children. In speech one must be
himself; his words should be in keeping with his character and
responsibilities. In v. 8 we are told that bribery is too often
successful. The gift (lit., "bribe") works. Edgar Jones writes:
"This is social realism with a vengeance."[32] Verse 9 says that
one who is forbearing is desirous of friendship, but he that re-
peateth ("harpeth on," ASV) a matter alienates "a close friend"
(Moffatt). A reproof entereth more ("sinks deeper," Moffatt)
into the sensitive heart of a good man than an hundred stripes
into a fool (10). In v. 11 the wicked are alerted to the risks
of rebellion against God or government. Verse 12 warns that

[31]*Op. cit.*, p. 210.   [32]*Op. cit.*, p. 155.

a **fool** is more dangerous than "a she-bear robbed of her cubs" (RSV).

5. *The Cost of Wisdom* (17:13-28)

It is bad enough to return evil for evil, but v. 13 speaks of the heinous sin of returning **evil for good.** The best time to stop a quarrel is in its **beginning** stages, not when the rivulet reaches floodtide (14). Verse 15 uses the language of the court and warns of the miscarriage of justice. **A price in the hand** (16) is a phrase not to be taken literally, because the Jewish teacher was forbidden to accept fees for his teaching. The **fool** is not ready to pay the price for God's way. Edgar Jones says it thus: "To obtain wisdom one must be morally receptive and religiously committed."[33] In 17 we see the value of lasting friendships. A true **friend** is a friend in fair and foul weather.[34] Verse 18 does not contradict 17, but warns against the abuse of friendship (see comments on 6:1-5).

The proud and contentious person will suffer for his evil attitudes. **He that exalteth his gate** (19) may well mean "he who opens wide his mouth" (Berk.). Note I Sam. 2:3; Mic. 7:5. Ungodliness also leads to misfortune (20). In 21 the pain of parenthood is seen as caused by a child who is morally and religiously rebellious (cf. v. 25; see comments on 10:1). Verse 22, telling us that a cheerful **heart** pays dividends, is as modern as psychosomatic therapy (cf. 3:8; 12:25). Verse 23 condemns bribery (cf. 8). In 24 the concentration of the godly is compared to the aimlessness of the sinner (cf. Phil. 3:13-14). For 25 see comment on 21. In v. 26 we have a warning against inappropriate and unjust procedures (cf. John 18:23). Verse 27 speaks of the value of disciplined speech. In 28 we are told that **even a fool** gains when he restrains his words.

6. *The Wise and Foolish* (18:1-24)

We have in v. 1 an exceedingly difficult Hebrew text. Some scholars see here a plea for social solidarity, important to the Hebrew people.[35] Wisdom is not a virtue to be exercised in

---

[33]*Ibid.*, p. 156.

[34]For a discussion of the word *friend* in Proverbs see Kidner, *op. cit.*, pp. 44-46; of *friendship*, see R. F. Horton, *op. cit.*, pp. 227-38.

[35]See the discussion on "The Evil of Isolation" by R. F. Horton, *op. cit.*, pp. 239-49.

isolation. "He who willfully separates and estranges himself [from God and man] seeks his own desire and pretext to break out against all wise and sound judgment" (Amp. OT). The **fool** is described as having **no delight in understanding** (2), only a desire to parade his moral deficiency. In v. 3 we see **contempt, dishonor,** and **disgrace** as the companions of sin. In contrast to this is the glory and honor of the man who walks with God (Isa. 6:3; Rom. 8:30). The **words** of such a good man are life-giving and their source inexhaustible (4; see comment on 10:11).

The warning of v. 5 is against legal injustice. It is not right to show partiality to the guilty or to deprive **the righteous** of justice. In 6-8 we have three proverbs on foolish and slanderous speech. The expression **his mouth calleth for strokes** (6) is translated, "His mouth invites a beating" (Amp. OT). Moffatt renders v. 8: "The words of a slanderer are like dainty morsels, swallowed and relished to the full." The lazy man and the destructive man are brothers of kindred spirit (9). He who creates no product is as bad as the man who destroys property. In v. 10 we are reminded that one may flee to a God of love for security just as a man may flee to a **strong tower** for shelter from a foe. The man of **wealth** imagines his money will give him security (11; cf. 10 and 10:15). The expression **in his own conceit** is translated "so he thinks" (Berk.).

Moffatt interprets 12,

> *Haughtiness ends in disaster:*
> *to be humble is the way to honour.*

Also see 15:33; 16:18-19.[36] Verse 13 is another proverb against hasty speech. On 14, Kidner aptly comments: "Short of outward resources, life is hard; short of inward, it is insupportable"[37] (cf. 12:25; 15:13). For any good life the desire to learn is indispensable (15). In v. 16 we see the use of gifts in cultivating friendships and in social amenities (cf. Gen. 32:20; I Sam. 25:27). The danger of abuse in the giving of gifts is pointed out in 15:27 and in 17:8, 23.

Reflecting the procedures of the court, v. 17 urges the importance of hearing both sides of a matter. The RSV translates it: "He who states his case first seems right until the other comes

---

[36]For helpful discussions on pride and humility see Rylaarsdam, *op. cit.,* pp. 66-67; R. F. Horton, *op. cit.,* pp. 179-90.

[37]*Op. cit.,* p. 129.

and examines him." Verse 18 suggests the casting of lots to settle disputes agreeably. Verse 19 warns that offenses are easily committed but difficult to dissolve. Moffatt interprets 20:

> A man must answer for his utterances
> and take the consequences of his words.

In 21 the power of the tongue for both good and evil is recognized. Verse 22 speaks of the blessing of a good wife (see comment on 12:4). A realistic description of the language of the rich and the poor is given in 23. In v. 24 two types of friends are suggested, though the Hebrew text is difficult and allows various interpretations. There are fair-weather friends who are interested mainly in social contacts, and there are those who are more dedicated and loyal than one's own brother (cf. 17:17; 27:10).

7. Couplets on Poverty and Wealth (19:1-17)

In v. 1 the poor with his simple honesty is contrasted with a fool who is perverse in his speech. Some scholars see this verse as an adaptation of 28:6. Others feel that the antithesis of 1 breaks down unless we see the fool as a rich fool, as in 28:6. It is not good to be without knowledge (2), especially a knowledge of God. The man who is without divine guidance sinneth, or misses the mark (cf. Judg. 20:16). In 3 the sinner is told to put the blame for his failure where it belongs—on his own foolishness. His heart fretteth (lit., is "angry or vexed") against the Lord. "He accuseth God in his heart" (LXX). The influence of wealth and the disadvantages of poverty are again stated in 4 (cf. 14:20; 18:23-24). Verse 5 warns against perjury (see 9 and comments on 14:5). In vv. 6-7 we see that wealth brings favor and friendships, but poverty results in being forgotten by relatives and fair-weather friends. Though he pursueth them with words (of entreaty), they give no heed to him.

The value of wisdom is stressed in 8. For v. 9 see comment on 5. In 10 the word delight is better translated "luxury." So we have two striking improprieties—a fool living in luxury and a slave exercising political power over princes. In 11 we are reminded that discretion (Heb., sekel; see comment on 13:15) brings restraint (cf. 14:17, 29) and a forgiving spirit (Mic. 7:18-19). Verse 12 calls for a realistic recognition of a king's moods.

A wayward son can ruin his father's happiness (cf. 10:1; 17:21, 25) and a nagging wife can destroy the peace of a home

(13). Toy quotes in this connection an Arab proverb: "Three things make a house intolerable: *tak* (the leaking through of rain), *nak* (a wife's nagging) and *bak* (bugs)."[38] In 14 the sage says that possessions may be a matter of **inheritance** but a good **wife** is a gift of God (see comments on 12:4). Indolence makes a man unaware of his best interests and results in **hunger** (15; see comments on 6:10). Obedience to God brings life, but sin results in spiritual death (16; see comment on 15:10). In 17 we are assured that kindness to **the poor** has its rewards (cf. Isa. 10:1-2; Amos 2:6-7; 4:1-5). We must not, however, misconstrue this proverb to make good deeds an atonement for sin (cf. Eph. 2:8-9).

8. *The Importance of Listening* (19:18-29)

In 18 the sage reminds us that withholding discipline when a child is young and impressionable is unfair to him. The words **Let not thy soul spare for his crying** are translated, "Do not set your heart on his destruction" (Berk.) The idea is that the overindulgent parent will by his leniency destroy his own child. In Proverbs the spoiling of a child is a sin against God and society, as well as against one's offspring. In 19 scholars recognize a most difficult Hebrew text and one subject to various interpretations. It is likely, however, a reminder that a man with an uncontrollable temper will get himself into much trouble and the person who tries to help him out of difficulty will have to **do it again.** Verse 20 contains a plea for responsible listening. The phrase **that thou mayest be wise in thy latter end** is excellently translated "that you may be wise the rest of your days" (Berk.).

The sovereignty of God is stressed in 21 (see comment on 16:1). Though the Hebrew text is exceedingly difficult in 22, some scholars see the word **desire,** or intention, as the key to its understanding (cf. Mark 12:41-44; II Cor. 8:12). **A poor man** who would like to help one in distress **is better** than a rich man who has ability to give aid but does not **desire** to do so. "A poor righteous man is better than a rich liar" (LXX). To know God and live for Him is a satisfying way (23)—a key truth in Proverbs (cf. 10:2-3; 14:27). In 24 we have a satire on the **slothful.** Says Greenstone: "The irony is against the lazy person who dips his hand into the dish to take out some food, but his laziness overcomes his hunger so that he refrains from putting the food into his mouth."[39] There is reference here perhaps to eating from a common dish (cf. Mark 14:20).

A fool learns by example (25); a wise man learns by reproof and instruction. For the meaning of the terms **scorner** and **simple** see comments on 1:4 and 1:22. In 26 an ungrateful son is depicted in his shameful mistreatment of his aged parents (cf. 28:7, 24). **Cease, my son, to hear the instruction that causeth to err** (27) suggests that there is both good and bad teaching. It may also be a warning that one should not listen to truth and then fail to act accordingly, for by doing so he only increases his guilt. In 28 we have another warning against distorting the truth (cf. 16:27; see comment on 14:5). Those who refuse to heed instruction shall not escape due punishment (29).

9. The Character of the Righteous (20:1-14)

Intoxicating drinks—**wine** and **strong drink** (1)—are personified as doing what men do under their influence. They become mockers at higher values, and "brawlers" (RSV), noisy and quarrelsome persons. Here is a strong condemnation of drunkenness. This indictment is given in fuller and more vivid language in 23:29-35.[40] **Wine** (Heb., *yayin*) is fermented grape juice; **strong drink** or mead (Heb. *shekar*) is a general term for all intoxicating beverages (cf. Isa. 28:7). Such drinks were forbidden to the priests (Lev. 10:9), to the Nazarites (Num. 6:3), and to the Rechabites (Jeremiah 35).

The fear resulting from the **anger of a king** is like the terror produced by **the roaring of a lion** (2; cf. 19:12). He that provokes a king **sinneth against his own soul,** or better, "He who makes him angry endangers his own life" (Berk.). In 3 there is a warning against quarrelsomeness, but "a fool quarrels with everyone" (Moffatt, see comment on 17:14). In 4 the sluggard's refusal to work appears to be due to cold weather. But the words **by reason of the cold** mean literally "in autumn," when the harvest is over and the time for plowing has come. The lazy man refuses to plow in plowing season; this is the reason his neighbors

---

[39]*Op. cit.,* p. 209.

[40]For differing points of view on the use of wine in the OT see Rylaarsdam, *op. cit.,* pp. 69-70, who sees the OT as teaching moderation rather than abstinence; see also R. F. Horton, *op. cit.,* pp. 275-87, who presents a strong case for abstinence.

later refuse to help him. Verse 5 suggests a search for motives: "The purpose in the heart of a man is like deep water; but a man of good sense will get it out" (BB). In 6 we have a contrast between profession and reality. In 7 the **integrity** of a righteous man is seen as an honorable heritage for **his children.**

An upright judge evaluates character. The word **scattereth** (8) is a verb used of winnowing grain. Kidner says: "The practiced eye of a true ruler sifts the chaff from the wheat; still surer is the Spirit of the Lord: Isaiah 11:3; I Corinthians 2:15."[41] Verse 9 stresses the universality of sin and the inadequacy of a human remedy. **Who can say, I have made my heart clean?** Clarke answers: "No man. But thousands can testify that the blood of Jesus Christ has cleansed them from all unrighteousness. And he is pure from his sin, who is justified freely through the redemption that is in Jesus."[42] On 10 see comment on 11:1. In 11 we see the conduct of **a child** as the revealer of his character. For the expression **hearing ear** (12) see comment on 15:31. **The seeing eye** here represents the entire person. So for obedience due to **hearing** and the understanding due to **seeing,** we are debtors to grace (cf. Eph. 2:8-10). For 13 see comments on 6:6-8. In 14 we have a reference to the usual practice of the Oriental markets. Toy says: "The purchaser disparages the ware, beats down the seller, and boasts of his cleverness."[43]

10. *Wisdom and Lasting Wealth* (20:15-30)

Wisdom is the most abiding wealth (15; see comments on 3:13-17 and 8:10-11). Verse 16 stresses the folly of standing **surety** for another (see comment on 6:1-5). The last part of 16 is better translated, "hold him in pledge when he gives surety for foreigners" (RSV). In 17 we have a proverb on the aftermath of sin (see notes on 5:4 and 9:17). Moffatt translates 18:

> *Take counsel when you form a plan,*
> *and have some policy when you make war.*

See comment on 11:14. In 19 we have a warning against gossip (see note on 11:13). For 20 see comments on 4:19 and 7:9. In 21 the sage stresses the forfeiture of God's blessings by those who obtain their **inheritance** by unjust means (cf. 13:11). Verse 22 is a reminder that God is in control of man's affairs; He is our

[41]*Op. cit.,* p. 137.   [42]*Op. cit.,* p. 757.
[43]*Op. cit.,* p. 388.

Saviour and Vindicator (cf. Rom. 12:17; I Pet. 3:9). For 23 see v. 10 and note on 11:1.

For 24 see comments on 16:1-2, 9. Edgar Jones well states: "This affirmation of God's grace and his ultimate control of human life is highly significant in a work which emphasizes the freedom and initiative of men. It underlines the presuppositions of religious faith and conviction underlying practical maxims."[44] Verse 25 stresses the danger of making rash vows. It is better for a person to count the cost than to make a vow hurriedly "and not until afterward inquire [whether he can fulfill it]" (Amp. OT). For v. 26 see note on 8. The wheel is the wheel of the threshing cart and is not to be taken literally, but rather as a symbol suggestive of punishment.

God has given to every man a living spirit (27)—conscience. It is literally "the breath of life" (cf. Gen. 2:7), through which God works in man's life. The expression inward parts is used for the total personality. In 28 the sage tells us that a king's justice must be tempered with mercy. In 29 we see strength as the glory of young men but wisdom as the glory of old age (cf. 16:31). The sage, however, would not deny that a young man should be righteous nor that an elderly man may enjoy strength. In 30 physical punishment is seen as having some moral effect, perhaps a deterrent from further sinning (cf. Ps. 119:67). The blueness of a wound refers to bruises from being struck. Moffatt translates it:

> Blows and bruises tell for good;
> they go deep into the very soul.

But only the stripes of the Suffering Servant can bring about our redemption (cf. Isa. 53:5).

11. The Wicked and Their Ways (21:1-12)

This chapter begins with an emphasis on the controlling hand of God in the affairs of men. A king's heart (1; choices) can be guided by God just as a farmer can direct irrigation water into different channels. For 2 see comment on 16:1-2. For 3 see notes on 15:8-9. In KJV the two halves of the couplet in 4 appear to be unrelated. In the first line an high look ("haughty eyes," Berk.), and a proud heart are denounced. In the second line the plowing, or the sinner's work that is not intended to glorify

[44]*Op. cit.*, p. 175.

God, is displeasing to Him (cf. I Cor. 10:31). The word **plowing** is often translated "lamp" (Vulg., LXX, RSV), suggesting by its symbolism that the false happiness and hope of the sinner are distasteful to God.

Verse 5 tells us that thoroughness in planning pays off, but the "get-rich-quick" scheme is condemned (cf. 13:11; 20:21). Wealth obtained by fraudulent means disappears into thin air and is hurtful to the obtainer; it is as if one set out deliberately to **seek death** (6; cf. 10:2; Jer. 17:11). Verse 7 is a companion to 5 and 6 and underscores the boomerang effect of sinful deeds. **Judgment** is better translated "justice." The alternatives of the wickedness of evil men and the righteousness of God's men are presented in 8 (cf. Psalm 1). On the phrase, **As for the pure, his work is right,** Deane and Taylor-Taswell comment: "The pure in heart will be right in action; he follows his conscience and God's law, and goes direct on his course without turning or hesitation."[45]

Peace with privation is better than contention with a **brawling woman** (9; cf. 19 and notes on 19:13-14). This saying is repeated in 25:24. Kidner says we have in 10 "an important truth about depravity: men can sin not merely from weakness but eagerly and ruthlessly"[46] (cf. 4:16). Sin also has a social impact; it affects the wicked man's **neighbour.** For 11 see comment on 19:25. Verse 12 consists of two unconnected lines and its interpretation is difficult. Toy says: "As the Heb. text stands the subject of the couplet must be God, the *righteous one* . . . a righteous man might be said to note the wicked, but could not be said to hurl him to ruin."[47] So it is God who brings the sinner to judgment. Jones and Walls think the point of 12 is "that the righteous take warning from the overthrow of the wicked."[48]

12. *The Treasures of the Wise* (21:13-21)

He that is heartless regarding **the cry of the poor** (13) should not expect to receive help from God or man (cf. 24:11-12; 25:21; also Matt. 25:31-46; Luke 16:19-31). In 14 we have another proverb on bribery but here its oft-observed results are realistically evaluated (cf. notes on 15:27 and 17:8). While the righteous rejoice in seeing justice done, it is a "dismay to evil doers" (15,

---

[45]*Op. cit.,* p. 405.   [46]*Op. cit.,* p. 143.
[47]*Op. cit.,* p. 402.   [48]*Op. cit.,* p. 533.

RSV). The outcome of the moral wanderer is expressed in 16; he is as good as **dead** (cf. 27:8; Ps. 119:176). In 17 there is a warning to the spendthrift and the overindulgent (cf. 20; also Amos 4:1-3; 6:3-6). In 18 we see the ultimate vindication of **the righteous.** Greenstone points out that the meaning is "not that the wicked is punished for the sin of the righteous, but that in the case of a general calamity, the righteous escapes and the wicked takes his place."[49] The evil from which the righteous man is spared comes to the wicked. For scriptural illustrations of this proverb see Esther 7:10 and Luke 16:25.

For 19 see 9 and notes on 19:13-14. In 20 we are reminded that the **wise** man uses material possessions thoughtfully but the fool squanders them. Those who seek **righteousness and mercy** (21) shall find them (cf. Matt. 5:6). In 22 wisdom is seen as better security than walled cities (cf. II Cor. 10:4; I John 5:4). For 23 see notes on 12:13 and 13:3. The scoffer is portrayed in 24. He **dealeth in proud wrath** ("acts with overbearing pride," Amp. OT). On vv. 25-26, Kidner aptly comments: "The sluggard lives in his world of wishing, which is his substitute for working. It can ruin him materially (25) and imprison him spiritually (26), for he can neither command himself nor escape himself."[50] In contrast to the sluggard is **the righteous** man of industry and liberality; he has ample for himself and something to share with others.

The sacrifice of the wicked (27) is unacceptable to God, especially when it is offered **with a wicked mind,** i.e., as a substitute for genuine repentance (see comments on 15:8-9). A reliable witness is one who testifies to what he hears (28) and sees (cf. 14:5; I John 1:1-3). The hardening of **his face** (29) is descriptive of the brazen front of a shamelessly impudent person (cf. Jer. 5:3; Ezek. 3:7). But the righteous man **directeth his way** (acts thoughtfully) on the basis of sound principle. The emphasis of 30 is that human **wisdom** and schemes cannot defeat the purposes of **the Lord** (cf. Acts 2:23; 4:27-28). Verse 31 condemns reliance on military might and material resources rather than on God (cf. Ps. 20:7; 33:17-22; Isa. 31:1-3).

13. The Worth of a Good Name (22:1-16)

A good name (1; reputation or character; cf. Eccles. 7:1; Luke 10:20; Acts 6:3) is more desirable than perishable treas-

---

[49]*Op. cit.*, p. 227.   [50]*Op. cit.*, p. 145.

ures. The equality of all men before **the Lord,** regardless of their
wealth, is underscored in 2 (cf. 14:31; 29:13). Of v. 3, Greenstone says: "The picture suggests some dangerous object lying
on the highway, which is evident to the prudent, but the inexperienced walks on it and is tripped by it."[51] For the meaning of
simple see note on 1:4. **Humility and the fear of the Lord** (4)
bring their rightful compensations (cf. 3:5-8; 21:21; Luke 14:11).
Verse 5 reminds us that the perverse person meets many obstacles on his way, but that the path of the righteous is unim-
peded (see comment on 13:15).

The importance of training children in their formative years
is expressed in 6. Some scholars see here an emphasis on voca-
tional training. The expression **in the way he should go** is literally "according to his way," i.e., aptitudes or inclinations. But
the Hebrew sage is likely speaking primarily of moral training.
The word for **train** is used elsewhere to "dedicate" a house (Deut.
20:5) and a temple (I Kings 8:63). Fritsch sees this verse as
expressing "one of the strong points of the Hebrew sages, viz.,
their insistence on the moral training of the child by his parents."[52] **And when he is old, he will not depart from it.** These
words are most assuring to faithful, devout parents. They are
not, however, to be understood as an absolute guarantee. Environment alone will not save our children. Necessary also to
make possible their salvation is the exercise of free choice on
their part in order to receive the ever-available grace of God.

In 7 we have another expression of economic realism (cf. 10:
15). Verse 8 gives us a lesson on sowing and reaping (see comment on 12:13-14). The words **The rod of his anger shall fail**
Greenstone interprets as meaning: "His power for doing evil
shall fail. The rod which the wicked holds over his victim will
not long endure."[53]

God's blessings are upon him who gives **bread to the poor**
(9; cf. 19:17; Deut. 15:9-10; II Cor. 9:7-8). In 10 we are reminded that **contention** will exist as long as **the scorner** is around
(cf. Matt. 18:17). Verse 11 is difficult to translate and may best
be rendered: "He who loves purity and the pure in heart, and
who is gracious in speech, will for the grace of his lips have the
king for his friend" (Amp. OT). Verse 12 reminds us that God
is on the side of truth and watches over His own (cf. Deut. 6:24;

[51]*Op. cit.,* p. 233.   [52]*Op. cit.,* IB, 4:907
[53]*Op. cit.,* p. 235.

Josh. 24:17). In 13 the lazy man voices a flimsy excuse for not working. He stays in his house because he might **be slain** by **a lion without.**

Another warning against the **strange women** (adulteresses) appears in 14 (see comments on 2:16-19; 5:7-14; and 7:6-23). **The rod of correction** (15) is seen as an accepted factor in the rearing of children (see note on 13:24). Various interpretations have been given to 16 because of the ambiguity of the Hebrew text. One of the most satisfactory translations reads: "He who oppresses the poor to get gain for himself, and he who gives to the rich will surely come to want" (Amp. OT).

Section III The Words of the Wise

Proverbs 22:17—24:34

In this portion of Proverbs we have a collection of moral and religious teachings presented in an intimate manner by the teacher to his pupil or son. This section resembles the first part of Proverbs (cc. 1—9) in that it usually consists of longer units than the two-line couplets of the preceding division (10:1—22:16).

Some scholars note the striking similarity of this portion of Proverbs to the wisdom literature of other nations and assume direct or indirect dependence of Israel's sages thereon. This assumption is especially true of the Egyptian document entitled "The Wisdom of Amen-em-opet [Amenemope]." For a discussion of this matter see "Proverbs and Other Wisdom Literature" in the Introduction.

A. Introduction, 22:17-21

With v. 17 we have the beginning of a distinct section of Proverbs appropriately titled the words of the wise. In his prophecy (18:18) Jeremiah recognized three groups of teachers in Israel: the priest, whose function was to give the Torah, which included both the written and the oral law; the wise men, who gave counsel; and the prophet, who proclaimed the word of God. The words of Israel's sages are recorded in this section. Their words are not merely pious platitudes, but voice the call of God found throughout Proverbs and in all Scripture. Fitted in thy lips (18) is better "are ready on thy lips" (RSV). Them that send unto thee (21) is understood as "all inquirers" (Moffatt).

In 17-21 we may see "The Call of God." (1) The plea for acceptance and obedience, 17; (2) The personal realization of God is first inwardly experienced and then outwardly expressed, 18; (3) The purpose of God's call is that we might fully trust Him, 19; (4) The product of knowing God is directed and changed lives, 20; (5) The profession of God is the witness others need, 21.

B. First Collection, 22:22—23:14

This collection begins with a warning against the exploitation of the poor. **Neither oppress the afflicted** (22) means not to use legal action against them. **In the gate** (22) refers to the recognized court of justice at the gate of the city (cf. Job 31:21). God will be the Advocate of the poor and will bring judgment upon their oppressors (23). The danger of wrong associations is stressed in vv. 24-25 (see notes on 1:10-19). The word **learn** (25; Heb., *alaph*) means to "learn by association." In 26-27 we have another warning against indiscreet surety (see comments on 6:1-5). The reason for the warning is:

> *For if you have nothing to pay,*
> *your very bed will be seized* (27, Moffatt).

A single couplet in 28 stresses the importance of respect for property rights in the Hebrew tradition. **The ancient landmark** refers to the stones which designated the boundaries of a person's property. These boundaries were regarded as sacred in the ancient world. This truth is underlined here in the wisdom literature (cf. 23:10-11; Job 24:2), and also in the law and the prophets (cf. Deut. 19:14; Hos. 5:10). Greedy King Ahab violated these sacred rights in taking Naboth's vineyard (I Kings 21). In 29 the capable and **diligent** are praised. While the word **diligent** is used for a scribe in Ps. 45:1 and Ezra 7:6, the Hebrews honored the industrious person whatever his trade or profession might be. A **diligent** man was honored by **kings**. The word **mean** in the last phrase of this verse is translated "obscure" (Moffatt) and "undistinguished" (Berk.).

Israel's sage urges in 23:1-3 the importance of proper etiquette in the presence of kings. **Put a knife to thy throat** (2) is likely an expression for self-restraint. Caution is urged in 3 because a king's **dainties** may be **deceitful meat**, i.e., "offered with questionable motives" (Amp. OT). In vv. 4-5 **riches** are seen to be as elusive as the **eagle** from the hunter (cf. Luke 12:20; I Tim. 6:7-10). The RSV translates 4:

> *Do not toil to acquire wealth;*
> *be wise enough to desist.*

In 6-8 we are warned to stay away from **him that hath an evil eye,** i.e., a miserly host. **But his heart is not with thee** (7) is translated "but is grudging the cost" (Amp. OT). Of the words,

519

The morsel . . . shalt thou vomit up, Greenstone says: "If you agree to dine with him, you will be so disgusted with his miserliness that the meal will nauseate you."[1]

We are not to cast our pearls before swine (9; see comments on 9:7-10). In vv. 10-11, God is described as the Protector of **the fatherless** and defenseless. The Lord is here called *goel,* originally a designation for the next of kin, who was obligated to redeem the land of an unfortunate relative (cf. Lev. 25:25; Num. 5:8; Ruth 4:1-8) or even avenge a murder (Num. 35:19). If the fatherless were without human relatives to defend them, God would be their *Goel* ("Champion," Moffatt).

The sage reminds us that godly wisdom has its price in acceptance and obedience (12; see notes on 1:2). Likewise the lessons in life's school are not without their demands (13-14). For the next generation to know God's way some discipline will be involved. The faithful **correction** of a **child** is not amiss but will rather **deliver his soul from hell** (see comments on 13:24 and 19:18). This admonition does not ignore free choice or divine grace, but it emphasizes the place of parents as partners with God in the redemptive task.

C. SECOND GROUP, 23:15—24:22

1. *Guidelines for Godly Living* (23:15-28)

This section begins with a warm personal appeal—**My son**—so characteristic of the first major division of Proverbs (cc. 1—9). The teacher rejoices in the progress of his pupil (16). The expression **my reins** is literally "my kidneys," but is better rendered "my soul" (RSV). Toy reminds us that the Hebrew people "regarded both the heart and the kidneys (on account of their physiological importance) as seats of the intellectual, moral and religious life, and the two terms are in this respect treated as synonyms."[2] The sage urges his pupil not to **envy sinners** but to continue **in the fear of the Lord** (17; see comments on 1:7). The outcome of a righteous man's life will be rewarding (18; see notes on 5:4 and 19:20).

In 19-21 drunkenness and gluttony are cited as detrimental practices capable of reducing a man to **rags** (see comments on 20:1 and 23:29-35). The descriptions **winebibbers** and **riotous eaters** (20) were later used by the enemies of Jesus (cf. Matt.

---

[1]*Op. cit.,* p. 245.   [2]*Op. cit.,* p. 433.

11:19; Luke 7:34). The pupil is urged to follow parental guidance (22-25), an underscoring of the fifth commandment by the teacher. Following this, the sage warns about adultery (26-28), a vice repeatedly dealt with in Proverbs (see notes on 2:16-19; 5:7-14; and 7:6-23).

2. *A Portrait of Drunkenness* (23:29-35)

Here the sage paints with unforgettable strokes the portrait of a drunkard—immoral, insensible, and irresponsible. As one views this portrait, a few questions beg for expression. If the use of the lighter wines of low alcohol content in the day of a primitive culture produced such miseries, who can estimate the tragic consequences of the use of distilled alcoholic beverages of high alcohol content in a society throbbing with the tensions of a complex culture and racing with the speed of the jet age? If the sage spoke so forcibly against drunkenness in his day, what would be his attitude regarding a drinking society in this day that produces its increasing millions of alcoholics? If the teacher saw drunkenness so damaging in his time of unmechanized travel, what would he say about alcohol and its part in the highway slaughter of our modern, high-speed transportation?

Smith-Goodspeed interprets 30b as "who go often to test the mixture."

Look not thou upon the wine when it is red (31). These words do not suggest moderation but rather total abstinence from intoxicating drinks. **Moveth itself aright** is better "glides down smoothly" (Moffatt). No one can possibly suffer the consequences of intoxication and the torments of alcoholism unless he drinks. Schloerb well states: "By picturing the unhappy condition of the intoxicated man, the sage hoped to provide the incentive for leaving the sparkling cup alone."[3]

Verse 35a may be read, "They may strike me but I feel no pain" (Smith Goodspeed).

3. *Wise Counsels to a Son* (24:1-22)

This chapter begins with a warning regarding the corrupting influence of evil associates (1-2; cf. 3:31; 23:17; 24:19; Ps. 37:1, 8). **Destruction** (2) would be "violence," and **mischief** would be "trouble." In 3-4 wisdom's advantages are extolled, whether

[3]*Op. cit.,* p. 915.

the meaning be literal or symbolic of a family or a man's character (cf. 9:1; 14:1). Wisdom, understanding, and knowledge as used here and throughout are roughly synonymous, and are used as such in poetic parallelism. They represent moral insight, the ability to relate aright to God, to man, and to life. Wisdom is needed for military strategy (5-6; see notes on 11:14). In 7 wisdom is seen as a treasure the fool has not paid the price to obtain, and thus he cannot speak in the gate (the public assembly of the elders; see comments on 1:20-23).

The person who schemes to do wrong is a mischievous person (8)—a troublemaker. The content and intent of the fool's plans are sinful. The phrase, The thought of foolishness is sin (9), is well translated, "Now sin is folly's scheme" (Moffatt). Men as well as God condemn the scorner who is an abomination. If a man gives in to discouragement in the day of adversity (10; temptation), he reveals the limitations of his strength and courage (10). In 11-12 we have a warning to all who selfishly avoid involvement in the troubles of others. The words drawn unto death (11) refer to those innocent persons condemned to death by political intrigue or who are otherwise in extreme danger. Verse 12 exposes the selfish motives of the uninvolved. It sweeps away a person's flimsy excuses for failing to show compassion and render help to the distressed (cf. 12:14; 24:29; Deut. 22:1-4).

In vv. 13-14, under the figure of eating honey and honeycomb, the teacher stresses the benefits of wisdom. There is personal delight—sweet to thy taste—in doing God's will (13; Ps. 19:10). Wisdom is rewarding for both the present and the future (14; see comments on 3:13). The wicked man (15) is warned against doing harm to the righteous. A just man falleth (16) into difficulty, not sin. Falleth (Heb., naphal) does not convey the idea of falling morally. Seven times is a Hebrew expression meaning "frequently or often." But the wicked shall fall into mischief; i.e., he is "crushed" (Moffatt) by his calamity. He does not have the inner resources to help him recuperate as does the righteous (cf. Ps. 34:19; Mic. 7:8).

Certainly the man of God should never gloat over the misfortunes that come to his enemies (17; cf. 17:5). Gloating over another's calamities is not pleasing to God and will incur his wrath (18). For a New Testament expression of this truth see Rom. 11:18-21. In 19-20 we are reminded not to envy sinners, for their apparent prosperity is not enduring—The candle of the

wicked shall be put out (see notes on 7:9 and 13:9). In 21-22
we have an admonition on the acceptance of constituted authority
(cf. Rom. 13:1-7; I Pet. 2:17). The phrase **with them that are
given to change** (21) is descriptive of revolutionaries or political
agitators who change their allegiance. Verse 22 is variously
translated, one of the best renderings being: "For their calamity
shall rise suddenly, and who knows the punishment and ruin
which both [the Lord and the king] will bring upon *the rebellious?"* (Amp. OT)

D. Additional Admonitions, 24:23-34

These things also (23) may mean, "Here are further words
from Israel's sages." In 23-26 the teachers stress impartiality in
the administration of justice. **Respect of persons** (partiality)
was forbidden in Hebrew law (cf. Lev. 19:15; Deut. 1:17; 16:19).
The expression **kiss his lips** (26) may mean that the person who
renders a right decision will win respect and affection. Kissing,
however, in a court of law seems inappropriate to some scholars.
They prefer to translate the word **kiss** as "equip." So the meaning of 26 would be that equipping one's lips with knowledge
enables him to give a **right answer.**

On 27, Edgar Jones comments: "The main import is that
marriage involves a due regard for the responsibilities of providing a home and a livelihood. These should be assured first;
then the marriage can have a secure foundation and a family
reared."[4] In 28 we have a warning to the false **witness** (see
comment on 14:5). In 29, Israel's sage speaks against the sin of
retaliation. This truth is amplified in the Sermon on the Mount
(Matt. 5:38-48). In 30-34 we have another indictment of the
sluggard (see notes on 6:6-11). The lazy man is warned:

> *Poverty will come upon you like a robber,*
> *and want like an armed man* (34, RSV).

---

[4]*Op. cit.*, p. 202.

Section **IV** *The Hezekiah Collection of Solomon's Proverbs*

Proverbs 25:1—29:27

For this collection of 137 Solomonic proverbs we are indebted to Hezekiah, perhaps the greatest of the reformer kings of Judah's history. Not only did Hezekiah lead his nation in spiritual renewal, but tradition ascribes to his reign a great literary revival. Doubtless Hezekiah was a man of literary interests (cf. II Kings 18:18, 37; Isa. 38:10-20). During his reign he sought to preserve the extant literary treasures of his people, especially those of Israel's greatest sage.

According to the title verse (25:1), Hezekiah's scribes **copied out** (literally, "removed from one document to another") these proverbs of Solomon. They were taken from some previous anthology (cf. I Kings 4:32). The sayings in this collection are similar to those of the first major section of Proverbs (10:1—22:16). We have here no lengthy discourses, no logical connection between many of the couplets, and no easy arrangement of contents. R. B. Y. Scott, however, has made a topical arrangement of this section.[1]

A. FIRST COLLECTION, 25:1—27:27

1. *Regarding Kings and the Court* (25:1-10)

For the import of 1 see the introductory paragraphs above. In 2-7 the sage casts the king in a favorable light, as God's vicegerent. While the ways **of God** (2) are inscrutable, **the honour of kings** rests in their ability to know what is going on in the kingdom. A king's wisdom is superior and not always understood by his people (3). As only from refined **silver** are the best vessels made, so only from the most worthy of servants can a king's righteous government **be established** (4-5). In 6-7 guidance is given for behavior **in the presence of** a king. Jesus

[1]"Proverbs—Ecclesiastes," *The Anchor Bible*, general eds. W. F. Albright and D. N. Freedman (Garden City, N.Y.: Doubleday & Co., Inc., 1965), p. 171.

used these truths in a parable to teach a lesson on proper life attitudes and the dangers of self-exaltation (cf. Luke 14: 7-11). In 8-10 the sage warns against hasty litigation. Such may lead to an adverse verdict and public embarrassment (8; cf. 17:14; Matt. 5:25). It is better to discuss such matters privately and to refrain from revealing things that would hurtfully involve others (9; Matt. 18:15). Secret (9) or slanderous words cannot be recalled and are spoken to one's **shame** (10).

2. *Four Beautiful Comparisons* (25:11-14)

A word . . . spoken at the right time and in an appropriate manner **is like apples of gold** "in a setting of silver" (11; Amp. OT). The acceptance of reproof or sound advice is as valuable as **an ornament of fine gold** (12). Cowles says of 13: "Ice-water in a hot summer day gives us the true sense of this figure. So is a reliable messenger to his employers. They can trust him and they are refreshed by his fidelity to his trust."[2] In 14 we have an indictment against boastful speech. Such speech is as disappointing as **clouds and wind without rain.** Thus the sage depicts a person who boasts of his generosity when actually he gives nothing.

3. *Varied Counsels on Conduct* (25:15-28)

Patience and gentleness in speech are surprisingly powerful weapons (cf. 15:1; 16:14, 32; I Pet. 3:15-16). **A soft tongue breaketh the bone,** or, "Soft speech breaks down the most bone-like resistance" (15, Amp. OT). In 16 we have a plea for self-control and moderation (cf. 27). Kidner aptly comments: "Since Eden, man has wanted the last ounce out of life, as though beyond God's 'enough' lay ecstasy, not nausea."[3] In 17 the principle of moderation is applied to one's social relationships. **A maul,** or "war club," **and a sword, and a sharp arrow** (18) are used to express the damaging power of **false** witnessing. The Hebrew of 19 allows two interpretations. It may suggest that one dare not place his confidence in an evil man. On the other hand, it may mean that the **unfaithful man** has no security in the testing time (cf. Job 8:13-15).

---

[2]*Proverbs, Ecclesiastes and The Song of Solomon* (New York: D. Appleton and Co., 1884), p. 168.

[3]*Op. cit.,* p. 159.

The triplet in 20 tells us that frivolity and sadness do not go together (cf. Dan. 6:18; Rom. 12:15). Variously rendered because of difficulties in the text, one of the best translations reads: "Like one who takes off a garment on a cold day, or like vinegar upon soda, so is a singer of songs to a heavy heart" (Berk.). In 21-22 the sage reminds us that the most effective revenge is to do good to one's **enemy**. New Testament expressions of this high ethical standard are found in the Sermon on the Mount (Matt. 5:44) and in the teachings of Paul (Rom. 12:20).

The evil of slander is pictured as the results of a **north wind** (23) that brings unpleasant **rain**. A **backbiting tongue** is literally "a tongue of secrecy," or talk behind one's back. Moffatt translates the verse:

> *North winds bring rain:*
> *slander brings angry looks.*

For 24 see comment on 21:9. Communication was inadequate in those early days, so **good news** (25) was always most welcome (cf. 25:13). In 26 we have a warning against the catastrophe of spiritual and moral defection. "Like a muddied fountain and a polluted spring is a righteous man who yields, falls down *and* compromises his integrity before the wicked" (Amp. OT). The first line of 27 expresses the thought of 16. The second line is difficult. One of the best renderings reads: "To eat much honey is not good, nor for men to seek their own glory" (Berk.). In lack of self-control there is great weakness. Such a man is like **a city** ... **without walls** (28; see note on 16:32).

4. About Fools and Their Folly (26:1-12)

This section, with the exception of 2, has been designated by Toy as the "Book of Fools—a string of sarcasms on the class most detested by the sages."[4] See comments on 1:7 and 22 for the meaning of the word "fool" in Proverbs. The **fool** (1) in public office is as inappropriate as **snow in** a Palestinian **summer** and as injurious as a **rain** during the **harvest** season (March to September). In 2 we are told that an undeserved **curse** will miss its mark. "As a sparrow wanders and a swallow flies about, so an unjustified curse does not alight" (Berk.). The fool responds not to counsel but to compulsion (3). In 4-5 we have seemingly

[4]*Op. cit.*, p. 471.

contradictory statements. Verse 4, however, warns against stooping to the level of a fool. Verse 5 urges us to rebuke the fool so that he might realize his folly.

In 6 the danger of sending a message by the hand of a fool is stressed (see note on 13:17). Scott translates 7: "A maxim quoted by fools is as limp as a lame man's legs."[5] Cowles says: "None but sensible men catch the true meaning of the real proverb and know how to speak it impressively."[6] The most likely meaning of 8 is that to give honour to a fool is as absurd as fastening a stone in a sling, so that it is useless. Verse 9 is a companion to 7. Edgar Jones says: "The meaning is that the drunkard cannot use a thorn stick without injury to himself any more than a fool is able to use a *mashal* [proverb] as a means of instruction."[7]

Perhaps the most obscure text in all of Proverbs is v. 10. Several of the Hebrew words have more than one meaning. Moffatt translates it thus: "An able man does everything himself: a fool hires the first passer-by." In 11 we see that the fool refuses to learn (cf. II Pet. 2:22). Verse 12 states that a man of conceit is worse than a fool (cf. 3:7; 29:20; Luke 18:11; Rom. 12:16; Rev. 3:17).

5. *The Sluggard* (26:13-16)

In these verses we have a satirical portrait of the indolent—a favorite target of Israel's sages. See comments on 6:6-11; 19:24; and 22:13. The figure seven in 16 represents an indefinite number.

6. *Various Scoundrels* (26:17-28)

A warning on meddling in the affairs of others is given in 17. Moffatt renders it: "He catches a passing dog by the ears who meddles with a quarrel not his own." Edgar Jones says: "The force of the comparison is that the dog in Palestine stood for danger and not domesticity since it ran wild in the streets."[8]

Verses 18-19 mean either that the practical joker who deceives his neighbour for his own amusement is condemned or the man is condemned who deceives his neighbor and then to save himself from the consequences says it was all in sport. In 20-21

⁵*Op. cit.*, p. 157.   ⁶*Op. cit.*, p. 173.
⁷*Op. cit.*, p. 212.   ⁸*Op. cit.*, p. 213.

the talebearer (malicious gossip) is condemned. For 22 see the identical proverb in 18:8 and the comment on it.

In 23-28 we have an arraignment of hypocritical speech and character. **Burning lips and a wicked heart** (23) are like an earthen vessel **covered** by a glaze of silver **dross,** giving the impression of solid silver (cf. Matt. 23:27). Hatred is the father of untruthful **lips** and continuing **deceit** (24). **Seven abominations in his heart** (25) depicts an evil heart (cf. Matt. 12:45). Sooner or later such hypocrisy results in public trial and exposure to **the whole congregation** (26; see note on 5:14). The boomeranging consequences of evil are expressed in 27. The man of evil intent who digs **a pit** for others and who rolls **a stone** up the hill to hurl down on others will be trapped by his own schemes (cf. Ps. 7:15; Eccles. 10:8). The words **a lying tongue hateth** (28) go to the very heart of the matter. The **lying tongue** and the **flattering mouth** are the outflow of a hateful and an unclean heart; they work **ruin** to both their object and their possessor.

7. *Truths for Today and Tomorrow* (27:1-22)

In 1 we are reminded that today and **tomorrow** are in the hands of God. Here the sage tells us that, since man's powers are limited, we must live continually in the fear of the Lord (see comments on 1:7). For New Testament expressions of this truth see Luke 12:16-21 and Jas. 4:13-16. A man should live, says Solomon, so that others will praise him rather than giving himself to **praise** from his **own lips** (2). It is easier to carry a load of **sand** or **stone** (3) than to bear the angry vexations of a fool. Jealousy is even more burdensome than **anger** (4). **Love** (5) should not be silent when the best interests of a friend can be served by a **rebuke.** The healthy rebuke of a sincere **friend,** though not pleasant to receive, is much better for one than the expressions of **an enemy** that are "lavish *and* deceitful" (Amp. OT).

The value of a healthy appetite is expressed in 7. With a spiritual hunger one can profit even from the bitter-tasting rebuke of 6. The hardship of the wanderer is expressed in 8. Perhaps we have here a reference to the fortunes of the wise men of Israel, who were travelling teachers. Verse 9 is difficult, and its renderings are many. One of the best reads: "As perfume and incense gratify the senses so a friend's cordiality strengthens one's spirit."[9] The triplet of 10 urges us not to forsake old family friends. **Better is a neighbour that is near** in the hour of emergency **than a brother** who is **far off.**

Responsibility and involvement on the part of the pupil are the teacher's joy (11; cf. I Thess. 2:19-20; 3:8; see note on 10:1). For 12 see the identical proverb of 22:3 and the comment there. For 13 see the similar couplet of 20:16 and the notes on **surety** (6:1-5). **A loud,** ostentatious profession of friendship, like the lavish kisses of an enemy (6), incur the suspicion of sinister purposes (14). For 15 see the similar couplet of 19:13 and the comments there. Scott ties 16 to 15 and his translation of 16 reads: "To try to restrain her is like trying to restrain the wind; one cries out that 'his hand is slippery.' "[10]

The impact of one's associates on his character is the theme of 17 (see comments on 1:10-19; cf. 13:20; 22:24-25). Social distinctions will not keep a faithful servant from being rewarded by **his master** (18). Greenstone makes this terse comment on 19: "Just as the reflection in the water depends on the degree of its purity and translucence, so the heart of man reflects his judgment of the other man's character."[11] Sinful man is restless and his desires are **never** fully **satisfied** (20; for the meaning of **hell** [*sheol*] and **destruction** [*abaddon*] see comment on 15:11). A man's character is tested, or put in the crucible, by the **praise** of others or by what he himself praises (21). **A fool** and his folly are inseparable, apart from the grace of God.

> *Crush a fool in a mortar with a pestle*
> *along with crushed grain,*
> *yet his folly will not depart from him* (22, RSV).

8. The Parable of the Shepherd (27:23-27)

In these verses the sage eulogizes the nomadic way of life, that characterized a large segment of Israel's people. For similar instructions to the farmer see Isa. 28:23-29. **Be thou diligent** reflects work well done as the theme of 23. **Riches** (24) are fleeting and one must not forget the values that are eternal (cf. 23:5; Job 20:28; Ps. 49:10). Here are words as relevant to the people of the space age as to the ancient shepherd of Israel. In 25-27 the shepherd is reminded that the things entrusted to

[9]Scott, *op. cit.*, p. 161.   [10]*Ibid.*, p. 162.
[11]*Op. cit.*, p. 289.

him require responsible care, if they are to be fruitful and useful. Diligence on man's part must be linked to providential care on God's part.

B. SECOND COLLECTION, 28: 1—29: 27

1. *The Wicked and the Righteous* (28:1-28)

A good conscience gives one courage (1). The word **bold** here means "confident, secure." Kidner says: "The straightforward man, like the lion, has no need to look over his shoulder. What is at his heels is not his past (Nu. 32:23) but his rear-guard: God's goodness and mercy (Ps. 23:6)."[12] An unstable government—**many . . . princes** (2)—is due to moral corruption, but righteous men preserve good government. "A wicked man who oppresses the needy is like a devastating rain which ruins the harvest" (3, Scott).[13] Evil men combine their efforts against **law** and order, but good men who **keep the law** oppose such conduct (4; cf. Rom. 1:18-32). While **evil men** do not know what is right, those who **seek the Lord** (5) are enlightened (cf. Ps. 119:100; Eccles. 8:5; John 7:17; I Cor. 2:15).

Honest poverty and right conduct are better than dishonest wealth (6; see note on 19:1). An undisciplined son is a disgrace (7; see note on 23:19-25). The word **riotous** (7) is "gluttonous" or "self-indulgent." "He who pays heed to instruction is a wise son; but the companion of profligates brings disgrace on his father" (Smith-Goodspeed). In 8 the sage reminds us that the greedy extortioner's gains **by usury** (see comment on 6:1-5) will eventually fall into the hands of one who is compassionate, and **will pity the poor.** In the parable of the pounds Jesus expressed a similar truth (Luke 19:24). The person who rejects God's will as revealed in **the law** (9) indicates his insincerity and cannot pray aright. The parable of the Pharisee and the publican is a New Testament parallel of this truth (Luke 18: 10-14). Misleading others is condemned in 10 (cf. Matt. 5:19; 18:6; 23:15). Such behavior boomerangs (see note on 26:27).

The **conceit of the rich** is the theme of 11. The arrogant man thinks that his business ability is an indication of his superior wisdom, but a **poor** man may see through this man's shortcomings and possess true wisdom and security (see note on 18:11). In 12

[12]*Op. cit.,* p. 168.   [13]*Op. cit.,* p. 164.

wicked and righteous leadership are contrasted. This verse is well translated: "When the [uncompromisingly] righteous triumph, there is a great glory and celebration; but when the wicked rise [to power], men hide themselves" (Amp. OT). In 13 we are reminded that God's mercy is dependent upon sincere repentance. The classic expressions of this truth are found in Ps. 32:1-4 and I John 1:6-9. Fear of the Lord (14) is seen as a guard against sin and its dreadful consequences. A wicked ruler (15) is compared to the wild beasts of the jungle. Toy captures the meaning of 16: "He who is oppressive is lacking in intelligence, he who hates unjust gain will live long."[14]

The RSV clarifies 17 thus:

If a man is burdened with the blood of another,
let him be a fugitive until death;
let no one help him (cf. Num. 35:31-34).

The way of God is profitable (18; cf. 10:9). An apt translation reads: "A man of blameless life is safe: pitfalls bring down the man of crooked courses" (Moffatt). A plea for diligence is expressed in 19 (see the similar proverb of 12:11). A faithful man (20) should expect to gain wealth only by hard work and not by hasty, get-rich-quick schemes (see note on 20: 21). The setting of 21 is that of the court of law. A judge must be impartial and must not accept even the smallest of bribes— a piece of bread (cf. 18:5; 24:23). In grasping for riches one often stoops to practices that result in inner moral and spiritual poverty; he also finds material gain elusive (22; cf. 23:4-5 and the note there). To have an evil eye is to be selfish.

In the long run honest rebuke is better than deceitful flattery (23). The son who robbeth his father or his mother (24), i.e., who tries to gain control of their property or squanders their resources, is classed with the destructive criminal (cf. Mark 7:11-12; I Tim. 5:4, 8). The proud man gets into difficulty, but the one who puts his trust in the Lord prospers (25; cf. Matt. 6:19-34). It is utter folly to trust alone in one's own capabilities; the wise man trusts in the Lord (26). The blessedness of giving is stressed in 27 (see notes on 11:24-29 and 22:9). He that hideth his eyes is the man who pays no attention to the poor. For 28 see comment on 12.

[14]Op. cit., p. 502.

2. God and the Reign of the Righteous (29:1-27)

The fate of the man who stubbornly refuses to learn and resists the truth is expressed in 1. For an elaboration of this theme see comments on 1:24-33. For 2 see notes on 28:12 and on 11:10-11. A wise son is the joy of his parents (3; see notes on 28:7 and 10:1). A wise **king** rules with **judgment** (justice) and refuses **gifts** (bribes and tribute money; 4; cf. 15:27). The deceitful flatterer becomes entangled in his own **net** (5; 26:28; 28:23). In 6 we have a contrast between the **evil man** who gets ensnared by sin and **the righteous** man who rejoices in his escape from such snares. The man of God has personal concern for **the poor** (7), but **the wicked** man refuses to accept any responsibility for the needy. For an example of the concern of the righteous see Job 29:12-17.

The sage sees **scornful men** (8) as morally and spiritually arrogant. Such men **bring a city into a snare**; literally, "fan the flames of a dispute until there is a blaze." Men of God, however, bring peace and harmony (cf. Jas. 3:13-18). Verse 9 is clearer in the language of RSV:

> If a wise man has an argument with a fool,
> the fool only rages and laughs,
> and there is no quiet.

An excellent rendering of 10 reads: "The bloodthirsty detest a blameless man but the upright are concerned for his welfare."[15] A foolish man has neither wisdom nor self-discipline, but a wise man controls his emotions (11; cf. 14:17, 29; 16:32; 25:28). The character of a ruler sets the moral tone of his kingdom—like king, like servant (12). The oppressed and the oppressor alike benefit from God's providential care—He gives light to the eyes of both (13). Jesus expressed this truth in Matt. 5:44-45.

The permanence of a king's reign depends upon his exercise of justice and on his moral character (14; cf. 16:12; 20:28; 25:5). In 15 we have a plea for the wholesome restraint of children. For 16 see the similar teaching of 2, also 28:12, 28. The discipline of children brings gratifying rewards to the parents (17; a companion to v. 15). Of 18, Jones and Walls say: "The law, the prophets and the wisdom literature meet in this verse. Where the revealed will of God, as expressed in His Word, is not kept

---

[15]Scott, *op. cit.*, p. 168.

constantly in view, His people break loose from their allegiance."[16] The slave, like the son, will need proper training and discipline (19). For 20 see the similar proverb of 26:12. In 21 we have a warning to the indulgent master. The thought is well captured by this rendering: "He who pampers his servant from a child will have him expecting the rights of a son afterward" (Amp. OT).

The folly of anger is the theme of 22. Not only does a violent temper stir up trouble; it also "is the cause of many a sin" (Moffatt). **Pride** and humility are contrasted again in 23 (cf. 11:2; see note on 16:18-19). In the choice of companions one may place himself in jeopardy (24). The **partner** of **a thief** shares the plunder but incurs guilt. Furthermore, he refuses to testify against the thief and thus commits perjury (cf. Lev. 5:1). **The fear of man,** or of what others think, can result in moral cowardice and sin (25; cf. Matt. 10:28; Mark 8:38). But by placing his confidence in God one **shall be safe;** literally, "set on high" (cf. 16:7; 18:10). God decides the destiny of every man, so undue reliance on human, and especially political, power is deplored by the sages (26). In the final verse of this section of Proverbs the conflict between good and evil is again set forth and the importance of moral choice underlined (27; see comments on 2:12-15).

---

[16]*Op. cit.*, p. 536.

Section V The Words of Agur

Proverbs 30:1-33

The chapter is entitled "The Words of Agur" from its opening
sentence. Nothing is known of **Agur the son of Jakeh** (1). He
may have been, like Job and Baalim, a non-Israelite who had
come to know the God of the Hebrew faith. He may have been
a respected non-Jewish teacher and possibly a contemporary
of Solomon. Some have conjectured that **Agur** was simply
another name for Solomon. More significant, however, than
Agur's exact identity is the fact that his words were considered
worthy of inclusion in the Book of Proverbs.

A. PERSONAL OBSERVATIONS, 30:1-9

1. *The Knowledge of God* (30:1-4)

The exact meaning of 1 is as uncertain as Agur's identity.
Some scholars see **Ithiel** and **Ucal** as favorite pupils of Agur.
Others translate these names in such a way as to symbolize
Agur's struggle to come to a knowledge of God. "I am wearied,
O God, I am wearied, O God, and spent" (Smith-Goodspeed).
In 2-3, Agur expresses his ignorance of God and his profound
sense of humility in his approach to God. He is not, however, a
skeptic, as some assert, but recognizes that God is not compre-
hended by human wisdom alone. Agur makes no claim to
superior **knowledge of the holy,** as others have done.

With five rhetorical questions he contrasts the Creator and
the creature (4). God is knowable, but He is also incompre-
hensibly great (cf. Job 11:7-8; 38—41; Ps. 104:1-5; Prov. 8:
24-29 and note there; Isa. 40:12; Rom. 11:33-35). In the light of
God's "majestic otherness" man is seen with all his finite limitations.

2. *The Revelation of God* (30:5-6)

These verses provide the answer to the probing questions
of 2-4. While the light of human intellect is inadequate to give an
understanding of God's being and His works, the inerrant self-
disclosure of God through His Word is within reach of all who
put their trust in him (5). God is fully reliable and **his words**

534

(6) need no appendages of human speculation to make them complete (Deut. 4:2; 12:32; Ps. 18:30; 84:11; 115:9-11).

3. *The Prayer of Agur* (30:7-9)

The burden of Agur's prayer is twofold. He prays humbly, first of all, that he will be able to maintain his godly integrity— **before I die** (7)—or literally, "all the days of my life." **Remove far from me vanity** (falsehood) **and lies** (8). He prays earnestly, in the second place, for the simple necessities of life—no more, no less. Such a petition anticipates the Lord's Prayer. Agur wants neither the dangers of prosperity nor the desperations of **poverty**. He desires nothing that would cause him to **deny** or blaspheme his Lord. Here is the golden mean applied to moral and spiritual concerns. Agur's aspirations might well be in the hearts and on the lips of us all.

B. NUMERICAL PROVERBS, 30:10-33

In this section we have the numerical proverbs (see 15, 18, 21, 24, 29) characteristic of the Hebrew gnomic literature. Israel's sages used devices such as numerical sequences, acrostic patterns, and various types of parallelisms to accentuate truths and to aid memorization.

1. *Against Slandering and Evildoers* (30:10-14)

In 10 we have a couplet that warns against slander (cf. Rom. 14:4). In 11-14 there are severe indictments of four classes of depraved persons—those who reject the claims of the family (11); the self-righteous (12); the contemptuous (13); and the cruel in word and deed (14).

2. *Four Insatiable Things* (30:15-16)

The **horseleach** (15) is rendered "leech" by most ancient and modern translators and commentators. Greenstone says: "The leech sucks the blood of its victim until it is glutted and falls off. Hence it became symbolic of greed, bloodthirstiness."[1] It is, therefore, a fitting symbol with which to introduce the four examples of insatiable things—**the grave, the barren womb, the dry earth**, and **fire**.

[1]*Op. cit.*, p. 321.

3. The Arrogant Son (30:17)

The body of a disrespectful son will not be given a decent burial but will serve as food for **ravens** and **eagles** (lit., "young vultures"). This graphic portrait the sage uses to emphasize the Hebrew's high regard for parental authority (cf. 23:22 and Exod. 20:12).

4. Four Incomprehensible Things (30:18-19)

Man can never fully understand the phenomena of nature, even in this age of a knowledge explosion. In his prescientific day the sage selected four examples of the mystery of nature (19).

5. The Shocking Adulteress (30:20)

After illustrating the mysteries of nature, the sage describes **an adulterous woman** who is at ease in her sin and totally indifferent to her immorality. Kidner says: "An act of adultery is as unremarkable to her as a meal."[2]

6. Four Intolerable Things (30:21-23)

Here four unbearable persons are described. Moffatt explains them as:

> a slave who rises to be king,
> a fool who makes a fortune,
> a plain girl who at last gets married,
> and a maid who supplants her mistress.

Such persons would bring chaos to a community or society, and Israel's sages "were the enemies of social and political revolution."[3]

7. Four Remarkable Little Things (30:24-28)

The sage who wrote these words was not enamored with bigness. He saw the significance and the productivity of little things such as **the ants** (25); **the conies** (26) or Syrian hyrax, somewhat comparable to the rabbit (ISBE); **the locusts** (27); and **the spider** (28) or "lizard" (Berk., RSV).

---

[2]Op. cit., p. 180.   [3]Rylaarsdam, op. cit., p. 92.

8. *Four Stately Things* (30:29-31)

Here the sage cites four examples of majestic bearing and power—the **lion;** the **greyhound** (the Heb. here is uncertain; it has been translated "war horse," BB; "fighting cock," Berk., and "strutting cock," RSV); the male **goat;** and the **king.** These are symbols of the power that God has given to His creatures.

9. *A Concluding Challenge* (30:32-33)

The conclusion, like the beginning, of this chapter deals with the virtue of humility. If one has been guilty of arrogant conduct or has contemplated such, he should face it. **Lay thine hand upon thy mouth** (32) is an expression suggesting the silent admission of blame (cf. Job 21:5; 40:4). Agur's final words comprise a plea for one to refuse to agitate **strife** (33) and an encouragement to "live peaceably with all men" (Rom. 12:18).

Section **VI** *The Words of Lemuel*

Proverbs 31:1-9

A. TITLE, 31:1

This section contains the instruction of a king's mother to her son. **King Lemuel** and **his mother** were likely non-Israelites, although nothing is known definitely regarding them. The lessons of the passage, however, are clear and significant. Toy calls this segment of Proverbs "a manual for kings and judges."[1]

B. WARNINGS AGAINST LUST AND STRONG DRINK, 31:2-7

The construction of 2 suggests both earnestness and loving concern. Moffatt renders it:

> Son of mine, heed what I say,
> listen, O son of my prayers, and obey.

Lemuel is her son and one whom she dedicated to the Lord (cf. I Sam. 1:11). She warns him, first of all, against sensual debauchery (3). Edgar Jones says: "The counsel is not mere prohibition but is given that the king may carry out his duties to the community. It means discipline for a fuller dedication."[2] She is eager for him to give his best to his responsibility as a king.

The ruler must not only be morally fit, but physically strong as well. So the honorable mother warns: **O Lemuel, it is not for kings to drink wine; nor for princes strong drink** (4) that **pervert** one's **judgment** (5). The sage, of course, recognizes the use of wine as a drug or medicine for certain distresses (6; cf. I Tim. 5:23) and as a sedative for criminals who are suffering (6-7). Rylaarsdam's observation is fitting: "Jesus' refusal to take the wine offered him on the cross (Mark 15:23) is probably reported in order to draw attention to his kingship, especially on the cross, and to his judgment over sin and death."[3]

C. RULE IN RIGHTEOUSNESS, 31:8-9

The concluding counsel of the king's mother is beamed at motivating her son to reign in righteousness, giving special at-

[1]*Op. cit.*, p. 538.   [2]*Op. cit.*, p. 245.
[3]*Op. cit.*, p. 92.

tention to **the poor** and underprivileged. She urged, **Open thy mouth** (8; "speak up," Berk.) for those who cannot speak for themselves. **Such as are appointed to destruction** is better "all who are left desolate" (RSV). Reflected in such counsel is the concern for social justice so frequently voiced by Israel's prophets (cf. Isa. 10:1-2; Amos 2:6-7; 4:1; 5:15).

Section VII The Virtuous Wife and Mother

Proverbs 31:10-31

In this final section we have a beautiful acrostic poem that is an immortal tribute to the virtuous wife and mother. The poem has been called the "Golden ABC of Womanhood." It contains twenty-two stanzas or couplets each beginning with a letter of the Hebrew alphabet.

This poem is a fitting climax to the Book of Proverbs. First of all, much has been said about the contentious woman (cf. 19:13; 21:9; 25:24; 27:15), so the sage pays tribute to one more noble. Secondly, there are repeated condemnations of the adulteress and sinful woman (cf. cc. 1—9; 22:14; 23:27; 29:3; 31:3). Now the sage presents the better portrait of commendable womanhood. Again, throughout Proverbs the mother's place in the training of children has been noted (cf. 1:8-9; 10:1; 17:25; 18:22; 19:14; 23:25; 28:24). In the closing words the sage underscores this great truth of the Hebrew family tradition.

Finally, the purpose of Proverbs is to help people come to know wisdom—the way of the Lord (see comments on 1:2-6). In the concluding poetical expression the sage portrays more than a wife of strength and character in a general sense. The poem is not simply a contrast to the contentious woman and the adulteress. It is more than a tribute to Hebrew womanhood. This wife and mother is an example of one who fulfills God's purposes for her life. It is in this respect that the ideal she exemplifies is within the reach of all.

A. Crowning Characteristics, 31:10-29

A wife so capable and strong in character is priceless—**far above rubies** (10). She is so unfailing in her devotion that **her husband . . . shall have no need of spoil** (11; "no lack of *honest* gain or need of *dishonest* spoil," Amp. OT). All that she does contributes to his well-being (12). She is unceasingly industrious (13-15). She has outstanding business ability (16-19). **The fruit of her hands** (16) is better "with her earnings" (Smith-Goodspeed). The phrases, **She girdeth her loins . . . and strengtheneth her arms** (17), are to be understood as her efforts to fasten her skirt and sleeves so that she is unhampered in her

540

work. **Her candle goeth not out by night** (18) does not mean that she works all night, but that there was plenty of oil in her house so that her lamp could burn through the night (cf. 13:9; Matt. 25:8). **The spindle** and **distaff** (19) were instruments used in the hand spinning of thread for weaving cloth.

This ideal wife is charitable and unselfish toward **the needy** (20). **All her household are clothed with scarlet** (21) indicates articles of luxury (cf. Exod. 25:4; II Sam. 1:24; Jer. 4:30). The word **scarlet** may also mean more than one garment. Williams says that color was not the issue. The rendering could well be that "all her household are clothed in double garments."[1] **Her own clothing** (22) was attractive and in good taste. This wife is a boon to **her husband** (23), who is a respected leader in the community (cf. 1:21; 24:7). Her industry results in profits for the family (24).

This mother has **strength and honour** (25); she is confident regarding the future of her home. She is gracious and kind in her instructions to her children and in her directives to her servants (26). She is tireless in her devotion to **her household** (27). She is respected and loved by **her children** and **her husband** (28). The writer concludes his eulogy:

Many women have done well,
But you have excelled them all (Smith-Goodspeed).

B. A CONCLUDING TRIBUTE, 31:30-31

In v. 30 we are reminded that **favour** (charm) and **beauty** are fleeting, but that a godly character is of lasting value. The husband of this good wife is urged to give her **the fruit of her hands** (31)—due recognition for her work, and also public acclaim.

Not all may possess the unusual gifts and resources of this outstanding wife and mother, but all may follow her as she followed the Lord. In this she is the exemplification of true wisdom. Thus Proverbs ends as it begins (1:7) with the challenge to take the way of wisdom, which is to fear the Lord always and live according to His purposes.

---

[1]Walter G. Williams, *Archaeology in Biblical Research* (New York-Nashville: Abingdon Press, 1965), p. 175.

Bibliography

I. COMMENTARIES

CLARKE, ADAM. *The Holy Bible with a Commentary and Critical Notes,* Vol. III. New York: Abingdon-Cokesbury Press, n.d.

COOK, F. C. *The Bible Commentary: Proverbs-Ezekiel.* Abridged and edited by J. M. FULLER. Grand Rapids, Michigan: Baker Book House, 1953.

COWLES, HENRY. *Proverbs, Ecclesiastes and The Song of Solomon* (Critical, Explanatory and Practical). New York: D. Appleton and Co., 1884.

DAVIES, G. HENTON; RICHARDSON, ALAN; WALLIS, CHARLES L. (eds.). *The Twentieth Century Bible Commentary.* Revised edition. New York: Harper and Brothers, Publishers, 1955.

DEANE, W. J., and TAYLOR-TASWELL, S. T. *Proverbs* (Exposition). "The Pulpit Commentary." Edited by H. M. D. SPENCE and JOSEPH S. EXELL. London and New York: Funk and Wagnalls Co., 1913.

FRITSCH, CHARLES T. "The Book of Proverbs" (Introduction and Exegesis). *The Interpreter's Bible.* Edited by GEORGE A. BUTTRICK, *et al.,* Vol. IV. New York: Abingdon Press, 1955.

GREENSTONE, JULIUS H. *Proverbs with Commentary.* Philadelphia: The Jewish Publication Society, 1950.

HARRIS, R. LAIRD. "Proverbs" (Introduction and Commentary). *The Wycliffe Bible Commentary.* Edited by CHARLES F. PFEIFFER and EVERETT F. HARRISON. Chicago: Moody Press, 1962.

HENRY, MATTHEW. *Commentary on the Whole Bible,* Vol. III. New York: Fleming H. Revell, n.d.

HORTON, R. F. *The Book of Proverbs.* "The Expositor's Bible." Edited by W. ROBERTSON NICOLL. New York: A. C. Armstrong and Son, 1903.

JONES, EDGAR. *Proverbs and Ecclesiastes.* "Torch Bible Commentaries." General editors, JOHN MARSH and ALAN RICHARDSON. New York: The Macmillan Co., 1961.

JONES, W. A. REES, and WALLS, ANDREW F. "The Proverbs" (Introduction and Commentary). *The New Bible Commentary.* Edited by F. DAVIDSON, *et al.* Grand Rapids, Mich.: Wm. B. Eerdmans Publishing Co., 1953.

KIDNER, DEREK. *The Proverbs* (An Introduction and Commentary). "The Tyndale Old Testament Commentaries." General editor, D. J. WISEMAN. London: The Tyndale Press, 1964.

KITCHEN, KENNETH A. "Proverbs." *The Biblical Expositor.* Consulting editor, CARL F. H. HENRY, Vol. II. Philadelphia: A. J. Holman Co., 1960.

MACLAREN, ALEXANDER. *Expositions of Holy Scripture,* Vol. III. Grand Rapids, Michigan: Wm. B. Eerdmans Publishing Co., 1938.

OESTERLEY, W. O. E. *The Book of Proverbs.* "Westminster Commentaries." Editors, WALTER LOCK and D. C. SIMPSON. London: Methuen and Co, 1929.

PEAKE, ARTHUR S. *Peake's Commentary on the Bible.* Edited by MATTHEW BLACK and H. H. ROWLEY. New York: Thomas Nelson and Sons, 1962.

RYLAARSDAM, J. COERT. *The Proverbs, Ecclesiastes, The Song of Solomon.* "The Layman's Bible Commentary," Vol. 10. Edited by BALMER H. KELLY, *et al.* Richmond, Va.: John Knox Press, 1964.

SCHLOERB, ROLLAND W. "The Book of Proverbs" (Exposition). *The Interpreter's Bible.* Edited by GEORGE A. BUTTRICK, *et al.,* Vol. IV. New York: Abingdon Press, 1955.

SCOTT, R. B. Y. "Proverbs—Ecclesiastes" (Introduction, Translation, and Notes). *The Anchor Bible.* General editors, W. F. ALBRIGHT and D. N. FREEDMAN. Garden City, New York: Doubleday & Company, Inc., 1965.

SPURGEON, C. H. *The Treasury of David,* Vol. V. London: Passmore and Alabaster, 1881.

TOY, CRAWFORD H. *A Critical and Exegetical Commentary on the Book of Proverbs.* "The International Critical Commentary." Edited by CHARLES A. BRIGGS, SAMUEL R. DRIVER, and ALFRED PLUMMER. New York: Charles Scribner's Sons, 1904.

WILLIAMS, GEORGE. *The Student's Commentary on the Holy Scriptures.* Grand Rapids, Michigan: Kregel Publications (5th edition), 1953.

II. OTHER BOOKS

ANDERSON, BERNHARD W. *Understanding the Old Testament.* Englewood Cliffs, New Jersey: Prentice-Hall, Inc., 1960.

ARCHER, GLEASON L., JR. *A Survey of Old Testament Introduction.* Chicago: Moody Press, 1964.

LINDSELL, HAROLD (Introductions, Annotations, Topical Headings, Marginal References, and Index Prepared and Edited by). *Harper Study Bible* (The Holy Bible—Revised Standard Version). New York: Harper & Row, Publishers, 1964.

PRITCHARD, JAMES B. (ed.). *Ancient Near Eastern Texts Relating to the Old Testament.* Princeton: Princeton University Press,· 1950.

PURKISER, W. T., *et al. Exploring the Old Testament.* Kansas City: Beacon Hill Press, 1955.

RHODES, ARNOLD B. *The Mighty Acts of God.* Richmond, Virginia: The Covenant Life Curriculum Press, 1964.

RYLAARSDAM, J. COERT. *Revelation in Jewish Literature.* Chicago: The University of Chicago Press, 1946.

THOMPSON, J. A. *The Bible and Archaeology.* Grand Rapids, Michigan: Wm. B. Eerdmans Publishing Co., 1962.

UNGER, MERRILL F. *Unger's Bible Handbook.* Chicago: Moody Press, 1966.

WILLIAMS, WALTER G. *Archaeology in Biblical Research.* New York: Abingdon Press, 1965.

YOUNG, EDWARD J. *An Introduction to the Old Testament.* Grand Rapids, Michigan: Wm. B. Eerdmans Publishing Co., 1950.

III. ARTICLES

BLACKMAN, E. C. "Mind, Heart." *A Theological Word Book of the Bible.* Editor, ALAN RICHARDSON. New York: The Macmillan Co., paperback edition, 1962, pp. 144-46.

BLANK, S. H. "Book of Proverbs." *The Interpreter's Dictionary of the Bible.* Edited by GEORGE BUTTRICK, *et al.* New York: Abingdon Press, 1962., Vol. K-Q, pp. 936-40.

——. "Wisdom." IDB, Vol. R-Z, pp. 852-61.

——. "Wisdom of Solomon." IDB, Vol. R-Z, pp. 861-63.

FRITSCH, CHARLES T. "The Gospel in the Book of Proverbs." *Theology Today,* Vol. VII, April, 1950—January, 1951. Editor, JOHN A. MACKAY. Princeton, N.J., pp. 169-83.

GILMORE, HAYDN L. "Biblical Proverbs: God's Transistorized Wisdom." *Christianity Today,* X, No. 22 (August 19, 1966), 6, 8.

HUBBARD, D. A. "Book of Proverbs." *New Bible Dictionary.* Editor, J. D. DOUGLAS. Grand Rapids, Michigan: Wm. B. Eerdmans Publishing Co., 1962, pp. 1049-50.

——. "Wisdom" and "Wisdom Literature." NBD, pp. 1333-35.

MILLER, MADELEINE S. and J. LANE. "Solomon," pp. 692-94; "Ezion-geber," p. 182; "Gezer," pp. 223-25; "Hiram," p. 262; "Megiddo," pp. 434-36; "Millo," pp. 445-46. *Harper's Dictionary of the Bible.* New York: Harper and Brothers, Publishers, 1956.

The Book of

ECCLESIASTES

or THE PREACHER

A. F. Harper

Introduction

A. NAME

In the opening verse of Ecclesiastes the author identifies himself as "the Preacher" (Heb., *Koheleth*). The word comes from a root which means "to assemble" and thus probably indicates one who gathers an assembly to address it, hence a speaker or preacher. In the Septuagint the Greek term *Ecclesiastes* was used and has been brought over into our English translations as the name of the book. The term designates "a member of the *ecclesia*, the citizens' assembly in Greece." In the early Christian era *ecclesia* was the term used for the Church.

B. AUTHORSHIP

Who was *Koheleth?* The language of 1:1 and the description of c. 2 seem to indicate King Solomon. The Solomonic authorship was accepted by both Jewish and Christian tradition down to comparatively recent times. Martin Luther seems to have been the first to deny it, and probably most Bible students would agree with him. Purkiser writes:

> In the first verse, it is ascribed to "the son of David, king in Jerusalem" . . . However, chapter 1:12 says, "I the Preacher *was* king over Israel in Jerusalem." Obviously, there never was a time in Solomon's life when he could have referred to his reign in the past tense. Chapter 2:4-11 also describes the works of Solomon's reign as something that was passed at the time of writing.
> Again, in 1:16, the writer says, "I . . . have gotten more wisdom than *all* they that have been before me in Jerusalem." The same thought is repeated in chapter 2:7. In the case of Solomon, only David had preceded him as king in Jerusalem. Again, it must be remembered that the Jews used the term "son" for any descendent; thus, Jesus is spoken of also as the "son of David."[1]

Among recent conservative scholars Young writes: "The author of the book, then, was one who lived in the postexilic period and who placed his words in the mouth of Solomon, thus

---

[1]*Know Your Old Testament* (Kansas City: Beacon Hill Press, 1947), pp. 149-50.

employing a literary device for conveying his message."[2] Hendry considers non-Solomonic authorship such a closed issue that he does not discuss it in his Introduction.[3] Those who reject Solomon as the author usually date the book from 400 to 200 B.C., some even later.

The strongest argument against accepting Solomonic authorship seems to be the presence in the text of Aramaic words that are not known to have been used in the time of Solomon. Archer, however, argues against the validity of this evidence, asserting that "the text of Ecclesiastes fits into no known period in the history of the Hebrew language . . . there is at present no sure foundation for dating this book upon linguistic grounds (although it is no more dissimilar to tenth century Hebrew than it is to fifth century or second century)."[4]

If Solomon be not the author, we must say at least that much in the book reflects his life and experiences.

C. INTERPRETATION

How shall we interpret the message of this book? The reader is soon impressed by apparently contradictory positions. A persisting theory holds that the book is a dialogue with opposing positions presented by different characters. If this view is held, the oft-repeated "vanity of vanities" would be the author's verdict on an outlook confined to the present world. Another favorite approach has been to trace a consistently pessimistic point of view to the original author and to explain opposing views as insertions by later editors who sought to correct overstatements and to make the book more consistent with the then current religious teaching.

The book does present vacillations between faith and pessimism. But these need not compel us to abandon a belief in the unity of Ecclesiastes. Are not such vacillations a natural consequence of half faith and half worldliness, whether in Solomon

[2]*An Introduction to the Old Testament* (Grand Rapids: Wm. B. Eerdmans Publishing Co., 1950), p. 340.

[3]"Ecclesiastes," *The New Bible Commentary*, ed. F. Davidson, *et al.* (Grand Rapids: Wm. B. Eerdmans Publishing Co., 1953), pp. 338-39.

[4]*A Survey of Old Testament Introduction* (Chicago: Moody Press, 1964), pp. 465-66. See here his explanation of the peculiar linguistic structure of Ecclesiastes.

himself or in the earth-centered life that the book depicts? Barton writes, "When a modern man realizes how many different conceptions and moods he can entertain, he finds fewer authors in a book like Qoheleth."[5]

If this book represents the struggle of a soul with dark doubts, it also reveals a man who came out on the positive side. Despite his pessimistic moods, life is as precious as a golden bowl (12:6), and the final answer to the quest for meaning is, "Fear God, and keep his commandments" (12:13).

D. Organization

Ecclesiastes is not a closely reasoned or logically organized book. It is more like a diary in which a man has recorded his impressions from time to time. Often it appears to express moods of the moment and emotional responses rather than a balanced philosophy of life. The mood is skeptical more often than not, and yet, as Paterson writes: "It would have been a great pity and a serious loss if a book that is meant to be the Bible of all men made no reference or failed to deal with the mood of scepticism which is common to all men."[6]

The structure of the book makes it so difficult to outline that many commentators do not attempt a logical pattern. In the outline here presented the author has been influenced by Archer[7] more than by any other one writer. At times the careful reader will note that a caption points to one significant thought in the section rather than summarizing all that is there.

Though the paragraphs are at times only loosely related to each other, they are all related to the theme of the book—perhaps this is true only because that theme is as broad as life itself!

[5]"Ecclesiastes," *The International Critical Commentary*, ed. C. A. Briggs, et al. (New York: Charles Scribner's Sons, 1908), p. 162.

[6]*The Book That Is Alive* (New York: Charles Scribner's Sons, 1954), p. 130.

[7]*Op. cit.*, pp. 460-62.

Outline

I. The Quest for Life's Meaning, 1:1—2:26
   A. Introduction, 1:1-11
   B. The Vanity of Human Experiences, 1:12—2:26

II. Coming to Terms with Life, 3:1—5:20
   A. Poem of an Orderly World, 3:1-8
   B. Frustration and Faith, 3:9-15
   C. The Problem of Moral Evil, 3:16-22
   D. Disappointments of Life, 4:1-16
   E. Worshipping God Rightly, 5:1-7
   F. Adjusting to Economic Problems, 5:8-20

III. No Satisfaction in Earthly Goods, 6:1—8:17
   A. Disappointments from Wealth and Family, 6:1-12
   B. Practical Wisdom in a Sinful World, 7:1-29
   C. Coming to Terms with an Imperfect World, 8:1-17

IV. Life's Injustices in God's Hands, 9:1—10:20
   A. Thoughts on Death, 9:1-18
   B. Wisdom and Folly, 10:1-20

V. How Best to Invest Life, 11:1-8
   A. Be Generous, 11:1-3
   B. Be Industrious, 11:4-6
   C. Be Joyful, 11:7-8

VI. Seeing Life Whole, 11:9—12:14
   A. Earthly Life in Perspective, 11:9—12:8
   B. Life in the Light of Eternity, 12:9-14

Section I The Quest for Life's Meaning

Ecclesiastes 1:1—2:26

A. INTRODUCTION, 1:1-11

1. Title of the Book (1:1)

In this opening verse the writer gives the inscription, or title of his book. He calls it **The words of the Preacher.** The Hebrew term is *Koheleth,* which comes from *kahal* and means one who assembles or collects a congregation. The Septuagint[1] translated the word as *Ecclesiastes,* which has come over into our English Bible as the name of the book. The translation is derived from *ecclesia,* the Greek word we render "church." The author thus thought of himself as a preacher or religious teacher.

But who is this preacher? If we take v. 1 at face value, he was King Solomon—for there was no other **son of David** who was **king in Jerusalem.** However, to take this verse literally leaves other passages of the book unexplained. For discussion of this problem see Introduction, "Authorship."

2. Theme of the Book (1:2-11)

a. The text (1:2-3). In 2-11 the Preacher outlines the theme of his "sermon." The text is, **Vanity of vanities; all is vanity** (2). The Hebrew word is *hebhel,* which means "vapor" or "breath." This reflects the transience of life, but the author means more. Life seems to be going nowhere. Various translators have used the terms **vanity,** *futility, fruitless, aimless,* and *empty.* From this point of view our lives are meaningless. The repetition, **vanity of vanities,** is the Hebrew way of increasing the force and thus expressing utter futility (cf. *servant of servants,* Gen. 9:25; and *holy of holies*). The writer omits no phase of life; **all** is vain and useless.

In what sense does the Preacher make this declaration? There are interpreters who see it as his prevailing mood, his fixed philosophy of life. It seems better to understand it as a judgment passed on men who see earthly life as man's only life (see Intro., "Interpretation").

[1]The Greek translation of the OT, often abbreviated LXX.

There are, of course, hours—and sometimes days and weeks —when the theme of Ecclesiastes expresses the mood of the soul. But these are hours and days of depression. They occur in times of loss and discouragement. Such moods are temporary emotional reactions which in time give way to a truer understanding of life. They become life-shaping attitudes and life-forming convictions only to the man whose whole life is **under the sun** (3), whose outlook is entirely worldly and secular. Such a man has ample reason to ask, **What profit hath a man of all his labour?**

"If we are not certain, it may be because we are living at too low a level. If we live for pleasure or for money or for fame, then spiritual realities must of necessity become nebulous and vague. To feel that we are immortal we must live like immortals. Gazing constantly into the trivial blinds the eyes to the splendour of the eternal, and working always for fading wreaths robs the heart of its belief in the crown of glory. To those who give themselves wholeheartedly to the service of mankind in the spirit of His Son, God communicates not only peace and joy, but an unconquerable conviction that when work here is finished, to die is gain" (Selected).

This is the high faith to which the Christian revelation points us. But the man for whom Koheleth speaks never achieved this faith as a fixed pattern of life. For him other facts usually loomed larger.

b. *Illustrations from nature* (1:4-8). If a man looks only at life's physical environment, he finds only the answers that the material world can give. Koheleth here shows four of those frustrating facts. The physical earth is more permanent than the earthly life of a man: **One generation passeth away, and another generation cometh: but the earth abideth for ever** (4). This earth is not destined to last forever (II Pet. 3:10), but it has outlasted the earthly lives of countless generations of men. If life here is all, the Preacher has a persuasive point.

The argument now turns to the cycles of the natural world, and the writer sees nothing but their monotony. **The sun** (5) rises only to set, and then **hasteth to his place** to rise again. **The wind** (6) blows **south** and the wind blows **north** (a reflection of the prevailing winds of Palestine) and then repeats the process. **All the rivers run** (7) to **the sea;** evaporation and rainfall return the waters to the land, and the rivers flow again where they flowed before.

Nature moves in a circle, and when one can see only the circle he goes mad. **All things are full of labour** (8)—unfathomable energy is expended and there is nothing different from before. It is an utterly senseless activity—"unspeakably tiresome" (Berk.). As an afterthought, the pessimistic mood sees here only futility in man's continuing powers of sense: **The eye is not satisfied with seeing, nor the ear filled with hearing.**

But why should a man be pessimistic about the world's recurring functions? When the sun shines, and the breezes blow, and the rain falls, conscious beings are blessed by them. Instead of seeing it all as senseless repetition, nature may be seen as alive, energetic, and vibrant. He who is pessimistic about the eyes that always see and the ears that always hear should face for a time the prospect of losing his sight or hearing. These provisions of God would then be seen clearly for the blessings that they are.

c. Sameness and weariness (1:9-11). One can scarcely contradict the facts that the writer points out in these verses. Most of the things that we do have been done by someone else before us—and most of them will be done again by many others following us. Let us admit that there are few experiences that can be called a **new thing under the sun** (9). Most of life's basic activities have **been already of old time, which was before us** (10). But so what? Do we demand that things must be new in order to be valuable? Certainly this is not the outlook of a collector of antiques!

We must remember that all of the old things are new to the new people who come into the world. Also old experiences gain new meaning for persons who are somehow renewed with a fresh enthusiasm for life. There are new lives, new days, possible new interests, new services, and new devotions that bring fresh meaning to life. Perhaps in failures of devotion and service may be found the key to the writer's mood. In 13 he tells us that he gave himself to understand his world. Knowledge is good, but God has never planned that we should be detached observers. Those who serve with the abandonment of devotion find meaning that is lost to the merely interested onlooker.

Does v. 11 contradict the argument of 9-10, and reveal Koheleth's pessimism as a mood instead of a rational position? The writer has argued that life is vain because nothing is new. Now he argues that life is vain because so little will be remembered!

Many things are forgotten—and for most of this we may be grateful—but also many things are remembered. The monuments that men build and the books they write preserve the memories of the past. Many of the things we cherish most are preserved in our memories here, and we believe will be with us in a conscious existence beyond the grave. Moreover, God does not forget (Ps. 56:8).

B. THE VANITY OF HUMAN EXPERIENCES, 1:12—2:26

This section is in autobiographical form. The writer tells of a personal life quest, but who is the writer? He says **I . . . was king over Israel in Jerusalem** (12). For answers see Introduction, "Authorship."

1. *The Intellectual Quest* (1:13-16)

Whether or not we accept Solomon as the author of the book, we must admit that this section is in keeping with the interests of Israel's third king. Here is the search of the iniquiring mind, the effort of the man who seeks to see life steadily and to see it whole—to **search out by wisdom concerning all things** (13). But the intellectual venture is not fully satisfying. The writer turned from it as "an unhappy business that God has given to the sons of men to be busy with" (13, RSV). In 16 he reasons that, if the king with all of his financial resources and intellectual gifts has failed to find satisfaction in his search, how can any man with lesser resources reach a different conclusion?

The frustrated Koheleth concludes that the intellectual efforts of life are **vanity and vexation of spirit** (14), because the **crooked cannot be made straight** (15) and all the things that are wrong **cannot be numbered**. We are finite. We must admit that we can always find more things wrong than we can make right. "We do, however, possess the power by the grace of God and the mystery of our own creative personalities to take the raw material of experience and our own always unfinished selves, and make of life an enterprise worthy of its cost and promise. The **crooked** can be **made straight**, in highways, in society, and in the soul; not always easily or soon, and always at a price. But we have no choice save to try it."[2]

---

[2]Gaius Glenn Atkins, "Ecclesiastes" (Exposition), *The Interpreter's Bible*, ed. George A. Buttrick, et al. (New York: Abingdon-Cokesbury Press, 1951), V, 32.

2. A Probe and a Discovery (1:17-18)

In 17 the Preacher reaffirms his effort to **know wisdom,** but adds a word about his study techniques. He tried to gain wisdom by understanding its opposites, **madness and folly.** This was not only an effort to experience all of the facts. Various commentators suggest that it was a deeper probe of the mind in a search for the principles by which one can distinguish **wisdom** from **madness and folly.** But Koheleth found that even a theory of knowledge can be a **vexation of spirit.**

There is truth in 18 that is discovered by a growing personality. The more knowledge one gains, the more gaps he discovers in what he knows, and the less satisfied he is with his development. "He who more than one life lives, more than one death must die." But who would want to avoid the pains of knowledge at the cost of remaining ignorant? Who would try to avoid the sorrows of lost loved ones by refusing to love? We gain as we go forward in the quest for life. To withdraw from the quest is to forfeit the goal.

3. A Test of Pleasure (2:1-3)

In his search for the highest good many a man has tried the paths of **pleasure (1), laughter (2),** and the stimulation of **wine (3).** The Preacher admits his own experiment with these forms of diversion, but quickly discovered that they are unworthy pursuits for a man. Entertainment serves a useful purpose as occasional diversion from the serious tasks of life, but happiness is not found in diversion. **Mirth . . . also is vanity** when one makes it his ultimate goal. **Laughter . . . what doeth it** to satisfy our deepest needs? And "to stimulate my body with wine" (3, Berk.)—even for a man who can handle it **with wisdom**—is not the road to satisfaction.[3]

4. A Test of Activity and Possessions (2:4-11)

Turning from entertainment to activity, the king lost himself for a while in constructive work. He built **houses (4),** planted **vineyards,** made **gardens and orchards (5),** and made **pools of**

[3]"They that think to give themselves to wine, and yet to acquaint their hearts with wisdom, will perhaps deceive themselves as much as they do that think to serve both God and mammon" (Matthew Henry, *Commentary on the Holy Bible* [Chicago: W. P. Blessing Company, n.d.], Vol. III, *ad loc.*).

water "to irrigate a plantation of growing trees" (6, Smith-Goodspeed). A man needs the labor of people to maintain economic ventures, so he "bought male and female slaves, and had slaves who were born in my house" (7, RSV). He had herds and flocks of **cattle;** and accumulated **silver and gold** (8). The **peculiar treasure of kings and of the provinces** was probably costly and unique gifts which came to the king from other heads of state (cf. I Kings 10:1-2, 10). The king was also a patron of the arts, surrounding himself with **men singers and women singers.** The last part of 8 is obscure in the Hebrew. Most modern translators understand it as a reference to sex satisfaction: "I acquired . . . the delights of men—mistresses galore" (Berk.).

All of this may be called the cultural effort. What he did and what he got were honorable and praiseworthy according to the standards of his society. He was the successful suburbanite of our culture—perhaps the millionaire governor. He had all that money could buy, and all that intelligence and fame could give: **My heart rejoiced in all my labour: and this was my portion** (10). This was his **portion**—but it was not enough— **all was vanity and vexation of spirit** (11). How could it be otherwise when it was all for himself? No wonder it failed to inspire him (Berk., fn.). Self-centered activity will not stand up under reflection; the activity must have a satisfying purpose.

5. Wisdom and Folly Compared (2:12-17)

If a man cannot find abiding happiness in activity and the accumulation of a fortune, can it be found in using the mind to its maximum? The writer now gave his thought **to behold wisdom . . . and folly** (12).[4] It does not take long to reach the conclusion of the Preacher, **Wisdom excelleth folly, as far as light excelleth darkness** (13). The **wise** man (14) uses his intelligence to guide him, **but the fool** walks in the dark night of ignorance. Man is better than an animal because he can live a thoughtful life.

But here the sandy foundation of all mere humanism becomes apparent. How much better is the **wise** man than **the fool** when their life-spans are the same? The relative values of earthly life

---

[4]The last half of 12 seems to be an afterthought of advice for the benefit of others who would seek satisfaction in personal gains: If King Solomon, with his resources, failed in this effort, what could lesser men hope to achieve?

seem more nearly equal if all of them end at the grave. For the thoroughgoing worldling there is not even the satisfaction of living on in the memories of men: **There is no remembrance of the wise more than of the fool** (16). The mind of the Preacher rebelled against this levelling of all the values that men hold most dear: **Therefore I hated life** (17). He was neither the first nor the last to sense the rightness of man's yearning for immortality. Addison wrote of Plato's argument:

> *It must be so,—Plato, thou reasonest well!*
> *Else whence this pleasing hope, this fond desire,*
> *This longing after immortality?*
> *Or whence this secret dread, and inward horror*
> *Of falling into naught? Why shrinks the soul*
> *Back on herself, and startles at destruction?*
> *'Tis the divinity that stirs within us;*
> *'Tis Heaven itself that points out an hereafter,*
> *And intimates eternity to man.*[5]

6. The Vanity of Accumulated Wealth (2:18-23)

In these six verses the writer reflects on the worthwhileness of his years spent in getting and hoarding wealth. What bothers him most is that he must **leave it unto the man that shall be after me** (18). **And who knoweth whether he shall be a wise man or a fool?** (19) Probably for a man who had gathered so diligently for himself it was natural to distrust others—even his own heirs. For **himself** read "myself"; this is the obvious meaning (cf. ASV).

History has often verified the basic facts underlying the Preacher's pessimism. Few sons have proved as effective in preserving fortunes as their fathers were in gathering them—it is often only "three generations from shirt sleeves to shirt sleeves." But these facts need not drive the **heart to despair** (20). They should rather guide us in the getting, spending, and bequeathing of our money.

If a man is so mad after money that **his heart taketh not rest in the night** (23), this is **vanity**. A satisfying life is more important than a fortune. If we can think of no better use for accumulated wealth than to leave it to be dissipated by irresponsible heirs, there is cause for pessimism regarding our labors. But the

[5]*Cato*, Act V, Sc. 1.

king could have used his wealth while he lived—used it for the good of his fellowman and for the advancement of the work of God. It is not wise for a good man to spend all of his life accumulating money and leave entirely to others the decisions on how to use it. Let a man in his lifetime invest and give as wisely and as generously as he accumulates. When he does so he has something for **all his labour, and of the vexation of his heart** (22). And if he has something to leave to his heirs, let him pray over the decisions and then act with faith in the next generation, whose character he has had a part in shaping.

7. The Blessings of Labor (2:24-26)

The king himself reached the conclusion that an all-out drive for wealth was sheer folly (23). A man should have enough to **eat and drink** (24), but he should also "enjoy himself as he does his work" (24, Moffatt). This is God's good plan for man.

Verse 25 in KJV correctly translates the Hebrew, but the translation does not fit the context. Most modern translations follow the Septuagint, e.g., Smith-Goodspeed, "For who can eat and who can enjoy apart from him?" Such an interpretation connects 24 and 26 into a meaningful sequence. We know that every good gift is from God (Jas. 1:17). It is He who has given appetite, the ability to taste, and the capacity to enjoy life.

In 26 the Preacher sums up what the Bible teaches about a moral universe: **God giveth to a man that is good . . . wisdom, and knowledge, and joy: but to the sinner he giveth travail.** Adam Clarke comments: "1. God gives *wisdom*—the knowledge of himself, light to direct in the way of salvation. 2. *Knowledge*—understanding to discern the operation of his hand; *experimental acquaintance* with himself, in the dispensing of his *grace* and the *gifts of his Spirit*. 3. *Joy;* a hundred days of ease for one day of pain; one thousand enjoyments for one privation; and to them that believe peace of conscience, and joy *in the Holy Ghost*."[6]

---

[6]*The Holy Bible with a Commentary and Critical Notes* (New York: Abingdon-Cokesbury Press, n.d.), Vol. III, *ad loc.*

Section II Coming to Terms with Life

Ecclesiastes 3:1—5:20

In this section the philosopher-preacher probes the facts of life as he finds them and relates them to the tenets of his faith in God.

A. POEM OF AN ORDERLY WORLD, 3:1-8

In the poetry[1] of this passage the Preacher expounds his text, **To every thing there is a season, and a time to every purpose under the heaven** (1). There are interpreters who see in the passage only an absolute fatalism (1-8), with man's unwilling surrender to it (9-15). Others see a recognition of God's sovereignty, complemented by man's freedom and ability to adjust his life to the requirements of God. Atkins writes: "The passage has a restrained majesty of movement, as though the river of life were two currents flowing between the same banks. There is a current of permission, so to speak, and a stream of prohibition. It is a part of the wisdom of life to know where to catch the flowing tide and not to waste hope and effort on what cannot— at that time at least—be done."[2] "God has ordained order, it is ours to observe it" (Berk., fn., *loc. cit.*).

These verses deal with man's actions rather than with aspects of the world of nature. For the most part their meaning is clear, though one should not always expect to find literal meanings in words used poetically. **A time to pluck up** (2) probably means to harvest or it may mean to dig up, i.e., to transplant, as is done with tomato plants. **A time to kill** (3) may refer to judicial execution, or to warfare. In view of 5, it may, however, mean more generally to destroy.[3] **A time to cast away** (6) probably means a time to share with others. **A time to love** (8) suggests

[1]Cf. the poetic form in Berk., RSV, *et al.*

[2]*Op. cit.*, p. 43.

[3]Cf. O. S. Rankin, "Ecclesiastes" (Exegesis), *The Interpreter's Bible*, ed. George A. Buttrick, *et al.* (New York: Abingdon-Cokesbury Press, 1956), V, 44, for a different Rabbinical interpretation of 5.

expressing our love to God and to our fellowman. **A time to hate** would be to hate evil and oppose wrong.

It is clear that man's life is not simple. It is a complex of interacting and changing forces that require one response now and a different response under different circumstances. We do not always like the changing scene but wisdom requires us to adjust to it. Looking back, we can say it is well that God has planned it so.

B. FRUSTRATION AND FAITH, 3:9-15

The man who lives for this world alone is never far from frustration. The writer voices again the question of 2:22: "What benefit does the workman get for that for which he wears himself out?" (9, Berk.) In v. 10, Koheleth declares, **I have seen the travail, which God hath given to the sons of men,** but in it he finds elements of value. **He hath made every thing beautiful in his time** (11; cf. Gen. 1:4, 12, 18, 21, 25, 31).

In 12-13 we get the same earthy answer that was given in 2:24: a man can only **eat and drink, and enjoy the good of all his labour.** But Koheleth's faith now begins to come to his aid. No matter what the complexities of life, **it is the gift of God** (13). A man is here not only to enjoy himself but **to do good in his life** (12). We can never hope to understand all the plan of God: **No man can find out the work that God maketh from the beginning to the end** (11). Nevertheless God's plan is dependable: **Nothing can be put to it, nor any thing taken from it** (14). Furthermore, God has made this kind of world and these circumstances of life in order **that men should fear** ("be reverent," Berk.) **before him.**

Verse 15 has been variously translated and interpreted. The first two clauses clearly declare the unchanging order of our universe. But what is the meaning of the last clause? It has been translated, "God seeks out what has passed by" (Berk.), and, "God seeks what has been driven away" (RSV). The words can be understood in the context simply as God's continuing action in His orderly universe. May it not with equal validity be understood as expressing the purpose of His universe—a parallel to the last clause of 14? If this be granted, we see God's universe and His activity as designed to draw men to himself—even those who have somehow been "passed by" and "driven away."

Verse 11 has also been the occasion for much difference of interpretation. **He hath set the world in their heart** has been translated, "He has put eternity into man's mind" (RSV), and, "He also has planted eternity in their heart" (Berk.). Is not this very hunger in the spirit of man as unchanging and recurrent as the rising sun? Is not this one of God's provisions to draw us to himself and to lift us above the concerns of our material world? "One great reason for our lack of satisfaction lies in this innate sense of the eternity of the inner self, which no earthly things and doings can fully meet."[4]

C. THE PROBLEM OF MORAL EVIL, 3:16-22

1. *God Has the Answer* (3:16-17)

The writer now turns from the meaning of life's complexities to a consideration of its moral contradictions. He saw that in the courts where there should have been **judgment** (justice), there was **wickedness** (16); where there ought to have been **righteousness**, there was **iniquity**. How can we reconcile the presence of evil in a world ruled by a righteous God? The answer of faith is that **God** will someday **judge the righteous and the wicked** (17; cf. Matt. 13:24-30, 36-43). Earlier in the chapter Koheleth expounded beautifully the balanced nature of life; there are a time and a place appropriate for every experience of man. Here that philosophy is by faith extended to resolve the problem of evil. **I said in mine heart, God** will in His own right time resolve this contradiction—right judgment shall be meted out to both **the righteous and the wicked.**

2. *Uncertainty of the Future Life* (3:18-22)

The clause **that God might manifest them** (18) may be understood as "God is testing them to show them that they are but beasts" (RSV). Some apply this verse to "the wicked" in 16-17, but it seems to belong to the more universal considerations that follow. **That which befalleth the sons of men befalleth beasts ... as the one dieth, so dieth the other ... all turn to dust again** (19-20). These are undeniable statements of fact concerning the body—but what of the spirit? The form of the following question seems clearly to betray uncertainty and feeble faith, "Who

[4]*The Berkeley Version*, fn., *loc. cit.*

knows whether the spirit of man goes upward?"[5] (21, Smith-Goodspeed) It is the blight of this question mark that leads to the time-serving conclusion, "So I saw the best thing for a man was to be happy in his work; that is what he gets out of life" (22, Moffatt). What had happened to the faith in the future expressed in 17? What happens to the nerve of faith and high endeavor whenever doubt regarding man's future life takes possession of one's spirit?

D. DISAPPOINTMENTS OF LIFE, 4:1-16

1. *Social Oppression* (4:1-3)

This section may validly be considered a continuation of the preceding discussion of the injustices of life. **So I returned** (1) perhaps means that the writer's thought turned again to the meditations of 3:16. When he entered deeply into the injustices of political and economic life, it appeared hopeless. There were **the tears of** the **oppressed,** and **no comforter** for them. **Power** was on the side of the oppressor, and no one to stand with the oppressed. Crushed by these inequities, the heart cries, It is better to be **dead** than **alive** (2). Still better off is he who has never been born and therefore has **not seen the evil work that is done under the sun** (3).

But desperate as many oppressive conditions are, this solution must be considered as an emotional mood of the moment—not a philosophy for life. The author himself contradicts his position when in 9:4 he asserts that "a living dog is better than a dead lion." Atkins comments: "Some faint shadow of that attitude falls, perhaps more often than we think, across the most fortunate: the wish that they had been spared the burden of life. And yet, life is a trust; and though there is no promise that it will be easy, enough is given to make it not only a brave adventure, but in its nobler accomplishments a challenge worth the labor and the cost, both for this shadowed world and for an enduring and spiritual order."[6]

---

[5]"On a frosty morning on the farm it is a repeated item of interest to see the breaths of persons and of animals; the first going upward, the other downward, as the 'Preacher' describes it. Perhaps he saw in it a hint of the ultimate destiny of the godly soul—heavenward" (Berk., fn., *loc. cit.*).

[6]*Op. cit.*, pp. 53-54.

2. The Enigma of Effort (4:4-6)

The KJV states that for **every right work . . . a man is envied of his neighbour** (4). The RSV and others interpret it, "All toil and all skill in work come from a man's envy of his neighbor." In either case, the place of competition and envy as life motives are overrated by our pessimistic Koheleth. These assertions are only half-truths—if that much. He who believes these dangerous falsehoods should look further and live better. There are men who are driven by the goad of competitive achievement, but are we to forget the millions who toil to supply the necessities of life for themselves? To provide comforts for those whom they love? To render a worthy stewardship to God, to whom they have dedicated all of life's energies?

To be envied because of one's achievements is bad, and to strive to achieve only in order to beat one's neighbor is worse. Both are **vanity and vexation of spirit.** But even so, activity is necessary to a good life; only **the fool foldeth his hands together** (5) and does nothing. **Eateth his own flesh** may mean destroys himself or perhaps lives off his relatives. In 6, Koheleth reveals his oft-repeated position that wisdom takes a middle ground, avoiding both extremes: "Better is one handful with quiet than two handfuls with trouble and striving after wind" (Smith-Goodspeed). Our Lord would support this advice against extreme and anxious activity in the effort to secure material gain (Matt. 6:25-34).

Atkins points out "one lovely phrase, *a handful of quietness.* Generals rest a marching army at intervals, for, say, fifteen minutes: only a handful of quietness, but it keeps the army marching. The faculty to seize a handful of quietness out of the stresses and strains of the world has healing and sustaining power. We call it relaxation. It is more than that. It is letting life rebaptize itself in the blessed and enduring, and so find rest. It quiets the perturbed spirit and anticipates the ultimate healing when 'the wicked cease from troubling, and . . . the weary are at rest' (Job 3:17)."[7]

3. The Evil of Aloneness (4:7-12)

Nearly any burden can be borne if there is a friend with whom to share it. Koheleth sees clearly that one of life's great

[7] *Ibid.,* p. 54.

evils occurs when **there is one alone** (8). The expression **there is not a second** means no partner. For a man to work and yet have no one—**neither child nor brother**—to inspire and give purpose to his toil **is a sore travail** indeed. For a satisfying life a man must have a worthy answer to the question, **For whom do I labour?** And that answer must be found beyond himself in family, in service to the needs of men, or in fulfilling the will of God for his life.

Over against the evils of isolation vv. 9-12 set forth the values of working together. Moffatt says, "Two are better than one; they come well off in all they undertake" (9). Matthew Henry comments, "Whatever service they do [for each other] it is returned to them another way."[8] Human fellowship and cooperation bring mutual helpfulness (10), warmth (11) and defense (12). **A threefold cord is not quickly broken** is a proverb suggesting that, if two are better than one, three are still better. For a man to have friends, he must show himself friendly. He who seeks to "do good in his life" (3:12) will seldom suffer the pangs of isolation.

4. The Brevity of Fame (4:13-16)

The significance of this section is not clear but it seems to be a meditation on the **vexation of spirit** (16) coming to a disillusioned ruler. Several contemporary commentators find in the story a reference to Joseph, the **poor and . . . wise child** (13) who came **out of prison . . . to reign** (14). If this be correct, **the second child** (15) may refer to Joseph as second only to Pharaoh (Gen. 41:43). **Born in his kingdom** (14) means born in the kingdom that would eventually be his.

The meaning of the paragraph may be that some things are better than others—a **wise child** is better **than an old and foolish king.** Nevertheless there is nothing—not even the experiences of the wise young ruler—that is very good in the long run. "I have seen all the living on earth side with such a youth . . . Yet later on men lost all interest in him! This too is vain and futile" (15-16, Moffatt).

E. WORSHIPPING GOD RIGHTLY, 5:1-7

One of the facts of life with which a man must reckon is that God is the Creator, man is the created, and we must thus

---

[8]*Op. cit.,* p. 596.

answer to God. Worship in face-to-face encounter is our most significant obligation and opportunity.

1. Be Reverent (5:1-3)

Keep thy foot (1) is excellently rendered by a current admonition, "Watch your step!"[9] There is genuine wisdom in our preacher's advice, but it must be modified by Jesus' revelation of the character of God. If we understand 1 to say, Be reverent in the presence of God, we give full and glad assent. God is high and holy; therefore reverent awe is always becoming in His presence. To be **ready to hear** indicates the attitude of receptivity. It is always better to listen to the Holy Spirit than to be too intent on telling God what we want Him to hear. Hearing may imply obedience; thus the translation: "To draw near to obey is better than that fools should offer sacrifice" (Smith-Goodspeed; cf. I Sam. 15:22). **The sacrifice of fools** would be any irreverent or insincere approach to God. Moffatt translates the last clause of 1, "All a fool knows is how to do wrong"—even in his worship.

Be not rash with thy mouth (2) suggests that respectful silence or reverent and thoughtful prayer is more appropriate than much speaking in patterned liturgical forms. "This proverb [v. 3] is to the effect that as excessive business leads to a night of dreams, so verbosity leads a man into talking nonsense (Heb. 'a fool's voice')."[10] Cf. Jas. 1:19, 26; 3:2-10.

2. Keep Your Vows (5:4-7)

A vow is essentially a contract with God. It is a commitment made by us to Him, and it is dangerous to be careless in keeping such promises. "When you vow a vow to God, do not delay paying it . . . Pay what you vow" (4, RSV). **Better is it that thou shouldest not vow, than that thou shouldest vow and not pay** (5). But "best of all is to pledge and to pay" (Berk., fn., *loc cit.*). Vows made to God in moments of confrontation with Him have power, if kept, to lift us to new levels of devotion and service; but a broken pledge to God jeopardizes our standing with Him and undermines the very structure of character (Deut. 23:21-23).

Thy flesh (6) means oneself; thus, "Let not your mouth bring you into sin" (Smith-Goodspeed). **The angel** probably

---

[9]G. S. Hendry, *op. cit.*, p. 542.   [10]O. S. Rankin, *op. cit.*, p. 57.

refers to the priest (Mal. 2:7), and thus to the pastor or any of God's human representatives. **To destroy the work of thine hands** would be to frustrate one's plans or to diminish the success of his undertakings. **On the multitude of dreams and many words** (7) see comment on v. 3.

Fear thou God (7) is very often a wholesome biblical exhortation to reverence God and obey Him. If so understood here, it is an appropriate summation of the whole section. However, Rankin[11] and others say that this is not an admonition to godly fear, but is a warning not to irritate a tyrant God. This interpretation seems consistent with much of the mood of vv. 1-7. God is so high and man so low (2) that it is best to avoid Him as much as possible. Verses 4-6 suggest a legalistic God who listens to no reason and allows for no mistakes. At this point Koheleth is no further than the halfway house in his journey from skepticism to faith. This is not the NT portrait of God nor the Christian view of man's relationship with Him. Jesus tells us that God is a Father, kind and reasonable. We are to love and obey Him, but within that relationship we should expect to find joyful fellowship in His presence—we may share with Him our joys, our mistakes, and our problems, whatever they may be. God is a Companion to be sought, not an austere power to be feared and shunned.

F. Adjusting to Economic Problems, 5:8-20

1. Exacting Civil Authorities (5:8-9)

Verses 8-9 seem to present a special aspect of the economic inequities of life. The RSV gives a clear interpretation of 8: "If you see in a province the poor oppressed and justice and right violently taken away, do not be amazed at the matter." There are two reasons suggested why we should not be surprised: (a) **He that is higher . . . regardeth;** i.e., in tax collections each higher official watches the one below and demands a plush accounting. **There be higher than they** may mean only that there is always some official higher up to be satisfied. However a legitimate interpretation is (b) that the phrase refers to God himself. "Looking up the ladder of authority we may, according to our vision, see only 'the powers that be,' or we may see above them Him who will 'judge the fatherless and the oppressed' (Ps. X.18)."[12]

---

[11]*Ibid.*, p. 58.   [12]C. S. Hendry, *op. cit.*, p. 542.

Verse 9 seems to suggest that, after all, income from the worker must pay for the costs of government, and even farmers exploited by **the king** are better off than farmers with no government; "A country prospers with a king who has control" (Moffatt). Social control is required for a settled agricultural community, and even more control is required where millions of people live in crowded cities.

2. Wealth Is a Mixed Blessing (5:10-12)

Koheleth says, Even though you are overtaxed and cannot accumulate wealth, do not be distressed about it. Wealth is, at best, a mixed blessing. To fix one's heart on gaining it until it becomes his chief concern is frustrating: **He that loveth silver shall not be satisfied with silver** (10). "Unless there is wealth in the soul, men go down to their graves with empty hands." Jesus bids us remember that "a man's life consisteth not in the abundance of the things which he possesseth" (Luke 12:15).

When goods increase, they are increased that eat them (11). "The more meat, the more mouths . . . The more men have, the better house they must keep, the more servants they must employ, the more guests they must entertain . . . and the more [spongers] they will havîng hanging on them."[13] Of what use is more money when it only demands more toil? The overeating of the rich and worry about their wealth rob them of sleep. But **a labouring man** (12) sleeps well, due to his physical toil and to his lack of cares.

3. Wealth Is Often Lost (5:13-17)

Koheleth here as elsewhere (2:21; 3:16; 4:13) seems to be reflecting on a particular case that he had observed, **a sore evil which I have seen under the sun** (13). This particular evil was a man whose **riches** were **kept** to his own **hurt.** In this case the hurt came because he lost his wealth "in an unfortunate enterprise" (14; Smith-Goodspeed). Having lost his wealth, the father had no legacy to leave to **a son.** The pronoun **he** (15) refers to the father rather than the son. The latter part of the verse repeats the obvious fact that hoarding of wealth is vain because a man can take **nothing of his labour** with him. **Naked shall he return** means that at the man's death there was left no tangible wealth

---

[13]Matthew Henry, *op. cit.*, p. 600.

to show for his life's work. Moffatt asks, "What does he gain by all his futile toil, spending his days in gloominess, privations, deep anxieties, distress, and fits of anger?" (16-17)

4. Hold Wealth Loosely (5:18-20)

Here is the Preacher's own considered judgment on the right attitude toward money. "Note! What I myself have seen to be preferable and fair is to eat and drink and to find enjoyment in all his labor at which he toils" (18, Berk.). This is as near as the pleasant-life formula of Ecclesiastes ever comes to being wholly true. A man had better enjoy his work and the fruits of his toil than to fret and worry about them. Even the man who has **riches and wealth** (19) should not become obsessed with them. Let a man keep interested, keep busy, and keep constructively occupied no matter how much wealth he has. But here again creeps in the writer's "almost morbid fascination of death."[14] The best reason he can give for activity is that a man "shall not often think of the brevity of his life" (Berk.).

The attitude of holding wealth loosely is good, but how much better is such an attitude when accompanied by radiant Christian faith! Rylaarsdam writes: "For Koheleth . . . all human values are relativized because none of them is the means to man's true end. In this respect he anticipates the view of Paul; what he lacks is the latter's clarity and conviction about this end and about the love and power of God by which it is given."[15] When this is a living part of a man's faith, God truly **answereth him in the joy of his heart** (20).

---

[14] J. Coert Rylaarsdam, "The Proverbs, Ecclesiastes, The Song of Solomon," *The Layman's Bible Commentary*, Vol. X, ed. Balmer H. Kelly, *et al.* (Richmond, Va.: John Knox Press, 1964), p. 114.

[15] *Ibid.*, pp. 114-15.

Section III No Satisfaction in Earthly Goods

Ecclesiastes 6:1—8:17

A. Disappointments from Wealth and Family, 6:1-12

Though c. 6 is here placed under a new division, it is related to the theme of c. 5. Verses 1-2 continue the Preacher's reflections on the disappointments of wealth. Both 1-2 and 3-6 are illustrations of the premise laid down in 5:18-19, that enjoyment is the gift of God, and that peace of mind is the highest good that life can afford.

1. Wealth Without Happiness (6:1-2)

Verse 1 introduces another evil which the author has **seen under the sun.** He observes that this **evil is common among men.** The Hebrew is more accurately translated "lies heavily upon men" (Amp. OT). The frustration of wealth without the sense of a worthy life is possible, of course, only to those who have wealth. Nevertheless it is **common among men** and women of means.

In 2:18-23 the problem was the wealthy man whose fortune might be dissipated by foolish heirs; in 5:13-17 it was the man of wealth who lost it. Here the evil is the man who has wealth but has no satisfaction in it—this is the meaning of **God giveth him not power to eat thereof** (2). The terms **riches, wealth, and honour** may be understood as money, property, and esteem. He who has these seems to have everything **that he desireth.** But without happiness these are in vain. A life full of things but without true happiness **is an evil disease.** Like the knowledge of a spreading cancer, it shrinks or destroys the normal joys of a man's existence.

2. Family Without Appreciation (6:3-6)

A large family and a long life were regarded as great blessings among the Hebrews. But even these can be worse than useless. **If a man beget an hundred children** (3) and **be not filled with good**—i.e., find no joy in them—what is the value of it? If a man **live many years** but **have no burial**—i.e., "an honorable burial, that testifies of the real love of his posterity"—what is the good of such a life? **Verses 3-5** show the writer's frequent use of comparisons. **An untimely birth** that never comes to conscious existence **is better** than a life that finds no worthy fulfillment. Though the stillborn child is born in vain, **departeth in darkness** (4), and is never given a **name,** his lot is preferable to a purposeless life. Never to have **seen the sun** (5) or to have **known any thing** is better than to have seen and known the deep disappointments that sometimes come from wealth and family.

Koheleth could see no value in a deeply disappointing earthly life because he had no high faith in life beyond the grave. **A thousand years twice told** (6) would be an earthly life twice as long as Methuselah's (cf. Gen. 5:27). The reasoning here is that, if there is no happiness in earthly life, the longer it continues, the worse it is. And when you have totaled the values of earthly existence, aren't you finished adding? **Do not all go to one place** —the silent, final grave? "Both the lifeless foetus and the man whose life has been long but wretched, are destined to Sheol, and the lifeless foetus is to be congratulated because it reaches the goal by a shorter and less agonizing way."[1]

3. *Some Further Frustrations* (6:7-9)

a. Earthly satisfaction versus spiritual desire (6:7). **All the labour of man** (the earthbound man) **is for his mouth** ("self-preservation and enjoyment," Amp. OT), **and yet the appetite** (spiritual hunger) **is not filled.** "All human life is a grasping after enjoyment, but after an enjoyment vain in itself, and affording no true satisfaction."[2]

b. Even wisdom is not enough (6:8). Here in a single verse Koheleth repeats the argument of 2:12-17 (see also comments there). The Preacher does not answer his own question. However, the implied position is that if living for the "mouth" (7) is not enough, neither is living by the mind. The basis for this conclusion is in 6—both "go to one place." The phrase **to walk before the living** is taken by Galling to mean "to live without thought of the morrow." He therefore thinks that the meaning is,

[1]George A. Barton, *op. cit.,* p. 130.

[2]Tayler Lewis, *Commentary on the Holy Scriptures,* ed. John Peter Lange, trans. Philip Schaff (Grand Rapids: Zondervan Publishing House, n.d.), p. 100.

"What advantage has the wise man over the fool, the man of understanding over him who lives thoughtlessly?"[3]

c. An unsatisfactory answer (6:9). Here Koheleth again reaches his unsatisfying answer—Make the best of it while you live. Because the wise man with his higher aims—**the wandering of the desire**—has nothing better than the pleasure-seeking fool, why make the effort? One had better be content with what comes easily and naturally. The **vanity and vexation of spirit** may well apply to the entire section (7-9); on the other hand, it may apply specifically to the unhappy conclusion of v. 9.

4. *Finite Man Against Fate* (6:10-12)

Here Koheleth sums up his pessimistic view of the whole human situation. **That which hath been . . . named** (10) means the whole of existence—and **it is known,** i.e., foreknown and predetermined. **Man is a finite creature and cannot contend with him** (God) **that is mightier than he.** Verse 11 asserts that man is so powerless against his Creator as to make the discussion of the matter futile. Verse 12 is a concluding cry in the dark: "Who can tell what is good for man in life, during the few days of his empty life that passes like a shadow? For who can tell a man what is to happen in this world when he is gone?" (Moffatt)

"How impressive throughout Ecclesiastes is the evidence that, while Solomon the prodigal is doing his utmost to prove that life is futile and not worth living, the Holy Spirit is using him to show that these conclusions are the tragic effect of living 'under the sun'—ignoring the Lord, away from God the Father, oblivious of the Holy Spirit—and yet face to face with the mysteries of life and nature!"[4] Atkins comments succinctly, "Unless there is wealth in the soul, men go down to their graves with empty hands."[5]

B. Practical Wisdom in a Sinful World, 7:1-29

This chapter contains a group of proverbs and other brief observations. They are tied together by the common theme of what makes good sense in our kind of world. The series is evoked by the question of 6:12, "What is good for man in this life?"

[3] Quoted by O. S. Rankin, *op. cit.,* p. 62.
[4] Amp. OT (12), fn.   [5] *Op. cit.,* p. 59.

1. A Basis for Wise Choices (7:1-4)

Verse 1 begins with a play on the Hebrew words: *Shem* **(name)** is better than *shemen* **(ointment)**. It is wise counsel that says, If you wish to have an effective life, live so that you build a good reputation. Opportunity in life often depends on the image of ourselves that exists in the minds of our associates. In the East men often use perfume to make themselves socially more acceptable. But for really significant acceptability **a good name** is better than **ointment.**

The remainder of this section points out that a serious approach to life is better than a gay mood. Life is a business rather than a party. To adopt this demeanor makes for the best decisions and the best reputation. **The day of death,** etc. (1) probably means: It is better to visit the bereaved than to attend a birthday party. This interpretation is supported by v. 2, **It is better to go to the house of mourning, than to go to the house of feasting.** Death is **the end of all men**—one experience that is common to all—and this fact puts a right perspective on many decisions. **The living** will therefore pay proper attention to it.

Sorrow is better than laughter (3) because times of sorrow cause us to think seriously. "In such cases most men try themselves at the tribunal of their own consciences, and resolve on amendment of life."[6] The statement, **By the sadness of the countenance the heart is made better,** suggests that "a good cry relieves emotional upheaval" (Berk., fn.). Because of these facts he who is wise is serious-minded:

The mind of the wise is in the house of mourning,
But the mind of fools is in the house of mirth (4, Smith-Goodspeed).

2. Some Pitfalls for Right Judgment (7:5-10)

Sound judgment consists in knowing what data to reject as much as in knowing what to accept. The Preacher here points out some things that a wise person will avoid.

This passage lends itself to a practical exposition under the topic "Biblical Advice to Wise People of God," using *a* to *f* below as divisions.

a. Don't take the wrong advice (7:5-6). Listen to dependable advisers, even when their counsel hurts. **The rebuke of the**

---

[6]Adam Clarke, *op. cit.,* p. 822.

wise (5) may hurt momentarily; but if they are wise, they rebuked us because we were wrong and needed to be set right. The song of fools may mean either flattery to avoid the truth that hurts or simply irresponsible opinions. Both are like the crackling of thorns under a pot (6)—they may be bright and merry but they cook no food.[7]

b. Don't let your judgment be warped by irrelevant circumstances (7:7). A man can make the wrong decisions and say the wrong things because of emotional pressures. We read of the children of Israel that "Moses was troubled because of them; for they made his spirit bitter, and he said unwise things" (Ps. 106: 32-33, BB). We are here cautioned that oppression "and extortion make a wise man foolish, and a bribe [gift] destroys the understanding and judgment" (Amp. OT).

c. Don't decide on the basis of incidentals (7:8a). Better is the end of a thing than the beginning thereof says to us, Make your decisions in view of basic purposes and goals; never mind about early and incidental reactions.

d. Don't be impatient (7:8b). Proud in spirit here probably means to be rash because one is in a hurry. Persistent patience has resolved many a problem that would not yield to immediate pressure. "It is better quietly to await the course of an affair until its issue, and not to judge and act until then, than to proceed rashly and with passionate haste, and bring upon one's self its bad consequences."[8]

e. Don't get upset (7:9). Don't get angry. Anger is always the enemy of clear thinking and sound judgment. Only fools let this enemy of the soul destroy their interpersonal relations and their reputations as responsible persons. Matthew Henry comments, "Be not soon angry . . . Be not long angry . . . He therefore that would approve himself so wise as not to give place to the devil, must not let the sun go down on his wrath, Eph. IV, 26, 27."[9]

f. Don't complain about the times (7:10). To peevishly complain that the former days were better than these is beneath a wise man's conduct. In the first place, even if true, it never contributes much to resolving today's problems. Moreover, we do not enquire wisely concerning this, because more often than

---

[7]The usual fuel was slow-burning, dry cow dung. It produced effective heat in contrast to the dry thornbushes that burned up in minutes.

[8]Tayler Lewis, op. cit., p. 106.   [9]Op. cit., p. 605.

not we have insufficient facts to form a correct judgment. So far as decision and action are concerned, "Today is ours, and today alone."

3. *Seek Wisdom* (7:11-12)

Perhaps some objector is imagined to challenge the Preacher by asking, What good is wisdom without money? The sages generally said that wisdom was better than wealth (Prov. 16:16). Koheleth declares:

> *Wisdom is as good as an inheritance,*
> *a real profit for mankind* (11, Moffatt).

To them that see the sun means to man in his earthly existence. Both **wisdom** (12) and **money** are valuable,

> *but knowledge does more good than money,*
> *it safeguards a man's life* (Moffatt).

Clarke comments, *"Money* is the means of supporting our animal life: but *wisdom*—the religion of the true God—gives *life to them that have it. Money* cannot procure the favor of God, nor give *life* to the soul."[10]

4. *Count on God* (7:13-14)

It seems probable that these two verses are linked with 11-12 (cf. paragraphing in *The Berkeley Version*). In the distribution of wealth, we are to **consider the work of God.** In His providence He puts money into the hands of few, but wisdom is within the reach of all. **Who can make that straight, which he hath made crooked?** is a figure declaring the sovereignty of God (cf. 1:15). Whatever He gives, it is wisdom for man **in the day of prosperity** to **be joyful** (14) and **in the day of adversity,** to **consider.** The expression **to the end that man should find nothing after him** means "to keep man from knowing what is to happen" (Moffatt).

"God interlaces his providences, and veils his providences, in order that, unable to see the future, we may learn to put our trust in Him rather than in any earthly good. . . . It therefore behoves a man . . . to take both crooked and straight, both evil and good from the hand of God, and to trust in Him whatever may befall."[11]

---

[10]*Op. cit.,* p. 823.

[11]Samuel Cox, "Ecclesiastes," *The Expositor's Bible* (New York: A. C. Armstrong and Son, 1903), p. 199.

5. Avoid Self-righteousness and Wickedness (7:15-18)

The argument in this passage supports a position somewhere between moral legalism on the one hand and outright moral license on the other. It is a plea for wisdom in ethical judgment. Koheleth lays down as a premise in 15 that just rewards for good and evil are not apparent in this life: **A just man . . . perisheth and a wicked man . . . prolongeth his life.** Verses 16-17 refer to the "rigidly pious," the overwise, and the extremely wicked. Since man does not have the wisdom of God he is counseled to temperate judgment and actions. **Be not righteous over much (16)** refers to the kind of pharisaical self-righteousness that our Lord so often condemned (cf. Matt. 5:20; Luke 5:32).[12] The **over wise** are those who pretend an absolute knowledge that has no tolerance for any difference of opinion. Extremes of this kind **destroy** one's influence for good and are displeasing to God.

Regarding **Be not over much wicked (17)** Clarke comments: "Do not multiply wickedness; do not add direct opposition to godliness to the rest of your crimes. Why should you provoke God to destroy you before your time?"[13]

After all his counsels of caution, Koheleth knows that a man must take a stand for right and against wrong. **It is good that thou shouldest take hold of this (18,** righteousness). Rankin explains 18c thus: "The God-fearer will fulfill his duties in every case or 'will preserve a worthy attitude' (Odeburg) to all men."[14]

6. Be Wise, but Remember You Are Human (7:19-20)

These verses seem to summarize and support the preceding argument, i.e., wisdom is good but no man is perfect. **Wisdom strengtheneth the wise (19)** "more than [they could be strengthened by] ten rulers or valiant generals who are in the city" (Amp. OT). The translation of 20 in KJV suggests support for the doctrine of the necessity of sinning. Such support is not present in the Hebrew. On a parallel passage from the lips of Solomon in I Kings 8:46, Clarke writes: "The original . . . *ki yechetu loch* . . . should be translated IF they shall sin against thee . . . *ki ein Adam asher lo yecheta,* for there is no man that

---

[12]"It cannot be supposed, except by those who are totally unacquainted with the nature of true religion, that a man may have *too much holiness, too much of the life of God in his soul!*" (Adam Clarke, *op. cit.,* p. 824).

[13]*Ibid.*   [14]*Op. cit.,* p. 67.

MAY not sin; i.e., there is . . . none that is not liable to transgress."[15] Moreover, the term **sinneth** may not refer here to sin in the sense of "a known violation of the will of God." Rankin interprets the verse, "There is no such thing as an absolutely good man, a man without moral fault."[16]

7. Ignore Unfair Criticism (7:21-22)

The wise counsel here is, Don't get upset over everything you hear; you can be sure that some people will criticize what you say and do; just remember that **thou thyself likewise hast criticized others.** "Let us examine how much truth there is in gossip about us, examine ourselves rather than tracing the gossipers" (Berk., fn.). There is great encouragement in remembering what the Bible asserts about unfair criticism—"And the Lord heard it" (Num. 12:2). If He has heard it, and if we belong to Him, we do not need to worry much about it.

8. Remember You Are Not Omniscient (7:23-24)

All this (23) refers back to the issues which have just been considered. Koheleth had earnestly tried to "see life steadily and to see it whole," but he was compelled to admit his limitations. Moffatt has an insightful translation: "I thought to become wise, but wisdom remained out of reach. Reality is beyond my grasp; deep it lies, very deep, and no one can lay hands upon the heart of things." The theme occurs again at 8:16-17 (cf. Job 11:7-8). "Though the wisdom that is essential to our salvation may be soon learned, through the teaching of the Spirit of wisdom, yet in wisdom itself there are extents and depths which none can reach or fathom."[17]

9. Remember the Evil in Men (7:25-29)

The author reminds us again of his careful investigation, **I applied mine heart to know** (25). Though it is impossible to plumb the depths of ultimate reality (23-24), one may know assuredly that **wickedness** is **folly**, and **foolishness** is **madness.** The worst of life's wickedness, Koheleth finds in the woman who uses her charms to enslave a man. She is "more bitter even than death—the woman who entangles men, whose heart is a net,

---

[15]*Op. cit.,* II, 416.   [16]*Op. cit.,* p. 66.
[17]Adam Clarke, *op. cit.,* p. 824.

whose clasp is a chain" (26, Moffatt). The man who **pleaseth God** may, by His help, escape; **but the sinner shall be taken by her.**

The writer does not assert that all woman are bad (cf. 9:9) but the percentage is high! **Counting one by one** (27), or as we would say, "putting two and two together," he reached his conclusion. He found **one good man among a thousand . . . but a good woman among all those have I not found** (28). If Solomon himself is not the author of this paragraph, both the situation and the mood fit him. How could his estimate of women be different? The one **thousand** women in his life (I Kings 11:1-4) were but his playthings and pawns. How could they react other than to use the only power of influence that they had over him? "Robbed of their natural dignity and use as helpmeets, condemned to be mere toys, trained only to minister to sense, what wonder if they have fallen below their due place and honour?"[18]

In 29 the writer softens his castigation somewhat by recognizing that there is a serious bent to evil in both men and women —**They have sought out many** "devices for evil" (Amp. OT). This is one of the few statements in the Bible regarding man's original innocence and his subsequent fall (cf. Berk., fn.).

C. COMING TO TERMS WITH AN IMPERFECT WORLD, 8:1-17

1. *Adjusting to the Inevitable* (8:1-9)

This section discusses wise conduct for one who lives under an autocratic government.

a. *An ode to wisdom* (8:1). Verse 1 is a little poem in praise of wisdom. It may have been a common saying in the time of the writer. Moffatt's translation is appealing.

> *Who is like a wise man?*
> *Who can explain things?*
> *Man's wisdom lights his face up,*
> *it transfigures even a rough countenance.*

The relevance of this verse as an introduction to the section becomes clearer when "we recall that the king was considered the wise man par excellence, inasmuch as his office and state gave him access to the secrets of God."[19]

---

[18]Samuel Cox, *op. cit.*, p. 204.   [19]J. Coert Rylaarsdam, *op. cit.*, p. 121.

b. It is wise to obey the king (8:2-6). **I counsel thee to keep the king's commandment** (2) anticipates Paul's guidance to Christians (Rom. 13:1-5). The counsel is the same although the reasons given are not identical. **In regard of the oath of God** (2) probably means one's oath of allegiance to the king (Barton), although it may have Paul's meaning of responsibility to obey civil authority because of one's loyalty to the will of God.

Verses 3-4 are a simple appeal on the basis of naked authority. **Be not hasty to go out of his sight** (3) is interpreted as, "Rebel not rashly against him" (Moffatt). **Stand not in an evil thing** perhaps means, "Do not mess with contrary matters, for he does as he pleases" (Berk.). Verse 4 says clearly, "Since the king's word prevails, who can say to him, 'What are you doing?' " (Berk.) The writer supports his advice by reminding us, **Whoso keepeth the king's commandment shall feel no evil thing** (5). In the face of impossible circumstances or unbending authority, one does well to compromise when moral issues are not involved. It is a wise prayer that asks, "Lord, help me to change what can be changed; teach me to accept what cannot be changed; and give me wisdom to know the difference."

Verses 5b-6 offer a still further reason for obedience even when the demands are unjust. "The wise heart knows there is a time of judgment coming, even though to-day men may be crushed under the king in misery; for all there is an hour of judgment" (Moffatt).

c. Life sometimes offers no choice (8:7-9). Verse 7 may be read in the context of what precedes. If so, it means that one never knows what a despotic king will do (Barton). It may, however, be seen in the wider philosophical meaning of 3:22 and 6:12, that we simply do not know what the future holds. This interpretation fits better with 9, where Koheleth lists other situations where man is at the mercy of forces beyond his control. **Man has no power . . . to retain the spirit**[20] (8; "the breath of life," Amp. OT); **there is no discharge** from the army that is based simply on the soldier's wish; **neither shall wickedness** be a "shield for wrongdoers" (Moffatt). These are the things that Koheleth has **seen** and to which he **applied** his **heart** (9) as he contemplated man's political situation where "one man has power over another to injure him" (9, Smith-Goodspeed).

---

[20]Some translate it "to restrain the wind" (Smith-Goodspeed and Moffatt). ASV and RSV follow KJV in making it a parallel construction with **power in the day of death.**

2. *The Struggle for Faith* (8:10-17)

In 1-9 the writer has dealt with adjusting to evil and oppression in rulers; but how does one reconcile the existence of this evil with his faith in a good and omnipotent God?

a. An assertion of faith (8:10-13). The Hebrew text of 10 is uncertain. In KJV **the wicked** are **forgotten in the city;** in RSV, following the Septuagint, "the wicked . . . were praised." This idea fits the context, while KJV violates it. The ASV has both preserved the words of the Hebrew and the meaning of the context thus: "So I saw the wicked buried, and they came to the grave; and they that had done right went away from the holy place, and were forgotten in the city; this also is vanity." For the **wicked** to be **buried** in honor and the righteous to be **forgotten in the city** violates the moral order; but Koheleth's faith rises above the problem, at least momentarily.

Verse 11 states a widely recognized fact. Punishment for sin seems so long delayed and therefore so unlikely to happen that the ungodly go on sinning, unrestrained by any fear. But in spite of the contradiction of appearances and the brazen attitude of the wicked, the writer declares his own faith. **Though a sinner do evil an hundred times, and his days be prolonged, yet surely I know that it shall be well with them that fear God . . . but it shall not be well with the wicked** (12-13; cf. Ps. 1:1-6). This is also the faith expressed by Lowell:

> *Truth forever on the scaffold, Wrong forever*
> *on the throne,—*
> *Yet that scaffold sways the future, and, be-*
> *hind the dim unknown,*
> *Standeth God within the shadow, keeping*
> *watch above his own.*

Which are as a shadow means that the wicked shall not prolong his life like a shadow that grows rapidly longer toward sunset.

b. When faith falters (8:14-15). Koheleth's fine faith expressed in 12-13 seems to fail him as a guide for life. His mind turns again to the inequities of 10 and he again becomes frustrated because **just men** are rewarded **according to the work of the wicked,** and the wicked receive what **the righteous** deserve (14). When Koheleth forgot God (12-13) and fixed his gaze on the earth (14), life sagged. The best he could advise was, **A man hath no better thing . . . than to eat, and to drink, and to be**

merry (15). This is the limit of the vision of an earthbound man, and it runs like a refrain through Ecclesiastes (3:22; 5:18). When there is no firm faith in a God of righteousness, there is little endeavor that goes beyond seeking a comfortable life **under the sun.**

c. *We walk by faith—if we walk* (8:16-17). The conclusion reached here is true, and it is helpful if one does not hold it as life's final truth. Koheleth declares that, although a man studies until he **neither day nor night seeth sleep with his eyes (16)**, yet he cannot understand the ultimate good of life—**the work that is done under the sun (17)**. This repeats the theme developed at length in 1:12—2:26, and stated again in 7:23-24. Koheleth wisely rejects the ultimate conclusion of the humanist: "A wise man may think he is coming on the secret, but even he will never find it" (17, Moffatt). As yet the writer "carries no lamp of Revelation in his hand. . . . For the present he will trust to Reason and Experience, and mark the conclusions to which these conduct when unaided by any direct light from Heaven."[21]

But the light of unaided reason does not shine far enough. If a man is to walk without stumbling, he must accept the added light of faith in the revelation of God's righteousness (cf. Isa. 55: 6-11). Koheleth had hold of the secret in 12-13 but he let it slip. After reason has shown us to its furthest limits, faith must go further to light the way. The spirit of man must live by this faith: "I know that my redeemer liveth, and that . . . at the latter day . . . shall I see God" (Job 19:25-26).

Verses 10-17 lend themselves to a sermonic treatment, "The Struggle for Faith." Sub-points *a*, *b*, and *c* develop the theme.

[21]Samuel Cox, *op. cit.*, p. 230.

Section **IV** *Life's Injustices in God's Hands*

Ecclesiastes 9:1—10:20

A. THOUGHTS ON DEATH, 9:1-18

1. Death Comes to All (9:1-3)

The Preacher recognizes that the lives of **the righteous, and the wise . . . are in the hand of God** (1), but he cannot say whether this is for good or ill. "Will he love them? Will he hate them? None can tell; anything may happen to them" (1, Moffatt).

Koheleth's almost insane obsession with death is again the paralysis that destroys his faith. No matter what a man is or does, he dies—**there is one event to the righteous, and to the wicked** (2). The terms **clean** and **unclean** probably refer to the keeping of ceremonial observances, as does also the contrast between the man who sacrifices and him who does not. "The profane man fares like the man whose oath is sacred" (Moffatt).

This is an evil among all things (3) probably means, "There is no evil like this in the world" (Moffatt). Such a frustration engenders **evil** in men's hearts and fills them with **madness** both **while they live, and after . . . they go to the dead.** Here is the spiritual turmoil of all whose faith gives them no vision beyond the grave, but whose very nature cries out for such faith.

2. Death Seems So Final! (9:4-6)

In a hasty, despondent moment Koheleth had said that death is better than life (4:1-3). But few men with health and sound mind will stand by that assertion. Koheleth doesn't. He now declares that **a living dog is better than a dead lion** (4),[1] because while a man lives, **there is hope,** and he also enjoys all the interests of conscious life. **But the dead know not any thing** (5). "Cut off from life, they know nothing of what passes **under the sun** (6). Their day of probation is ended, and therefore they can have no farther **reward** (5) in living a holy life; nor can they be

---

[1] "This is a telling sentence for those of us who feel our inadequacies; we are alive; we may accomplish what the greatest thinkers and doers, now dead, cannot now accomplish on earth" (Berk., fn.).

581

liable to any farther punishment for crimes in a state of probation, that being ended."[2]

3. Enjoy Life While You Can (9:7-10)

Here the author repeats (cf. 2:24; 3:12, 22; 5:18; 8:15) his philosophy of life—the highest philosophy normally attainable by a man who has no faith in a righteous God and in a conscious life beyond the grave. **Bread** and **wine** were the accepted means of sustenance and enjoyment. **God now accepteth thy works** (7) has been variously interpreted as: (a) Enjoy life because this is what God has planned for man to do; (b) Since you serve God and your works are acceptable to Him, you may count on a satisfying life; (c) Since you can't know God's will and ways, make the most of what you can understand and enjoy. The third view seems most consistent with the context. **Garments** of **white** (8) were the normal clothing for the courts and for festive occasions. Oil on the **head** was a symbol of joy (cf. Ps. 23:5; 45:7).

While Koheleth's philosophy of life is earthbound, it is neither gluttonous nor sensual; it is simply the good neighbor existence of the average suburban home. There is plenty to eat, good clothing and cosmetics, a congenial marriage with **the wife whom thou lovest** (9), and an active involvement in one's work and hobbies—**Whatsoever thy hand findeth to do, do it with thy might** (10). By many it is considered "the good life," but it has nagging limitations that compel one to label it **vanity . . . vanity.** Even the happiest marriage is only for **the days . . . given thee under the sun,** and neither profession nor hobbies extend beyond **the grave, whither thou goest.**

There is serious truth in 10 even for the Christian who believes in immortality. Earthly life is a probation which offers some opportunities that end at the grave. The truth of Ecclesiastes is reflected in the words of Annie Coghill:

> Work, for the night is coming . . .
> When man's work is o'er.

Jesus himself reminds us that limitation of time gives urgency to our tasks: "I must work the works of him that sent me, while it is day: the night cometh, when no man can work" (John 9:4).

---

[2]Adam Clarke, *op. cit.*, p. 829

4. *Even the Wise Cannot Win* (9:11-12)

In 1-2 it was said that both the righteous and the wise were subject to the same fate as the wicked. Koheleth has dealt with the righteous (2-10) and now turns to consider the wise. Thoughtful men have always believed that intelligence and knowledge are advantages in life, but Koheleth is in frustrated intellectual rebellion. He declares that **the race is not to the swift, nor the battle to the strong . . . time and chance happen to them all** (11). The term **chance** means evil chance or misfortune. Among these misfortunes **time** (time cut short by death) is the worst. Even the wisest **knoweth not his time** (12), but like fish **taken in a net or birds . . . caught in the snare**, death **falleth suddenly upon** him.

The truth is that Koheleth was right—but only half right. The swift win more races than the slow—but they don't win every race. There are forces in life that are subject to intelligence and human power, but there are elements affecting human destiny that God has reserved to His own control. It is ours to learn which are which, to manage those placed within our control, and to accept with reverent awe and loving obedience the forces that a sovereign God has reserved to himself.

5. *Wisdom Is Better than Force* (9:13-18)

Koheleth himself knew the relative value of wisdom, though he stated his case for chance and death (11-12) so vigorously that one could miss his qualifications which follow. Again our political philosopher recalled a historical incident in which the significance **seemed great** (13) to him (cf. 4:13-16). **A little city** (14) with **few** resources for defense was saved from the attack of **a great king** because they **found in it a poor wise man** (15). Here wisdom proved its own worth. Though the man was **poor** and apparently unrecognized as a leader, yet his wise suggestions commended themselves to his people **and he by his wisdom delivered the city.**

But poor, pessimistic Koheleth can't let a strong, optimistic fact stand untarnished; he must point out "the fly in the ointment"—**No man remembered that same poor man.** Nevertheless the worth of wisdom wins out: **Wisdom is better than strength** (16), even if **the poor man's wisdom is despised, and his words are not heard.**

Koheleth reflects that the quiet **words of wise men** are better than the loud talk **of him that ruleth among fools** (17), and also that **wisdom is better than weapons of war** (18). Verses 17-18 comprise a four-line stanza that Koheleth either composed or quoted because it expressed his thoughts so well. Moffatt renders it:

> *Wise words heard in quiet far excel*
> *shouts from a ringleader of revellers.*
> *Wisdom is better than weapons of war;*
> *often a single error spoils good strategy.*

B. WISDOM AND FOLLY, 10:1-20

1. *A Little Folly Can Ruin a Life* (10:1-4)

Although here treated under a separate heading, this section is closely related to the close of c. 9. Verse 1 expands the last clause of 9:18. The literal translation "flies of death" has striking connotations. One sin can undo much good, and one poor judgment can weaken or destroy a lifelong **reputation for wisdom and honour** (1).

a. The nature of folly (10:1-3). Verse 2 returns to the idea of exalting wisdom begun in 1:16-18. The **wise man's heart** (2) is his judgment. The **right hand** stands for light and righteousness while the **left** represents darkness and wrong. Even on a casual stroll a fool's **wisdom faileth him, and he saith to every one that he is a fool** (3).

How does one identify the lack of wisdom in himself and in others? How does he correct it? Wisdom means good judgment; sound judgment involves knowing the right facts and putting them together in right relationships. No man can be wise who is either ignorant or hasty in judgment. **He saith to every one that he is a fool** may mean that a fool's actions and words advertise his foolishness. If so, the advertising is done (a) by talking too much and thinking too little, (b) by quick judgments without considering all the facts, (c) by having quick and firm opinions on every subject, (d) by acting as though he is always right and others are always wrong. Moffatt translates 3:

> *Even on a walk the fool shows lack of sense,*
> *for he calls everyone a fool.*

b. *The folly of a quick resignation* (10:4). This verse discusses a special instance where a little folly can quickly ruin a life.

If a ruler's temper rises against you,
  do not resign your position,
for composure may remedy serious mistakes (Berk.)

The advice is, If you have a place of employment and service, and feel you should try to keep it, don't resign. Weather the storm, wait to decide, or leave the initiative and decision to others. This verse has been called "wisdom for the under man" (cf. Prov. 10:12; 15:1; 25:15) but it has in it the virtue recommended by Him who said, "Blessed are the meek: for they shall inherit the earth" (Matt. 5:5).

2. *Folly and Wisdom in High Places* (10:5-20)

a. *Appointment of incompetent leaders* (10:5-7). There is probably a psychological rather than a logical progression from 4 to 5. In 4, Koheleth had been warning against folly in the presence of an angry ruler. This suggested to him an instance of folly **which proceedeth from the ruler** (5). It is the evil of appointing incompetent men to responsible positions and keeping wise leaders from positions of influence (cf. Prov. 19:10; 30:21-22). Such an evil may exist in elective systems as well as under appointive procedures. The problem faces all who have responsibility for selecting wise leaders—for wisdom in leaders is the place where wisdom counts most. The Hebrew suggests that this **evil** may sometimes be unintentional.[3] It is nevertheless an evil. The writer here equates **the rich** (6) and **princes** (7) with the wise. In his day riding **upon horses** was a mark of prestige and honor; **walking** was the lot of the good, but perhaps incompetent, man.

b. *The wisdom of action* (10:8-11). The central truth of these sayings is that there are dangers in any significant actions that one takes—digging a **pit** or tearing out a **hedge** (8), removing **stones** or cutting **wood** (9). Nevertheless, action must be taken (cf. 11:4-6), even though there are dangers. These can be largely avoided through proper foresight—**Wisdom is profitable**

[3]Cf. Barton, *op. cit.*, p. 170; also Moffatt and Smith-Goodspeed.

to direct (10). However, such wisdom must be exercised before decisions are made or actions taken—

> *If the snake bites before the charming,*
> *then the charmer's skill does not benefit* (11, Berk.).

The proverb is comparable to ours about locking the barn door after the horse has been stolen.

Some interpreters see here appropriate retribution for the evil actions of digging a pit to snare another, breaking through a hedge to steal, and removing stones to alter property lines. Although this interpretation is possible, it does not seem to fit the context.

Again, the connection of the passage with the preceding section is psychological. The accidental error of wrong appointments (5-7) suggests expansion on the idea of dangers especially relevant to persons with administrative responsibilities. The Hebrew reflected in 11b of KJV seems to relate the verse to 12-15—the **babbler** (11) and **the lips of a fool** (12). Most modern versions follow the ASV in attaching it to 8-11, "Then is there no advantage to the charmer" (cf. Berk. above).

c. *The nature of folly—continued* (10:12-15). These verses seem to continue a consideration of the destructive nature of folly (cf. 1-3). Verse 12 is a typical antithetical proverb in which the second part stands in contrast to the first:

> *The words of a wise man's mouth are gracious,*
> *But the lips of the fool destroy him* (Smith-Goodspeed).

This section may be a general observation on folly, but placed here between 1-11 and 16-20 it would seem to have special relevance to rulers.

Wisdom and foolishness are seen to be revealed in one's speech. A current quip says, "A fool may be mistaken for a wise man if he keeps his mouth shut; but open it and he removes all doubt." Verse 13 seems to indicate a progressive deterioration:

> *The beginning of the words of his mouth is folly,*
> *and the end of his speech is perverse stupidity* (Berk.)

In 14 we see a familiar theme in Ecclesiastes. A fool is not only **full of words** but he prattles about the meaning of life—**what shall be; and what shall be after him**—which even a wise man cannot know. Verse 15 has proved difficult for the translators.

The first part seems to indicate the confusion to himself of the fool's actions, "The toil of a fool wearies him" (RSV). Of the last part Clarke writes: "I suppose this to be a proverb: 'He knows nothing; he does not know his way to the next village'."[4] It is a disparaging remark like our own, "He doesn't have sense enough to come in out of the rain."

d. Unworthy leaders (10:16-19). From the general evil of the man who is a fool, Koheleth turns to the deeper tragedy of a people whose rulers are unworthy. **Woe to thee, O land!** (16) is a form of malediction sometimes found in the wisdom literature (cf. 4:10), and often in the prophets (e.g., Isa. 5:8-23; Jer. 50:27; Hos. 7:13; Amos 6:1).[5] **When thy king is a child** has been interpreted literally, but the meaning is probably broader, including irresponsible rulers who act like children. To feast **in the morning** was to turn the day into confusion (cf. Isa. 5:11; Acts 2:15), and to put personal pleasure ahead of official duty. **The morning** was the usual time for dispensing justice in the courts of the East (Jer. 21:12).

Verse 17 contrasts with 16 and exhibits a use of the beatitude (blessing) common in the wisdom literature (cf. Ps. 1:1; Prov. 3:13; 8:34). **The son of nobles** seems to equate the wellborn with the able. However, it may have a meaning that is more than literal, i.e., "a son of nobles—not merely in blood, but in virtue, the true nobility."[6] The last half of the verse has been rendered: "And your officials feast at the proper time, for strength, and not for drunkenness!" (Amp. OT)

Verses 17-19 appear to be three proverbs either coined or borrowed by Koheleth to support his discussion of rulers. In 18 indolent rulers are condemned for letting the state fall into ruin. There may be a play on words in 18b: *Falling hands make a falling house,* the falling of hands being a synonym for idleness (Barton; cf. Prov. 10:4).

In 19 there are reflected the attitudes that ruin rulers. Perhaps the evils increase in the order listed:

> *Men feast for merry-making,*
> *and they drink for revelry—*
> *and money does it all!* (Moffatt)

---

[4]*Op. cit.,* p. 833.   [5]Rylaarsdam, *op. cit.,* p. 128.

[6]A. R. Fausset, *A Commentary Critical and Explanatory on the Old and New Testaments,* by Robert Jamieson, A. R. Fausset, and David Brown (Grand Rapids: Zondervan Publishing House, one vol., n.d.), p. 412.

e. *Even bad government has value* (10:20). This may be simply a caution of prudence—**Curse not the king nor the rich** (those with authority). The advice may be simply to keep yourself out of trouble. Careless talk is dangerous and has a way of getting back to the people talked about. Among the ancients birds were considered to have supernatural powers. This may be the origin of the proverb, **A bird of the air shall carry the voice.** Cf. our expression of mysterious communication, "A little bird told me."

But beyond the above interpretation there may be more than prudence here. Koheleth elsewhere urges support for established government (8:1-5). This is in accord with NT teaching (Rom. 13:1-7).

Section V How Best to Invest Life

Ecclesiastes 11:1-8

Koheleth is coming toward the close of his exploration of the meaning and purpose of life. He has faced frequent frustration and often settled for pessimism or mediocrity, but his final conclusions are optimistic and worthy.

A. BE GENEROUS, 11:1-3

The author has earlier dealt with the self-centered life (5:10-12; 6:1-6). It does not pay; therefore live generously. Life is uncertain and much of it is not subject to our control; nevertheless generosity and helpfulness are better than selfishness. **Cast thy bread upon the waters** (1) is a figure of speech. Some would explain it as sowing rice seed from a boat in the shallow waters of a flooded field. Others see engaging in business—committing your grain to the hazardous shipping of the Mediterranean. Under either figure the action suggests the hazard as well as the promise of the generous life—investment based on faith in God's laws of sowing and reaping. The Targum understands it as giving bread to poor sailors.[1] Verse 2 is best understood as further exhortation to generous sharing. **Give . . . to seven, and also to eight** is a vivid way of saying, Give to many. Even though you do not know **what evil shall be upon the earth,** generous living is better than a life of selfishness.

Verse 3a may suggest God's generosity as further motivation to the unselfish life (cf. Matt. 5:44-45). **Where the tree falleth, there it shall be** (3b) clearly suggests the element of unchangeable fate. But the context of the entire chapter suggests that Koheleth may here be speaking of the inevitable results of human choices. The kind of life you live determines the kind of person you will be. God's later judgment and the facts of later life bid one make right choices from youth onward (cf. 9 and 12:1).

Some commentators understand 1-3 to be only prudent economic advice in an uncertain and unmanageable world. But to

[1]Adam Clarke, *op. cit.*, p. 834.

accept this view detaches the passage from the high spiritual counsel of 11: 7—12: 7.

B. Be Industrious, 11: 4-6

Koheleth here resumes a theme considered in 10: 8-9. The good life requires decision and action. There are uncertainties and dangers, but he who waits for full knowledge and perfect security will never venture. **He that observeth the wind,** i.e., waits until there is no wind to disturb the even scattering of his seed, **shall not sow (4).** Also **he that regardeth the clouds**—to be sure that his grain, when cut, will not get wet[2]—**shall not reap.**

In v. 5 we are reminded that there are always factors known only to God in any decision that we make. The meaning of **the way of the spirit** must be decided by the context, since the word may mean either "spirit" or "wind." Several modern translations make it "wind" and thus relate it to 4. Moffatt puts it into poetry:

> *As you know not how the wind blows,*
> *nor how a babe within the womb grows,*
> *so you cannot know how God works,*
> *God who is in everything.*[3]

The advice of 6 is a clear summary of both the conclusion and the reasoning:

> *In the morning sow your seed,*
> *And till the evening give your hand no rest;*
> *For you know not which shall prosper, this or that,*
> *Or whether both alike shall be good* (Smith-Goodspeed).

C. Be Joyful, 11: 7-8

Early in the book Koheleth said that death was better than life (4: 2-3). Later he admits that life is better than death (9: 4). Now he acknowledges that life can be a thing of at least subdued joy: **Truly the light is sweet, and a pleasant thing it is for the eyes to behold the sun (7).** A man should live joyfully all of his life but he should remember that he will not live here always. There comes an end to life here, and Koheleth has little expec-

[2]Barton, *op. cit.*, p. 183.

[3]Cf. RSV and Smith-Goodspeed for an alternate interpretation.

tation of any life beyond the grave. Let a man "consider the days of darkness, for they will be many. All that comes is nothingness" (8, Berk.).

In c. 11 there is "A Message to the Young": (1) Live generously, 1-3; (2) Live industriously, 4-6; (3) Live joyfully, 7-10; (4) Live in view of tomorrow, 3b, 8b, 9b.

Section **VI** *Seeing Life Whole*

Ecclesiastes 11:9—12:14

In this closing section Koheleth gives a summary statement of conclusions reached in his quest for the meaning of life. He is still a pessimist but at least he has all of the essential elements in view—youth, old age, death, and man's responsibility to "fear God, and keep his commandments."

A. EARTHLY LIFE IN PERSPECTIVE, 11:9—12:8

1. *Youth, Death, and Accountability to God* (11:9—12:1a)

Wisdom requires that all facts be rightly considered in reaching a conclusion. The facts of life are (a) the energies and joys of youth, (b) the inevitable decline of natural energies in old age, (c) the certainty of death, and (d) man's accountability to God for his stewardship of life. Life's highest good must be decided in view of these facts.

In youth life's energies and joys are so real that it is difficult to take the other three into account; therefore the Preacher must give God's counsel. One can and should enjoy life. **Rejoice, O young man, in thy youth . . . and walk in the ways of thine heart** (9). Hendry writes that one should "accept youth with its blessings and opportunities in the sober recognition that youth and age alike are of God's appointment."[1] Yet there is more: **But know thou, that for all these things God will bring thee into judgment.** Karl Barth reminds us that here is "the great But" in which God's revealed plan for man's probation is crystallized.[2] Therefore life's most important counsel is given, **Remember now thy Creator in the days of thy youth** (12:1). The **vanity of childhood and youth** (11:10) is simply that they do not last for all of life. They are futile only in the sense that they are not final.

Adam Clarke suggests the following exposition of this section: (1) You are not your own; (2) Remember your Creator; (3) Remember Him in your youth; (4) Remember Him now.[3]

---

[1]*Op. cit.*, p. 545.   [2]Quoted by Hendry, *ibid.*

[3]*Op. cit.*, p. 836.

2. Old Age (12:1b-5)

The **evil days** (1) here refer to old age, not to death, as in 11:8. The evil of these days lies in their misery and limitations (cf. II Sam. 19:33-35). **I have no pleasure in them** refers to life's earlier experiences that gave one joy. In all of literature no one has so movingly pictured old age. Here indeed is "the music of mortality." The text is obscure in places and the language is the imagery of the poet. Agreement on the interpreta- tion of some phrases has not been achieved, but the general meaning is clear and beautiful in nearly any of the translations.

Old age is pictured as a time of fading light and the dark days of winter. **The clouds** (2) suggest depression and **the rain** may speak of tears (Amp. OT). "Luster and joy, warmth and sunshine, have gone."[4] **The keepers of the house** (3) are the arms that grow weak and the hands that **tremble.** The **strong men** are the legs that are bent with age. **The grinders** is a figure of speech for the teeth. The literal translation is "grinding-maids"; it refers to the Eastern custom of grain grinding by the women. **The windows** that are **darkened** would be the eyes that no longer see.

Rankin[5] understands all of 4 to refer to growing deafness. Thus **the doors** are the ears[6] that, when closed, **shut out the sounds in the streets.** The **sound of the grinding** is the customary sound of life in the home. The **voice of the bird** is the birdlike, high-pitched voice of the deaf.[7] For the deaf, "all the notes of song sink low" (Smith-Goodspeed).

In 5 the figure of the house is dropped but the description of old age continues. **That which is high** depicts fear of heights because of unsteadiness, dizziness, or shortness of breath. **Fears . . . in the way** suggest the dangers of a walk due to lack of agility and liability to falling. The flourishing (white-blossomed) **almond tree** is a poetic figure for graying hair. **The grasshopper shall be a burden** is usually understood to mean that even a small object is difficult to carry.[8] **Desire shall fail** is more literally

---

[4]Rankin, op. cit., p. 84.   [5]Ibid., p. 85.

[6]On the basis of OT figures some interpreters understand **the doors** to be the lips (cf. Ps. 141:3; Mic. 7:5).

[7]Others relate this phrase to the wakefulness of the aged who tend to "get up with the birds."

[8]Adam Clarke, contra, observes: "But probably the words refer to the man himself, who, bent at the loins, and his arms hanging down, exhibits some caricature of the animal [insect] in question" (op. cit., p. 337).

translated "the coper-berry is ineffectual" (Smith-Goodspeed). In Koheleth's time this berry was used to stimulate the sexual urge; *The Berkeley Version* therefore says the "manly urge is gone" (fn.). A broader meaning, and a fact true to life, is suggested by KJV, i.e., that all natural appetites fail to function as they did in the prime of life. Moffatt fittingly concludes this description of the latter end of life:

> *So man goes to his long, long home,*
> *and mourners pass along the street.*

But we should remember some of the things that Koheleth left out. Atkins reminds us, "If old age is unhaunted by too many regrets and fears, it may well be a gracious period of tranquility, with treasures of memory, the compensations of children's children, blessed comradeship of mind and spirit—and rest. Like the late afternoon of a summer's day, when the shadows have grown long but the light lingers, and there are small bird notes in the treetops, and twilight is peace. It may indeed be more; it may be the season for reaping and storing the final harvest of life."[9]

3. Death Is a Part of Life (12:6-8)

As surely as night follows day, death follows old age. Although the thought of 6 follows naturally from 5b, the connective **or ever** (6; before) goes back to v. 1: "Remember now thy Creator . . . before **the silver cord be loosed.**" The image of **the golden bowl** may come from the Temple furniture, where such a vessel supplied the flame-sustaining oil for the lamps of the candlestick (cf. Zech. 4:2-3). However, here the picture is of a **golden bowl** suspended by a **silver cord.** The cord is cut; the bowl falls and is **broken** (crushed). The next two figures represent life as an essential medium for continuing existence. It is a **pitcher** without which one cannot drink from a **fountain,** or a **wheel** without which he cannot draw water from the **cistern.**

All of these figures represent earthly life as ending suddenly and without the possibility of being regained—the cord is cut; the bowl is crushed; the pitcher and the wheel are broken. Koheleth next clearly reflects the Bible record of man's creation (cf. Gen. 2:7): **Then shall the dust return to the earth as it** was: **and the spirit shall return unto God who gave it** (7). For the last time Ecclesiastes voices the verdict upon a life that a man believes to end at the grave, "Utterly vain . . . everything is vain!" (8, Moffatt)

In 1-7 we find the divine admonition, "Remember Now Thy Creator." (1) Remember Him in the days of youth, 1; (2) Remember Him before old age comes, 2-5; (3) Remember Him before you are called to meet God, 6-7.

B. LIFE IN THE LIGHT OF ETERNITY, 12:9-14

These closing verses are a commendation of the writer and a summation of his thought. Some commentators assume that they were added by a disciple, but such an assumption is not necessary. There is no change in the vocabulary or style;[10] and other inspired writers have commended the counsel that they themselves gave (cf. I Cor. 7:25).

1. *Koheleth as a Teacher* (12:9-12)

The preacher (9) was not only **wise** but he also sought to be a teacher—to share his wisdom with others. **Because** is better rendered "besides" or "further." It is implied that he wrote other teachings not included in this book: "He composed, and sought out, and arranged many proverbs" (Smith-Goodspeed). The phrase **sought to find out acceptable words** (10) reflects a writer's concern for his craftmanship. He knew that "a word fitly spoken is like apples of gold in a setting of silver" (Prov. 25:11, RSV). But as a true man of God **the preacher** never let his style obscure his message; what he wrote was **words of truth.**

These words were **as goads, and as nails;** i.e., they had "penetrating brevity . . . inciting and searching influence"[11] (cf. Heb. 4:12). **Masters of assemblies** is better translated as "collected sayings" (Berk., Amp. OT). "The expression **one shepherd** refers not to Koheleth or Solomon but to God, who is the fountainhead of wisdom."[12] Because these words are given under divine inspiration, the writer moves with full confidence to his exhortation: **By these, my son, be admonished** (12). There have been **many books** written and **much study** given to discover the meaning of life. But apart from revelation these lead only

---

[10]Hendry, *op. cit.*, p. 546.   [11]Lewis, *op. cit.*, p. 167.
[12]Rankin, *op. cit.*, p. 87.

to **a weariness of the flesh.** God's man knows the importance of the intellect (9:17-18) but he is also aware of its limitations (8:17).

2. God's Answer to Man's Search (12:13-14)

The closing mood of Ecclesiastes is, What is already written is enough, so **let us hear the conclusion of the whole matter** (13). That declaration speaks clearly of divine revelation. There is a **God** in heaven before whom men should **fear.** He has given us **his commandments,** which we are expected to **keep . . . this is the whole duty of man**—and the duty of every man (cf. ASV, fn.).

God is a holy God, and He is concerned with ethical holiness in men. He shall **bring every work into judgment (14)**—even **every secret thing.** Every act and every thought of man shall be judged on the basis of whether it was **good** or **evil.**

Koheleth presents a search for man's highest good. Again and again his best answer, based on this world only, is, Live as comfortably as possible. But even in this world achievement of worthy goals is better than mere comfort.

> *Not enjoyment, and not sorrow,*
> *Is our destined end or way;*
> *But to act, that each tomorrow*
> *Find us farther than today.*[13]

Jesus tells us that both our comforts and our exertions find their meaning and their place as we submit our whole lives to God. "Seek ye first the kingdom of God, and his righteousness; and all these things shall be added unto you" (Matt. 6:33).

---

[13]H. W. Longfellow, "A Psalm of Life."

Bibliography

I. COMMENTARIES

ATKINS, GAIUS GLENN. "Ecclesiastes" (Exposition). *The Interpreter's Bible.* Edited by GEORGE BUTTRICK, *et al.,* Vol. V. New York: Abingdon-Cokesbury Press, 1956.

BARTON, GEORGE A. "Ecclesiastes." *The International Critical Commentary.* Edited by C. A. BRIGGS, *et al.* New York: Charles Scribner's Sons, 1908.

CLARKE, ADAM. *The Holy Bible with a Commentary and Critical Notes,* Vol. III. New York: Abingdon-Cokesbury Press, n.d.

COX, SAMUEL. "Ecclesiastes." *The Expositor's Bible.* New York: A. C. Armstrong and Son, 1903.

FAUSSET, A. R. *A Commentary Critical and Explanatory on the Old and New Testaments,* by ROBERT JAMIESON, A. R. FAUSSET, and DAVID BROWN. Grand Rapids: Zondervan Publishing House. One vol., n.d.

HENDRY, G. S. "Ecclesiastes." *The New Bible Commentary.* Edited by F. DAVIDSON, *et al.* Grand Rapids, Mich.: Wm. B. Eerdmans Publishing Co., 1953.

HENRY, MATTHEW. *Commentary on the Holy Bible.* Chicago: W. P. Blessing Co. Vol. III, n.d.

LEWIS, TAYLER. "Ecclesiastes." *Commentary on the Holy Scriptures.* Edited by JOHN PETER LANGE. Translated by PHILIP SCHAFF. Grand Rapids: Zondervan Publishing House, n.d.

RANKIN, O. S. "Ecclesiastes" (Exegesis). *The Interpreter's Bible.* Edited by GEORGE A. BUTTRICK, *et al.,* Vol. V. New York: Abingdon-Cokesbury Press, 1956.

RYLAARSDAM, J. COERT. "The Proverbs, Ecclesiastes, The Song of Solomon." *The Layman's Bible Commentary,* Vol. X. Edited by BALMER H. KELLY, *et al.* Richmond, Va.: John Knox Press, 1964.

II. OTHER BOOKS

ARCHER, GLEASON L., JR. *A Survey of Old Testament Introduction.* Chicago: Moody Press, 1964.

PATERSON, JOHN. *The Book That Is Alive.* New York: Charles Scribner's Sons, 1954.

PURKISER, W. T., *et al. Exploring the Old Testament.* Kansas City: Beacon Hill Press, 1955.

——. *Know Your Old Testament.* Kansas City: Beacon Hill Press, 1947.

RYLAARSDAM, J. COERT. *Revelation in Jewish Wisdom Literature.* Chicago: The University of Chicago Press, 1946.

YOUNG, EDWARD J. *An Introduction to the Old Testament.* Grand Rapids: Wm. B. Eerdmans Publishing Co., 1950.

THE SONG OF
SOLOMON

A. F. Harper

Introduction

THE SONG OF SOLOMON and an alternate title, "The Song of Songs," are both derived from the first verse of the book. The heading "Song of Songs" is a literal translation of the Hebrew *Shir hashirim*. This language lays emphasis upon superlative quality—the song is thus described as the best or most excellent song (cf. Gen. 9:25; Exod. 26:33; Eccles. 1:2). In the Vulgate (Latin Bible) the book is called Canticles.

In the Hebrew Scriptures, the Song of Solomon is the first of five short books called the Rolls (*Megilloth*). The other four are Ruth, Lamentations, Ecclesiastes, and Esther. Each of these was read at one of the great annual Jewish festivals, the Song of Songs being used at the Passover season.

A. LITERARY FORM

The Song is an example of Hebrew lyric poetry; hence the modern-language translations cast it in poetic form (cf. Berk., RSV, Moffatt). This ancient Hebrew verse had no rhyme or meter as in our Western form. There is in it a balance and rhythm of thought rather than of sounds or syllables. The lines are arranged so that the thought is expressed in different ways, by repetition, by amplification, by contrast or response,[1] as in 8:6:

> *Love is strong as death;*
> *jealousy is cruel as the grave:*
> *the coals thereof . . . coals of fire,*
> *. . . a most vehement flame.*

B. INTERPRETATION

Commentators are agreed that the Song of Solomon is a poem with love as its theme, but beyond this there are wide differences of interpretation.

Allegorical. From the time of the Talmud (ca. A.D. 150 to 500) it was common among the Jews to regard this book as an allegorical song of God's love for His chosen people. Following

[1]W. T. Purkiser, *et al., Exploring the Old Testament* (Kansas City, Mo.: Beacon Hill Press, 1957), pp. 210-13.

this pattern Christians have seen in it a picture of Christ's love for the Church. J. Hudson Taylor, following Origen, found in it a description of the believer's relationship to his Lord.[2]

It is natural that the allegorical interpretation has found adherents among devout and scholarly men from earliest times until the present. Steadfast earthly love is our most precious and meaningful human relationship. We know that our relationship with God ought to be at least as fine as this, and so we borrow our best human pictures in the attempt to describe the divine-human love and response.

But in spite of all that has been said in favor of an allegorical interpretation of the book, this view has a fatal flaw. Adam Clarke, dean of Wesleyan commentators, is among those who point out this weakness.

> Were this mode of interpretation [the allegorical] to be applied to the Scriptures in general, (and why not, if legitimate here?) in what a state would religion soon be! Who could see any thing certain, determinate, and fixed in the meaning of the Divine oracles, when *fancy* and *imagination* must be the standard interpreters? God has *not* left his word to man's will in this way. . . . nothing [should be] received as the doctrine of the Lord but what may be derived from those *plain words* of the Most High. . . .
> Allegory, metaphor, and figures in general, where the design is clearly indicated, which is the case with all those employed by the sacred writers, may come in to *illustrate* and more forcibly apply Divine truth; but to extort celestial meanings from *a whole book*, where no such *indication* is given, is most certainly not the way to arrive at the knowledge of the true God, and of Jesus Christ whom he has sent.[3]

Contrary to the opinion of some, it seems questionable that the allegorical interpretation among the Jews was a factor in the inclusion of the Song in the canon of the OT. The canon was finally ratified about the close of the first century A.D., and the earliest known allegorical interpretations appear in the Talmud (second to fifth centuries). Gottwald says: "It is probable that the allegorical interpretation followed canonicity, rather than preceded it."[4] It is true that Origen and other Church fathers held to the allegorical interpretation of the Song. But Origen applied this same method to other books of the Bible, and we no

[2]*Union and Communion* (London: Morgan and Scott, n.d.).

[3]Adam Clarke, *The Holy Bible with a Commentary and Critical Notes* (New York: Abingdon-Cokesbury Press, n.d.), III, 845.

[4]IDB, IV, 422.

longer accept this kind of interpretation as valid for them. Why should it be necessary to do so for the Song of Solomon?

Meek writes, "The allegorical interpretation could make the book mean anything that the fertile imagination of the expositor was able to devise, and in the end, its very extravagances were its undoing, so that it has now all but disappeared."[5]

Literal. On such premises as noted above it seems clear that the allegorical method must be rejected as an unacceptable way to interpret the Bible. We therefore have left only such methods as permit us to take the clear sense of the words as written to give us their meaning. On this basis, the Song of Solomon is talking about the human love of a man and a woman. It was this love that was missing from man's life when God said, "It is not good that the man should be alone; I will make an help meet for him" (Gen. 2:18). But even when taking the literal meaning of the Song, there is a variety of interpretations.

Cultic. With the discovery of ancient Near Eastern cult liturgies a theory sprang up that explained the Song of Songs as a pagan ritual that had been secularized or even accommodated to the worship of Jehovah. But as Gottwald points out, "There are formidable problems," if one accepts this interpretation.[6]

Lyrical. Among contemporary commentators it has been common to explain the Canticles as a collection of love lyrics describing physical beauty (*wasfs*), sung at Syrian weddings, and perhaps at other times when the lover yearned to express his affection for his beloved. This view may account for the origin of some passages in the Song but it fails to explain the evidences of unity in the book.[7]

Three characters. This view seems to have been advanced first by Ibn Ezra, made popular by J. F. Jacobi (1771), and given in careful detail by Heinrich Ewald (1826).[8] Though rejecting the view himself, Meek writes: "If the book is to be interpreted literally, there must be two beloveds, a king and a shepherd."[9]

---

[5]"The Song of Songs" (Exegesis), *The Interpreter's Bible*, ed. George A. Buttrick, *et al.* (New York: Abingdon Press, 1956), V, 93.

[6]See Gottwald's full discussion (IDB, IV, 423).

[7]W. J. Cameron, "The Song of Solomon," *The New Bible Commentary*, ed. Francis Davidson, *et al.* (Grand Rapids, Michigan: Wm. B. Eerdmans Publishing Co., 1956), p. 547.

[8]Meek, *op. cit.*, p. 93.   [9]*Ibid.*, p. 94.

In 1891 Driver wrote: "According to . . . [this] view . . . accepted by the majority of modern critics and commentators, there are three principal characters, viz. Solomon, the Shulamite maiden, and her shepherd lover."[10] This position has been defended and developed currently by Terry[11] and Pouget.[12]

According to the three-character interpretation, the young woman was the only daughter among several brothers belonging to a widowed mother living at Shunem (see map 3). She fell in love with a handsome young shepherd and they became engaged. Meanwhile King Solomon on a summer visit to the neighborhood was attracted by the girl's beauty and grace. She was abducted, or under an impulse of the moment (cf. 6:12) came of her own accord with the king's servants to Solomon's court. Here the king sought to woo her but was rejected. Pressing his case, Solomon tried to dazzle her with his pomp and splendor. But all of his promises of jewels, prestige, and the highest position among his wives failed to win the girl's affections. She steadfastly declared her love for her country sweetheart. Finally, recognizing the depth and noble character of her love, Solomon released the girl from his court. Accompanied by her beloved shepherd, she left the court and returned to her humble country home.

If this interpretation be accepted, the theme of the book is faithfulness in love rather than exclusively conjugal love, as in any two-character explanation.

Although there are problems in this interpretation, they are not unanswerable. The view has been held by many competent Bible scholars and commends itself to the writer as the best basis for outlining and explaining the contents of the book. In taking this position, it must be admitted that the decisions as to who is speaking are entirely subjective. Every verse in the book is put into some speaker's mouth in the form of direct discourse. There is, however, no indication at any point that tells the reader who is speaking. The outline followed in this commentary reflects major agreement among commentators who accept the three-character interpretation. There are of course minor differences even between those who agree on the major divisions. In these

[10]*An Introduction to the Literature of the Old Testament* (New York: Charles Scribner's Sons, 1891), p. 410.

[11]*The Song of Songs* (New York: Eaton and Mains, n.d.).

[12]Translated by Joseph L. Lilly, C.M., *The Canticle of Canticles* (The Declan X. McMullen Company, Inc., 1948).

604

instances the author accepts responsibility for choice between the alternatives.

C. Authorship

Since opinions differ so widely as to interpretation, it is natural that there is little agreement among scholars regarding the author.

The traditional view, based on 1:1, is that the book was written by King Solomon. But the language of the verse can be correctly understood to mean either *by* Solomon, *for* Solomon, or *about* Solomon.

Many scholars reject the traditional view on the grounds that the book contains Aramaic words that were not current in Israel during the time of Solomon. In answer one can say that, in view of Israel's contact with the outside world, such terms could easily have been known and used at this period.[13]

If one accepts the three-character interpretation assumed in this commentary, Solomon's authorship is challenged on psychological grounds. It is argued that King Solomon would not be likely to tell the story of his rejection by this girl with whom he had been enamored. But is it not tenable that a man with King Solomon's philosophical mind and moods could have written the Song as we have it? It is not likely that he would have done so immediately. But could not an older and a wiser Solomon, looking back on these experiences, have been moved to write the account? Is there not a frame of reference, especially in later life, from which one can appreciate the powerful drives of physical attraction, acknowledge the joys of human love, and at the same time give higher value to a steadfast loyalty that puts integrity above the allure of royalty and wealth? If it were psychologically possible for the king to relinquish in honor the girl whom he might have kept by force, it does not seem impossible for the same man to have written the story. Sampey writes: "The beauty and power of the book seemed to later students and editors to make the writing worthy of the gifted king whose fame as a composer of both proverbs and songs was handed on to later times (I Kings 4:32)."[14]

What shall we conclude? Two recent conservative scholars disagree. Woudstra (though not accepting the three-character

---

[13]The problem is made more complex by the fact that there are nearly 50 words in this short book of 117 verses that occur nowhere else in the Bible (Kerr, *op. cit.*, p. 106).

[14]ISBE, V, 2831.

interpretation) writes: "There is no sufficient ground to deviate from this historic position [Solomon's authorship]."[15] Cameron asserts, "If Ewald is followed in holding that there is a shepherd lover . . . belief in the authorship of Solomon is scarcely tenable and it is impossible to name the writer."[16]

D. Date

The dating of the book depends on one's view of its authorship. If Solomon wrote the Song, it dates from the tenth century B.C. Those who seek to date it by the occurrence of foreign words in the text range from 700 B.C. to 300 B.C.

[15]"Song of Solomon," *The Wycliffe Bible Commentary,* ed. Charles F. Pfeiffer and Everett F. Harrison (Chicago: Moody Press, 1962), p. 595.

[16]*Op. cit.,* p. 547.

Outline

I. Name and Identification, 1:1

II. Awakening to Reality, 1:2-4a

III. The King's First Visit, 1:4b—2:7
  A. Shulammith and the Maidens, 1:4b-8
  B. Solomon and Shulammith, 1:9—2:7

IV. A Visit and a Dream, 2:8—3:5
  A. The Beloved's Visit, 2:8-17
  B. First Dream of the Beloved, 3:1-5

V. The King Again a Suitor, 3:6—5:1
  A. The Royal Procession, 3:6-11
  B. The King's Second Proposal, 4:1—5:1

VI. A Song of the Beloved, 5:2—6:3
  A. Shulammith's Second Dream, 5:2-8
  B. Shulammith's Song of Her Beloved, 5:9—6:3

VII. The King's Supreme Proposal, 6:4—8:4
  A. Ardent Wooing, 6:4-10
  B. Effective Refusal, 6:11-12
  C. Appeal of the Maidens, 6:13—7:5
  D. Passion Aflame, 7:6-9
  E. A Cry for True Love, 7:10—8:4

VIII. Reunion and Reflection, 8:5-14
  A. Shulammith's Eulogy of Love, 8:5-7
  B. A Reminder and a Response, 8:8-12
  C. Love's Reward at Last, 8:13-14

Section I Name and Identification

The Song of Solomon 1:1

The phrase **song of songs** is the Hebrew mode for expressing superlatives. It is a form comparable to Lord of Lords and holy of holies. To the writer, this song was the best in the book!

The clause **which is Solomon's** has been used as evidence that Solomon wrote the book. However, the text does not give strong proof because the words may mean either by, for, or about Solomon. See Introduction, "Authorship."

Section II Awakening to Reality

The Song of Solomon 1:2-4a

The Shulamite (6:13) maiden is here presumed to be arriving at the summer home of the king, situated at the foot of the Lebanon Mountains (see map 3), in a garden enclosed by a latticework trellis. It is the spring of the year.

The maiden had been abducted from her home, or perhaps had consented while in a confused state of mind to accompany the king's chariot. See 6:12, which has been translated,

Ere I was aware, my soul's fancy
seated me in a princely chariot of my people (Berk.).

As the chariot comes to a halt, Shulammith is surrounded by "the daughters of Jerusalem" (5), members of the king's harem at this summer home. As she realizes her situation, a great longing

608

for her betrothed sweeps over her and she cries out, **Let him kiss me with the kisses of his mouth** (2).

The maidens seek to reassure Shulammith that her charms assure her own future:

> *For better are thy loves than wine.*
> *In fragrance thy ointments are good;*
> *As ointment shall thy name be poured out;*
> *Therefore maidens love thee* (Terry).

But in fear and in vain the girl calls after the departing charioteer, "Draw me after you, let us make haste" (4, RSV). The chariot moves on and Shulammith is left to face what she must.

Section III *The King's First Visit*

The Song of Solomon 1:4b—2:7

This episode occurs in one of the apartments for women in the country residence of the king. Here it has been planned for Solomon first to meet the Shulamite.

A. SHULAMMITH AND THE MAIDENS, 1:4b-8

Shulammith and the **daughters of Jerusalem** (5; members of the king's harem) appear at first to be the only ones present. The girl exclaims with incredulity and shock, **The king hath brought me into his chambers** (4). To this her companions reply with encouragement:

> *We will exult and rejoice in you;*
> *we will extol your love more than wine;*
> *rightly do they love you* (4, RSV).

The conversation continues in dialogue form:[1]

[1]This is the only book of the Bible that has all of its content put into the mouths of speakers.

Shulammith: **I am black, but comely,**
                 O ye daughters of Jerusalem (5).

Maidens (interrupting): "Dark as are the tents of Kedar,
                 lovely as the curtains of Solo-
                 mon" (Berk.).

In 6 the girl implores her companions not to stare at her
because of her dark skin. She explains that her brothers **were
angry** with her and as punishment put her out under the hot
Palestinian sun to work in the **vineyards.** The expression **Mine
own vineyard have I not kept** refers to her own complexion and
person.

1. *Cry for Her Distant Lover* (1:7)

Memories of the home surroundings awaken pangs of longing and she cries out in anguish:

Tell me, you whom deep in my soul I love,
  where you pasture your flock,
    where you have it lie down at midday
for why should I be as a veiled woman (the garb
  of the harlot, cf. Gen. 28:15),
    wandering among the flocks of your companions? (Berk.)

2. *Response of a Scornful Harem* (1:8)

Disgusted that Shulammith should prefer a rustic shepherd
to the attentions of the king, one of the maidens speaks sharply
and sarcastically:

  If thou knowest not, most beautiful of women,
  Follow the tracks of the flock,
  And go pasture thy goats
  Near the shepherds' tents (Pouget)

One cannot predict what would have happened as a result of this
beginning of a quarrel in the harem had not Solomon himself
appeared on the scene.

B. SOLOMON AND SHULAMMITH, 1:9—2:7

1. *Compliments and Promises* (1:9-11)

The king first pays the girl a high compliment on her beauty
and grace, likening her to "a mare of Pharaoh's chariots" (9,

610

Berk.). This is hardly a compliment in Western taste, but in Eastern lands it would express the highest admiration. Clarke cites a comparable instance from Greek literature: "The golden Helen, tall and graceful, appears as distinguished among us as the furrow in the field, the cypress in the garden, or the *Thessalian horse in the chariot*."[2] **Pharaoh's chariots** were a royal type as distinguished from lesser kinds. In 10 the king pays special attention to the girl's facial features:

> *Thy cheeks are comely with plaits of hair,*
> *Thy neck with strings of jewels* (ASV).

In 11 the royal suitor promises more and costlier jewels: "We will have golden beads strung round you, studded with silver" (Moffatt).

2. A First Signal of Refusal (1:12-14)

This paragraph is to be understood as Shulammith's first reminder to the king that his attentions are not welcomed because her love has been pledged to another. The key expressions are **his table** (12; Heb., "couch") in contrast to a possible "our couch," and the emphasis upon **my wellbeloved** (13). The meaning seems to be that while the king was in his proper place and she was in her rightful situation with her betrothed, her physical charms were outgoing and inviting. But under existing relationships her **spikenard** gave forth no perfume. In 13-14 the girl declares her love with abandon—but it is for another. She carries the thought of her beloved in her heart just as she wore on her bosom a bag of myrrh.

Terry envisions the girl shrinking from Solomon's advances, and translates her words:

> *Until the king was among its surroundings,*
> *My nard gave out its fragrance.*
> *A bag of myrrh is my love to me,*
> *Upon my bosom it shall remain.*
> *A bunch of cypress flowers is my love to me,*
> *Among the vineyards of En-gedi.*

[2]*Op. cit.*, p. 856.

3. *Further Pursuit and Evasion* (1:15—2:7)

a. Dialogue (1:15—2:2). Enamored with Shulammith, and refusing to accept her reluctance, the king presses his case:

> *How fair you are, my dear,*
> *how fair with dove-like eyes!*

But the girl replies as though speaking to one far away, **Behold, thou art fair, my beloved, yea, pleasant** (16). The next words, **Our bed is green,** have reference "to the shady greensward, on which she and her lover had been accustomed to repose and converse. Like all the imagery that follows, it contains a delicate reminder that she loves the fields and the woods, not the attractions of kings' houses."[3]

Verse 17 suggests the imagery of the open forest in which the siding and roof of the house consist of the living trees. In 2:1 the girl again identifies herself with a simpler way of life than that to be found in a king's court.

> *I am* (only) *a rose* (Heb., crocus) *of Sharon,*
> *a lily of the valleys* (RSV).

But the enamored royal suitor responds, If you are only a lily,

> *Like a lily among thorns*
> *Is my beloved among the youthful maidens* (Pouget).

The older allegorical interpretations assigned the words of 2:1 to the Beloved, and they were thus applied to our Lord. In this setting the verse has given inspiration for the gospel songs "Jesus, Rose of Sharon" and "The Lily of the Valley."

b. Love with honor (2:3-7). In 3-4, Shulammith again seeks to turn aside the king's ardor by telling of her love for **my beloved among the sons** (3). She chose **the apple tree** as a figure to suggest the pleasant surroundings of her first and true love. In 3b there is probably an allusion to the God-ordained combination of protection and deep joys in marriage. Having likened her betrothed to the apple tree, she sighs:

> *I yearn to sit down in its shade,*
> *And its fruit is sweet to my palate* (Pouget).

---

[3]Terry, *op. cit.*, p. 23.

Assuming in 4 that the Shulamite continues to think of the rural setting as her **banqueting house,** Pouget translates it:

> *He had me enter his hut*
> *And the flag he unfurled above me was love.*

Some assume that in 5-7 Shulammith continues speaking to the king. Others understand that the king withdrew at this point and the words were spoken only to the **daughters of Jerusalem** (7). In either case, the girl bursts into an impassioned plea. Exhausted by the emotional strain, she asks for **flagons** (Heb., cakes of raisins) and **apples** (5) to strengthen her physically. **I am sick of love** is better translated, "I am sick from love" (ASV).

In 6 older interpreters distinguished "the left hand as the hand of providence and the right as the hand of grace."[4] In view of the context, however, there seems to be here a clear reference to love's embrace (cf. 8:3). The sentiment is equivalent to "He is the only one who shall ever embrace me with a lover's freedom."[5]

The personal interpretation reflected in KJV, **Stir not up, nor awake my love** (7), is rejected by several newer translations in favor of an impersonal statement about the passion of love. *The Berkeley Version* has it:

> *Do not awaken nor stir up love,*
> *until love itself shall please.*

Morgan saw here a clear word of Bible warning, especially to young people.[6] God has given the emotions of conjugal love. They are given for man's happiness and well-being. But they make this contribution to life only when given expression at the time and under the circumstances that God has ordained. God's warning is, Don't arouse passion until it is right to do so—accompanied by true love and within the bonds of marriage. **By the roes, and by the hinds of the field** is a form of rustic adjuration or oath. The **roes** and **hinds** are figures sometimes found in Eastern poetry to express womanly beauty.

---

[4]Cameron, *op. cit.,* p. 550.   [5]Terry, *op. cit.,* p. 25.
[6]*Living Messages of the Bible, Genesis to Malachi* (New York: Fleming H. Revell Co., 1911), p. 80.

Section IV   A Visit and a Dream

The Song of Solomon 2: 8—3: 5

A. The Beloved's Visit, 2: 8-17

In these verses we have a description by the Shulamite of a visit from her shepherd lover while she was held captive in the king's summer house. It may be understood as historical narrative but it seems more probable that we have here a soliloquy. The girl's "heart and thoughts are with her absent lover; her lively imagination brings him near, and she seems to hear his voice as at former times, and sings to herself"[1] the song of these verses.

1. The Lover's Approach (2: 8-9)

The young woman here describes the course of her beloved as he approaches the enclosure. We need to remember that it was not a wall but some sort of latticework. **The voice of** (8) is better translated "Hark!" or "Listen." Moffatt renders the verses:

> Listen, it is my darling,
>   there he is, coming to me,
> leaping across the mountains,
>   bounding over the hills!
> There he stands behind our wall,
>   gazing through the window,
>   glancing through the lattice!

2. The Beloved's Entreaty (2: 10-14)

The dramatic quality of 10a is caught by Pouget, "My beloved is about to speak to me; he speaks to me!" We have here a love song of sheer beauty, couched in the language of the awakening spring season. In the eyes of love, nature becomes all alive with significance. As a description of springtime the passage is unexcelled, and reflects the unique interest in nature found in the book.

We are introduced to flocks and vineyards, to kids and shepherds' tents, to myrrh and clusters of henna blossoms, to doves and

[1]Terry, op. cit., p. 26.

614

little foxes, to fir trees and cedars, to the rose of Sharon and the
lily of the valleys, to raisin cakes and apples, to young stags and
gazelles, to the vineyards in blossom and to the clefts in the rocks,
to flocks of goats and to the hinds of the field, to the wood of
Lebanon, to myrrh and frankincense and fragrant perfumes, to oils
and spices and pomegranates, to saffron and calamus and cinnamon, to nectar and the flowing streams of Lebanon. . . . The beauty
of nature is everywhere revealed.[2]

In Palestine **the winter** (11) is the season of clouds and
heavy **rain.** But in the spring the warm sun calls forth new
life from the moist earth. **The turtle** (12) is better the turtledove,
a migratory bird that appears in Palestine the second week in
April (cf. Jer. 8:7). **Putteth forth** (13) means "ripeneth" (ASV).
This variety of figs remains green on the trees during the winter
months and ripens rapidly in the spring. The **tender grape** would
be the grape blossoms.

But the new life in nature only creates the mood of the
lover; his plea is for his beloved: **Arise, my love, my fair one,
and come away** (13). In 14, Shulammith hears her beloved calling her **my dove** (cf. 1:15). The girl confined behind the latticework is likened to the **dove . . . in the** inaccessible **clefts of the
rock.** Here is pleading love:

Let me hear your voice, let me see your face;
for your voice is sweet, and your face is lovely (Berk.).

3. *Shulammith's Response* (2:15-17)

In response to her beloved's entreaty, the girl turns her face
toward him and sings two little songs.

a. *The little foxes* (2:15). There may be here an oblique
reference to some previous lovers' quarrel that had occurred between them. Perhaps it was even the occasion for the Shulamite's momentary petulant willingness to leave her home and
accompany the king's servants to his country residence. (See
Intro., "Interpretation"; also comments on 1:2.) Others see in
the foxes a reference to the king's attentions to her that threatened the **tender grapes** of their own romance which had reached
only the time of betrothal.

Nearly all expositors find here a universal truth in personal relationships. And here is the source of the proverb, "It is

[2]Kerr, *op. cit.,* p. 101.

615

the little foxes that spoil the vines." To despise little things in the relationships of love is to show oneself utterly ignorant of important facts of life. It is little things that often account for happiness or for sorrow—a little remembrance, or a little forgetfulness. What is true in our relations with each other is equally true in our relationships with God. "And how numerous the little foxes are! Little compromises with the world; disobedience to the still small voice in little things; little indulgences of the flesh to the neglect of duty; little strokes of policy; doing evil in little things that good may come; and the beauty, and the fruitfulness of the vine are sacrificed."[3]

b. *Pledge of love* (2:16-17). Now the quarrel is over, apologies have been made, and there is no longer a barrier between the lovers: **My beloved is mine, and I am his** (16). The expression, **He feedeth among the lilies,** is to be understood as "He enjoys all of my affection." Here a feeling of anxiety arises. Fearful for her lover's safety if he lingers, she bids him hurry away. But she wishes him to return soon, when evening comes:

> *Until the day begins to cool*
> *and the shadows lengthen,*
> *turn, my lover, and be as a gazelle, or a young hart,*
> *upon the mountains that separate us* (17, Berk.).

It is uncertain whether **the mountains of Bether** refers to a real place—perhaps Bithron beyond Jordan—or whether we have a psychological figure for "mountains of separation." In either case here is reflected the discipline of waiting. In the immediate context it is waiting for the time of reunion and the consummation of marriage. In the broader sense it is steadfastness and patience in the necessary waiting for any desired end or worthy goal that now eludes us.

B. First Dream of the Beloved, 3:1-5

In this action Shulammith and the women are again together in the apartment of the king's summer home. She tells them how her love for her shepherd sweetheart fills her dreams. **By night** (1) is plural in the Hebrew, indicating that this was more than a single dream. Her dreams **by night** reflected her thoughts

[3]Taylor, *op. cit.,* pp. 53-54.

by day. Moffatt catches her mood of longing and frustration in v. 1.

> *Night after night in bed*
> *I dreamed I sought my beloved,*
> *and sought him in vain.*

In her dreams Shulammith had expressed her determination: **I will rise now . . . I will seek him whom my soul loveth** (2). The expression **broad ways** refers to street intersections. The spaces were broader at the gates and crossings than in the narrow streets of the cities, and so there was perhaps more likelihood that the one she sought would be among the crowds gathered there. **The watchmen** (3) moved quietly about the city checking suspicious-looking persons.

This dream, as most such dreams of love, had a happy ending. Shulammith **found him** for whom her heart yearned. She **would not let him go** (4) until she had **brought him** to her **mother's house** for the consummation of their marriage. The reference to the house of the mother suggests that the mother was a widow. Fausset writes: "In the East one large apartment often serves for the whole family; so the bride here speaks of her mother's apartment as her own."[4]

The refrain of 5 (cf. 2:7 and 8:4) "is not an anticlimax to the reunion of the two lovers in the dream. Rather, it indicates recognition of the fact that because of the effects which love can have, it must be handled with the utmost care and should not be aroused before its proper time."[5] Shulammith appeals to the women not to try further to arouse in her the passion of love for the king when there is only one for whom she has pure affection. The italicized **my** has been added to KJV and makes the reference seem personal, when in fact the girl is stating a universal principle, "Do not awaken nor stir up love until it please" (Berk., cf. comments on 2:7).

---

[4]Robert Jamieson, A. R. Fausset, and David Brown, *A Commentary, Critical and Explanatory on the Old and New Testaments*, I and II (Grand Rapids, Michigan: Zondervan Publishing House, n.d.), 420.

[5]Woudstra, *op. cit.*, p. 599.

Section V   The King Again a Suitor

The Song of Solomon 3: 6—5: 1

A. THE ROYAL PROCESSION, 3: 6-11

This paragraph describes a royal procession that brings Solomon and the Shulamite together. Pouget assumes that Solomon rides in the litter and comes to the summer residence to renew his suit for the girl's love.[1] Terry interprets the scene in reverse and has Shulammith riding in the litter from the summer residence into Jerusalem (see map 3), where she is again to meet the king.[2] The expression **cometh out of the wilderness** (6) lends credence to Terry's view. The whole procedure is designed to overwhelm the girl with the glory of King Solomon. The speeches seem to have been made by the "maidens of Jerusalem" who accompany the Shulamite.

Verse 6 is perhaps a rhetorical question by the maidens designed to impress the girl. The grammar indicates that **who** should be neuter. Smith-Goodspeed renders the question:

> *What is this coming up from the wilderness,*
>   *like columns of smoke,*
> *Perfumed with myrrh and frankincense,*
>   *made from all kinds of merchants' spices?*

Verses 7-8 give the reply from the maidens themselves. The **bed** (7) was a litter or palanquin—a couch or chair carried by poles on the shoulders of bearers. It was **Solomon's** because he owned it and had sent it for the Shulamite. The girl and her companions were protected on the journey by **threescore valiant men.** The **fear in the night** (8) would be from Arab marauders, who often attacked and robbed such processions of the wealthy.

Verses 9-10 are a further effort to glorify Solomon and to condition the girl to accept his proposal. **The wood** (9) was from **Lebanon,** her own northern Palestine—perhaps this litter had been made especially for her and for this special journey. Pouget translates 10:

[1]*Op. cit.,* p. 179.   [2]*Op. cit.,* p. 32.

618

> *He made its columns of silver;*
> *Its back is of gold;*
> *Its seat of purple.*
> *Inside is embroidery, work of love,*
> *Done by the Daughters of Jerusalem.*

Reference to the work of **love** by **the daughters of Jerusalem** was probably intended to say to Shulammith: "Every woman loves the king; any girl who is brought to the palace joyfully accepts his proposal." Immediately after this appeal by the maidens the procession has arrived at the palace. The chamberlain of the king calls upon the girl and her attendants:

> *Go forth, O daughters of Zion,*
> *and behold King Solomon,*
> *with the crown with which his mother crowned him*
> *on the day of his wedding,*
> *on the day of the gladness of his heart* (11, RSV).

B. The King's Second Proposal, 4:1—5:1

The scene is probably a room in the Jerusalem palace where the king is waiting for Shulammith. He seeks to win her by his splendor and words of loving admiration.

1. *Solomon's First Song* (4:1-5)

Cameron writes: "This is a song, after the pattern of the 'wasf,' commonly sung at Syrian marriages still. It was sometimes imitated, where only a love song was intended. It is a type of description appreciated in the East, though it may not in all respects commend itself to Western taste."[3]

The king speaks his appreciation for the girl's beauty: **Behold, thou art fair, my love; behold, thou art fair** (1). From this fervent expression of admiration he goes on to compliment her features and figure. Her eyes are like **doves' eyes**—lustrous even behind her veil. The long, dark tresses, flowing down across her neck and shoulders, are as beautiful **as a flock of** black **goats** lying along the slope of **mount Gilead**. Her **teeth** (2) are as white and perfect as **a flock of sheep** after being washed in preparation for shearing. The **twins** refer to the upper and lower teeth. **None is barren** says that none are missing. Moffatt renders it:

[3]*Op. cit.*, p. 551.

> *Paired together in rows,*
> *not one a-wanting.*

Solomon continued his praise:

> *Your lips are as a scarlet thread,*
> *and your mouth is very comely.*
> *Your cheeks are as halves of a pomegranate*
> *gleaming behind your veil* (3, Berk.).

The Hebrew word means **temples** but probably both temple and cheek were included. We might have said "as pretty and smooth as an apple." **The tower of David** (4) to which the girl's **neck** is likened is not now known but was apparently well-known at the time. The king compares the circular jewels of her necklace to the bright brass **shields** hung around the walls of the **armoury.** Woudstra comments on 5: "The breasts of the bride are youthfully tender like fawns of a gazelle. Feeding among the lilies suggests the well-formed body of the bride from which the breasts arise."[4]

2. Shulammith's Demurrer (4:6)

"At this point Shulammith looks away, as if she would fain withdraw, and she gives utterance, aside, to a deep sigh for her mountain home. She has no response for the king's admiration. . . . To her, the heights of Lebanon, and Amanah, and Shinar, and Hermon, are far more attractive than Solomon in all his glory."[5] She sighs:

> *Until the day breathes cool, and the shadows flee,*
> *I would, for my part, walk to the mountain of myrrh,*
> *And to the hill of frankincense* (6, Terry).

3. Solomon's Second Song (4:7-15)

In the words of v. 1, the enamored king renews his suit, **Thou art . . . fair, my love** (7). But here he goes further, **Thou art all fair . . . there is no spot in thee.** In response to the girl's yearning for her native hills, he pleads—and casts reflection upon her uncivilized mountain home (see map 3):

> *Come with me from Lebanon, my bride;*
> *come with me from Lebanon.*

---

[4]*Op. cit.,* p. 600.   [5]Terry, *op. cit.,* p. 37.

Depart from the peak of Amana,
from the peak of Senir and Hermon,
from the dens of lions,
from the mountains of leopards (8, RSV).

In a torrent of desire the gifted Solomon continues to pour out his love song:

You have ravished my heart, my sister, my bride,
you have ravished my heart with one glance of your eyes,
with a single bead of your necklace.
How sweet is your love, my sister, my bride;
How much more delicious is your love than wine;
and the fragrance of your ointments
than all the rich spices.
Your lips drop honey, my bride,
honey and milk are under your tongue;
and the fragrance of your garments is like
the fragrance of Mount Lebanon (9-11, Berk.).

The fragrance of Lebanon (11) from its shrubs, trees, and flowers may well have been proverbial (cf. Hos. 14: 6-7).

At 12 the torrential outpouring is checked momentarily by a gesture from the Shulamite. She again looks away, as if not hearing his words of love and admiration. He pauses, seeing that her heart has been given to another. Rylaarsdam comments on 12: "She is the pure bride, the virginal 'garden locked' who invites her one and only beloved."[6]

But the song is checked only momentarily. The king's ardor reasserts itself and the song again rises to a crescendo. The figure of a garden in 12a is expanded in 13-14, and the figure of the fountain is carried further in 15. Thy plants (13) speaks of the girl's attractions. "These are the subject through verses 13-15, and the exotic plants of the king's garden are appropriately employed by him as images of the maiden's loveliness, and remind us of his traditional familiarity with all manner of trees, and plants, and flowers. See I Kings IV, 33."[7] Moffatt interprets these verses as follows:

---

[6]"The Proverbs, Ecclesiastes, The Song of Solomon," *The Layman's Bible Commentary*, ed. Balmer H. Kelly, et al. (Richmond, Virginia: John Knox Press, 1964), X, 152.

[7]Terry, *op. cit.*, p. 39.

Your charms are a pomegranate paradise—
with henna and roses,
and spikenard and saffron,
with cassia and cinnamon,
all sorts of frankincense,
with myrrh and with eaglewood,
all the best spices!
You are the fountain of my garden,
a well of fresh water,
like streams from Lebanon.

4. Rejection and Invitation (4:16)

It is the Shulamite who speaks. Her words and inflections are intended to close the door to the king's ardor. She "uses the image of the garden to express delicately her wish to be with her beloved."[8]

Awake, O north wind;
and come, thou south;
blow upon my garden,
that the spices thereof may flow out.
Let my beloved come into his garden,
and eat his pleasant fruits.

5. Inclined to Use Force (5:1)

Terry understands this verse as follows: "The king becomes greatly excited by the words of Shulammith, and, impatient and presumptuous, he utters the following, as if to consummate his wishes by his own authority.

I have come to my garden, my sister-spouse;
I have plucked my myrrh with my spice,
I have eaten my honeycomb with my honey,
I have drunk my wine with my milk.
Eat, O comrades!
Drink, yea, drink abundantly, O lovers![9]

But despite this outburst, Solomon senses his rebuff and leaves to resume his suit for Shulammith on another occasion.

[8]Robert H. Pfeiffer, "The Song of Songs," *The Abingdon Bible Commentary*, ed. by Frederick Carl Eiselen, Edwin Lewis, and David G. Downey (New York: Abingdon-Cokesbury Press, 1929), p. 625.

[9]*Op. cit.*, pp. 40-41.

Section VI A Song of the Beloved

The Song of Solomon 5: 2—6: 3

In this section the Shulamite is still in Jerusalem at the palace. The women of the court are with her again.

A. Shulammith's Second Dream, 5: 2-8

We have here the account of a dream from which Shulammith had recently awakened. She imagines that her absent lover had come seeking her in vain. The words, "I slept, but my heart was awake" (2, RSV), reflect how fine a line sometimes divides consciousness from slumber. The concerns of the girl's every waking moment reflected themselves in her dreams.

Constantly yearning for the sound of that familiar voice, she heard it in her sleep: **Open to me, my sister, my love** (2). Having travelled far through the night, his **head is filled** (wet) **with dew** and he asks for warmth and shelter.

If 3 be understood as a part of the dream, it is probable that the Shulamite is still blaming herself for their separation. The flimsy excuses in the dream that she gave for not admitting him may reflect her unjustifiable part in the lovers' quarrel alluded to in 2:15. Verse 4 reflects the continued effort of the beloved for a reconciliation, and Shulammith's tardy response to those efforts. **By the hole of the door** is a correct translation, though RSV and Berkeley have probably given the true intent with the rendering "put his hand on the latch." **My bowels were moved for him** is better, "My heart yearned for him" (Moffatt).

Verses 5-6 reflect the girl's true attitude toward her beloved. She **rose up to open** (5) to him. "The best proof a bride could give her lover of welcome was to anoint herself . . . *profusely* with the *best* perfumes."[1] This was what Shulammith did, until from **her hands** the **myrrh** dripped **upon the handles of the lock**. But extravagant as her welcome was, it came too late— **My beloved had withdrawn himself, and was gone** (6). The next statement, **My soul failed when he spake,** may refer back to the lover's request in 2. It may with equal validity be translated, "when he turned away"; and this fits the context better.

[1]Fausset, *op. cit.*, p. 423.

625

Another appropriate rendering is, "My soul had failed him when he spoke" (Berk.). Now desperate to atone for earlier failure, she cries, **I sought him, but I could not find him; I called him, but he gave me no answer.**

> *For of all sad words of tongue or pen,*
> *The saddest are these: "It might have been!"*[2]

In her dream the Shulamite went so far in taking the initiative to recover her beloved that **the watchmen** (7) thought her an evil woman prowling the streets at night. They **smote her** and **took away her veil.** Here the dream broke off—but not the heart longing behind the dream. Having exhausted her personal resources at this point, she enlists the aid of others:

> *O maidens of Jerusalem, I charge you,*
> *if you find my darling,*
> *tell my darling this,*
> *that I am lovesick* (8, Moffatt).

B. Shulammith's Song of Her Beloved, 5:9—6:3

At 1:8 (see comments there) and again at 5:8 we see the effect of standing alone for a chosen cause. The "daughters of Jerusalem" could not understand why any woman would reject the attentions of the king in preference for the love of a shepherd. They themselves had accepted Solomon's harem as a way of life. At first (1:8) they had been only scornful of the Shulamite's loyalty. But now they sought to find out her reasons: **What is thy beloved more than another beloved, O thou fairest among women?** (9) Steadfastness in devotion gave her opportunity to tell others of her beloved, who to her was "altogether lovely" (16). Instead of mistreating the young woman, "they become sympathetically interested in her love. They want to know who this shepherd is that she dares prefer to the king."[3]

1. The Perfect Human Form (5:10-16)

Love can see no fault in its beloved, and Shulammith could see nothing but perfection in her shepherd lover. "What the Apollo Belvedere is in the sculptor's art, this word picture is in Oriental poetry."[4] The description here is from head to toe in

[2]John Greenleaf Whittier, "Maud Muller."
[3]Pouget, *op. cit.*, p. 185.   [4]Terry, *op. cit.*, p. 44.

contrast to 7:1-5, which is from foot to head. **White** (10) should be read "bright" or "radiant." The RSV renders the verse:

My beloved is all radiant and ruddy,
distinguished among ten thousand.

The **fine** (pure) **gold** (11) represents the nobility that radiates from his head and face. His hair is becomingly curly and **black as a raven.** Twice before (1:15 and 4:1) we have seen this comparison to **the eyes of doves** (12). The expression **doves by the rivers** suggests a "picture of exquisite delight; their quick movements seem to make them twinkle with joy."[5] **Washed with milk, and fitly set** refers to the dark brown iris and black pupil set against the white of the eyes.

The comparison of **cheeks** to **a bed of spices** (13) refers to his perfumed beard, which was customary. **His lips** were like the red **lilies** of Palestine, and his breath was like **sweet smelling myrrh.** In 14-15, Shulammith moves on to describe other features of her Beloved's body. "As in statuary to the artist, here the partly undraped figure is suggestive only of beauty, free from indelicacy."[6] Moffatt translates 14-15:

His fingers are golden tapers
tipped with topaz pink,
his body is wrought of ivory
blue-veined with sapphire,
his limbs are marble columns
resting on sockets of gold,
he towers to the eye like Lebanon,
as lordly as a cedar.

Verse 16 may be simply the end of Shulammith's description of her beloved's figure, or it may be understood as her personal reaction to her idealization of him. **His mouth** is literally "his palate," the organ of speech. Hence RSV translates, "His speech is most sweet." **He is altogether lovely** is literally, "All of him is desirableness."[7] Moffatt therefore seems to reflect accurately the girl's probable expression of satisfied love:

His kisses are utterly sweet—
he is all a delight!
And that is my darling, my dear,
O maidens of Jerusalem!

---

[5]*Ibid.*   [6]Fausset, *op. cit.,* p. 424.
[7]Cameron, *op. cit.,* p. 553.

2. An Interested Inquiry (6:1-3)

The inquiry comes from one or more of the "daughters of Jerusalem." The question, **Whither is thy beloved gone?** (1) is directly related to 5:6, where the girl's dream told of her lost lover; it is also related to 5:8, where the women were charged to give him a message if they found him. The interested women desire to help in the search, but Shulammith claims her beloved as exclusively her own.

In 4:12-15 and in 5:1, Shulammith has been called a garden. It seems reasonable therefore that v. 2 refers to the mutual love she and her beloved have already known, and to an expected reunion when their marriage will be consummated. **I am my beloved's, and my beloved is mine** (3), has overtones of the Christian wedding vows, ". . . and keep me only unto thee so long as we both shall live."

Section VII The King's Supreme Proposal

The Song of Solomon 6:4—8:4

A. ARDENT WOOING, 6:4-10

At this point the scene changes and Solomon visits the Shulamite again, once more seeking to win her affection.

1. The King's Praise (6:4-7)

As one skilled in the art of making love, Solomon compliments the girl's beauty and expresses his affection: **Thou art beautiful, O my love** (4). The comparison was to **Tirzah**, a lovely city of Shulammith's own beloved northern Palestine, and to **Jerusalem**, the capital city where she was then residing. The name **Tirzah** signifies beautiful or delightful, and **Jerusalem** was called "the perfection of beauty" (cf. Ps. 48:1-2).

The reference to **Tirzah** is frequently cited as evidence against the authorship of Solomon. It is argued that (a) the author must have been a writer from the northern kingdom, because no southern author would compare Tirzah favorably with Jerusalem. It is urged that (*b*) in Solomon's time Tirzah was not the capital of the north, as was Jerusalem in the south. But such evidence is at best inferential. As Cameron says, "All that is required [to justify the comparison] is a town remarkable for strength and beauty."[1] And if Solomon be the author, what would be more natural than for him to try to please the Shulamite by such a reference to her beloved homeland?

It is difficult to understand 4*b*-5*a* as part of a lover's suit, but in the exact setting of this song it appears natural. Shulammith's cool stare must have momentarily checked the king's ardor. Her integrity presented a formidable obstacle to him. Adeney speaks of the last part of 4 as "Solomon's expression of awe for the terrible purity and constancy of the Shulamite."[2] The first part of 5 is often explained as a request for the girl to **turn away thine eyes** because their enchantment had **overcome** the suitor. Gray and Adams seem closer to facts when they write, "This dread of the heroine's eyes is incredible if she were his exultant bride, but intelligible if she is resisting his devotion."[3]

But the royal suitor is not accustomed to being denied. He renews his fulsome praise. Verses 5*b*-7 repeat the king's earlier compliments. See comments on 4:1-3.

2. *Be My Queen* (6:8-10)

Apparently the king sensed that he was getting nowhere in his customary invitation for the girl to join his court as one of the harem. He therefore offers her a special place: "One only is my dove, my perfect one" (9, Terry). Solomon had many more wives and **concubines** than here indicated (I Kings 11:1-3). However, no special significance is to be made of the figures, as indeed is suggested by the expression **and virgins without number** (8). The king simply declared that Shulammith was more attractive than all of the beautiful women at his court. She had been **the only one of her mother** (9), and she should be the only one for the king.

[1] *Op. cit.,* p. 553.

[2] "The Song of Solomon and the Lamentations of Jeremiah," *The Expositor's Bible,* ed. W. Robertson Nicoll (New York: A. C. Armstrong and Son, 1903), p. 34.

[3] *Bible Commentary* (Grand Rapids, Michigan: Zondervan Publishing House, n.d.), III, 71.

Adding compliment to compliment, Solomon tells the girl that **the daughters** (her rivals in the court) **saw her, and blessed her.** Even **the queens and the concubines,** who would normally be jealous, **praised her.** In 10, Solomon seems to be quoting the women.

> *Who is this (they say), that looks forth like the morning,*
> *Beautiful as the white moon, clear as the warm sun,*
> *Awe-inspiring as the bannered host?* (Terry)

These words appear to have been spoken by the women when they first saw the Shulamite looking **forth** from the curtains of Solomon's litter that brought her to Jerusalem (see comments on 3:6-11).

B. EFFECTIVE REFUSAL, 6:11-12

The reference to her forced presence in Jerusalem stirs Shulammith to fear as she recalls the circumstances of her abduction. She rejects the king's suit by reminding him that she is a captive subject of his attentions. On that spring day, she recalls,

> *Down I went to the walnut-bower,*
> * to see the green plants of the dale,*
> * to see if the vines were a-budding,*
> * and the pomegranates in flower* (11, Moffatt).

From that point on she had been unwillingly detained by the servants of the king. "I know not [how] my soul put me into the chariots of Amminadib" (12, Terry). **Ammi-nadib** has never been identified and the meaning of the Hebrew is uncertain. There appears to be a sarcastic rebuff for the enamored king in the translation:

> *Before I knew it, my fancy set me*
> * in the chariot of my ardent lover* (Smith-Goodspeed).

C. APPEAL OF THE MAIDENS, 6:13—7:5

The action here is difficult to trace, though it is clear that the Shulamite is the one being addressed. Perhaps as the girl made her cynical thrust at the king she started to leave the room in indignation. Again (see comment on 3:10) the maidens sought to intercede in behalf of their master and king: **Return, return,**

O Shulamite; return, return, that we may look upon thee (13). The girl replied, **What will ye see in the Shulamite?**

It is probable that the last sentence of 13 is the answer of the maidens to this question. **Two armies** may be understood as a proper name. The ASV translates it as "the dance of Mahanaim." This was the place where Jacob was met by the angels (Gen. 32:1-2). The maidens "mean that the dancing of Shulammith would be an angelic sight, like that of Jacob when the angels met him. In accordance with that thought, the women at once proceed to say (or sing as a chorus) how admirable her appearance in the dance would be."[4]

> *How beautiful are your feet in sandals,*
> *O maiden of queenly form!*
> *Your rounded thighs are a jeweled chain,*
> *   the work of a master craftsman.*
> *Your navel is as a rounded bowl*
> *   in which mingled wine is never lacking;*
> *your belly as a heap of wheat, set about with lilies.*
> *Your breasts are as two fawns, the twins of a gazelle;*
> *Your neck is as a tower of ivory,*
> *   your eyes as pools of Heshbon by*
> *   the gate of Bath-rabbim.*
> *Your nose is as a tower of Lebanon,*
> *   looking down upon Damascus.*
> *Your head crowns you as Mount Carmel;*
> *   your flowing locks are purple,*
> *A king is caught in their tresses* (Berk., 1-5).

This is a description of the human form from foot to head. In 5:10-15 it was from head to foot. **A round goblet** (2) suggests **liquor.** "And so the chorus, having mentioned the beautiful waist . . . adds the words which follow in the general sense of . . . Give thyself up to all the delights which become a form so admirable."[5] "Heaps **of wheat,** decorated with flowers, were placed in parallel rows on Eastern threshing floors."[6] **Like two young roes** (3) suggests breasts that were "beautiful and delicate, and exactly matching."[7] Old **ivory** (4) was believed to be the most beautiful color the body could have. The figure of the **pools in Heshbon**

---

[4]Terry, *op. cit.*, p. 49.   [5]*Ibid.*, p. 50.

[6]Cameron, *op. cit.*, p. 554.   [7]Gray and Adams, *op. cit.*, p. 66.

was meant to describe the **eyes** as clear, deep, quiet, and full. **Thy nose** may refer to the face, and the figure of speech would indicate a courageous countenance. The glossy splendor of the black hair so much admired in the East sometimes has a sheen **like purple (5)**. The figure of a lover caught and **held in the** tresses of his beloved is common in Eastern poetry.

Such uninhibited reveling in physical charms strikes the Western mind as indiscreet. And yet Woudstra reminds us that "our God, who created the magnificence of nature, with its almost infinite variety, also created the human body in such a way that it is a marvel of his handiwork. Physical beauty and the pure desire of husband and wife (and bridegroom and bride) for each other are God-given gifts to man. It is the perversion of these gifts that is base (cf. Rom. 1:26-27), and therefore to be condemned."[8]

D. PASSION AFLAME, 7:6-9

Following the passion-kindling song of the women, the king makes a final approach to the Shulamite. In proof of the assertion that he was held captive by her beauty, Solomon exclaims, **How fair and how pleasant art thou, O love, for delights!** (6) She was all that any man could desire. "*Tamar*, the word for **palm (7)**, was commonly a girl's name, this tall and graceful tree being regarded as a type of female beauty."[9] The words **of grapes** are not in the original; it is probable that **clusters** of dates were meant.

In 8 the king expresses his desire to embrace Shulammith and to fully enjoy her love and beauty. It seems apparent that he was perilously close to taking by force what he could not gain by consent. Moffatt translates:

> *Methinks I will climb that palm,*
> *taking hold of the boughs!*

The impassioned plea continued:

> *Oh may your breasts be clusters of fruit,*
> *and your breath sweet as an apple!*
> *May your kisses be exquisite wine*
> *that slips so smoothly down,*
> *gliding over the lips and the teeth!* (8-9, Moffatt)

---

[8]*Op. cit.*, p. 602.   [9]Cameron, *op. cit.*, p. 554

E. A Cry for True Love, 7:10—8:4

These wild emotions must be checked without destroying herself and the king. Taylor, following the allegorical interpretation, made a comment regarding the Church, but it could be equally true of Shulammith, the faithful: "Grace has made her like the palm tree, the emblem alike of uprightness and of fruitfulness."[10] Again the girl took recourse to her most effective strategy in turning aside the king's advances. She "suddenly interrupts the king, takes up the sentiment that . . . [falls] from his lips, and gives it a reference to her own lover, whom she calls upon to come and lead her away to her home among the vineyards."[11]

The language of the Shulamite is just as clear in its intent as was the infatuated outburst of the king. But here it is pure and chaste because expressed within God's planned framework of true love and marriage. In moving words she declares her devotion.

> *I belong to my beloved, and his desire is for me.*
> *Come, my beloved, let us go out into the fields,*
>   *let us lodge among the hennas* [cf. 4:13].
> *Let us rise and go early to the vineyards;*
> *let us see whether the vines have now budded,*
>   *whether the blossoms have already opened*
>   *and the pomegranates are come into flower;*
> *there will I give you my love* (10-12, Berk.).

The mandrakes (13) were thought by the ancients to "stimulate sexual desire (as well as induce conception; cf. Gen. 30:14-16). Hence mandrakes are called love apples. The plant gave forth a strong smell which was pleasing to people in the east."[12] The **pleasant fruits** is probably a metaphor referring to the girl's love which she promised in 12.

Verses 8:1-4 seem to be a continuation of 7:10-13. "In ancient Israel, as in the Arab world today, a public display of affection between lovers is severely condemned. For a woman to flout custom in this manner is to forfeit her good name. This singer knows that well enough."[13] If you were only **my brother** (1), she says, I could kiss you in public without arousing suspi-

---

[10]*Op. cit.,* p. 97.   [11]Terry, *op. cit.,* p. 52.
[12]Woudstra, *op. cit.,* p. 603.   [13]Rylaarsdam, *op. cit.,* p. 158.

cion or giving offense. Shulammith desires to bring her beloved to her **mother's house** (2), where her mother **would instruct** her as to how she might best please him. **Spiced wine and juice of my pomegranate** are probably further metaphors for the girl's affections. Verses 3-4 are repeated from 2:6-7. See comments there.

Apparently Solomon made no further advances, for to the end of the book we hear nothing more from him or from the women of his court. Convinced at last that he could not win the Shulamite's affection—and perhaps shamed by her steadfast loyalty—he released her from custody. Thus God's Word reflects the encouraging fact that the influence of a good and strong person can steady a weaker one and save an impulsive individual from low living.

Section **VIII** *Reunion and Reflection*

The Song of Solomon 8:5-14

A. SHULAMMITH'S EULOGY OF LOVE, 8:5-7

1. *The Setting* (8:5)

The closing scene of the Song is in a country place near the home of the Shulamite. The question of v. 5, as questions elsewhere in the book, is designed to focus attention on a new situation. It may have been a literary device of the author, though Terry puts the inquiry, **Who is this that cometh?** in the mouth of one of the brothers. The phrase **leaning upon her beloved** permits us to assume that the Shulamite and her beloved were reunited upon her release by Solomon and that he accompanied her from Jerusalem to her home.

Nearing her home they pass the spot where love had first kindled between them. The beloved spoke gently: "Under the apple tree I awakened you" (Berk.). The spot was doubly sacred to Shulammith because there she had also been born. Birth in the open was common at that time.

2. The Song (8:6-7)

The girl's response poured from her heart. What had begun between them there "under the apple tree," she would have confirmed forever. **Set me as a seal upon thine heart, as a seal upon thine hand** (6). This **seal** would be a signet worn on the hand or arm as a memorial of a person greatly loved. It would perhaps be comparable to the significance of our wedding ring. Shulammith implores, Put me in your heart as well as on your hand.

There is poetry of high order in 6-7:

Love is strong as death;
Jealousy (ardent love) *is cruel* (retentive) *as the grave:*
The flashes thereof are flashes of fire,
A very flame of the Lord.
Many waters cannot quench love,
Neither can the floods drown it:
If a man would give all the substance
 of his house for love,
It would utterly be rejected.[1]

There was **jealousy** (6) in the kind of love that Shulammith knew. She could not endure the thought of having a less interest from her beloved than her relation to him required. She was giving him her whole self—her all—and could not be content with only a part of his love in return. **A most vehement flame** is translated, "A very flame of Jehovah" (ASV). This is the only place that the name of God appears in the book. "But the Shulamite has good reason for claiming God to be on her side in the protection of her love from cruel wrong and outrage."[2] Her love was God-given and true. If a man tried to buy it with **all the substance of his house** (7)—as Solomon had—he would be **utterly** spurned. And here was a girl whose conduct had proved the truth of her words.

---

[1] Adapted from Taylor, *op. cit.*, pp. 112, 115.
[2] Gray and Adams, *op. cit.*, p. 76.

B. A REMINDER AND A RESPONSE, 8: 8-12

Verses 8-9 are the words of the brothers (cf. 1:6 and Intro., "Three characters"); perhaps one asks the question in 8 and another replies in 9. Recognizing the probability of the imminent marriage of Shulammith, they intimate that she may need some older-brother advice and interference. The description **a little sister, and she hath no breasts** (8) is clearly a suggestion that they consider her immature. **The day when she shall be spoken for** would be the day of her marriage plans. In reply a brother declares, **If she be a wall** (9; i.e., chaste and resisting all efforts of unworthy lovers), **we will build her a palace of silver** (arrange a worthy marriage). On the other hand **if she be a door** (easily open to all offers of love), **we will inclose her** (build a protecting wall around her).

Shulammith replies with justifiable spirit that her recent experiences are sufficient answer to every question her brothers have raised. All of her reply in 10-12 seems to refer to those experiences. A marginal reading in ASV puts 10 in the past tense:

> *I was a wall, and my breasts*
> *like the towers thereof.*

Shulammith here asserts both her faithfulness and her maturity. The clause **then was I** (10) seems a clear reference to the time when Solomon sought to win her affections. **In his eyes** (Solomon's) she was as one that was seeking a husband; for this is the meaning of a woman finding **favour** (peace). The phrase is equivalent to finding rest (cf. Ruth 1:9 and 3:1).

Verses 11-12 appear to be a reference to the many women in Solomon's court, under the metaphor of **a vineyard** (11). The **keepers** would be the "daughters of Jerusalem" (1:5; Solomon's wives and concubines). Each one was obliged to bring to the king such **fruit** as was proper from her presence in his vineyard. The valuation which he—and they—placed upon the questionable privilege was high, **a thousand pieces of silver**. The location of **Baal-hamon** is unknown.

In 12, Shulammith declares her joy at being free from Solomon's vineyard and being in full possession of her own.

> *I keep my vineyard to myself:*
> *you are welcome to your silver, Solomon,*
> *welcome to your fruit, you keepers!* (12, Moffatt)

C. Love's Reward at Last, 8:13-14

In 13, Shulammith's beloved speaks. His salutation, **Thou that dwellest in the gardens,** picks up her own figure, "My vineyard . . . is before me" (12). His request is the yearning of the newly married to be together alone on the wedding trip:

> *My companions are listening for your voice;*
> *let me hear it* (RSV).

Shulammith's reply reflects the true lover's equal eagerness for the long awaited consummation,

> *Come quickly . . . beloved . . . like a gazelle,*
> *or like a young hart upon mountains of spices* (14, Berk.).

"This last verse is to be understood as a fragment of song which Shulammith has been wont to sing for the delight of her lover in former days, and which she knows is specially pleasing to him. . . . With this song of the maiden, the drama ends, and the two lovers, arm in arm, pass from the scene, conscious that true love has triumphed. She clings as a signet-ring to his arm, and he knows that her love for him is 'strong as death.' "[3]

And so closes this strange book. It is different from any other in the Bible; but it is in the Bible. We believe that God inspired him who wrote it and those who gave it a place in the canon of Scripture. It is a book about love between a man and a woman—one of God's gracious gifts to us. With the hymn-writer we sing:

> *For the joy of human love*
> .   .   .   .
> *Lord of all, to Thee we raise*
> *This our hymn of grateful praise.*[4]

---

[3]Terry, *op. cit.*, p. 60.
[4]Folliott S. Pierpont, "For the Beauty of the Earth."

Bibliography

I. COMMENTARIES

ADENEY, WALTER F. "The Song of Solomon and the Lamentations of Jeremiah." *The Expositor's Bible*. Edited by W. ROBERTSON NICOLL. New York: A. C. Armstrong and Son, 1903.

CAMERON, W. J. "The Song of Solomon." *The New Bible Commentary*. Edited by FRANCIS DAVIDSON, *et al*. Grand Rapids, Michigan: Wm. B. Eerdmans Publishing Co., 1956.

CLARKE, ADAM. *The Holy Bible with a Commentary and Critical Notes*, Vol. IV. New York: Abingdon-Cokesbury Press, n.d.

GRAY, JAMES COMPER, and ADAMS, GEORGE M. *Bible Commentary*, Vol. III. Grand Rapids, Michigan: Zondervan Publishing House, n.d.

JAMIESON, ROBERT, FAUSSET, A. R., BROWN, DAVID. *A Commentary, Critical and Explanatory on the Old and New Testaments*, Vols. I and II. Grand Rapids, Michigan: Zondervan Publishing House, n.d.

KERR, HUGH THOMPSON, and KERR, HUGH THOMPSON, JR. "The Song of Songs" (Exposition). *The Interpreter's Bible*. Edited by GEORGE A. BUTTRICK, *et al*., Vol. V. New York: Abingdon Press, 1956.

MEEK, THEOPHILE, J. "The Song of Songs" (Exegesis). *The Interpreter's Bible*. Edited by GEORGE A. BUTTRICK, *et al*., Vol. V. New York: Abingdon Press, 1956.

PFEIFFER, ROBERT H. "The Song of Songs." *The Abingdon Bible Commentary*. Edited by FREDERICK CARL EISELEN, EDWIN LEWIS, and DAVID G. DOWNEY. New York: Abingdon-Cokesbury Press, 1929.

POUGET, WILLIAM, and GUITTON, JEAN. *The Canticle of Canticles*. Translated by JOSEPH L. LILLY, C.M. The Declan X. McMullen Company, Inc., 1948.

RYLAARSDAM, J. COERT. "The Proverbs, Ecclesiastes, The Song of Solomon." *The Layman's Bible Commentary*. Edited by BALMER H. KELLY, *et al*., Vol. 10. Richmond, Virginia: John Knox Press, 1964.

TERRY, MILTON S. *The Song of Songs*. New York: Eaton and Mains, n.d.

WOUDSTRA, SIERD. "Song of Solomon." *The Wycliffe Bible Commentary*. Edited by CHARLES F. PFEIFFER and EVERETT F. HARRISON. Chicago: Moody Press, 1962.

II. OTHER BOOKS

DRIVER, S. R. *An Introduction to the Literature of the Old Testament*. New York: Charles Scribner's Sons, 1891.

MORGAN, G. CAMPBELL. *Living Messages of the Bible, Genesis to Malachi*. New York: Fleming H. Revell Co., 1911.

PURKISER, W. T., *et al*. *Exploring the Old Testament*. Kansas City, Mo.: Beacon Hill Press, 1957.

SIMEON, CHARLES. *Expository Outlines on the Whole Bible*, Vol. 7. Grand Rapids, Michigan: Zondervan Publishing House (reprint), 1956.

TAYLOR, J. HUDSON. *Union and Communion*. London: Morgan and Scott, n.d.

III. ARTICLES

GOTTWALD, N. K. "Song of Songs." *The Interpreter's Dictionary of the Bible*. Edited by GEORGE A. BUTTRICK, *et al.*, Vol. IV. New York: Abingdon Press, 1962.

SAMPEY, JOHN RICHARD. "Song of Songs." *The International Standard Bible Encyclopedia*. Edited by JAMES ORR, *et al.*, Vol. V. Grand Rapids, Michigan: Wm. B. Eerdmans Publishing Co., 1943.

Map 1

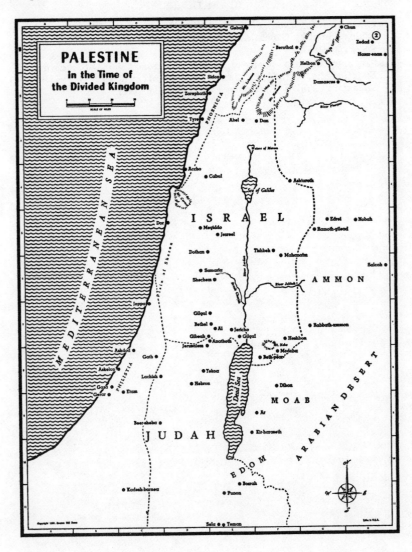

PALESTINE

in the Time of
the Divided Kingdom

Map 2

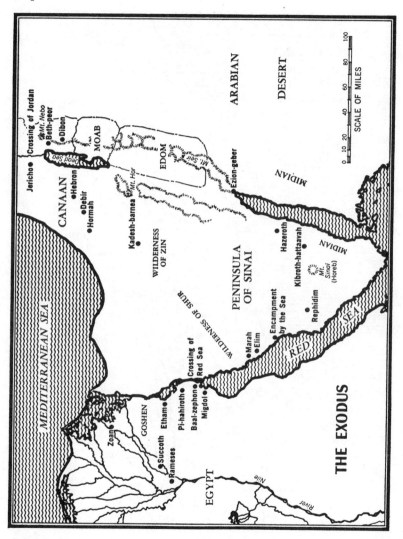

Map 3

PALESTINE
in the Time
of the Judges
0   10   20   30
SCALE OF MILES

MEDITERRANEAN SEA

SYRIA

Hobah

Sidon
PHOENICIA
Mt. Lebanon

Damascus   River Abana

Zarephath

Mt. Hermon

River Pharpar

Tyre   Dan

Beth-rehob

Heleph
Kedesh

Achzib   Hazor
ASHER   Zebulun   Waters of Merom

Golan

Accho

ZEBULUN   NAPHTALI

MANASSEH

Sea of Galilee

Kitron   Aphek

Plain of Esdraelon
Mt. Carmel   River Kishon   Mt. Tabor

River Yarmuk

Dor
Megiddo   Endor
ISSACHAR   Shunem
Jezreel   Beth-barah
Beth-shean   Jordan River
Dothan   Jabesh-gilead
GILEAD

Edrei

Ramoth-gilead

Dion

Kerioth

MANASSEH   Samara
Mt. Ebal
Pirathon   Shechem
Mt. Gerizim   River Kerith
EPHRAIM   Zaretan   Succoth
Joppa   Shiloh   Adam
DAN   Gilgal   Ephraim
Bethel
Beth-horon   Mizpeh   Ai   Michmash
Ekron   Ajalon   BENJAMIN   Jericho   Shittim   Elealah
Makkedah   Beth-shemesh   Gibeon   Ramah   Gilgal   Heshbon
Kirjath-jearim   Jerusalem   Mt. Nebo
Ashdod   Timnath   Bethlehem   Brook   Beth-peor   Baal-meon
Askelon   Gath   Azekah   Kidron
Adullam   Hareth   Tekoa   REUBEN   Bezer
Eglon   Hebron
JUDAH   Dibon
Gaza   Lachish   Engedi   River Arnon
Gerar   Debir   Carmel
Zanoah   Maon
Sharuhen   Hazor   Arad
Beer-sheba   Moladah   Kir
Ziklag   MOAB

Manahaim   Salcah
GAD
River   Mt. Gilead
Jabbok
Penuel
Rabbath-ammon

AMMON

Bered

Rehoboth   SIMEON

Dead Sea